Reading Culture

Reading Culture Companion Website

Reading Culture Online is a book-specific Companion Website designed to support *Reading Culture,* 5/E, by Diana George and John Trimbur. The Companion Website is an extension, and not a replication, of the book, and is designed to facilitate travel between the book and the world wide web. Material on the world wide web will be seen as culture in its own right, and careful consideration is given to different subjects such as evaluation of web design, chat room culture, newsgroups, and so on. The Student Resources section contains chapter summaries, as well as features like those in the book: Checking out the Web, Visual Culture, and Mining the Archive. The Instructor Resources section of the website contains cultural studies links, rhetoric and writing links, alternate syllabi, collaborative group projects, and additional field-work resources. You can visit the website at www.ablongman.com/george.

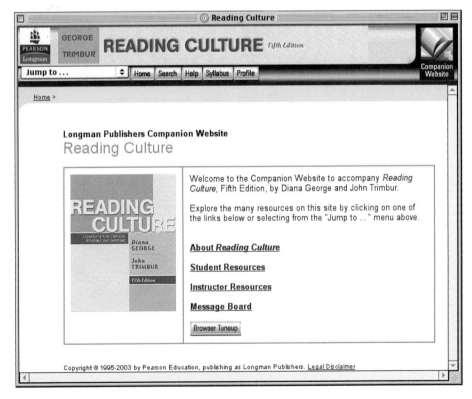

Reading Culture

CONTEXTS FOR CRITICAL READING AND WRITING

Fifth Edition

Diana George
Michigan Technological University

John Trimbur
Worcester Polytechnic Institute

PEARSON
Longman

New York San Francisco Boston
London Toronto Sydney Tokyo Singapore Madrid
Mexico City Munich Paris Cape Town Hong Kong Montreal

Senior Vice President and Publisher: Joseph Opiela
Senior Acquisitions Editor: Lynn M. Huddon
Development Manager: Janet Lanphier
Development Editor: Katharine Glynn
Executive Marketing Manager: Ann Stypuloski
Senior Supplements Editor: Donna Campion
Media Supplements Editor: Nancy Garcia
Production Manager: Ellen MacElree
Project Coordination, Text Design, and Electronic Page Makeup: Electronic Publishing Services Inc., NYC
Cover Design Manager: Wendy Ann Fredericks
Cover Designer: Kay Petronio
Photo Researcher: Photosearch Inc.
Manufacturing Manager: Dennis J. Para
Printer and Binder: Quebecor World
Cover Printer: Phoenix Color Corps.

For permission to use copyrighted material, grateful acknowledgment is made to the copyright holders on pp. 575–579, which are hereby made part of this copyright page.

Library of Congress Cataloging-in-Publication Data

Reading culture : contexts for critical reading and writing / [edited by] Diana George, John
    Trimbur.--5th ed.
        p. cm.
    Includes bibliographical references and index.
    ISBN 0-321-12220-8 (pbk.)
    1. College readers. 2. English language--Rhetoric--Problems, exercises, etc. 3. Critical
thinking--Problems, exercises, etc. 4. Academic writing--Problems, exercises, etc. I.
George, Diana, II. Trimbur, John.

PE1417.R38 2004
808'.0427--dc21

                                                                2003043398

Please visit our website at http://www.ablongman.com/george

ISBN 0-321-12220-8

3 4 5 6 7 8 9 10—QWT—06 05 04

Culture is ordinary;
that is where we must start

Raymond Williams

Contents

CHAPTER 4   Images   **173**

CHAPTER 7   Storytelling   **312**

CHAPTER 8   Work   **357**

CHAPTER 9   American History   **405**

CHAPTER 10   Living in a Postcolonial World   **491**

Visual Resources

Page Design

Parodies and Rewrites

Performance Art

Photographs

Posters

Product Design

Public Health Messages

Web Pages

Alternate Contents

Literary Genres

Preface

Every edition of *Reading Culture* has opened with these words from Raymond Williams: "Culture is ordinary; that is where we must start." We start, then, with the world that surrounds us and the experience of everyday life. In *Reading Culture*, we ask students to look at culture as a way of life that organizes social experience and shapes the identities of individuals and groups. We will be using the term *culture* in this textbook to talk about how people make sense of their worlds and about the values, beliefs, and practices in which they invest their energies and allegiances. We want to provide students with reading and writing assignments so they can understand how their familiar ways of life fit into the diverse, mass-mediated, multicultural realities of contemporary America.

Reading Culture assumes that students are already immersed in a wealth of cultural information and that their experiences of everyday life can usefully be brought to attention as material for reflection and deliberation. The reading and writing assignments in *Reading Culture* are designed to promote a critical distancing so that students can begin to observe and evaluate as well as participate in contemporary America. To this end, *Reading Culture* asks students to read in two ways. First we ask students to read carefully and critically the range of writing about culture we have assembled here. We ask them to identify the purposes and assumptions writers bring to the study of culture and the rhetorical patterns they use to enact their aims. Second, we ask students to read the social world around them, to identify the patterns of meaning in the commonplace, and to put into words the familiar experiences of everyday life that often go without saying.

Reading Culture is organized into ten chapters. The first chapter, "Reading the News," introduces students to the study of culture by looking at the American news media. The chapter includes critical strategies for reading the news on television, in print, and over the Internet, as well as a sequence of reading and writing activities about the events of September 11, 2001.

The chapters that form the main part of *Reading Culture*, as in past editions, are arranged under several broad topics. "Generations" and "Schooling" explore the personal experience of growing up and going to school. "Images," "Style," and "Public Space" emphasize the visual dimension of culture—in the popular media, in design and packaging, and in the way public space is planned, legislated, and used. The next three chapters, "Storytelling," "Work," and "American History" investigate narratives Americans tell themselves, the experience of the workplace, and the meaning of the past in contemporary America. The final chapter, "Living in a Postcolonial World," examines the movement of people, cultures, and languages in an era of globalization.

In the third edition of *Reading Culture*, we included two new features—Visual Culture and Fieldwork—that are now standard in the textbook. In each chapter, a Visual Culture section presents strategies for analyzing and interpreting films, photographs, television shows, ads, public health messages, page design, signs in public places, and other forms of visual communication. In addition, most chapters include a Fieldwork section that provides ways of studying culture through interviews, participant observation, questionnaires, oral histories, and other forms of on-site research.

The fourth edition introduced Mining the Archives, Perspectives, and instructions on Reading the Web. These features have also been carried over into the fifth edition, in many cases revised to accommodate new readings and assignments.

Reading Culture is designed to be used flexibly and creatively. Instructors may wish to ask students to work on the chapters in *Reading Culture* as they are arranged, but this is only one possible order.

The *Reading Culture* Companion Website, located at http://www.ablongman.com/george, and the Instructor's Manual also provide a wealth of resources for instructors wishing to extend their students' investigations on any of the chapter topics or individual readings.

New to the Fifth Edition

This fifth edition includes new and expanded features to help students investigate contemporary and past cultures. These additions come in large part from discussions we've had with writing teachers who have used previous editions of *Reading Culture*.

- *Color and Visual Culture.* This is the first edition of *Reading Culture* in four-color. The use of color adds a new dimension to the material we present for visual study, and accordingly we have expanded the Visual Culture features and developed additional Visual Essays for many chapters. We have also expanded the number of assignments that ask students to create their own visual compositions.

- *Two new chapters.* Chapter 1, "Reading the News," serves the same purposes as opening chapters in past editions—namely, to set up a case study of how to "read" culture and to introduce critical reading and writing strategies. What's new is the focus on the news media and a short case study of how the news covered the events of September 11, 2001.

  Chapter 10, "Living in a Postcolonial World," reframes multicultural America from a global perspective to investigate issues of language, power, and knowledge that arise at the borders of nations and cultures. The new case study in the chapter, "The Politics of World English," asks students to consider English in its global context.

- *Classic Readings.* Most chapters now include a Classic Reading in the study of culture. These selections offer students a perspective on how the issues raised in each chapter have been written about in the past by men and women whose thinking we still return to—writers and thinkers such as James Agee, Roland Barthes, Margaret Mead, and W.E.B. Du Bois.

- *Checking Out the Web.* The fifth edition of *Reading Culture* has expanded the Checking Out the Web feature so that each chapter offers several Internet assignments to choose from.

The readings in *Reading Culture* draw on a variety of resources, including popular press features, academic scholarship, and news reports. Each reading selection is introduced by a headnote that provides a context for the reading and a Suggestion for Reading that directs students to notice particular themes or rhetorical features in the selection. The reading selections are followed by Suggestions for Discussion, which raise issues for students to talk about in class or in small collaborative groups. The Suggestions for Writing ask students to consider a range of angles on the issues presented in the reading selections. Typically these writing assignments ask students to interpret a key point or passage in the reading selection, to relate the reading selection to their own experience, and to connect the reading to other readings and to the cultural realities of contemporary America.

The fifth edition of *Reading Culture* offers opportunities extending across chapters to work with visual literacy, multiculturalism, and microethnography. The work you do with this text will, however, depend on your needs and your students' interests. We think that with this edition, *Reading Culture* has become a more flexible resource for teaching writing and critical reading and for asking students to write about, and in the culture of, contemporary America.

Acknowledgments

There are a number of people we want to thank for their insight and advice. Lynn Huddon and Katharine Glynn provided the editorial support for this edition. We appreciate as well the careful readings we received by reviewers of this book:

Patricia Cullinan, *Truckee Meadows Community College;* Ruth Elowitz, *Santa Rosa Junior College;* Teresa Flynn, *Colorado State University;* Patricia A. Moody, *Syracuse University;* Robert G. Roth, *Middlesex County College;* Kenneth Womack, *Pennsylvania State University–Altoona.*

We want to thank the teachers who have used the first four editions of *Reading Culture.* The feedback, suggestions, and insights they have offered us over the years have enabled us to see the book in new ways and to plan the fifth edition with their ideas in mind. We also thank our companions Chuck Harris and Lundy Braun for their ongoing patience and faith that we could complete this work one more time. We thank our students at Michigan Technological University and Worcester Polytechnic Institute, and Clare Trimbur, Lucia Trimbur, and Catherine Trimbur for the best confirmation of our intentions we could possibly receive: they recognized themselves and their peers in this project and let us know that the cultural resources we are seeking to tap are vitally important to students in contemporary America.

We dedicate this book to the late Jim Berlin whose work challenged a generation of teachers and students to turn their attention to the small things of everyday life—those ways of living and communicating that constitute a culture.

Diana George

John Trimbur

Introduction

culture: *education, enrichment, erudition, learning, wisdom,*
breeding, gentility, civilization, colony, community, crowd, folks,
group, settlement, society, staff, tribe, background, development,
environment, experience, past, schooling, training, upbringing,
customs, habits, mores, traditions

The British cultural historian Raymond Williams has written that culture "is one of the two or three most complicated words in the English language." This is so, Williams explains, because the term *culture* has acquired new meanings over time without losing the older meanings along the way. Therefore, writers sometimes use the term *culture* in quite different and incompatible ways. Even a simple list of synonyms, such as the one that opens this chapter, can illustrate the truth of Williams's observation.

For some, culture refers to great art in the European tradition—Beethoven's symphonies, Shakespeare's plays, Picasso's paintings, or Jane Austen's novels. Culture in that tradition refers to something that you read; something that you see in a museum, an art gallery, or a theater; or something that you hear in a concert hall. It is often called "high culture" and is closely linked to the idea of becoming cultured—of cultivating good taste and discriminating judgment. A cultured person, according to this sense of the term, is someone who has achieved a certain level of refinement and class.

We encounter this use of the term frequently. For example, advertisers who want their products to seem high class will draw on this idea of culture, as in the Absolut Vodka campaign that pays homage to such artists as Vermeer, Rubens, and Modigliani.

Those who equate culture with high art would most likely not consider rock musicians such as Jimi Hendrix and Nirvana or pop stars such as Marilyn Monroe or Madonna to belong in the domain of culture. Nor would they include popular entertainment such as *The Sopranos, The Oprah Show, Monday Night Football*, the *National Enquirer*, the latest Harlequin romance, or NASCAR stock car racing in that category. In making a distinction between high and low art, those with this view of culture are largely interested in the classics and in keeping serious art separate from popular culture.

Other people, however, take an alternative approach to the study of culture. Instead of separating high from low art, they think of culture in more inclusive terms. For them, *culture* refers not only to the literary and artistic works that critics have

1

ABSOLUT HOFMEKLER.
HOMAGE TO JAN VERMEER

Ori Hofmeker is an artist on the staff of *Penthouse* magazine. For this ad campaign, he was asked to reproduce works of old masters, inserting an Absolut bottle in the ad as though it belonged in the original. Richard Lewis, *The Absolut Story*

called masterpieces but also to the way of life that characterizes a particular group of people at a particular time. Developed at the turn of the nineteenth century by anthropologists, though it has now spread into common use, this view of *culture* offers a way to think about how individuals and groups organize and make sense of their social experience—at home, in school, at work, and at play. Culture includes all the social institutions, patterns of behavior, systems of belief, and kinds of popular entertainment that create the social world in which people live. Taken this way, culture means not simply masterpieces of art, music, and literature, but a people's lived experience—what goes on in the everyday lives of individuals and groups.

Reading Culture explores the interpretation of contemporary American culture and how cultural ideas and ideals are communicated in the home, the workplace, at school, and through the media. When we use the term *culture* in this book, we are using a definition that is much closer to the second definition mentioned above than to the first. We think that the distinction between high and low art is indeed an important one, but not because high art is necessarily better or more "cultured" than popular entertainment. What interests us is how the two terms are used in an ongoing debate about the meaning of contemporary culture in the United States—about what languages should be taught in the schools, the way media interpret daily events, or the quality of Americans' popular tastes. We will ask you to explore these issues in the following chapters to see how arguments over media or schooling or national identity tell stories of contemporary U.S. culture.

In short, the purpose of this book is not to bring you culture or to make you cultured but to invite you to become more aware of the culture you are already living. According to the way we will be using the term, culture is not something you can go out and get. Rather, culture means all the familiar pursuits and pleasures that shape people's identities and that enable and constrain what they do and what they might become. Our idea is to treat contemporary American culture as a research project—to help you understand these ways of life from the inside as you live and observe them.

Reading Culture

The following chapters offer opportunities to read, research, and write about contemporary culture. The reading selections present writers who have explored central facets of American culture and offer information and ideas for you to draw on as you do your own work of reading and writing about culture. Each chapter raises a series of questions about how American culture organizes social experience and how Americans understand the meaning and purpose of their daily lives.

In these chapters, we will be asking you to think about how the writers find patterns in U.S. culture and how they position themselves in relation to contemporary cultural realities. We will be asking you to read not only to understand what the writers are saying but also to identify what assumptions they are making about cultural topics such as schooling, the media, or national identity. We also will be asking you to do another kind of reading, where the text is not the printed word but the experience of everyday life in contemporary America. We will be asking you to read culture—to read the social world around you, at home and in classrooms, at work and at play, in visual images and public places.

Reading a culture means finding patterns in the familiar. In many respects, of course, you are already a skilled reader of culture. Think of all the reading that you do in the course of a day. You read the textbooks assigned in your courses and the books and magazines you turn to for pleasure. But you also read a variety of other "texts." You read the logos on clothes people wear, the cars they drive, and the houses they live in to make guesses about their social status or about how you will relate to them. You read the way social experience is organized on your campus to determine who your friends will be, who the preppies are, the jocks, the geeks. You read all kinds of visual images in the media not only for the products advertised or the entertainment offered but for the lifestyles that are made attractive and desirable. Most of your reading takes place as you move through the daily reality of contemporary American life, and it often takes place below the threshold of consciousness. Often, people just take this kind of reading for granted.

To read culture means *not* taking for granted such readings of everyday life. Reading culture means bringing forward for analysis and reflection those commonplace aspects of everyday life that people normally think of as simply being there, a part of the natural order of things. Most likely you do some of that kind of reading when you stop to think through an ad or a history lesson or anything that makes you connect what you are seeing or reading with other ideas coming your way every day. Very likely, you do not accept without question all that you see and read. You probably turn a skeptical eye to much of it. Still, to read culture, you will have to be more consistent as you learn to bring the familiar back into view so that you can begin to understand how people organize and make sense of their lives. To read culture in this way is to see that American culture is not simply passed down from generation to generation in a fixed form but is a way of life through which individuals and groups are constantly making their own meanings in the world of contemporary America.

We are all influenced by what cultural critics call "mainstream culture," whether we feel part of it or not. Everyone to one extent or another (and whether they embrace or reject its tenets) is shaped by what is sometimes called the "American way of life" and the value that it claims to place on hard work, fair play, individual success, romantic love, family ties, and patriotism. This is, undoubtedly, the most mass-mediated culture in human history, and it is virtually impossible to evade the dominant images of America past and present—whether of the Pilgrims gathered at that mythic scene of the first Thanksgiving or of retired pro football players in a Miller Lite commercial.

Yet for all the power of the "American way of life" as it is presented by schools, the mass media, and the culture industry, U.S. culture is hardly monolithic or homogeneous. It is diverse, divided along the lines of race, class, gender, language, ethnicity, age, occupation, region, politics, economics, and religion. In part because of that diversity, the culture of contemporary America is constantly in flux. To read culture, therefore, is to see not only how its dominant cultural expressions shape people but also how individuals and groups shape culture—how their responses to and interpretations of contemporary America rewrite its meanings according to their own purposes, interests, and aspirations.

In 1958 Raymond Williams wrote the essay "Culture Is Ordinary," explaining why he thought that culture is not limited to high art or a university degree. It is also embodied in our ordinary, everyday ways of understanding how to make a life in the world. Read the following excerpt from "Culture Is Ordinary," and use the Suggested Assignment that follows it to begin your own investigation of culture in America.

CULTURE IS ORDINARY

Raymond Williams

Raymond Williams (1921–1988) has been called Britain's foremost culture theorist and public intellectual. In this excerpt, Williams tells of coming from a working-class village in Wales, where he was born and raised, to Trinity College, Cambridge, as a scholarship student. Williams writes several times in this selection that "culture is ordinary."

SUGGESTION FOR READING As you read, notice those places in which Williams explains different meanings of the word *culture* and how he describes his own encounters with the different ways people identify what it means *to be cultured.*

The bus stop was outside the cathedral. I had been looking at the Mappa Mundi, with its rivers out of Paradise, and at the chained library, where a party of clergymen had got in easily, but where I had waited an hour and cajoled a verger before I even saw the chains. Now, across the street, a cinema advertised the *Six-Five Special* and a cartoon version of *Gulliver's Travels*. The bus arrived, with a driver and a conductress deeply absorbed in each other. We went out of the city, over the old bridge, and on through the orchards and the green meadows and the fields red under the plough. Ahead were the Black Mountains, and we climbed among them, watching the steep fields end at the grey walls, beyond which the bracken and heather and whin had not yet been driven back. To the east, along the ridge, stood the line of grey Norman castles; to the west, the fortress wall of the mountains. Then, as we still climbed, the rock changed under us. Here, now, was limestone, and the line of the early iron workings along the scarp. The farming valleys, with their scattered white houses, fell away behind. Ahead of us were the narrower valleys: the steel-rolling mill, the gasworks, the grey terraces, the pitheads. The bus stopped, and the driver and conductress got out, still absorbed. They had done this journey so often, and seen all its stages. It is a journey, in fact, that in one form or another we have all made.

I was born and grew up halfway along that bus journey. Where I lived is still a farming valley, though the road through it is being widened and straightened, to carry the heavy lorries to the north. Not far away, my grandfather, and so back through the generations, worked as a farm labourer until he was turned out of his cottage and, in his fifties, became a roadman. His sons went at thirteen or fourteen on to the farms, his daughters into service. My father, his third son, left the farm at fifteen to be a boy porter on the railway, and later became a signalman, working in a box in this valley until he died. I went up the road to the village school, where a curtain divided the two classes—Second to eight or nine,

First to fourteen. At eleven I went to the local grammar school, and later to Cambridge.

Culture is ordinary: that is where we must start. To grow up in that country was to see the shape of a culture, and its modes of change. I could stand on the mountains and look north to the farms and the cathedral or south to the smoke and the flare of the blast furnace making a second sunset. To grow up in that family was to see the shaping of minds: the learning of new skills, the shifting of relationships, the emergence of different language and ideas. My grandfather, a big hard labourer, wept while he spoke, finely and excitedly, at the parish meeting, of being turned out of his cottage. My father, not long before he died, spoke quietly and happily of when he had started a trade-union branch and a Labour Party group in the village, and, without bitterness, of the 'kept men' of the new politics. I speak a different idiom, but I think of these same things.

Culture is ordinary: that is the first fact. Every human society has its own shape, its own purposes, its own meanings. Every human society expresses these, in institutions, and in arts and learning. The making of a society is the finding of common meanings and directions, and its growth is an active debate and amendment under the pressures of experience, contact, and discovery, writing themselves into the land. The growing society is there, yet it is also made and remade in every individual mind. The making of a mind is, first, the slow learning of shapes, purposes, and meanings, so that work, observation and communication are possible. Then, second, but equal in importance, is the testing of these in experience, the making of new observations, comparisons, and meanings. A culture has two aspects: the known meanings and directions, which its members are trained to; the new observations and meanings, which are offered and tested. These are the ordinary processes of human societies and human minds, and we see through them the nature of a culture: that it is always both traditional and creative; that it is both the most ordinary common meanings and the finest individual meanings. We use the word culture in these two senses: to mean a whole way of life—the common meanings; to mean the arts and learning—the special processes of discovery and creative effort. Some writers reserve the word for one or other of these senses; I insist on both, and on the significance of their conjunction. The questions I ask about our culture are questions about our general and common purposes, yet also questions about deep personal meanings. Culture is ordinary, in every society and in every mind.

(1958)

SUGGESTIONS FOR DISCUSSION

1. Raymond Williams says that culture consists of both "known meanings and directions" and "new observations and meanings." What does he mean by these two aspects of culture? List examples of each aspect of culture. Compare your list with those of your classmates. Discuss the principles of selection in the lists.

2. Williams "insists" on the "significance" of the "conjunction" between two senses of culture—what he calls a "whole way of life" and the "special processes of discovery and creative effort." What is this "conjunction"?

3. In the opening paragraph, Williams describes the bus trip from Cambridge, where he attended university, to the Black Mountains in Wales, where he grew up. He says this is a "journey…that in one form or another we have all made." What does he mean? What does this journey tell us about culture?

SUGGESTED ASSIGNMENT

Work together with a group of classmates. Think of as many instances as you can where the terms *culture* or *cultured* appears. For example, when do you hear other people (family, friends, coworkers, neighbors, teachers, and so on) use the terms? When do you use them yourself? Where have you seen the terms in written texts or heard them used on radio and television or in the movies? Make a list of occasions when you have encountered or used the terms. Categorize the various uses of the terms. Are they used in the same way in each instance or do their meanings differ? Explain your answer. How do you account for the similarities and differences in the use of the terms? Compare the results of your group discussion with the results of other groups.

CHAPTER 1

Reading the News

Self-Portrait with Newsboy by Lewis W. Hine. The J. Paul Getty Museum, Los Angeles. ©The J. Paul Getty Museum

A newspaper should have no friends.

—Joseph Pulitzer

One of the basic troubles with radio and television news is that both instruments have grown up as an incompatible combination of show business, advertising and news. Each of the three is a rather bizarre and demanding profession. And when you get all three under one roof, the dust never settles.

—Edward R. Murrow

And, that's the way it is.

—Veteran CBS anchor Walter Cronkite's nightly sign-off

When two highjacked passenger planes crashed into New York's World Trade Center on September 11, 2001, the news media scrambled to maintain round-the-clock coverage of events as they unfolded. That meant both sorting out the facts and keeping the audience involved. As was true during such dramatic events as the Kennedy assassination, the Challenger Shuttle disaster of 1985, and the Persian Gulf War of 1991, after the World Trade Center attack, radio and television provided live, on-the-spot reporting that brought listeners and viewers directly to the news scene while video replays broadcasted the story over and over. People in the United States and all over the world wanted to make sense of the event—to know what was going on, who was involved, and why.

The job of the news media is to report what is happening in the world. That task requires more than organizing a series of events in the order they occurred. Reporting the news involves selection and interpretation. Whether it is in hourly updated

Internet news sites, nightly television news programs, daily newspapers, or weekly news magazines, the news media select which events to report and which aspects of those stories to emphasize.

News reporters, moreover, inevitably interpret events for readers and viewers, giving them a way to understand the motives, forces, and conflicts that underlie what happened. In the case of 9/11, the news media quickly framed the story with headlines such as "America's New War," "America Under Attack," and "A New Day of Infamy." This angle tied the day's events to the December 7, 1942, Japanese attack on Pearl Harbor and America's entrance into World War II.

The events of 9/11 have turned subsequently into President George W. Bush's "war on terrorism" and continue to dominate the news media, shaping news stories of all sorts. Some stories are predictable, such as the coverage of the U.S. military campaign in Afghanistan, plans for "homeland security," and the debate about whether to launch a preemptive strike against Saddam Hussein's regime in Iraq. But other stories are related in less obvious ways. Reports of economic downturns and corporate scandal, features on racial profiling and discrimination against Muslims, even movie reviews and celebrity interviews are linked to September 11 and the ongoing war against terrorism. Because this story has so much influence, it is a good case study for learning what it means to read the news.

Of course, "reading the news" means reading all kinds of news—everything from sports to celebrity to business to local news. This chapter looks at how the news media shapes news for viewers, readers, and Internet users. It begins with an overview of what constitutes news and what audiences expect from the news. In the sections that follow, you will have the opportunity to examine television news, newspapers, news magazines, and Internet news sources. Using the events of 9/11, you will explore how journalists themselves talk about the way a serious news event has been handled. Throughout the chapter, you will be directed to gather first-hand information on what audiences think, how different media communicate the news, and how to read stories about the news. All of this work prepares you for the chapters that follow in *Reading Culture*.

Thinking About the News

In their introduction to *The Elements of Journalism,* Bill Kovach and Tom Rosenstiel write that citizens can expect journalists to stick to these principles:

1. Journalism's first obligation is to the truth.
2. Its first loyalty is to citizens.
3. Its essence is a discipline of verification.
4. Its practitioners must maintain an independence from those they cover.
5. It must serve as an independent monitor of power.
6. It must provide a forum for public criticism and compromise.
7. It must strive to make the significant interesting and relevant.
8. It must keep the news comprehensive and proportional.
9. Its practitioners must be allowed to exercise their personal conscience.

The principles in this list reveal a basic faith in the potential power of the press. In the United States, although citizens and media critics may well complain about the quality of news reporting, they traditionally have defended the freedom of the press guaranteed in the Bill of Rights. In fact, journalism has often considered itself a watchdog on democracy (principles 5 and 6 above)—independent of government and big business, presenting the facts, making independent judgments, and having "no friends," as Joseph Pulitzer said should be the case with a newspaper.

At the same time, critics of contemporary journalism maintain that the press has become much too close to special interests to exercise that watchdog role (see principles 1, 2, and 4). These critics point to the fact that the news media—including newspapers, news magazines, television networks, and Internet sites—are owned by corporate conglomerates such as AOL Time Warner and media tycoons such as Rupert Murdoch. They argue, furthermore, that these news media rely as much on entertaining as informing their readers and viewers by emphasizing the sensationalistic side of the news and highlighting celebrities, scandals, and lifestyles.

To gauge how people view the news today, do this exercise with classmates:

Exercise 1.1

1. Form a group with three or four classmates. Each group member can use the following questions to interview five to ten friends, classmates from other courses, coworkers, teachers, and/or family members about the news. Use written questions so people can answer on paper or via e-mail, or ask the questions in person and record the answers in a notebook. If possible, interview people from different age groups and walks of life.

    Do you read a daily newspaper? What is it? How often? Why?

    Do you listen to news on the radio?

    Do you read a weekly news magazine such as *Time* or *Newsweek*?

    If you watch news on television would you consider yourself:

      ☐ A regular viewer?

      ☐ An occasional viewer?

      ☐ Someone who only watches when a major story breaks?

    Are there other sources you rely on for news? What are they?

    Which news sources do you trust to give you accurate reports?

    Which news sources do you consider biased, incomplete, or frivolous?

    Look at this list of journalistic principles. Do you think they are observed by the news media today? Are some but not other principles practiced?

    Journalism's first obligation is to the truth.

    Its first loyalty is to citizens.

    Its essence is a discipline of verification.

    Its practitioners must maintain an independence from those they cover.

    It must serve as an independent monitor of power.

    It must provide a forum for public criticism and compromise.

    It must strive to make the significant interesting and relevant.

    It must keep the news comprehensive and proportional.

    Its practitioners must be allowed to exercise their personal conscience.

    Age:

      ☐ 16–23   ☐ 24–35   ☐ 35–45   ☐ 45–60   ☐ over 60

- Gender:

    ☐ male   ☐ female

- Profession: With your group, summarize the findings of your interviews. Tally how many people were interviewed and note their age, gender, and profession. Where do the people you interviewed get their news—television, radio, newspapers, news magazines, the Internet? Do these news sources vary depending on age, gender, or profession? How do people seem to assess the accuracy of the news? How did they respond to the list of journalistic principles? What patterns do you see in how people assess the accuracy and bias in the news and whether they think the news media stick to journalistic principles?

2. Report your findings in class. Compare them with the findings of other groups. What do you see as the significance of these findings?

Reading Television News

This section offers strategies for reading and analyzing television news. First we look at the content of evening network news programs and the audience that watches them. That is followed by a discussion of the identifying visual and verbal codes that identify programs as news programs, a distinct type of television show that differs in fundamental ways from everything else on the air.

The task of television news programming—at least according to the networks that produce news shows—is to inform citizens, entertain viewers, and advertise to consumers, all at the same time. There is little question that television news is a commercial enterprise and that the ratings (or percentage of viewers who watch a news program) matter. Therefore news programmers seek the widest audience by combining hard news about the important national and international events of the day with soft news about lifestyle, celebrities, and entertainment.

The exact combination of hard and soft news will vary, depending in large part on the type of news show. The traditional mainstays of television news—national network news and local news—themselves differ in important respects. National network news, with well-known anchors Tom Brokaw, Peter Jennings, and Dan Rather, claim the greatest authority of the news programs and have extensive resources to send reporters anywhere in the world to cover breaking stories or to develop special investigative feature stories. Local news typically features a limited amount of national and international stories, along with local news, weather, sports, and lifestyle features.

The advent of cable television has made possible for the first time continuous news programming; networks such as CNN, CNBS, and MSNBC have round-the-clock coverage of national and international news as well as separate segments on financial, health, legal, sports, and entertainment news. With its on-the-spot coverage, CNN gained public recognition initially during the Persian Gulf War of 1991. Since then, cable news has become a fixture in American life, and the networks are likely to be playing nonstop in such places as airports, hotel lobbies, and health clubs.

Other types of news programs include news magazines such as *60 Minutes, 20/20,* and *Nightline,* which show investigative reporting and interviews; news commentary such as *Crossfire* or Chris Matthew's *Hardball;* and interview shows such as *Larry King Live* and *Connie Chung Tonight.* Information and entertainment tend to blur together in these types of news shows—to create what is often called "infotainment."

Terms to Keep in Mind as You Read Television News

Hard News. Hard news consists of the important events of the day in international, national, and local affairs. Hard news tends to focus on serious issues with real consequences. Reports on the presidential election in Brazil, a train crash in India, antiwar demonstrations in London, a nation-wide strike in South Africa, hurricane damage in the Caribbean, terrorist threats to abortion clinics in the United States, and the indictment of the mayor of Providence for racketeering are all examples of hard news. Hard news may also include reporting on the law, business, science, and education when the story has wide interest, such as the Supreme Court decision on school vouchers, the corporate scandals at Enron, or new studies on global warming and environmental exposure and breast cancer. Sometimes the hard news overlaps with celebrity news, as in the case of the O.J. Simpson murder trial or the death of Princess Diana.

Soft News. Soft news is meant to entertain as well as to inform viewers by focusing on celebrities, the entertainment world, and lifestyle. Soft news tends to emphasize the human interest side of things—sometimes with an eye out for scandal and the sensational: another Hollywood star with a drinking problem checks into rehabilitation, the family squabble over whether to freeze baseball legend Ted Williams's body, the upcoming tour of the Rolling Stones as a test of the aging rockers, or the latest drugs to hit the rave scene. Soft news can also emphasize heartwarming aspects of the news: third graders raising money to send to an Afghani elementary school, a teenage boy rescuing two people trapped in a burning car, or neighbors helping a black family repaint its house after vandals had spray-painted racist slogans on it.

Feature Stories. Feature stories can be based on either hard or soft news. Features are different from news stories in the way they can go beyond reporting the events of the day to presenting more in-depth background, interviews, and analysis. Some feature stories try to get behind the news to reveal trends and underlying patterns. Feature stories might focus on the debate about mammography in medical circles, the controversy over the hunting rights of Native Americans in Alaska, or the European movement against genetically modified food. Major investigative feature stories sometimes run in two- or three-part series.

Breaking News. Breaking (sometimes called "developing") news refers to events that are just unfolding. Television news teams will sometimes interrupt regularly scheduled programming to announce an important piece of breaking news such as election results, a national leader rushed to the hospital, or the 9/11 attacks.

Continuing News. Continuing news refers to ongoing stories that unfold over a period of time and spin off related stories. For example, several stories grew out of the World Trade Center attack as continuing news stories—reports on which families received compensation and why, debates about how or whether to rebuild the World Trade Center, congressional investigations into what the FBI and CIA knew before 9/11, and proposed legislation to allow airline pilots to carry guns.

What Is News? Analyzing Content and Audience

The question of whether or not a story is newsworthy is a perennial one in television news programming. What counts as news on television depends on the station or network, the type of news show, its audience, and whether the primary focus is to entertain or to inform.

In the following viewing exercise, you analyze evening news programming on the major networks ABC, CBS, and NBC to obtain insight into three areas. First, by noticing how news shows select and interpret the major events of the day, you will see how some events, such as the war on terrorism and the collapse of major corporations such as Enron and World.com in the summer of 2002, influence news programming not only in headline stories but also in related features.

Second, by examining the content of the evening network news, including the commercials, you can draw inferences about who the intended audience is and how the news show addresses viewers' age, interests, and social position.

And third, by investigating what appears on the evening news, you can begin to formulate your own conclusions about the meaning of news programming—and respond to the critics who claim that by reducing the coverage of hard news, television news programming has become increasingly frivolous and has defaulted on its journalistic responsibilities.

Exercise 1.2

1. Choose for this project the evening news on one of the major networks—ABC, CBS, or NBC. It will help if you can tape the evening news in its entirety. Construct an outline of the news show by doing the following:

   ▢ Identify the exact title of the news program. Note date and time of the broadcast.

   ▢ Record the headlines that appear at the beginning of the news.

   ▢ Organize your outline by segments, using commercial breaks as the boundaries for the segments. Note that these segments are often titled. Record the titles that appear on the screen or that the anchor uses.

   ▢ Time each story.

   ▢ Note the program sponsors that appear during commercial breaks.

   Sample Outline of a News Program

   ABC World News Tonight with Peter Jennings
   July 15, 2002, 6:30–7:00 Eastern Daylight Time

   Headlines (00:52)
   Homeland security plan
   Alan Greenspan talks to Congress on corporate greed
   National security and the whales
   Women and menopause—A Closer Look
   Sound as a weapon—On the Cutting Edge

   Segment 1—Top Stories
   (00:53) Homeland security plan summarized
   (01:39) Congressional reaction
   (01:39) Americans Spying on their neighbors. Report on Operation Tips
   (02:01) Alan Greenspan reporting on the economy
   (00:19) Report on World.com and severance pay for workers
   (00:23) Summary of the proposed Corporate Accountability Bill

(01:50) In overseas news, Attack on Israeli civilians by Palestinians (on-screen title: AMBUSH)
(00:14) Report on interview with Saddam Hussein
(00:14) IRA Apology for killing civilians over the years (on-screen title: IRA APOLOGY)
(00:38) Promos for Closer Look and Cutting Edge features
(02:12) Commercial Break: Toyota; Mylanta; Shout laundry product; Liquid PlumR; Immodium anti-diarrhea medicine

Segment 2—National Briefing
(00:16) Report on gas masks being issued to Aniston, Alabama residents living near a chemical weapons incinerator
(00:16) Report on Ted Williams's will
(00:12) Allen Iverson turns himself in to the police
(01:55) Whales vs. Sonar for Navy; Military vs. Environmentalists (update from a two-year-old story)
(00:24) World Trade Center designs revealed (memorial vs. business)
(00:20) Promos for Closer Look and Cutting Edge features
(02:51) Commercial Break: State Farm Insurance; Nexium prescription gastric drug; Best Western ad featuring retired couple; Bayer Women's aspirin; Miracle Ear hearing aid; Dulcolax laxative; Tinamed plantar wart patch; promo for next day's news (Botox Parties)

Segment 3—Closer Look
(03:00) Report on medical findings related to hormone replacement therapy and menopause
(00:09) Promo for on-line chat with one of the experts for the Closer Look segment
(00:09) Promo for Cutting Edge story
(03:12) Commercial Break: Starkist; Celebrex prescription arthritis drug; Orville Redenbacher popcorn; Publisher's Clearinghouse; Best Western; Maalox; Allstate retirement funds; promo for ABC's evening lineup

Segment 4—On the Cutting Edge
(02:38) Sonic guns
(00:03) Sign-off

2. Use your outline to write a brief summary of the program's content. Use the following questions to help you focus your summary.

   ▪ What were the top stories introduced at the beginning of the broadcast?

   ▪ How many hard news stories appeared in the broadcast compared with soft news stories such as human interest, lifestyle, celebrity, or entertainment? How much time was given to hard news and how much time to soft news?

   ▪ Which stories are given the most time and which are brief notes?

   ▪ How much international news is broadcast in relation to national news and how much time is allotted to each?

   ▪ What kinds of stories dominate national news? What kinds of stories dominate international news?

   ▪ How much time do commercials take?

Sample Summary
On July 15, 2002, *ABC World News Tonight with Peter Jennings* featured three kinds of stories: stories related to terrorism and homeland security, stories featuring financial news, and stories featuring medical reports on hormone replacement therapy for women past menopause. This night, the programming was dominated by stories relating to the military or to threats on the country. Almost all of the hard news stories, for example, were about homeland security. Two feature stories also focused on the military or on weapons.

Of the thirty minutes set aside for this program, 2:13 were devoted either to headlines at the beginning of the show or to promotions throughout announcing what stories would be coming up after the commercial breaks.

Commercials took up 8:25.

Of the remaining eighteen-plus minutes, approximately ten minutes were spent on hard news and less than one minute on two soft news headlines. This included about ten minutes on headline stories primarily covering homeland security and finance; 1:08 on "national news briefs," including one on Ted Williams and one on Allen Iverson, which I would call soft news; and 2:30 on international news, both reports on conflicts between Israel and Palestine.

Nearly eight minutes were taken up with feature stories, including 4:55 on two military and weaponry stories and 3:00 on a medical story.

It is also interesting to note that one thirty-eight-second promotion for upcoming feature stories was ten seconds longer than two of the international briefings, which were only fourteen seconds each.

3. Now consider the target audience for the news program. Take into account the stories in the broadcast and the commercials that aired during the time you watched. Use this information to write a one-page analysis of the target audience for this program.

Sample Audience Analysis

The target audience for *ABC World News Tonight* on July 15, 2002, is middle-aged adults, probably professionals, and many near retirement. That conclusion is based on the fact that, by far, the largest number of products advertised are aimed at a fifty-five and over age group. These include ads for retirement and long-term care insurance, senior discounts at motels, and several pharmaceutical products that treat gastric problems, high blood pressure, and menopause or premenstrual syndrome. Those commercials account for more than eight minutes of the thirty-minute broadcast.

In addition, six minutes or more of the broadcast are devoted to stories about threats to retirement funds and to hormone replacement therapy for postmenopausal women. In other words, at least half of the time of this broadcast goes to some message—either news or commercial—directed at this older audience.

4. Work together in groups or as a whole class on this last part. Enter types of news in the outlines you and your classmates made into a chart like the one reprinted here.

EVENING NEWS TOPICS OVER TIME

ALL NETWORKS	1977 (%)	1987 (%)	1997 (%)	DATE
Hard News	67	58	41	
Celebrity News	2	3.3	7.7	
Crime/Law/Courts	8	6.8	13	
Business/Economy	5.5	11.1	7.4	
Science and Technology	3.5	4.5	5.8	
Lifestyle Features	13.5	16.2	24.8	
TOTAL	100	100	100	

With your classmates, examine the data you have gathered and recorded in the chart. What percentage of the news is hard news? What percentage is devoted to other types of news?

How do the percentages compare with earlier surveys of the evening news? What trends do you see? How have the major events of the day influenced the news program you watched? After you have examined your data and discussed how current events have shaped choices for programmers, write an analysis of what constitutes "the evening news" for the major television networks.

Analyzing Visual and Verbal Codes

Understanding how television news works requires paying attention to visual and verbal codes. A code is a system of signs that conveys meaning. Words, numbers, images, even body language can act as a code. Visual codes such as corporate logos identify companies, trademarks identify consumer brands, and male and female icons identify rest rooms. Codes are also used to organize information, such as the periodic table in chemistry or maps of continents and countries. And codes can be used for persuasive purposes. Consider, for example, the way the "V for Victory" sign of World War II (holding up the forefinger and middle finger to form a V) became a peace sign in the 1960s.

The codes of television news are the ways television sends messages to viewers so that they recognize what they see on the news as real events that have taken place in the world. Television is a multimodal form of communication that simultaneously uses more than one kind (or mode) of communication to represent the reality of the news. In the case of television news, viewing involves putting together sight and sound—or the visual, verbal, and aural codes that identify this type of program.

Notice, for example, the music that introduces and closes the evening news. It is brief but dramatic—like an announcement that says, "Pay attention. Something serious and important is about to happen." The music works in conjunction with the news anchor's voice—usually serious and low (even if the anchor is a woman)—and with the headlines and video footage that appear on the screen. It all happens together and so quickly that you may notice only that the evening news just came on. These are common television news codes that work together to take viewers into the special domain of the nightly news show.

In the comic strip *This Modern World*, shown on p. 16, the cartoonist Tom Tomorrow draws on readers' familiarity with the codes of television news programming to make a satiric point.

The comic strip has reproduced such codes of television news as the "talking heads" of anchorman Biff and special correspondent Wanda in close-up behind the news desk, looking straight into the camera and talking authoritatively to the audience. That is the look Tom Tomorrow expects his readers to recognize, even if they don't realize it, in his parody of news commentary.

Visual Codes

Set and screen design. The set and screen design refers to both the physical setting of the news show and the graphics that appear on the screen. The set of *ABC World News Tonight,* for example, is designed to focus viewers' attention on anchorman Peter Jennings sitting behind a semicircular desk in a news room, with a stylized blue world map as background. When the camera pulls away at the end of the broadcast, it shows Jennings surrounded by a crew at individual computer terminals. The design

of the set is simple, as though to demonstrate the seriousness of working journalists but with the main visual emphasis on Jennings as the anchor and star of the show. By contrast, *CNN Live* and *CNN Headline News* both feature busy screens with weather, stock quotes, sports scores, and headlines or news promos running continuously across the bottom of the screenwhile the anchor is delivering the news. *CNN Headline News,* in fact, made a point of redesigning its screen to mimic a Web page, suggesting, perhaps, that it identifies its viewing audience as being Internet savvy.

Spatial arrangement. Spatial arrangement refers to how people are placed within the camera frame—or the area you can see on your television screen. A news anchor, for example, is normally at the center of the screen, pictured sitting behind a news desk, a talking head who speaks directly to the camera—and the viewer. This spatial arrangement emphasizes the stability and authority of the anchor as a trusted source of the news.

Sometimes, news reports use a split screen, which shows the anchor asking questions on one side of the screen and a reporter on location or an interview subject on the other side. The use of a split screen both adds visual variety and makes news reporting more dynamic by picturing a conversational exchange.

Camera space. Camera space means how close you are as a viewer to what appears on the screen. Camera space indicates the social intimacy or distance between the viewer and what is represented on the screen—whether a close-up (head and shoulders), a medium close-up (chest, head, shoulders), a medium shot (waist on up), a full shot (head to toes), or a wide shot (the entire set or stage). In general, the closer the camera is to the subject, the more intimate the feeling, whereas the more distant the camera is from a subject, the less intimate.

News anchors are typically shot in medium close-up. When, for example, you see Dan Rather behind his news desk, you usually see his chest, head, and shoulders, which is a respectful, formal, and not too intimate social distance.

The movement of the camera can alter the social distance established on the screen. When, for example, the camera moves in for a close-up of a news anchor, viewers sense they are being brought closer to the source of the news because something important is being said. By the same token, when the camera pans to a wide shot of the news room at the end of the program, it distances the viewer and signifies visually the close of the show.

Sequence of visuals. The sequence of visuals refers to the order in which images appear on the screen. The sequence of visuals in a news report can suggest meanings and relationships that may not be stated explicitly but take place nonetheless through a process of visual association.

Take, for example, the relationships implied in the following four visual elements that appeared sequentially in a news story on a school shooting—first, the headline, "Another School Shooting," and a picture of a handgun; second, video footage of the high school student accused of the shooting walking into a courtroom handcuffed and in prison uniform; third, an on-site interview with a tearful student at the high school where the shooting occurred; and fourth, a medium close-up of a psychiatrist seated behind a desk explaining possible motives in school shootings.

As the camera moves from the headline and picture of a gun to a shot of the teenage boy in court, the implied logic is to associate the gun with the boy. In turn, the movement from the boy in court to the crying high school student associates the boy in prison uniform and handcuffs with the cause of the tears, and the psychiatrist in the final part of the sequence appears as an expert capable of bringing some order and explanation to an otherwise chaotic situation.

Medium shot   Close-up

FIGURE 1.1

Verbal Codes

Headlines. Headlines identify the key stories selected as the news of the day. Television news programs typically use brief headlines at the top or bottom of the screen to interpret the news. For example, during the war in Afghanistan, the headline "America Strikes Back!" framed the military campaign in relation to 9/11. Similarly, the headline "Corporate Greed" at the top of a story gives viewers a slant on the motives of CEOs and other business executives.

Voice-over. Voice-over is a narrator speaking off-camera while scenes from a news report are shown on-screen. Viewers typically ascribe a high degree of authority to voice-over narration, just as readers do to the omniscient narrator in novels and short stories. The disembodied speech of voice-over suggests that the viewer is listening to someone able to see and explain everything that is going on.

On-location reporting. Reporting on-location brings the credibility of the eyewitness to news stories. A news reporter on the streets of Jerusalem, London, or Johannesburg or a weather reporter standing in wind and rain gives viewers the experience of being where the news is breaking. The language an on-location reporter uses can be less formal and more speculative than the language used in the studio, taking on a sense of urgency or uncertainty in the face of unfolding events.

Subtitles. Subtitles are written translations of what the on-screen speaker is saying when the speaker is using a language other than English or is speaking English with an accent that news producers think their audience will find difficult to understand. In both cases, the use of subtitles identifies the speaker as someone outside the U.S. mainstream, which can affect his or her credibility.

Exercise 1.3

Choose a cable or network news broadcast and analyze the visual and verbal codes. Tape the show so that you can watch it several times. (You can use the same news program you taped for the Exercise on page 12.) Choose at least one story or segment, and make a detailed outline of the story's verbal and visual codes.

Below is a sample of the kinds of notes you might take while watching for visual and verbal codes. These verbal and visual codes have been detailed from the headlines segment and from the top story in the broadcast.

Sample Outline of Visual and Verbal Codes

ABC World News Tonight with Peter Jennings
July 15, 2002

Headlines (53 seconds)
Visual: Graphic depicting Homeland Security Report cover. Fades to Bush at microphone speaking to a group.
Voice-over: "On *World News Tonight,* the president's latest ideas to protect the country from terrorism. Red teams and quarantines and having Americans spy on one another."
Visual: Dollar bills fading to image of Alan Greenspan talking. Title "corporate greed" in top right of screen while a hand fans out a stack of paper money.
Voice-over: "The chairman of the federal reserve on the subject of greed in corporate America. Using language *everyone* can understand."
Visual: Warship on the ocean with a sonar screen that fades to a swimming whale overlaying the left half of the image; the title "whales & warships" in the lower right quadrant of the screen. The left side of the screen then brings the whale image back into focus while the warship fades into the background. The whale is now beached and apparently dead.
Voice-over: "National security and the whales. The navy has permission to use a very powerful sonar that may be harmful to the creatures of the sea."

Visual: Left half of screen has a close-up of a prescription medicine bottle being opened and pills pouring into a hand. That blends into the right side of the screen with women walking down a crowded street. That compound image fades into the title: *A Closer Look.*

Voice-over: "Millions of women confused by the recent reports on menopause. We'll take a closer look at whether women should reconsider how they're being treated."

Visual: Cartoon graphic of men shooting sonic beams first at the camera and then the cartoon turns to reveal sonic beams being shot at a cartoon figure and knocking him down. The graphic fades to the title: *Cutting Edge.*

Voice-over: "And, sound as a weapon. The sonic bullets that knock you to your knees. Technology, on the cutting edge."

Story 1 with transition into Story 2: (1 minute 13 seconds)
Visual Sequence:

1. Peter Jennings, seated behind desk in medium close-up. The camera slowly moves in to close-up while he announces the first story, Operation Tip.
2. Series of graphics summarizing the Bush plan.
3. Jennings behind desk as a transition to video of
4. Bush behind microphone announcing his plan.
5. Back to Jennings, who asks for commentary and report from Linda Douglas on Congress's reaction.
6. Shift to split screen with Douglas on left, Jennings on right. Both are facing the camera, though Jennings is looking slightly to the left where the split screen shows Douglas.
7. Shift to Douglas filling screen in close-up, on location in Washington, as she announces the congressional response and the related story.

Verbal: Series of graphics with summary of Operation Tip. Titles include "Create 'red teams' that think like terrorists" and "Have states toughen their quarantine laws." Jennings reads these in voice-over as they are displayed on-screen.

In his transition to Linda Douglas's report, Jennings calls the plan a "hugely ambitious project which is going to be extremely expensive."

Write a brief (one- to two-page) description of the visual and verbal codes of the broadcast you watched.

Sample Verbal/Visual Code Description

The ABC news program I watched looked like a typical news report common on the networks. It began with a brief introduction of the headlines of the day and the feature stories that would fill out the program and moved directly to Peter Jennings behind his desk.

Peter Jennings introduces the main stories of the night in a talking heads composition. The set behind him is barely visible but is simply a blue world map of some sort. The focus is on Jennings.

The camera moves from medium close-up to close-up when Jennings is talking directly to the television audience. This gives him the authority to speak as the source of information. Jennings is probably in his midforties, dressed conservatively in a blue suit and tie. He wears his hair short and looks very formal and serious sitting behind the anchor desk.

Most of the visuals throughout this newscast seemed to be intended more to hold viewer interest than anything else. In Story 1, for example, the visuals function primarily as backdrop, though the video of Bush at the microphone does serve to connect him directly to the homeland security plan. Any image of the American president announcing a plan that he wants supported gives a very official look to a story. It almost seems, then, that the story is more about Bush than the plan itself, especially since this part of the story only lasted a little over a minute.

Once Jennings turns the story over to another reporter, the series of graphics that summarize Operation Tip are primarily composed of titles such as "Have states toughen their quarantine laws" that seem to highlight the sensational parts of the plan. Because Peter Jennings reads these in voice-over, they get quite a bit of weight. And Jennings concludes the report by saying that the plan is a "hugely ambitious project which is going to be extremely expensive." That seems to be partial reporting and partial editorializing.

Verbal codes seem most important in the Headlines segment of our outline in which words such as "Corporate Greed" appear on-screen as titles to define one story. Voice-overs during the Headline segment emphasized the sensational. Sentences such as "Red teams and quarantines and having Americans spy on one another," "Whales vs. warships," and "Millions of women confused" are spoken in a very dramatic voice almost as if these are all breaking news stories.

In general, the program follows a typical pattern: Peter Jennings introduces the story and then turns it over to an on-location reporter. That reporter tells the longer part of the story as graphics highlighting specific words such as "Ambush" or "Confused" frame the story and shape the way the audience might respond to it. The camera then returns to Jennings, who either summarizes the story, comments on it, or introduces the next story.

Very few of the stories were long. The longest story was the Closer Look segment, which featured information on hormone replacement therapy. It lasted three minutes, plus another twenty-five seconds or so either promoting that story or announcing an on-line chat on the topic at ABC.com. The only thing longer than this story was one commercial break.

This program concluded with a long story about a new weapon that knocks criminals down "with sound." That was the Cutting Edge portion of the news, a feature that reports on new technologies. This was the only place on the broadcast that used cartoon graphics; they were of men with sonic guns shooting at cartoon people targets. Their guns would shoot circles of sound at the criminals, who would fall down like video game characters. The cartoon graphics might have been used to suggest that this is a future technology, one still in the planning stage, but it holds promise for personal and national defense.

Share with several classmates the visual/verbal outline and description summary you wrote. As you read each others' outlines and descriptions, what differences do you notice? How do the shows resemble one another? How do they differ?

Once you have completed your investigations and discussions with classmates, write an essay examining the ways that verbal and visual codes work together in any segment of the news program you watched. What story do they combine to tell? Is the visual just the backdrop of the story or does it represent an unfolding event? How does the anchor or the on-location reporter frame the story? How would the story read if the sound were turned off and you only had the visual and what was printed on the screen?

Reading Newspapers

Washington Post editors Leonard Downie, Jr., and Robert. G. Kaiser have argued that, although September 11, 2001, was a day of television, September 12 belonged to newspapers. The *Washington Post* sold a million copies on September 12, 2001, over 150,000 more than it usually sells. Other major papers experienced a similar increase in sales, some printing and selling fifty percent more papers than usual. If viewers were glued to their television screens round-the-clock on September 11, on September 12 they wanted to read the kind of coverage that newspapers provide.

This incident raises interesting questions about the differences between television and print news. One difference has to do with the sheer amount of news presented daily in the two media. Network evening news shows, for example, typically broadcast less than fifteen minutes of hard news in their daily thirty-minute time slots. Moreover, a typical *NBC Nightly News* program contains about 3,600 words, whereas an issue of the *New York Times* or the *Washington Post* contains roughly 100,000 words a day.

There are also important differences in the scope of news coverage. Although the cable news networks such as CNN and MSNBC offer continuous coverage, they do not cover the range of national and international stories that are in major newspapers such as the *New York Times, Washington Post, St. Louis Post-Dispatch, Chicago Tribune, Miami Herald,* and *Los Angeles Times.*

These differences in the amount and scope of news coverage point to key differences in the expectations of newspaper readers compared with those of television viewers. People turn to television for updates, daily headlines, sports, and weather. In times of crisis, they expect television news to provide ongoing coverage of events such as the attack on the World Trade Center. But for in-depth coverage with background information, analysis, and commentary, people rely on newspapers.

This does not mean that all newspapers are the same. In fact, there are different types of newspapers, with different readerships. For our purposes, we'll look at three types—local newspapers, newspapers with national circulation, and tabloids.

Local newspapers have a readership based in a town, city, or region. These newspapers typically feature news of local interest, such as stories on the school budget, the zoning board, and the mayoral race, along with international and national news taken from the Associated Press, the *New York Times,* or *Washington Post* wire services. Newspapers with national circulation, such as the *New York Times, Washington Post, Wall Street Journal,* and *USA Today,* are read throughout the United States. The *Wall Street Journal* presents the news from a probusiness perspective, whereas *USA Today,* at least in the opinion of its critics, offers a lite version of the news. The *New York Times* and *Washington Post* are considered by many to be the pillars of respectable, influential, and responsible journalism, with a national audience of educated, well-informed readers in business, government, and the professions.

The third type of newspaper is the tabloid. Though often scorned for emphasizing gossip, crime, and scandal—and in the case of the *National Enquirer* and *Weekly World,* for being outright crackpot—daily news tabloids such as the *New York Daily News* and *Boston Herald* offer a popular alternative for their working-class and lower middle-class readership that presents a sensationalistic and sometimes antiauthoritarian slant on the news.

The following two sections examine the visual composition of front pages in newspapers and the images they project and provide guidelines for following a news stories from reading print news.

The Look of the Front Page: Analyzing Visual Design

Readers recognize different types of newspapers—and decide which to read—in part by their visual design. The visual design of a newspaper's front page is meant to send a message about its identity and intended readership. Based on visual cues, readers make assumptions about the authority, credibility, seriousness, and respectability of the newspaper. Tabloids, for example, are easily identified by their front page graphics and sensationalistic screamer headlines, whereas newspapers with national circulation, such as the *New York Times, Washington Post,* and *Wall Street Journal,* project a more conservative and respectable image, with less graphics, more restrained headlines, and visual emphasis on the columns of newsprint.

By the end of the twentieth century, the *New York Times* had reduced the number of columns on its front page from eight to six and had added color to front-page photos. Although traditionalists objected to such changes, the *New York Times* was in many respects following the lead of *USA Today,* the national daily that broke with the conventional look of newspapers by featuring less print, shorter news stories, more white space, more and larger pictures, and lots of color to attract a younger, media-savvy readership. In recent years, many local and national newspapers have been redesigned to heighten their visual appeal and compete with television and the Internet.

Guidelines for Analyzing the Visual Design of Front Pages

Page layout. Draw a sketch of one of the front pages reprinted on the opposite page that identifies each separate visual element. Label these elements. Are they headlines, photos or other graphics, news stories, weather reports, sports scores, previews of stories inside the paper, short features (such as "On this day 50 years ago" or "Fact of the day"), or something else? This sketch should help you see how much space is devoted to hard news (whether local, national, or international) and how much to other features. Notice too how many news stories there are, how they are positioned on the page, and how their layout gives them greater or less emphasis.

Gray space. Gray space is the amount of unbroken text that appears on the page. The greater the gray space, the denser a page will seem. Gray space often indicates longer, more in-depth news reporting. Notice how much gray space appears on the front page and how it affects the apparent seriousness and credibility of the newspaper.

Graphics-to-text ratio. Pages with more graphics have less gray space and hence a more open, less dense feeling. Use your sketch of the front page layout to get a rough estimate of the graphic-to-text ratio. Consider what readership would prefer a less dense page with more graphics, such as a tabloid or *USA Today*, and what readership would prefer front pages with less graphics and more gray space, such as the *Wall Street Journal*.

Use of color. The use of color gives front pages a contemporary look, whereas black and white signifies more traditional news formats. Notice how, or whether, color is used, not just in news photos but also in headings and borders that highlight features.

Print fonts. The size and type of fonts used in headlines, stories, and captions contribute to the overall visual design of the front page. For example, big, bold headlines that extend across the front of a newspaper signal something important, catastrophic, or surprising. Notice how or whether the print fonts vary on the front page. If they do vary, how does this direct readers' attention?

Exercise 1.4

1. Work with a group of your classmates. Use the guidelines to analyze the visual design of the front pages reprinted here, or bring in front pages of your own. Consider how each of the front pages selects the news of the day and what inferences you can draw about their intended readership. Compare the front pages. Based on the visual design of these pages, how do they differ in terms of credibility and respectability? How would you describe the image they project? What are the most important visual cues that establish this image?

2. Take an issue of the *Wall Street Journal* and redesign its front page to look like a tabloid. It won't be possible to include all the stories on the *Wall Street Journal*'s front page, so you'll have to select those that will appeal most to tabloid readers. Consider how to rewrite the headlines and include more graphics to give the stories a sensationalistic tabloid look.

Continuing News: Covering a Story

Major news stories such as 9/11 and the war on terrorism generate a wide range of coverage. Newspapers report events as they take place—the attack on the World Trade Center, the war in Afghanistan, and the debate in Congress about whether to

launch a preemptive military strike against Iraq. But national newspapers such as the *New York Times* and *Washington Post* as well as local ones also provide other types of coverage, such as analysis of policymaking, feature stories based on investigative reporting or the human interest side of the latest news, editorials that state the official position of a newspaper, op-ed commentary in which regular columnists and others express their views, and letters to the editor.

Newspapers are typically divided into sections—news, arts and lifestyle, business, and sports. These sections may cover major news stories from their specific angles—for example, the business section reports on the war on terrorism's consequences on oil prices or the arts section's stories on architectural proposals for redesigning the space where the World Trade Center once stood.

The following exercise asks you to follow a major news story and see how different types of newspapers have covered it not only in news reporting but also in the other parts of a newspaper.

Exercise 1.5

For this project, pick a major news story. Follow its coverage in three to five newspapers over the course of about a week. Use a local newspaper, your school newspaper, and national newspapers.

1. Write down the headlines each newspaper uses to announce the story.

2. Note the section in which the story appears in each newspaper.

3. Which papers offer analysis of the event or feature stories covering different angles on the event? What aspects of the event do these analyses or features highlight?

4. Are there editorials or op-ed pieces that provide commentary on the news event? What perspectives on the news story do these provide?

5. Are there letters to the editor that offer readers' opinions? How do they compare with the newspaper's official editorial position and op-ed perspectives?

6. Taking all of this coverage into account, write a report on how the news story is covered in the newspapers.

Reading News Magazines

Weekly news magazines such as *Time, Newsweek,* and *U.S. News and World Report* combine the reporting, analysis, and commentary of print journalism with the visual emphasis of television news. Founded in 1923, *Time* pioneered the type of news coverage and graphic design still used in weekly news magazines in the United States and around the world. This format generally features national and international stories in the front of the magazine, followed by sections on business, technology, health, ideas, religion, lifestyle, music, theater, movies, books, and sports (not all of which will necessarily appear in any single issue). News magazines also have regular columnists who provide analysis and commentary on recent events, with the last page reserved for celebrated writers such as Anna Quindlan and George F. Will.

Weekly news magazine provide news coverage that differs in interesting ways from the daily reporting of newspapers. Because the magazines appear once a week, their news staffs have more time to cover the news and more events to select from when they decide on the combination of stories in that week's issue. News magazines give readers a different slant on the news by combining investigative reporting from the news scene with analysis and commentary. Readers expect news magazines to cover the most important news of the week, and accordingly, the magazines have a good deal of influence in setting what counts as news, key trends, and big issues. For many readers, the cover story on a copy of *Time* and *Newsweek* defines the news of the day—and it could be anything from the latest events in the Middle East to the controversy about genetically modified food to the latest trend in Hollywood films.

A quick glance shows how news magazines differ from newspapers visually. The magazines use glossy paper and teams of photographers, graphic designers, and illustrators to promote visual interest and involvement on the reader's part. High production values, the use of color, and imaginative page layouts give *Time* and *Newsweek* their distinctive look. The visual emphasis of the news magazines is evident in a text-graphic ratio that devotes extensive space to a wide range of images. The page is designed to be seen and looked at, and media analysts have suggested that in this regard, the design of news magazines encourages browsing as much as reading.

The next two sections analyze two characteristics of weekly news magazines: the two-page spread and the cover story.

Analyzing Visual Design: The Two-Page Spread

News magazines do not just report the news. They add another dimension by visualizing it. News magazines have always relied extensively on photographs to bring readers to the news scene and photo essays to tell a story in pictures. Photographs remain a key part of the news magazines' repertoire in, for example, the annual news-in-pictures issue.

Just as important, news magazines use space across pages to combine graphics with text. The visual features in two-page spreads generally serve as separate sources of information that mix maps, graphs, time lines, charts, bulleted lists, and illustrations. "Parched Land," shown on p. 26, is a typical example that appeared in *Time* magazine, September 16, 2002, accompanying a news story on the drought of 2001–2002.

Exercise 1.6	**1.** Draw a sketch of the spread design used in "Parched Land." Identify each separate visual unit. Indicate the type of information and the visual display (map, graph, chart, etc.) that presents it.
	2. Consider the use of color coding on the maps. How does this coding contribute to the visual display of information?
	3. How does the experience of reading "Parched Land" differ from reading written text? What can visual features such as "Parched Land" do that written text can't do? What can written texts do that visual displays of information can't do?
	4. Choose a familiar news story, trend, or issue as the basis for a two-page spread and sketch a design. Decide what information you want to convey and the type of visual display best suited to present it. (You don't necessarily need to have the information at hand to do this assignment.)

Cover Stories: Putting a Face on the News

Whether you're browsing a newsstand or looking for something to read in the dentist's office, it's the picture on the cover of a magazine that's likely to catch your eye. For news magazines, these pictures could come from the scene of a breaking story like a school shooting or from a softer news story like a feature on teen depression.

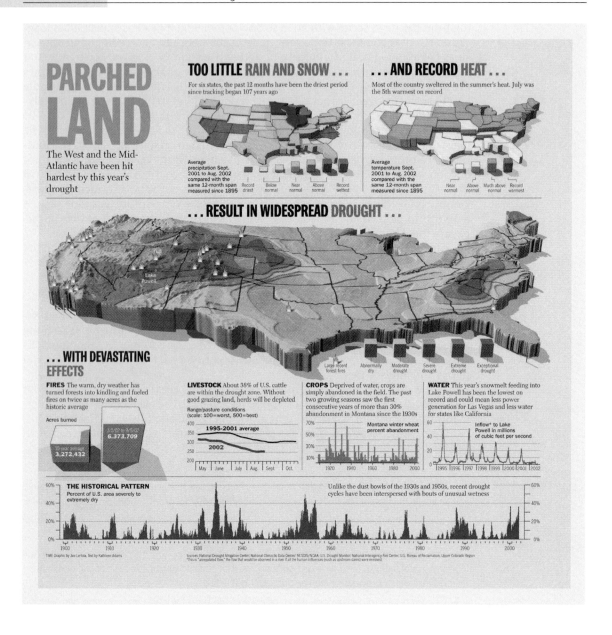

PARCHED LAND

The West and the Mid-Atlantic have been hit hardest by this year's drought

TOO LITTLE RAIN AND SNOW . . .

For six states, the past 12 months have been the driest period since tracking began 107 years ago

Average precipitation Sept. 2001 to Aug. 2002 compared with the same 12-month span measured since 1895

Record driest | Below normal | Near normal | Above normal | Record wettest

. . . AND RECORD HEAT . . .

Most of the country sweltered in the summer's heat. July was the 5th warmest on record

Average temperature Sept. 2001 to Aug. 2002 compared with the same 12-month span measured since 1895

Near normal | Above normal | Much above normal | Record warmest

. . . RESULT IN WIDESPREAD DROUGHT . . .

Lake Powell

Large recent forest fires | Abnormally dry | Moderate drought | Severe drought | Extreme drought | Exceptional drought

. . . WITH DEVASTATING EFFECTS

FIRES The warm, dry weather has turned forests into kindling and fueled fires on twice as many acres as the historic average

Acres burned

1/1/02 to 9/5/02 6,373,709
10-year average 3,272,432

LIVESTOCK About 38% of U.S. cattle are within the drought zone. Without good grazing land, herds will be depleted

Range/pasture conditions (scale: 100=worst, 500=best)

1995-2001 average
2002

May | June | July | Aug. | Sept. | Oct.

CROPS Deprived of water, crops are simply abandoned in the field. The past two growing seasons saw the first consecutive years of more than 30% abandonment in Montana since the 1930s

Montana winter wheat percent abandonment

1920 1940 1960 1980 2000

WATER This year's snowmelt feeding into Lake Powell has been the lowest on record and could mean less power generation for Las Vegas and less water for states like California

Inflow* to Lake Powell in millions of cubic feet per second

1995 1996 1997 1998 1999 2000 2001 2002

THE HISTORICAL PATTERN
Percent of U.S. area severely to extremely dry

Unlike the dust bowls of the 1930s and 1950s, recent drought cycles have been interspersed with bouts of unusual wetness

1900 1910 1920 1930 1940 1950 1960 1970 1980 1990 2000

TIME Graphic by Joe Lertola. Text by Kathleen Adams

Sources: National Drought Mitigation Center; National Climatic Data Center/ NESDIS/NOAA; U.S. Drought Monitor; National Interagency Fire Center; U.S. Bureau of Reclamation, Upper Colorado Region
*This is "unregulated flow," the flow that would be observed in a river if all the human influences (such as upstream dams) were removed.

Still, the staple of news magazine covers is the picture of the person who puts a face on the week's major events and issues.

There has long been a kind of public recognition (or in some cases, notoriety) that goes with making the cover of *Time* magazine. Who is on the cover of *Time* matters, and a list of who has appeared the most often and who the first woman or African American was provides windows into the mainstream media's sense of what is newsworthy. Nowhere is this so true as in the annual Man of the Year issue, for which *Time* selects the person who embodies the most important news of the year. Shown on the opposite page are *Time* Man of the Year covers from four decades.

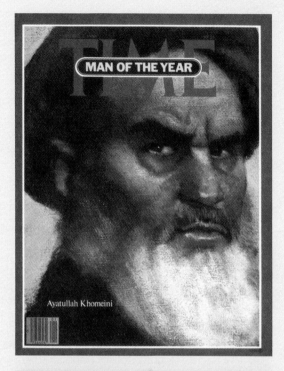

1. Divide into four groups, with each group responsible for a decade of *Time*'s Man of the Year covers, starting with the first in the 1930s . You should be able to find copies of *Time* in your college or public library, in bound volumes, microfilm, or microfiche. Review the covers from your decade, paying particular attention to the story inside that provides a rationale for *Time*'s choice.

2. Prepare a report (oral or written, depending on your teacher's direction) on the decade of *Time* covers you researched. Identify the different people who were selected as Man of Year over the decade. Explain what the selection might indicate about the important events or issues of the day. Note any patterns you see. Consider the criteria of selection. What does *Time* seem to think is newsworthy? Who or what is left out?

Reading News on the Web

On September 11, 2001, Internet news sites experienced record log-ins. From all over the world, at their office desks, in their homes, in library cubicles, and anywhere they had access to the Web, people were logging on. They were looking for as much information as they could find, and the same audience surge that had people watching television news round-the-clock and buying newspapers the next day drove those with an Internet connection to turn to the World Wide Web, which could barely handle the traffic, especially in the first hours after the attack on the World Trade Center.

One of the most powerful beliefs about the Internet is that it is possible to find any thing, any time. And to some extent, this is true. The Internet is a vast warehouse, a powerful network, an unending stream of information. What isn't true, however, is that the Internet has all of the information anyone could need at all times and on every topic, or that there is one central space where all of the information is gathered, catalogued, and easy to locate, read, watch, listen to, or download.

In fact, it might be more accurate to think of the Internet as a library without a consistent catalogue system, with many different librarians having wildly different interests and budgets, with a row of booksellers off to the side trying to get your attention to sell you something, with a garage sale going on in the middle, and with books and papers sitting wherever there's an available space.

There are places on the 'Net where material is carefully catalogued and easy to get to. Many newspapers have their own Web sites, though their electronic archives vary from paper to paper, depending on when they began putting things on the Web and whether they include all the articles published in their papers. So, unlike the microfilms of newspapers available in school libraries (which include copies of everything from front page stories to editorials to advertisements), a newspaper's Web archive may have only certain articles.

Other sites on the Web offer alternative news. Matthew Drudge's www.drudgereport.com prides itself in publishing news reports and gossip the mainstream press avoids. Some Web sites, such as http://www.moveon.org, combine analysis of the war on terrorism with antiwar appeals and petitions. And there is on-line news satire at sites such as www.theonion.com. These sites all take advantage of one reason people go to the Internet: to read opinions and get information they cannot easily find in mainstream news sources.

Internet news is truly multimodal; it brings several different forms of communication together by making video, audio files, and print available to its users. You can watch it, listen to it, and read it. And it allows for on-line discussions that enable users to converse with each other, sharing opinions and asking for information. More than anything else, the Internet lets anyone with a connection and the time—whether institutions or those people who simply want their own space on the 'Net—to publish their work.

The exercises that follow focus your attention on news as it is happening on the Internet and on the people logging in to get their news on a computer terminal.

Exercise 1.8

News reports on the Web come in several ways. Some are simple headlines such as the abbreviated headlines along the right-hand side of the yahoo.com home page. If you click on one of those headline links, you will be sent to the first paragraph of the story and to related stories from wire sources and from several newspapers across the country. That page will also have earlier report links for the same story, possibly video to open and watch, and a link to hit if you want to read the rest of the story.

More typical news pages are those sponsored by news organizations. Nationally known newspapers such as the *New York Times* or the *Chicago Tribune* have sites linked to the paper. These sites will reproduce the front page of the day and provide links to stories. Other sites such as CNN News and MSNBC or ABC News also have sites that act as extensions of their television broadcasts. In fact, many newspapers and television broadcasts remind readers and viewers that if they want further information on a subject covered in the broadcast, they can go to the Web site, where they will find more stories and sometimes an on-line chat with an expert.

1. Choose a site that has a corresponding news source either in television or in print.

2. Take preliminary notes on the two. How is the Web site similar to the newspaper or television broadcast? What is different? Pay attention not only to the information presented but also to how it is presented and how an audience accesses that information. (If you conducted surveys in this chapter, turn to those surveys for more information on how people get their news.)

3. For one day, get the news from both sources—for example, *NBC Nightly News* and MSNBC or the *New York Times* in print and the same paper on the Web. Refine your preliminary notes to include specific examples from that day's news.

4. Use the information you found and the notes you took to write a comparison of the two news sources. What advantages and disadvantages does each have? Is the news different at the two sources? Which source do you prefer? Why?

Exercise 1.9

The September 11 attack prompted an outpouring of talk on the Internet as people tried to make sense of what happened and of their feelings about what ought to happen next. Analyzing the talk that appears on message boards, chat rooms, readers' forums, and e-mail links can give you further clues to the purposes of a Web site, the kind of visitors it wants to attract, and the type of on-line discussion it wants to foster.

1. Search a site featuring on-line chat about this topic. There are many, including a site called www.itshappening.com, where users can, as the site's ad claims, "rant about current events."

2. Print at least one thread of a current conversation so that you can read it carefully. Use that printout as the basis for a written analysis of talk on the Web. In it, notice what kinds of issues or comments contributors seem to respond to most quickly or with most passion. How does the anonymity of the Web allow contributors to say things they might not say if they were face to face? What seems to have prompted the various writers to talk on the Web? Does the conversation thread offer a wide range of opinions, or does one position seem to emerge stronger than others?

Reading Web Sites

One of the attractions of the Web is that anyone with an Internet connection and some technical knowledge can put up a site. There is little question that, despite the growing commercialization of the Web, it still provides broad access to the means of communication and a new forum for discussion and debate. At the same time, it is also important to understand that the information and perspectives that show up on the Web are largely unregulated—and can range from the thoroughly reliable to the utterly crackpot. That's part of the creative and chaotic anarchy of the Web that makes it so interesting and so much fun. But it also means that Web users need to learn to read in a new way so that they can assess the various sites they visit—to identify who put them up, what their purposes are, and what can be expected from them in terms of the reliability of the information and ideas they contain.

WHAT TO LOOK FOR

Though there is great variation among Web site designs, several standard features have emerged that offer you a way to analyze Web sites. Here are things to look for in any Web site. You can use these features as clues to determine who put up the Web site, what its purposes are, how reliable and up to date its information is, and what its biases and attitudes are.

URL

The header at the top of your screen gives you the Web page address, or URL (Uniform Resource Locator). You can find out a good deal about a Web site from the URL alone. Take, for example, the URL for *re: constructions*, a site put together by faculty and students at MIT in response to the September 11 attacks: http://web.mit.edu/cms/reconstructions

There are two parts to the URL: the host name "web.mit.edu" and the file path "cms/reconstructions." The host name tells you the address of the server where the page is located (Web), the organization that put up the Web page (mit), and the domain (edu). Domain names identify the kinds of organizations that sponsor Web sites: ".edu" refers to educational institutions, ".org" to nonprofit organizations, ".gov" to government agencies, ".mil" to the military, and ".com" and ".net" to commercial enterprises. The file path enables a browser to find a particular page within a Web site. In this case, the address means that the host is the Web server at the Massachusetts Institute of Technology. Its file path takes you to MIT's Program in Comparative Media Studies, which created the site, to the site's home page, which is entitled *re: constructions. reflections on humanity and media after tragedy*.

Organizational Logo and Title

Web pages often feature an organization's logo or a common header at the top of each page. This feature helps to unify a Web site visually and to identify the sponsoring organization from page to page. The MIT site, for example, makes the theme easy to identify by featuring the logo at top center of each linking page. In some pages, however, it is difficult or impossible to tell who is sponsoring the Web site.

Links

Links appear as text or graphics to help you navigate from place to place, both within a particular Web site and to Web pages at other sites. They may appear at the top or bottom of the page or both places. Many Web sites, such as the *re: constructions* site, include a menu of links. In this case, the menu appears at the bottom of the home page and in a left-hand column on each linking page. But wherever they appear, links offer clues about the purpose of the site because they indicate the range and type of information and opinion the Web site considers relevant. Notice, for example, the inferences you can draw by looking at the links in the MIT site.

Signature and Credits

Signatures give the name and often the e-mail address of the person who maintains the Web page, information on when the Web page was established, when it was last updated, and those who have contributed to it. Sometimes people and organizations include further information such as their e-mail address, postal address, and phone number. Often this information is on the home page. In the MIT site, this kind of information appears in the linked page "introduction," where the reason for the site is explained and the *re: constructions* Editorial Team is listed.

Advertising

As the Web becomes increasingly commercialized, more and more advertising appears. The type of products and services advertised can help give you a sense of the kind of Web site you're visiting, much as you can draw some inferences about how magazines see themselves and their readers from their

(continues)

Reading Web Sites *(continued)*

ads. The absence of advertising, as in the case of Web sites such as MIT's, can also offer you information on how the organization or institution wants to relate to its readers.

WHAT CAN YOU DO AT THE SITE?

The possibilities that Web sites offer readers can give you further information to assess the site. Some, such as many of the 9/11 memorials, want you simply to read the text and see the graphics that have been put up on the page as though you are visiting an actual shrine. Others give you more options—to navigate the site or follow links to other Web sites. Some invite you to sign a guest book, send e-mail, fill out surveys, enter contests, watch animation and videos, listen to music, or take part in message-board discussions. Commercial sites, of course, want you to buy something. Consider whether the Web site you're visiting provides you with choices about where you can go and whether it invites you to participate interactively. What purpose do these possibilities serve? What kind of relationship does the site seem to want to establish with people who visit it?

Reading About the News—The Case of 9/11

Now that you have looked at how the news is reported on television, in newspapers and weekly news magazines, and on-line, you are ready to investigate and enter into the debates over how the media handled what by any measure was a major news story: the events of September 11, 2001. We have chosen three different discussions of that event and the media's representation of it. Much of this discussion centers on whether or not the media strayed from the journalistic principles presented earlier in this chapter, especially principles of fairness and accuracy.

Preparing to Read

Before you begin reading the excerpts below, look back at the nine principles of journalism listed on p. 8. After reviewing that list, write a brief informal statement on what you assume should be the role of the news media in a free society. Consider, for example, which of those principles you assume should always be at work in news reporting and which you regard as idealistic or even unnecessary. Your own position on these matters will come into play as you read and respond to these pieces.

Reading Strategies

Although you may be familiar with many of the reading strategies described below because you have used them throughout your education, it is useful to review them. All of them involve writing, and all can help you both to read more carefully and to write your way into the texts you are reading as you develop your own analysis and your position on the issues.

◼ *Underlining or highlighting:* Most students underline or highlight what they are assigned to read—whether it's a textbook, a journal article, or a novel. The purpose is to catch the key points or memorable passages so that you can return to them easily when you need to study for a test or write a paper. This strategy works best if you keep in mind that you are looking for key points or noteworthy moments in the writing. If you underline or highlight too much of a reading selection, the strategy isn't likely to work well at all.

◼ *Annotating.* Sometimes as students underline, they also write comments in the margins. This practice, annotation, is a more active kind of reading than underlining because it provides readers with a written record of their experience of the text. It offers readers a technique to write their way into the text. Annotations might include one- or two-word paraphrases of the content, notes on how the writer has structured the piece of writing ("key supporting evidence" or "refutes opposing views"), reactions ("I've never seen that"), or questions about difficult passages.

◼ *Summarizing.* Not many students who underline or annotate take the next step to summarize. This is unfortunate because summarizing allows you to spend time thinking through what you have read. Summarizing builds on underlining and annotating by providing you with a brief account, in your own words, of what you have been reading. This strategy can be enormously useful for difficult material.

◼ *Exploratory writing.* Exploratory writing offers a way to think out loud—on paper—about what you have been reading. It allows you to go beyond summary and annotation and begin to make decisions about what you have read, what it connects to, how it helps you understand issues, or how it seems to confuse an issue. With exploratory writing, you can experiment with ways of explaining and justifying your own reactions so that others will take them seriously, even if they don't agree. Exploratory writing can be personal in tone, but it isn't private. It is a level between the reactions you recorded in those annotations ("this is truly idiotic" or "I couldn't agree more") and the public voice you eventually will need to assume in a more formal, deliberative essay.

◼ *Synthesis.* When you do research, you must do more than explore your own responses to what different writers have said about a topic and how they have said it. You also need to compare how these writers have written on the same topic, how they have positioned themselves in different ways in relation to what other writers have argued, or how they have identified a different set of issues to address within the topic. Comparing writers' positions and perspectives to see how they work in relation to one another is *synthesis.* Synthesis literally means to combine several separate elements or substances to create something new. To synthesize the arguments from two or more writers, look for places where the writers share common ground, where they depart from one another, and how one writer's position might help you understand the other writer's position.

Reading and Writing Exercises

The following reading and writing exercises have been developed as a sequence, but they do not have to be completed in this order. These are flexible strategies that can be combined in several ways.

Exercise 1.10   Read Downie and Kaiser's "News Values" and Rutenberg's "Fox Portrays a War of Good and Evil, and Many Applaud." Note that we have highlighted, annotated, and summarized the Downie and Kaiser piece. Underline or highlight, annotate, and summarize the Rutenberg article.

NEWS VALUES

Leonard Downie, Jr., and Robert G. Kaiser

Leonard Downie, Jr., and Robert G. Kaiser have worked for the *Washington Post* since the early 1960s. During that time, Downie has been an investigative reporter, an editor for the *Post's* Watergate coverage, a foreign correspondent, and managing editor. In 1991, he succeeded Ben Bradlee as the *Washington Post* executive editor. Kaiser has been a local, national, and foreign correspondent as well as a national news and managing editor. He currently serves as a *Post* associate editor and senior correspondent.

The following passage is excerpted from their book-length investigative report on the American press, *The News About the News: American Journalism in Peril* (2002).

The 1990s were not a happy decade for American journalism. A few fine news organizations continued to thrive, but many more suffered. *How?* The pressures from owners to make more profit undermined good journalism; frivolous subjects often displaced more important topics; celebrities became more important newsmakers than presidents and potentates. Many in the news business thought traditional news values were in grave jeopardy.

Connection to 9/11 Then, on September 11, 2001, the news media were transformed. Confronted by a national catastrophe, reporters, editors, and producers, columnists and anchors, even the proprietors, all knew what to do. *I'm not sure about this* They tossed aside commercial considerations to give Americans vivid, thorough, responsible and informative coverage of the biggest story of modern times. Readers and viewers devoured the coverage, watching and reading more news than they ever had before.

Those terrorist attacks had a profound effect on America's news organizations. Sandy Mims Rowe, editor of the *Portland* Oregonian, described it: "To have this affirmation of our importance to the democracy, and of our readers' need for detailed, comprehensive, intelligent information, will spur editors to do what we should have been doing all along.... We have blamed all of the trash that's been out there on our readers, and on our customers, and said that's what they want. But I don't buy that." Peter Jennings of ABC, heartened by the renewed interest in serious foreign news, said the coverage of the terrorist attacks and public reaction to it "should give us a new look at life." *Jennings' predictions*

Not surprisingly, the best news organizations did the best job covering this story, but nearly everyone in the news business made a memorable effort to serve readers and viewers. Seventy-five of the Gannett Company's ninety-seven newspapers published extra editions on the day of the terrorist attacks, and devoted many extra pages to the story in the days that followed. Network television showed no commercials for four days, an expensive decision. The journalism was not uniformly excellent, but the best news values did prevail. *Really?*

The juxtaposition between alternative sets of values about journalism was stark. For much of the 1980s and 1990s, American news organizations had drifted toward softer, sillier, less significant journalism in a society that didn't seem to

protest. Then an unanticipated national catastrophe reminded both the providers and consumers of news that good journalism was not

just appealing, but absolutely necessary. Suddenly the choices between hard and soft, silly
and serious news came into clear focus.

Sample Summary

Downie and Kaiser contend that the September 11 attacks had a transforming effect on the
news media. Despite the bad practice news organizations had fallen into by the end of the twentieth century, when a serious story had to be covered, the news media "knew what to do." They
ignored pressure from commercial interests and covered the story in a thorough and responsible way. Downie and Kaiser quote news people such as Peter Jennings who are convinced that
this event should mark a turning point in the way journalists do their work in the future. Their
conclusion, in this passage, is that American news, which "had drifted toward softer, sillier, less
significant journalism" was shaken awake by the events of September 11, 2001.

In the sample, our highlights and annotations help us summarize Downie and
Kaiser. We did not include our reactions to the article because reactions are more appropriate for an exploratory writing that records a response to what is written. We also
incorporated brief quotes into our summary. By quoting a few short passages, you are
reminding yourself of those parts of a reading that you find the most important.

As you compose a comparable summary of the Rutenberg article, incorporate
brief quotes into your writing. Rutenberg's article is a critique of television news and
especially Fox television news. In your underlinings and annotations, pay attention
to how Rutenberg sets up his argument and how the language he has chosen might
shape public opinion.

FOX PORTRAYS A WAR OF GOOD AND EVIL, AND MANY APPLAUD

Jim Rutenberg

Jim Rutenberg is a business correspondent for the *New York Times*. This article appeared in
the *Times* on December 3, 2001, nearly two months after intense television coverage of the
attacks had begun.

1 Osama bin Laden, according to Fox News Channel anchors, analysts and correspondents, is "a
dirtbag," "a monster" overseeing a "web of hate."
His followers in Al Qaeda are "terror goons." Tal-
iban fighters are "diabolical" and "henchmen."

Ever since the terrorist attacks on Sept. 11,
the network has become a sort of headquarters
for viewers who want their news served up with
extra patriotic fervor. In the process, Fox has
pushed television news where it has never gone

before: to unabashed and vehement support of a
war effort, carried in tough-guy declarations
often expressing thirst for revenge.

The network, owned by the News Corporation of Rupert Murdoch, has always had a reputation—one it disavows—of being politically
conservative. But its demeanor since Sept. 11 has
surprised even its critics. The network is encouraging correspondents and writers to tap into
their anger and let it play out in a way that

reminds some rivals and press critics of the war drumbeat of the old Hearst papers and the ideologically driven British tabloids.

The usual anchor role of delivering the news free of personal opinion has been altered to include occasional asides. On a recent edition of the network's 5 p.m. program, "The Big Story," the anchor, John Gibson, said that military tribunals were needed to send the following message to terrorists: "There won't be any dream team for you. There won't be any Mr. Johnnie hand-picking jurors and insisting that the headgear don't fit, you must acquit. Uh-uh. Not this time, pal."

5   Geraldo Rivera, now a Fox war correspondent in Afghanistan, has said that he would consider killing Osama bin Laden himself if he came across him. (In a live transmission from Taliqan on Thursday, he acknowledged carrying a gun for self defense.)

So far, the journalistic legacy of this war would seem to be a debate over what role journalism should play at a time of war. The Fox News Channel is the incarnation of a school of thought that the morally neutral practice of journalism is now inappropriate.

It has thrown away many of the conventions that have guided television journalism for half a century, and its viewers clearly approve. The network's average audience of 744,000 viewers at any given moment is 43 percent larger than it was at this time last year—helped along by a sizable increase in distribution.

On some days, Fox draws an audience even larger than the audience of CNN, part of AOL Time Warner; CNN is available in nine million more homes. In prime time, Fox draws a larger average audience than CNN even more often, a challenge to CNN that could become stronger as Fox's distribution grows.

The style and success of Fox News have already had an effect. Last month, CNN, showing concern about being outflanked by its competitor, took the extraordinary step of ordering its correspondents to mention the Sept. 11 attacks during any showing of civilian casualties in Afghanistan.

10   Like the rest of the country, television journalism has engaged in a good bit of soul-searching since Sept. 11. Faced with covering a direct, large-scale attack on American soil, people at the other television networks have debated the merits of wearing American flag lapel pins in front of cameras and the danger of letting emotions get in the way of objective reporting. Others, like executives at the Reuters news agency, have cautioned writers and editors about using the word "terrorist."

Such hand-wringing has become fodder for conservative press critics. But Fox has not been saddled with such problems.

The network's motto is "fair and balanced," a catch phrase drafted to imply that it is objective while its competitors carry a liberal bias. But in this conflict, Fox executives say, to be unequivocally fair and balanced is to participate in the worst kind of cultural relativism. Giving both sides equal credence is to lose touch with right and wrong, they contend.

Fox denies that its reports are tinged with ideology. They simply reflect the new realities facing the nation, the network says.

"What we say is terrorists, terrorism, is evil, and America doesn't engage in it, and these guys do," said Roger Ailes, the Fox News chairman. "Yet, suddenly, our competition has discovered 'fair and balanced,' but only when it's radical terrorism versus the United States."

15   Fox does not suffer from the same affliction as competitors who are "uncomfortable embracing a good-versus-evil canvas," argued John Moody, the Fox senior vice president in charge of news. That, he said, is a relic of the Vietnam War and Watergate, watershed eras that infused journalism with an outmoded, knee-jerk suspicion of government.

The Fox News mantra of "be accurate, be fair, be American," Mr. Moody said, is appropriate for the times.

Brit Hume, the anchor of "Special Report," Fox's 6 p.m. news program, said he had avoided giving too much weight to reports about civilian casualties in Afghanistan.

"O.K., war is hell, people die," he said. "We know we're at war. The fact that some people are dying, is that really news? And is it news to be treated in a semi-straight-faced way? I think not."

The network says it has also shied away from showing too many reports looking into the genesis of Muslim hostility toward the United States.

20   Instead, Fox's reports simply take that hostility as a given. On Thursday, for instance, while introducing a segment about the popularity of American films in Islamic countries, a Fox anchor, Shepard Smith, said, "They hate what we stand for, so why do they love our movies so much?"

Mr. Ailes said the network held the government accountable when necessary. He said, for instance, that the network's top-rated talk show host, Bill O'Reilly, had regularly railed against Attorney General John Ashcroft (as ineffectual and overly secretive) and Gen. Tommy R. Franks, the commander of United States forces in Afghanistan (as being hamhanded at public relations).

"We are not anti-the United States," Mr. Ailes said. "We just do not assume that America's wrong first." But David Westin, the president of ABC News, said it was important for his journalists to maintain their neutrality in times of war. "The American people right now need at least some sources for their news where they believe we're trying to get it right, plain and simply," he said, "rather than because it fits with any advocacy we have."

It may be a good time to have that position. A survey released on Wednesday by the Pew Research Center of 1,500 adult Americans found that 30 percent wanted their newscasters to take a pro-American stance during their reports.

Two executives at two networks were reluctant to argue against Fox's position that the rest of the media coverage of the war had relied on misguided evenhandedness, saying that could invite accusations of insufficient patriotism in the current climate. Mr. Westin added, "Our people don't have to lead the American people to the conclusion they should reach about these horrible terrorist acts."

25   Alex S. Jones, the director of the Joan Shorenstein Center on the Press, Politics and Public Policy at Harvard University, said that by reporting the news with such an American perspective, Fox News was failing to explain the evolution of the other side's motivation against the United States.

"I think people need to understand what's going on on the other side of the equation, how the U.S. is viewed by its critics," he said.

Mr. Ailes said the Fox network did as much of that as was necessary.

"Look, we understand the enemy—they've made themselves clear: they want to murder us," he said. "We don't sit around and get all gooey and wonder if these people have been misunderstood in their childhood. If they're going to try to kill us, that's bad."

In the final analysis, Mr. Ailes said, "I don't believe that democracy and terrorism are relative things you can talk about, and I don't think there's any moral equivalence in those two positions." He added: "If that makes me a bad guy, tough luck. I'm still getting the ratings."

SUGGESTIONS FOR DISCUSSION

1. Compare with other members of your class the summary you have written of Rutenberg's critique of Fox News. To what extent are the summaries your classmates have written similar? To what extent do they differ? If they differ, how do you account for those differences? Don't assume that one summary is necessarily better or more accurate than another. Instead, try to identify the principles of selection each writer has used. Discuss how others' summaries change or add to your own understanding of what the author is saying in his article.

2. With a group of your classmates, look back at the underlinings and annotations you made in this article. What details, language choices, or incidents seem to each of you particularly striking or crucial for following the argument?

3. Explain what Rutenberg sees as the problem with the Fox news motto to "be accurate, be fair, be American." Go back to the statement you wrote on the role of a free press at the beginning of this section. How would you say your attitudes about the news influence the way you read Rutenberg or Downie and Kaiser? To what extent do these writers complicate your position or convince you to change anything you might have written?

Exercise 1.11 Read William Uricchio's "Television Conventions," underlining and annotating as you read. Respond to the article in an exploratory writing.

Here is a sample of exploratory writing, written in response to the article "News Values" by Leonard Downie, Jr., and Robert G. Kaiser. Notice how the exploratory writing is a much more immediate and personal response to the ideas represented in the article.

Sample Exploratory Writing

Downie and Kaiser would have us believe that one event can change the way an entire industry does its business. Maybe it can. If any event could do that, it would have to be something as catastrophic as 9/11. I'm not sure I'm convinced, though. Can journalism really go from being "silly," like they say, to being serious and responsible in just one day? What happens when the ratings drop or the ad revenues fall off? Won't they just go back to whatever draws the biggest audience?

And, I wonder who they mean when they say that the "best news organizations did the best job covering this story." Do they mean the major networks or just some of the networks, or do they mean newspapers? They work for the *Washington Post*, so they probably mean newspapers, but that isn't entirely clear. I'd like to know more about what they have in mind when they talk about the best job covering a story. I do think they are right, though, in that last sentence, that choices really came into focus over that event. I'm not sure, though, that everybody took the high road.

As you can see from this sample, exploratory writing does just that—it explores the reader's attitudes about a reading selection, it opens possible directions for further research and examination, and it allows the reader to begin moving toward a position on the subject at hand.

When you do exploratory writing, feel free to take some of the ideas the writer has raised and run with them, even if it seems that this will take you far afield from the reading. You may choose to dwell at length on a particular detail or incident in the reading that strikes you, even if it isn't the main point you'd identify in a summary. You may find that a particular reading selection reminds you of something you know or something you've read in a different context. It can be valuable to record this kind of connection.

TELEVISION CONVENTIONS

William Uricchio

William Uricchio is Professor of Comparative Media Studies at MIT in Cambridge and Professor of Comparative Media History at Utrecht University in the Netherlands. This article was written on September 16, 2001, for the MIT Web site responding to the events of September

11, *re: constructions. reflections on humanity and media after tragedy.* In an introductory sentence, Uricchio calls this commentary a few thoughts "on conventions of the televisual sort—formats genres, and recurrent patterns in form and content."

1 I learned about the attack on the WTC while calling the US Embassy in the Netherlands. "Aren't you watching television?" asked my incredulous speaking partner. "There's been a horrible accident at the World Trade Center." I tuned in and sure enough, during those first uncertain minutes before suspicion was even possible, it seemed as if a passenger jet had somehow crashed into the tower. And then, before my eyes, a second jet hit and the penny dropped: this was indeed a calculated act of terrorism, one moreover, with the eyes of the world focused upon it. The news about the attack on the Pentagon followed; then reports (now discredited) about a car bomb at the State Department; the Pennsylvania crash (or was it an in-air explosion?); a phantom fifth passenger jet; and reports about staffers running from the White House...

Before long, CNN was sporting a new graphic—"Attack on America"; the image of the jet penetrating the second WTC tower was in heavy rotation; and a nation (and probably a good bit of the world) watched in horror as the towers collapsed. Within the course of a few hours, the unthinkable had occurred and news coverage shifted from responding to uncertain events to imposing form and meaning upon them. Graphic form, rhythmic form (the footage of the jet smashing into the second tower repeated up to 30 times per hour), and increasingly, narrative form—all gave coherence to events that were still difficult to comprehend. As if a story set in Batman's Gotham, a simple narrative of good versus evil emerged, and as in Batman's universe, evil could be embodied in only a limited number of characters. Bin Laden quickly (and perhaps appropriately—but at the time it was anything but clear) helped to complete the narrative, providing evil with a face and name.

The quick transformation of unpredictable live events into familiar narrative patterns, it can be argued, produces a certain comfort; but it also frames the event, establishing specific ways

of thinking about the situation, together with an inclination towards narrative resolution. The framing of the story as an "Attack on America" and the insistence upon almost exclusively domestic coverage was a choice. It precluded other sorts of framing such as "an attack on the West" which might have appeared had we seen the spontaneous street demonstrations of shocked and saddened people in Berlin, Copenhagen, Paris, London, and other parts of the world. The "world" part of the WTC accounted for over 1000 now missing "foreigners," and the functions of many of the businesses within it were emphatically global. But ours was an American story. And the choice of an antagonist who embodies the antithesis of our values (a multi-millionaire who has rejected consumerism, a terrorist who seems deeply religious) helped to mute the complexity of the 18 or so terrorists who destroyed themselves along with their helpless victims. Bin Laden's casting helped to keep narrative causality elegantly simple: evil.

While I am not in a position to dispute this attribution, the point I want to make is that this sort of narrative inscription comes easily to our culture's use of television, and it brings with it a simplicity (or is it clarity?) of narrative logic that is muddied, even spoiled by complex questions about history, foreign policy, or representation that yield real insight. By September 15, news coverage carried the graphic "America at War" accompanied by subdued martial theme music (an element conspicuously absent for the first two days or so). And although we are being prepared for a long and difficult war, the image of finding 'em, smoking 'em out of their holes, and running 'em down has the same elegantly simple appeal as the original framing of the story.

5   Conventions can be understood in numerous ways. They embody work routines, allowing television production staff to turn from the stress of covering live events to the predictability of recycling taped sequences. They embody micro-narratives

common to the larger culture, whether the battle between good and evil, or moral balance through retribution, or the ultimate transcendence of the good guy. And they effectively contain complex and unruly details, in the process encouraging us to suppress unnecessary questions (but in the process, blocking us from insight and understanding). They frame issues in terms of the known and familiar, and in the process, direct our thinking (and our actions) in predictable ways. The dangers of this organizing strategy, particularly when confronting complex issues or when dealing with the unknown are profound indeed.

This is not to say that all program conventions are dangerous. Indeed, some can be quite useful. As TV anchors and hosts of breakfast shows interviewed survivors, replayed telephone messages spoken by now dead WTC office workers, and asked how it felt when they learned that their partners or parents were dead, one could see the familiar imprint of the "confessional" television genre. OK—many of the questions seemed poorly chosen, and the construction of emotion moments somewhat contrived. But the episodes worked their charm like the best of talk-TV. Although not to everyone's taste, programs such as *Oprah* help people to come to terms with a variety of difficult issues. Those exposing their souls as well as the viewing public seem to benefit. The formula has trav-

eled well, and most European countries have national variants of these programs (there is a body of literature on these programs—see for example, Sonia Livingstone and Peter Lunt, *Talk on Television*, Routledge 1994). The point is that they provide a vernacular, a way for people to work through complex emotional issues, and in the case of the attack on the Pentagon and WTC, a way to humanize and make felt the abstraction of numbers. The banality (and downright stupidity) of some of the questions notwithstanding, this use of a broader televisual convention has helped a public feel the enormity of the loss caused by the attack.

The pain of losing loved ones remains a trauma that few of us will escape. But the vicious and arbitrary way that so many died in New York, Washington and Pennsylvania is horrifying in a very different way. Carried by a medium so often filled with simulated images of death and destruction, horror of this magnitude easily reads as spectacle. Flattened on the small screen and consumed in our livingrooms far from the sounds, smells and dust of lower Manhattan, the images seem fantastic, even surreal. Somehow it seems only appropriate that talkshow conventions, televisual forms designed to embrace the most banal of human situations, be used to puncture this distance, and move us from gawking spectators into a more empathetic mode of engagement.

SUGGESTIONS FOR DISCUSSION

1. Uricchio writes that even though imposing a familiar narrative or story on an event can produce a certain comfort, it also serves to "frame," or establish fixed ways of thinking about an event or situation. What does he mean by that? What, if anything, is the real problem with that way of telling a news story of this magnitude? If the media weren't framing this event as "America Under Attack" with good guys, bad guys, and a potential resolution, how else might it be reported?

2. With a group of your classmates, compare the exploratory piece you have each written in response to this selection. How do your responses differ? In what ways are they similar? What about Uricchio's article might account for the ways you and members of your group have responded?

3. Near the end of his article, Uricchio compares some of the interviews with survivors and their families with the conventions of talk show interviews. He says that the use of this particular convention "has helped a public feel the enormity of the loss caused by the attack." How do you respond to that claim?

Exercise 1.12	Reread Uricchio, summarize it, and then write a synthesis of the articles by Downie and Kaiser, Rustenberg, and Uricchio. In your synthesis, pay attention to the way each of these arguments touches on the discussions of the others. How would you say, for example, that some of Uricchio's comments place him in alliance with Downie and Kaiser as well as with Rutenberg? Where does he depart from them?

In preparation for this assignment, reread the articles, but also go back and look at those portions of the articles you have underlined as well as at the annotations you have written in margins. If you have summarized articles, those summaries will help you see what each of these writers is doing in his separate discussion. Think of a synthesis as a place where you report on a conversation: Who said what? Where does each writer stand on the issues? What seems interesting or different? How do their arguments compare with and contrast with one another?

In a synthesis, you are trying to get a handle on how a topic or issue has been discussed by others. Don't offer your opinion on the issues or the way these writers have handled the issues. In a synthesis, you simply want to focus on analyzing how different writers have presented a position or an argument. Set forth the terms and shape of the public conversation so that, eventually, you will be able to position yourself or other writers within that conversation.

Writing About the News

Your ideas about how the news is reported have likely begun to form as you watched news programming, read newspapers and weekly news magazines, checked out news coverage on the Internet, and read what the critics have said. Now it is time for you to formulate a position on your own. Below are suggestions for writing assignments, but the paper you write will be determined primarily by your own interests and the turn your thinking has taken as you have done the work throughout this chapter.

SUGGESTIONS FOR WRITING

1. Much of the discussion about television news—and especially about the coverage of 9/11—is about whether or not television is actually covering the news or simply competing for a viewing audience, thereby putting too much emphasis on soft news that features celebrities, scandal, entertainment, and lifestyles. Review the viewing notes you took, the chart you and your classmates made, and the readings in this section, and write your own analysis of the state of television news. Consider in your analysis what television news does best as well as what seems lacking in television coverage of the news.

2. If you are interested in doing Internet research on issues surrounding the media coverage of 9/11, you will discover that several Web sites continue to be active. Remember that Internet sites are notoriously fleeting things. Those sites sponsored by news organizations, national museums, and libraries, however, tend to be much more stable. The Pew Charitable Trust, for example, maintains several sites devoted both to coverage of 9/11 and to research projects dealing with the media. On September 15, that organization published a report entitled "How Americans Used the Internet after the Terror Attack." The report can be found on

the Pew's Internet and American Life site at http://www.pewinternet.org. The Pew Trust also maintains a September 11 archive of television, newspaper, Web conversations, Web pages, and other pieces of information linked to 9/11. Those archives can be found at http://september11.archive.org, which is likely to remain active for a long time. Use these sites or sites like them to learn how the press continues to treat the events of 9/11. What are the issues as they are currently represented on the Internet, in archives, and in memorials? If you have some knowledge of putting together a site, you can even devise a Web site of your own to address these issues. Make sure your site has a central purpose or argument and that the material you choose for it adds to the information already out or offers a different way of understanding all of that information.

3. William Uricchio writes that there is an impulse in a news report to make it into a "story," that is, to find a compelling narrative, heroes, villains, and ultimately, a resolution to the conflict. Uricchio is also suggesting that reporters may be trying to find a neat way of tying up the ends and of keeping their audiences satisfied. Review the current major news stories. Choose one to follow in several media—television, radio, newspaper, news magazine, Internet—and examine that story for the narrative that seems to be emerging from it. What is lost when the press sticks to one particular narrative? What other narratives might be written from this story?

Conclusion

What you have been doing in the assignments throughout this chapter amounts to a kind of cultural analysis of the news. The assignments have asked you to rely on your own observations, learn firsthand what others think, read what critics and analysts have written, and write your position on or analysis of those issues. As you have read, taken notes, summarized, and synthesized others' writing, you have been analyzing how writers seek to shape public opinion and how the news media represent what is happening in American culture. This amounts to a cultural analysis of the role of the news media at a moment of crisis in American life and thought.

Throughout the chapters that follow, we will be presenting further opportunities to do this kind of cultural analysis—to read and write your way into some of the meanings of contemporary U.S. culture. The work you do will be informed by what others have written, but it will also rely on your own knowledge of the culture you live in and on the observations you will be able to make from your own fieldwork. At times, you will be asked to go beyond analysis to produce your own texts. You are, after all, not only a reader of culture but a user and producer of that culture.

CHAPTER 2 Generations

TV happiness shared by all the family!

Reprinted by permission, Motorola

This is not your father's Oldsmobile. This is the new generation—of Olds.

—1990 television commercial
for Oldsmobile

America is a nation of immigrants, and it is common to distinguish between first and second generations—between those who first traveled to and settled in the United States from Europe, Asia, Africa, or Latin America and their children who were born here. The two generations are biologically related to each other as well as to older generations as far back as people can trace their ancestry. Yet first-generation and second-generation Americans often differ in the way they live their lives, in the hopes they have for themselves and their children, and in the ties they feel to the traditions and customs of their places of ancestry.

People are also members of a historical generation that is formed by a common history and common experiences shared by others their age. To be a member of a generation in cultural terms, then, is to belong both to a family you are related to biologically and to a group of people you are related to historically.

In this chapter, you will be asked to read, think, and write about what it means to be a member of and a participant in your historical generation. Whether you are straight out of high school or returning to college after some time off, it can be valuable for you to consider how your own personal experience has been shaped by growing up at a particular moment in a particular historical generation.

The term *generation* denotes change. It suggests new life and new growth—new styles, new values, and new ways of living. Americans hear generational voices all the time in everyday conversation, when young people tell their parents not to be "so old-fashioned" and their parents reply, "It wasn't like that when we were growing up." Advertisers too, as the Oldsmobile commercial at the beginning of this chapter indicates, like to make consumers believe that the new generation of goods—cars, stereos, computers, household appliances—is smarter, better designed, and more high tech than its predecessors.

Each generation produces its own way of speaking and its own forms of cultural expression. Cultural historian Raymond Williams says that "no generation speaks quite the same language as its predecessor." Young people, for example, use their own slang to recognize friends, to distinguish between insiders and outsiders, to position themselves in relation to the older generation. Whether you say "whatever," "awesome," or "far out"; the kind of music that you like to listen to; the way you dance; your style of dress; where you go to hang out— reveals something about you and your relation to the constantly changing styles of youth culture in contemporary America.

How a generation looks at itself is inevitably entangled in the decisive historical events, geopolitical changes, and popular entertainment of its day. The Depression, World War II, the Vietnam War, the Reagan years, and the "new prosperity" of the 1990s have each influenced a generation profoundly. To understand what it means to belong to your generation, you will need to locate your experience growing up as a member of your generation in its historical times—to see how your generation has made sense of its place in American history and its relation to past generations.

From the invention of the American teenager and juvenile delinquency in movies such as *Rebel Without a Cause* and *The Wild One* in the 1950s to grunge rock and MTV in the 1990s, American media have been fascinated by each new generation of young people. Each generation seems to have its own characteristic mood or identity that the media try to capture in a label— the "lost" generation of the Jazz Age in the 1920s, the "silent" generation of the Eisenhower years in the 1950s, the "baby boomers" of the 1960s, the "yuppies" of the 1980s, or the "slackers" of the 1990s. When people use these labels, they are not only referring to particular groups of people but are also calling up a set of values, styles, and images, a collective feeling in the air. When thinking about your generation, look at how the media have represented it and how these media representations have entered into your generation's conception of itself.

This is not to say that everyone in the same generation has the same experience and the same feelings. A generation is not a monolithic thing. In fact, every generation is divided along the same lines of race, class, gender, and ethnicity that divide the wider society. But a generation is not simply a composite of individuals either. To think about the mood of your generation—the sensibility that suffuses its lived experience—you will need to consider how the character of your generation distinguishes it from generations of the past, even if that character is contradictory or inconsistent.

Reading the Culture of Generations

This chapter begins with three reading selections. They each present a different writing strategy that examines the relationship between generations. In the first, "Kiswana Browne," a chapter from the novel *The Women of Brewster Place,* Gloria Naylor uses fiction to explore the differences and continuities between an African American mother and her daughter. In the next selection, Dave Marsh writes a memoir recounting a moment of revelation while listening to Smoky Robinson sing "You Really Got a Hold on Me." The third reading, "Youth and American Identity," an excerpt from Lawrence Grossberg's longer study *It's a Sin,* takes a broader, more analytical perspective on the way post–World War II America invested its hopes in the younger generation as the living symbol of national identity and the American Dream.

The next three selections look at conflicts, differences, and misunderstandings between generations. In "Teenage Wasteland," Donna Gaines writes as a sympathetic reporter who investigates a teenage suicide pact and the response of local officials in Bergenfield, New Jersey. Thomas Hine's "Goths in Tomorrowland" explores the fragmentation of teenage subcultures and the alienation of young people from adult society. "Gen X's Enduring Legacy: The Internet," by Mike Pope, looks at the world of cyberculture as a generational divide.

The following pair of readings, "Perspectives: Before and After 9/11," asks you to consider the impact of September 11, 2001, on a generation's sense of itself. The first reading, Arlie Russell Hochschild's "Gen (Fill in the Blank): Coming of Age, Seeking an Identity" appeared before September 11. The second selection, "Generation 9-11" by Barbara Kantrowitz and Keith Naughton, appeared in *Newsweek* two months after. Taken together, they give you an opportunity to think about historical events as defining moments in the life of a generation.

The Classic Reading in this chapter is Allen Ginsberg's anthem of the Beat Generation of the 1950s, "Howl."

As you read, think, talk, and write about the interpretations presented in this chapter, consider how you would characterize your own generation. What styles of cultural expression mark your generation from your predecessors? What is your generation's sense of itself? How is your generation portrayed in the media? Perhaps when you have completed your work, you will find a way to define the particular mood and character of your generation.

KISWANA BROWNE

Gloria Naylor

Gloria Naylor's highly acclaimed novel *The Women of Brewster Place* (1980) tells the stories of several African American women who live in a housing project in an unnamed city. "Kiswana Browne" presents a powerful account of the encounter between a mother and daughter that explores both their generational differences and the aspirations that they hold in common. Naylor's story reveals how the much-publicized generation gap of the 1960s is never simply a matter of differences in politics and lifestyle but rather is complicated by the intersecting forces of race, class, and gender. The cultural shift signified by Kiswana's change of name represents both a break with the past and, as Kiswana discovers, a continuation of her family's resistance to racial oppression.

SUGGESTION FOR READING   As you read, underline and annotate the passages where the story establishes conflict between the two characters and where (or whether) it resolves the conflict.

1   From the window of her sixth-floor studio apartment, Kiswana could see over the wall at the end of the street to the busy avenue that lay just north of Brewster Place. The late-afternoon shoppers looked like brightly clad marionettes as they moved between the congested traffic, clutching their packages against their bodies to guard them from sudden bursts of the cold autumn wind. A portly mailman had abandoned his cart and was bumping into indignant window-shoppers as he

puffed behind the cap that the wind had snatched from his head. Kiswana leaned over to see if he was going to be successful, but the edge of the building cut him off from her view.

A pigeon swept across her window, and she marveled at its liquid movements in the air waves. She placed her dreams on the back of the bird and fantasized that it would glide forever in transparent silver circles until it ascended to the center of the universe and was swallowed up. But the wind died down, and she watched with a sigh as the bird beat its wings in awkward, frantic movements to land on the corroded top of a fire escape on the opposite building. This brought her back to earth.

Humph, it's probably sitting over there crapping on those folks' fire escape, she thought. Now, that's a safety hazard....And her mind was busy again, creating flames and smoke and frustrated tenants whose escape was being hindered because they were slipping and sliding in pigeon shit. She watched their cussing, haphazard descent on the fire escapes until they had all reached the bottom. They were milling around, oblivious to their burning apartments, angrily planning to march on the mayor's office about the pigeons. She materialized placards and banners for them, and they had just reached the corner, boldly sidestepping fire hoses and broken glass, when they all vanished. A tall copper-skinned woman had met this phantom parade at the corner, and they had dissolved in front of her long, confident strides. She plowed through the remains of their faded mists, unconscious of the lingering wisps of their presence on her leather bag and black fur-trimmed coat. It took a few seconds for this transfer from one realm to another to reach Kiswana, but then suddenly she recognized the woman.

"Oh, God, it's Mama!" She looked down guiltily at the forgotten newspaper in her lap and hurriedly circled random job advertisements. By this time Mrs. Browne had reached the front of Kiswana's building and was checking the house number against a piece of paper in her hand. Before she went into the building she stood at the bottom of the stoop and carefully inspected the

condition of the street and the adjoining property. Kiswana watched this meticulous inventory with growing annoyance but she involuntarily followed her mother's slowly rotating head, forcing herself to see her new neighborhood through the older woman's eyes. The brightness of the unclouded sky seemed to join forces with her mother as it high-lighted every broken stoop railing and missing brick. The afternoon sun glittered and cascaded across even the tiniest fragments of broken bottle, and at that very moment the wind chose to rise up again, sending unswept grime flying into the air, as a stray tin can left by careless garbage collectors went rolling noisily down the center of the street.

Kiswana noticed with relief that at least Ben wasn't sitting in his usual place on the old garbage can pushed against the far wall. He was just a harmless old wino, but Kiswana knew her mother only needed one wino or one teenager with a reefer within a twenty-block radius to decide that her daughter was living in a building seething with dope factories and hang-outs for derelicts. If she had seen Ben, nothing would have made her believe that practically every apartment contained a family, a Bible, and a dream that one day enough could be scraped from those meager Friday night paychecks to make Brewster Place a distant memory.

5   As she watched her mother's head disappear into the building, Kiswana gave silent thanks that the elevator was broken. That would give her at least five minutes' grace to straighten up the apartment. She rushed to the sofa bed and hastily closed it without smoothing the rumpled sheets and blanket or removing her nightgown. She felt that somehow the tangled bedcovers would give away the fact that she had not slept alone last night. She silently apologized to Abshu's memory as she heartlessly crushed his spirit between the steel springs of the couch. Lord, that man was sweet. Her toes curled involuntarily at the passing thought of his full lips moving slowly over her instep. Abshu was a foot man, and he always started his lovemaking from the bottom up. For that reason Kiswana changed the color of the polish on her toenails every

week. During the course of their relationship she had gone from shades of red to brown and was now into the purples. I'm gonna have to start mixing them soon, she thought aloud as she turned from the couch and raced into the bathroom to remove any traces of Abshu from there. She took up his shaving cream and razor and threw them into the bottom drawer of her dresser beside her diaphragm. Mama wouldn't dare pry into my drawers right in front of me, she thought as she slammed the drawer shut. Well, at least not the bottom drawer. She may come up with some sham excuse for opening the top drawer, but never the bottom one.

When she heard the first two short raps on the door, her eyes took a final flight over the small apartment, desperately seeking out any slight misdemeanor that might have to be defended. Well, there was nothing she could do about the crack in the wall over that table. She had been after the landlord to fix it for two months now. And there had been no time to sweep the rug, and everyone knew that off-gray always looked dirtier than it really was. And it was just too damn bad about the kitchen. How was she expected to be out job-hunting every day and still have time to keep a kitchen that looked like her mother's, who didn't even work and still had someone come in twice a month for general cleaning. And besides…

Her imaginary argument was abruptly interrupted by a second series of knocks, accompanied by a penetrating, "Melanie, Melanie, are you there?" Kiswana strode toward the door. She's starting before she even gets in here. She knows that's not my name anymore.

She swung the door open to face her slightly flushed mother. "Oh, hi, Mama. You know, I thought I heard a knock, but I figured it was for the people next door, since no one hardly ever calls me Melanie." Score one for me, she thought.

"Well, it's awfully strange you can forget a name you answered to for twenty-three years," Mrs. Browne said, as she moved past Kiswana into the apartment. "My, that was a long climb. How long has your elevator been out? Honey, how do you manage with your laundry and gro-

ceries up all those steps? But I guess you're young, and it wouldn't bother you as much as it does me." This long string of questions told Kiswana that her mother had no intentions of beginning her visit with another argument about her new African name.

10   "You know I would have called before I came, but you don't have a phone yet. I didn't want you to feel that I was snooping. As a matter of fact, I didn't expect to find you home at all. I thought you'd be out looking for a job." Mrs. Browne had mentally covered the entire apartment while she was talking and taking off her coat.

"Well, I got up late this morning. I thought I'd buy the afternoon paper and start early tomorrow."

"That sounds like a good idea." Her mother moved toward the window and picked up the discarded paper and glanced over the hurriedly circled ads. "Since when do you have experience as a fork-lift operator?"

Kiswana caught her breath and silently cursed herself for her stupidity. "Oh, my hand slipped—I meant to circle file clerk." She quickly took the paper before her mother could see that she had also marked cutlery salesman and chauffeur.

"You're sure you weren't sitting here moping and day-dreaming again?" Amber specks of laughter flashed in the corner of Mrs. Browne's eyes.

15   Kiswana threw her shoulders back and unsuccessfully tried to disguise her embarrassment with indignation.

"Oh, God, Mama! I haven't done that in years—it's for kids. When are you going to realize that I'm a woman now?" She sought desperately for some womanly thing to do and settled for throwing herself on the couch and crossing her legs in what she hoped looked like a nonchalant arc.

"Please, have a seat," she said, attempting the same tones and gestures she'd seen Bette Davis use on the late movies.

Mrs. Browne, lowering her eyes to hide her amusement, accepted the invitation and sat at the window, also crossing her legs. Kiswana saw immediately how it should have been done. Her celluloid poise clashed loudly against her mother's quiet dignity, and she quickly uncrossed her legs. Mrs. Browne turned her head toward the window and pretended not to notice.

"At least you have a halfway decent view from here. I was wondering what lay beyond that dreadful wall—it's the boulevard. Honey, did you know that you can see the trees in Linden Hills from here?"

20   Kiswana knew that very well, because there were many lonely days that she would sit in her gray apartment and stare at those trees and think of home, but she would rather have choked than admit that to her mother.

"Oh, really, I never noticed. So how is Daddy and things at home?"

"Just fine. We're thinking of redoing one of the extra bedrooms since you children have moved out, but Wilson insists that he can manage all that work alone. I told him that he doesn't really have the proper time or energy for all that. As it is, when he gets home from the office, he's so tired he can hardly move. But you know you can't tell your father anything. Whenever he starts complaining about how stubborn you are, I tell him the child came by it honestly. Oh, and your brother was by yesterday," she added, as if it had just occurred to her.

So that's it, thought Kiswana. That's why she's here.

Kiswana's brother, Wilson, had been to visit her two days ago, and she had borrowed twenty dollars from him to get her winter coat out of lay-away. That son-of-a-bitch probably ran straight to Mama—and after he swore he wouldn't say anything. I should have known, he was always a snotty-nosed sneak, she thought.

25   "Was he?" she said aloud. "He came by to see me, too, earlier this week. And I borrowed some money from him because my unemployment checks hadn't cleared in the bank, but now they have and everything's just fine." There, I'll beat you to that one.

"Oh, I didn't know that," Mrs. Browne lied. "He never mentioned you. He had just heard that Beverly was expecting again, and he rushed over to tell us."

Damn. Kiswana could have strangled herself.

"So she's knocked up again, huh?" she said irritably.

Her mother started. "Why do you always have to be so crude?"

30   "Personally, I don't see how she can sleep with Willie. He's such a dishrag."

Kiswana still resented the stance her brother had taken in college. When everyone at school was discovering their blackness and protesting on campus, Wilson never took part; he had even refused to wear an Afro. This had outraged Kiswana because, unlike her, he was dark-skinned and had the type of hair that was thick and kinky enough for a good "Fro." Kiswana had still insisted on cutting her own hair, but it was so thin and fine-textured, it refused to thicken even after she washed it. So she had to brush it up and spray it with lacquer to keep it from lying flat. She never forgave Wilson for telling her that she didn't look African, she looked like an electrocuted chicken.

"Now that's some way to talk. I don't know why you have an attitude against your brother. He never gave me a restless night's sleep, and now he's settled with a family and a good job."

"He's an assistant to an assistant junior partner in a law firm. What's the big deal about that?"

"The job has a future, Melanie. And at least he finished school and went on for his law degree."

35   "In other words, not like me, huh?"

"Don't put words into my mouth, young lady. I'm perfectly capable of saying what I mean."

Amen, thought Kiswana.

"And I don't know why you've been trying to start up with me from the moment I walked in. I didn't come here to fight with you. This is your first place away from home, and I just wanted to see how you were living and if you're doing all right. And I must say, you've fixed this apartment up very nicely."

"Really, Mama?" She found herself softening in the light of her mother's approval.

40   "Well, considering what you had to work with." This time she scanned the apartment openly.

"Look, I know it's not Linden Hills, but a lot can be done with it. As soon as they come and paint, I'm going to hang my Ashanti print over the couch. And I thought a big Boston Fern would go well in that corner, what do you think?"

"That would be fine, baby. You always had a good eye for balance."

Kiswana was beginning to relax. There was little she did that attracted her mother's approval. It was like a rare bird, and she had to tread carefully around it lest it fly away.

"Are you going to leave that statue out like that?"

45   "Why, what's wrong with it? Would it look better somewhere else?"

There was a small wooden reproduction of a Yoruba goddess with large protruding breasts on the coffee table.

"Well," Mrs. Browne was beginning to blush, "it's just that it's a bit suggestive, don't you think? Since you live alone now, and I know you'll be having male friends stop by, you wouldn't want to be giving them any ideas. I mean, uh, you know, there's no point in putting yourself in any unpleasant situations because they may get the wrong impressions and uh, you know, I mean, well…" Mrs. Browne stammered on miserably.

Kiswana loved it when her mother tried to talk about sex. It was the only time she was at a loss for words.

"Don't worry, Mama." Kiswana smiled. "That wouldn't bother the type of men I date. Now maybe if it had big feet…" And she got hysterical, thinking of Abshu.

50   Her mother looked at her sharply. "What sort of gibberish is that about feet? I'm being serious, Melanie."

"I'm sorry, Mama." She sobered up. "I'll put it away in the closet," she said, knowing that she wouldn't.

"Good," Mrs. Browne said, knowing that she wouldn't either. "I guess you think I'm too picky, but we worry about you over here. And you refuse to put in a phone so we can call and see about you."

"I haven't refused, Mama. They want seventy-five dollars for a deposit, and I can't swing that right now."

"Melanie, I can give you the money."

55   "I don't want you to be giving me money— I've told you that before. Please, let me make it by myself."

"Well, let me lend it to you, then."

"No!"

"Oh, so you can borrow money from your brother, but not from me."

Kiswana turned her head from the hurt in her mother's eyes. "Mama, when I borrow from Willie, he makes me pay him back. You never let me pay you back," she said into her hands.

60   "I don't care. I still think it's downright selfish of you to be sitting over here with no phone, and sometimes we don't hear from you in two weeks—anything could happen—especially living among these people."

Kiswana snapped her head up. "What do you mean, these people. They're my people and yours, too, Mama—we're all black. But maybe you've forgotten that over in Linden Hills."

"That's not what I'm talking about, and you know it. These streets—this building—it's so shabby and rundown. Honey, you don't have to live like this."

"Well, this is how poor people live."

"Melanie, you're not poor."

65   "No, Mama, *you're* not poor. And what you have and I have are two totally different things. I don't have a husband in real estate with a five-figure income and a home in Linden Hills—*you* do. What I have is a weekly unemployment check and an overdrawn checking account at United Federal. So this studio on Brewster is all I can afford."

"Well, you could afford a lot better," Mrs. Browne snapped, "if you hadn't dropped out of college and had to resort to these dead-end clerical jobs."

"Uh-huh, I knew you'd get around to that before long." Kiswana could feel the rings of anger begin to tighten around her lower backbone, and they sent her forward onto the couch. "You'll never understand, will you? Those bourgie schools were counterrevolutionary. My place was in the streets with my people, fighting for equality and a better community."

"Counterrevolutionary!" Mrs. Browne was raising her voice. "Where's your revolution now,

Melanie? Where are all those black revolutionaries who were shouting and demonstrating and kicking up a lot of dust with you on that campus? Huh? They're sitting in wood-paneled offices with their degrees in mahogany frames, and they won't even drive their cars past this street because the city doesn't fix potholes in this part of town."

"Mama," she said, shaking her head slowly in disbelief, "how can you—a black woman—sit there and tell me that what we fought for during the Movement wasn't important just because some people sold out?"

70   "Melanie, I'm not saying it wasn't important. It was damned important to stand up and say that you were proud of what you were and to get the vote and other social opportunities for every person in this country who had it due. But you kids thought you were going to turn the world upside down, and it just wasn't so. When all the smoke had cleared, you found yourself with a fistful of new federal laws and a country still full of obstacles for black people to fight their way over—just because they're black. There was no revolution, Melanie, and there will be no revolution."

"So what am I supposed to do, huh? Just throw up my hands and not care about what happens to my people? I'm not supposed to keep fighting to make things better?"

"Of course, you can. But you're going to have to fight within the system, because it and these so-called 'bourgie' schools are going to be here for a long time. And that means that you get smart like a lot of your old friends and get an important job where you can have some influence. You don't have to sell out, as you say, and work for some corporation, but you could become an assemblywoman or a civil liberties lawyer or open a freedom school in this very neighborhood. That way you could really help the community. But what help are you going to be to these people on Brewster while you're living hand-to-mouth on file-clerk jobs waiting for a revolution? You're wasting your talents, child."

"Well, I don't think they're being wasted. At least I'm here in day-to-day contact with the problems of my people. What good would I be

after four or five years of a lot of white brainwashing in some phony, prestige institution, huh? I'd be like you and Daddy and those other educated blacks sitting over there in Linden Hills with a terminal case of middle-class amnesia."

"You don't have to live in a slum to be concerned about social conditions, Melanie. Your father and I have been charter members of the NAACP for the last twenty-five years."

75   "Oh, God!" Kiswana threw her head back in exaggerated disgust. "That's being concerned? That middle-of-the-road, Uncle Tom dumping ground for black Republicans!"

"You can sneer all you want, young lady, but that organization has been working for black people since the turn of the century, and it's still working for them. Where are all those radical groups of yours that were going to put a Cadillac in every garage and Dick Gregory in the White House? I'll tell you where."

I knew you would, Kiswana thought angrily.

"They burned themselves out because they wanted too much too fast. Their goals weren't grounded in reality. And that's always been your problem."

"What do you mean, my problem? I know exactly what I'm about."

80   "No, you don't. You constantly live in a fantasy world—always going to extremes—turning butterflies into eagles, and life isn't about that. It's accepting what is and working from that. Lord, I remember how worried you had me, putting all that lacquered hair spray on your head. I thought you were going to get lung cancer—trying to be what you're not."

Kiswana jumped up from the couch. "Oh, God, I can't take this anymore. Trying to be something I'm not—trying to be something I'm not, Mama! Trying to be proud of my heritage and the fact that I was of African descent. If that's being what I'm not, then I say fine. But I'd rather be dead than be like you—a white man's nigger who's ashamed of being black!"

Kiswana saw streaks of gold and ebony light follow her mother's flying body out of the chair. She was swung around by the shoulders and made to face the deadly stillness in the angry woman's eyes. She was too stunned to cry out from the pain of the long fingernails that dug into her shoulders, and she was brought so close to her mother's face that she saw her reflection, distorted and wavering, in the tears that stood in the older woman's eyes. And she listened in that stillness to a story she had heard from a child.

"My grandmother," Mrs. Browne began slowly in a whisper, "was a full-blooded Iroquois, and my grandfather a free black from a long line of journeymen who had lived in Connecticut since the establishment of the colonies. And my father was a Bajan who came to this country as a cabin boy on a merchant mariner."

"I know all that," Kiswana said, trying to keep her lips from trembling.

85   "Then, know this." And the nails dug deeper into her flesh. "I am alive because of the blood of proud people who never scraped or begged or apologized for what they were. They lived asking only one thing of this world—to be allowed to be. And I learned through the blood of these people that black isn't beautiful and it isn't ugly—black is! It's not kinky hair and it's not straight hair—it just is.

"It broke my heart when you changed your name. I gave you my grandmother's name, a woman who bore nine children and educated them all, who held off six white men with a shotgun when they tried to drag one of her sons to jail for 'not knowing his place.' Yet you needed to reach into an African dictionary to find a name to make you proud.

"When I brought my babies home from the hospital, my ebony son and my golden daughter, I swore before whatever gods would listen—those of my mother's people or those of my father's people—that I would use everything I had and could ever get to see that my children were prepared to meet this world on its own terms, so that no one could sell them short and make them ashamed of what they were or how they looked—whatever they were or however they looked. And Melanie, that's not being white or red or black—that's being a mother."

Kiswana followed her reflection in the two single tears that moved down her mother's cheeks until it blended with them into the woman's copper skin. There was nothing and then so much that she wanted to say, but her throat kept closing up every time she tried to speak. She kept her head down and her eyes closed, and thought, Oh, God, just let me die. How can I face her now?

Mrs. Browne lifted Kiswana's chin gently. "And the one lesson I wanted you to learn is not to be afraid to face anyone, not even a crafty old lady like me who can outtalk you." And she smiled and winked.

90   "Oh, Mama, I…" and she hugged the woman tightly.

"Yeah, baby." Mrs. Browne patted her back. "I know."

She kissed Kiswana on the forehead and cleared her throat. "Well, now, I better be moving on. It's getting late, there's dinner to be made, and I have to get off my feet—these new shoes are killing me."

Kiswana looked down at the beige leather pumps. "Those are really classy. They're English, aren't they?"

"Yes, but, Lord, do they cut me right across the instep." She removed the shoe and sat on the couch to massage her foot.

95   Bright red nail polish glared at Kiswana through the stockings. "Since when do you polish your toenails?" she gasped. "You never did that before."

"Well…" Mrs. Browne shrugged her shoulders, "your father sort of talked me into it, and, uh, you know, he likes it and all, so I thought, uh, you know, why not so…" And she gave Kiswana an embarrassed smile.

I'll be damned, the young woman thought, feeling her whole face tingle. Daddy into feet! And she looked at the blushing woman on her couch and suddenly realized that her mother had trod through the same universe that she herself was now traveling. Kiswana was breaking no new trails and would eventually end up just two feet away on that couch. She stared at the woman she had been and was to become.

"But I'll never be a Republican," she caught herself saying aloud.

"What are you mumbling about, Melanie?" Mrs. Browne slipped on her shoe and got up from the couch.

100   She went to get her mother's coat. "Nothing, Mama. It's really nice of you to come by. You should do it more often."

"Well, since it's not Sunday, I guess you're allowed at least one lie."

They both laughed.

After Kiswana had closed the door and turned around, she spotted an envelop sticking between the cushions of her couch. She went over and opened it up; there was seventy-five dollars in it.

"Oh, Mama, darn it!" She rushed to the window and started to call to the woman, who had just emerged from the building, but she suddenly changed her mind and sat down in the chair with a long sigh that caught in the upward draft of the autumn wind and disappeared over the top of the building.

SUGGESTIONS FOR DISCUSSION

1. Gloria Naylor tells this story from Kiswana Browne's point of view. How would the story be different if Naylor had chosen to tell it from Kiswana's mother's point of view? What would be gained? What lost?

2. Consider how Naylor has organized this story—how she establishes a central conflict, leads up to the story's climax, and finally resolves the conflict. Does this type of plot seem familiar? Does the story achieve closure or does it seem open ended? What kinds of satisfaction do readers derive from plots such as this one? What, if anything, do such plots leave out or ignore?

3. Is Naylor making a judgment, whether implicit or explicit, of her characters? Explain your answer.

SUGGESTIONS FOR WRITING

1. Take the perspective of either Kiswana Browne or her mother and write an essay that explains how the character you have chosen sees the other. If you wish, write the essay in the voice of the character. Or you may choose to comment on the character's perceptions of the other and their generational differences in your own voice. In either case, be specific in your use of detail to define generational differences between the two women.

2. On one level, the chapter "Kiswana Browne" seems to be concerned with a generation gap between Kiswana and her mother. At the same time, other factors—race, class, and gender—affect the way generational differences are played out between the two characters. Write an essay that explains to what extent the chapter presents a version of the generation gap and to what extent other factors determine what happens between Kiswana and her mother. Do Kiswana and her mother have things in common, as well as generational differences? How do these factors influence the outcome of the story?

3. "Kiswana Browne" tells of the encounter between a young woman and her family and explores generational differences that have to do with issues such as lifestyle, names, and politics. Can you think of an encounter that you have had with your parents, or that someone you know has had with his or her parents, that involves such telling generational conflicts? (The conflict should be something that highlights differences in generational attitudes, values, or styles—not just "normal" disagreements about using the car or what time curfew should be.) Write an essay that explores such a conflict and explains what generational differences are at stake.

FORTUNATE SON

Dave Marsh

Dave Marsh is one of today's leading rock-and-roll critics. He is the author of books on Bruce Springsteen, Elvis Presley, and The Who. The following selection introduces *Fortunate Son* (1985), a collection of Marsh's shorter critical essays and reviews. In his introduction, Marsh offers a memoir—a remembering—of his adolescence in Pontiac, Michigan, and how listening to rock and roll as a teenager in a working-class community led him to question "not just racism but all the other presumptions that ruled our lives."

SUGGESTION FOR READING Notice that Marsh has divided his memoir into two parts. Part I tells the story of why Marsh's family moved from Pontiac to the suburbs, but Part II is about living in Pontiac before the move. As you read, consider why Marsh has organized his memoir this way. How does Part II comment on what takes place in Part I? Where does Marsh explain the moment of revelation—or epiphany—that stands at the center of his memories?

INTRODUCTION I

> This old town is where I learned about lovin'
> This old town is where I learned to hate
> This town, buddy, has done its share of shoveling
> This town taught me that it's never too late
>
> *Michael Stanley, "My Town"*

1   When I was a boy, my family lived on East Beverly Street in Pontiac, Michigan, in a two-bedroom house with blue-white asphalt shingles that cracked at the edges when a ball was thrown against them and left a powder like talc on fingers rubbed across their shallow grooves. East Beverly ascended a slowly rising hill. At the very top, a block and a half from our place, Pontiac Motors Assembly Line 16 sprawled for a mile or so behind a fenced-in parking lot.

Rust-red dust collected on our windowsills. It piled up no matter how often the place was dusted or cleaned. Fifteen minutes after my mother was through with a room, that dust seemed thick enough for a finger to trace pointless, ashy patterns in it.

The dust came from the foundry on the other side of the assembly line, the foundry that spat angry cinders into the sky all night long. When people talked about hell, I imagined driving past the foundry at night. From the street below, you could see the fires, red-hot flames shaping glowing metal.

Pontiac was a company town, nothing less. General Motors owned most of the land, and in one way or another held mortgages on the rest. Its holdings included not only the assembly line and the foundry but also a Fisher Body plant and on the outskirts, General Motors Truck and Coach. For a while, some pieces of Frigidaires may even have been put together in our town, but that might just be a trick of my memory, which often confuses the tentacles of institutions that monstrous.

5   In any case, of the hundred thousand or so who lived in Pontiac, fully half must have been employed either by GM or one of the tool-and-die shops and steel warehouses and the like that supplied it. And anybody who earned his living locally in some less directly auto-related fashion was only fooling himself if he thought of independence.

My father worked without illusions, as a railroad brakeman on freight trains that shunted boxcars through the innards of the plants, hauled grain from up north, transported the finished Pontiacs on the first leg of the route to almost anywhere Bonnevilles, Catalinas, and GTOs were sold.

Our baseball and football ground lay in the shadow of another General Motors building. That building was of uncertain purpose, at least to me. What I can recall of it now is a seemingly reckless height—five or six stories is a lot in the flatlands around the Great Lakes—and endless walls of dark greenish glass that must have run from floor to ceiling in the rooms inside. Perhaps this building was an engineering facility. We didn't know anyone who worked there, at any rate.

Like most other GM facilities, the green glass building was surrounded by a chain link fence with barbed wire. If a ball happened to land on the other side of it, this fence was insurmountable. But only very strong boys could hit a ball that high, that far, anyhow.

Or maybe it just wasn't worth climbing that particular fence. Each August, a few weeks before the new models were officially presented in the press, the finished Pontiacs were set out in the assembly-line parking lot at the top of our street. They were covered by tarpaulins to keep their design changes secret—these were the years when the appearance of American cars changed radically each year. Climbing *that* fence was a neighborhood sport because that was how you discovered what the new cars looked like, whether fins were shrinking or growing, if the new hoods were pointed or flat, how much thinner the strips of whitewall on the tires had grown. A weird game, since everyone knew people who could have told us, given us exact descriptions, having built those cars with their own hands. But climbing that fence added a hint of danger, made us feel we shared a secret, turned gossip into information.

10   The main drag in our part of town was Joslyn Road. It was where the stoplight and crossing guard were stationed, where the gas station with the condom machine stood alongside a short-order restaurant, drugstore, dairy store, small groceries and a bakery. A few blocks down, past the green glass building, was a low brick building set back behind a wide, lush lawn. This building, identified by a discreet roadside sign, occupied a long block or two. It was the Administration Building for all of Pontiac Motors—a building for executives, clerks, white-collar types. This building couldn't have been more than three-quarters of a mile from my house, yet even though I lived on East Beverly Street from the time I was two until I was past fourteen, I knew only one person who worked there.

In the spring of 1964, when I was fourteen and finishing eighth grade, rumors started going around at Madison Junior High. All the buildings on our side of Joslyn Road (possibly east or west of Joslyn, but I didn't know directions then—there was only "our" side and everywhere else) were about to be bought up and torn down by GM. This was worrisome, but it seemed to me that our parents would never allow that perfectly functioning neighborhood to be broken up for no good purpose.

One sunny weekday afternoon a man came to our door. He wore a coat and tie and a white shirt, which meant something serious in our part of town. My father greeted him at the door, but I don't know whether the businessman had an appointment. Dad was working the extra board in those years, which meant he was called to work erratically—four or five times a week, when business was good—each time his nameplate came to the top of the big duty-roster board down at the yard office. (My father didn't get a regular train of his own to work until 1966; he spent almost twenty years on that extra board, which meant guessing whether it was safe to answer the phone every time he actually wanted a day off—refuse a call and your name went back to the bottom of the list.)

At any rate, the stranger was shown to the couch in our front room. He perched on that old gray davenport with its wiry fabric that bristled and stung against my cheek, and spoke quite earnestly to my parents. I recall nothing of his features or of the precise words he used or even of the tone of his speech. But the dust motes that hung in the air that day are still in my memory, and I can remember his folded hands between his spread knees as he leaned forward in a gesture of complicity. He didn't seem to be selling anything; he was simply stating facts.

He told my father that Pontiac Motors was buying up all the houses in our community from Tennyson Street, across from the green glass building, to Baldwin Avenue—exactly the boundaries of what I'd have described as our neighborhood. GM's price was more than fair; it doubled what little money my father had paid in the early fifties. The number was a little over ten thousand dollars. All the other houses were going, too; some had already been sold. The entire process of tearing our neighborhood down would take about six months, once all the details were settled.

15   The stranger put down his coffee cup, shook hands with my parents and left. As far as I know, he never darkened our doorstep again. In the back of my mind, I can still see him through the front window cutting across the grass to go next door.

"Well, *we're* not gonna move, right, Dad?" I said. Cheeky as I was, it didn't occur to me this wasn't really a matter for adult decision-making—or rather, that the real adults, over at the Administration Building, had already made the only decision that counted. Nor did it occur to me that GM's offer might seem to my father an opportunity to sell at a nice profit, enabling us to move some place "better."

My father did not say much. No surprise. In a good mood, he was the least taciturn man alive, but on the farm where he was raised, not many words were needed to get a serious job done. What he did say that evening indicated that we might stall awhile—perhaps there would be a slightly better offer if we did. But he exhibited no doubt that we would sell. And move.

I was shocked. There was no room in my plans for this…rupture. Was the demolition of our home and neighborhood—that is, my life—truly inevitable? Was there really no way we could avert it, cancel it, *delay* it? What if we just plain *refused to sell*?

Twenty years later, my mother told me that she could still remember my face on that day. It must have reflected extraordinary distress and confusion, for my folks were patient. If anyone refused to sell, they told me, GM would simply build its parking lot—for that was what would replace my world—around him. If we didn't sell, we'd have access privileges, enough space to get into our driveway and that was it. No room to play, and no one there to play with if there had been. And if you got caught in such a situation and didn't like it, then you'd really be in a fix, for the company wouldn't keep its double-your-

money offer open forever. If we held out too long, who knew if the house would be worth anything at all. (I don't imagine that my parents attempted to explain to me the political process of condemnation, but if they had, I would have been outraged, for in a way, I still am.)

My dreams always pictured us as holdouts, living in a little house surrounded by asphalt and automobiles. I always imagined nighttime with the high, white-light towers that illuminated all the other GM parking lots shining down upon our house—and the little guardhouse that the company would have to build and man next door to prevent me from escaping our lot to run playfully among the parked cars of the multitudinous employees. Anyone reading this must find it absurd, or the details heavily derivative of bad concentration-camp literature or maybe too influenced by the Berlin Wall, which had been up only a short time. But it would be a mistake to dismiss its romanticism, which was for many months more real to me than the ridiculous reality—moving to accommodate a *PARKING LOT*—which confronted my family and all my friends' families.

20   If this story were set in the Bronx or in the late sixties, or if it were fiction, the next scenes would be of pickets and protests, meaningful victories and defeats. But this isn't fiction—everything set out here is as unexaggerated as I know how to make it—and the time and the place were wrong for any serious uproar. In this docile midwestern company town, where Walter Reuther's trip to Russia was as inexplicable as the parting of the Red Sea (or as forgotten as the Ark of the Covenant), the idea that a neighborhood might have rights that superseded those of General Motors' Pontiac division would have been regarded as extraordinary, bizarre and subversive. Presuming anyone had had such an idea, which they didn't—none of my friends seemed particularly disturbed about moving, it was just what they would *do*.

So we moved, and what was worse, to the suburbs. This was catastrophic to me. I loved the city, its pavement and the mobility it offered even to kids too young to drive. (Some attitude for a Motor City kid, I know.) In Pontiac, feet or a bicycle could get you anywhere. Everyone had cars, but you weren't immobilized without them, as everyone under sixteen was in the suburbs. In the suburb to which we adjourned, cars were *the* fundamental of life—many of the streets in our new subdivision (not really a neighborhood) didn't even have sidewalks.

Even though I'd never been certain of fitting in, in the city I'd felt close to figuring out how to. Not that I was that weird. But I was no jock and certainly neither suave nor graceful. Still, toward the end of eighth grade, I'd managed to talk to a few girls, no small feat. The last thing I needed was new goals to fathom, new rules to learn, new friends to make.

So that summer was spent in dread. When school opened in the autumn, I was already in a sort of cocoon, confused by the Beatles with their paltry imitations of soul music and the bizarre emotions they stirred in girls.

Meeting my classmates was easy enough, but then it always is. Making new friends was another matter. For one thing, the kids in my new locale weren't the same as the kids in my classes. I was an exceptionally good student (quite by accident—I just read a lot) and my neighbors were classic underachievers. The kids in my classes were hardly creeps, but they weren't as interesting or as accessible as the people I'd known in my old neighborhood or the ones I met at the school bus stop. So I kept to myself.

25   In our new house, I shared a room with my brother at first. We had bunk beds, and late that August I was lying sweatily in the upper one, listening to the radio (WPON-AM, 1460) while my mother and my aunt droned away in the kitchen.

Suddenly my attention was riveted by a record. I listened for two or three minutes more intently than I have ever listened and learned something that remains all but indescribable. It wasn't a new awareness of music. I liked rock and roll already, had since I first saw Elvis when I was six, and I'd been reasonably passionate about the Ronettes, Gary Bonds, Del Shannon, the Crystals, Jackie Wilson, Sam Cooke, the Beach Boys and those first rough but sweet

notes from Motown: the Miracles, the Temptations, Eddie Holland's "Jamie." I can remember a rainy night when I tuned in a faraway station and first heard the end of the Philadelphia Warriors' game in which Wilt Chamberlain scored a hundred points and then found "Let's Twist Again" on another part of the dial. And I can remember not knowing which experience was more splendid.

But the song I heard that night wasn't a new one. "You Really Got a Hold on Me" had been a hit in 1963, and I already loved Smokey Robinson's voice, the way it twined around impossibly sugary lines and made rhymes within the rhythms of ordinary conversation, within the limits of everyday vocabulary.

But if I'd heard those tricks before, I'd never understood them. And if I'd enjoyed rock and roll music previously, certainly it had never grabbed me in quite this way: as a lifeline that suggested—no, insisted—that these singers spoke *for* me as well as to me, and that what they felt and were able to cope with, the deep sorrow, remorse, anger, lust and compassion that bubbled beneath the music, I would also be able to feel and contain. This intimate revelation was what I gleaned from those three minutes of music, and when they were finished and I climbed out of that bunk and walked out the door, the world looked different. No longer did I feel quite so powerless, and if I still felt cheated, I felt capable of getting my own back, some day, some way.

TRAPPED II

It seems I've been playing your game way too long
And it seems the game I've played has made you
   strong

Jimmy Cliff, "Trapped"

That last year in Pontiac, we listened to the radio a lot. My parents always had. One of my most shattering early memories is of the radio blasting when they got up—my mother around four-thirty, my father at five. All of my life I've hated early rising, and for years I couldn't listen to country music without being reminded almost painfully of those days.

30   But in 1963 and 1964, we also listened to WPON in the evening for its live coverage of city council meetings. Pontiac was beginning a decade of racial crisis, of integration pressure and white resistance, the typical scenario. From what was left of our old neighborhood came the outspokenly racist militant anti–school busing movement.

The town had a hard time keeping the shabby secret of its bigotry even in 1964. Pontiac had mushroomed as a result of massive migration during and after World War II. Some of the new residents, including my father, came from nearby rural areas where blacks were all but unknown and even the local Polish Catholics were looked upon as aliens potentially subversive to the community's Methodist piety.

Many more of the new residents of Pontiac came from the South, out of the dead ends of Appalachia and the border states. As many must have been black as white, though it was hard for me to tell that as a kid. There were lines one didn't cross in Michigan, and if I was shocked, when visiting Florida, to see separate facilities labeled "White" and "Colored," as children we never paid much mind to the segregated schools, the lily-white suburbs, the way that jobs in the plants were divided up along race lines. The ignorance and superstition about blacks in my neighborhood were as desperate and crazed in their own way as the feelings in any kudzu-covered parish of Louisiana.

As blacks began to assert their rights, the animosity was not less, either. The polarization was fueled and fanned by the fact that so many displaced Southerners, all with the poor white's investment in racism, were living in our community. But it would be foolish to pretend that the situation would have been any more civilized if only the natives had been around. In fact the Southerners were often regarded with nearly as much condescension and antipathy as blacks— race may have been one of the few areas in which my parents found themselves completely in sympathy with the "hillbillies."

Racism was the great trap of such men's lives, for almost everything could be explained by it, from unemployment to the deterioration of community itself. Casting racial blame did much more than poison these people's entire concept of humanity, which would have been plenty bad enough. It immobilized the racist, preventing folks like my father from ever realizing the real forces that kept their lives tawdry and painful and forced them to fight every day to find any meaning at all in their existence. It did this to Michigan factory workers as effectively as it ever did it to dirt farmers in Dixie.

35   The great psychological syndrome of American males is said to be passive aggression, and racism perfectly fit this mold. To the racist, hatred of blacks gave a great feeling of power and superiority. At the same time, it allowed him the luxury of wallowing in self-pity at the great conspiracy of rich bastards and vile niggers that enforced workaday misery and let the rest of the world go to hell. In short, racism explained everything. There was no need to look any further than the cant of redneck populism, exploited as effectively in the orange clay of the Great Lakes as in the red dirt of Georgia, to find an answer to why it was always the *next* generation that was going to get up and out.

Some time around 1963, a local attorney named Milton Henry, a black man, was elected to Pontiac's city council. Henry was smart and bold—he would later become an ally of Martin Luther King, Jr., of Malcolm X, a principal in the doomed Republic of New Africa. The goals for which Henry was campaigning seem extremely tame now, until you realize the extent to which they haven't been realized in twenty years: desegregated schools, integrated housing, a chance at decent jobs.

Remember that Martin Luther King would not take his movement for equality into the North for nearly five more years, and that when he did, Dr. King there faced the most strident and violent opposition he'd ever met, and you will understand how inflammatory the mere presence of Milton Henry on the city council was. Those council sessions, broadcast live on WPON, invested the radio with a vibrancy and vitality that television could never have had. Those hours of imprecations, shouts and clamor are unforgettable. I can't recall specific words or phrases, though, just Henry's eloquence and the pandemonium that greeted each of his speeches.

So our whole neighborhood gathered round its radios in the evenings, family by family, as if during wartime. Which in a way I guess it was—surely that's how the situation was presented to the children, and not only in the city. My Pontiac junior high school was lightly integrated, and the kids in my new suburban town had the same reaction as my Floridian cousins: shocked that I'd "gone to school with niggers," they vowed they would die—or kill—before letting the same thing happen to them.

This cycle of hatred didn't immediately elude me. Thirteen-year-olds are built to buck the system only up to a point. So even though I didn't dislike any of the blacks I met (it could hardly be said that I was given the opportunity to know any), it was taken for granted that the epithets were essentially correct. After all, anyone could see the grave poverty in which most blacks existed, and the only reason ever given for it was that they liked living that way.

40   But listening to the radio gave free play to one's imagination. Listening to music, that most abstract of human creations, unleashed it all the more. And not in a vacuum. Semiotics, the New Criticism, and other formalist approaches have never had much appeal to me, not because I don't recognize their validity in describing certain creative structures but because they emphasize those structural questions without much consideration of content: And that simply doesn't jibe with my experience of culture, especially popular culture.

The best example is the radio of the early 1960s. As I've noted, there was no absence of rock and roll in those years betwixt the outbreaks of Presley and Beatles. Rock and roll was a constant for me, the best music around, and I had loved it ever since I first heard it, which was about as soon as I could remember hearing anything.

In part, I just loved the sound—the great mystery one could hear welling up from "Duke

of Earl," "Up on the Roof," "Party Lights"; that pit of loneliness and despair that lay barely concealed beneath the superficial bright spirits of a record like Bruce Channel's "Hey Baby"; the nonspecific terror hidden away in Del Shannon's "Runaway." But if that was all there was to it, then rock and roll records would have been as much an end in themselves—that is, as much a dead end—as TV shows like *Leave It to Beaver* (also mysterious, also—thanks to Eddie Haskell—a bit terrifying).

To me, however, TV was clearly an alien device, controlled by the men with shirts and ties. Nobody on television dressed or talked as the people in my neighborhood did. In rock and roll, however, the language spoken was recognizably my own. And since one of the givens of life in the outlands was that we were barbarians, who produced no culture and basically consumed only garbage and trash, the thrill of discovering depths within rock and roll, the very part that was most often and explicitly degraded by teachers and pundits, was not only marvelously refreshing and exhilarating but also in essence liberating—once you'd made the necessary connections.

It was just at this time that pop music was being revolutionized—not by the Beatles, arriving from England, a locale of certifiable cultural superiority, but by Motown, arriving from Detroit, a place without even a hint of cultural respectability. Produced by Berry Gordy, not only a young man but a *black* man. And in that spirit of solidarity with which hometown boys (however unalike) have always identified with one another, Motown was mine in a way that no other music up to that point had been. Surely no one spoke my language as effectively as Smokey Robinson, able to string together the most humdrum phrases and effortlessly make them sing.

45   That's the context in which "You Really Got a Hold on Me" created my epiphany. You can look at this coldly—structurally—and see nothing more than a naked marketing mechanism, a clear-cut case of a teenager swaddled in and swindled by pop culture. Smokey Robinson wrote and sang the song as much to make a buck

as to express himself; there was nothing of the purity of the mythical artist about his endeavor. In any case, the emotion he expressed was unfashionably sentimental. In releasing the record, Berry Gordy was mercenary in both instinct and motivation. The radio station certainly hoped for nothing more from playing it than that its listeners would hang in through the succeeding block of commercials. None of these people and institutions had any intention of elevating their audience, in the way that Leonard Bernstein hoped to do in his *Young People's Concerts* on television. Cultural indoctrination was far from their minds. Indeed, it's unlikely that anyone involved in the process thought much about the kids on the other end of the line except as an amorphous mass of ears and wallets. The pride Gordy and Robinson had in the quality of their work was private pleasure, not public.

Smokey Robinson was not singing of the perils of being a black man in this world (though there were other rock and soul songs that spoke in guarded metaphors about such matters). Robinson was not expressing an experience as alien to my own as a country blues singer's would have been. Instead, he was putting his finger firmly upon a crucial feeling of vulnerability and longing. It's hard to think of two emotions that a fourteen-year-old might feel more deeply (well, there's lust…), and yet in my hometown expressing them was all but absolutely forbidden to men. This doubled the shock of Smokey Robinson's voice, which for years I've thought of as falsetto, even though it really isn't exceptionally high-pitched compared to the spectacular male sopranos of rock and gospel lore.

"You Really Got a Hold on Me" is not by any means the greatest song Smokey Robinson ever wrote or sang, not even the best he had done up to that point. The singing on "Who's Loving You," the lyrics of "I'll Try Something New," the yearning of "What's So Good About Goodbye" are all at least as worthy. Nor is there anything especially newfangled about the song. Its trembling blues guitar, sturdy drum pattern, walking bass and call-and-response voice arrangement are not very different from many of the other Miracles records of that period. If there is a single instant in the record which is unforgettable by itself, it's probably the opening lines: "I don't like you/But I love you…"

The contingency and ambiguity expressed in those two lines and Robinson's singing of them was also forbidden in the neighborhood of my youth, and forbidden as part and parcel of the same philosophy that propounded racism. Merely calling the bigot's certainty into question was revolutionary—not merely rebellious. The depth of feeling in that Miracles record, which could have been purchased for 69¢ at any K-Mart, overthrew the premise of racism, which was that blacks were not as human as we, that they could not feel—much less express their feelings—as deeply as we did.

When the veil of racism was torn from my eyes, everything else that I knew or had been told was true for fourteen years was necessarily called into question. For if racism explained everything, then without racism, not a single commonplace explanation made any sense. *Nothing* else could be taken at face value. And that meant asking every question once again, including the banal and obvious ones.

For those who've never been raised under the weight of such addled philosophy, the power inherent in having the burden lifted is barely imaginable. Understanding that blacks weren't worthless meant that maybe the rest of the culture in which I was raised was also valuable. If you've never been told that you and your community are worthless—that a parking lot takes precedence over your needs—perhaps that moment of insight seems trivial or rather easily won. For anyone who was never led to expect a life any more difficult than one spent behind a typewriter, maybe the whole incident verges on being something too banal for repetition (though in that case, I'd like to know where the other expressions of this story can be read). But looking over my shoulder, seeing the consequences to my life had I not begun questioning not just racism but all of the other presumptions that ruled our lives, I know for certain how and how much I got over.

That doesn't make me better than those on the other side of the line. On the other hand, I won't trivialize the tale by insisting upon how fortunate I was. What was left for me was a raging passion to explain things in the hope that others would not be trapped and to keep the way clear so that others from the trashy outskirts of barbarous America still had a place to stand—if not in the culture at large, at least in rock and roll.

Of course it's not so difficult to dismiss this entire account. Great revelations and insights aren't supposed to emerge from listening to rock and roll records. They're meant to emerge only from encounters with art. (My encounters with Western art music were unavailing, of course, because every one of them was prefaced by a lecture on the insipid and worthless nature of the music that I preferred to hear.) Left with the fact that what happened to me did take place, and that it was something that was supposed to come only out of art, I reached the obvious conclusion. You are welcome to your own.

SUGGESTIONS FOR DISCUSSION

1. Marsh uses the Smokey Robinson and the Miracles' song "You Really Got a Hold on Me" to anchor his memoir. In fact, it is Marsh's recollection of listening to this song that provides the grounds for the "intimate revelation" or "epiphany" that Marsh sets up at the end of Part I and then explains more fully in Part II. What exactly is this revelation, and how does it emerge from Marsh's experience of listening to rock and roll?

2. In Marsh's view, racism is connected to the powerlessness felt by members of the white working-class community in Pontiac. Explain that connection. What does Marsh mean when he talks about racism as the "great trap"? How does Marsh's understanding of racism divide him from the older generation in Pontiac?

3. Marsh explains that rock-and-roll singers "spoke for as well as to me." Can you think of other examples of singers speaking for you or for some other individual or group? Explain what the singer gave voice to in your own or others' experience.

SUGGESTIONS FOR WRITING

1. Dave Marsh's memoir about growing up in Pontiac, Michigan, serves as the introduction to a collection of his essays and reviews of rock and roll. In this sense, the introduction is meant to present his reasons for writing about rock and roll. At the end of the memoir, Marsh says: "I reached the obvious conclusion. You are welcome to your own." Write an essay that explains what conclusions Marsh reaches and why. Do his conclusions seem persuasive to you? Assess how well Marsh enables you to understand his perspective on growing up in Pontiac. What conclusions do you draw?

2. One of the striking features of Dave Marsh's memoir about growing up in Pontiac is his attention to class. As Marsh shows, the sense of powerlessness rock and roll spoke to in his experience grows out of the relation between his working-class community in Pontiac and the dominant economic interests in society, represented by General Motors. Depending on class position, people's feelings can range from the sense of powerlessness that Marsh describes to the persistent anxieties of the middle classes about maintaining their socioeconomic status to the self-confidence of the economically secure and their sense of entitlement to society's rewards. Write an essay that analyzes how the class character of your family and the community in which you grew up has shaped your own sense of power or powerlessness and your expectations about what you are entitled to in life. Note whether there are significant differences in expectations between generations. If there are, how would you explain them? If not, how would you explain the continuity between generations?

3. As you have seen, Marsh uses the Smokey Robinson song "You Really Got a Hold on Me" to trigger the central revelation of the memoir, the moment when "the veil of racism was torn from my eyes" and everything "was necessarily called into question." Use an

encounter that you have had with a song, an album, a live performance, a movie, or some other form of popular culture to write a memoir explaining such a moment of insight in your experience. The revelation doesn't have to change everything, as it does for Marsh, but it does need to indicate something notable—a new outlook, a shift in attitude, a discovery of one sort or another—that you can link to your encounter. Following Marsh's example, your task is to tell a story in sufficient detail that explains how and why the encounter had such a powerful impact on you. What was it that gave the song, album, movie, or other thing such force? What was it about the circumstances at the time that made you especially open to such influence?

YOUTH AND AMERICAN IDENTITY

Lawrence Grossberg

Lawrence Grossberg is the Morris Davis Professor of Communication at the University of North Carolina–Chapel Hill. A cultural critic who writes about popular culture and rock music, his essays have been collected in two volumes, *Bringing It All Back Home* (1997) and *Dancing in Spite of Myself* (1997). This selection appears in the latter volume. It is taken from "It's a Sin: Essays on Postmodernism, Politics, and Culture," a study of the connections between politics and popular culture in the Reagan era. In the following excerpt, Grossberg explains how after World War II, young people came to be seen as a living symbol of a unified national identity.

SUGGESTION FOR READING As you read, notice that Lawrence Grossberg has organized this section from his longer essay in a problem-and-solution format. To follow Grossberg's line of thought, underline and annotate the passages where he defines what he sees as the problem of American national identity and where he explains how American young people were represented as the solution in the post–World War II period.

1   The meaning of "America" has always been a problem. Except for rare moments, Americans have rarely had a shared sense of identity and unity. Rather, the United States has always been a country of differences without a center. The "foreign" has always been centrally implicated in our identity because we were and are a nation of immigrants. (Perhaps that partly explains why Americans took up anti-communism with such intensity—here at least was an "other," a definition of the foreign, which could be construed as non-American, as a threatening presence which defied integration.) It is a nation without a tradition, for its history depends upon a moment of founding violence which almost entirely eradicated the native population, thereby renouncing any claim to an identity invested in the land. And despite various efforts to define some "proper" ethnic and national origin, it is precisely the image of the melting pot, this perpetual sense of the continuing presence of the other within the national identity, that has defined the uniqueness of the nation. It is a nation predicated upon differences, but always desperately constructing an imaginary unity. The most common and dominant solution to this in its history involved constituting the identity of the United States in the future tense; it was the land of possibility, the "beacon on the hill," the new world, the young nation living out its "manifest destiny." Perhaps the only way in which the diversity of populations and regions could be held together was to imagine itself constantly facing frontiers. It is this perpetual ability to locate and conquer new frontiers, a sense embodied within "the American dream" as a recurrent theme, that has most powerfully defined a national sense of cultural uniqueness.

After what the nation took to be "its victory" in the second world war it anxiously faced a depressing contradiction. On the one hand, the young nation had grown up, taking its "rightful" place as the leader of the "free world." On the other hand, what had defined its victory—its very identity—depended upon its continued sense of difference from the "grown-up" (i.e., corrupt, inflexible, etc.) European nations. It was America's openness to possibility, its commitment to itself as the future, its ability to reforge its differences into a new and self-consciously temporary unity, that had conquered the fascist threat to freedom. The postwar period can be described by the embodiments of this contradiction: it was a time of enormous conservative pressure (we had won the war protecting the American way; it was time to enjoy it and not rock the boat) and a time of increasingly rapid change, not only in the structures of the social formation but across the entire surface of everyday life. It was a time as schizophrenic as the baby boom generation onto which it projected its contradictions. Resolving this lived dilemma demanded that America still be located in and defined by a future, by an American dream but that the dream be made visible and concrete. If the dream had not yet been realized, it would be shortly. Thus, if this dream were to effectively define the nation in its immediate future, if there was to be any reality to this vision, it would have to be invested, not just in some abstract future, but in a concrete embodiment of America's future, i.e., in a specific generation. Hence, the American identity was projected upon the children of those who had to confront the paradox of America in the postwar years. But if the dream was to be real for them, and if it were to be immediately realizable, people would have to have children and have children they did! And they would have to define those children as the center of their lives and of the nation; the children would become the justification for everything they had done, the source of the very meaning of their lives as individuals and as a nation.

The baby-boom created an enormous population of children by the mid-fifties, a population which became the concretely defined image of the nation's future, a future embodied in a specific generation of youth who would finally realize the American dream and hence become its living symbol. This was to be "the best fed, best dressed, best educated generation" in history, the living proof of the American dream, the realization of the future in the present. The American identity slid from a contentless image of the future to a powerful, emotionally invested image of a generation. America found itself by identifying its meaning with a generation whose identity was articulated by the meanings and promises of youth. Youth, as it came to define a generation, also came to define America itself. And this generation took up the identification as its own fantasy. Not only was its own youthfulness identified with the perpetual youthfulness of the nation, but its own generational identity was defined by its necessary and continued youthfulness. But youth in this equation was not measured simply in terms of age; it was an ideological and cultural signifier, connected to utopian images of the future and of this generation's ability to control the forces of change and to make the world over in its own images. But it was also articulated by economic images of the teenager as consumer, and by images of the specific sensibilities, styles and forms of popular culture which this generation took as its own (hence, the necessary myth that rock and roll was made by American youth). Thus, what was placed as the new defining center of the nation was a generation, an ideological commitment to youth, and a specific popular cultural formation. Obviously, this "consensus" constructed its own powerfully selective frontier: it largely excluded those fractions of the population (e.g., black) which were never significantly traversed by the largely white middle class youth culture. Nevertheless, for the moment, the United States had an identity, however problematic the very commitment to youth was and would become, and it had an apparently perpetually renewable national popular; it had a culture which it thought of as inherently American and which it identified with its own embodied image of itself and its future.

But this was, to say the least, a problematic solution to America's search for an identity, not merely because any generation of youth has to grow up and, one assumes, renounce their youthfulness, but also because "youth" was largely, even in the fifties, an empty signifier. As [Carolyn] Steedman says, "children are always episodes in someone else's narratives, not their own people, but rather brought into being for someone else's purpose." Youth has no meaning except perhaps its lack of meaning, its energy, its commitment to openness and change, its celebratory relation to the present, and its promise of the future. Youth offers no structure of its own with which it can organize and give permanence to a national identity. That is, youth itself, like America, can only be defined apparently in a for-ever receding future. How could this generation possibly fulfill its own identity and become the American dream—become a future which is always as yet unrealized and unrealizable? How could a generation hold on to its own self-identity as youthful, and at the same time, fulfill the responsibility of its identification with the nation? What does it mean to have constructed a concrete yet entirely mobile center for a centerless nation? Perhaps this rather paradoxical position explains the sense of failure that characterizes the postwar generations, despite the fact that they did succeed in reshaping the cultural and political terrain of the United States.

SUGGESTIONS FOR DISCUSSION

1. Define the problem of American national identity as Grossberg poses it early in this selection. How and in what sense did American young people become a "solution" to this "problem" in the post–World War II period?

2. Grossberg notes that the national commitment to youth set up its own "powerfully selective frontier," excluding, among others, young African Americans. Examine the claim that Grossberg makes here that the image of youth in the popular imagination after World War II was largely a white middle-class one—marked in the media as white "teenagers" but "black youth." Explain why you do or do not find the claim persuasive. What further evidence could you offer, one way or the other? If you agree with the claim, does it still hold true?

3. At the end of this selection, Grossberg suggests that youth is a "problematic solution to America's search for identity." What makes the solution problematic? What is the "sense of failure that characterizes the postwar generations, despite the fact that they did succeed in reshaping the cultural and political terrain of the United States"?

SUGGESTIONS FOR WRITING

1. Lawrence Grossberg quotes Carolyn Steedman's remark that "children are always episodes in someone else's narratives, not their own people, but rather brought into being for someone else's purposes." Apply this quote to your own experience growing up. Write an essay that explains how your life might be seen as an "episode" in "someone else's narrative." Take into account the hopes your parents and other significant adults invested in you and your future.

2. Grossberg opens this selection by saying that "the United States has always been a country of differences without a center." He describes American national identity as one "predicated upon differences, but always desperately constructing an imaginary unity." Write an essay that explains how you would describe America's national identity. To do this, consider whether you see a "shared sense of identity and unity" or whether, as Grossberg suggests, American identity should be characterized according to its diversity and the "continuing presence of the other within the national identity."

3. Gloria Naylor in "Kiswana Browne," Dave Marsh in "Fortunate Son," and Lawrence Grossberg in "Youth and American Identity" have written of the issue of generational identity, though in quite different ways. Naylor has written a fictional account, which is a chapter from her novel *The Women of Brewster Place;* Marsh has written a memoir

based on his own experience; and the selection from Grossberg's "It's a Sin" takes an analytical perspective on the emotional and cultural investments made in American youth in the post–World War II period. Because each of these writers uses such a different writing strategy, he or she is likely to have different effects on his or her readers. Write an essay that compares the writing strategies. What do you see as the advantages and disadvantages of each writer's attempt to address the issue of generational identity? What effects are the writers' various strategies likely to have on readers?

TEENAGE WASTELAND

Donna Gaines

Donna Gaines writes regularly for the *Village Voice.* She also writes regularly for *Rolling Stone* and *SPIN.* She holds a Ph.D. in sociology, has worked as a social worker with teenagers, and teaches at Barnard College. The following selection is taken from Gaines's book *Teenage Wasteland* (1990), an investigative report on the suicide pact carried out by four "heavy metal" kids in the working-class suburbs of northern New Jersey in 1987. Gaines does not believe in the traditional neutrality of the reporter toward her subjects but instead aligns herself with the "burnouts" and takes on the task of telling their side of the story.

SUGGESTION FOR READING   This selection is set on the first anniversary of the suicide pact—a time of reckoning with the event and what it meant for the Bergenfield community. Notice how Gaines treats the explanations of "why they did it" offered by various adults, journalists, and officials.

III

1   On the first anniversary of the suicide pact, a number of special follow-up news reports aired on local and national television. We saw many of the same faces—officials, loyal students of Bergenfield High School, mental health administrators. Over the year the town had gained a certain moral authority—it had survived the suicide pact as well as the media invasion. The community had learned something and had grown. By now, Bergenfield's representatives also knew how to work media.

On WABC's *Nightline,* we would learn of Bergenfield's "new awareness," its comprehensive battery of preventive services. We would see signs advertising "help" posted in store windows all over town, wherever kids might hang around. There was a hot line, and Bergenfield police were getting special training for suicide calls. Bergenfield High School would implement a "peer leadership" program. Parents would get involved at the school. There was an aggressive youth out-

reach program. The town would take pride in itself as a model for other towns to follow. Officials would seek out federal and state funding so that these programs could continue to help Bergenfield's youth. The town had been successful with its rational responses to a serious social problem. This is how Bergenfield would present itself to the television world.

On a local news program, there was a brief clip of a follow-up visit to Bergenfield High, on the anniversary of the suicide pact. Wholesome and alert students selected to represent the school sat around a table with their principal, Lance Rosza, and reiterated what had become *the* story about the Bergenfield suicide pact. The four kids "had nothing to do with the school." They had "chosen" to drop out. They committed suicide because they had "personal problems."

Police lieutenant Donald Stumpf, who had also served as school board president, admitted that Bergenfield was "weak on dropouts." A juvenile officer, Stumpf noted that once the kids drop out, "they go to never-neverland." Maybe that's where they came from, since the school took every opportunity to point out that it had nothing to do with its students' dropping out. Suddenly the "burnouts" appeared in this state of social dislocation, as if by magic. They had no involvement with the school or the town. By choice they turned their backs on all the available support, concern, and care. They were self-made outcasts, disengaged atoms floating in space somewhere over Bergenfield. There was no discussion of the process, only the product.

5   In the end, Bergenfield High School would be vindicated by its more devoted students, honored for its "involvement" with potential dropouts and their families. Supposedly, the town's "new awareness" and the preventive services had paid off: a few dropouts had been saved, or at least temporarily reprogrammed. In fact, Bergenfield officials had implemented programs so successfully they were now deemed worthy of replication in communities across America. And finally, everybody agreed Lisa, Cheryl, Tommy Rizzo, and Tommy Olton had committed suicide because they had *personal problems*.

Once the event was understood, explained under the banner of *personal problems,* entire sets of questions could be logically excluded. Yes, the four kids did have personal problems. But maybe there was more to it than that.

Some explanations for "why they did it" were formulated with compassion and sincerity, others were handed down contemptuously, callously. There was no organized conspiracy to keep "the burnouts'" own story silent. But it was kept silent—it was now outside the discourse which framed the event. In a sense, the burnouts' story, their view of things, was evacuated from the social text.

Once we all agreed that the four kids had banded together in a suicide pact because they had *personal problems,* we no longer needed to ask what "the burnouts" were alienating themselves from. Or what role their identification as "burnouts" played in the way they felt about themselves, their families, their school, or their town.

With the suicide pact explained away as the result of *personal problems,* it would be reasonable to believe that aided by Satan, drugs, and rock & roll, four "troubled losers" pulled each other down, deeper and deeper, into an abyss of misery until they finally idled themselves out of it.

10   If we understood the Bergenfield suicide pact as the result of *personal problems,* we would then have to remove the event from its social context. And once we did that, the story according to "the burnouts" would never be known; it would be buried with the four kids.

There were other reasons why "the burnouts" themselves weren't being heard. First, they had little access to the media. They weren't likely to be on hand when Bergenfield High School authorities needed bright, articulate youth to represent the school or the town to reporters. "Alienated youth" don't hang around teachers or shrinks any longer than they have to.

Second, to the chagrin of their caretakers, "burnouts" aren't particularly "verbal." The basic life-world shared by teenage suburban metalheads is action-oriented: best understood in context, through signs and symbols in motion. It would be hard to convey one's thoughts and feelings to reporters in the succinct lines that make up the news.

In the beginning "the burnouts" did talk to reporters, but things got twisted around—"the papers got the story all fucked up"—and besides, they really hated hearing their friends and their town maligned by strangers. So they clammed right up.

The kids everybody called burnouts understood this: Once you open the door, they've got you. You're playing their language game. Whatever you say can be held against you. At the very least, it changes meaning once it's out of the context created by you and your friends. Better to keep it to yourself. So programs existed in Bergenfield but "the burnouts" didn't dare use them. They may have been outcasts, but they weren't stupid. They knew to avoid trouble.

15   Kids who realize that they are marginal fear reprisals. Over and over again I was asked not to

mention names. And no pictures. As a rule, teenagers love performing for the media. It's a game that lets adults think they understand "kids today," and it's fun. But "the burnouts" were now media wise. They knew better. They wanted complete control or they weren't saying shit.

So by design and by default, nobody really got to hear what "the burnouts" had to say. Like any other alienated youth since the conceptualization of "youth" as a social category, they don't like to talk to adults. About anything. After the suicide pact a few "burnouts" told reporters they were reluctant to confide in school guidance counselors because the counselors might tell their parents and "they'd be punished or even sent to a psychiatric hospital."

The idea of troubled youth doing themselves in was especially disturbing to a town that boasted over thirty active programs for its youth prior to the suicide pact of March 11. Yet Lieutenant Stumpf noted that the Bergenfield kids who most needed the services would not make use of them.

Authorities had acknowledged that the more "alienated" or "high-risk" youth of Bergenfield would not voluntarily involve themselves with the town's services. But the kids weren't talking about what it was that held them back, why they weren't looking to confide in the adults.

In the local papers, experts called in to comment on the tragedy referred to this as "the conspiracy of silence"—the bond of secrecy between teenage friends. While there was some acknowledgment that this reflected kids' terror of "getting in trouble," nobody questioned whether or not this fear might be rational.

20   Yet it was becoming clear that for Bergenfield's marginally involved youth, the idea of going to see a school guidance counselor or really "opening up" to parents, shrinks, and even clergy was inconceivable. It was apparent that even if they had done nothing wrong, they felt guilty.

On those rare occasions when "burnouts" spoke to reporters, it was obvious that any brush with authority carried the promise of trouble, fear of punishment, of getting snagged for *something*. Enemy lines were drawn. "Burnouts" articulated little confidence that they could be understood by their appointed caretakers, and they assumed that fair treatment was unlikely. Even being able to relate on any level of natural comfort was out of the question.

By now it was also apparent that the "burnouts," as a clique, as carriers of a highly visible "peer-regulated" subculture, posed a threat to the hegemony of parents, teachers, and other mandated "agents of socialization" in Bergenfield. The initial blaming of the suicide victims' friends for whatever had gone wrong did take some of the pressure off the parents and the school. This was predictable—after all, "Where'd you learn that from, your friends?" is a well-traveled technique adults use to challenge and suppress a kid's dissenting view.

While some "burnouts" did complain to reporters about feeling neglected by the town, the school, and their parents, some were just as happy to be left alone. This was a loosely connected network of friends and acquaintances who appeared to live in a world of their own, almost discontinuous from the rest of the town.

Readings of youth, from the *Rebel Without a Cause* 1950s to *The River's Edge* 1980s, have explored the young person's long-standing critique of the adult world: Nobody talks about what is really going on. Especially not parents, and never at school. The "burnouts" seemed to understand that very well. Yet the "insularity" of this group of outcasts frustrated adults everywhere. It annoyed them as much as "explosive inside views" might have titillated them.

25   These kids were actively guarding their psychic space because the adults controlled everything else. Yet the experts on the scene continued to urge the "burnouts" to purge. Forget about it. It's no secret, you give them an inch and they'll take a self. Bergenfield's alienated youth population already had a different way of seeing things. How *could* they reach out and speak up? When every day up until the suicide pact, and shortly thereafter, they were encouraged to suppress what *they* perceived to be reality? When living means having to deny what you feel, disassociating yourself to survive, you better stay close to your friends or you could start to believe the bull-

shit. Yes, the "burnouts" carried the news, they knew the truth. They all understood what that "something evil in the air" was. Alone, it made them crazy. Together, it made them *bad*.

SUGGESTIONS FOR DISCUSSION

1. Donna Gaines notes that school officials, mental health workers, and others from Bergenfield explained the suicide pact as the result of "personal problems." Why do you think this explanation became the dominant response to the suicides? Why would this explanation appeal to those in positions of authority? What, in Gaines's view, does this explanation of the suicides evade?

2. Gaines puts considerable emphasis on the suspicion of the "burnouts" toward the media, schools, and the world of adults in general. How does she explain this suspicion? To what extent does it seem reasonable or unreasonable?

3. The media have sensationalized teenage suicide by linking it to heavy-metal music and Satanism. Groups such as Black Sabbath, Ozzy Osbourne, Iron Maiden, Judas Priest, and Metallica have been blamed for instigating suicides among heavy-metal fans. At the same time, teens such as the Bergenfield "burnouts" in part define their group identity as "metalheads"—which sets up a classic case of young people versus adults. What do you know about heavy-metal music? Do you listen to it or know people who do? Why has heavy-metal music become so controversial? Work with two or three other students to answer these questions. Pool the information that you have about heavy-metal music. If you are not familiar with the music, you may want to interview a heavy-metal fan.

SUGGESTIONS FOR WRITING

1. One of Gaines's key points is that adults' tendency to explain the suicides as the result of "personal problems" evades some deeper questions about what it is the "burnouts" are alienated from and how their identities as "burnouts" shape their relations to each other, their families, their schools, and their communities. She wants us to think about them, in other words, not as isolated individuals but as a social phenomenon—a coherent subculture of "metalheads." Take Gaines's point seriously by using it to analyze a group or subculture of alienated teenagers you know something about. Follow Gaines's model for this assignment by writing an account that is sympathetic to troubled or marginalized young people. Imagine that your task is to explain to readers why the group of young people is alienated from the official system and what holds together their subculture.

2. The media have been fascinated by teenage suicide and its sensationalistic connection to heavy-metal music and Satanism. Write a report that explains how adult culture represents heavy-metal music and what, in your view, is at stake for the relationship between generations.

   You might, for example, visit the Web site of the Parents Music Resource Group, which was established by Tipper Gore to monitor teenage listening preferences. Or you might investigate the 1990 trial in which a $6.2 million product liability suit charged Judas Priest with inspiring the suicides of two Nevada teenagers. (*Reader's Guide to Periodical Literature* should provide you with the sources that you need.)

3. Gaines says that "burnouts" in Bergenfield systematically avoided social services and youth programs directed at "high-risk" young people. Their suspicion of adult culture was simply too high. Write an essay that explains what kinds of programs might succeed. How could they overcome young people's fears and suspicions? You don't have to limit yourself to the Bergenfield "burnouts" for this assignment. Draw on your knowledge, observations, and experience with troubled young people in other settings.

GOTHS IN TOMORROWLAND

Thomas Hine

Thomas Hine is well known for his writing about architecture and design. He is the author of *Populuxe* (1987), a book on American design in the 1950s and 1960s, and *The Total Package* (1995), a study of brand names and packaging. The following selection comes from his most recent book, *The Rise and Fall of the American Teenager* (1999). Hine explores the diversity of teen culture and its relation to adult society.

SUGGESTION FOR READING Hine begins with an anecdote about the goth "invasion" of Disneyland in 1997 and the "zero tolerance" policy adopted by Disney's security forces. Notice that Hine wants to do more than just tell his story. He sees in it a larger issue about how the "mere presence of teenagers threatens us." As you read, keep in mind this general theme of the alienation of teenagers from adult society, how adults enforce it, and how teenagers maintain it.

I feel stupid and contagious.

Kurt Cobain, "Smells Like Teen Spirit" (1991)

1   In the summer of 1997, the security forces at Disneyland and the police in surrounding Ana-heim, California, announced a "zero tolerance" policy to fend off a new threat.

Hordes of pale, mascaraed goths—one of the many tribes of teendom—were invading. It was an odd onslaught. Unlike their barbarian namesakes, they weren't storming the gates of the walled Magic Kingdom. They had yearly passes, purchased for $99 apiece. Many of them had not even been goths when their parents dropped them off at the edge of the parking lot. Rather, they changed into their black some-times gender-bending garments, applied their white makeup accented with black eyeliner and gray blush-on. The punkier among them acces-sorized with safety pins and other aggressively ugly, uncomfortable-looking pierceables. And most important of all, they reminded them-selves to look really glum. Once inside, they headed for Tomorrowland, Disneyland's most unsettled neighborhood, and hogged all the benches.

It was a sacrilege. Disneyland, said those who wrote letters to the editor, is supposed to be "the happiest place on earth," and these young people with their long faces clearly didn't belong. The presence of sullen clusters of costumed teens showed, some argued, that Disney had given up its commitment to family values. It was no longer possible to feel safe in Disneyland, came the complaints, and that was about the last safe place left.

Actually, the safety of Disneyland was part of the attraction for the goth teens. They told reporters that their parents bought them season passes because the theme park's tight security would assure nothing bad would happen to them. In the vast sprawl of Orange County, Cali-fornia, there are very few safe places where teens are welcome, and Disneyland has always been one of them.

Those who complained spoke of the goths as if they were some sort of an alien force, not just white suburban California teenagers. Only a few years earlier, they had been kids who were delighted to go with their parents to meet Mickey. And only a few years from now, they will be young adults—teaching our children, cleaning our teeth, installing our cable televi-sion. But now they insist on gloom. And the adult world could not find a place for them—even in Tomorrowland.

5   Unlike Minnesota's Mall of America—which became a battleground for gang warfare trans-

planted from Minneapolis and which eventually barred unescorted teenagers from visiting at night—the perceived threat to Disneyland was handled in a low-key way. Teenagers were arrested for even the tiniest infractions outside the park and forced by security guards to follow Disneyland's quite restrictive rules of decorum within the park. After all, the theme park's administrators had an option not available to government; they could revoke the yearly passes. While Disneyland doesn't enforce a dress code for its visitors, it can keep a tight rein on their behavior.

Yet, despite its lack of drama, I think the situation is significant because it vividly raises many of the issues that haunt teenagers' lives at the end of the twentieth century. It is about the alienation of teenagers from adult society, and equally about the alienation of that society from its teenagers. The mere presence of teenagers threatens us.

It is also a story about space. How, in an environment devoid of civic spaces, do we expect people to learn how to behave as members of a community? And it is about the future. Is a meaningful tomorrow so far away that young people can find nothing better to do than engage in faux-morbid posturing? (Even Disney's theme parks are losing track of the future; they are converting their Tomorrowlands into nostalgic explorations of how people used to think about the future a century and more ago.)

And even its resolution—a stance of uneasy tolerance backed by coercion and force—seems symptomatic of the way Americans deal with young people now.

Inevitably, a lack of perspective bedevils efforts to recount the recent past, but the problem is more than that. The last quarter of the twentieth century has, in a sense, been about fragmentation. Identity politics has led to a sharpening of distinctions among the groups in the society, and a suspicion of apparent majorities. Postmodern literary theory warns us to mistrust narratives. Even advertising and television, which once united the country in a common belief in consumption, now sell to a welter of micromarkets. Thus we are left without either a common myth, or even the virtual common ground of *The Ed Sullivan Show*.

10   It seems crude now to speak of teenagers and think of the white middle-class, heterosexual young people that the word "teenager" was originally coined to describe. The "echo" generation of teenagers, whose first members are now entering high school, is about 67 percent non-Hispanic white, 15 percent black, 14 percent Hispanic, and 5 percent Asian or American Indian. The proportion of Hispanic teens will grow each year, and the Census Bureau also reports significantly greater numbers of mixed-race teens and adoptees who are racially different from their parents.

Even the word "Hispanic" is a catch-all that conceals an enormous range of cultural difference between Mexicans, Cubans, Puerto Ricans, Dominicans, and other groups whose immigration to the United States has increased tremendously during the last quarter century. Urban school systems routinely enroll student populations that speak dozens of different languages at home.

Differences among youth do not simply involve differences of culture, race, income, and class—potent as these are. We now acknowledge differences in sexual orientation among young people. Today's students are also tagged with bureaucratic or medical assessments of their abilities and disabilities that also become part of their identities.

There are so many differences among the students at a high school in Brooklyn, Los Angeles, or suburban Montgomery County, Maryland, that one wonders whether the word "teenager" is sufficient to encompass them all. Indeed, the terms "adolescent" and "teenager" have always had a middle-class bias. In the past, though, working-class youths in their teens were already working and part of a separate culture. Now that the work of the working class has disappeared, their children have little choice but to be teenagers. But they are inevitably different from those of the postwar and baby boomer eras because they are growing up in a more heterogeneous and contentious society.

What follows, then, is not a single unified narrative but, rather, a sort of jigsaw puzzle. Many pieces fit together nicely. Others seem to be missing. It's easier to solve such a puzzle if you know what picture is going to emerge, but if I were confident of that, I wouldn't be putting you, or myself, to such trouble.

These discussions do have an underlying theme: the difficulty of forging the sort of meaningful identity that Erik Erikson described at mid-century. But if we look for a picture of the late-twentieth-century teenager in these fragments, we won't find it. That's because we're expecting to find something that isn't there.

15   The goths who invaded Tomorrowland are examples of another kind of diversity—or perhaps pseudo-diversity—that has emerged gaudily during the last two decades. These are the tribes of youth. The typical suburban high school is occupied by groups of teens who express themselves through music, dress, tattoos and piercing, obsessive hobbies, consumption patterns, extracurricular activities, drug habits, and sex practices. These tribes hang out in different parts of the school, go to different parts of town. Once it was possible to speak of a youth culture, but now there is a range of youth subcultures, and clans, coteries, and cliques within those.

In 1996 a high school student asked fellow readers of an Internet bulletin board what groups were found in their high schools. Nearly every school reported the presence of "skaters," "geeks," "jocks," "sluts," "freaks," "druggies," "nerds," and those with "other-colored hair," presumably third-generation punks. There were also, some students reported, "paper people," "snobs," "band geeks," "drama club types" (or "drama queens"), "soccer players" (who aren't counted as jocks, the informant noted),

"Satanists," "Jesus freaks," "industrial preps," "techno-goths," and "computer dweebs." Several took note of racial and class segregation, listing "blacks," "Latinos," "white trash," and "wannabe blacks." There were "preppies," who, as one writer, possibly a preppie herself noted, "dress like the snobs but aren't as snobbish." "Don't forget about the druggie preps," another writer fired back.

This clearly wasn't an exhaustive list. Terms vary from school to school and fashions vary from moment to moment. New technologies emerge, in-line skates or electronic pagers for instance, and they immediately generate their own dress, style, language, and culture.

The connotations of the technologies can change very quickly. Only a few years ago, pagers were associated mostly with drug dealers, but now they've entered the mainstream. Pagers became respectable once busy mothers realized that they could use them to get messages to their peripatetic offspring. Young pager users have developed elaborate codes for flirtation, endearment, assignation, and insults. They know that if 90210 comes up on their pager, someone's calling them a snob, and if it's 1776, they're revolting, while if it's 07734, they should turn the pager upside down and read "hELLO."

Most of the youth tribes have roots that go back twenty years or more, though most are more visible and elaborate than they once were. Many of these tribes are defined by the music they like, and young people devote a lot of energy to distinguishing the true exemplars of heavy metal, techno, alternative, or hip-hop from the mere poseurs. Hybrid and evolutionary versions of these cultures, such as speed metal, thrash, or gangsta rap make things far more confusing.

20   One thing that many of these subcultures have in common is what has come to be known as modern primitivism. This includes tattooing, the piercing of body parts, and physically expressive and dangerous rituals, such as the mosh pits that are part of many rock concerts. Young peo-

ple use piercing and tattoos to assert their maturity and sovereignty over their bodies.

"Can this be child abuse?" Sally Dietrich, a suburban Washington mother, asked the police when her thirteen-year-old son appeared with a bulldog tattooed on his chest. "I said, 'What about destruction of property?' He's my kid.'" Her son was, very likely, trying to signal otherwise. Nevertheless, Dietrich mounted a successful campaign to bar tattooing without permission in the state of Maryland, one of many such restrictions passed during the 1990s.

It may be a mistake to confuse visible assertions of sexual power with the fact of it. For example, heavy-metal concerts and mosh pits are notoriously male-dominated affairs. And the joke of MTV's "Beavis and Butt-head" is that these two purported metalheads don't have a clue about how to relate to the opposite sex. Those whose costumes indicate that they have less to prove are just as likely to be sexually active.

In fact, visitors to Disneyland probably don't need to be too worried about the goths, a tribe which, like many of the youth culture groups, has its roots in English aestheticism. As some goths freely admit, they're pretentious, and their morbid attitudes are as much a part of the dress-up games as the black clothes themselves.

The goth pose provides a convenient cover. For some males, it gives an opportunity to try out an androgynous look. The costumes, which emphasize the face and make the body disappear, may also provide an escape for young women and men who fear that they're overweight or not fit. Black clothes are slimming, and darkness even more so. "Until I got in with goths, I hadn't met other people who are depressed like I am and that I could really talk to," said one young woman on an Internet bulletin board. Another said being a goth allowed her relaxation from life as a straight-A student and a perfect daughter.

25   Although young people recognize an immense number of distinctions among the tribes and clans of youth culture and are contemptuous of those they regard as bogus, most adults cannot tell them apart. They confuse thrashers with metalheads and goths because they all wear black. Then they assume that they're all taking drugs and worshipping Satan.

The adult gaze is powerful. It classes them all as teenagers, whether they like it or not. The body alterations that young people use to assert that they are no longer children successfully frighten grown-ups, but they also convince them these weird creatures are well short of being adults. The ring through the lip or the nipple merely seems to demonstrate that they are not ready for adult responsibility. What they provoke is not respect but restrictions.

Tribes are about a yearning to belong to a group—or perhaps to escape into a disguise. They combine a certain gregariousness with what seems to be its opposite: a feeling of estrangement. The imagery of being alone in the world is not quite so gaudy as that of modern primitivism, yet it pervades contemporary youth culture.

While youthful exploration of the 1920s, 1940s, 1950s, or 1960s often took the form of wild dancing, more recently it has been about solitary posing. This phenomenon is reflected, and perhaps encouraged, by MTV, which went on the air in 1981. In contrast with the rudimentary format of *American Bandstand,* in which the viewer seemed simply to be looking in on young people having fun dancing with one another, MTV videos tend to be more about brooding than participation. They are highly subjective, like dreams or psychodramas. They connect the viewer with a feeling, rather than with other people.

And while the writhing, leaping, and ecstatic movement of the mosh pit seems to be an extreme form of *American Bandstand*-style participation, it embodies a rather scary kind of community. One's own motions have little relationship to those of others. And there's substantial risk of injury. The society implied by the dance is not harmonious and made up of couples. Rather, it is violent and composed of isolated individuals who are, nevertheless, both seeking and repulsing contact with others. If this sounds like a vision of American society as a whole, that's not surprising. Figuring out what things are really like is one of the tasks of youth. Then they frighten their elders by acting it out.

30   When a multinational company that sells to the young asked marketing psychologist Stan Gross to study teenagers around the country, he concluded after hundreds of interviews and exercises that the majority of young people embraced an extreme if inchoate individualism. Most believe that just about every institution they come in contact with is stupid. When asked to choose an ideal image for themselves, the majority selected a picture that depicted what might be described as confident alienation. The figure sits, comfortably apart from everything, his eyes gazing out of the image at something unknown and distant.

Such studies are done, of course, not to reform the young but to sell to them. And the collective impact of such knowledge of the young has been the proliferation of advertising that encourages young people not to believe anything—even advertising—and to express their superiority by purchasing the product that's willing to admit its own spuriousness.

The distance between spontaneous expression and large-scale commercial exploitation has never been shorter. Creators of youth fashion, such as Nike, go so far as to send scouts to the ghetto to take pictures of what young people are wearing on the streets and writing on the walls. Nike seeks to reflect the latest sensibilities, both in its products and its advertising. The company feeds the imagery right back to those who created it, offering them something they cannot afford as a way of affirming themselves.

One result of this quick feedback is that visual symbols become detached from their traditional associations and become attached to something else. Rappers, having made droopy pants stylish in the suburbs, began to wear preppie sportswear, and brand names like Tommy Hilfiger and Nautica became badges of both WASP and hip-hop sensibilities. Thus, even when the fashions don't change, their meaning does. Such unexpected shifts in the meaning of material goods cannot be entirely manipulated by adults. But marketers have learned that they must be vigilant in order to profit from the changes when they come.

More overtly than in the past, many of today's young are looking for extreme forms of expression. This quest is just as apparent in sports, for example, as in rock culture. The 1996 Atlanta Olympics began with an exhibition of extreme cycling and extreme skating. These and other extreme sports, categorized collectively as "X-Games," have become a cable television fixture because they draw teenage males, an otherwise elusive audience. "Extreme" was one of the catchwords of the 1990s, and it became, by 1996, the most common word in newly registered trade names, attached either to products aimed at youth or which sought to embody youthfulness.

35   Young people are caught in a paradox. They drive themselves to extremes to create space in which to be themselves. Yet the commercial machine they think they're escaping is always on their back, ready to sell them something new.

SUGGESTIONS FOR DISCUSSION

1. Thomas Hine uses the opening anecdote about goth teens and Disneyland to announce the theme of this passage. As Hine presents it, what is this story meant to represent about the relations between teenagers and adults? What further examples and evidence does Hine offer in the rest of the selection to reinforce his point?

2. Hine suggests that the terms *teenager* and youth *culture* no longer have one common meaning. If anything, he sees a diversity of teenagers and "tribes of youth" defined by

different styles of dress, music, body ornamentation, extracurricular activity, drug use, and sexual practices as well as racial and ethnic markers. Consider your high school and college. What "tribes" are represented? Develop a classification of the various groups. What do you see as the leading ways in which groups of young people define themselves? What are the meanings of the identities they take on? What are the relationships among the various groups?

3. Hine points to a social dynamic in which "extreme" forms of cultural expressions, such as tatooing, body piercing, music, and sports, are meant to affirm group identities but, from an adult perspective, only reinforce the view that young people "are not ready for adult responsibility." What is the lure, for young people, of such extreme expressions? How, from the perspective of adults, do the various forms of extreme style and behavior get lumped together?

SUGGESTIONS FOR WRITING

1. Write an essay that classifies the various groups (or "tribes") of youth culture at the high school you attended or your college. Describe the leading groups, their styles, behaviors, values, and attitudes. After providing an overview of the groups, explain their relationship to each other and to the adult society that surrounds them.

2. Hine suggests that some of the groupings of youth culture represent a threat to adult society. Consider what Hine thinks is the source of this fear. Why would adults be so worried about young people? What exactly is at stake in the fears and anxieties of the older generation?

3. At the end of this selection, Hine says that young people are "caught in a paradox": No matter how much they rebel against adult society to create a space for themselves, the "commercial machine" they're trying to escape from reincorporates their cultural styles in the form of new products and merchandise. Do you think this is a reasonable assessment? Why or why not? Write an essay that explains your answer—and whether you think young people can establish their own way of doing things, independent of the market and the workings of adult society.

GEN X'S ENDURING LEGACY: THE INTERNET

Mike Pope

Mike Pope is the letters editor of the *Tallahasee Democrat.* The following column of opinion appeared as an op-ed piece in several newspapers across the country on November 13, 2001. Pope is trying to come to terms with the meaning of his generation, which has been labeled, he says, in "our cultural vocabulary," as "Generation X." In demographic terms, Generation X refers to those born between 1963 and 1981. The real question Pope poses is the meaning of this generation—how it views itself and how others view it. Pope makes the Internet the key defining feature that separates his generation from the generation of baby boomers that came before.

SUGGESTION FOR READING As you read, observe how Mike Pope notes the "transformations" Generation X has gone through in the public eye. In an interesting stroke, he also links the first George H.W. Bush administration (1988–1992) to the second George W. Bush administration (2000–) to provide historical context.

1   It's been 10 years since Douglas Coupland introduced "Generation X" into our cultural vocabulary; many people my age still wince at the phrase. To many folks born between 1963 and 1981, the phrase seems more like a marketing ploy than a rallying cry.

"How can we sell them our product," the overpaid executives muse. "None of our silly marketing tricks are working on them, so let's tap into their sense of existential cynicism and unending pessimism."

Witness Coca-Cola's advertising strategy for OK Soda that featured slogans such as "Don't be fooled into thinking there has to be a reason for everything" and "What's the point of OK? Well, what's the point of anything?" (Incidentally, there is a very elaborate theory circulating on the Internet that the CIA and conservative editor William Kristol worked together on the marketing strategy of OK to brainwash young people into being "neoconservatives.")

During the last 10 years, the reputation of Generation X has undergone several transformations. In the beginning, many viewed us as whining slackers, lost in a sea of economic mediocrity. The first Bush recession had saddled us with wage stagnation, unchecked corporate greed, an enormous Cold War national debt, a glut of low-wage service jobs and the skyrocketing cost of college and home ownership. (In case you are wondering, I'm still paying off my student loan and I don't own a house.)

5   But then something dramatic happened to Generation X: the Internet. It changed how we viewed ourselves and how the world viewed us. Suddenly, baffled baby boomers were asking us how to e-mail their friends or download Beatles tunes. Low-wage service jobs gave way to high-tech industry jobs. Irony became hip.

Giddy with revolutionary fever and ungodly amounts of caffeine, Generation X finally had something to do. And boy did we do it—for 18 hours a day. Blessed with this new communication medium and an opportunity to do something truly radical, we formed bold start-up companies and ordered expensive, ergonomically designed office furniture.

Then, of course, the bottom fell out of the market and now you can buy ergonomically designed office furniture secondhand. As we Gen Xers like to say, "Whatever."

As the second Bush recession continues to tighten its grip and the sins of the CIA have blessed us with gas masks and sky marshals, Internet companies such as Netradio continue to fold (the Minneapolis-based corporation closed this month, laying off 50 employees). The age of irony is over. Nobody wants to buy banner ads anymore.

For the past 10 years, the phrase "Generation X" has been loaded with cynical subtext and subtle derision. It has graced the market strategies of Fortune 500 companies and fueled academic complaints about "self-absorption and materialism." It has downloaded itself onto the hard drive of America and America has responded, "Whatever."

10   Okay, so maybe we oversold the Internet by promising that the old media would soon be obsolete. Maybe the recently outdated New Economy works from many of the economic paradigms of the Old Economy. Maybe we shouldn't expend so much of our energy crying into our lattes.

But during the past 10 years, Generation X has imbued the world with its enduring legacy: the Internet. History may not reward us as the "greatest" generation, but it's no small accomplishment to revolutionize communication, education and commerce. Sure the Internet bubble may have burst—for now. But don't dismiss the possibility that Internet IPOs will once again burst upon the scene, just like the Old Economy theory of "economic cycles" predicts.

And don't be so quick to dismiss irony. It will make a comeback.

SUGGESTIONS FOR DISCUSSION

1. This piece relies on readers recognizing immediately the term *Generation X*. Mike Pope gives a couple of ways to understand Generation X as it changes in meaning. Begin by describing your own sense of what Generation X means. Who are these people? In what sense are they a generation? What are the most visible representations of Generation X (think of music, movies, TV shows, and advertising). Now compare this understanding of Generation X with Pope's. How do they differ? How are they similar? How can you account for differences and similarities?

2. Pope says that one of the distinguishing features of Generation X is its sense of irony. What does this mean? Consider Pope's examples of how advertisers picked up on this sense of irony.

3. The generational divide—what separates Generation X from the baby boomers (born between 1946 and 1962)—in Pope's view is the Internet. What is the impact of the Internet? Is it just a matter of knowing how to e-mail or download music? Is there another step to take here to explain how the Internet shapes the lived experience of Generation X?

SUGGESTIONS FOR WRITING

1. Pope notes that "Gen Xers like to say, 'Whatever.'" Write an essay that explains the attitude behind the use of the word "Whatever." Or substitute another term that somehow embodies the attitude of a generation.

2. Write an essay about the influence of the Internet on generations in contemporary America. Think here in terms not only of whether people of different generations can easily operate the Internet but also on their experience of it.

3. Imagine you've been asked to write an essay called "Generation Y's Enduring Legacy:" What would you put on the other side of the colon? Think of Generation Yers as those born after 1981 who are the late teens and early twenty-year-olds today. Your task, much as Pope defines his, is to distinguish this generation from the one that preceded it.

PERSPECTIVES   Before and After 9/11

As everyone is aware, the terrorist acts of September 11, 2001, loom as a defining moment in American culture. It's easy to see what has taken place subsequently—George W. Bush's "war against terrorism," a heightened awareness of the vulnerability of the United States to attack, the military campaign in Afghanistan, and perhaps a new sense of how the United States is interconnected to world politics. At publication time, the Bush administration has just invaded Iraq. These are the geopolitical realities of our time.

These two readings focus on the domestic scene—to raise questions about young people's understanding of what 9/11 means for their generation and its sense of identity. As Arlie Russell Hochschild notes in "Gen (Fill in the Blank): Coming of Age, Seeking an Identity," Americans who grew up in the 1930s, 1940s, and 1960s were "branded by large events—the Depression, World War II, Vietnam—and the collective moods they aroused." To see how 9/11 has affected the "collective mood" of a generation, consider first Hochschild's article, which appeared in the *New York Times* on March 8, 2000, well before 9/11, and second, the excerpt from "Generation 9/11" by Barbara Kantrowitz and Keith Naughton, two months after the terrorist attacks. Both readings rely on the notion of a defining moment in the life of a generation. These two views of the current generation offer a way for you to assess how 9/11 has influenced a generation.

GEN (FILL IN THE BLANK): COMING OF AGE, SEEKING AN IDENTITY

Arlie Russell Hochschild

Arlie Russell Hochschild is a professor of sociology at the University of California, Berkeley, where she codirects the Center for Working Families; she is also the author of such sociological studies as *The Time Bind: When Work Becomes Home and Home Becomes Work* (2001) and *The Managed Heart: Commercialization of Human Feelings* (1985). This article appeared in a special section of the *New York Times* on "Generations" on March 8, 2000.

SUGGESTION FOR READING Arlie Russell Hochschild, unlike the other writers in this chapter, provides a definition of the idea of a generation based on sociologist Karl Mannheim's classic 1927 essay, "The Problem of Generations." As Hochschild notes, according to Mannheim, "a generation is a cohort of people who feel the impact of a powerful historical event and develop a shared consciousness about it." As you read, pay attention to how Hochschild uses this definition to analyze the generation of twenty- and thirty-year-olds and how she finds, in the absence of a large historical crisis in the life of this generation before 9/11, an underlying trend.

1 "I'm not part of the 1960's generation," said Sandy de Lissovoy. "I don't feel part of Gen X or Gen Y. I'm sure not part of the 'Me Generation.' Who made up that term? I hate it. What's really in front of me is my computer, but even with it, I'm between the generation that barely tolerates computers and the one that treats them like a member of the family."

Mr. de Lissovoy, a 29-year-old graphic designer in San Francisco, was expressing as well as anyone the feelings that, as a sociology professor, I frequently hear during office hours. At this moment he was having a hard time defining his generation. He raised his eyebrows quizzically, smiled and said, "Call me the @ Generation One and a Half."

Can we make up our generation, as Mr. de Lissovoy playfully did, or is it imposed upon us, like it or not?

These are questions that the German sociologist Karl Mannheim took up in his classic 1927 essay, "The Problem of Generations." Is a generation a collection of people born in the same span of years? No, he thought, that is a cohort, and many cohorts are born, come of age and die without becoming generations. For Mannheim, a generation is a cohort of people who feel the impact of a powerful historical event and develop a shared consciousness about it. Not all members of a generation may see the event the same way, and some may articulate its defining features better than others. But what makes a generation is its connection to history.

5   Americans who came of age in the 1930's, 40's and 60's have been branded by large events—the Great Depression, World War II, Vietnam—and the collective moods they aroused. But from the 70's through the 90's, history's signal events happened elsewhere. Communism collapsed, but not in the United States. Wars raged in Rwanda, the Balkans and elsewhere, but they had little effect here. The forces in the United States have been social and economic, and they have shifted the focus to personal issues—matters of lifestyle that are shaped by consumerism, the mass media and an increasing sense of impermanence in family and work.

"There is no overarching crisis or cause for our generation," Mr. de Lissovoy said. "It's more a confusing, ambiguous flow of events. There's a slow, individual sorting out to do."

But underneath this confusing, ambiguous flow of events is a trend toward a more loosely jointed, limited-liability society, the privatizing influence of that trend and the crash-boom-bang of the market, which, in the absence of other voices, is defining generations left and right.

People in their 20's and early 30's are often called Gen X'ers, a term derived from a novel by Douglas Coupland. The book, "Generation X," was followed by a film, "Slacker," directed by Richard Linklater, about a group of overeducated, underemployed oddballs who drop to the margins of society. But for Jim Kreines, a 32-year-old graduate student of philosophy at the University of Chicago, the label fit loosely, if at all.

When I asked him what generation he belonged to, Mr. Kreines replied, "I'm not sure I care enough to argue about this." He had read the Coupland book and seen the film. But did the Gen X'er label apply to him? He was not sure it mattered.

10   Many Gen X'ers may be trying to sort out a certain cultural sleight of hand. They feel luckier than previous generations because they enjoy many more options. In the 50's, said Charles Sellers, a 28-year-old urban planner in Portland, Ore., there was only one choice. "If you were a woman you were a housewife," he said. "If you were a man you married and supported your family. Today, except for the Mormons, Americans have a long cultural menu to choose from. If you're a woman, you can be a single woman, a career woman, a lesbian, a single mom by choice, a live-in lover, a married-for-now wife, a married-forever wife. And the same for work: I'm on my third career."

But the wider menu of identities comes with a decreasing assurance that any particular identity will last. This is because a culture of deregulation has slipped from our economic life into our cultural life. Gen X'ers, at least in the middle class, can be more picky in finding "just the right mate" and "just the right career." But once you've found them, you begin to wonder if you can you keep them.

In his book *The New Insecurity*, Jerald Wallulis, a philosopher at the University of South Carolina, observed that in the last 30 years, people have shifted the way they base their identity: from marriage and employment to marriage-ability and employability. Old anchors no longer hold, and a sense of history is lost. For the generations of the 80's and 90's, this rootlessness is their World War II, their Vietnam. And it presents a more difficult challenge than the one faced by the 60's generation.

Mr. de Lissovoy's parents divorced when he was a baby and now live on opposite coasts. Consider, too, the shifting family ties of a 27-year-old computer programmer in Silicon Valley, who asked that her name be withheld. "My mother divorced four times and is living on uncertain terms with her fifth," she said, "so I'm not sure if she'll stay with him either. I haven't gotten attached to any of my stepdads. My dad remarried four times, too, only now he's married to a woman I like."

When her parents divorced, she spent every other weekend with her father. "My dad was glad to see me, but I'd have to remind him of the name of my best friends," she said. "He didn't know what mattered to me. After a while it just got to be dinner and a video, and after that, I didn't feel much like going to his apartment."

15   Talking about her love life, she said: "If I meet someone I really like, I become shy and tied up in knots. I can't talk about anything personal." It was as if she did not dare to begin a relationship for fear of ending it.

After the parents of another young woman divorced, her father married a woman as young as his daughter, and is very involved with his new, young children who are the same age as his grandchildren. Now, when his daughter tries to arrange a visit between her father and his grandchildren, he is often too pinched for time to see them. His daughter feels hurt and angry—first to miss out on a father, then a grandfather.

Reflecting on these generational jumbles, Mr. de Lissovoy commented: "Today's hype is that 'You can get it if you really want it'—a mate, career and love still sells a lot of tickets. We're the Generation of Individual Choice. Which? Which? Which? But the bottom can fall out from some of those choices. And in the end, we're orphans.

We're supposed to take care of ourselves. That's our only choice."

Not every young person I have talked with has felt so adrift. The 20-somethings of the 90's have more material resources than their predecessors—ample job opportunities, for example.

Still, Mr. de Lissovoy's feelings reflect something true about America these days. Despite the recent economic miracle, we are experiencing a care deficit. Social services have been cut; hospitals release patients 24 hours after surgery to recover at home. But who is home to do the caring? Two-thirds of mothers are working. One-quarter of households are headed by single mothers; they need help, too. Paradoxically, American individualism and pride in self-sufficiency lead us to absorb rather than resist this deficit: "Care? Who needs care? I can handle it," thus adding one problem to another.

20   If in previous decades large historic events drew people together and oriented them to action, the recent double trend toward more choice but less security leads the young to see their lives in more individual terms. Big events collectivize, little events atomize. So with people facing important but private problems, and thinking in individual, not collective, terms, the coast became clear in the 80's and 90's for the marketplace to stalk into this cultural void and introduce generation-defining clothes, music and videos.

Generations X and Y function as market gimmicks nowadays. The market dominates not just economic life, as the economist Robert Kuttner argues in "Everything for Sale," but our cultural life as well. It tells us what a generation is—a Pepsi generation, a Mac generation, an Internet generation. And a magazine about shoot-'em-up computer games calls itself *NextGen*.

Advertisers are appealing to children over the heads of their parents. Juliet B. Schor, an economics lecturer at Harvard, suggests that the younger generation is the cutting edge of a full-blown market culture. More than $2 billion is spent on advertising directed at them, 20 times the amount spent a decade ago. Most of the advertising is transmitted through television; it is estimated that youngsters increased their viewing time one hour a day between 1970 and 1990. Three out of five children ages 12 to 17 now have a TV in their bedroom. Advertisers are trying to enlist children against their parents' better judgment, Dr. Schor said recently, and overworked parents sometimes give in and go along. If Dr. Schor is correct, Generation Y might be defined even more than Generation X by what its members buy than by what they do or who they are.

Marketing strategists, meanwhile, are turning over all the generations faster, slicing and dicing the life cycle into thinner strips. In the computer industry, an advertising generation is nine months; in the clothing industry, a season. In department stores, between the displays for girls in their preteens and teens, is a new age, "tweens." The identity promised by a style or a brand name for one generation is marked off from an increasing number of others. And the styles continually replace old with new.

This creates a certain consumer logic. Older consumers buy what makes them feel young, while young consumers, up to a point, buy what makes them feel older. So the preteenager will buy the tween thing while the teenager will buy the 20-something jacket, and the 40-year-old will browse in the racks for 30-year-olds.

25   To be sure, every American decade has fashion marketeers define generational looks and sounds, but probably never before have they so totally hijacked a generation's cultural expression. Allison Pugh, a 33-year-old married mother of two and a graduate student in sociology at the University of California at Berkeley, said: "I definitely feel like people just two or three years younger than me are the beginning of another generation. But I can only say why by pointing to superficial things, like how many pierces they have, how high their shoes are and what kind of music they listen to. I roomed with a girl just two years younger and she listened to Smashing Pumpkins, Nirvana and Hole. I was 'old'—as in out of it—even just a few years out of college. I started to sound like my mother: 'That's not music; what is that noise?' "

Like Ms. Pugh, Mr. de Lissovoy is considered old to the generation at his heels. He is wired, but feels ambivalent about it. "What I don't like is disposability, hyperspeed, consumption," he said. "I'd like to reduce these. What I want more of is face-to-face interaction, a value on repair, families living nearby each other. I'd love to live in a multigenerational, multiracial cohousing project. And a more leisurely pace of life. I want some pretty old-fashioned things."

The 60's generation is hitting 60, and with some computer nerds striking it rich, 60's-era protests are not defining the new generation. But that era's flame is not dead. In front of a large gathering at the Pauley ballroom on the Berkeley campus a few months ago, the Mario Savio Young Activist Award for 1999—named after the leader of the 1964 Free Speech Movement—was given to Nikki Bas, a 31-year-old American of Filipino descent who coordinates Sweatshop Watch, a campaign against the poor pay and working conditions of third-world workers who make football uniforms and other clothing sold on American college campuses. Mr. de Lissovoy remembers hearing about Mr. Savio from his 60's activist mother, but he does not know Nikki Bas, is no longer a student and is under time pressure at work. So he is not signing up.

Still, from a distance he watched the protests in Seattle against the World Trade Organization late last year, and they kindled a sense of the importance of history that he feels the market is driving out. "I hated the mindless anarchists who broke shop windows," he said. "But the other protesters who went there to speak up against mega-corporations running the show, and for the family farm, local communities, monarch butterflies and sea turtles—they are taking the long view of the planet. We usually think it's the older generation that wants to preserve the past, and it's the young who don't mind tearing things up. In Seattle, the young environmentalists had their eye on history, and it was the old who had an eye on their pocketbooks."

Ultimately, market generations are generations of things, and they can make us forget generations of people. "My generation doesn't know how globalization will turn out," Mr. de Lissovoy said. "But we won't see how globalization is messing us up if we've forgotten how the world used to be. Whichever way, we don't see that what we are doing is forgetting the past. And we're nobodies without a sense of history."

30   He recalled how baseball caps with X's became popular with teenagers, especially in Detroit, after Spike Lee's film on Malcolm X came out. "When a TV interviewer asked a kid about the X on his cap, he didn't know who Malcolm X was," Mr. de Lissovoy said. "He didn't even know he was a person. We need to appreciate the work it takes to get us where we are. Otherwise we aren't anywhere."

GENERATION 9-11

Barbara Kantrowitz and Keith Naughton

Barbara Kantrowitz and Keith Naughton are writers for *Newsweek*. This article appeared in the November 12, 2001 edition, almost exactly two months after the terrorist attacks. Here is an excerpt from the article, the opening section that presents the view that "kids who grew up with peace and prosperity are facing their defining moment." The rest of the article consists of reporting on what happened at the University of Michigan in the days immediately following 9/11.

SUGGESTION FOR READING   Notice that Barbara Kantrowitz and Keith Naughton use roughly the same idea of a generation that Arlie Russell Hochschild does—an age group that finds its collective identity in a decisive historical moment. As you read, pay attention to how Kantrowitz and Naughton set up the problem of generational identity.

1   It was a sleepy, gray afternoon—a challenge to any professor. And for the first few minutes of class last week, University of Michigan sociologist David Schoem had some trouble rousing the 18 freshmen in his seminar on "Democracy and Diversity." One student slurped yogurt while another stretched his arms wide and yawned. A few others casually took notes. But the lassitude ended abruptly when Schoem switched the discussion to America's war on terrorism. For the rest of the hour, the students argued passionately and articulately about foreign policy, racism and media coverage. Then, New Yorker Georgina Levitt offered one view that stopped the debate cold. "September 11 has changed us more than we realize," she said. "This just isn't going to go away."

At Michigan and campuses all around the country, the generation that once had it all—peace, prosperity, even the dot-com dream of retiring at 30—faces its defining moment. College students are supposed to be finding their place in the world, not just a profession but also an intellectual framework for learning and understanding the rest of their lives. After the terrorist attacks, that goal seems more urgent and yet more elusive than ever. In the first week, they prayed together, lit candles and mourned. Now they're packing teach-ins and classes on international relations, the Mideast, Islamic studies, even Arabic. Where they once dreamed of earning huge bonuses on Wall Street, they're now thinking of working for the government, maybe joining the FBI or the CIA. They're energized, anxious, eager for any information that will help them understand—and still a little bit in shock.

It's too soon to tell whether 2001 will be more like 1941, when campuses and the country were united, or 1966, the beginning of a historic rift. So far, there have been only scattered signs of a nascent antiwar movement; at Michigan and other campuses, students' views are in sync with the rest of the country's. In the NEWSWEEK Poll conducted last week, 83 percent of young Americans said they approved of President George W. Bush's job performance and 85 percent favored the current military action. These figures are consistent across all age groups. But students also understand that the future is increasingly unpredictable and that long-held beliefs and assumptions will be severely tested in the next few years. "Our generation, as long as we've had an identity, was known as the generation that had it easy," says Greg Epstein, 24, a graduate student in Judaic studies at Michigan. "We had no crisis, no Vietnam, no Martin Luther King, no JFK. We've got it now. When we have kids and grandkids, we'll tell them that we lived through the roaring '90s, when all we cared about was the No. 1 movie or how many copies an album sold. This is where it changes."

What will they make of their moment? It's always tricky to generalize about a generation, but before September 11, American college students were remarkably insular. Careers were their major concern both during the high-tech boom (how to cash in) and after (how to get a job). According to the annual survey of college freshmen conducted by UCLA's Higher Education Research Institute, only 28.1 percent of last year's freshman class reported following politics, compared with a high of 60.3 percent in 1966. Nationwide, campus activism has been low key through the 1990s. That was true even at Michigan, the birthplace of SDS and a hotbed of antiwar protest during Vietnam. Alan Haber, a 65-year-old peace protester and fixture on the Ann Arbor campus since his own student days in the 1960s, says that before September 11, there was no central issue that ignited everyone, just a lot of what he describes as "little projects": protests against sweatshops or nuclear weapons. He thinks that may change as these campus activists begin questioning the U.S. military efforts. "This situation," he says, "bangs on the head and opens a heart."

5   Despite their perceived apathy and political inexperience, this generation may be uniquely qualified to understand the current battle. "I think they realize more than the adults that this is a clash of cultures," says University of Pennsylvania president Judith Rodin, "something we haven't seen in a thousand years." While their parents' high-school history lessons concentrated almost exclusively on Western Europe, they've learned about Chinese

dynasties, African art, even Islam. They are more likely than their parents to have dated a person from another culture or race, and to have friends from many economic and ethnic backgrounds. Their campuses as well are demographically very different from those of a generation ago. "It's gone from a more elite institution to more of a microcosm of the population," says David Ward, president of the American Council on Education, a national association of colleges and universities.

Others argue that this spirit of tolerance can have a downside, particularly now. When author David Brooks, who wrote a widely discussed Atlantic Monthly article on rampant pre-professionalism at Princeton last year, returned there after September 11, he found a surging interest in global affairs and issues of right and wrong—but also a frustration with the moral relativism of much of the curriculum (see this week's Web Exclusive at Newsweek.MSNBC.com). One student told him that he had been taught how to deconstruct and dissect, but never to construct and decide.

SUGGESTIONS FOR DISCUSSION

1. Written before 9/11, Arlie Russell Hochschild calls attention to the fact that twenty- and thirty-year-olds in the 1990s did not face a defining historical event such as the Depression, World War II, or Vietnam. Nonetheless, she suggests that "underneath this confusing, ambiguous flow of events is a trend toward a more loosely jointed, limited-liability society, the privatizing influence of that trend and the crash-boom-bang of the market" as the defining feature of a generation. What exactly does she mean by this trend? In what sense does it produce a shared consciousness, just as the historical events she lists have done for earlier generations? Think here in particular of how marketing creates generations.

2. Barbara Kantrowitz and Keith Naughton's "Generation 9-11" seems to assume that September 11, 2001, represents a defining historical moment in the life of a generation. Notice, however, that they leave the meaning of this defining moment open-ended, asking "whether 2001 will be more like 1941, when campuses and the country were united, or 1966, the beginning of a historic rift." Clearly, they are using 1941 to refer to the bombing of Pearl Harbor and the onset of U.S. involvement in World War II, on one hand, and 1966 to refer to beginnings of an antiwar movement and the deep split in the American public over the Vietnam War, on the other. You are reading this excerpt several years after 9/11. Looking back, to what extent does that defining moment of September 11, 2001, now resemble 1941 or 1966? Consider whether these historical analogies are helpful at all in understanding the impact of 9/11. Are there other, different historical precedents that might be clarifying?

3. What is your view of the influence of 9/11? Is it a defining moment? If so, how? If not, why not?

SUGGESTIONS FOR WRITING

1. Read Barbara Kantrowitz and Keith Naughton's entire article in the November 12, 2001 *Newsweek*. Jot down your own account of what happened in your school or community immediately following 9/11. But don't stop there. Step back and ask, from your own perspective several years later, what the meaning of those events is. Write an essay that both describes what happened around 9/11 and what you now see as its meaning.

2. Arlie Russell Hochschild links two notions—personal choice and personal insecurity. Write an essay that begins by explaining what she means by this linkage. Give examples from your own experience or draw on what you've read and what you know. To what extent does the link help to explain the collective mood of a generation?

3. Update the two readings. Write an essay that explains the impact of 9/11 on your generation.

CLASSIC READING

HOWL

Allen Ginsberg

Allen Ginsberg(1926–97) is one of the greatest American poets of the twentieth century. Drawing on Walt Whitman and William Blake for inspiration, Ginsberg wrote "Howl" over a period of time in 1955 and 1956. It quickly became both the anthem of the Beat Generation and the source of an obscenity court case (in which "Howl" was judged "legal" in 1957). Ginsberg subsequently published books of poetry such as *Planet News* (1963), *The Fall of America* (1971), and *Plutonian Ode* (1980). Along with Jack Kerouac's novel *On the Road*, "Howl" defines the sensibility of the Beat Generation of the 1950s and forms a key link to Bob Dylan, the antiwar movement, and the counterculture of the 1960s.

SUGGESTION FOR READING "Howl" is divided into three parts. Notice that Part I is actually one long sentence, linked by clauses that begin with "who." Part II focuses on Moloch, the pagan deity in the Old Testament to whom children were sacrificed. Part III uses direct address—to Carl Solomon, to whom the poem is dedicated: "I am with you in Rockland," the mental institution where Ginsberg met Solomon (and where perhaps the theme "the best minds of my generation destroyed by madness" begins).

I

1   I saw the best minds of my generation destroyed by madness, starving hysterical naked,

dragging themselves through the negro streets at dawn looking for an angry fix,

angelheaded hipsters burning for the ancient heavenly connection to the starry dynamo in the machinery of night,

who poverty and tatters and hollow-eyed and high sat up smoking in the supernatural darkness of cold-water flats floating across the tops of cities contemplating jazz,

5   who bared their brains to Heaven under the El and saw Mohammedan angels staggering on tenement roofs illuminated,

who passed through universities with radiant cool eyes hallucinating Arkansas and Blake-light tragedy among the scholars of war,

who were expelled from the academies for crazy & publishing obscene odes on the windows of the skull,

who cowered in unshaven rooms in underwear, burning their money in wastebaskets and listening to the Terror through the wall,

who got busted in their pubic beards returning through Laredo with a belt of marijuana for New York,

10   who ate fire in paint hotels or drank turpentine in Paradise Alley, death, or purgatoried their torsos night after night

with dreams, with drugs, with waking nightmares, alcohol and cock and endless balls,

incomparable blind streets of shuddering cloud and lightning in the mind leaping toward poles of Canada & Paterson, illuminating all the motionless world of Time between,

Peyote solidities of halls, backyard green tree cemetery dawns, wine drunkenness over the rooftops, storefront boroughs of teahead joyride neon blinking traffic light, sun and moon and tree vibrations in the roaring winter dusks of Brooklyn, ashcan rantings and kind king light of mind,

who chained themselves to subways for the endless ride from Battery to holy Bronx on benzedrine until the noise of wheels and children brought them down shuddering mouth-wracked and battered bleak of brain all drained of brilliance in the drear light of Zoo,

15   who sank all night in submarine light of Bickford's floated out and sat through the stale beer afternoon in desolate Fugazzi's, listening to the crack of doom on the hydrogen jukebox,

who talked continuously seventy hours from park to pad to bar to Bellevue to museum to the Brooklyn Bridge,

a lost battalion of platonic conversationalists jumping down the stoops off fire escapes off windowsills off Empire State out of the moon,

yacketayakking screaming vomiting whispering facts and memories and anecdotes and eyeball kicks and shocks of hospitals and jails and wars,

whole intellects disgorged in total recall for seven days and nights with brilliant eyes, meat for the Synagogue cast on the pavement,

20   who vanished into nowhere Zen New Jersey leaving a trail of ambiguous picture postcards of Atlantic City Hall,

suffering Eastern sweats and Tangerian bone-grindings and migraines of China under junk-withdrawal in Newark's bleak furnished room,

who wandered around and around at midnight in the railroad yard wondering where to go, and went, leaving no broken hearts,

who lit cigarettes in boxcars boxcars boxcars racketing through snow toward lonesome farms in grandfather night,

who studied Plotinus Poe St. John of the Cross telepathy and bop kabbalah because the cosmos instinctively vibrated at their feet in Kansas,

25   who loned it through the streets of Idaho seeking visionary indian angels who were visionary indian angels,

who thought they were only mad when Baltimore gleamed in supernatural ecstasy,

who jumped in limousines with the Chinaman of Oklahoma on the impulse of winter midnight streetlight smalltown rain,

who lounged hungry and lonesome through Houston seeking jazz or sex or soup, and followed the brilliant Spaniard to converse about America and Eternity, a hopeless task, and so took ship to Africa,

who disappeared into the volcanoes of Mexico leaving behind nothing but the shadow of dungarees and the lava and ash of poetry scattered in fireplace Chicago,

30   who reappeared on the West Coast investigating the FBI in beards and shorts with big pacifist eyes sexy in their dark skin passing out incomprehensible leaflets,

who burned cigarette holes in their arms protesting the narcotic tobacco haze of Capitalism,

who distributed Supercommunist pamphlets in Union Square weeping and undressing while the sirens of Los Alamos wailed them down, and wailed down Wall, and the Staten Island ferry also wailed,

who broke down crying in white gymnasiums naked and trembling before the machinery of other skeletons,

who bit detectives in the neck and shrieked with delight in policecars for committing no crime but their own wild cooking pederasty and intoxication,

35   who howled on their knees in the subway and were dragged off the roof waving genitals and manuscripts,

who let themselves be fucked in the ass by saintly motorcyclists, and screamed with joy,

who blew and were blown by those human seraphim, the sailors, caresses of Atlantic and Caribbean love,

who balled in the morning in the evenings in rosegardens and the grass of public parks and cemeteries scattering their semen freely to whomever come who may,

who hiccuped endlessly trying to giggle but wound up with a sob behind a partition in a Turkish Bath when the blond & naked angel came to pierce them with a sword,

40   who lost their loveboys to the three old shrews of fate the one eyed shrew of the heterosexual dollar the one eyed shrew that winks out of the womb and the one eyed shrew that does nothing but sit on her ass and snip the intellectual golden threads of the craftsman's loom,

who copulated ecstatic and insatiate with a bottle of beer a sweetheart a package of cigarettes a candle and fell off the bed, and continued along the floor and down the hall and ended fainting on the wall with a vision of ultimate cunt and come eluding the last gyzym of consciousness,

who sweetened the snatches of a million girls trembling in the sunset, and were red eyed in the morning but prepared to sweeten the snatch of the sunrise, flashing buttocks under barns and naked in the lake,

who went out whoring through Colorado in myriad stolen night-cars, N.C., secret hero of these poems, cocksman and Adonis of Denver— joy to the memory of his innumerable lays of girls in empty lots & diner backyards, moviehouses' rickety rows, on mountaintops in caves or with gaunt waitresses in familiar roadside lonely petti- coat upliftings & especially secret gas-station solipsisms of johns, & hometown alleys too,

who faded out in vast sordid movies, were shifted in dreams, woke on a sudden Manhattan, and picked themselves up out of basements hun- gover with heartless Tokay and horrors of Third Avenue iron dreams & stumbled to unemploy- ment offices,

45   who walked all night with their shoes full of blood on the snowbank docks waiting for a door in the East River to open to a room full of steam- heat and opium,

who created great suicidal dramas on the apartment cliff-banks of the Hudson under the wartime blue floodlight of the moon & their heads shall be crowned with laurel in oblivion,

who ate the lamb stew of the imagination or digested the crab at the muddy bottom of the rivers of Bowery,

who wept at the romance of the streets with their pushcarts full of onions and bad music,

who sat in boxes breathing in the darkness under the bridge, and rose up to build harpsi- chords in their lofts,

50   who coughed on the sixth floor of Harlem crowned with flame under the tubercular sky sur- rounded by orange crates of theology,

who scribbled all night rocking and rolling over lofty incantations which in the yellow morn- ing were stanzas of gibberish,

who cooked rotten animals lung heart feet tail borsht & tortillas dreaming of the pure veg- etable kingdom,

who plunged themselves under meat trucks looking for an egg,

who threw their watches off the roof to cast their ballot for Eternity outside of Time, & alarm clocks fell on their heads every day for the next decade,

55   who cut their wrists three times successively unsuccessfully, gave up and were forced to open antique stores where they thought they were growing old and cried,

who were burned alive in their innocent flannel suits on Madison Avenue amid blasts of leaden verse & the tanked-up clatter of the iron regiments of fashion & the nitroglycerine shrieks of the fairies of advertising & the mustard gas of sinister intelligent editors, or were run down by the drunken taxicabs of Absolute Reality,

who jumped off the Brooklyn Bridge this actu- ally happened and walked away unknown and for- gotten into the ghostly daze of Chinatown soup alleyways & firetrucks, not even one free beer,

who sang out of their windows in despair, fell out of the subway window, jumped in the filthy Passaic, leaped on negroes, cried all over the street, danced on broken wineglasses bare- foot smashed phonograph records of nostalgic European 1930s German jazz finished the whiskey and threw up groaning into the bloody toilet, moans in their ears and the blast of colos- sal steamwhistles,

who barreled down the highways of the past journeying to each other's hotrod-Golgotha jail- solitude watch or Birmingham jazz incarnation,

60   who drove crosscountry seventytwo hours to find out if I had a vision or you had a vision or he had a vision to find out Eternity,

who journeyed to Denver, who died in Den- ver, who came back to Denver & waited in vain, who watched over Denver & brooded & loned in Denver and finally went away to find out the Time, & now Denver is lonesome for her heroes,

who fell on their knees in hopeless cathe- drals praying for each other's salvation and light and breasts, until the soul illuminated its hair for a second,

who crashed through their minds in jail wait- ing for impossible criminals with golden heads and the charm of reality in their hearts who sang sweet blues to Alcatraz,

who retired to Mexico to cultivate a habit, or Rocky Mount to tender Buddha or Tangiers to boys or Southern Pacific to the black locomotive or Harvard to Narcissus to Woodlawn to the daisychain or grave,

65 who demanded sanity trials accusing the radio of hypnotism & were left with their insanity & their hands & a hung jury,

who threw potato salad at CCNY lecturers on Dadaism and subsequently presented themselves on the granite steps of the madhouse with shaven heads and harlequin speech of suicide, demanding instantaneous lobotomy,

and who were given instead the concrete void of insulin Metrazol electricity hydrotherapy psychotherapy occupational therapy pingpong & amnesia,

who in humorless protest overturned only one symbolic pingpong table, resting briefly in catatonia,

returning years later truly bald except for a wig of blood, and tears and fingers, to the visible madman doom of the wards of the madtowns of the East,

70 Pilgrim State's Rockland's and Greystone's foetid halls, bickering with the echoes of the soul, rocking and rolling in the midnight solitude-bench dolmen-realms of love, dream of life a nightmare, bodies turned to stone as heavy as the moon,

with mother finally ******, and the last fantastic book flung out of the tenement window, and the last door closed at 4 A.M. and the last telephone slammed at the wall in reply and the last furnished room emptied down to the last piece of mental furniture, a yellow paper rose twisted on a wire hanger in the closet, and even that imaginary nothing but a hopeful little bit of hallucination—

ah, Carl, while you are not safe I am not safe, and now you're really in the total animal soup of time—

and who therefore ran through the icy streets obsessed with a sudden flash of the alchemy of the use of the ellipse the catalog the meter & the vibrating plane,

who dreamt and made incarnate gaps in Time & Space through images juxtaposed, and trapped the archangel of the soul between 2 visual images and joined the elemental verbs and set the noun and dash of consciousness together jumping with sensation of Pater Omnipotens Aeterna Deus

75 to recreate the syntax and measure of poor human prose and stand before you speechless and intelligent and shaking with shame, rejected yet confessing out the soul to conform to the rhythm of thought in his naked and endless head,

the madman bum and angel beat in Time, unknown, yet putting down here what might be left to say in time come after death,

and rose reincarnate in the ghostly clothes of jazz in the goldhorn shadow of the band and blew the suffering of America's naked mind for love into an eli eli lamma lamma sabacthani saxophone cry that shivered the cities down to the last radio

with the absolute heart of the poem of life butchered out of their own bodies good to eat a thousand years.

II

What sphinx of cement and aluminum bashed open their skulls and ate up their brains and imagination?

80 Moloch! Solitude! Filth! Ugliness! Ashcans and unobtainable dollars! Children screaming under the stairways! Boys sobbing in armies! Old men weeping in the parks!

Moloch! Moloch! Nightmare of Moloch! Moloch the loveless! Mental Moloch! Moloch the heavy judger of men!

Moloch the incomprehensible prison! Moloch the crossbone soulless jail-house and Congress of sorrows! Moloch whose buildings are judgment! Moloch the vast stone of war! Moloch the stunned governments!

Moloch whose mind is pure machinery! Moloch whose blood is running money! Moloch whose fingers are ten armies! Moloch whose breast is a cannibal dynamo! Moloch whose ear is a smoking tomb!

Moloch whose eyes are a thousand blind windows! Moloch whose skyscrapers stand in the long streets like endless Jehovahs! Moloch whose factories dream and croak in the fog! Moloch whose smokestacks and antennae crown the cities!

85   Moloch whose love is endless oil and stone! Moloch whose soul is electricity and banks! Moloch whose poverty is the specter of genius! Moloch whose fate is a cloud of sexless hydrogen! Moloch whose name is the Mind!

Moloch in whom I sit lonely! Moloch in whom I dream Angels! Crazy in Moloch! Cocksucker in Moloch! Lacklove and manless in Moloch!

Moloch who entered my soul early! Moloch in whom I am a consciousness without a body! Moloch who frightened me out of my natural ecstasy! Moloch whom I abandon! Wake up in Moloch! Light streaming out of the sky!

Moloch! Moloch! Robot apartments! invisible suburbs! skeleton treasuries! blind capitals! demonic industries! spectral nations! invincible madhouses! granite cocks! monstrous bombs!

They broke their backs lifting Moloch to Heaven! Pavements, trees, radios, tons! lifting the city to Heaven which exists and is everywhere about us!

90   Visions! omens! hallucinations! miracles! ecstasies! gone down the American river!

Dreams! adorations! illuminations! religions! the whole boatload of sensitive bullshit!

Breakthroughs! over the river! flips and crucifixions! gone down the flood! Highs! Epiphanies! Despairs! Ten years' animal screams and suicides! Minds! New loves! Mad generation! down on the rocks of Time!

Real holy laughter in the river! They saw it all! the wild eyes! the holy yells! They bade farewell! They jumped off the roof! to solitude! waving! carrying flowers! Down to the river! into the street!

III

Carl Solomon! I'm with you in Rockland where you're madder than I am

95   I'm with you in Rockland where you must feel very strange

I'm with you in Rockland where you imitate the shade of my mother

I'm with you in Rockland where you've murdered your twelve secretaries

I'm with you in Rockland where you laugh at this invisible humor

I'm with you in Rockland where we are great writers on the same dreadful typewriter

100   I'm with you in Rockland where your condition has become serious and is reported on the radio

I'm with you in Rockland where the faculties of the skull no longer admit the worms of the senses

I'm with you in Rockland where you drink the tea of the breasts of the spinsters of Utica

I'm with you in Rockland where you pun on the bodies of your nurses the harpies of the Bronx

I'm with you in Rockland where you scream in a straightjacket that you're losing the game of the actual pingpong of the abyss

105   I'm with you in Rockland where you bang on the catatonic piano the soul is innocent and immortal it should never die ungodly in an armed madhouse

I'm with you in Rockland where fifty more shocks will never return your soul to its body again from its pilgrimage to a cross in the void

I'm with you in Rockland where you accuse your doctors of insanity and plot the Hebrew socialist revolution against the fascist national Golgotha

I'm with you in Rockland where you will split the heavens of Long Island and resurrect your living human Jesus from the superhuman tomb

I'm with you in Rockland where there are twentyfive thousand mad comrades all together singing the final stanzas of the Internationale

110   I'm with you in Rockland where we hug and kiss the United States under our bedsheets the United States that coughs all night and won't let us sleep

I'm with you in Rockland where we wake up electrified out of the coma by our own souls' airplanes roaring over the roof they've come to drop angelic bombs the hospital illuminates itself imaginary walls collapse O skinny legions run outside O starry-spangled shock of mercy the eternal war is here O victory forget your underwear we're free

I'm with you in Rockland in my dreams you walk dripping from a sea-journey on the highway across America in tears to the door of my cottage in the Western night

SUGGESTIONS FOR DISCUSSION

1. After you've read "Howl," write for five minutes or so. What is your overall reaction to the poem? Pick out two or three especially striking lines or images in the poem. Now, meet in a group of four or five. Compare your reactions to the poem. How would you account for differences and similarities? What lines or images did you and other group members pick out? What do these selections from the poem reveal about it?

2. As noted above Moloch (in Part II) is a pagan deity in the Old Testament who demands the sacrifice of children. How does the sacrifice of children form a major theme in the poem?

3. "Howl" defined the sensibility of a generation. What poem, song, or other form of cultural expression does that work today?

SUGGESTIONS FOR WRITING

1. "Howl" is filled with anxiety, fear, desire, and hope. Write an essay that sorts out the conflicting feelings in the poem.

2. Who would or could write a version of "Howl" today?

3. Write your own version of "Howl." Begin with "I have seen the best minds of my generation…" and go from there. Write a poem or an essay, as you see fit.

CHECKING OUT THE WEB

1. As Michael Pope suggests in "Gen X's Enduring Legacy: The Internet," the meanings ascribed to Generation X have changed over time. Do a Web search using "Generation X" as the keywords. Surf through several sites, paying attention to the representation of Generation X that comes to the surface. What meanings and characteristics of the generation appear in each? What do they have in common? What differences do you see? How would you account for these differences and similarities?

2. The readings in this chapter reveal how adults represent young people. To get a sense of how young people today represent themselves on-line, check out a number of teen e-zines. YO: Youth Outlook at http://www.youthoutlook.org and About Teens at http://www.aboutteens.org are places to start, but there are many others e-zines for youth and college-age students. How do teens and college students represent themselves, their concerns, and their interests?

3. Allen Ginsberg was a spokesman for the Beat Generation of the 1950s. You've read his poem "Howl." Do a Web search to put the poem in the historical context of the Beat Generation and bring the results to class.

The identity of a generation takes shape in part through the movies. Since the 1950s, movies about teenagers and youth culture have explored generational identities and intergenerational conflicts. In *The Wild One, Blackboard Jungle,* and *Rebel Without a Cause* (the1950s); *The Graduate* and *Easy Rider* (the1960s); *Saturday Night Fever* and *American Graffiti* (the 1970s); *River's Edge, The Breakfast Club,* and *Fast Times at Ridge-mont High* (the 1980s); and *Do the Right Thing, Boyz'n the Hood, Slackers,* and *Clerks* (the1990s), to name some of the best-known movies, Hollywood and independent filmmakers have fashioned influential representations of young people.

This section considers how movies represent various youth cultures and their relations to adult culture. Think about what the term *representation* means. A key term in cultural analysis, it is more complex than it appears. At first glance, it seems to mean simply showing what is there, reflecting life as it occurs. But the complexity comes in because the medium of representation—whether language or moving images—has its own codes and conventions that shape the way people see and understand what is being shown. By the same token, representation is not just the result of a writer's or filmmaker's intentions. Readers and viewers make sense of the codes and conventions of representation in different ways, depending on their interests and social position. So to think about the representation of youth cultures in films in a meaningful way, consider how the images of youth culture in film have been filtered through such conventions as the feature film, the Hollywood star system, and the available stock of characters and plots viewers will recognize and respond to.

JUVENILE DELINQUENCY FILMS

James Gilbert

James Gilbert is an American historian at the University of Maryland. The following selection is taken from Gilbert's book *A Cycle of Outrage: America's Reaction to Juvenile Delinquency in the 1950s* (1988). Here, Gilbert traces the emergence in the 1950s of juvenile delinquency films and popular responses to them. This selection consists of the opening paragraph of Gilbert's chapter "Juvenile Delinquency Movies" and his analysis of *The Wild One, Blackboard Jungle,* and *Rebel Without a Cause.*

SUGGESTION FOR READING Notice how Gilbert sets up his dominant theme in the opening paragraph, when he explains that widespread public concern with juvenile delinquency presents Hollywood with "dangerous but lucrative possibilities." Take note of how Gilbert defines these "possibilities" in the opening paragraph and then follow how he traces this theme through his discussion of the three films.

Whereas, shortly after the screening of this movie the local police had several cases in which the use of knives by young people were involved and at our own Indiana Joint High School two girls, while attending a high school dance, were cut by a knife wielded by a teen-age youth who by his own admission got the idea from watching *Rebel Without a Cause.*

Now Therefore Be It Resolved by the Board of Directors of Indiana Joint High School that said Board condemns and deplores the exhibition of pictures such as *Rebel Without a Cause* and any other pictures which depict abnormal or subnormal behavior by the youth of our country and which tend to deprave the morals of young people.

Indiana, Pennsylvania, Board of Education to the MPAA, January 9, 1956

1   The enormous outpouring of concern over juvenile delinquency in the mid-1950s presented the movie industry with dangerous but lucrative possibilities. An aroused public of parents, service club members, youth-serving agencies, teachers, adolescents, and law enforcers constituted a huge potential audience for delinquency films at a time when general audiences for all films had declined. Yet this was a perilous subject to exploit, for public pressure on the film industry to set a wholesome example for youth remained unremitting. Moreover, the accusation that mass culture caused delinquency—especially the "new delinquency" of the postwar period—was the focus of much contemporary attention. If the film industry approached the issue of delinquency, it had to proceed cautiously. It could not present delinquency favorably; hence all stories would have to be set in the moral firmament of the movie Code. Yet to be successful, films had to evoke sympathy from young people who were increasingly intrigued by the growing youth culture of which delinquency seemed to be one variant.

Stanley Kramer's picture, *The Wild One,* released in 1953, stands in transition from the somber realism of "film noir" pessimism and environmentalism to the newer stylized explorations of delinquent culture that characterized the mid-1950s. Shot in dark and realistic black and white, the film stars Marlon Brando and Lee Marvin as rival motorcycle gang leaders who invade a small California town. Brando's character is riven with ambiguity and potential violence—a prominent characteristic of later juvenile delinquency heroes. On the other hand, he is clearly not an adolescent, but not yet an adult either, belonging to a suspended age that seems alienated from any recognizable stage of development. He appears to be tough and brutal, but he is not, nor, ultimately, is he as attractive as he might have been. His character flaws are appealing, but unnerving. This is obvious in the key symbol of the film, the motorcycle trophy which he carries. He has not won it as the towns-

people assume; he has stolen it from a motorcycle "scramble." Furthermore, he rejects anything more than a moment's tenderness with the girl he meets. In the end, he rides off alone, leaving her trapped in the small town that his presence has so disrupted and exposed. The empty road on which he travels leads to similar nameless towns; he cannot find whatever it is he is compelled to seek.

Brando's remarkable performance made this film a brilliant triumph. Its moral ambiguity, however, and the very attractiveness of the alienated hero, meant that the producers needed to invoke two film code strategies to protect themselves from controversy. The first of these was an initial disclaimer appearing after the titles: "This is a shocking story. It could never take place in most American towns—but it did in this one. It is a public challenge not to let it happen again." Framing the other end of the film was a speech by a strong moral voice of authority. A sheriff brought in to restore order to the town lectures Brando on the turmoil he has created and then, as a kind of punishment, casts him back onto the lonesome streets.

Aside from Brando's stunning portrayal of the misunderstood and inarticulate antihero, the film did not quite emerge from traditional modes of presenting crime and delinquency: the use of black and white; the musical score with its foreboding big-band sound; the relatively aged performers; and the vague suggestions that Brando and his gang were refugees from urban slums. Furthermore, the reception to the film was not, as some might have predicted, as controversial as what was to come. Of course, there were objections—for example, New Zealand banned the film—but it did not provoke the outrage that the next group of juvenile delinquency films inspired.

5   The film that fundamentally shifted Hollywood's treatment of delinquency was *The Blackboard Jungle,* produced in 1955, and in which traditional elements remained as a backdrop for contemporary action. The movie was shot in

black and white and played in a slum high school. But it clearly presented what was to become the driving premise of subsequent delinquency films—the division of American society into conflicting cultures made up of adolescents on one side and adults on the other. In this film the delinquent characters are portrayed as actual teenagers, as high school students. The crimes they commit are, with a few exceptions, crimes of behavior such as defying authority, status crimes, and so on. Of most symbolic importance is the transition in music that occurs in the film. Although it includes jazz numbers by Stan Kenton and Bix Beiderbecke, it is also the first film to feature rock and roll, specifically, "Rock Around the Clock" played by Bill Haley.

The story line follows an old formula of American novels and films. A teacher begins a job at a new school, where he encounters enormous hostility from the students. He stands up to the ringleader of the teenage rowdies, and finally wins over the majority of the students. In itself this is nothing controversial. But *Blackboard Jungle* also depicts the successful defiance of delinquents, who reject authority and terrorize an American high school. Their success and their power, and the ambiguous but attractive picture of their culture, aimed at the heart of the film Code and its commitment to uphold the dignity of figures and institutions of authority.

Still cautious, the studio opened the film with a disclaimer. It also used a policeman as a voice of authority who explained postwar delinquency in this way: "They were six years old in the last war. Father in the army. Mother in a defense plant. No home life. No Church life. No place to go. They form street gangs....Gang leaders have taken the place of parents."

Despite this protective sermonizing, the film aroused substantial opposition. It did so for many reasons, but principally because it pictured a high school with unsympathetic administrators and teachers in the grip of teenage hoodlums. Given contemporary fears of just such a situation, and the belief that such was the case throughout the

United States, the film's realistic texture was shocking. But other elements distressed some audiences. For example, the leading adolescent character is a black student, played with enormous sympathy and skill by Sidney Poitier. And the clash of cultures and generations, which later became standard in juvenile delinquency films, was in this, its first real expression, stated with stark and frightening clarity. For example, in one crucial scene, a teacher brings his precious collection of jazz records to school to play for the boys, hoping, of course, to win them over. His efforts to reach out to them fail completely. The students mock and despise his music and then destroy his collection. They have their own music, their own culture, and their own language.

Public response to *Blackboard Jungle* provided a glimpse of the audience division between generations and cultures. Attending a preview of the film, producer Brooks was surprised, and obviously delighted, when young members of the audience began dancing in the aisles to the rock and roll music. This occurred repeatedly in showings after the film opened. But other reactions were more threatening. For example in Rochester, New York, there were reports that "young hoodlums cheered the beatings and methods of terror inflicted upon a teacher by a gang of boys" pictured in the film. But box office receipts in the first few weeks indicated a smash hit, and in New York City the first ten days at Loew's State theater set a record for attendance.

Nevertheless, the film caused an angry backlash against the film industry. Censors in Memphis, Tennessee, banned it. It was denounced by legal organizations, teachers, reviewers like Bosley Crowther of the *New York Times,* and even by the Teenage Division of the Labor Youth League (a communist organization). The National Congress of Parents and Teachers, the Girl Scouts, the D.A.R., and the American Association of University Women disapproved it. The American Legion voted *Blackboard Jungle* the movie "that hurt America the most in foreign countries in 1955." And the Ambassador to Italy, Clare Booth Luce, with State Department approbation, forced the film's withdrawal from the Venice Film Festival.

10   Following swiftly on this commercial success was *Rebel Without a Cause*, a very different sort of film, and perhaps the most famous and influential of the 1950s juvenile delinquency endeavors. Departing from the somber working-class realism of *Blackboard Jungle*, *Rebel* splashed the problem of middle-class delinquency across America in full color. Moreover, its sympathy lay entirely with adolescents, played by actors James Dean, Natalie Wood, and Sal Mineo, who all live wholly inside the new youth culture. Indeed, this is the substantial message of the film: each parent and figure of authority is grievously at fault for ignoring or otherwise failing youth. The consequence is a rebellion with disastrous results.

Once the script had been developed, shooting began in the spring of 1955, during the height of the delinquency dispute and following fast on the heels of the box-office success of *Blackboard Jungle*. Warner Brothers approved a last minute budget hike to upgrade the film to color. In part this was a response to the box office appeal of the star, James Dean, whose *East of Eden* was released to acclaim in early April.

When it approved the film, the Code Authority issued two warnings. Geoffrey Shurlock wrote to Jack Warner in March 1955: "As you know, we have steadfastly maintained under the requirements of the Code that we should not approve stories of underage boys and girls indulging in either murder or illicit sex." He suggested that the violence in the picture be toned down. Furthermore, he noted: "It is of course vital that there be no inference of a questionable or homosexual relationship between Plato [Sal Mineo] and Jim [James Dean]." A follow-up commentary suggested the need for further changes in the area of violence. For example, Shurlock noted of the fight at the planetarium: "We suggest merely indicating that these high-school boys have tire chains, not showing them flaunting them."

Despite these cautions, the film, when it was released, contained substantial violence: the accidental death of one of the teenagers in a "chickie run"; the shooting of another teenager; and Plato's death at the hands of the police. Furthermore, there remained strong echoes of Plato's homosexual interest in Jim.

The film also took a curious, ambiguous position on juvenile delinquency. Overtly, it disapproved, demonstrating the terrible price paid for misbehavior. Yet the film, more than any other thus far, glorified the teenage life-styles it purported to reject. Adult culture is pictured as insecure, insensitive, and blind to the problems of youth. Teenagers, on the other hand, are portrayed as searching for genuine family life, warmth, and security. They choose delinquency in despair of rejection by their parents. Indeed, each of the three young heroes is condemned to search for the emotional fulfillment that adults deny: Dean for the courage his father lacks; Natalie Wood (as his girlfriend) for her father's love; and Plato for a family, which he finds momentarily in Dean and Wood. Instead of being securely set in adult society, each of these values must be constructed outside normal society and inside a new youth-created world. What in other films might have provided a reconciling finale—a voice of authority—becomes, itself, a symbol of alienation. A policeman who befriends Dean is absent at a decisive moment when he could have prevented the tragic ending. Thus no adults or institutions remain unscathed. The ending, in which adults recognize their own failings, is thus too sudden and contrived to be believable. It is as if the appearance of juvenile delinquency in such a middle-class setting is impossible to explain, too complex and too frightening to be understood in that context.

15   And also too attractive, for the film pictures delinquent culture as an intrusive, compelling, and dangerous force that invades middle-class homes and institutions. The producers carefully indicated that each family was middle class, although Plato's mother might well be considered wealthier than that. Teenage, delinquent culture, however, has obvious working-class origins,

symbolized by souped-up jalopies, levis, and T-shirts that became the standard for youth culture. In fact, when Dean goes out for his fateful "chickie run," he changes into T-shirt and levis from his school clothes. Furthermore, the film presents this delinquent culture without judgment. There is no obvious line drawn between what is teenage culture and what is delinquency. Is delinquency really just misunderstood youth culture? The film never says, thus reflecting public confusion on the same issue.

A second tactic of the filmmakers posed a philosophic problem about youth culture and delinquency. This emerges around the symbol of the planetarium. In the first of two scenes there, Dean's new high school class visits for a lecture and a show. The lecturer ends his presentation abruptly with a frightening suggestion—the explosion of the world and the end of the universe. He concludes: "Man existing alone seems an episode of little consequence." This existential reference precedes the rumble in which Dean is forced to fight his new classmates after they puncture the tires of his car. The meaning is clear: Dean must act to establish an identity which his parents and society refuse to grant him. This is a remarkable translation of the basic premise of contemporary Beat poets, whose solitary search for meaning and self-expression tinged several of the other initial films in this genre also.

Another scene at the planetarium occurs at night, at the end of the film. The police have pursued Plato there after he shoots a member of the gang that has been harassing Dean. Dean follows him into the building, and, in a reprise of the earlier scene, turns on the machine that lights the stars and planets. The two boys discuss the end of the world. Dean empties Plato's gun, and the confused youth then walks out of the building. The police, mistaking his intent, gun him down. Once again tragedy follows a statement about the ultimate meaninglessness of life.

By using middle-class delinquency to explore questions of existence, this film undeniably contested the effectiveness of traditional family and community institutions. There is even the hint that Dean, Wood, and Mineo represent the possibility of a new sort of family; but this is only a fleeting suggestion. In the end it is family and community weakness that bring tragedy for which there can be no real solution. Without the strikingly sympathetic performances of Dean, Wood, and Mineo, this picture might have fallen under the weight of its bleak (and pretentious) message. As it was, however, *Rebel Without a Cause* was a box office smash, and Dean's short, but brilliant career was now assured.

As with *Blackboard Jungle,* the MPAA was the focus of furious reaction to the film. Accusations of copycat crimes, particularly for a stabbing in Indiana, Pennsylvania, brought condemnations and petitions against "pictures which depict abnormal or subnormal behavior by the youth of our country and which tend to deprave the morals of young people." The MPAA fought back against this accusation in early 1956 as Arthur DeBra urged an investigation to discover if the incident at the Indiana, Pennsylvania, high school had any relationship to the "juvenile delinquency situation in the school and community." As one writer for the *Christian Science Monitor* put it, "the new Warner Brothers picture will emerge into the growing nationwide concern about the effects on youth of comics, TV, and movies." This prediction was based upon actions already taken by local censors. The Chicago police had ordered cuts in the film, and the city of Milwaukee banned it outright.

20   On the other hand, much of the response was positive. As *Variety* noted in late 1955, fan letters had poured in to Hollywood "from teenagers who have identified themselves with the characters; from parents who have found the film conveyed a special meaning; and from sociologists and psychiatrists who have paid tribute to the manner in which child-parent misunderstanding is highlighted."

Quite clearly, the film became a milestone for the industry. It established youth culture as a fitting subject for films, and created some of the most pervasive stereotypes that were repeated in later films. These included the tortured, alienated, and misunderstood youth and intolerant parents and authority figures. It did not, however, lead to more subtle explorations of the connections between youth culture and delinquency. If anything, the opposite was true. For one thing, Dean was killed in an auto accident shortly after this enormous success. Furthermore, it was probably the seriousness of *Blackboard Jungle* and *Rebel* that provoked controversy, and the movie industry quickly learned that it could attract teenage audiences without risking the ire of adults if it reduced the dosage of realism. Thus the genre deteriorated into formula films about teenagers, made principally for drive-in audiences who were not particular about the features they saw.

SUGGESTIONS FOR DISCUSSION

1. Gilbert notes that *Rebel Without a Cause* became a "milestone" for the film industry, establishing youth culture as a fitting (and profitable) subject and creating stereotypes of alienated youth and intolerant adults that recurred in later movies. Consider to what extent these stereotypes continue to appear in movies. How would you update their appearance since the 1950s? List examples of movies that use the conventionalized figures of alienated youth and intolerant adults. What continuity do you see over time? In what ways have the portrayals changed?

2. Gilbert says that by "using middle-class delinquency to explore questions of existence," *Rebel Without a Cause* "contested the effectiveness of traditional family and community institutions." Explain what Gilbert means. Can you think of other films that "contest" family and community institutions?

3. Watch the three films Gilbert discusses—*The Wild One, Blackboard Jungle,* and *Rebel Without a Cause.* Working together with a group of classmates, first summarize Gilbert's discussion of how each film handles the dilemma of evoking viewers' sympathy for young people while in no way presenting delinquency in a favorable light. Next, develop your own analysis of how (or whether) each film creates sympathy for young people in their confrontations with the adult world. To what extent do you agree with Gilbert's line of analysis? Where do you differ with or want to modify his analysis?

SUGGESTED ASSIGNMENT

Pick a film or group of films that in some way characterizes a generation of young people. For example, analyze how *The Graduate* captures something important about youth in the 1960s. Or look at how a cluster of three or four films portrays the "twentysomething" generation of the 1990s. Or you can follow *Newsweek*'s example in "Raging Teen Hormones" and put together a time line that reveals some trend in youth films. (Notice how the thermometer registers how "hot" the film is.)

Write an analysis of how the film or films represent youth. Do not decide whether the portrayal is accurate, but analyze how it constructs a certain image of youth culture and what might be the significance of the representation.

Raging Teen Hormones

Contemporary teen films are much more explicit than such classics as "Splendor in the Grass" (though maybe not as erotic). A survey of some recent landmarks.

Fast Times at Ridgemont High
1982 *Casual nudity, sex scenes and profanity: big hit*

The Breakfast Club
1985 *Talkathon featured minimal skin. Dirty mouths earned R rating anyway.*

Ferris Bueller's Day Off
1986 *Teens play hooky, attend ball game, parade. Wholesome to the max.*

Heathers
1989 *Do what with a chainsaw? R rating for black comedy about teen suicide.*

Clueless
1995 *Heroine is 'a virgin who can't drive.' Jane Austen plot brought PG-13.*

Here are some suggestions to help you examine how a film represents youth culture:

- *How does the film portray young people?* What in particular marks them as "youth"? Pay particular attention to the characters' clothing, hairstyles, body posture, and ways of speaking.
- *How does the film mark young people generationally?* Are the characters part of a distinctive youth subculture? How would you characterize the group's collective identity? What is the relation of the group to the adult world and its institutions? What intergenerational conflicts figure in the film?
- *How does the film portray a particular historical moment or decade?* What visual clues enable viewers to locate the era of the film? What historical events, if any, enter into the film?
- *How does the sound track contribute to the representation of youth culture that is projected by the film?*
- *How do the stars of the film influence viewers' perceptions of youth culture?* Do they enhance viewers' sympathies? Are the main characters cultural icons like James Dean or Marlon Brando?

FIELDWORK   Ethnographic Interviews

Music is one of the keys to generational identities. Songs carry the emotional power to define for their listeners what it means to be alive at a particular moment. Singers and musicians evoke generations and decades—Frank Sinatra's emergence as a teen idol in the big band era of the 1940s; Elvis Presley, Little Richard, Buddy Holly, and early rock and roll in the 1950s; the Beatles, Rolling Stones, Bob Dylan, Motown, and the Memphis sound of Aretha Franklin and Otis Redding in the 1960s; the funk of Parliament and War, disco, and punk bands such as the Clash and Sex Pistols in the 1970s; the megastars Bruce Springsteen, Madonna, and Michael Jackson, the rap of Public Enemy and NWA, alternative, and the grunge groups of the 1980s and 1990s.

One way to figure out how people experience their lives as part of a generation is to investigate what music means to them. The fieldwork project in this chapter investigates how people across generations use music daily to create, maintain, or subvert individual and collective identities. The method is the ethnographic interview, a nondirective approach that asks people to explain how they make sense of music in their lives. "Ethnographic" means literally graphing—getting down in the record—the values and practices of the ethnos, the tribe or group.

MY MUSIC

Susan D. Craft, Daniel Cavicchi, and Charles Keil

The following three ethnographic interviews come from the Music in Daily Life Project in the American Studies program at the State University of New York at Buffalo. The project's goal was to use open-ended ethnographic interviews to find out what music means to people and how they integrate music into their lives and identities. Two undergraduate classes conducted the interviews and began with the question, "What is music about for you?" (The classes settled on this question "so as not to prejudge the situation" and to give the respondents "room to define music of all kinds in their lives.") Then the interviews were edited, organized by age group, and published in the book *My Music* (1993). The interviews that follow come from people from three generations—ages fifteen, thirty-three, and fifty-seven, respectively.

SUGGESTION FOR READING Keep in mind that the interviews you are reading were not scripted but are the result of interviewers' on-the-spot decisions. As you read, notice how the interviewers ask questions and when they ask for more details or redirect the conversation.

EDWARDO

Edwardo is fifteen years old and is enrolled in an auto mechanics program at a vocational high school.

Q: What kind of music do you like to listen to?

A: Basically, I listen to anything. I prefer rap and regular…R and B and rock.

Q: What groups do you listen to when you get a choice?

A: When I'm by myself, I listen to rap like Eric B, MC Hammer, and KRS I. People like that. When I'm with my friends, I listen to Ozzie, and Pink Floyd, Iron Maiden, Metallica. You know, groups like that.

Q: Why do you listen to different stuff when you're by yourself? Different than when you're with your friends?

A: Usually when I'm over at their house they have control of the radio, and they don't like to listen to rap that much.

Q: What kind of things do you do when you are listening to music by yourself?

A: I lip-synch it in the mirror. I pretend I'm doing a movie. Kind of embarrassing, but I do that. And I listen to it while I'm in the shower. And…that's about all.

Q: Would you like to be a professional musician?

A: Kind of. Yeah.

Q: If you pictured yourself as a musician, how would you picture yourself? What kind of music would you play?

A: I'd probably rap. If I didn't, I'd like to play the saxophone.

Q: When you're walking along, do you ever have a song going through your head? Do you have specific songs that you listen to and, if not, do you ever make up songs?

A: Yes. I rap a lot to myself. I make up rhymes and have one of my friends give it a beat. Sometimes we put it on tape. Sometimes we don't.

Q: Could you give me an example of some of the stuff you have put together on your own?

A: I made up one that goes something like, "Now I have many mikes/stepped on many floors./Shattered all the windows/knocked down all the doors." That's just a little part of it. This is hard for me. I'm nervous.

Q: So what kind of things do you try to put together in your songs? What kinds of things do you try to talk about in your songs?

A: I make up different stories. Like people running around. Sometimes I talk about drugs and drinking. Most of the time I just brag about myself.

Q: Do you have any brothers and sisters who listen to the same sort of stuff?

A: Yes. My older brother…he's the one who got me into rap. We're originally from the Bronx, in New York, and he doesn't listen to anything else. My cousin, he listens to heavy metal but he's kind of switched to late-seventies, early-seventies rock. He listens to Pink Floyd and all them, so I listen with him sometimes. I listen with my friends. That's about all.

Q: How long have you been listening to rap?

A: For about seven or eight years.

Q: What kind of stuff were you listening to before that?

A: Actually, I don't remember. Oh yeah. We used to live in California and I was listening to oldies…like the Four Tops and all them. In California…the Mexicans down there, they only listen to the oldies and stuff like that.

Q: Why would you say you changed to rap?

A: When I came down here, everything changed. People were listening to different kinds of music and I was, you know, behind times. So I just had to switch to catch up.

Q: So you would say that your friends really influence you and the kind of music you listen to by yourself?

A: Yeah. I would say that.

Q: When you're listening to music by yourself, what kinds of things go through your mind? Are you concentrating on the words or what?

A: Sometimes I think about life, and all the problems I have. Sometimes I just dwell on the lyrics and just listen to the music.

Q: Do you ever use music as a way to change your mood? If you're really depressed, is there a record you put on?

A: No. Usually when I listen to music and it changes me is when I'm bored and I don't have anything to do or I just get that certain urge to listen to music.

RALPH

Ralph is thirty-three years old, an experienced truck driver working as a bus driver for a city transit authority when he was interviewed by a male friend.

I was weaned on the music of the fifties. My musical taste began to form in about…well, my first record album was Chubby Checker's "Let's Do the Twist"…that was 1961. I begged my mom for it. I saw it up at a grocery store here; I had to have it. So she bought it for me. I really dug that.

I still really dig those old rhythm and blues bands back then. I was mainly a product of the Beatles–Rolling Stones–Dave Clark Five era. You know, I never really cared for the Rolling Stones when they first came out. My big group was the Dave Clark Five. I thought they were it until I heard they died in a plane crash somewhere in France, which was a big rumor of the day; but two or three weeks later we found out they didn't die.

I was a Beatles generation kid. I can still remember most of the lyrics of most of the songs they put out. It's a result of constant repetition of

it being drummed into my head constantly…just as I'm sure that like somebody who was born in the seventies…David Bowie…I'm sure that a teenager in the seventies would know the words to his songs—"Ziggy Stardust," the early Bowie stuff.

Did the Beatles direct me? Yes, they had some influence on my life. I hate to admit it, but they did. They always painted a rosy picture when I was growing up. It was all love and peace, the flower-child movement. But at that time someone who had a big influence on my musical life was my big brother. He was bringing home stuff like the Supremes at the A-Go-Go…blues…which I really think is the Lord's music. Today you can't find it anymore; there is very little of it coming out, if any.

Today's music just depresses me; it's like the doldrums between 1973 to about 1978…before the new pop or new wave scene arrived…the punkies, the pop stars. I can see things leading that way now too with all this techno-pop. Basically I was into jazz at the time; that's when I got my jazz influences with Monk, Bird, and Coltrane. I used to listen to those people heavily back in the early 1970s. I really loved groups like the Mahavishnu Orchestra. I love jazz fusion and Jeff Beck, but there's some people I really don't care for…Pat Metheny. I never cared for him; why, I don't know. Maybe he has no character in his guitar. It's like a bland speed shuffle. Whereas people like Larry Coryell and John McLaughlin and Jeff Beck, Jan Akkerman…it's just so distinct…their own personal signature. But guys like Pat Metheny and that guy who played with Chick Corea, Al Dimeola, they just don't sign their work; it's all just mumbo-jumbo to me. Other people like them; they sell, right? I don't know; that's my personal taste. I really appreciated any band with a truly outstanding guitarist, somebody you can say: Ah, now this is *him*…I really appreciate that, the signatures.

I like to hear music that I'm not going to hear anyplace else; judge it for myself. Another phase of my life I went through, I really appreciated the blues. From about '67 to '72 was really my blues era, when I was in college. Of course, a lot of people were blues addicts then. Everybody was getting drafted for Vietnam...the blues were very popular back then. You had a lot of English blues groups coming out, like the original Fleetwood Mac, Peter Green...who I thought was a phenomenal blues guitar player, phenomenal!...different groups like the Hedgehogs. A lot of groups shucked it off and went commercial; that really turned me off to them. I also happen to like Beach Boy music...all a rip-off of black history, all a rip-off of black music...but white fun...black fun translated into white fun. Surf music was big around '65 or '66. I'll admit it; we were punks.

Ah, let's see...punk. Where did punk start out? Malcolm McLaren? Malcolm McDowell in *Clockwork Orange*?...when he played the ultimate punk, Alex? Was it Richard Hell in 1974 in New York City with ripped T-shirts and safety pins? Punk is kind of a quaint way of expressing yourself. It hasn't come to murder yet; I wonder if it's gonna come down to murder-rock? You've got savage beating and stuff like that; I wonder if it's ever going to get there. It'll be interesting to see where it goes in the future...looking ahead.

These days I like to go into a bar with a quality jukebox...go in there, dump some quarters in the box, and listen to the old songs.

STEVE

Steve is fifty-seven years old and works as a salesman. He was interviewed by his daughter.

Q: Dad, what does music do for you?

A: What does music do for me? Well, music relaxes me. In order for me to explain, I have to go back and give you an idea exactly how my whole life was affected by music. For example, when I was five or six years old, my mother and father had come from Poland, so naturally all music played at home was ethnic music. This established my ethnic heritage. I had a love for Polish music. Later on in life, like at Polish weddings, they played mostly Polish music...since we lived in Cheektowaga and there is mostly Polish people and a Polish parish. My love for Polish music gave me enjoyment when I was growing up and it carried on all these years to the present time.

But naturally as I got educated in the English language I started going to the movies. I was raised during the Depression and, at that time, the biggest form of escape was musicals...people like Dick Powell, Ruby Keeler, Eddie Cantor, Al Jolson, and Shirley Temple. These were big stars of their day and in order to relax and forget your troubles...we all went through hard times...everybody enjoyed musicals, they were the biggest thing at that time. A lot of musicals were shows from Broadway so, as I was growing up in the Depression and watching movie musicals, I was also getting acquainted with hit tunes that came from Broadway. In that era, Tin Pan Alley was an expression for the place where all these song writers used to write and compose music, and these songs became the hits in the musicals.

Later on these writers went to the movies and it seemed as if every month there was a new hit song that everyone was singing. Some of the writers, like Irving Berlin, Gershwin, Jerome Kern, Harry Warren, and Sammy Kahn...some of these songs are the prettiest songs that were ever written. Even though I never played a musical instrument or was a singer, I was like hundreds of thousands of people in my era who loved music. In fact, radio was very popular at that time, so you heard music constantly on the radio, in the musicals, and all my life I could sing a song all the way through, knowing the tune *and knowing the words*.

Later on in life, when we get to W.W. II, music used to inspire patriotism, and also to bring you closer to home when overseas. For example, one place that just meant music was the Stage Door Canteen in Hollywood. All the stars of the movies and musicals used to volunteer their services and entertain everybody. Later on, as these stars went overseas and performed for the G.I.s, I had a chance to see a lot of these stars in person—stars that I really enjoyed, seeing their movies and listening to their music. So it was like bringing home to overseas. Of course, there was a lot of patriotic songs that stirred us...we were young...say, the Air Force song like

"Praise the Lord and Pass the Ammunition." There was sentimental songs like "There'll Be Blue Birds Over the White Cliffs of Dover," "I Heard a Nightingale Sing Over Berkeley Square." But it was actually music that helped you through tough times like W.W. II, the way music helped you feel better during the Depression…in days that I was younger.

When I came back from overseas…now I'm entering the romantic part of my life, in my early twenties…it was the era of the big bands. One of the greatest events in music history were bands like Glenn Miller and Benny Goodman, the Dorsey Brothers and Sammy Kaye…big bands were popular at the time you used to go to local Candy Kitchens and play the jukebox, and, just like some of the songs said, it was a wonderful time to be with your friends. Good clean entertainment; you listen to the jukebox, dance on the dance floor.

In the big band era, we get into the popular singers who used to sing with the big bands. They went on their own and the era of the ballads was born, and to me this was my favorite era of music in my life. I'll mention some of the big singers just to give you an idea of what I mean—singers like Bing Crosby, Frank Sinatra, Doris Day, Margaret Whiting, Jo Stafford, and Perry Como.

The time of your life when you meet the "girl of your dreams." I was fortunate that we had the Canadiana. It was just like the Love Boat of its time. They used to have a band, and you used to be able to dance on the dance floor. If they didn't have a dance band that night, they would play records, and you could listen to music riding on the lake at night under the stars and moon. It was unbelievable, that particular part of life. It's a shame the younger people of today couldn't experience, not only the boat, but a lot of the things we went through. We thought it was tough at that time, but it was the music that really made things a lot happier and the reason why it's so easy for someone like myself to hear a song and just place myself back in time, at exactly where I was. Was I in the Philippines, or

Tokyo, or on the boat? What were the songs that were playing when I first met my wife, what were they playing when I was a young recruit in the Air Force? All I have to do is hear the songs and it'll just take me back in time and I will relive a lot of the parts of my life and, of course, you only remember the good parts! (laughing) You don't remember the bad.

Music to me is very important. One thought that I wanted to mention, about going back in time: when I was just five or six years old, my parents, because they were from the old country, played Polish music, so that when I did meet the girl I was going to marry…every couple has a favorite song and ours was one that was very popular at that time…it was a Polish song to which they put American lyrics. The song was "Tell Me Whose Girl You Are," and I think it was because my wife and I came from a Polish background that Polish music was still a very important part of our life.

Q: What music really did for you was to make you get through bad times and made you think of good things mostly, right?

A: Well, yes, and I would say that music became part of my personality. I use music to not only relax, I use it to relieve tension. About thirty percent of the time I am singing, and it has become part of my personality because it has given me a certain amount of assurance. Not only does it relax me but I think it also bolsters my confidence in being a salesman where you have to always be up. You can't be depressed. Otherwise, you're just going to waste a day. I think music to me is also something that bolsters my spirit.

Q: Does music amplify your mood or does it change your mood? For example, when you're in a depressed mood do you put on something slow or something happy to get you out of that mood?

A: Well, when I was single, if my love life wasn't going right, I used to play sad songs. Well, I guess like most young kids when their love life isn't going right they turn to sad music. I know that after I'm married and have children and more experience, if I get in a depressed mood then I switch to happier music to change the mood.

Q: What do you think about today's music?

A: (laughing) I could give you enough swear words....No, seriously, I will answer you. I can do it right off the top of my head because I was in a restaurant this morning and I heard a song being played on the radio, which was supposedly a big hit by a new big star. Supposedly this fellow is just as big as Michael Jackson. I think his name is Prince, singing "All Night Long" [Lionel Richie], and, my God when I heard that record where they kept repeating the words over and over, I said to myself, "God, how terrible it is that these kids are not getting benefit of the music that we had when I was younger," because I can take one phrase and write a modern song. I could do the lyrics. And I'm not musical. Say, "Let's Go Mud Wrestling Tonight, Let's Go Mud Wrestling Tonight, You and I, Let's Go Mud Wrestling Tonight. We will be in the mud, we will be in the mud. After the day is over, it's night so Let's Go Mud Wrestling Tonight!"

I really felt very sorry because I realize that the music that I'm telling you about now...music of my era...not only gave me relaxation, not only gave me a certain amount of stimulation...the lyrics of the songs actually educated me. I would say thirty percent of what I know about life today was gleaned from songs. You remember what you learned from a song. Today I heard Paul Robeson singing "Ol' Man River," and I remember seeing the movie with Paul Robeson—the best singer of all time, and the story where it had a mixed marriage, things going on now...the problems of the black people. He sang, "take me away from the White Man Boss." That phrase stuck in my mind because as I heard the song today...and this song was sung thirty or forty years ago...I had also read in the editorial page why Reagan isn't the best candidate for the blacks because they are losing a lot of what they have gained, and I began to realize what a long struggle these people are having.

Q: So, in other words, some of the music you listen to taught you about the people singing it and gave you knowledge...?

A: Well, not only taught me about the people singing, but about life in general, conditions. For example, during the Depression there was a big hit, "Brother Can You Spare A Dime?" and the words went, "...once I built a railroad...now I'm asking for a hand-out."

It wasn't just the person singing the song but the times. For example, during the war era we sang songs that were not only patriotic, but they taught us a lot about what we were fighting for, what was so important about saving America. In a lot of cases, the songs weren't written by the religious but they had some religious overtones and brought in some sense of faith.

SUGGESTIONS FOR DISCUSSION

1. Edwardo's responses to the interviewer's questions are much shorter than Ralph's or Steve's. One senses the pressure that the interviewer must have felt to keep the conversation going. Ralph's interview, though, is one long response. Steve's contains an extended statement that is followed by question and answer. Take a second look at the questions that the interviewers ask of Edwardo and Steve. What do their purposes seem to be? Try to get a sense of how and why the interviewer decided to ask particular questions. What alternatives, if any, can you imagine?

2. Notice that the interviewees do not fall easily into one distinct musical subculture. Each talks about a range of music. How do Edwardo, Ralph, and Steve make sense of these various forms of musical expression?

3. Each of the interviewees relates his musical tastes to particular social groups or moments in time. How do they connect music to their relationship with others and/or their memories of the past?

Fieldwork Project

Work with two or three other students on this project. Each group member should interview three people of different ages to get a range of responses across generations. Use the opening question "What is music about for you?" from the Music in Daily Life project. Tape and transcribe the interview.

As a group, assemble and edit a collection of the interviews and write an introduction that explains the purpose of the interviews and their significance. Refer to "A Note on Interviewing" on the opposite page.

Editing

An edited interview is not simply the transcribed tape recording. It's important to capture the person's voice, but you also want the interview to be readable. Taped interviews can be filled with pauses, um's and ah's, incomplete or incoherent thoughts, and rambling associations. It is standard practice to "clean up" the interview, as long as doing so does not distort or change the subject's meanings. Cleaning up a transcript may include editing at the sentence level, but you may also leave out some of the taped material if it is irrelevant.

Writing an Introduction

In the introduction to the edited interviews, explain your purpose in asking people about the role that music plays in their lives. Follow this with some observations and interpretations of the results. Remember that the interviews have a limited authority. They don't "prove" anything about the role of music in daily life and the formation of individual or group identity. But they can be suggestive—and you will want to point out how and why.

The Music in Daily Life Project emphasizes the verbs you can use to describe people's relationship to music:

> Is this person *finding* music to explore and express an identity or being *invaded* by music to the point of identity diffusion, *using* music to solve personal problems, *consuming* music to fill a void and relieve alienation and boredom, *participating* in musical mysteries to feel fully human, *addicted* to music and evading reality, *orienting* via music to reality?

As you can see, each verb carries a different interpretation.

A Note on Interviewing

- *Choosing subjects.* Choose carefully. The three subjects you choose don't have to be big music buffs, but you will get your best interviews from people who are willing to talk about their likes, dislikes, memories, and associations.

- *Preparing your subject.* Make an appointment for the interview, and be on time. Tell your subject how long you will be spending and why you want this information.

- *Preparing yourself.* Before the interview, make a list of questions you want to ask. Most questions should be open-ended—they should not lead to a yes or no response. Just keep in mind that your goal is to listen, so you'll want to give your subject plenty of time to talk.

- *Conducting the interview.* Remember that in many respects, you control the agenda because you scheduled the interview and have determined the questions. The person you interview will be looking for guidance and direction. You are likely to have choices to make during the interview. The guidelines used by the Music in Daily Life Project note the following situation:

  > Somebody says, "I really love Bruce Springsteen and his music, can't help it, I get weepy over 'Born in the USA,' you know? But sometimes I wonder if I haven't just swallowed the hype about his being a working-class hero from New Jersey with the symbolic black guy by his side, you know what I mean?" and then pauses, looking at you for some direction or an answer. A choice to make.

  The choice concerns which thread in the conversation to follow—the person's love for Springsteen or his feeling of being hyped by the working-class hero image. You could do several things at this point in the interview. You could just wait for the person to explain, or you could say, "Tell me a little more about that," and hope the person will decide on which thread to elaborate. Or you could ask a direct question—"Why do you love Springsteen's music so much?" "What makes you weepy about 'Born in the USA'?" "Why do you think you're being hyped?" (Notice that each of these questions involves a choice that may take the interview in a different direction.)

  The point here is that a good interviewer must listen carefully during the interview. The goal is not to dominate but to give the subject some help in developing his or her ideas. Your task as an interviewer is to keep the conversation going.

- *Get Permission.* If you plan to use the subject's name in class discussion or a paper, get permission and make arrangements to show your subject what you have written.

Life Magazine

During the 1940s and 1950s, *Life* was the most popular general magazine in the United States, with an estimated readership of twenty million. Founded as a weekly in 1936, *Life* was the first American magazine to give a prominent place to the photoessay—visual narratives of the week's news as well as special features about American life and culture. If anything, *Life* taught generations of Americans what events in the world looked like, bringing them the work of such noted photographers as Robert Capa, Margaret Bourke-White, and W. Eugene Smith in photojournalistic accounts of the farm crisis and labor conflicts during the Great Depression and of battle-front situations during World War II.

In another sense, *Life* also taught Americans what the world should look like. After World War II, *Life* regularly featured families in postwar America, ordinary people in their new suburban homes, driving new cars on America's newly built freeway systems to work, school, and church. Perhaps no other source offers such a rich archive of what domestic life was supposed to be in the 1940s and 1950s in these pictorial representations of white, middle-class nuclear families.

To get a sense of how *Life* pictured America in the early postwar period, check out the December 3, 1945 issue and the news story "U.S. Normalcy: Against the Backdrop of a Troubled World *Life* Inspects an American City at Peace." Published just four months after World War II ended, the article juxtaposed images of international instability (the beginnings of the Cold War, the Nuremburg Trials, and child refugees in war-torn Europe and China) and of domestic turmoil (industrial strikes and unemployment) with the concerns of people in Indianapolis returning "their minds and energies to work, football games, automobile trips, family reunions and all the pleasant trivia of the American way of life."

Most college and public libraries have *Life* in their collection. Take a look through several issues. You will find many family portraits. You could develop various projects from this photojournalistic archive about family values in the postwar period, the role of women as homemakers, representations of teenagers, and the relation of domestic life to the Cold War. Keep in mind that the photoessays on the American family not only provide slices of life from the 1940s and 1950s but they also codify Americans' understanding of the ideal family and the American dream. Remember too that audiences did not read these photoessays on the family in isolation from advertisements and other photoessays. You might want to consider the overall flow of *Life* and how its messages about the family are connected to other messages.

Finally, you might think about why there is no longer a general magazine such as *Life* that claims to picture the "American way of life." The magazine industry today is thriving by attracting specialized readerships based on such interests as computers, skateboarding, mountain biking, and indie rock. The era of such general national magazines as *Life, Look, Colliers,* and the *Saturday Evening Post* has clearly been replaced by niche marketing and subcultural 'zines. What does this proliferation of specialized magazines suggest to you about the current state of American culture?

CHAPTER 3 | Schooling

Courtesy of Teachers College, Columbia University

I wish first that we should recognize that education is ordinary; that it is, before everything else, the process of giving to the ordinary members of society its full common meanings, and the skills that will enable them to amend these meanings, in the light of their personal and common experience.

—Raymond Williams, *Culture Is Ordinary*

By the time you read this chapter, you will likely have spent a considerable amount of time in school. Most Americans between the ages of five and seventeen or eighteen are full-time students whose daily lives revolve around their schooling. From the moment people enter school until the time they drop out, leave temporarily, graduate from high school, or go on to college, their intellectual and cultural growth is intimately connected to going to school and learning how to be students. Because so much of growing up takes place in them, schools are key agents of acculturation in America, the place where the younger generation not only learns how to read, write, and do mathematics but also gets its upbringing in literature, history, and civics. One of the purposes of all this schooling is to transmit bodies of knowledge from one generation to the next, and classrooms are the place where this intergenerational communication normally occurs, from teacher to student.

Americans have always put a lot of faith in schools to educate the younger generation—to prepare them for the work of the future and to teach them what it means to be an American, a good citizen, and a productive member of society. But it is precisely because Americans put so much faith—and invest so many resources—in schooling that they worry and argue incessantly about what the schools are—or should be—accomplishing. Over the past decade, there has been mounting dissatisfaction with and criticism of the American education system at the elementary, secondary, and college levels. Educational reformers have noted a variety of problems—ranging from declining standardized test scores and the "literacy crisis" to unimaginative teaching, passive learning, and outdated or irrelevant curriculum to skyrocketing college costs and the loss of careers in science, engineering, and mathematics. Critics have called attention to male biases in the curriculum and the neglect of race, ethnicity, and class in the study of history, culture, and literature. Others have argued that the way schools test and reward achievement favors middle-class students over working-class and poor students, whites over blacks, and males over females.

As a student, you are at the center of much of this controversy, and you are in a unique position to comment on schooling in your life and in the lives of others. The purpose of this chapter is to offer you opportunities to read, think, and write about the role of schooling in America today. You are invited to explore the world of schooling to identify how it has influenced you as a student, a learner, and a person. You will be asked in the reading and writing assignments to recall classroom episodes from your past and observe classroom life in the present. You will work your way from examining the everyday practices of schooling to contemplating the mission and function of education in contemporary America. The writers in this chapter will give you an idea of some of the questions educators are currently asking about schooling in America. By engaging in the educational issues raised by the reading and writing assignments, you can begin to develop your own analysis of the role of schooling.

One way to begin is to ask what sounds like a very simple and innocent question: What have you learned in school? The answers, however, may not be simple at all. Consider the formal curriculum you have studied—the subjects you have taken, the teachers who have instructed you, and the knowledge you have acquired. Think about why American schools teach what they do, why academic subjects are organized as they are, and what assumptions about the nature and function of education have shaped the formal curriculum.

The experience of going to school involves more than learning the content of the courses. It is a way of life that shapes the students' sense of themselves and their life chances. Many people remember their first day in school because it marks, quite literally, the transition from home and play to classroom life and the world of schoolwork. The kind of knowledge students acquire when they learn how to be students and go to school forms what educators call the "hidden curriculum." This part of the curriculum is just as structured as the lessons students study in the formal curriculum. The difference is that in the hidden curriculum, the content remains unstated and is acted out in practice. The hidden curriculum, therefore, refers to all the unspoken beliefs and procedures that regulate classroom life—the rules of the game no one writes down but that teachers and students have internalized in their expectations about each other.

Students begin to learn the hidden curriculum in the early grades, when they learn how to sit still, pay attention, raise their hands to be called on, follow directions, perform repetitive tasks, and complete work on time. Students learn what pleases teachers and what doesn't, what they can say to teachers and what they ought to keep to themselves. One of the functions of American schools has been to instill in the younger generation the habits of discipline, punctuality, hard work, and the wise use of time—to teach them, as the old adage goes, that "there is a time for work and a time for play." The hidden curriculum could be described as a training ground where students learn to work for grades and other symbolic rewards, to take tests and believe in their accuracy and fairness.

Examining the hidden curriculum offers a useful way to look at classroom life, in part because it demands that you research, bring into view, and question the kinds of things that take place in school that teachers and students seem to take for granted. Why, for example, is the school day divided as it is, and what is the effect of moving from subject to subject in fifty-minute intervals? Why do students sit in rows? Who has the right to speak in class? Who gets called on by the teacher? Why do teachers ask questions when they already know the answer? You will be asked in the reading and writing assignments to research questions such as these, to bring the hidden curriculum's unstated norms to light, and to assess their effects on students and on the role schooling plays in American culture.

Reading the Culture of Schooling

The reading and writing assignments in this chapter will ask you to draw on your memories of schooling and your current position as a student—to be a partici-pant–observer of the education you are currently experiencing. The opening selec-tion in the chapter—"What High School Is," Theodore R. Sizer's critical analysis of the typical high school day—offers some interesting leads to think about the goals of education at your high school or college. Sizer's portrait of a high school day comes from a longer study, *Horace's Compromise,* which offers a program to reform high school education. The next reading, however, Leon Botstein's "Let Teenagers Try Adulthood," suggests that high schools can't be reformed but should be abol-ished and replaced.

The Perspectives section that follows looks at the controversy over school vouch-ers and whether public moneys should go toward tuition in private schools. This sec-tion consists of the opinions of Supreme Court justices, who divided five for and four against the constitutionality of the voucher system in the Cleveland public schools, along with editorials supporting and opposing the ruling.

The selection from Mike Rose recounts the struggles and aspirations of return-ing adult learners and raises troubling questions about how schooling labels and stig-matizes people as being intellectually deficient—blaming the victim for school failure that has deeper social and political roots. Then Margaret Finders's "Note-Passing: Struggles for Status" shows how junior high school girls use reading and writing out-side the official curriculum. She traces one form of hidden literacy and how it (along with writing graffiti, yearbook signing, and reading teen 'zines) maintains social net-works and hierarchies.

The last two reading selections—Min-zhan Lu's "From Silence to Words: Writ-ing as Struggle" and June Jordan's "Nobody Mean More to Me Than You and the Future Life of Willie Jordan"—examine the relationship between the language of home and community and the language of the classroom.

The Classic Reading in this chapter is Lisa Delpit's groundbreaking critique of writ-ing process teaching, "Skills and Other Dilemmas of a Progressive Black Educator."

What emerges from the reading and writing assignments in this chapter is a pic-ture of schooling as a means of sorting out students to prepare them for their future roles in society. How this sorting out takes place—how tracking assigns some stu-dents to college preparatory courses and others to vocational programs, how some students learn to be successful in school while others fail, how schooling confirms or undermines individual students' self-confidence—these are some of the questions you will be invited to explore. Your position as a participant–observer gives you a useful vantage point to raise such questions from the inside, to ask about the meaning of your own education and the role of schooling in American culture.

WHAT HIGH SCHOOL IS

Theodore R. Sizer

Theodore R. Sizer has been chairman of the education department at Brown University; headmaster of Phillips Academy, Andover; and dean of the Graduate School of Education at Harvard. The following selection is the opening chapter from *Horace's Compromise,* Sizer's book-length study of American high schools. Sizer's book takes a critical look at high schools—at overworked teachers, undermotivated students, and the "assembly-line" educational practices that process people rather than educate them. Originally published in 1984, Sizer's study was one of a number of national reports that appeared in the 1980s and raised serious questions about the quality of American education. This reading selection looks at how the school day is organized and what it means to students to "take subjects."

SUGGESTION FOR READING As you read, notice that Sizer gives a full account of Mark's day before stepping back to generalize about its significance. Underline and annotate this selection to indicate where Sizer begins to analyze the meaning of Mark's day and how Sizer goes on to develop a critical analysis of the typical high school day.

1 Mark, sixteen and a genial eleventh-grader, rides a bus to Franklin High School, arriving at 7:25. It is an Assembly Day, so the schedule is adapted to allow for a meeting of the entire school. He hangs out with his friends, first outside school and then inside, by his locker. He carries a pile of textbooks and notebooks; in all, it weighs eight and a half pounds.

From 7:30 to 8:19, with nineteen other students, he is in Room 304 for English class. The Shakespeare play being read this year by the eleventh grade is *Romeo and Juliet.* The teacher, Ms. Viola, has various students in turn take parts and read out loud. Periodically, she interrupts the (usually halting) recitations to ask whether the thread of the conversation in the play is clear. Mark is entertained by the stumbling readings of some of his classmates. He hopes he will not be asked to be Romeo, particularly if his current steady, Sally, is Juliet. There is a good deal of giggling in class, and much attention paid to who may be called on next. Ms. Viola reminds the class of a test on this part of the play to be given next week.

The bell rings at 8:19. Mark goes to the boys' room, where he sees a classmate who he thinks is a wimp but who constantly tries to be a buddy. Mark avoids the leech by rushing off. On the way, he notices two boys engaged in some sort of transaction, probably over marijuana. He pays them no attention. 8:24. Typing class. The rows of desks that embrace big office machines are almost filled before the bell. Mark is uncomfortable here: typing class is girl country. The teacher constantly threatens what to Mark is a humiliatingly girl future: "Your employer won't like these erasures." The minutes during the period are spent copying a letter from a handbook onto business stationery. Mark struggles to keep from looking at his work; the teacher wants him to watch only the material from which he is copying. Mark is frustrated, uncomfortable, and scared that he will not complete his letter by the class's end, which would be embarrassing.

Nine tenths of the students present at school that day are assembled in the auditorium by the 9:18 bell. The dilatory tenth still stumble in, running down aisles. Annoyed class deans try to get the mob settled. The curtains part; the program is a concert by a student rock group. Their electronic gear flashes under the lights, and the five boys and one girl in the group work hard at being casual. Their movements on stage are studiously at three-quarter time, and they chat with one another as though the tumultuous screaming of their schoolmates were totally inaudible. The girl balances on a stool; the boys crank up the music. It is very soft rock, the sanitized lyrics surely cleared with the assistant principal. The girl sings, holding the mike close to her mouth, but can scarcely be heard. Her light voice is tentative, and the lyrics indecipherable. The guitars, amplified, are tuneful, however, and the drums are played with energy.

5   The students around Mark—all juniors, since they are seated by class—alternately slouch in their upholstered, hinged seats, talking to one another, or sit forward, leaning on the chair backs in front of them, watching the band. A boy near Mark shouts noisily at the microphone-fondling singer, "Bite it...ohhh," and the area around Mark explodes in vulgar male laughter, but quickly subsides. A teacher walks down the aisle. Songs continue, to great applause. Assembly is over at 9:46, two minutes early.

9:53 and biology class. Mark was at a different high school last year and did not take this course there as a tenth-grader. He is in it now, and all but one of his classmates are a year younger than he. He sits on the side, not taking part in the chatter that goes on after the bell. At 9:57, the public address system goes on, with the announcements of the day. After a few words from the principal ("Here's today's cheers and jeers..." with a cheer for the winning basketball team and a jeer for the spectators who made a ruckus at the gymnasium), the task is taken over by officers of ASB (Associated Student Bodies). There is an appeal for "bat bunnies." Carnations are for sale by the Girls' League. Miss Indian American is coming. Students are auctioning off

their services (background catcalls are heard) to earn money for the prom. Nominees are needed for the ballot for school bachelor and school bachelorette. The announcements end with a "thought for the day. When you throw a little mud, you lose a little ground."

At 10:04 the biology class finally turns to science. The teacher, Mr. Robbins, has placed one of several labeled laboratory specimens—some are pinned in frames, other swim in formaldehyde—on each of the classroom's eight laboratory tables. The three or so students whose chairs circle each of these benches are to study the specimen and make notes about it or drawings of it. After a few minutes each group of three will move to another table. The teacher points out that these specimens are of organisms already studied in previous classes. He says that the period-long test set for the following day will involve observing some of these specimens— then to be without labels—and writing an identifying paragraph on each. Mr. Robbins points out that some of the printed labels ascribe the specimens' names different from those given in the textbook. He explains that biologists often give several names to the same organism.

The class now falls to peering, writing, and quiet talking. Mr. Robbins comes over to Mark, and in whispered words asks him to carry a requisition form for science department materials to the business office. Mark, because of his "older" status, is usually chosen by Robbins for this kind of errand. Robbins gives Mark the form and a green hall pass to show to any teacher who might challenge him, on his way to the office, for being out of a classroom. The errand takes Mark four minutes. Meanwhile Mark's group is hard at work but gets to only three of the specimens before the bell rings at 10:42. As the students surge out, Robbins shouts a reminder about a "double" laboratory period on Thursday.

Between classes one of the seniors asks Mark whether he plans to be a candidate for schoolwide office next year. Mark says no. He starts to explain. The 10:47 bell rings, meaning that he is late for French class.

10   There are fifteen students in Monsieur Bates's language class. He hands out tests taken the day before: "*C'est bien fait, Etienne...c'est mieux, Marie...Tch, tch, Robert...*" Mark notes his C + and peeks at the A − in front of Susanna, next to him. The class has been assigned seats by M. Bates; Mark resents sitting next to prissy, brainy Susanna. Bates starts by asking a student to read a question and give the correct answer. "*James, question un.*" James haltingly reads the question and gives an answer that Bates, now speaking English, says is incomplete. In due course: "*Mark, question cinq.*" Mark does his bit, and the sequence goes on, the eight quiz questions and answers filling about twenty minutes of time.

"Turn to page forty-nine. *Maintenant, lisez après moi...*" and Bates reads a sentence and has the class echo it. Mark is embarrassed by this and mumbles with a barely audible sound. Others, like Susanna, keep the decibel count up, so Mark can hide. This I-say-you-repeat drill is interrupted once by the public address system, with an announcement about a meeting for the cheerleaders. Bates finishes class, almost precisely at the bell, with a homework assignment. The students are to review these sentences for a brief quiz the following day. Mark takes notes of the assignment, because he knows that tomorrow will be a day of busywork in French class. Much though he dislikes oral drills, they are better than the workbook stuff that Bates hands out. Write, write, write, for Bates to throw away, Mark thinks.

11:36. Down to the cafeteria, talking noisily, hanging out, munching. Getting to Room 104 by 12:17: U.S. history. The teacher is sitting cross-legged on his desk when Mark comes in, heatedly arguing with three students over the fracas that had followed the previous night's basketball game. The teacher, Mr. Suslovic, while agreeing that the spectators from their school certainly were provoked, argues that they should neither have been so obviously obscene in yelling at the opposing cheerleaders nor have allowed Coke cans to be rolled out on the floor. The three students keep saying that "it isn't fair." Apparently they and some others had been assigned "Saturday mornings" (detentions) by the principal for the ruckus.

At 12:34, the argument appears to subside. The uninvolved students, including Mark, are in their seats, chatting amiably. Mr. Suslovic climbs off his desk and starts talking: "We've almost finished this unit, chapters nine and ten...." The students stop chattering among themselves and turn toward Suslovic. Several slouch down in their chairs. Some open notebooks. Most have the five-pound textbook on their desks.

Suslovic lectures on the cattle drives, from north Texas to railroads west of St. Louis. He breaks up this narrative with questions ("Why were the railroad lines laid largely east to west?"), directed at nobody in particular and eventually answered by Suslovic himself. Some students take notes. Mark doesn't. A student walks in the open door, hands Mr. Suslovic a list, and starts whispering with him. Suslovic turns from the class and hears out this messenger. He then asks, "Does anyone know where Maggie Sharp is?" Someone answers, "Sick at home"; someone else says, "I thought I saw her at lunch." Genial consternation. Finally Suslovic tells the messenger, "Sorry, we can't help you," and returns to the class: "Now, where were we?" He goes on for some minutes. The bell rings. Suslovic forgets to give the homework assignment.

15   1:11 and Algebra II. There is a commotion in the hallway: someone's locker is rumored to have been opened by the assistant principal and a narcotics agent. In the five-minute passing time, Mark hears the story three times and three ways. A locker had been broken into by another student. It was Mr. Gregory and a narc. It was the cops, and they did it without Gregory's knowing. Mrs. Ames, the mathematics teacher, has not heard anything about it. Several of the nineteen students try to tell her and start arguing among themselves. "O.K., that's enough." She hands out the day's problem, one sheet to each student. Mark sees with dismay that it is a single, complicated "word" problem about some train that, while traveling at 84 mph, due west, passes a car

that was going due east at 55 mph. Mark struggles: Is it $d = rt$ or $t = rd$? The class becomes quiet, writing, while Mrs. Ames writes some additional, short problems on the blackboard. "Time's up." A sigh; most students still writing. A muffled "Shit." Mrs. Ames frowns. "Come on, now." She collects papers, but it takes four minutes for her to corral them all.

"Copy down the problems from the board." A minute passes. "William, try number one." William suggests an approach. Mrs. Ames corrects and cajoles, and William finally gets it right. Mark watches two kids to his right passing notes; he tries to read them but the handwriting is illegible from his distance. He hopes he is not called on, and he isn't. Only three students are asked to puzzle out an answer. The bell rings at 2:00. Mrs. Ames shouts a homework assignment over the resulting hubbub.

Mark leaves his books in his locker. He remembers that he has homework, but figures that he can do it during English class the next day. He knows that there will be an in-class presentation of one of the *Romeo and Juliet* scenes and that he will not be in it. The teacher will not notice his homework writing, or won't do anything about it if she does.

Mark passes various friends heading toward the gym, members of the basketball teams. Like most students, Mark isn't an active school athlete. However, he is associated with the yearbook staff. Although he is not taking "Yearbook" for credit as an English course, he is contributing photographs. Mark takes twenty minutes checking into the yearbook staff's headquarters (the classroom of its faculty adviser) and getting some assignments of pictures from his boss, the senior who is the photography editor. Mark knows that if he pleases his boss and the faculty adviser, he'll take that editor's post for the next year. He'll get English credit for his work then.

After gossiping a bit with the yearbook staff, Mark will leave school by 2:35 and go home. His grocery market bagger's job is from 4:45 to 8:00, the rush hour for the store. He'll have a snack at 4:30, and his mother will save him some supper to eat at 8:30. She will ask whether he has any homework, and he'll tell her no. Tomorrow, and virtually every other tomorrow, will be the same for Mark, save for the lack of the assembly; each period then will be five minutes longer.

20   Most Americans have an uncomplicated vision of what secondary education should be. Their conception of high school is remarkably uniform across the country, a striking fact, given the size and diversity of the United States and the politically decentralized character of the schools. This uniformity is of several generations' standing. It has, however, two appearances, each quite different from the other, one of words and the other of practice, a world of political rhetoric and Mark's world.

A California high school's general goals, set out in 1979, could serve equally well most of America's high schools, public and private. This school had as its ends:

- Fundamental scholastic achievement…to acquire knowledge and share in the traditionally accepted academic fundamentals…to develop the ability to make decisions, to solve problems, to reason independently, and to accept responsibility for self-evaluation and continuing self-improvement.
- Career and economic competence
- Citizenship and civil responsibility
- Competence in human and social relations
- Moral and ethical values
- Self-realization and mental and physical health
- Aesthetic awareness
- Cultural diversity

In addition to its optimistic rhetoric, what distinguished this list is its comprehensiveness. The high school is to touch most aspects of an adolescent's existence—mind, body, morals, values, career. No one of these areas is given especial prominence. School people arrogate to themselves an obligation to all.

An example of the wide acceptability of these goals is found in the courts. Forced to present a detailed definition of "thorough and efficient education," elementary as well as secondary, a West Virginia judge sampled the best of conventional wisdom and concluded that

> there are eight general elements of a thorough and efficient system of education: (a) Literacy, (b) The ability to add, subtract, multiply, and divide numbers, (c) Knowledge of government to the extent the child will be equipped as a citizen to make informed choices among persons and issues that affect his own governance, (d) Self-knowledge and knowledge of his or her total environment to allow the child to intelligently choose life work—to know his or her options, (e) Work-training and advanced academic training as the child may intelligently choose, (f) Recreational pursuits, (g) Interests in all creative arts such as music, theater, literature, and the visual arts, and (h) Social ethics, both behavioral and abstract, to facilitate compatibility with others in this society.

25   That these eight—now powerfully part of the debate over the purpose and practice of education in West Virginia—are reminiscent of the influential list, "The Seven Cardinal Principles of Secondary Education," promulgated in 1918 by the National Education Association, is no surprise. The rhetoric of high school purpose has been uniform and consistent for decades. Americans agree on the goals for their high schools.

That agreement is convenient, but it masks the fact that virtually all the words in these goal statements beg definition. Some schools have labored long to identify specific criteria beyond them; the result has been lists of daunting pseudospecificity and numbing earnestness. However, most leave the words undefined and let the momentum of traditional practice speak for itself. That is why analyzing how Mark spends his time is important: from watching him one uncovers the important purposes of education, the ones that shape practice. Mark's day is similar to that of other high school students across the country, as similar as the rhetoric of one goal statement to others'. Of course, there are variations, but the extent of consistency in the shape of school routine for a large and diverse adolescent population is extraordinary, indicating more graphically than any rhetoric the measure of agreement in America about what one does in high school, and, by implication, what it is for.

The basic organizing structures in schools are familiar. Above all, students are grouped by age (that is, freshman, sophomore, junior, senior), and all are expected to take precisely the same time—around 720 school days over four years, to be precise—to meet the requirements for a diploma. When one is out of his grade level, he can feel odd, as Mark did in his biology class. The goals are the same for all, and the means to achieve them are also similar.

Young males and females are treated remarkably alike; the schools' goals are the same for each gender. In execution, there are differences, as those pressing sex discrimination suits have made educators intensely aware. The students in metalworking classes are mostly male; those in home economics, mostly female. But it is revealing how much less sex discrimination there is in high schools than in other American institutions. For many young women, the most liberated hours of their week are in school.

School is to be like a job: you start in the morning and end in the afternoon, five days a week. You don't get much of a lunch hour, so you go home early, unless you are an athlete or are involved in some special school or extracurricular activity. School is conceived of as the children's workplace, and it takes young people off parents' hands and out of the labor market during prime-time work hours. Not surprisingly, many students see going to school as little more than a dogged necessity. They perceive the day-to-day routine, a Minnesota study reports, as one of "boredom and lethargy." One of the students summarizes: School is "boring, restless, tiresome, puts ya to sleep, tedious monotonous, pain in the neck."

30   The school schedule is a series of units of time: the clock is king. The base time block is about fifty minutes in length. Some schools, on what they call modular scheduling, split that fifty-minute block into two or even three pieces. Most

schools have double periods for laboratory work, especially in the sciences, or four-hour units for small numbers of students involved in intensive vocational or other work-study programs. The flow of all school activity arises from or is blocked by these time units. "How much time do I have with my kids" is the teacher's key question.

Because there are many claims for those fifty-minute blocks, there is little time set aside for rest between them, usually no more than three to ten minutes, depending on how big the school is and, consequently, how far students and teachers have to walk from class to class. As a result, there is a frenetic quality to the school day, a sense of sustained restlessness. For the adolescents, there are frequent changes of room and fellow students, each change giving tempting opportunities for distraction, which are stoutly resisted by teachers. Some schools play soft music during these "passing times," to quiet the multitude, one principal told me.

Many teachers have a chance for a coffee break. Few students do. In some city schools where security is a problem, students must be in class for seven consecutive periods, interrupted by a heavily monitored twenty-minute lunch period for small groups, starting as early as 10:30 A.M. and running to after 1:00 P.M. A high premium is placed on punctuality and on "being where you're supposed to be." Obviously, a low premium is placed on reflection and repose. The student rushes from class to class to collect knowledge. Savoring it, it is implied, is not to be done much in school, nor is such meditation really much admired. The picture that these familial patterns yield is that of an academic supermarket. The purpose of going to school is to pick things up, in an organized and predictable way, the faster the better.

What is supposed to be picked up is remarkably consistent among all sorts of high schools. Most schools specifically mandate three out of every five courses a student selects. Nearly all of these mandates fall into five areas—English, social studies, mathematics, science, and physical education. On the average, English is required

to be taken each year, social studies and physical education three out of the four high school years, and mathematics and science one or two years. Trends indicate that in the mid-eighties there is likely to be an increase in the time allocated to these last two subjects. Most students take classes in these four major academic areas beyond the minimum requirements, sometimes in such special areas as journalism and "yearbook," offshoots of English departments.

Press most adults about what high school is for, and you hear these subjects listed. *High school? That's where you learn English and math and that sort of thing.* Ask students, and you get the same answers. High school is to "teach" these "subjects."

35   What is often absent is any definition of these subjects or any rationale for them. They are just there, labels. Under those labels lie a multitude of things. A great deal of material is supposed to be "covered"; most of these courses are surveys, great sweeps of the stuff of their parent disciplines.

While there is often a sequence *within* subjects—algebra before trigonometry, "first-year" French before "second-year" French—there is rarely a coherent relationship or sequence *across* subjects. Even the most logically related matters—reading ability as a precondition for the reading of history books, and certain mathematical concepts or skills before the study of some physics—are only loosely coordinated, if at all. There is little demand for a synthesis of it all; English, mathematics, and the rest are discrete items, to be picked up individually. The incentive for picking them up is largely through tests and, with success at these, in credits earned.

Coverage within subjects is the key priority. If some imaginative teacher makes a proposal to force the marriage of, say, mathematics and physics or to require some culminating challenges to students to use several subjects in the solution of a complex problem, and if this proposal will take "time" away from other things, opposition is usually phrased in terms of what may be thus forgone. If we do that, we'll have to give up colonial history. We won't be able to get to programming. We'll not be able to read *Death of a Salesman*. There isn't time. The protesters usually win out.

The subjects come at a student like Mark in random order, a kaleidoscope of worlds: algebraic formulae to poetry to French verbs to Ping-Pong to the War of the Spanish Succession, all before lunch. Pupils are to pick up these things. Tests measure whether the picking up has been successful.

The lack of connection between stated goals, such as those of the California high school cited earlier, and the goals inherent in school practice is obvious and, curiously, tolerated. Most striking is the gap between statements about "self-realization and mental and physical growth" or "moral and ethical values"—common rhetoric in school documents—and practice. Most physical education programs have neither the time nor the focus really to ensure fitness. Mental health is rarely defined. Neither are ethical values, save at the negative extremes, such as opposition to assault or dishonesty. Nothing in the regimen of a day like Mark's signals direct or implicit teaching in this area. The "schoolboy code" (not ratting on a fellow student) protects the marijuana pusher, and a leechlike associate is shrugged off without concern. The issue of the locker search was pushed aside, as not appropriate for class time.

40   Most students, like Mark, go to class in groups of twenty to twenty-seven students. The expected attendance in some schools, particularly those in low-income areas, is usually higher, often thirty-five students per class, but high absentee rates push the actual numbers down. About twenty-five per class is an average figure for expected attendance, and the actual numbers are somewhat lower. There are remarkably few students who go to class in groups much larger or smaller than twenty-five.

A student such as Mark sees five or six teachers per day; their differing styles and expectations are part of his kaleidoscope. High school staffs are highly specialized; guidance counselors rarely teach mathematics, mathematics teachers rarely teach English, principals rarely do any classroom instruction. Mark, then, is known a little bit by a number of people, each of whom sees him in one specialized situation. No one may know him as a "whole person"— unless he becomes a special problem or has special needs.

Save in extracurricular or coaching situations, such as in athletics, drama, or shop classes, there is little opportunity for sustained conversation between student and teacher. The mode is a one-sentence or two-sentence exchange: *Mark, when was Grover Cleveland president?* Let's see, was 1890...or something...wasn't he the one...he was elected twice, wasn't he?...*Yes...Gloria, can you get the dates right?* Dialogue is strikingly absent, and as a result the opportunity of teachers to challenge students' ideas in a systematic and logical way is limited. Given the rushed, full quality of the school day, it can seldom happen. One must infer that careful probing of students' thinking is not a high priority. How one gains (to quote the California school's statement of goals again) "the ability to make decisions, to solve problems, to reason independently, and to accept responsibility for self-evaluation and continuing self-improvement" without being challenged is difficult to imagine. One certainly doesn't learn these things merely from lectures and textbooks.

Most schools are nice places. Mark and his friends enjoy being in theirs. The adults who work in schools generally like adolescents. The academic pressures are limited, and the accommodations to students are substantial. For example, if many members of an English class have jobs after school, the English teacher's expectations for them are adjusted, downward. In a word, school is sensitively accommodating, as long as students are punctual, where they are supposed to be, and minimally dutiful about picking things up from the clutch of courses in which they enroll.

This characterization is not pretty, but it is accurate, and it serves to describe the vast majority of American secondary schools. "Taking subjects" in a systematized, conveyer-belt way is what one does in high school. That this process is, in substantial respects, not related to the rhetorical purposes of education is tolerated by most people, perhaps because they do not really either believe in those ill-defined goals or, in their heart of hearts, believe that schools can or should even try to achieve them. The students are happy taking subjects. The parents are happy, because that's what they did in high school. The rituals, the most important of which is graduation, remain intact. The adolescents are supervised, safely and constructively most of the time, during the morning and afternoon hours, and they are off the labor market. That is what high school is all about.

SUGGESTIONS FOR DISCUSSION

1. The portrait of Mark that begins this selection, as Sizer notes, is a composite blending of several real students and real high schools—"somewhere," Sizer says, "between precise journalism and nonfiction fiction." Sizer's portrait of Mark's school day must appear to be typical and recognizable for it to be persuasive and credible. Does Sizer achieve the kind of typicality he is trying for? Draw on your own experience and observations in high school to decide whether this is a fair portrait and what, if anything, it leaves out.

2. Sizer says, "Press most adults about what high school is for, and you hear these subjects listed. *High school? That's where you learn English and math and that sort of thing.*" How does Sizer answer his question, what is high school for? How would you answer it? Explain how you would account for differences and similarities between Sizer's answer and your own.

3. Do you agree with Sizer that there is a "lack of connection between stated goals" of high school education and "the goals inherent in school practice?" Sizer gives some examples of stated goals, such as the general goals for California high schools and the goals presented by a West Virginia judge, but he doesn't say what the "goals inherent in school practice" might be. Decide what these unstated goals are and how they determine what actually takes place in the daily routines of American high schools.

SUGGESTIONS FOR WRITING

1. At the end of this selection, Sizer says "'Taking subjects' in a systematized, conveyer-belt way is what one does in high school." A few lines later he says, "students are happy taking subjects." Do you agree with Sizer? Are high school students, in your experience, happy "taking subjects," or do they feel something is missing? Write an essay that develops your own position. Begin by summarizing what Sizer views as "conveyer-belt" education. Then explain to what extent and why you agree or disagree with his sense that students are happy "taking subjects."

2. Sizer says, "Most schools are nice....The academic pressures are limited, and the accommodations to students are substantial. For example, if many members of an English class have jobs after school, the English teacher's expectations for them are adjusted, downward." Write an essay that describes the expectations of teachers in the high school you attended and explains what influence those expectations have had on you as a student, a learner, and a person. Take into account whether teachers' expectations varied and whether they held the same expectations for all students.

3. Use Sizer's composite portrait of Mark's school day as a model to write a portrait of a typical day at the high school you attended or your college. You can draw on your own experience and memories, but keep in mind that Sizer's portrait is a made-up character, not a real person. Similarly, in this writing task, you'll need to invent your own typical student and his or her experience of the school day.

LET TEENAGERS TRY ADULTHOOD

Leon Botstein

Leon Botstein is the president of Bard College and author of *Jefferson's Children: Education and the Promise of American Culture* (1997). The following selection appeared on the Op Ed page of the *New York Times* in May 1999, shortly after the school shootings in Littleton, Colorado. Botstein uses the shootings at Columbine High School to give a sense of urgency to his argument that "American high schools are obsolete and should be abolished." As you will see, however, the case he makes does not depend on the Littleton events alone. In Botstein's view, there are larger reasons for recognizing that high school is a failure not worth reforming.

SUGGESTION FOR READING Botstein makes his main point—namely that high schools are out of date and should be abolished—in the opening sentence. As you read, mark the reasons he offers to support this position.

1   The national outpouring after the Littleton shootings has forced us to confront something we have suspected for a long time: the American high school is obsolete and should be abolished. In the last month, high school students present and past have come forward with stories about cliques and the artificial intensity of a world defined by insiders and outsiders, in which the insiders hold sway because of superficial definitions of good looks and attractiveness, popularity, and sports prowess.

The team sports of high school dominate more than student culture. A community's loyalty to the high school system is often based on the extent to which varsity teams succeed. High school administrators and faculty members are often former coaches, and the coaches themselves are placed in a separate, untouchable category. The result is that the culture of the inside elite is not contested by the adults in the school. Individuality and dissent are discouraged.

But the rules of high school turn out not to be the rules of life. Often the high school outsider becomes the more successful and admired adult. The definitions of masculinity and femininity go through sufficient transformation to make the game of popularity in high school an embarrassment. No other group of adults young or old is confined to an age-segregated environment, much like a gang in which individuals of the same age group define each other's world. In no workplace, not even in colleges or universities, is there such a narrow segmentation by chronology.

Given the poor quality of recruitment and training for high school teachers, it is no wonder that the curriculum and the enterprise of learning hold so little sway over young people. When puberty meets education and learning in modern America, the victory of puberty masquerading as popular culture and the tyranny of peer groups based on ludicrous values meet little resistance.

5   By the time those who graduate from high school go on to college and realize what really is at stake in becoming an adult, too many opportunities have been lost and too much time has been wasted. Most thoughtful young people suffer the high school environment in silence and in their junior and senior years mark time waiting for college to begin. The Littleton killers, above and beyond the psychological demons that drove them to violence, felt trapped in the artificiality of the high school world and believed it to be real. They engineered their moment of undivided attention and importance in the absence of any confidence that life after high school could have a different meaning.

Adults should face the fact that they don't like adolescents and that they have used high school to isolate the pubescent and hormonally active adolescent away from both the picture-book idealized innocence of childhood and the more accountable world of adulthood. But the primary reason high school doesn't work anymore, if it ever did, is that young people mature substantially earlier in the late 20th century than they did when the high school was invented. For example, the age of first menstruation has dropped at least two years since the beginning of this century, and not surprisingly, the onset of sexual activity has dropped in proportion. An institution intended for children in transition now holds young adults back well beyond the developmental point for which high school was originally designed.

Furthermore, whatever constraints to the presumption of adulthood among young people may have existed decades ago have now fallen away. Information and images, as well as the real and virtual freedom of movement we associate with adulthood, are now accessible to every fifteen- and sixteen-year-old.

Secondary education must be rethought. Elementary school should begin at age four or five and end with the sixth grade. We should entirely abandon the concept of the middle school and junior high school. Beginning with the seventh grade, there should be four years of secondary education that we may call high school. Young people should graduate at sixteen rather than eighteen.

They could then enter the real world, the world of work or national service, in which they would take a place of responsibility alongside older adults in mixed company. They could stay at home and attend junior college, or they could go away to college. For all the faults of college, at least the adults who dominate the world of colleges, the faculty, were selected precisely because they were exceptional and different, not because they were popular. Despite the often cavalier attitude toward teaching in college, at least physicists know their physics, mathematicians know and love their mathematics, and music is taught by musicians, not by graduates of education schools, where the disciplines are subordinated to the study of classroom management.

10   For those sixteen-year-olds who do not want to do any of the above, we might construct new kinds of institutions, each dedicated to one activity, from science to dance, to which adolescents could devote their energies while working together with professionals in those fields.

At sixteen, young Americans are prepared to be taken seriously and to develop the motivations and interests that will serve them well in adult life. They need to enter a world where they are not in a lunchroom with only their peers, estranged from other age groups and cut off from the game of life as it is really played. There is nothing utopian about this idea; it is immensely practical and efficient, and its implementation is long overdue. We need to face biological and cultural facts and not prolong the life of a flawed institution that is out of date.

SUGGESTIONS FOR DISCUSSION

1. First, make a list of the reasons Botstein gives to support his view that "high school doesn't work anymore." Next, notice that what he calls "the primary reason" appears in paragraph six. Consider why he has organized his reasons in the order they appear. How does the order of reasons lead readers from one point to the next? What assumptions about schooling and American teenagers is Botstein asking readers to share?

2. Both Botstein and Theodore Sizer in the preceding selection, "What High School Is," are highly critical of American high schools. Their critiques, however, are quite different ones. Compare the analyses they offer of American high schools. What in particular do they focus on? Are they looking at the same things and drawing different conclusions, or do their differences begin with the things they are analyzing? How do these differences in perspective set up Botstein to argue for abolishing high school but Sizer to argue for reforming it?

3. Like Botstein, Thomas Hine in "Goths in Tomorrowland" (Chapter 2) is concerned about the alienation of American teenagers from adult society. Read (or reread) the selection

from Hine. Compare the perspectives Hine and Botstein offer on the age segregation of American teenagers. What do they see as the larger implications of teenagers' alienation from adult society? Do you share their concern? Explain why or why not. Take into account what, if anything, you can say in favor of the kind of age segregation that takes place in high school.

SUGGESTIONS FOR WRITING

1. Write a letter to the editor of the *New York Times* that responds to Botstein's Op Ed piece. You can agree or disagree with his proposal to abolish American high schools or you can provide a different perspective on the issues of schooling he raises. In any case, explain your reasons for agreeing or the significance of the perspective you offer. To get a sense of the tone to use in such a letter and the approach to readers, take a look at some of the letters in a recent edition.

2. Assume that Botstein's plan to restructure American education actually takes place. In the new system, young people will leave secondary school at age sixteen. Some, as Botstein notes, will enter the world of work or national service, while others will go to college. For still others, however, "new kinds of institutions, each dedicated to one activity, from science to dance, to which adolescents could devote their energies while working together with professionals in those fields" will be developed. Develop your own proposal for one of these "new kinds of institutions." Include a rationale that explains why you think the particular activity the institution focuses on is worthwhile, what young people would do, and what the outcome might be.

3. Write an essay that develops your own position on what both Botstein and Thomas Hine write about as the age segregation of young people in high school. First, explain the perspective each offers and the consequences they believe follow from age segregation. Then, explain your own point of view on the issue, indicating whether you think their concern about the alienation of teenagers from adult society is a justifiable one.

PERSPECTIVES   School Vouchers

School vouchers emerged in the 1990s as one of the most controversial issues in American education, culminating in 2002 with a narrow Supreme Court decision in favor of the school voucher program in Cleveland, Ohio. The idea of school vouchers is a simple one: the government provides parents in poorly performing public school districts with tuition grants they can use to send their children to private schools. For some, school voucher programs are a reasonable reform that offers poor parents an alternative to failing public schools, such as those in Cleveland. For others, school voucher programs not only violate church–state separation (referred to in the Supreme Court decision as the Establishment Clause of the First Amendment) by using public funds to support religious schooling but such programs also undermine the role and mission of public education in American life.

Below are two sets of readings on the school voucher debate. The first set contains excerpts from the Supreme Court's decision and dissent. These readings are followed by two newspaper editorials that appeared when the ruling was announced in July 2002.

SUPREME COURT MAJORITY OPINION AND DISSENTING VIEWS

Whether the school vouchers program in Cleveland, Ohio, was constitutional was hotly debated in the Supreme Court in 2002, resulting in a five to four vote in favor of the program. As is often true in such controversial legal cases, to get their views on the record, justices wrote concurrences and dissents to the majority opinion. The following excerpts are taken from the majority opinion of the Supreme Court written by Chief Justice Rehnquist, a concurring view written by Justice Thomas, and two dissenting views written by Justices Breyer and Stevens.

SUGGESTION FOR READING As you read these judicial opinions, imagine them as a kind of dialogue in which a position—the majority opinion—is laid out and then others respond to it. Begin by underlining the reasons Chief Justice Rehnquist offers in support of the majority opinion. Notice next how Justice Thomas adds to Rehnquist's argument and then how Justices Breyer and Stephens seek to refute Rehnquist's line of judicial reasoning.

FROM THE OPINION, BY CHIEF JUSTICE REHNQUIST

1 The State of Ohio has established a pilot program designed to provide educational choices to families with children who reside in the Cleveland City School District. The question presented is whether this program offends the Establishment Clause of the United States Constitution. We hold that it does not.

There are more than 75,000 children enrolled in the Cleveland City School District. The majority of these children are from low-income and minority families. Few of these families enjoy the means to send their children to any school other than an inner-city public school. For more than a generation, however, Cleveland's public schools have been among the worst performing public schools in the nation. In 1995, a Federal District Court declared a "crisis of magnitude" and placed the entire Cleveland school district under state control....

It is against this backdrop that Ohio enacted, among other initiatives, its Pilot Project Scholarship Program. The program provides financial assistance to families in any Ohio school district that is or has been "under federal court order requiring supervision and operational management of the district by the state superintendent." Cleveland is the only Ohio school district to fall within that category.

The program provides two basic kinds of assistance to parents of children in a covered district. First, the program provides tuition aid for students in kindergarten through third grade, expanding each year through eighth grade, to attend a participating public or private school of their parent's choosing. Second, the program provides tutorial aid for students who choose to remain enrolled in public school.

5 The tuition aid portion of the program is designed to provide educational choices to parents who reside in a covered district. Any private school, whether religious or nonreligious, may participate in the program and accept program students so long as the school is located within the boundaries of a covered district and meets state-wide educational standards.

Participating private schools must agree not to discriminate on the basis of race, religion, or ethnic background, or to "advocate or foster unlawful behavior or teach hatred of any person or group on the basis of race, ethnicity, national origin, or religion." Adjacent public schools are eligible to receive a $2.250 tuition grant for each program student accepted in addition to the full amount of per-pupil state funding attributable to each additional student.

All participating schools, whether public or private, are required to accept students in accordance with rules and procedures established by the state superintendent. Tuition aid is distributed to parents according to financial need. Families with incomes below 200 percent of the poverty line are given priority and are eligible to receive 90 percent of private school tuition up to $2,250. For these lowest-income families, participating private schools may not charge a parental co-payment greater than $250. For all other families, the program pays 75 percent of tuition costs, up to $1,875, with no co-payment cap. Where tuition aid is spent depends solely upon where parents who receive tuition aid choose to enroll their child. If parents choose a private school, checks are made payable to the parents who then endorse the checks over to the chosen school....

The program has been in operation within the Cleveland City School District since the 1996–1997 school year. In the 1999–2000 school year, 56 private schools participated in the program, 46 (or 82 percent) of which had a religious affiliation. None of the public schools in districts adjacent to Cleveland have elected to participate. More than 3,700 students participated in the scholarship program, most of whom (96 percent) enrolled in religiously affiliated schools. Sixty percent of these students were from families at or below the poverty line. In the 1998–1999 school year, approximately 1,400 Cleveland public school students received tutorial aid. This number was expected to double during the 1999–2000 school year.

The Establishment Clause of the First Amendment, applied to the states through the 14th Amendment, prevents a state from enacting laws that have the "purpose" or "effect" of advancing or inhibiting religion. There is no dispute that the program challenged here was enacted for the valid secular purpose of providing educational assistance to poor children in a demonstrably failing public school system. Thus, the question presented is whether the Ohio program nonetheless has the forbidden "effect" of advancing or inhibiting religion.

10   To answer that question, our decisions have drawn a consistent distinction between government programs that provide aid directly to religious schools, and programs of true private choice, in which government aid reaches religious schools only as a result of the genuine and independent choices of private individuals. While our jurisprudence with respect to the constitutionality of direct aid programs has "changed significantly" over the past two decades, our jurisprudence with respect to true private choice programs has remained consistent and unbroken.

Respondents suggest that even without a financial incentive for parents to choose a religious school, the program creates a "public perception that the state is endorsing religious practices and beliefs." But we have repeatedly recognized that no reasonable observer would think a neutral program of private choice, where state aid reaches religious schools solely as a result of the numerous independent decisions of private individuals, carries with it the imprimatur of government endorsement.

Any objective observer familiar with the full history and context of the Ohio program would reasonably view it as one aspect of a broader undertaking to assist poor children in failed schools, not as an endorsement of religious schooling in general.

In sum, the Ohio program is entirely neutral with respect to religion. It provides benefits directly to a wide spectrum of individuals, defined only by financial need and residence in a particular school district. It permits such individuals to exercise genuine choice among options public and private, secular and religious. The program is therefore a program of true private choice. In keeping with an unbroken line of decisions rejecting challenges to similar programs, we hold that the program does not offend the Establishment Clause.

FROM THE CONCURRENCE, BY JUSTICE THOMAS

1 Frederick Douglass once said that "education...means emancipation. It means light and liberty. It means the uplifting of the soul of man into the glorious light of truth, the light by which men can only be made free." Today many of our inner-city public schools deny emancipation to urban minority students. Despite this Court's observation nearly 50 years ago in Brown v. Board of Education that "it is doubtful that any child may reasonably be expected to succeed in life if he is denied the opportunity of an education," (1954) urban children have been forced into a system that continually fails them. These cases present an example of such failures. Besieged by escalating financial problems and declining academic achievement, the Cleveland City School District was in the midst of an academic emergency when Ohio enacted its scholarship program.

The dissents and respondents wish to invoke the Establishment Clause of the First Amendment, as incorporated through the 14th, to constrain a state's neutral efforts to provide greater educational opportunity for underprivileged minority students. Today's decision properly upholds the program as constitutional, and I join it in full....

Although one of the purposes of public schools was to promote democracy and a more egalitarian culture, failing urban public schools disproportionately affect minority children most in need of educational opportunity. At the time of Reconstruction, blacks considered public education "a matter of personal liberation and a necessary function of a free society." Today, however, the promise of public school education has failed poor inner-city blacks. While in theory providing education to everyone, the quality of public schools varies significantly across districts. Just as blacks supported public education during Reconstruction, many blacks and other minorities now support school choice programs because they provide the greatest educational opportunities for their children in struggling communities. Opponents of the program raise formalistic concerns about the Establishment Clause but ignore the core purposes of the 14th Amendment. While the romanticized ideal of universal public education resonates with the cognoscenti who oppose vouchers, poor urban families just want the best education for their children, who will certainly need it to function in our high-tech and advanced society.

FROM THE DISSENT, BY JUSTICE BREYER

1 I believe that the Establishment Clause's concern for protecting the nation's social fabric from religious conflict poses an overriding obstacle to the implementation of this well-intentioned school voucher program. And by explaining the nature of the concern, I hope to demonstrate why, in my view, "parental choice" cannot significantly alleviate the constitutional problem....

School voucher programs finance the religious education of the young. And, if widely adopted, they may well provide billions of dollars that will do so. Why will different religions not become concerned about, and seek to influence, the criteria used to channel this money to religious schools? Why will they not want to examine the implementation of the programs that provide this money to determine, for example, whether implementation has biased a program toward or against particular sects, or whether recipient religious schools are adequately fulfilling a program's criteria? If so, just how is the state to resolve the resulting controversies without provoking legitimate fears of the kinds of religious favoritism that, in so religiously diverse a nation, threaten social dissension?

Consider the voucher program here at issue. That program insists that the religious school accept students of all religions. Does that criterion treat fairly groups whose religion forbids them to do so? The program also insists that no participating school "advocate or foster unlawful behavior or teach hatred of any person or group on the basis of race, ethnicity, national origin, or religion." And it requires the state to "revoke the registration of any school if, after a hearing, the superintendent determines that the school is in violation" of the program's rules. As one amicus argues, "it is difficult to imagine a more divisive activity" than the appointment of state officials as referees to determine whether a particular religious doctrine "teaches hatred or advocates lawlessness."

How are state officials to adjudicate claims that one religion or another is advocating, for example, civil disobedience in response to unjust laws, the use of illegal drugs in a religious ceremony, or resort to force to call attention to what it views as an immoral social practice? What kind of public hearing will there be in response to claims that one religion or another is continuing to teach a view of history that casts members of other religions in the worst possible light? How will the public react to government funding for schools that take controversial religious positions on topics that are of current popular interest— say, the conflict in the Middle East or the war on terrorism? Yet any major funding program for primary religious education will require criteria. And the selection of those criteria, as well as their application, inevitably pose problems that are divisive. Efforts to respond to these problems not only will seriously entangle church and state, but also will promote division among religious groups, as one group or another fears (often legitimately) that it will receive unfair treatment at the hands of the government. I recognize that other nations, for example Great Britain and France, have in the past reconciled religious school funding and religious freedom without creating serious strife. Yet British and French societies are religiously more homogeneous— and it bears noting that recent waves of immigration have begun to create problems of social division there as well.

5   In a society as religiously diverse as ours, the court has recognized that we must rely on the Religion Clauses of the First Amendment to protect against religious strife, particularly when what is at issue is an area as central to religious belief as the shaping, through primary education, of the next generation's minds and spirits....

In a society composed of many different religious creeds, I fear that this present departure from the court's earlier understanding risks creating a form of religiously based conflict potentially harmful to the nation's social fabric. Because I believe the Establishment Clause was written in part to avoid this kind of conflict, and for reasons set forth by Justice Souter and Justice Stevens, I respectfully dissent.

FROM THE DISSENT, BY JUSTICE STEVENS

1   Is a law that authorizes the use of public funds to pay for the indoctrination of thousands of grammar school children in particular religious faiths a "law respecting an establishment of religion" within the meaning of the First Amendment? In answering that question, I think we should ignore three factual matters that are discussed at length by my colleagues.

First, the severe educational crisis that confronted the Cleveland City School District when Ohio enacted its voucher program is not a matter that should affect our appraisal of its constitutionality. In the 1999–2000 school year, that program provided relief to less than five percent of the students enrolled in the district's schools.

The solution to the disastrous conditions that prevented over 90 percent of the student body from meeting basic proficiency standards obviously required massive improvements unrelated to the voucher program. Of course, the emergency may have given some families a powerful motivation to leave the public school system and accept religious indoctrination that they would otherwise have avoided; but that is not a valid reason for upholding the program.

Second, the wide range of choices that have been made available to students within the public school system has no bearing on the question whether the state may pay the tuition for students who wish to reject public education entirely and attend private schools that will provide them with a sectarian education.

5   The fact that the vast majority of the voucher recipients who have entirely rejected public education receive religious indoctrination

at state expense does, however, support the claim that the law is one "respecting an establishment of religion." The state may choose to divide up its public schools into a dozen different options and label them magnet schools, community schools, or whatever else it decides to call them, but the state is still required to provide a public education and it is the state's decision to fund private school education over and above its traditional obligation that is at issue in these cases.

Third, the voluntary character of the private choice to prefer a parochial education over an education in the public school system seems to me quite irrelevant to the question whether the government's choice to pay for religious indoctrination is constitutionally permissible. Today, however, the court seems to have decided that the mere fact that a family that cannot afford a private education wants its children educated in a parochial school is a sufficient justification for this use of public funds.

For the reasons stated by Justice Souter and Justice Breyer, I am convinced that the court's decision is profoundly misguided. Admittedly, in reaching that conclusion I have been influenced by my understanding of the impact of religious strife on the decisions of our forbears to migrate to this continent, and on the decisions of neighbors in the Balkans, Northern Ireland, and the Middle East to mistrust one another.

Whenever we remove a brick from the wall that was designed to separate religion and government, we increase the risk of religious strife and weaken the foundation of our democracy. I respectfully dissent.

"GIVE VOUCHERS A TRY" AND "THE WRONG RULING ON VOUCHERS"

The Providence Sunday Journal *and the* New York Times

Newspaper editorials represent the official position of the publication and not just the opinion of an individual writer. For this reason, editorials are not signed. In this instance, the *Providence Sunday Journal* sided with the majority opinion in favor of the school voucher program in Cleveland, and the *New York Times* opposed it.

SUGGESTION FOR READING   As you read the two editorials, notice how each positions itself in relation to the Supreme Court's decision. Consider how each editorial supports or refutes the court's legal reasoning and what additional arguments each editorial presents.

"GIVE VOUCHERS A TRY", *THE PROVIDENCE SUNDAY JOURNAL*

1 The U.S. Supreme Court's ruling in favor of a Cleveland school-voucher program is a sensible decision, and may very well have a salutary effect on public education. Here is why.

To begin with, it should be understood what the program entails. It permits parents of children in failing public schools to use modest vouchers to let them enroll their children in private or parochial schools. These are opportunities always available to affluent parents, but not to poor families, who are the beneficiaries of the Cleveland program. Families are not required to accept vouchers, nor are they directed to apply their voucher funds to particular schools. Parents are free to consider the alternatives—failing public schools or private alternatives—and make their own choices.

We cannot say whether the system is bound to succeed; we can only say that it is a sensible innovation that deserves a chance. And that is all the Supreme Court has done: given it a chance. The fact is that innumerable inner-city public school systems in America are failing the children they are meant to serve, and no amount of money seems to budge the bureaucracies and teachers' unions determined to preserve the status quo.

A voucher system gives low-income families a new opportunity to obtain a decent education for their children, and may give failing public schools a competitive challenge. Some might even rise to the occasion and reform themselves—thanks to vouchers.

5   It should also be understood what the voucher system is not. It is not an assault on public education in America. It is an attempt to improve some public schools by rescuing children trapped in abysmal systems and remind officials at failing schools of their basic mission. Where public schools succeed—that is, in most of America—parents gladly send their children to them. Nor do vouchers violate the separation of church and state. That parents tend to choose parochial schools has more to do with the high cost of secular private education, and the relatively low cost of religious-oriented schools, than any bid to establish religion in America.

As for the question of taxpayers subsidizing religious schools, vouchers are scarcely intended to fatten the endowments of parochial schools, most of which operate admirably on a shoestring. And it should be remembered that the federal government already "subsidizes" religious institutions in the form of research grants, academic scholarships, and the like.

That a student from Rhode Island might attend Providence College, a Catholic institution, with the help of a federal Pell Grant does not mean that America is about to become a theocracy.

"THE WRONG RULING ON VOUCHERS", *THE NEW YORK TIMES*

1   The country has been waiting for several years now to see how the Supreme Court would rule on school vouchers. Yesterday, in a 5-to-4 decision, the court issued a sweeping ruling upholding Cleveland's school voucher program. It was a bad decision on constitutional grounds, and a bad one for American education.

In theory, Cleveland's voucher program allows children to use state stipends to go to any school they want. In practice, the choice it offers them is between a failing public school system and the city's parochial schools. This is not a choice that the Constitution intended public tax money to underwrite.

The problem with the Cleveland program begins with the size of the stipends, which are capped at $2,250. That is far less than most private schools cost. But it is just right for parochial schools where, for a variety of reasons, tuition is far lower. Not surprisingly, fully 96.6 percent of students end up taking their vouchers to religiously affiliated schools.

Once students enroll in those schools, they are subjected to just the sort of religious training the First Amendment forbids the state to underwrite. In many cases, students are required to attend Mass or other religious services. Tax dollars go to buy Bibles, prayer books, crucifixes and other religious iconography. It is hard to think of a starker assault on the doctrine of separation of church and state than taking taxpayer dollars and using them to inculcate specific religious beliefs in young people.

5   The majority argues that the Cleveland program does not, as a technical matter, violate the First Amendment because it is parents, not the government, who are choosing where the money goes. But given the reality of education in Cleveland, parents do not have the wealth of options that would make their selection of religious schools meaningful. And in any case, the money ultimately comes from taxpayers, and therefore should not be directed—by whatever route—to finance religious training.

This ruling does as much damage to education as it does to the First Amendment. A common argument for vouchers is that they improve public schools by forcing them to compete for students. What is holding the public schools back, however, is not lack of competitive drive but the resources to succeed. Voucher programs like Cleveland's siphon off public dollars, leaving struggling urban systems with less money for skilled teachers, textbooks and computers. They also skim off some of the best-performing students, and the most informed and involved parents, from public schools that badly need their expertise and energy.

Yesterday's decision also undermines one of the public school system's most important functions: teaching democracy and pluralism. In public schools, Americans of many backgrounds learn together. In the religious schools that Cleveland taxpayers are being forced to sponsor, Catholics are free to teach that their way is best, and Jews, Muslims and those of other faiths can teach their co-religionists that they have truth on their side. As Justice John Paul Stevens wrote in dissent, "Whenever we remove a brick from the wall that was designed to separate religion and government, we increase the risk of religious strife and weaken the foundation of our democracy." This court has removed many bricks.

SUGGESTIONS FOR DISCUSSION

1. Analyze the line of reasoning in the majority opinion. Part of Chief Justice Rehnquist's task is to explain how the school voucher system in Cleveland does not violate ("offend") the Establishment Clause (the principle of church–state separation). How does he do this? What role does he give to "parental choice"? How is Justice Thomas's concurrence similar to Rehnquist's reasoning? What further reasons does Thomas offer? How would you characterize the underlying values and assumptions in the majority opinion?

2. Analyze the line of reasoning in the dissent. Notice that Justice Breyer begins by asserting that "'parental choice' cannot ameliorate the constitutional issue" of church–state separation. Why, in his view, is this so? In Justice Stevens's dissent, what are the three "factual matters" he thinks should be ignored? Why? How will ignoring them strengthen his position? Taken together, what do the dissenting opinions indicate the result of the school voucher program might be? Is this a reasonable prediction? What do their values and assumptions seem to be—and how do they differ from the majority?

3. Analyze the line of reasoning in the two editorials. What does the main strategy of support for vouchers seem to be in "Give Vouchers a Try"? What are the main reasons for opposing the majority opinion in "The Wrong Ruling on Vouchers"? Compare the line of reasoning in the editorials with the line of reasoning in the judicial opinions. What do you see as the main differences? How would you account for these differences?

SUGGESTIONS FOR WRITING

1. Write an essay that explains the significance of the debate over school vouchers. Draw on the Supreme Court Justices' opinions, the two newspaper editorials, class discussion, and your own analysis of the controversy. Although you have no doubt developed your own ideas about school vouchers, put the emphasis on giving your readers a way to understand the controversy and what is at stake instead of on whether they should support or oppose the Supreme Court decision. Step back from the arguments offered for or against the ruling in favor of school vouchers so that you can put the debate in context by pointing out what you think the main issues for education in America are, where these issues come from, and what implications they might have for the future.

2. Organize a formal debate. Divide the class in half. One side will support the majority opinion and the other will oppose it. (For this assignment, it doesn't matter what your own opinion is.) Each group should prepare a ten-minute opening statement that presents its position of support or dissent and decide on one member to make the presentation. Take notes during the two presentations. Once the opening statements have been made, return to your group to prepare a five-minute rebuttal of the other group's presentation, discussing what the other side's main reasons are and what effective refutations might be.

Make sure the rebuttal you design is in keeping with what your group presented in the opening statement. Choose someone to present it. After each side has presented its rebuttals, meet together as a class to consider what you learned in the debate. Did it deepen your understanding of the school vouchers issue? Why or why not? What do you see as the advantages of arguing for or against in a formal debate? What are the limitations?

3. Write an editorial that supports or opposes the Supreme Court decision. Now is the chance to have your own say and to explain what you think about the ruling. Use the two editorials as models. Notice that both make it clear early on exactly how they stand on the issue. Both also make it easy for readers to see how the reasons and examples in the editorial connect to its position on school vouchers.

CROSSING BOUNDARIES

Mike Rose

Mike Rose is a professor of education at UCLA. He has worked for the past twenty years teaching and tutoring children and adults from what he calls America's "educational underclass" — working-class children, poorly educated Vietnam vets, underprepared college students, and adults in basic literacy programs. The following selection is from the chapter "Crossing Boundaries" in Rose's award-winning book, *Lives on the Boundary* (1989). This book is an intensely personal account of Rose's own life growing up in a Los Angeles ghetto and his struggles as an educator to make schooling more accessible to children and adults labeled "remedial," "illiterate," and "intellectually deficient." As the following selection indicates, throughout *Lives on the Boundary,* Rose is especially interested in the "politics and sociology of school failure."

SUGGESTION FOR READING The following selection is separated into three parts. To help you think about how these parts combine to form a whole (or whether they do), underline and annotate as you read and note the focus of each section and how it provides a commentary on the other sections.

I myself I thank God for the dream to come back to school and to be able to seek the dream I want, because I know this time I will try and make my dream come true.

1   Each semester the staff of the Bay Area literacy program we're about to visit collects samples of their students' writing and makes books for them. You can find an assortment on an old bookshelf by the coordinator's desk. The booklets are simple: mimeographed, faint blue stencil, stapled, dog-eared. There are uneven drawings on the thin paper covers: a bicycle leaning against a tree, the Golden Gate Bridge, an Aubrey Beardsley sketch. The stories are about growing up, raising children, returning—sadly or with anticipation—to hometowns, to Chicago or St. Louis or to a sweep of rural communities in the South. Many of the stories are about work: looking for work, losing work, wanting better work. And many more are about coming back to school. Coming back to school. Some of these writers haven't been in a classroom in thirty years.

The stories reveal quite a range. Many are no longer than a paragraph, their sentences simple and repetitive, tenuously linked by *and* and *then* and *anyway*. There are lots of grammar and spelling errors and problems with sentence boundaries—in a few essays, periods come where commas should be or where no punctuation is needed at all: "It was hard for me to stay in school because I was allway sick. and that was verry hard for me." Or, "I sound better. now that my boys are grown." Papers of this quality are written, for the most part, by newcomers, people at the end of their first semester. But other papers—quite a few, actually—are competent. They tend to come from those who have received a year or more of instruction. There are still problems with grammar and sentence fragments and with spelling, since the writers are using a wider, more ambitious vocabulary. Problems like these take longer to clear up, but the writers are getting more adept at rendering their experience in print, at developing a narrative, at framing an illustration, at turning a phrase in written language:

> The kitchen floor was missing some of its tiles and had not been kissed with water and soap for a long time.
> The [teacher] looked for a moment, and then said, "All the students wishing to be accounted for, please be seated."
> A minute went by, then a tough looking Mexican boy got up, and walked to the teacher with a knife in his hand. When he got to the desk he said, "I'm here teacher! My name is Robert Gomez." With that he put the knife away, and walked over and found a seat.
> Back in the jaws of despair, pain, and the ugly scars of the defeated parents he loved. Those jaws he had struggled free of when he had moved out and away when he was eighteen years old.
> ...the wind was howling, angry, whirling.

A few new students also created such moments, indicators of what they'll be able to do as they become more fluent writers, as they develop some control over and confidence in establishing themselves on paper:

> [I used to have] light, really light Brown eyes, like Grasshopper eyes. which is what some peoples used to call me. Grasshopper, or Grasshopper eyes....I decided one Day to catch a Grasshopper. and look at its eye to be sure of the color.
> It was early in the morning just before dawn. Big Red, the sun hasn't showed its face in the heaven. The sky had that midnight blue look. The stars losing their shine.

There are about eight or ten of these stapled collections, a hundred and fifty or so essays. Five

years' worth. An archive scattered across an old bookcase. There's a folding chair close by. I've been sitting in it for some time now, reading one book, then another, story after story. Losing track. Drifting in and out of lives. Wondering about grasshopper eyes, about segregated schools, wanting to know more about this journey to the West looking for work. Slowly something has been shifting in my perception: the errors—the weird commas and missing letters, the fragments and irregular punctuation—they are ceasing to be slips of the hand and brain. They are becoming part of the stories themselves. They are the only fitting way, it seems, to render dislocation—shacks and field labor and children lost to the inner city—to talk about parents you long for, jobs you can't pin down. Poverty has generated its own damaged script, scars manifest in the spelling of a word.

5   This is the prose of America's underclass. The writers are those who got lost in our schools, who could not escape neighborhoods that narrowed their possibilities, who could not enter the job market in any ascendent way. They are locked into unskilled and semiskilled jobs, live in places that threaten their children, suffer from disorders and handicaps they don't have the money to treat. Some have been unemployed for a long time. But for all that, they remain hopeful, have somehow held onto a deep faith in education. They have come back to school. Ruby, the woman who wrote the passage that opens this section, walks unsteadily to the teacher's desk—the arthritis in her hip goes unchecked—with a paper in her hand. She looks over her shoulder to her friend, Alice: "I ain't givin' up the ship this time," she says and winks, "though, Lord, I might drown with it." The class laughs. They understand.

It is a very iffy thing, this schooling. But the participants put a lot of stock in it. They believe school will help them, and they are very specific about what they want: a high school equivalency, or the ability to earn seven dollars an hour. One wants to move from being a nurse's aide to a licensed vocational nurse, another needs to read and write and compute adequately enough to be self-employed as a car painter and body man.

They remind you of how fundamentally important it is—not just to your pocket but to your soul as well—to earn a decent wage, to have a steady job, to be just a little bit in control of your economic life. The goals are specific, modest, but they mean a tremendous amount for the assurance they give to these people that they are still somebody, that they can exercise control. Thus it is that talk of school and a new job brings forth such expansive language, as soaring as any humanist's testament to the glory of the word: "I thank God to be able to seek the dream I want...." For Ruby and her classmates the dream deferred neither dried up like a raisin in the sun, nor has it exploded. It has emerged again—for it is so basic—and it centers on schooling. "I admire and respect knowledge and those that have it are well blessed," writes another student. "My classmates are a swell group because they too have a dream and they too are seeking knowledge and I love them for that."

Sitting in the classroom with Ruby, Alice, and the rest, you think, at times, that you're at a revival meeting. There is so much testifying. Everybody talks and writes about dreams and goals and "doing better for myself." This is powerful, edifying—but something about it, its insistence perhaps, is a little bit discordant. The exuberance becomes jittery, an almost counterphobic boosting and supporting. It is no surprise, then, that it alternates with despair. In their hearts, Ruby and her classmates know how tenuous this is, how many times they've failed before. Somebody says something about falling down. Sally says, "I've felt that too. Not falling down on my legs or knees, but falling down within me." No wonder they sermonize and embrace. It's not just a few bucks more a week that's at stake; literacy, here, is intimately connected with respect, with a sense that they are not beaten, the mastery of print revealing the deepest impulse to survive.

When they entered the program, Ruby and Alice and Sally and all the rest were given several tests, one of which was a traditional reading inventory. The test had a section on comprehen-sion—relatively brief passages followed by multiple-choice questions—and a series of sections that tested particular reading skills: vocabulary, syllabication, phonics, prefixes and roots. The level of the instrument was pretty sophisticated, and the skills it tested are the kind you develop in school: answering multiple-choice questions, working out syllable breaks, knowing Greek and Latin roots, all that. What was interesting about this group of test takers was that—though a few were barely literate—many could read and write well enough to get along and, in some cases, to help those in their communities who were less skilled. They could read, with fair comprehension, simple news articles, could pay bills, follow up on sales and coupons, deal with school forms for their kids, and help illiterate neighbors in their interactions with the government. Their skills were pretty low-level and limited profoundly the kinds of things they could read or write, but they lived and functioned amid print. The sad thing is that we don't really have tests of such naturally occurring competence. The tests we do have, like the one Ruby and the others took, focus on components of reading ability tested in isolation (phonetic discrimination, for example) or on those skills that are school-oriented, like reading a passage on an unfamiliar topic unrelated to immediate needs: the mating habits of the dolphin, the Mayan pyramids. Students then answer questions on these sorts of passages by choosing one of four or five possible answers, some of which may be purposely misleading.

To nobody's surprise, Ruby and her classmates performed miserably. The tasks of the classroom were as unfamiliar as could be. There is a good deal of criticism of these sorts of reading tests, but one thing that is clear is that they reveal how well people can perform certain kinds of school activities. The activities themselves may be of questionable value, but they are interwoven with instruction and assessment, and entrance to many jobs is determined by them. Because of their centrality, then, I wanted to get some sense of how the students went about taking the tests. What happened as they tried to meet the test's demands? How was it that they failed?

10   My method was simple. I chose four students and had each of them take sections of the test again, asking them questions as they did so, encouraging them to talk as they tried to figure out an item.

The first thing that emerged was the complete foreignness of the task. A sample item in the prefixes and roots section (called Word Parts) presented the word "<u>un</u>happy," and asked the testtaker to select one of four other words "which gives the meaning of the underlined part of the first word." The choices were *very, glad, sad, not.* Though the person giving the test had read through the instructions with the class, many still could not understand, and if they chose an answer at all, most likely chose *sad,* a synonym for the whole word *unhappy.*

Nowhere in their daily reading are these students required to focus on parts of words in this way. The multiple-choice format is also unfamiliar—it is not part of day-to-day literacy—so the task as well as the format is new, odd. I explained the directions again—read them slowly, emphasized the sample item—but still, three of the four students continued to fall into the test maker's trap of choosing synonyms for the target word rather than zeroing in on the part of the word in question. Such behavior is common among those who fail in our schools, and it has led some commentators to posit that students like these are cognitively and linguistically deficient in some fundamental way: They process language differently, or reason differently from those who succeed in school, or the dialect they speak in some basic way interferes with their processing of Standard Written English.

Certainly in such a group—because of malnourishment, trauma, poor health care, environmental toxins—you'll find people with neurolinguistic problems or with medical difficulties that can affect perception and concentration. And this group—ranging in age from nineteen to the mid-fifties—has a wide array of medical complications: diabetes, head injury, hypertension, asthma, retinal deterioration, and the unusual sleep disorder called narcolepsy. It would be naive to deny the effect of all this on reading and writing. But as you sit alongside these students and listen to them work through a task, it is not damage that most strikes you. Even when they're misunderstanding the test and selecting wrong answers, their reasoning is not distorted and pathological. Here is Millie, whose test scores placed her close to the class average—and average here would be very low just about anywhere else.

Millie is given the word "<u>kilo</u>meter" and the following list of possible answers:

   a. thousand
   b. hundred
   c. distance
   d. speed

15   She responds to the whole word—*kilometer*—partially because she still does not understand how the test works, but also, I think, because the word is familiar to her. She offers *speed* as the correct answer because: "I see it on the signs when I be drivin'." She starts to say something else, but stops abruptly. "Whoa, it don't have to be 'speed'—it could be 'distance.'"

"It could be 'distance,' couldn't it?" I say.

"Yes, it could be one or the other."

"Okay."

"And then again," she says reflectively, "it could be a number."

20   Millie tapped her knowledge of the world—she had seen *kilometer* on road signs—to offer a quick response: *speed.* But she saw just as quickly that her knowledge could logically support another answer (*distance*), and, a few moments later, saw that what she knew could also support a third answer, one related to number. What she lacked was specific knowledge of the Greek prefix *kilo,* but she wasn't short on reasoning ability. In fact, reading tests like the one Millie took are constructed in such a way as to trick you into relying on commonsense reasoning and world knowledge—and thereby choosing a wrong answer. Take, for example, this item:

Cardio<u>gram</u>

   a. heart
   b. abnormal
   c. distance
   d. record

Millie, and many others in the class, chose *heart*. To sidestep that answer, you need to know something about the use of *gram* in other such words (versus its use as a metric weight), but you need to know, as well, how these tests work.

After Millie completed five or six items, I had her go back over them, talking through her answers with her. One item that had originally given her trouble was "<u>extra</u>ordinary": a) "beyond"; b) "acute"; c) "regular"; d) "imagined." She had been a little rattled when answering this one. While reading the four possible answers, she stumbled on "imagined": "I...im..."; then, tentatively, "imaged"; a pause again, then "imagine," and, quickly, "I don't know that word."

I pronounce it.

25 She looks up at me, a little disgusted: "I said it, didn't I?"

"You did say it."

"I was scared of it."

Her first time through, Millie had chosen *regular*, the wrong answer—apparently locking onto *ordinary* rather than the underlined prefix *extra*—doing just the opposite of what she was supposed to do. It was telling, I thought, that Millie and two or three others talked about words scaring them.

When we came back to "<u>extra</u>ordinary" during our review, I decided on strategy. "Let's try something," I said. "These tests are set up to trick you, so let's try a trick ourselves." I take a pencil and do something the publishers of the test tell you not to do: I mark up the test booklet. I slowly begin to circle the prefix *extra*, saying, "This is the part of the word we're concerned with, right?" As soon as I finish she smiles and says "beyond," the right answer.

30 "Did you see what happened there?" I said. "As soon as I circled the part of the word, you saw what it meant."

"I see it," she says. "I don't be thinking about what I'm doing."

I tell her to try what I did, to circle the part of the word in question, to remember that trick, for with tests like this, we need a set of tricks of our own.

"You saw it yourself," I said.

"Sure did. It was right there in front of me—cause the rest of them don't even go with 'extra.'"

35 I had been conducting this interview with Millie in between her classes, and our time was running out. I explained that we'd pick this up again, and I turned away, checking the wall clock, reaching to turn off the tape recorder. Millie was still looking at the test booklet.

"What is this word right here?" she asked. She had gone ahead to the other, more difficult, page of the booklet and was pointing to "<u>ego</u>centric."

I take my finger off the recorder's STOP button. "Let's circle it," I say. "What's that word? Say it."

"Ego."

"What's that mean?"

40 "Ego. Oh my." She scans the four options—*self, head, mind, kind*—and says "self."

"Excellent!"

"You know, when I said 'ego,' I tried to put it in a sentence: 'My ego,' I say. That's *me*."

I ask her if she wants to look at one more. She goes back to "cardio<u>gram</u>," which she gets right this time. Then to "<u>therm</u>ometer," which she also gets right. And "<u>bi</u>focal," which she gets right without using her pencil to mark the prefix. Once Millie saw and understood what the test required of her, she could rely on her world knowledge to help her reason out some answers.

Cognitive psychologists talk about task representation, the way a particular problem is depicted or reproduced in the mind. Something shifted in Millie's conception of her task, and it had a powerful effect on her performance.

45 It was common for nineteenth-century American educators to see their mission with the immigrant and native-born urban poor as a fundamentally moral one. Historian Michael Katz quotes from the Boston school committee's description of social and spiritual acculturation:

> taking children at random from a great city, undisciplined, uninstructed, often with inveterate forwardness and obstinacy, and with the

inherited stupidity of centuries of ignorant ancestors; forming them from animals into intellectual beings, and...from intellectual beings into spiritual beings; giving to many their first appreciation of what is wise, what is true, what is lovely and what is pure.

In our time, educators view the effects of poverty and cultural dislocation in more enlightened ways; though that moralistic strain still exists, the thrust of their concern has shifted from the spiritual to the more earthly realm of language and cognition. Yet what remains is the disturbing tendency to perceive the poor as *different* in some basic way from the middle and upper classes—the difference now being located in the nature of the way they think and use language. A number of studies and speculations over the past twenty-five years has suggested that the poor are intellectually or linguistically deficient or, at the least, different: They lack a logical language or reason in ways that limit intellectual achievement or, somehow, process information dysfunctionally. If we could somehow get down to the very basic loops and contours of their mental function, we would find that theirs are different from ours. There's a huge literature on all this and, originating with critics like linguist William Labov, a damning counterliterature. This is not the place to review that work, but it would be valuable to consider Millie against the general outlines of the issue.

Imagine her in a typical classroom testing situation. More dramatically, imagine her in some university laboratory being studied by one or two researchers—middle class and probably white. Millie is a strong woman with a tough front, but these would most likely be uncomfortable situations for her. And if she were anxious, her performance would be disrupted: as it was when she didn't identify *imagined*—a word she pronounced and knew—because she was "scared of it." Add to this the fact that she is very much adrift when it comes to school-based tests: She simply doesn't know how to do them. What would be particularly damning for her would be the fact that, even with repeated instruction and illustration, she failed to catch on to the way the test worked. You can see how an observer would think her unable to shift out of (inadequate) performance, unable to understand simple instructions and carry them out. Deficient or different in some basic way: nonlogical, nonrational, unable to think analytically. It would be from observations like this that a theory of fundamental cognitive deficiency or difference would emerge.

We seem to have a need as a society to explain poor performance by reaching deep into the basic stuff of those designated as other: into their souls, or into the deep recesses of their minds, or into the very ligature of their language. It seems harder for us to keep focus on the politics and sociology of intellectual failure, to keep before our eyes the negative power of the unfamiliar, the way information poverty constrains performance, the effect of despair on cognition.

"I was so busy looking for 'psychopathology,'..." says Robert Coles of his early investigations of childhood morality, "that I brushed aside the most startling incidents, the most instructive examples of ethical alertness in the young people I was getting to know." How much we don't see when we look only for deficiency, when we tally up all that people can't do. Many of the students in this book display the gradual or abrupt emergence of an intellectual acuity or literate capacity that just wasn't thought to be there. This is not to deny that awful limits still exist for those like Millie: so much knowledge and so many procedures never learned; such a long, cumbersome history of relative failure. But this must not obscure the equally important fact that if you set up the right conditions, try as best you can to cross class and cultural boundaries, figure out what's needed to encourage performance, that if you watch and listen, again and again there will emerge evidence of ability that escapes those who dwell on differences.

50   Ironically, it's often the reports themselves of our educational inadequacies—the position papers and media alarms on illiteracy in America—that help blind us to cognitive and linguistic

possibility. Their rhetorical thrust and their metaphor conjure up disease or decay or economic and military defeat: A malignancy has run wild, an evil power is consuming us from within. (And here reemerges that nineteenth-century moral terror.) It takes such declamation to turn the moneyed wheels of government, to catch public attention and entice the givers of grants, but there's a dark side to this political reality. The character of the alarms and, too often, the character of the responses spark in us the urge to punish, to extirpate, to return to a precancerous golden age rather than build on the rich capacity that already exists. The reports urge responses that reduce literate possibility and constrain growth, that focus on pathology rather than on possibility. Philosophy, said Aristotle, begins in wonder. So does education.

SUGGESTIONS FOR DISCUSSION

1. What motivates students such as Ruby, Alice, Sally, and Millie to return to school? What assumptions do they seem to make about the effects of education? Are these assumptions realistic? How do they compare with the assumptions you and your classmates make about the effects of education? Explain what you see as differences and similarities.

2. How does Rose explain poor performance and failure in school? Don't settle for generalizations such as "poverty and cultural dislocation." Look closely at how Rose analyzes Millie's experience with questions on a reading comprehension test. Do you find Rose's explanations persuasive? What do these explanations imply about the nature and function of schooling in America?

3. Rose says that "nineteenth-century American educators" looked at their "mission" as a "fundamentally moral one." Later he suggests that such a "moralistic strain still exists" in the way Americans think about education and that it can "spark in us the urge to punish, to extirpate, to return to a precancerous golden age." What is the nature of the "moral terror" Rose talks about? Do you agree with him? Draw upon your experience in school to respond to this question.

SUGGESTIONS FOR WRITING

1. Write an essay that explains what Mike Rose sees as causes of failure in school. Compare his explanation with your own views on what causes students to fail. Draw on your own experience and what you have observed.

2. Most students have been "punished" at some point or another during their schooling. Write an essay that tells the story of a time when you were (or someone you know was) "punished" in school. What did you do? Did you break a rule? Was the rule fair? Was the "punishment" just or unjust? Your story should tell about what happened and how you felt about it. Then use the story to reflect on what the incident reveals about life in school and how students encounter and deal with the "rules" of schooling.

3. Rose says that "reports [of]...our educational inadequacies—the position papers and media alarms on illiteracy in America—" reduce "literate possibility and constrain growth." Write an essay that considers Rose's claim that such reports "focus on pathology rather than on possibility." You'll need to find a report or a media account of literacy and American education. You can draw on reports from the past, such as A Nation at Risk (1993), which you can find in the library, or more recent ones on-line. Web sites, such as Edweek (www.edweek.org/) and the American Federation of Teachers (www.AFT.org/edissues/standards99/index.htm), feature recent reports. Or you can use media accounts, such as Newsweek's classic cover story "Why Johnny Can't Write" (December 1975) or more recent reporting on the "reading wars." (You can find overviews of the "reading wars" in "Reading: The First Skill" by Nick Anderson and Duke

Helfand in the *Los Angeles Times*, September 13, 1998, and in "School from Start to Finish; Reading Wars, Take 2" by Karin Chenoweth in the *Washington Post*, May 16, 1999.) In any event, examine carefully the report or media coverage to see how it describes an educational or literacy "crisis" and explains the causes and solutions. Use Rose's idea that reports too often rely on metaphors "of disease or decay or economic or military defeat" to analyze the report. In the broadest sense, Rose is arguing that educational reports are alarmist and use fear to persuade readers. Is there a sense in which this is true of the report you're analyzing? If so, how? If not, what feeling does the report or media account try to tap in readers? How can you tell? Use examples from the report or media account to explain.

NOTE-PASSING: STRUGGLES FOR STATUS

Margaret J. Finders

Margaret J. Finders is associate professor of English and education at Purdue University. The following selection is taken from her study *Just Girls: Hidden Literacies and Life in Junior High* (1997). In her study, Finders focuses on how a group of popular junior high girls (the "social queens") use reading and writing outside the official school curriculum—signing yearbooks, passing notes, writing bathroom graffiti, and reading teen 'zines. These "hidden literacies," Finders says, play key roles for these young women in defining their sense of self and maintaining group loyalties.

SUGGESTION FOR READING Notice that Finders first describes the formal features of notes, then explains the social functions they perform, and finally generalizes three themes that emerge from "note-passing as a ritualized event." As you read, consider how her presentation of note-passing sets up the generalizations with which this passage ends.

1 Note-writing as a genre did not allow for much individual expression or originality. The girls all protested indignantly whenever I suggested such a notion: "You can write whatever you want." Yet the following notes illustrate the standards required for the genre of note-writing.

> Lauren,
>
> Yo! What's up? Not much here. I'm in math and it is BORING. Did you know that I like Nate a lot. But he'd probably never go out with me caz I'm too ugly. AND FAT. Oh, well though. I'm still going to try and get him to go with me caz I like him. I hope he goes with me before the football game Friday. I want to be going with him at the game. Are you and Ricky going to the game? I want to go somewhere after that. Maybe you could come over or I could come to your house. Don't show this to anyone. W-B [Write Back] Maggie

> Lauren,
>
> Hey. What's up? You don't need to ask Bill for me cause he won't go and he's just that way I guess. You can try but I know he's not going to go. Well I'm almost positive. I'm in social studies and I just got busted caz I had none of my homework done. Fun. My handwriting majorly Sucks. I hate it. Go to *Body Guard* at the mall and I'll say you need a ride home. Then you can spend the night at my house. Call me tonight. I will be at my mom's. S.S. [Stay Sweet or Stay Sexy] Carrie.

Notes regularly began with a common salutation, "Hey, what's up?" followed by a reference to where the note was written—"I'm in math." "I'm in social studies." Because notes were always written in school, this move positioned the queen in opposition to the institutional power by boldly announcing an act of defiance during one particular class and then adding a condemning judgment such as, "It's so boring." In this move, queens perceived themselves as powerful by defying authority. Yet that power was somewhat diffused as they often embedded in the body of the note a reference to themselves as inadequate: too fat, too ugly, my handwriting sucks. Often in notes, messages closed with "Sorry So Sloppy," which were sometimes shortened to S.S.S. For the most part, extreme care was taken to write neatly, at time dotting the i's with circles or hearts.

The content of notes was generally about making social arrangements for after-school activities and for requesting help in making romantic contacts. The notes carried highly coded messages such as N.M.H. (not much here) that limited the readership to those who were inside the circle of friends. The closing, as well, was most often highly coded—B.F.F. (best friends forever) W-B (write back)—to provide an insider quality to those who knew the codes. Britton (1970), noting the "with-it" language of adolescents, argues for the necessity of "drawing together members of a group or the set, and keeping outsiders out" (p. 235). The meaning behind S.S.S. evolved over time. At first it meant "Sorry So Sloppy," but over the course of the seventh-grade year, it came to carry a completely different meaning: "Stay Sweet and Sexy." The evolution of this one code illustrates the demands embedded within shifting social roles from girl to adolescent.

Although notes generally followed a standard format, a few did contain important unknown information such as the appropriate time to receive a call, an apology for flirting with a boyfriend, or guarded information about family problems. The queens attempted to control the circulation of their notes and regularly added to their messages, "Don't show this to anyone." For the most part, notes created boundaries around a group of friends. By creating a tangible document, girls created proof of their memberships.

5   As stated previously, girls all voiced the opinion that "you just write whatever you want," yet when someone outside the intimate circle of friends wrote a note to one of the most popular girls, she was criticized. As one girl described it, "Look at that. She doesn't even know how to write right." These teens were criticized for not recognizing or following the rules and rituals on note-writing, a primary rule being that notes could be passed only to friends of equal social status. The unstated rules of adhering to established social hierarchies were clearly enforced. If, for example, a girl did not know her place in the social hierarchy and wrote a note to a more popular girl, she became the object of ridicule and laughter within the higher circle.

This need for social sorting at the junior high was visible to teachers. Debra Zmoleck described the practice in this way:

> I think part of the way junior high kids feel good about themselves is they've got to have that ego, you know, it's a pecking order. They've got to have somebody that's down there that all the other chickens peck at, you know. And I don't know why, I guess it's just part of junior high.

The "pecking order" to which Debra referred was often documented in literate practices. Literacy was a tool used to document and maintain social position. In private interviews, Angie and Lauren both made statements in accord with Tiffany's own self-assessment.

> I don't write notes much so now I don't get 'em. Lauren gets the most because she writes the most. She's the most popular. Me, not so much.

Tiffany lost status because she didn't write as many notes as other girls and slowly over time received fewer and fewer, marking her as less popular. On the other hand, Lauren was perceived to be the most popular girl among her network of friends because "she has the most notes." She also received more notes from boys, which further served to document her high status among her friends.

In the fall of seventh grade, the number of notes passed increased until mid-November when a plateau was reached; January saw a sharp decline. When asked about this decline, the queens all relayed the fact that there just wasn't as much to write about; yet the events that they had written about all year—social arrangements, sports, and boys—had not decreased in their interest or in their activity. I contend that note-passing had served its purpose—to sort and select a hierarchy among the queens who had just entered a new arena in the fall. Arriving from different sixth-grade classrooms, the queens used literacies in the new school context to negotiate entry into new friendship networks. Through print sources, they maintained familiar ties in this strange new world, connecting at first with old sixth-grade friends and then negotiating their ways into other social groups. By January, new social positions were securely established, and note-passing decreased because jockeying for position was no longer an option for gaining status or entry into the social queens' network.

10   Note-passing was clearly a gendered activity. It functioned to control male voices and to try out women's voices. Circulation of notes was controlled exclusively by girls. Girls decided who was entitled to see, receive, or write a note. Boys did not write notes to boys, and they wrote to girls only when they were invited or instructed to do so by a girl directly or through a channeling system, where one girl wrote to another girl who would then write to a boy, thereby granting him permission to write to the first girl. This act of literacy bestowed power and control of romantic interactions exclusively to females. The hierarchical arrangement placed power firmly in the hands of the social queens, who controlled and regulated which boys wrote or received notes.

To guard the circulation of messages, the queens informed me that learning to fold a note properly was vital to ensure that it would not open if it were dropped. Notes were folded into small triangles or squares with edges tucked in, serving as a lock to protect messages from unauthorized eyes. Such skill in intricate folding was also used to gain status within the inner circle. One's knowledge of elaborate folds signaled one as a member in good standing. Again, literacy served to document status within the circle of

friends. If one queen learned a new and extremely complex fold, she received high praise and then attained the honored position of teacher, instructing others in how to fold.

Note-folding was a crucial skill because passing the note was a fine game that required a small, streamlined object. A note could have no rough edges to catch in a pocket lining, and it must be easily manipulated in the palm of one hand in order to avoid detection as it slipped from hand to hand boldly under the nose of a teacher. Passing notes from one of the social queens to another under the sharp scrutiny of a teacher was seen by these girls as an act of defiance and a behavior to be admired. Girls wrote, circulated, and responded to notes while reading aloud, participating in classroom discussions, and completing written work. A girl, for instance, could participate in a large-group discussion while writing and then passing notes without skipping a beat as she actively engaged in the classroom discussion. Designed to fool the teacher into thinking one was paying attention, such a game documented allegiance to peers. Ironically, a queen had to pay extremely close attention to keep the game going in her favor, yet this game was played to make the teacher appear foolish and the teen powerful.

Whenever the risk became heightened by a teacher's reprimands or threats of posting notes on classroom walls, notes became a greater avenue of status-building. When the risks were greatest, girls began lacing their texts with obscene language to up the ante, for to have one such note confiscated would mean not only a disruption at school but disruption at home as well.

More often than not, the content of the note was inconsequential; meaning was conveyed in the passing of the note rather than within the text itself. The act of passing the note during class relayed the message, an act of defiance of adult authority. The message was modified not through words but through the creative manipulation of the passing. The closer one was to the teacher physically when the note was written or delivered, the more powerful the message. By mid-November, after the girls had grown to trust me, they would often dig into their pockets and notebooks and hand me unopened notes. They did not need to read the notes because the message was implicit in the process of passing: in clues such as who sent, who received, who was present during the passing, and how the note was transported.

15   After I examined note-passing as a ritualized event, several themes emerged: (1) Writing is a social event; (2) special status is ascribed to the girl who received the most notes, especially from boys; and (3) meaning often resides in the act of passing a note. Note-passing was a tool used to document and maintain social position. For the most part, notes were used to bestow power and patrol boundaries around a group of friends.

SUGGESTIONS FOR DISCUSSION

1. As Finders says in an earlier section, her study of junior high girls focuses on what Shirley Brice Heath calls "literacy events" — "any occasion in which a piece of writing is integral to the nature of participants' interactions and their interpretative processes." Finders is interested in how "literacy events" take place, the social functions they perform, and the meanings they have for participants. Consider the conclusions about the social role of reading and writing that Finders draws from this brief analysis of note-passing. How does her view of reading and writing differ from that of the official curriculum? What, if anything, does her perspective have to offer about reading and writing that you won't find in textbooks and classroom lessons?

2. Unlike the official curriculum, where students read and write on demand, note-passing is "self-sponsored" literacy, where the impetus comes from the student instead of the teacher. Make a list of the many kinds of self-sponsored reading and writing that you do or have done in the past. Finders pays particular attention to yearbook signing, note-passing, graffiti writing, and reading teen 'zines. These are not the only forms of reading and writing that fall outside the official curriculum. Others include writing journals, diaries, letters, e-mails, songs, poems, stories, raps, or petitions and reading magazines about sports, computers, cars, music, or other subjects and popular novels (romance, science fiction, horror, mystery, and so on). Compare the list you compile with those of two or three other students. What do you see as the social functions of such self-sponsored literacy? In what sense do you and others use these forms of reading and writing to define a sense of self and maintain friendship or interest groups?

3. As Finders points out, note-passing involves certain risks. It takes place as an unsanctioned act of reading and writing outside the official curriculum. It is also done in opposition to the rules of schooling and, to be successful, must evade notice by the teacher. For Finders and other researchers who pay attention to what students actually do in school, note-passing is just one instance among many of how young people defy adult authority to carry on their own business. What other examples of such defiant behavior can you think of from your own experience or that you observed in junior high and high school? What risks were involved? What were the rewards from the students' point of view? What do you see as the implications?

SUGGESTIONS FOR WRITING

1. Write an essay on the functions of note-passing in school classrooms. Draw on you own experience and what you know and have observed about classroom life. You don't have to limit yourself to note-passing in junior high and high school. Note-passing takes place in college too, and it may be interesting to look at the role it plays there and whether it differs in function from note-passing in earlier education.

2. Consider the kinds of self-sponsored reading and writing you engage in. In what ways do they differ from what you are asked to do in school? Write an essay that focuses on

one type of self-sponsored writing that is particularly important to you. Take into account the purposes this form of writing serves for you. To what extent are these purposes different from and similar to school-sanctioned purposes? Explain what you see as the significance of these differences and similarities.

3. It's a truism that students like to challenge the adult authority of schooling. Everyone can think of examples of how they or other students defied the powers that be in school, whether overtly or in more hidden ways. Choose a particularly revealing example of how you or another student or group of students sought to get away with something in school. First describe what happened and then analyze its meaning and significance. In your analysis, don't settle for easy generalizations such as the truism that young people will test limits and rebel against the older generation. Get inside the event from the student perspective. What exactly was at stake for the student or group of students? How did the act of resisting or evading authority assert the identity and social allegiances of the student or students involved?

FROM SILENCE TO WORDS: WRITING AS STRUGGLE

Min-Zhan Lu

Min-Zhan Lu teaches English at the University of Wisonsin, Milwaukee. She has written many important articles about literacy and the teaching of writing as well as a memoir, *Shanghai Quartet* (2001). The article included here, "From Silence to Words: Writing as Struggle," appeared in the journal *College English* in 1987.

SUGGESTION FOR READING Min-Zhan Lu's literacy narrative uses autobiography to raise larger issues about the possible tensions between "home" and "school" languages. In a large part of the selection, Lu tells the story of her experience growing up in China. Sometimes, though, she steps back to make sense of what happened. As you read, note those passages where Lu explains what she sees as the significance of her struggle with writing.

Imagine that you enter a parlor. You come late. When you arrive, others have long preceded you, and they are engaged in a heated discussion....You listen for a while, until you decide that you have caught the tenor of the argument; then you put in your oar. Someone answers; you answer him; another comes to your defense; another aligns himself against you, to either the embarrassment or gratification of your opponent, depending upon the quality of your ally's assistance. However, the discussion is interminable. The hour grows late, you must depart. And you do depart, with the discussion still vigorously in progress.

Kenneth Burke, The Philosophy of Literary Form

Men are not built in silence, but in word, in work, in action-reflection.

Paulo Freire, Pedagogy of the Oppressed

1 My mother withdrew into silence two months before she died. A few nights before she fell silent, she told me she regretted the way she had raised me and my sisters. I knew she was referring to the way we had been brought up in the midst of two conflicting worlds—the world of home, dominated by the ideology of the Western humanistic tradition, and the world of a society dominated by Mao Tse-tung's Marxism. My mother had devoted her life to our education, an education she knew had made us suffer political

persecution during the Cultural Revolution. I wanted to find a way to convince her that, in spite of the persecution, I had benefited from the education she had worked so hard to give me. But I was silent. My understanding of my education was so dominated by memories of confusion and frustration that I was unable to reflect on what I could have gained from it.

This paper is my attempt to fill up that silence with words, words I didn't have then, words that I have since come to by reflecting on my earlier experience as a student in China and on my recent experience as a composition teacher in the United States. For in spite of the frustration and confusion I experienced growing up caught between two conflicting worlds, the conflict ultimately helped me to grow as a reader and writer. Constantly having to switch back and forth between the discourse of home and that of school made me sensitive and self-conscious about the struggle I experienced every time I tried to read, write, or think in either discourse. Eventually, it led me to search for constructive uses for such struggle.

From early childhood, I had identified the differences between home and the outside world by the different languages I used in each. My parents had wanted my sisters and me to get the best education they could conceive of—Cambridge. They had hired a live-in tutor, a Scot, to make us bilingual. I learned to speak English with my parents, my tutor, and my sisters. I was allowed to speak Shanghai dialect only with the servants. When I was four (the year after the Communist Revolution of 1949), my parents sent me to a local private school where I learned to speak, read, and write in a new language—Standard Chinese, the official written language of New China.

In those days I moved from home to school, from English to Standard Chinese to Shanghai dialect, with no apparent friction. I spoke each language with those who spoke the language. All seemed quite "natural"—servants spoke only Shanghai dialect because they were servants; teachers spoke Standard Chinese because they were teachers; languages had different words because they were different languages. I thought of English as my family language, comparable to the many strange dialects I didn't speak but had often heard some of my classmates speak with their families. While I was happy to have a special family language, until second grade I didn't feel that my family language was any different than some of my classmates' family dialects.

5   My second grade homeroom teacher was a young graduate from a missionary school. When she found out I spoke English, she began to practice her English on me. One day she used English when asking me to run an errand for her. As I turned to close the door behind me, I noticed the puzzled faces of my classmates. I had the same sensation I had often experienced when some stranger in a crowd would turn on hearing me speak English. I was more intensely pleased on this occasion, however, because suddenly I felt that my family language had been singled out from the family languages of my classmates. Since we were not allowed to speak any dialect other than Standard Chinese in the classroom, having my teacher speak English to me in class made English an official language of the classroom. I began to take pride in my ability to speak it.

This incident confirmed in my mind what my parents had always told me about the importance of English to one's life. Time and again they had told me of how my paternal grandfather, who was well versed in classic Chinese, kept losing good-paying jobs because he couldn't speak English. My grandmother reminisced constantly about how she had slaved and saved to send my father to a first-rate missionary school. And we were made to understand that it was my father's fluent English that had opened the door to his success. Even though my family had always stressed the importance of English for my future, I used to complain bitterly about the extra English lessons we had to take after school. It was only after my homeroom teacher had "sanctified" English that I began to connect English with my education. I became a much more eager student in my tutorials.

What I learned from my tutorials seemed to enhance and reinforce what I was learning in my classroom. In those days each word had one meaning. One day I would be making a sentence at school: "The national flag of China is red." The next day I would recite at home, "My love is like a red, red rose." There seemed to be an agreement between the Chinese "red" and the English "red," and both corresponded to the patch of color printed next to the word. "Love" was my love for my mother at home and my love for my "motherland" at school; both "loves" meant how I felt about my mother. Having two loads of homework forced me to develop a quick memory for words and a sensitivity to form and style. What I learned in one language carried over to the other. I made sentences such as, "I saw a red, red rose among the green leaves," with both the English lyric and the classic Chinese lyric—red flower among green leaves—running through my mind, and I was praised by both teacher and tutor for being a good student.

Although my elementary schooling took place during the fifties, I was almost oblivious to the great political and social changes happening around me. Years later, I read in my history and political philosophy textbooks that the fifties were a time when "China was making a transition from a semi-feudal, semi-capitalist, and semi-colonial country into a socialist country," a period in which "the Proletarians were breaking into the educational territory dominated by Bourgeois Intellectuals." While people all over the country were being officially classified into Proletarians, Petty-bourgeois, National-bourgeois, Poor-peasants, and Intellectuals, and were trying to adjust to their new social identities, my parents were allowed to continue the upper middle-class life they had established before the 1949 Revolution because of my father's affiliation with British firms. I had always felt that my family was different from the families of my classmates, but I didn't perceive society's view of my family until the summer vacation before I entered high school.

First, my aunt was caught by her colleagues talking to her husband over the phone in English.

Because of it, she was criticized and almost labeled a Rightist. (This was the year of the Anti-Rightist movement, a movement in which the Intellectuals became the target of the "socialist class-struggle.") I had heard others telling my mother that she was foolish to teach us English when Russian had replaced English as the "official" foreign language. I had also learned at school that the American and British Imperialists were the arch-enemies of New China. Yet I had made no connection between the arch-enemies and the English our family spoke. What happened to my aunt forced the connection on me. I began to see my parents' choice of a family language as an anti-Revolutionary act and was alarmed that I had participated in such an act. From then on, I took care not to use English outside home and to conceal my knowledge of English from my new classmates.

10   Certain words began to play important roles in my new life at the junior high. On the first day of school, we were handed forms to fill out with our parents' class, job, and income. Being one of the few people not employed by the government, my father had never been officially classified. Since he was a medical doctor, he told me to put him down as an Intellectual. My homeroom teacher called me into the office a couple of days afterwards and told me that my father couldn't be an Intellectual if his income far exceeded that of a Capitalist. He also told me that since my father worked for Foreign Imperialists, my father should be classified as an Imperialist Lackey. The teacher looked nonplussed when I told him that my father couldn't be an Imperialist Lackey because he was a medical doctor. But I could tell from the way he took notes on my form that my father's job had put me in an unfavorable position in his eyes.

The Standard Chinese term "class" was not a new word for me. Since first grade, I had been taught sentences such as, "The Working class are the masters of New China." I had always known that it was good to be a worker, but until then, I had never felt threatened for not being one. That fall, "class" began to take on a new meaning for me. I noticed a group of Working-class students and teachers at school. I was made to understand that because of my class background, I was excluded from that group.

Another word that became important was "consciousness." One of the slogans posted in the school building read, "Turn our students into future Proletarians with socialist consciousness and education!" For several weeks we studied this slogan in our political philosophy course, a subject I had never had in elementary school. I still remember the definition of "socialist consciousness" that we were repeatedly tested on through the years: "Socialist consciousness is a person's political soul. It is the consciousness of the Proletarians represented by Marxist Mao Tse-tung's thought. It takes expression in one's action, language, and lifestyle. It is the task of every Chinese student to grow up into a Proletarian with a socialist consciousness so that he can serve the people and the motherland." To make the abstract concept accessible to us, our teacher pointed out that the immediate task for students from Working-class families was to strengthen their socialist consciousnesses. For those of us who were from other class backgrounds, the task was to turn ourselves into Workers with socialist consciousnesses. The teacher never explained exactly how we were supposed to "turn" into Workers. Instead, we were given samples of the ritualistic annual plans we had to write at the beginning of each term. In these plans, we performed "self-criticism" on our consciousnesses and made vows to turn ourselves into Workers with socialist consciousnesses. The teacher's division between those who did and those who didn't have a socialist consciousness led me to reify the notion of "consciousness" into a thing one possesses. I equated this intangible "thing" with a concrete way of dressing, speaking, and writing. For instance, I never doubted that my political philosophy teacher had a socialist consciousness because she was from a steelworker's family (she announced this the first day of class) and was a Party member who wore grey cadre suits and talked like a philosophy textbook. I noticed other things about her. She had beautiful eyes and spoke Standard Chinese with such a pure accent that I thought she should be a film star. But I was embarrassed that I had noticed things that ought not to have been associated with her. I blamed my observation on my Bourgeois consciousness.

At the same time, the way reading and writing were taught through memorization and imitation also encouraged me to reduce concepts and ideas to simple definitions. In literature and political philosophy classes, we were taught a large number of quotations from Marx, Lenin, and Mao Tse-tung. Each concept that appeared in these quotations came with a definition. We were required to memorize the definitions of the words along with the quotations. Every time I memorized a definition, I felt I had learned a word: "The national red flag symbolizes the blood shed by Revolutionary ancestors for our socialist cause"; "New China rises like a red sun over the eastern horizon." As I memorized these sentences, I reduced their metaphors to dictionary meanings: "red" meant "Revolution" and "red sun" meant "New China" in the "language" of the Working class. I learned mechanically but eagerly. I soon became quite fluent in this new language.

As school began to define me as a political subject, my parents tried to build up my resistance to the "communist poisoning" by exposing me to the "great books"—novels by Charles Dickens, Nathaniel Hawthorne, Emily Brontë, Jane Austen, and writers from around the turn of the century. My parents implied that these writers represented how I, their child, should read and write. My parents replaced the word "Bourgeois" with the word "cultured." They reminded me that I was in school only to learn math and science. I needed to pass the other courses to stay in school, but I was not to let the "Red doctrines" corrupt my mind. Gone were the days when I could innocently write, "I saw the red, red rose among the green leaves," collapsing, as I did, English and Chinese cultural traditions. "Red" came to mean Revolution at school, "the Commies" at home, and adultery in *The Scarlet Let-*

ter. Since I took these symbols and metaphors as meanings natural to people of the same class, I abandoned my earlier definitions of English and Standard Chinese as the language of home and the language of school. I now defined English as the language of the Bourgeois and Standard Chinese as the language of the Working class. I thought of the language of the Working class as someone else's language and the language of the Bourgeois as my language. But I also believed that, although the language of the Bourgeois was my real language, I could and would adopt the language of the Working class when I was at school. I began to put on and take off my Working class language in the same way I put on and took off my school clothes to avoid being criticized for wearing Bourgeois clothes.

15   In my literature classes, I learned the Working-class formula for reading. Each work in the textbook had a short "Author's Biography": "X X X, born in 19- in the province of X X, is from a Worker's family. He joined the Revolution in 19-. He is a Revolutionary realist with a passionate love for the Party and Chinese Revolution. His work expresses the thoughts and emotions of the masses and sings praise to the prosperous socialist construction on all fronts of China." The teacher used the "Author's Biography" as a yardstick to measure the texts. We were taught to locate details in the texts that illustrated these summaries, such as words that expressed Workers' thoughts and emotions or events that illustrated the Workers' lives.

I learned a formula for Working-class writing in the composition classes. We were given sample essays and told to imitate them. The theme was always about how the collective taught the individual a lesson. I would write papers about labor-learning experiences or school-cleaning days, depending on the occasion of the collective activity closest to the assignment. To make each paper look different, I dressed it up with details about the date, the weather, the environment, or the appearance of the Master-worker who had taught me "the lesson." But as I became more and more fluent in the generic voice of the Working-class

Student, I also became more and more self-conscious about the language we used at home.

For instance, in senior high we began to have English classes ("to study English for the Revolution," as the slogan on the cover of the textbook said), and I was given my first Chinese–English dictionary. There I discovered the English version of the term "class-struggle." (The Chinese characters for a school "class" and for a social "class" are different.) I had often used the English word "class" at home in sentences such as, "So and so has class," but I had not connected this sense of "class" with "class-struggle." Once the connection was made, I heard a second layer of meaning every time someone at home said a person had "class." The expression began to mean the person had the style and sophistication characteristic of the Bourgeoisie. The word lost its innocence. I was uneasy about hearing that second layer of meaning because I was sure my parents did not hear the word that way. I felt that therefore I should not be hearing it that way either. Hearing the second layer of meaning made me wonder if I was losing my English.

My suspicion deepened when I noticed myself unconsciously merging and switching between the "reading" of home and the "reading" of school. Once I had to write a report on *The Revolutionary Family,* a book about an illiterate woman's awakening and growth as a Revolutionary through the deaths of her husband and all her children for the cause of the Revolution. In one scene the woman deliberated over whether or not she should encourage her youngest son to join the Revolution. Her memory of her husband's death made her afraid to encourage her son. Yet she also remembered her earlier married life and the first time her husband tried to explain the meaning of the Revolution to her. These memories made her feel she should encourage her son to continue the cause his father had begun.

I was moved by this scene. "Moved" was a word my mother and sisters used a lot when we discussed books. Our favorite moments in novels were moments of what I would now call internal conflict, moments which we said "moved" us. I remember that we were "moved" by Jane Eyre when she was torn between her sense of ethics, which compelled her to leave the man she loved, and her impulse to stay with the only man who had ever loved her. We were also moved by Agnes in *David Copperfield* because of the way she restrained her love for David so that he could live happily with the woman he loved. My standard method of doing a book report was to model it on the review by the Publishing Bureau and to dress it up with detailed quotations from the book. The review of *The Revolutionary Family* emphasized the woman's Revolutionary spirit. I decided to use the scene that had moved me to illustrate this point. I wrote the report the night before it was due. When I had finished, I realized I couldn't possibly hand it in. Instead of illustrating her Revolutionary spirit, I had dwelled on her internal conflict, which could be seen as a moment of weak sentimentality that I should never have emphasized in a Revolutionary heroine. I wrote another report, taking care to illustrate the grandeur of her Revolutionary spirit by expanding on a quotation in which she decided that if the life of her son could change the lives of millions of sons, she should not begrudge his life for the cause of Revolution. I handed in my second version but kept the first in my desk.

20   I never showed it to anyone. I could never show it to people outside my family, because it had deviated so much from the reading enacted by the jacket review. Neither could I show it to my mother or sisters, because I was ashamed to have been so moved by such a "Revolutionary" book. My parents would have been shocked to learn that I could like such a book in the same way they liked Dickens. Writing this book report increased my fear that I was losing the command over both the "language of home" and the "language of school" that I had worked so hard to gain. I tried to remind myself that, if I could still tell when my reading or writing sounded incorrect, then I had retained my command over both languages. Yet I could no longer be confident of my command over either language because I had discovered that when I was not careful—or

even when I was—my reading and writing often surprised me with its impurity. To prevent such impurity, I became very suspicious of my thoughts when I read or wrote. I was always asking myself why I was using this word, how I was using it, always afraid that I wasn't reading or writing correctly. What confused and frustrated me most was that I could not figure out why I was no longer able to read or write correctly without such painful deliberation.

I continued to read only because reading allowed me to keep my thoughts and confusion private. I hoped that somehow, if I watched myself carefully, I would figure out from the way I read whether I had really mastered the "languages." But writing became a dreadful chore. When I tried to keep a diary, I was so afraid that the voice of school might slip in that I could only list my daily activities. When I wrote for school, I worried that my Bourgeois sensibilities would betray me.

The more suspicious I became about the way I read and wrote, the more guilty I felt for losing the spontaneity with which I had learned to "use" these "languages." Writing the book report made me feel that my reading and writing in the "language" of either home or school could not be free of the interference of the other. But I was unable to acknowledge, grasp, or grapple with what I was experiencing, for both my parents and my teachers had suggested that, if I were a good student, such interference would and should not take place. I assumed that once I had "acquired" a discourse, I could simply switch it on and off every time I read and wrote as I would some electronic tool. Furthermore, I expected my readings and writings to come out in their correct forms whenever I switched the proper discourse on. I still regarded the discourse of home as natural and the discourse of school alien, but I never had doubted before that I could acquire both and switch them on and off according to the occasion.

When my experience in writing conflicted with what I thought should happen when I used each discourse, I rejected my experience because it contradicted what my parents and teachers had taught me. I shied away from writing to avoid what I assumed I should not experience. But trying to avoid what should not happen did not keep it from recurring whenever I had to write. Eventually my confusion and frustration over these recurring experiences compelled me to search for an explanation: how and why had I failed to learn what my parents and teachers had worked so hard to teach me?

I now think of the internal scene for my reading and writing about *The Revolutionary Family* as a heated discussion between myself, the voices of home, and those of school. The review on the back of the book, the sample student papers I came across in my composition classes, my philosophy teacher—these I heard as voices of one group. My parents and my home readings were the voices of an opposing group. But the conversation between these opposing voices in the internal scene of my writing was not as polite and respectful as the parlor scene Kenneth Burke has portrayed (see epigraph). Rather, these voices struggled to dominate the discussion, constantly incorporating, dismissing, or suppressing the arguments of each other, like the battles between the hegemonic and counter-hegemonic forces described in Raymond Williams's *Marxism and Literature* (108–14).

25   When I read *The Revolutionary Family* and wrote the first version of my report, I began with a quotation from the review. The voices of both home and school answered, clamoring to be heard. I tried to listen to one group and turn a deaf ear to the other. Both persisted. I negotiated my way through these conflicting voices, now agreeing with one, now agreeing with the other. I formed a reading out of my interaction with both. Yet I was afraid to have done so because both home and school had implied that I should speak in unison with only one of these groups and stand away from the discussion rather than participate in it.

My teachers and parents had persistently called my attention to the intensity of the discussion taking place on the external social scene. The story of my grandfather's failure and my father's

success had from my early childhood made me aware of the conflict between Western and traditional Chinese cultures. My political education at school added another dimension to the conflict: the war of Marxist-Maoism against them both. Yet when my parents and teachers called my attention to the conflict, they stressed the anxiety of having to live through China's transformation from a semi-feudal, semi-capitalist, and semi-colonial society to a socialist one. Acquiring the discourse of the dominant group was, to them, a means of seeking alliance with that group and thus of surviving the whirlpool of cultural currents around them. As a result, they modeled their pedagogical practices on this utilitarian view of language. Being the eager student, I adopted this view of language as a tool for survival. It came to dominate my understanding of the discussion on the social and historical scene and to restrict my ability to participate in that discussion.

To begin with, the metaphor of language as a tool for survival led me to be passive in my use of discourse, to be a bystander in the discussion. In Burke's "parlor," everyone is involved in the discussion. As it goes on through history, what we call "communal discourses"—arguments specific to particular political, social, economic, ethnic, sexual, and family groups—form, re-form and transform. To use a discourse in such a scene is to participate in the argument and to contribute to the formation of the discourse. But when I was growing up, I could not take on the burden of such an active role in the discussion. For both home and school presented the existent conventions of the discourse each taught me as absolute laws for my action. They turned verbal action into a tool, a set of conventions produced and shaped prior to and outside of my own verbal acts. Because I saw language as a tool, I separated the process of producing the tool from the process of using it. The tool was made by someone else and was then acquired and used by me. How the others made it before I acquired it determined and guaranteed what it produced when I used it. I imagined that the more experienced and powerful members of the community were the ones responsible for making the tool. They were the ones who participated in the discussion and fought with opponents. When I used what they made, their labor and accomplishments would ensure the quality of my reading and writing. By using it, I could survive the heated discussion. When my immediate experience in writing the book report suggested that knowing the conventions of school did not guarantee the form and content of my report, when it suggested that I had to write the report with the work and responsibility I had assigned to those who wrote book reviews in the Publishing Bureau, I thought I had lost the tool I had earlier acquired.

Another reason I could not take up an active role in the argument was that my parents and teachers contrived to provide a scene free of conflict for practicing my various languages. It was as if their experience had made them aware of the conflict between their discourse and other discourses and of the struggle involved in reproducing the conventions of any discourse on a scene where more than one discourse exists. They seemed convinced that such conflict and struggle would overwhelm someone still learning the discourse. Home and school each contrived a purified space where only one discourse was spoken and heard. In their choice of textbooks, in the way they spoke, and in the way they required me to speak, each jealously silenced any voice that threatened to break the unison of the scene. The homogeneity of home and of school implied that only one discourse could and should be relevant in each place. It led me to believe I should leave behind, turn a deaf ear to, or forget the discourse of the other when I crossed the boundary dividing them. I expected myself to set down one discourse whenever I took up another just as I would take off or put on a particular set of clothes for school or home.

Despite my parents' and teachers' attempts to keep home and school discrete, the internal conflict between the two discourses continued whenever I read or wrote. Although I tried to suppress the voice of one discourse in the name of the other, having to speak aloud in the voice I had just silenced each time I crossed the boundary kept both voices active in my mind. Every "I think…" from the voice of home or school brought forth a "However…" or a "But…" from the voice of the opponents. To identify with the voice of home or school, I had to negotiate through the conflicting voices of both by restating, taking back, qualifying my thoughts. I was unconsciously doing so when I did my book report. But I could not use the interaction comfortably and constructively. Both my parents and my teachers had implied that my job was to prevent that interaction from happening. My sense of having failed to accomplish what they had taught silenced me.

30   To use the interaction between the discourses of home and school constructively, I would have to have seen reading or writing as a process in which I worked my way towards a stance through a dialectical process of identification and division. To identify with an ally, I would have to have grasped the distance between where he or she stood and where I was positioning myself. In taking a stance against an opponent, I would have to have grasped where my stance identified with the stance of my allies. Teetering along the "wavering line of pressure and counter-pressure" from both allies and opponents, I might have worked my way towards a stance of my own (Burke, *A Rhetoric of Motives* 23). Moreover, I would have to have understood that the voices in my mind, like the participants in the parlor scene, were in constant flux. As I came into contact with new and different groups of people or read different books, voices entered and left. Each time I read or wrote, the stance I negotiated out of these voices would always be at some distance from the stances I worked out in my previous and my later readings or writings.

I could not conceive such a form of action for myself because I saw reading and writing as an expression of an established stance. In delineating the conventions of a discourse, my parents and teachers had synthesized the stance they saw as typical for a representative member of the community. Burke calls this the stance of a "god" or the "prototype"; Williams calls it the "official" or "possible" stance of the community. Through the metaphor of the survival tool, my parents and teachers had led me to assume I could automatically reproduce the official stance of the discourse I used. Therefore, when I did my book report on *The Revolutionary Family,* I expected my knowledge of the official stance set by the book review to ensure the actual stance of my report. As it happened, I began by trying to take the official stance of the review. Other voices interrupted. I answered back. In the process, I worked out a stance approximate but not identical to the official stance I began with. Yet the experience of having to labor to realize my knowledge of the official stance or to prevent myself from wandering away from it frustrated and confused me. For even though I had been actually reading and writing in a Burkean scene, I was afraid to participate actively in the discussion. I assumed it was my role to survive by staying out of it.

Not long ago, my daughter told me that it bothered her to hear her friend "talk wrong." Having come to the United States from China with little English, my daughter has become sensitive to the way English, as spoken by her teachers, operates. As a result, she has amazed her teachers with her success in picking up the language and in adapting to life at school. Her concern to speak the English taught in the classroom "correctly" makes her uncomfortable when she hears people using "ain't" or double negatives, which her teacher considers "improper." I see in her the me that had eagerly learned and used the discourse of the Working class at school. Yet while I was torn between the two conflicting worlds of school and home, she moves with seeming ease from the conversations she hears over the dinner table to her teacher's words in the classroom. My husband and I are proud of the good work she does at school. We are glad she is spared the kinds of conflict between home and school I experienced at her age. Yet as we watch her becoming more and more fluent in the language of the classroom, we wonder if, by enabling her to "survive" school, her very fluency will silence her when the scene of her reading and writing expands beyond that of the composition classroom.

For when I listen to my daughter, to students, and to some composition teachers talking about the teaching and learning of writing, I am often alarmed by the degree to which the metaphor of a survival tool dominates their understanding of language as it once dominated my own. I am especially concerned with the way some composition classes focus on turning the classroom into a monological scene for the students' reading and writing. Most of our students live in a world similar to my daughter's, somewhere between the purified world of the classroom and the complex world of my adolescence. When composition classes encourage these students to ignore those voices that seem irrelevant to the purified world of the classroom, most students are often able to do so without much struggle. Some of them are so adept at doing it that the whole process has for them become automatic.

However, beyond the classroom and beyond the limited range of these students' immediate lives lies a much more complex and dynamic social and historical scene. To help these students become actors in such a scene, perhaps we need to call their attention to voices that may seem irrelevant to the discourse we teach rather than encourage them to shut them out. For example, we might intentionally complicate the classroom scene by bringing into it discourses that stand at varying distances from the one we teach. We might encourage students to explore ways of practicing the conventions of the discourse they are learning by negotiating through these conflicting voices. We could also encourage them to see themselves as responsible for forming or transforming as well as preserving the discourse they are learning.

35   As I think about what we might do to complicate the external and internal scenes of our students' writing, I hear my parents and teachers saying: "Not now. Keep them from the wrangle of

the marketplace until they have acquired the discourse and are skilled at using it." And I answer: "Don't teach them to 'survive' the whirlpool of crosscurrents by avoiding it. Use the classroom to moderate the currents. Moderate the currents, but teach them from the beginning to struggle." When I think of the ways in which the teaching of reading and writing as classroom activities can frustrate the development of students, I am almost grateful for the overwhelming complexity of the circumstances in which I grew up. For it was this complexity that kept me from losing sight of the effort and choice involved in reading or writing with and through a discourse.

WORKS CITED

Burke, Kenneth. *The Philosophy of Literary Form: Studies in Symbolic Action.* 2nd ed. Baton Rouge: Louisiana State UP, 1967.

––––– *A Rhetoric of Motives.* Berkeley: U of California P, 1969.

Freire, Paulo. *Pedagogy of the Oppressed.* Trans. M. B. Ramos. New York: Continuum, 1970.

Williams, Raymond. *Marxism and Literature.* New York: Oxford UP, 1977.

SUGGESTIONS FOR DISCUSSION

1. In the opening paragraph, Lu notes that her understanding of her own education was "so dominated by memories of confusion and frustration" that she was unable to speak about them to her dying mother. How does Lu go on to explain what rendered her confused, frustrated, and silent? Does she want the reader to see her silence as peculiar to her own life or illustrative of something that affects many people?

2. Lu says that part of her problem was that she had adopted a view of language as a "tool for survival." Explain what she means by the term "tool for survival" and why she thinks it caused her to be passive and unable to participate in public discussions.

3. In place of the metaphor of language as a "tool for survival," Lu wants to substitute a metaphor of multiple "voices in my mind" contending for her allegiance and attention. Explain what Lu means by these contending voices. Then test the metaphor of "voices in my mind" according to your own experience in and out of school. Can you think of instances in which you felt a struggle between the language of school and the language of home or some other group? How did you resolve or negotiate the struggle?

SUGGESTIONS FOR WRITING

1. Use Min-zhan Lu's essay as a model to think about how you became aware of the type of reading that is valued in English classes. Your experience will differ from Lu's, but all students in some fashion or another come to grips with English teachers' expectations about what they should find in the assigned reading . Write an essay that explains your own understanding of what English teachers are looking for when you read literature, whether poems, plays, short stories, or novels. What are you supposed to notice and admire? What kinds of analyses are you supposed to perform when you read literary texts? Consider how this type of schooled reading fits with the way you read literature on your own. To what extent do you read for the same purposes that are called for when you are assigned literary works in school? How would you explain the differences and similarities?

2. Lu describes her experience learning to write in China under an educational regime in which only certain forms of written expression were acceptable. The U.S. educational system is more open than the system in China when Lu was a schoolgirl. Nonetheless, there are certain conventions and formulas in place in American schools that students must observe when they write papers. Write an essay that explains your own experience in high school English classrooms writing themes and papers. Take into account how you were taught to write. Did your teachers introduce you to process writing or the five-paragraph theme? Did you exchange papers with other students to do peer response and

review? What was the effect of these expectations and classroom practices on your development as a writer?

3. Lu's essay and the following selection by June Jordan, "Nobody Mean More to Me Than You and the Future Life of Willie Jordan," raise questions about the way people perceive spoken and written language, particularly in terms of how it conforms to standard usage and grammatical correctness. Notice in Lu's essay how, in the final section, her daughter is bothered by people who "talk wrong." Read (or reread) Jordan's essay with an eye to how people respond to nonstandard forms such as Black English. Can you think of an example from school or elsewhere when nonstandard, unofficial, or incorrect uses of language were judged unfavorably—as a sign of lack of intelligence or low social status? Write an essay that explains what was at stake in such an instance.

NOBODY MEAN MORE TO ME THAN YOU AND THE FUTURE LIFE OF WILLIE JORDAN

June Jordan

June Jordan (1936–2002) was a poet, playwright, essayist, and professor of English at the University of California, Berkley. The following selection, "Nobody Mean More to Me Than You and the Future Life of Willie Jordan," opens *On Call*, a collection of Jordan's political essays published in 1985. In this essay, Jordan weaves two stories together, one concerning a class she taught on Black English and the other concerning Willie Jordan, a young black student in the class trying to come to terms with injustice in South Africa while facing the death of his brother through police brutality at home in Brooklyn. Jordan's story of how her students discovered the communicative power and clarity of Black English forms the backdrop for Willie Jordan's struggle to articulate his own understanding of oppressive power.

SUGGESTION FOR READING   Notice that there are many voices speaking in this essay—not just June Jordan the essayist and teacher but also Alice Walker in *The Color Purple*, Jordan's students studying and translating Black English, and Willie Jordan in the essay that closes the selection. Underline and annotate passages to indicate who is speaking and where the voice shifts.

1   Black English is not exactly a linguistic buffalo; as children, most of the thirty-five million Afro-Americans living here depend on this language for our discovery of the world. But then we approach our maturity inside a larger social body that will not support our efforts to become anything other than the clones of those who are neither our mothers nor our fathers. We begin to grow up in a house where every true mirror shows us the face of somebody who does not belong there, whose walk and whose talk will never look or sound "right," because that house was meant to shelter a family that is alien and hostile to us. As we learn our way around this environment, either we hide our original word habits, or we completely surrender our own voice, hoping to please those who will never respect anyone different from themselves: Black English is not exactly a linguistic buffalo, but we should understand its status as an endangered species, as a perishing, irreplaceable system of community intelligence, or we should expect its extinction, and, along with that, the extinguishing of much that constitutes our own proud, and singular, identity.

What we casually call "English," less and less defers to England and its "gentlemen." "English" is no longer a specific matter of geography or an element of class privilege; more than thirty-three countries use this tool as a means of "intranational communication."[1] Countries as disparate as Zimbabwe and Malaysia, or Israel and Uganda, use it as their non-native currency of convenience. Obviously, this tool, this "English," cannot function inside thirty-three discrete societies on the basis of rules and values absolutely determined somewhere else, in a thirty-fourth other country, for example.

In addition to that staggering congeries of non-native users of English, there are five countries, or 333,746,000 people, for whom this thing called "English" serves as a native tongue.[2] Approximately 10 percent of these native speakers of "English" are Afro-American citizens of the U.S.A. I cite these numbers and varieties of human beings dependent on "English" in order, quickly, to suggest how strange and how tenuous is any concept of "Standard English." Obviously, numerous forms of English now operate inside a natural, an uncontrollable, continuum of development. I would suppose "the standard" for English in Malaysia is not the same as "the standard" in Zimbabwe. I know that standard forms of English for Black people in this country do not copy that of Whites. And, in fact, the structural differences between these two kinds of English have intensified, becoming more Black, or less White, despite the expected homogenizing effects of television[3] and other mass media.

Nonetheless, White standards of English persist, supreme and unquestioned, in these United States. Despite our multi-lingual population, and despite the deepening Black and White cleavage within that conglomerate, White standards control our official and popular judgments of verbal proficiency and correct, or incorrect, language skills, including speech. In contrast to India, where at least fourteen languages co-exist as legitimate Indian languages, in contrast to Nicaragua, where all citizens are legally entitled to formal school instruction in their regional or tribal languages, compulsory education in America compels accommodation to exclusively White forms of "English." White English, in America, is "Standard English."

5   This story begins two years ago. I was teaching a new course, "In Search of the Invisible Black Woman," and my rather large class seemed evenly divided among young Black women and men. Five or six White students also sat in attendance. With unexpected speed and enthusiasm we had moved through historical narration of the 19th century to literature by and about Black women, in the 20th. I then assigned the first forty pages of Alice Walker's *The Color Purple,* and I came, eagerly, to class that morning:

"So!" I exclaimed, aloud. "What did you think?" How did you like it?"

The students studied their hands, or the floor. There was no response. The tense, resistant feeling in the room fairly astounded me.

At last, one student, a young woman still not meeting my eyes, muttered something in my direction:

"What did you say?" I prompted her.

10   "Why she have them talk so funny. It don't sound right."

"You mean the language?"

Another student lifted his head: "It don't look right, neither. I couldn't hardly read it."

At this, several students dumped on the book. Just about unanimously, their criticisms targeted the language. I listened to what they wanted to say and silently marvelled at the similarities between their casual speech patterns and Alice Walker's written version of Black English.

But I decided against pointing to these identical traits of syntax, I wanted not to make them self-conscious about their own spoken language—not while they clearly felt it was "wrong." Instead I decided to swallow my astonishment. Here was a negative Black reaction to a prize-winning accomplishment of Black literature that White readers across the country had selected as a best seller. Black rejection was aimed at the one irreducibly Black element of Walker's work: the language—Celie's Black English. I wrote the opening lines of *The Color Purple* on the blackboard and asked the students to help me translate these sentences into Standard English:

You better not never tell nobody but God. It'd kill your mommy.

Dear God,

    I am fourteen years old. I have always been a good girl. Maybe you can give me a sign letting me know what is happening to me.

    Last spring after Little Lucious come I heard them fussing. He was pulling on her arm. She say it too soon, Fonso. I aint well. Finally he leave her alone. A week go by, he pulling on her arm again. She say, Naw, I ain't gonna. Can't you see I'm already half dead, an all of the children.[4]

15   Our process of translation exploded with hilarity and even hysterical, shocked laughter: The Black writer, Alice Walker, knew what she was doing! If rudimentary criteria for good fiction include the manipulation of language so that the syntax and diction of sentences will tell you the identity of speakers, the probable age and sex and class of speakers, and even the locale—urban/rural/southern/western—then Walker had written, perfectly. This is the translation into Standard English that our class produced:

Absolutely, one should never confide in anybody besides God. Your secrets could prove devastating to your mother.

Dear God,

    I am fourteen years old. I have always been good. But now, could you help me to understand what is happening to me?

    Last spring, after my little brother, Lucious, was born, I heard my parents fighting. My father kept pulling at my mother's arm. But she told him, "It's too soon for sex, Alfonso. I am still not feeling well." Finally, my father left her alone. A week went by, and then he began bothering my mother, again: pulling her arm. She told him, "No, I won't! Can't you see I'm already exhausted from all of these children?"

(Our favorite line was "It's too soon for sex, Alfonso.")

Once we could stop laughing, once we could stop our exponentially wild improvisations on the theme of Translated Black English, the students pushed to explain their own negative first reactions to their spoken language on the printed page. I thought it was probably akin to the shock of seeing yourself in a photograph for the first time. Most of the students had never before seen a written facsimile of the way they talk. None of the students had ever learned how to read and write their own verbal system of communication: Black English. Alternatively, this fact began to baffle or else bemuse and then infuriate my students. Why not? Was it too late? Could they learn how to do it, now? And, ultimately, the final test question, the one testing my sincerity: Could I teach them? Because I had never taught anyone Black English and, as far as I knew, no one, anywhere in the United States, had ever offered such a course, the best I could say was "I'll try."

He looked like a wrestler.

He sat dead center in the packed room and, every time our eyes met, he quickly nodded his head as though anxious to reassure, and encourage me.

20   Short, with strikingly broad shoulders and long arms, he spoke with a surprisingly high, soft voice that matched the soft bright movement of his eyes. His name was Willie Jordan. He would have seemed even more unlikely in the context of Contemporary Women's Poetry, except that ten or twelve other Black men were taking the course, as well. Still, Willie was conspicuous. His extreme fitness, the muscular density of his presence underscored the riveted, gentle attention that he gave to anything anyone said. Generally, he did not join the loud and rowdy dialogue flying back and forth, but there could be no doubt about his interest in our discussions. And, when he stood to present an argument he'd prepared,

overnight, that nervous smile of his vanished and an irregular stammering replaced it, as he spoke with visceral sincerity, word by word.

That was how I met Willie Jordan. It was in between "In Search of the Invisible Black Women" and "The Art of Black English." I was waiting for departmental approval and I supposed that Willie might be, so to speak, killing time until he, too, could study Black English. But Willie really did want to explore contemporary women's poetry and, to that end, volunteered for extra research and never missed a class.

Towards the end of that semester, Willie approached me for an independent study project on South Africa. It would commence the next semester. I thought Willie's writing needed the kind of improvement only intense practice will yield. I knew his intelligence was outstanding. But he'd wholeheartedly opted for "Standard English" at a rather late age, and the results were stilted and frequently polysyllabic, simply for the sake of having more syllables. Willie's unnatural formality of language seemed to me consistent with the formality of his research into South African apartheid. As he projected his studies, he would have little time, indeed, for newspapers. Instead, more than 90 percent of his research would mean saturation in strictly historical, if not archival, material. I was certainly interested. It would be tricky to guide him into a more confident and spontaneous relationship both with language and apartheid. It was going to be wonderful to see what happened when he could catch up with himself, entirely, and talk back to the world.

September, 1984: Breezy fall weather and much excitement! My class, "The Art of Black English," was full to the limit of the fire laws. And in Independent Study, Willie Jordan showed up weekly, fifteen minutes early for each of our sessions. I was pretty happy to be teaching, altogether!

I remember an early class when a young brother, replete with his ever-present porkpie hat, raised his hand and then told us that most of what he'd heard was "all right" except it was "too clean." "The brothers on the street," he con-

tinued, "they mix it up more. Like 'fuck' and 'motherfuck.' Or like 'shit.'" He waited. I waited. Then all of us laughed a good while, and we got into a brawl about "correct" and "realistic" Black English that led to Rule 1.

25   Rule 1: *Black English is about a whole lot more than mothafuckin.*

As a criterion, we decided, "realistic" could take you anywhere you want to go. Artful places. Angry places. Eloquent and sweetalkin places. Polemical places. Church. And the local Bar & Grill. We were checking out a language, not a mood or a scene or one guy's forgettable mouthing off.

It was hard. For most of the students, learning Black English required a fallback to patterns and rhythms of speech that many of their parents had beaten out of them. I mean beaten. And, in a majority of cases, correct Black English could be achieved only by striving for incorrect Standard English, something they were still pushing at, quite uncertainly. This state of affairs led to Rule 2.

Rule 2: *If it's wrong in Standard English it's probably right in Black English, or, at least, you're hot.*

It was hard. Roommates and family members ridiculed their studies, or remained incredulous, "You studying that shit? At school?" But we were beginning to feel the companionship of pioneers. And we decided that we needed another rule that would establish each one of us as equally important to our success. This was Rule 3.

30   Rule 3: *If it don't sound like something that come out somebody mouth then it don't sound right. If it don't sound right then it ain't hardly right. Period.*

This rule produced two weeks of compositions in which the students agonizingly tried to spell the sound of the Black English sentence they wanted to convey. But Black English is, preeminently, an oral/spoken means of communication. And spelling don't talk. So we needed Rule 4.

Rule 4: *Forget about the spelling. Let the syntax carry you.*

Once we arrived at Rule 4 we started to fly, because syntax, the structure of an idea, leads you to the world view of the speaker and reveals her values. The syntax of a sentence equals the structure of your consciousness. If we insisted that the language of Black English adheres to a distinctive Black syntax, then we were postulating a profound difference between White and Black people, per se. Was it a difference to prize or to obliterate?

There are three qualities of Black English—the presence of life, voice, and clarity—that intensify to a distinctive Black value system that we became excited about and self-consciously tried to maintain.

1. *Black English has been produced by a pre-technocratic, if not anti-technological, culture:* More, our culture has been constantly threatened by annihilation or, at least, the swallowed blurring of assimilation. Therefore, our language is a system constructed by people constantly needing to insist that we exist, that we are present. Our language devolves from a culture that abhors all abstraction, or anything tending to obscure or delete the fact of the human being who is here and now/the truth of the person who is speaking or listening. Consequently, there is no passive voice construction possible in Black English. For example, you cannot say, "Black English is being eliminated." You must say, instead, "White people eliminating Black English." The assumption of the presence of life governs all of Black English. Therefore, overwhelmingly, all action takes place in the language of the present indicative. And every sentence assumes the living and active participation of at least two human beings, the speaker and the listener.

2. *A primary consequence of the person-centered values of Black English is the delivery of voice:* If you speak or write Black English, your ideas will necessarily possess that otherwise elusive attribute, voice.

3. *One main benefit following from the person-centered values of Black English is that of clarity:* If your idea, your sentence, assumes the presence of at least two living and active people, you will make it understandable, because the motivation behind every sentence is the wish to say something real to somebody real.

35   As the weeks piled up, translation from Standard English into Black English or vice versa occupied a hefty part of our course work.

Standard English (hereafter S.E.): "In considering the idea of studying Black English those questioned suggested—"

(What's the subject? Where's the person? Is anybody alive in here, in that idea?)

Black English (hereafter B.E.): "I been asking people what you think about somebody studying Black English and they answer me like this:"

But there were interesting limits. You cannot "translate" instances of Standard English preoccupied with abstraction or with nothing/nobody evidently alive, into Black English. That would warp the language into uses antithetical to the guiding perspective of its community of users. Rather you must first change those Standard English sentences, themselves, into ideas consistent with the person-centered assumptions of Black English.

Guidelines for Black English

1. *Minimal number of words for every idea:* This is the source for the aphoristic and/or poetic force of the language; eliminate every possible word.

2. *Clarity:* If the sentence is not clear it's not Black English.

3. *Eliminate use of the verb* to be *whenever possible:* This leads to the deployment of more descriptive and, therefore, more precise verbs.

4. *Use* be *or* been *only when you want to describe a chronic, ongoing state of things.*
   He *be* at the office, by 9: (He is always at the office by 9.)
   He *been* with her since forever.

5. *Zero copula:* Always eliminate the verb *to be* whenever it would combine with another verb, in Standard English.
   S.E.: She is going out with him.
   B.E.: She going out with him.

6. *Eliminate* do *as in:*

    S.E.: What do you think? What do you want?

    B.E.: What you think? What you want?

7. Rules number 3, 4, 5, and 6 provide for the use of the minimal number of verbs per idea and, therefore, greater accuracy in the choice of verb.

8. *In general, if you wish to say something really positive, try to formulate the idea using emphatic negative structure.*

    S.E.: He's fabulous.

    B.E.: He bad.

9. *Use double or triple negatives for dramatic emphasis.*

    S.E.: Tina Turner sings out of this world.

    B.E.: Ain nobody sing like Tina.

10. *Never use the* ed *suffix to indicate the past tense of a verb.*

    S.E.: She closed the door.

    B.E.: She close the door. Or, she have close the door.

11. *Regardless of intentional verb time, only use the third person singular, present indicative, for use of the verb* to have, *as an auxiliary.*

    S.E.: He had his wallet then he lost it.

    B.E.: He have him wallet then he lose it.

    S.E.: We had seen that movie.

    B.E.: We seen that movie. Or, we have see that movie.

12. *Observe a minimal inflection of verbs:* Particularly, never change from the first person singular forms to the third person singular.

    S.E.: Present Tense Forms: He goes to the store.

    B.E.: He go to the store.

    S.E.: Past Tense Forms: He went to the store.

    B.E.: He go to the store. Or, he gone to the store. Or, he been to the store.

13. *The possessive case scarcely ever appears in Black English:* Never use an apostrophe ('s) construction. If you wander into a posses-

sive case component of an idea, then keep logically consistent: ours, his, theirs, mines. But, most likely, if you bump into such a component, you have wandered outside the underlying world view of Black English.

    S.E.: He will take their car tomorrow.

    B.E.: He taking they car tomorrow.

14. *Plurality:* Logical consistency, continued: If the modifier indicates plurality then the noun remains in the singular case.

    S.E.: He ate twelve doughnuts.

    B.E.: He eat twelve doughnut.

    S.E.: She has many books.

    B.E.: She have many book.

15. *Listen for, or invent, special Black English forms of the past tense, such as:* "He losted it. That what she felted." If they are clear and readily understood, then use them.

16. *Do not hesitate to play with words, sometimes inventing them:* e.g. "astropotomous" means huge like a hippo plus astronomical and, therefore, signifies real big.

17. *In Black English, unless you keenly want to underscore the past tense nature of an action, stay in the present tense and rely on the overall context of your ideas for the conveyance of time and sequence.*

18. *Never use the suffix* -ly *form of an adverb in Black English.*

    S.E.: The rain came down rather quickly.

    B.E.: The rain come down pretty quick.

19. *Never use the indefinite article* an *in Black English.*

    S.E.: He wanted to ride an elephant.

    B.E.: He wanted to ride him a elephant.

20. *Invariant syntax:* in correct Black English it is possible to formulate an imperative, an interrogative, and a simple declarative idea with the same syntax:

    B.E.: You going to the store?

    You going to the store.

    You going to the store!

40   Where was Willie Jordan? We'd reached the mid-term of the semester. Students had formu-

lated Black English guidelines, by consensus, and they were now writing with remarkable beauty, purpose, and enjoyment:

I ain hardly speakin for everybody but myself so understan that.

Kim Parks

Samples from student writings:

Janie have a great big ole hole inside her. Tea Cake the only thing that fit that hole....

That pear tree beautiful to Janie, especial when bees fiddlin with the blossomin pear there growin large and lovely. But personal speakin, the love she get from starin at that tree ain the love what starin back at her in them relationship. (Monica Morris)

Love a big theme in, *They Eye Was Watching God*. Love show people new corners inside theyself. It pull out good stuff and stuff back bad stuff....Joe worship the doing uh his own hand and need other people to worship him too. But he ain't think about Janie that she a person and ought to live like anybody common do. Queen life not for Janie. (Monica Morris)

In both life and writin, Black womens have varietous experience of love that be cold like a iceberg or fiery like a inferno. Passion got for the other partner involve, man or women, seem as shallow, ankle-deep water or the most profoundest abyss. (Constance Evans)

Family love another bond that ain't never break under no pressure. (Constance Evans)

You know it really cold/When the friend you/Always get out the fire/Act like they don't know you/When you in the heat. (Constance Evans)

Big classroom discussion bout love at this time. I never take no class where us have any long arguin for and against for two or three day. New to me and great. I find the class time talkin a million time more interestin than detail bout the book. (Kathy Esseks)

As these examples suggest, Black English no longer limited the students, in any way. In fact, one of them, Philip Garfield, would shortly "translate" a pivotal scene from Ibsen's *A Doll's House,* as his final term paper.

Nora: I didn't gived no shit. I thinked you a asshole back then, too, you make it so hard for me save mines husband life.

Krogstad: Girl, it clear you ain't any idea what you done. You done exact what I once done, and I losed my reputation over it.

Nora: You asks me believe you once act brave save you wife life?

Krogstad: Law care less why you done it.

Nora: Law must suck.

Krogstad: Suck or no, if I wants, judge screw you wid dis paper.

Nora: No way, man. (Philip Garfield)

But where was Willie? Compulsively punctual, and always thoroughly prepared with neat typed compositions, he had disappeared. He failed to show up for our regularly scheduled conference, and I received neither a note nor a phone call of explanation. A whole week went by. I wondered if Willie had finally been captured by the extremely current happenings in South Africa: passage of a new constitution that did not enfranchise the Black majority, and militant Black South African reaction to that affront. I wondered if he'd been hurt, somewhere. I wondered if the serious workload of weekly readings and writings had overwhelmed him and changed his mind about independent study. Where was Willie Jordan?

One week after the first conference that Willie missed, he called: "Hello, Professor Jordan? This is Willie. I'm sorry I wasn't there last week. But something has come up and I'm pretty upset. I'm sorry but I really can't deal right now."

I asked Willie to drop by my office and just let me see that he was okay. He agreed to do that. When I saw him I knew something hideous had happened. Something had hurt him and scared him to the marrow. He was all agitated and stammering and terse and incoherent. At last, his sadly jumbled account let me surmise, as follows: Brooklyn police had murdered his unarmed, twenty-five-year-old brother, Reggie Jordan. Neither Willie nor his elderly parents knew what to do about it. Nobody from the press was interested. His folks had no money. Police ran his family around and around, to no point.

And Reggie was really dead. And Willie wanted to fight, but he felt helpless.

With Willie's permission I began to try to secure legal counsel for the Jordan family. Unfortunately, Black victims of police violence are truly numerous, while the resources available to prosecute their killers are truly scarce. A friend of mine at the Center for Constitutional Rights estimated that just the preparatory costs for bringing the cops into court normally approaches $180,000. Unless the execution of Reggie Jordan became a major community cause for organizing and protest, his murder would simply become a statistical item.

Again, with Willie's permission, I contacted every newspaper and media person I could think of. But the Bastone feature article in *The Village Voice* was the only result from that canvassing.

Again, with Willie's permission, I presented the case to my class in Black English. We had talked about the politics of language. We had talked about love and sex and child abuse and men and women. But the murder of Reggie Jordan broke like a hurricane across the room.

There are few "issues" as endemic to Black life as police violence. Most of the students knew and respected and liked Jordan. Many of them came from the very neighborhood where the murder had occurred. All of the students had known somebody close to them who had been killed by police, or had known frightening moments of gratuitous confrontation with the cops. They wanted to do everything at once to avenge death. Number One: They decided to compose a personal statement of condolence to Willie Jordan and his family, written in Black English. Number Two: They decided to compose individual messages to the police, in Black English. These should be prefaced by an explanatory paragraph composed by the entire group. Number Three: These individual messages, with their lead paragraph, should be sent to *Newsday*.

50 The morning after we agreed on these objectives, one of the young women students appeared with an unidentified visitor, who sat through the class, smiling in a peculiar, comfortable way.

Now we had to make more tactical decisions. Because we wanted the messages published, and because we thought it imperative that our outrage be known by the police, the tactical question was this: Should the opening, group paragraph be written in Black English or Standard English?

I have seldom been privy to a discussion with so much heart at the dead beat of it. I will never forget the eloquence, the sudden haltings of speech, the fierce struggle against tears, the furious throwaway, and useless explosions that this question elicited.

That one question contained several others, each of them extraordinarily painful to even contemplate. How best to serve the memory of Reggie Jordan? Should we use the language of the killer—Standard English—in order to make our ideas acceptable to those controlling the killers? But wouldn't what we had to say be rejected, summarily, if we said it in our own language, the language of the victim, Reggie Jordan? But if we sought to express ourselves by abandoning our language wouldn't that mean our suicide on top of Reggie's murder? But if we expressed ourselves in our own language wouldn't that be suicidal to the wish to communicate with those who, evidently, did not give a damn about us/Reggie/police violence in the Black community?

At the end of one of the longest, most difficult hours of my own life, the students voted, unanimously, to preface their individual messages with a paragraph composed in the language of Reggie Jordan. "*At least we don't give up nothing else. At least we stick to the truth: Be who we been. And stay all the way with Reggie.*"

55 It was heartbreaking to proceed, from that point. Everyone in the room realized that our decision in favor of Black English had doomed our writings, even as the distinctive reality of our Black lives always has doomed our efforts to "be who we been" in this country.

I went to the blackboard and took down this paragraph dictated by the class:

You Cops!
 We the brother and sister of Willie Jordan, a fellow Stony Brook student who the brother of

the dead Reggie Jordan. Reggie, like many brother and sister, he a victim of brutal racist police, October 25, 1984. Us appall, fed up, because that another senseless death what occur in our community. This what we feel, this, from our heart, for we ain't stayin' silent no more.

With the completion of this introduction, nobody said anything. I asked for comments. At this invitation, the unidentified visitor, a young Black man, ceaselessly smiling, raised his hand. He was, it so happens, a rookie cop. He had just joined the force in September and, he said, he thought he should clarify a few things. So he came forward and sprawled easily into a posture of barroom, or fire-side, nostalgia:

"See," Officer Charles enlightened us, "most times when you out on the street and something come down you do one of two things. Over-react or under-react. Now, if you under-react then you can get yourself kilt. And if you over-react then maybe you kill somebody. Fortunately it's about nine times out of ten and you will over-react. So the brother got kilt. And I'm sorry about that, believe me. But what you have to understand is what kilt him: Over-reaction. That's all. Now you talk about Black people and White police but see, now, I'm a cop myself. And (big smile) I'm Black. And just a couple months ago I was on the other side. But it's the same for me. You a cop, you the ultimate authority: the Ultimate Authority. And you on the street, most of the time you can only do one of two things: over-react or under-react. That's all it is with the brother. Over-reaction. Didn't have nothing to do with race."

That morning Officer Charles had the good fortune to escape without being boiled alive. But barely. And I remember the pride of his smile when I read about the fate of Black policemen and other collaborators, in South Africa. I remember him, and I remember the shock and palpable feeling of shame that filled the room. It was as though that foolish, and deadly, young man had just relieved himself of his foolish, and deadly, explanation, face to face with the grief of Reggie Jordan's father and Reggie Jordan's mother. Class ended quietly. I copied the para-graph from the blackboard, collected the individual messages and left to type them up.

Newsday rejected the piece.

The Village Voice could not find room in their "Letters" section to print the individual messages from the students to the police.

None of the TV news reporters picked up the story.

Nobody raised $180,000 to prosecute the murder of Reggie Jordan.

Reggie Jordan is really dead.

I asked Willie Jordan to write an essay pulling together everything important to him from that semester. He was still deeply beside himself with frustration and amazement and loss. This is what he wrote, unedited, and in its entirety:

Throughout the course of this semester I have been researching the effects of oppression and exploitation along racial lines in South Africa and its neighboring countries. I have become aware of South African police brutalization of native Africans beyond the extent of the law, even though the laws themselves are catalyst affliction upon Black men, women and children. Many Africans die each year as a result of the deliberate use of police force to protect the white power structure.

Social control agents in South Africa, such as policemen, are also used to force compliance among citizens through both overt and covert tactics. It is not uncommon to find bold-faced coercion and cold-blooded killings of Blacks by South African police for undetermined and/or inadequate reasons. Perhaps the truth is that the only reasons for this heinous treatment of Blacks rests in racial differences. We should also understand that what is conveyed through the media is not always accurate and may sometimes be construed as the tip of the iceberg at best.

I recently received a painful reminder that racism, poverty, and the abuse of power are global problems which are by no means unique to South Africa. On October 25, 1984 at approximately 3:00 p.m. my brother, Mr. Reginald Jordan, was shot and killed by two New York City policemen from the 75th precinct in the East New York section of Brooklyn. His life ended at the age of twenty-five. Even up to this current point in time the Police Department has failed to provide my family, which consists of five brothers, eight sisters, and two parents, with a plausible reason for Reggie's death. Out of the many stories that were given to my family by the Police Department, not one of them seems to hold water. In fact, I honestly believe that the Police Department's assessment of my brother's murder is nothing short of ABSOLUTE BULLSHIT, and thus far no evidence had been produced to alter perception of the situation.

Furthermore, I believe that one of three cases may have occurred in this incident. First, Reggie's death may have been the desired outcome of the police officer's action, in which case the killing was premeditated. Or, it was a case of mistaken identity, which clarifies the fact that the two officers who killed my brother and their commanding parties are all grossly incompetent. Or, both of the above cases are correct, i.e., Reggie's murderers intended to kill him and the Police Department behaved insubordinately.

Part of the argument of the officers who shot Reggie was that he had attacked one of them and took his gun. This was their major claim. They also said that only one of them had actually shot Reggie. The facts, however, speak for themselves. According to the Death Certificate and autopsy report, Reggie was shot eight times from point-blank range. The Doctor who performed the autopsy told me himself that two bullets entered the side of my brother's

head, four bullets were sprayed into his back, and two bullets struck him in the back of his legs. It is obvious that unnecessary force was used by the police and that it is extremely difficult to shoot someone in his back when he is attacking or approaching you.

After experiencing a situation like this and researching South Africa I believe that to a large degree, justice may only exist as rhetoric. I find it difficult to talk of true justice when the oppression of my people both at home and abroad attests to the fact that inequality and injustice are serious problems whereby Blacks and Third World people are perpetually short-changed by society. Something has to be done about the way in which this world is set up. Although it is a difficult task, we do have the power to make a change.

Willie J. Jordan Jr.
EGL 487, Section 58, November 14, 1984

It is my privilege to dedicate this book to the future life of Willie J. Jordan Jr., August 8, 1985.

NOTES

1. *English Is Spreading, But What Is English?* A presentation by Prof. S. N. Sridhar, Department of Linguistics, SUNY, Stony Brook, April 9, 1985: Dean's Convocation Among the Disciplines.
2. Ibid.
3. *New York Times*, March 15, 1985, Section One, p. 14: Report on Study by Linguists at the University of Pennsylvania.
4. Alice Walker, *The Color Purple* (New York: Harcourt Brace Jovanovich, 1982), p. 11.

SUGGESTIONS FOR DISCUSSION

1. How does June Jordan intertwine the story of her class on Black English and the story of Willie Jordan? Would these stories have the same impact if they were presented separately? What, if anything, does Jordan accomplish by weaving them together?

2. Reread the passages where Jordan's students translate the opening of *The Color Purple* into Standard English and the scene from *A Doll's House* into Black English. Describe the qualities of black expression that get lost in the first case and added in the second.

3. What are the advantages and disadvantages of Jordan's students' decision to write the preface to their individual messages to the police in Black English?

SUGGESTIONS FOR WRITING

1. Write an essay that explains the point June Jordan is making about the relationship between Black English and Standard English and what she thinks ought to be taught in school and why. Compare with your own views of what Jordan says on how language should be taught in American schools.

2. Write an essay that explains what you see as the advantages and disadvantages of Jordan's students' decision to compose the introduction to their letters to the police in Black English. Arrive at your own evaluation of their decision, but before you do, it may help to explain how and in what sense the decision they had to make was a difficult one.

3. Choose a passage of dialogue in a novel or play you know well in which the speakers are speaking Standard English. Using Phil Garfield's translation of a scene from *A Doll's House* into Black English as a model, translate the passage into some form of non-Standard English—whether the spoken language of your neighborhood, the vernacular of youth culture, or the dialect of a region.

CLASSIC READING

SKILLS AND OTHER DILEMMAS OF A PROGRESSIVE BLACK EDUCATOR

Lisa Delpit

Lisa Delpit holds the Benjamin E. Mays Chair of Urban Educational Leadership at Georgia State University and has received the prestigious MacArthur "genius" fellowship and the award for Outstanding Contribution to Education from the Harvard Graduate School of Education. Originally published in the *Harvard Educational Review* in 1986, "Skills and Other Dilemmas of a Progressive Black Educator" began, Delpit says, "as a letter to a University of Alaska colleague to lay out my concerns with the writing project movement and to detail the frustrations many teachers of color felt at being excluded from educational dialogue—in this case, the dialogue about literacy instruction." Delpit's article was an instant classic and is the most recent of the Classic Readings in this edition of *Reading Culture*.

SUGGESTION FOR READING As you read, pay attention to how Delpit identifies the "dilemmas" that are central to this article. Notice in particular how things seem to come to a head at the conference in Philadelphia. When you have finished reading, write a short statement that explains Delpit's "dilemmas" and how she resolves them.

1   Why do the refrains of progressive educational movements seem lacking in the diverse harmonies, the variegated rhythms, and the shades of tone expected in a truly heterogeneous chorus? Why do we hear so little representation from the multicultural voices which comprise the present-day American educational scene?

These questions have surfaced anew as I begin my third year of university "professoring" after having graduated from a prestigious university known for its progressive school of education. My family back in Louisiana is very proud about all of that, but still they find me rather tedious. They say things like, "She just got here and she's locked up in that room with a bunch of papers talking about she's gotta finish some article. I don't know why she bothers to come home." Or, "I didn't ask you about what any research said, what do *you* think?!"

I once shared my family's skepticism of academia. I remember asking myself in the first few months of my graduate school career, "Why is it these theories never seem to be talking about me?" But by graduation time many of my fellow minority students and I had become well trained: we had learned alternate ways of viewing the world, coaxed memories of life in our communities into forms which fit into the categories created by academic researchers and theoreticians, and internalized belief systems that often belied our own experiences.

I learned a lot in graduate school. For one thing I learned that people acquire a new dialect most effectively through interaction with speakers of that dialect, not through being constantly corrected. Of course, when I was growing up, my mother and my teachers in the pre-integration, poor black Catholic school that I attended corrected every other word I uttered in their effort to coerce my Black English into sometimes hypercorrect Standard English forms acceptable to black nuns in Catholic schools. Yet, I learned to speak and write in Standard English.

5   I also learned in graduate school that people learn to write not by being taught "skills" and grammar, but by "writing in meaningful contexts." In elementary school I diagrammed thousands of sentences, filled in tens of thousands of blanks, and never wrote any text longer than two sentences until I was in the tenth grade of high school. I have been told by my professors that I am a good writer. (One, when told about my poor community and segregated, skill-based schooling, even went so far as to say, "How did you *ever* learn how to write?") By that time I had begun to wonder myself. Never mind that I had learned—and learned well—despite my professors' scathing retroactive assessment of my early education.

But I cannot blame graduate school for all the new beliefs I learned to espouse. I also learned a lot during my progressive undergraduate teacher training. There, as one of the few black education students, I learned that the open classroom was the most "humanizing" of learning environments, that children should be in control of their own learning, and that all children would read when they were ready. Determined to use all that I had learned to benefit black children, I abandoned the cornfields of Ohio, and relocated to an alternative inner-city school in Philadelphia to student-teach.

Located on the border between two communities, our "open-classroom" school deliberately maintained a population of 60 percent poor black kids from "South Philly," and 40 percent well-to-do white kids from "Society Hill." The black kids went to school there because it was their only neighborhood school. The white kids went to school there because their parents had learned the same kinds of things I had learned about education. As a matter of fact, there was a waiting list of white children to get into the school. This was unique in Philadelphia—a predominantly black school with a waiting list of white children. There was no such waiting list of black children.

I apprenticed under a gifted young kindergarten teacher. She had learned the same things that I had learned, so our pairing was most opportune. When I finished my student teaching, the principal asked me to stay on in a full-time position.

The ethos of that school was fascinating. I was one of only a few black teachers, and the other black teachers were mostly older and mostly "traditional." They had not learned the kinds of things I had learned, and the young white teachers sometimes expressed in subtle ways that they thought these teachers were— how to say it—somewhat "repressive." At the very least they were "not structuring learning environments in ways that allowed the children's intellect to flourish": they focused on "skills," they made students sit down at desks, they made students practice handwriting, they corrected oral and written grammar. The subtle, unstated message was, "They just don't realize how smart these kids are."

10   I was an exception to the other black teachers. I socialized with the young white teachers and planned shared classroom experiences with them. I also taught as they did. Many people told me I was a good teacher: I had an open classroom; I had learning stations; I had children write books and stories to share; I provided games and used weaving to teach math and fine motor skills. I threw out all the desks and added carpeted open learning areas. I was doing what

I had learned, and it worked. Well, at least it worked for some of the children.

My white students zoomed ahead. They worked hard at the learning stations. They did amazing things with books and writing. My black students played the games; they learned how to weave; and they threw the books around the learning stations. They practiced karate moves on the new carpets. Some of them even learned how to read, but none of them as quickly as my white students. I was doing the same thing for all my kids—what was the problem?

I taught in Philadelphia for six years. Each year my teaching became less like my young white friends' and more like the other black women's who taught at the school. My students practiced handwriting; I wrote on the board; I got some tables to replace some of the thrown-out desks. Each year my teaching moved farther away from what I had learned, even though in many ways I still identified myself as an open-classroom teacher. As my classroom became more "traditional," however, it seemed that my black students steadily improved in their reading and writing. But they still lagged behind. It hurt that I was moving away from what I had learned. It hurt even more that although my colleagues called me a good teacher, I still felt that I had failed in the task that was most important to me—teaching black children and teaching them well. I could not talk about my failure then. It is difficult even now. At least I did not fall into the trap of talking about the parents' failures. I just did not talk about any of it.

In 1977 I left Philadelphia and managed to forget about my quandary for six and a half years—the one and a half years that I spent working in an administrative job in Louisiana and the five years I spent in graduate school. It was easy to forget failure there. My professors told me that everything I had done in Philadelphia was right; that I was right to shun basals; that I was right to think in terms of learner-driven and holistic education; that, indeed, I had been a success in Philadelphia. Of course, it was easy to forget, too, because I could develop new

focal points. I could even maintain my political and moral integrity while doing so—graduate school introduced me to all *sorts* of oppressed peoples who needed assistance in the educational realm. There were bilingual speakers of any number of languages; there were new immigrants. And if one were truly creative, there were even whole countries in need of assistance—welcome to the Third World! I could tackle someone else's failures and forget my own.

In graduate school I learned about many more elements of progressive education. It was great. I learned new "holistic" teaching techniques—integrating reading and writing, focusing on meaning rather than form. One of the most popular elements—and one, I should add, which I readily and heartily embraced—was the writing process approach to literacy. I spent a lot of time with writing process people. I learned the lingo. I focused energy on "fluency" and not on "correctness." I learned that a focus on "skills" would stifle my students' writing. I learned about "fast-writes" and "golden lines" and group process. I went out into the world as a professor of literacy armed with the very latest, research-based and field-tested teaching methods.

All went well in my university literacy classes. My student teachers followed my lead and shunned limited "traditional" methods of teaching. They, too, embraced holistic processes and learned to approach writing with an emphasis on fluency and creative expression.

But then I returned to Philadelphia for a conference. I looked up one of my old friends, another black woman who was also a teacher. Cathy had been teaching for years in an alternative high school. Most of the students in her school, and by this time in the entire Philadelphia system, were black. Cathy and I had never taught together but had worked together on many political committees and for many radical causes. We shared a lot of history, *and* a lot of philosophies. In fact, I thought we were probably in agreement on just about everything, especially everything having to do with education. I was astounded to discover our differences.

Cathy invited me to dinner. I talked about my new home, about my research in the South Pacific, and about being a university professor. She brought me up to date on all the gossip about radicals in Philly and on the new committees working against apartheid. Eventually the conversation turned to teaching, as it often does with teachers.

Cathy began talking about the local writing project based, like those in many other areas, on the process approach to writing made popular by the Bay Area Writing Project. She adamantly insisted that it was doing a monumental disservice to black children. I was stunned. I started to defend the program, but then thought better of it, and asked her why she felt so negative about what she had seen.

She had a lot to say. She was particularly adamant about the notion that black children had to learn to be "fluent" in writing—had to feel comfortable about putting pen to paper—before they could be expected to conform to any conventional standards. "These people keep pushing this fluency thing," said Cathy. "What do they think? Our children have no fluency? If they think that, they ought to read some of the rap songs my students write all the time. They might not be writing their school assignments but they sure are writing. Our kids *are* fluent. What they need are the skills that will get them into college. I've got a kid right now—brilliant. But he can't get a score on the SAT that will even get him considered by any halfway decent college. He needs *skills*, not *fluency*. This is just another one of those racist ploys to keep our kids out. White kids learn how to write a decent sentence. Even if they don't teach them in school, their parents make sure they get what they need. But what about our kids? They don't get it at home and they spend all their time in school learning to be *fluent*. I'm sick of this liberal nonsense."

20   I returned to my temporary abode, but found that I had so much to think about that I could not sleep. Cathy had stirred that part of my past I had long avoided. Could her tirade be related to the reasons for my feelings of past failures? Could I have been a pawn, somehow, in some kind of perverse plot against black success? What did those black nuns from my childhood and those black teachers from the school in which I taught understand that my "education" had hidden from me? Had I abrogated my responsibility to teach all of the "skills" my black students were unlikely to get at home or in a more "unstructured" environment? These were painful thoughts.

The next day at the conference I made it my business to talk to some of the people from around the country who were involved in writing process projects. I asked the awkward question about the extent of minority teacher involvement in these endeavors. The most positive answer I received was that writing process projects initially attracted a few black or minority teachers, but they soon dropped out of the program. None came back a second year. One thoughtful woman told me she had talked to some of the black teachers about their noninvolvement. She was pained about their response and still could not understand it. They said the whole thing was racist, that the meetings were racist, and that the method itself was racist. They were not able to be specific, she added, but just felt they, and their ideas, were excluded.

I have spent the last few months trying to understand all that I learned in Philadelphia. How could people I so deeply respect hold such completely different views? I could not believe that all the people from whom I had learned could possibly have sinister intentions towards black children. On the other hand, all of those black teachers could not be completely wrong. What was going on?

When I asked another black teacher in another city what she thought of her state's writing project, she replied in a huff, "Oh, you mean the white folks' project." She went on to tell me a tale I have now heard so many times. She had gone to a meeting to learn about a "new" approach to literacy. The group leaders began talking about the need for developing fluency, for first getting anything down on paper, but as soon as this teacher asked when children were to be taught the technical skills of writing standard prose, leaders of the group began to lecture her on the danger of a skills orientation in teaching literacy. She never went back.

In puzzling over these issues, it has begun to dawn on me that many of the teachers of black children have their roots in other communities and do not often have the opportunity to hear the full range of their students' voices. I wonder how many of Philadelphia's teachers know that their black students are prolific and "fluent" writers of rap songs. I wonder how many teachers realize the verbal creativity and fluency black kids express every day on the playgrounds of America as they devise new insults, new rope-jumping chants and new cheers. Even if they did hear them, would they relate them to language fluency?

25   Maybe, just maybe, these writing process teachers are so adamant about developing fluency because they have not really had the opportunity to realize the fluency the kids already possess. They hear only silence, they see only immobile pencils. And maybe the black teachers are so adamant against what they understand to be the writing process approach because they hear their students' voices and see their fluency clearly. They are anxious to move to the next step, the step vital to success in America—the appropriation of the oral and written forms demanded by the mainstream. And they want it to happen quickly. They see no time to waste developing the "fluency" they believe their children already possess. Yes, they are *eager* to teach "skills."

Of course, there is nothing inherent in the writing process approach itself which mitigates against students' acquiring standard literacy skills; many supporters of the approach do indeed concern themselves with the technicalities of writing in their own classrooms. However, writing process advocates often give the impression that they view the direct teaching of skills to be restrictive to the writing process at best, and at worst, politically repressive to students already oppressed by a racist educational system. Black

teachers, on the other hand, see the teaching of skills to be essential to their students' survival. It seems as if leaders of the writing process movement find it difficult to develop the vocabulary to discuss the issues in ways in which teachers with differing perspectives can hear them and participate in the dialogue. Progressive white teachers seem to say to their black students, "Let me help you find your voice. I promise not to criticize one note as you search for your own song." But the black teachers say, "I've heard your song loud and clear. Now, I want to teach you to harmonize with the rest of the world." Their insistence on skills is not a negation of their students' intellect, as is often suggested by progressive forces, but an acknowledgment of it: "You know a lot; you can learn more. Do It Now!"

I run a great risk in writing this—the risk that my purpose will be misunderstood; the risk that those who subject black and other minority children to day after day of isolated, meaningless, drilled "subskills" will think themselves vindicated. That is not the point. Were this another paper I would explain what I mean by "skills"—useful and usable knowledge which contributes to a student's ability to communicate effectively in standard, generally acceptable literary forms. And I would explain that I believe that skills are best taught through meaningful communication, best learned in meaningful contexts. I would further explain that skills are a necessary but insufficient aspect of black and minority students' education. Students need technical skills to open doors, but they need to be able to think critically and creatively to participate in meaningful and potentially liberating work inside those doors. Let there be no doubt: a "skilled" minority person who is not also capable of critical analysis becomes the trainable, low-level functionary of the dominant society, simply the grease that keeps the institutions which orchestrate his or her oppression running smoothly. On the other hand, a critical thinker who lacks the "skills" demanded by employers and institutions of higher learning can aspire to financial and social status only within the disenfranchised underworld.

Yes, if minority people are to effect the change which will allow them to truly progress we must insist on "skills" *within the context of* critical and creative thinking.

But that is for another paper. The purpose of this one is to defend my fellow minority educators at the same time I seek to reestablish my own place in the progressive educational arena. Too often minority teachers' voices have been hushed: a certain paternalism creeps into the speech of some of our liberal colleagues as they explain that our children must be "given voice." As difficult as it is for our colleagues to hear our children's existing voices, it is often equally difficult for them to hear our own. The consequence is that all too often minority teachers retreat from these "progressive" settings grumbling among themselves, "There they go again." It is vitally important that non-minority educators realize that there is another voice, another reality; that many of the teachers whom they seek to reach have been able to conquer the educational system *because* they received the kind of instruction that their white progressive colleagues are denouncing.

What am I suggesting here? I certainly do not suggest that the writing process approach to literacy development is wrong or that a completely skills-oriented program is right. I suggest, instead, that there is much to be gained from the interaction of the two orientations and that advocates of both approaches have something to say to each other. I further suggest that it is the responsibility of the dominant group members to attempt to hear the other side of the issue; and after hearing, to speak in a modified voice that does not exclude the concerns of their minority colleagues.

30   It is time to look closely at elements of our educational system, particularly those elements we consider progressive; time to see whether there is minority involvement and support, and if not, to ask why; time to reassess what we are doing in public schools and universities to include other voices, other experiences; time to seek the diversity in our educational movements that we talk about seeking in our classrooms. I would advocate that university researchers, school districts, and teachers try to understand the views of their minority colleagues and constituents, and that programs, including the country's many writing projects, target themselves for study. Perhaps ethnographies of various writing projects, with particular attention given to minority participation and nonparticipation, would prove valuable. The key is to understand the variety of meanings available for any human interaction, and not to assume that the voices of the majority speak for all.

I have come to believe that the "open-classroom movement," despite its progressive intentions, faded in large part because it was not able to come to terms with the concerns of poor and minority communities. I truly hope that those who advocate other potentially important programs will do a better job.

SUGGESTIONS FOR DISCUSSION

1. Lisa Delpit seems to be torn between what she has learned in progressive education programs and what she hears from fellow black educators. What exactly is the tension Delpit feels? What seem to be the main issues? What is the significance of these issues for teaching and educational policy?

2. Delpit acknowledges that she runs a "great risk" of being misunderstood. What does she worry readers might misunderstand? What does she do to reduce the risk of misunderstanding?

3. It is likely that you and your classmates have had experience with both a "writing process" approach and a "skills-oriented" approach to literacy development. Drawing on your own experiences, what do you see as the strengths and weaknesses of each approach? Consider Delpit's case for their interaction. What would this interaction look like concretely?

SUGGESTIONS FOR WRITING

1. Write an analysis of the differing claims of process and skills that set up Delpit's "dilemmas." Your task here is not to side with one or the other approach but to identify and explain their underlying assumptions. Consider, on the one hand, what writing process advocates must assume to hold that teaching skills directly restricts individual development and is politically repressive. On the other hand, consider what the black teachers Delpit talks to must assume to think that the indirect teaching of writing process advocates is at best "liberal nonsense" and at worst racist. What is dividing the two groups? What is at stake in this division?

2. Assume, as Delpit does, that "skills are best taught through meaningful communication, best learned in meaningful contexts." This sounds sensibly balanced but remains somewhat abstract, the subject, as Delpit says, of another paper. Write an essay that takes on this work of developing more fully and more concretely how skills might best be taught and learned. First, explain what the issue of skills is, as Delpit sees it. Then invent an assignment or two for a high school or college writing class that integrates the learning of skills into a meaningful context. Identify the skill you want to teach and how you tie it to critical and creative thinking.

3. Delpit says that black teachers "see the teaching of skills to be essential to their students' survival." The positive spin that Delpit gives here to the idea of survival differs considerably from Min-zhan Lu's sense that "the metaphor of language as a tool for survival led me to be passive in my use of discourse, to be a bystander in the discussion." Write an essay that compares their differing uses of the term *survival*. Do they mean the same thing by the term or do their conceptions differ? What might explain why one invests the term with positive, enabling qualities while the other makes it a limiting condition? What do you see as the significance of these differing uses?

CHECKING OUT THE WEB

1. Visit the Web sites of several colleges. Include different types of institutions—state universities, state colleges, community colleges, elite private universities, small private liberal arts colleges, engineering schools, and so on. Using this information, write a report (or present orally to class) on what you see as the profile of these various schools. What do the Web sites emphasize? How do the schools distinguish themselves from each other? What is the main selling point to get students to apply? Think about the structure of American higher education—who goes where to college, why, and what are the outcomes?

2. The debate about school vouchers is taking place on-line as well as in print. Check out several Web sites by entering "school vouchers" into a search engine. What is the range of opinion you find there? What perspectives can you identify that don't appear in the readings?

3. In 1996, the Oakland, California, school board voted to recognize Ebonics as the language of African American students. Do a Web search to find out more about this decision and the controversy that ensued. What do you see as the main issues in the debate?

Picturing Schooldays

Visual images of teachers and children can be found in many places and put to many uses. A photograph of a one-room schoolhouse, for example, recaptures the early days of American schooling and summons up nostalgia for tight-knit communities of the past. By the same token, Norman Rockwell's paintings of school scenes summon up pictures of lost innocence—a time when students were well behaved and learned the three R's from strict but benevolent teachers. More recently, images of school have been used to illustrate the plight of American education, to argue for uniforms or dress codes, and to advertise new educational products.

Viewing images of schooling releases fond and not-so-fond emotional associations. Nearly everyone can remember what it was like to be in school and what their relationships were like with teachers and peers. The way people make sense of images of schooling, however, depends on more than just their personal experience. The composition of the images also provides cues about how to respond to them.

This section investigates the composition of photographs of school—to see how the pictures represent teachers and students and to examine their relationship to each other and to the institution of schooling. In particular, the section looks at how the composition of photographs uses **vectors** to establish relationships among the people in a photograph and **perspective** to establish the viewer's attitude toward what the photo represents.

Vectors

When viewers look at visual images of schooling, such as the photographs assembled below, they turn these images into a story about what the people are doing and what their relationship is to each other. Because the photograph itself is a still shot, it can't record action that occurs over time. Accordingly, viewers have to fill in the story themselves based on their familiarity with the scene pictured and the cues they take from the photograph.

To see how the composition of a photograph enables the viewer to fill in the story, look at how the people and things in the photo are connected by vectors, or the diagonal lines a viewer's eyes follow from one element of the photograph to another.

Take, for example, the first photograph—Francis Benjamin Johnston's picture of schoolchildren at the Hampton Institute saluting the American flag. The viewer recognizes the flag salute right away because it is such a familiar part of schooling and civic life. (What may be puzzling is why the students' arms are outstretched in salute. The outstretched arm—or Roman salute—was the conventional way of saluting the flag until World War II, when it was changed because it reminded people of the Nazi salute to Hitler.) But the photograph also contains visual cues that enable the viewer to recognize this familiar gesture. Notice in the schematic drawing how the outstretched arms and eyelines of the schoolchildren create a vector that connects them to the image of the flag and cues viewers to the interaction taking place.

Francis Benjamin Johnston
"Pledging Allegiance."

Vectors in
"Pledging Allegiance."

Perspective

Perspective is the angle of sight—or point of view—that a photograph offers a viewer.
Viewers' attitudes toward what is represented in a photograph will vary depending
on perspective.

1. **Frontal** angle promotes a high level of involvement and the sense that viewers are directly engaged with the image.

Wallace Kirkland. "Jane Addams Reading
at Hull House, Chicago, 1930's."

2. **Oblique** angle gives viewers a sense of detachment, as though they are simply
   looking on as a bystander.

3. **High** angle, in which the camera looks down on the people in the photo, gives
   the viewer a sense of power.

4. **Low** angle, in which the camera looks up, makes the people in the photo seem
   powerful.

SUGGESTIONS FOR DISCUSSION

1. Francis Benjamin Johnston's photograph of the schoolchildren saluting the flag at Hampton Institute can be an unsettling one that may provoke mixed feelings. How is the viewer to respond to the photo? How do the outstretched arms, and their now unavoidable association with the Hitler salute, influence the viewer's attitude to the photograph? Is the viewer being asked to admire the students' patriotism and the sense of order depicted, or does the image cast the students as victims of an authoritarian system? Could both, in some sense, be true? How does the fact that the students are African Americans at an all-black school in the time of segregated education enter into your response?

2. Notice how the children are grouped in the photo of Jane Addams. What do these groupings suggest about the children's relationship to each other and to the teacher? What vectors connect the participants, and what story do they tell? Follow the eyelines. What are the children observing? Do their eyelines point to an important focus of attention, or are they turned down to the children's work? Do the students look at each other? Is the teacher's gaze the dominant vector in the image?

3. In the Microsoft ad shown on the next page, the use of frontal perspective seems to bring viewers directly into the classroom. Compare the frontal perspective in the Microsoft ad with the oblique perspective of the classroom photo at the opening of this chapter. What effects on viewers' attitudes are these differing perspectives likely to have? Consider also

how the text in the upper right corner and the line drawings superimposed on the photo shape the message viewers are likely to take from the ad. How would reading the photo of the classroom be different without the text and drawings?

SUGGESTED ASSIGNMENT

What photographic image could tell the story of your classroom and the prevailing relationships among the students and between the teacher and the students? For this project, work in a group with two or three other students to take a photograph of your classroom.

When composing a photographic image, consider the following questions. How would students and the teacher be distributed and grouped in space? What vectors, or eyelines, would connect them? How would you want to position the viewer in relation to the classroom? How would you frame a shot that creates the point of view and angle of sight that you want for the viewer?

When you have decided on the shot you want, take the picture. This may involve posing students and the teacher in particular ways or asking them to do certain things. Everyone in class needs to cooperate on this project—whether you are taking the picture or being its subject.

When all the groups have developed the photos, bring them to class and discuss to what extent they portray different and similar stories. Identify the main vectors in each and how they establish the key relationships among the participants. Consider, too, how the photos create points of view and degrees of involvement on the viewer's part.

Microsoft ad. Used with permission from Microsoft Corporation

FIELDWORK   Classroom Observation

Most students know that being successful in school means understanding what teachers value and what they expect from students. This is sometimes called "psyching out" a teacher, and students learn to be good at it. They do this by evaluating the formal requirements of the course (e.g., reading assignments, labs, homework, tests, papers), by observing what takes place in the classroom (e.g., lectures, discussion, films, group work), and by learning the teacher's personality and eccentricities.

The purpose of this project is to investigate what it takes to be successful in a course in which you are enrolled and to draw some conclusions about the nature of teaching and learning. The method used is participant/observation. You are asked, in effect, to observe yourself, your teacher, and other students and to take detailed notes on what you do in and out of class.

Several weeks will be needed for this project so that you can accumulate a sufficient amount of entries in your field log to make your observations reliable and conclusions possible.

Field Log

As a participant–observer, you need to keep a field log on the classes; reading assignments; papers; exams; sections or labs, if pertinent; study groups; and informal conversations outside of class.

Background

When you start this project, write a statement that summarizes what you know about the course at this time. Ask yourself the following questions:

1. *Why are you taking the class?* To fulfill a requirement, for personal interest, for some other motivation?

2. *Read the syllabus:* How does it describe the content of the course and what you will learn? What are the assignments? How will the course grade be determined?

3. *Describe the format of the class:* What size is the class? In what kind of room does it meet? Does it look like it will be mostly lecture, discussion, a combination of the two, something else? Keep track of attendance patterns. Note where students sit to see if patterns develop.

4. *From what you can tell so far, what will you need to do to get the grade you want?*

Field Notes

Field notes consist of the observations you record during and outside of class. Use these questions:

1. *Where do you sit in class?* Why?

2. *How do you actually spend your time in class?* Taking notes, doodling, engaging in class discussion, looking around, writing notes to other students, day-

dreaming, talking to other students, working on something for another class, reading a newspaper or magazine?

3. *What does the teacher do in class?* Is it the same thing every day or does it change? How does the teacher run the class? Do individual class meetings have a routine format? Is there a set schedule (e.g., lecture Monday, discussion Wednesday, film Friday)? Who talks?

4. *What do other students do?*

5. *What do you do outside of class?* Keep track of the time devoted to various activities: reading assignments, reviewing or rewriting notes, studying for tests (alone or with others), attending lab sessions or section meetings, doing research, writing papers, meeting with the teacher or assistant, talking informally with other students about the class, and so on.

Analysis

Review your notes and look for patterns and key points. Here are some questions to consider:

1. *Compare what you know now about the course with what you wrote earlier on in your field log:* Have your responses changed? Does the course syllabus give an accurate forecast of what to expect, or have you become aware in other ways of the "real" requirements of the class? Have you changed your mind about the grade you think you might get?

2. *What kinds of patterns emerge from notes on what you do in class?* Do you do the same thing in every class, or does your activity vary? Have you changed what you do in class consciously? If so, why?

3. *Has the work returned to you so far (homework, tests, quizzes, papers, etc.) confirmed or revised what you thought it would take to do well in the course?* What have you learned about the teacher's expectations and preferences?

4. *How does the work you do outside of class figure in?* Could you skip class and still do well? Do you do all the work or only certain assignments? Do you have a system for deciding what to do and not do? If so, how did you develop it? Do you meet with or talk to the teacher, the teaching assistant, or other students about the class?

5. *What patterns emerge from your observations of other students?*

6. *What are the main differences and similarities in the courses you have observed?* What is their significance?

Writing the Report

For this project, use a version of the standard format for reports.

Introduction

Explain what you are investigating and the purpose of your research. Identify the class you observed, its enrollment, usual attendance, course requirements, and any other pertinent information. It can help readers to summarize this information in a diagram that accompanies your Introduction. (See Table 3.1.)

TABLE 3.1

DESCRIPTIONS OF COURSES OBSERVED

STUDENT	COURSE TITLE	ENROLLMENT AND % USUAL ATTENDANCE	COURSE REQUIREMENTS AND STUDENT INTERPRETATIONS OF THEM (MC = MULTIPLE CHOICE)
Worth	Anthropology	90 (60%)	Pass 2 MC midterms = take notes, attend, study notes; 1-pg. extra credit paper.
	Common Medicines	150 (90%)	2 MC tests: drug names, uses = memorize, memorize; good notes are critical; final cramming will not do here.
	International Studies: Africa	55 (90%)	4 short ans. tests; 6-pg. paper. Study ugly stuff like population distribution.
	Art History	100 (95%)	Midterm and Final, both essay. Memorize names and dates; concepts not a problem.
Cynthia	Anthropology	76 (60%)	Read for weekly quizzes, watch films, pass MC midterm and final. 1-pg. book review for extra credit.
	Intellectual Trad. of the West (Medieval)	25 (90%)	Write 4 papers, essay midterm and final. Read, attend.
	Sociology	400 (50%)	3 MC tests. Read, take notes, watch films.
Alycia	Intellectual Trad. of the West (Medieval)	25 (80%)	1 paper; midterm, final with take-home essay. 150–200 pp./wk. reading.
	Critical Literature	22 (60–75%)	3 papers; response ¶s. 15–60 min. reading/night to practice analyzing.
	Law	20 (95%)	10 1-page papers; research on topic about church and state.
John	Astronomy	105 (60%)	MC tests. Attend, read text, extra credit for 1000-word report.
	Psychology	155 (70–75%)	MC tests. Attend, read text, extra credit for being a subject in dept. experiments.
	Basic Acting II	9 (100%)	Perform 2 scenes, one monologue; attend 3 plays, review 2 of them.
Brandt	Calculus	35 (80%)	Problem sets. Take notes; geometrically interpret concepts; review and keep up.
	Chemistry	450 (70%)	Problems sets and MC test; read to get high grades on tests.
	History of Science	20 (97%)	Essay midterm and final; paper. Take notes & refer to them when reading; research final paper (use Wr. 210 skills); do well on final by catching up.

Method

Explain how you gathered data.

Observations

Summarize key points from your field log to establish patterns and to characterize your participation in the course. (See the sample Observations.)

Conclusions

Derive inferences and generalizations from your observations. (See sample Conclusions.)

OBSERVATIONS AND CONCLUSIONS FROM "CROSS-CURRICULAR UNDERLIFE: A COLLABORATIVE REPORT ON WAYS WITH ACADEMIC WORDS"

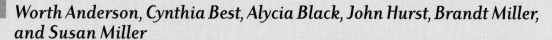

Worth Anderson, Cynthia Best, Alycia Black, John Hurst, Brandt Miller, and Susan Miller

The following Observations and Conclusions come from a longer article written by a group of undergraduates at the University of Utah in an independent study course under the direction of Susan Miller, a faculty member in English and a prominent writing theorist. Following an introductory section, the article consists of observations and conclusions written by the various members of the research group.

SAMPLE OBSERVATIONS

Art History

1   On the first day of class, the professor urged us all to drop, said she was willing to dispense drop cards to everyone, launched into a lecture that filled the time, handed out a syllabus, and reminded us that it was not too late to drop. I promptly named her "Madame Battleaxe."

It got worse. She was the embodiment of objectivist theories: "There are these facts. They constitute Truth. I will speak. You will listen. You will emerge with Truth." She spoke quickly, had some funky uses for the word "sensuous." I take notes very poorly, so I just sat and listened. A friend who sat beside me and played stenographer was frustrated by this, but for me I did better by just listening.

I realized that I was having trouble memorizing dates on pictures, so I went to see her. We got to talking about Charles V, and amazingly, I liked her. She reassured me about the test, and explained how highly she valued coherent writing, composed with an eye to history. I decided that she considered herself a historian, so her audience values would be in that community.

After our meeting, I was far more tolerant of her in class. On the midterm and final I wrote much more than anyone else, and emerged both times with the top grade. Serving up what she wanted worked.

Sociology

5 The teacher basically taught lecture one day— film one day—lecture one day....I believe that it's good to develop a routine, but not a rut! At first people groaned when they found out we were going to be watching another film. Once the students realized how the class would be taught, they began walking out during the films and lectures. One day I counted twenty-two people who walked out during a film. Later, the students developed a different routine. They would come to class and stay only if there was a film (so they could answer the test questions). But they would leave if the teacher was lecturing because they felt they could get more from reading the book.

The teacher lectured from an outline of key words on the overhead projector. Several people commented that his lectures were hard to follow, but I thought they weren't too difficult because he followed the book. In fact, at times he read straight from it! The professor had the habit of leaning on the lectern while he lectured and placing his hand on his chin. (It almost covered his mouth!) One day I observed, "Five people walked out of the lecture early. I assume from the time that had elapsed that it was after they'd copied the outline. I noticed people who simply copied the outline of key words and then just sat there in a kind of stupor."

In such a large class I noticed diverse student behaviors. One day during the film, as I counted the twelve people who left early, the girl to my left did homework for another class, the guy in front

of me ate yogurt, and the guy to my right organized his Franklin Day Planner. I rarely took notes on the films because they were irrelevant, but some people took notes anyway. One girl's notes consisted of "Boring ≫ ≫ ≫ Big Time!"

Calculus

I would go early to hear students discuss assignments and compare solutions to take-home quizzes, but this seemed almost a formality rather than a concern over concepts. When the professor began to work rapidly on the board, the lead flew across my notebook. She may not be exceptionally exciting, but unless you pay attention, you get lost fast. There was only moderate interaction between students and instructor by way of questions. Amazingly few questions are raised about such complex material.

There were several overlapping communities of student interaction in this class. Although it was a small class, there were many students whose names I didn't know, and could barely recognize by sight. I think this was because math is an independent discipline. You only need to interact with a few students to find the right answer. I took notes the whole time. After class, I would talk to students who could explain concepts like double integration a little better than what I had understood.

10   Math is a very sequential subject. When I had had trouble understanding the last assignment, I knew it would only compound with a new one. Today's concepts would be based on what we learned yesterday, which was based on the day before. Students had a tough time when they hadn't been here. Dr. A. covers the new material by relating it to yesterday's material, which makes it easier. Dr. A. becomes a narrator

for the strange mathematical figures that appear on the board.

When Dr. A. explained what kind of questions there would be on tests, she sometimes let us use a "cheat sheet," so we knew it would be hard. I would meet with other students to study.

SAMPLE CONCLUSIONS

A.

In ITW, I learned both on my own and in class. I learned as I read the assignments alone, and then my knowledge was expanded when the professor expounded on the material. Sections of this course are taught by teachers from different disciplines, so students who take more than one part of the sequence learn about ideas and about professors' specific fields. This section was actually "taught." The history professor who taught it connected ideas to historical background. But in Sociology, I learned the most from the text. The instructor's lectures were helpful, but I gained very little from the films. Ironically though, I preferred the films to the lectures. As I wrote one day, "I enjoyed the film simply because I didn't have to listen to another lecture." Anthropology was not "taught." The professor simply spouted facts each day. In considering where the learning occurred here, I've decided I learned most from the text. The films were informative and very helpful, but they were never shown at the right times. I really struggled with the professor's lectures, yet I learned from my notes because that's the only place that certain material was given.

School is a contract between a student and a teacher. Each must share a mutual respect for the other for learning to occur. In my liberal education courses, the teachers were not as concerned about the classes as they should have been. I got the impression that these teachers were being punished. They were bored because the material was so fundamental to their disciplines. But to the students, the material is new. If the professor shows excitement and projects a positive attitude, students will tend to be more interested in learning. Large classes require more effort from both students and teachers.

B.

Generally, the crucial part of learning in any classroom is digging up what the professor expects. I find that all classes require exceptional note-taking and analytical reading. Not all classes "require" attendance; in some I learn more from reading than from going to class. Poorly attended classes are those where the professor reads the text and gives no additional information. Well attended classes are taught by professors who enjoy the subject and make the students feel comfortable with it.

15 Although most of the students' learning must be done outside of class, an attitude toward learning is developed in the classroom. The professor's role is crucial because the students will be as active as the teacher is. Many of my peers say that the average student counts on having at least one "blow-off" class. If a teacher is strict, the students will make greater efforts and follow the teacher's guidelines. If a teacher is dull and doesn't include fun tidbits or allow us to express varying views, the students will find the material dull and difficult to study. But if the professor is excited, encourages us to voice different opinions, and interacts with us, the students will be excited about the subject and have an easier time.

MINING THE ARCHIVE

Textbooks from the Past

A Doll for Jane

"Hello, Father," said Dick.

"Jane will have a birthday soon.

Please get a new doll for Jane.

Get a baby doll that talks.

Please get a doll that talks."

One way to get a sense of schooling in an earlier time is to take a look at that period's textbooks. Two of the most famous and popular series were designed to teach reading: *McGuffey's Eclectic Readers,* used by millions of American children during the nineteenth century, and the Dick and Jane primers, used from the 1930s to the 1960s. Each series offers a fascinating view of how elementary school students learned to read as well as the kinds of social values transmitted through the reading lessons. On the one hand, the McGuffey readers were anthologies of essays, poems, speeches, and stories filled with moral advice, patriotic ideas, and religious instruction. Heavily didactic in tone, the content of the readers was meant to be morally uplifting. The Dick and Jane readers, on the other hand, created a child's world of fun and surprise. Dick and Jane, along with their little sister, Sally, dog, Spot, and kitten, Puff, lived in an American dream of white picket-fenced suburban homes, loving parents, laughter, and security. Most college and large public libraries will have copies of *McGuffey's Eclectic Reader* and some will have Dick and Jane readers as well. You can also find selections from the two textbook series in Elliot J. Gorn, ed., *The McGuffey Readers: Selections from the 1879 Edition* (Boston: Bedford, 1998) and Carol Kismaric and Marvin Heiferman, *Growing Up with Dick and Jane: Learning and Living the American Dream* (San Francisco: Collins Publishers, 1996). Researching these textbooks can lead to writing projects that focus on a range of topics. Below are a few examples; take these or design your own:

- nineteenth-century reading instruction
- the Protestant middle-class values of the McGuffey readers
- gender stereotypes in Dick and Jane
- the postwar American dream in the Dick and Jane primers

CHAPTER 4 Images

New York, c. 1940. © Helen Levitt. Courtesy Laurence Miller
Gallery, New York

In no other form of society in history has there been such a concentration of images, such a density of visual messages.
—John Berger, *Ways of Seeing*

It is in fact hard to get the camera to tell the truth.
—James Agee, *A Way of Seeing. Photographs by Helen Levitt*

We are surrounded daily by the visual message. On billboards, in magazines, on television, in film and video, on our computer screens, and in nearly every public and private space, images of all sorts compete for our attention. They carry messages from corporate advertisers, nonprofit organizations, public and private institutions, and friends and family, and they ask us to buy, to give, to believe, to subscribe, to respond, to understand, to act.

The image that conveys a message is hardly a new phenomenon. For centuries the images people created—paintings, drawings, designs, sketches, icons—did not simply decorate the insides of caves, temples, churches, palaces, and the like but they also recorded family and community history; taught lessons in religion, culture, and politics; and even gave directions to locations.

173

New to the experience of the image are the vast numbers and many kinds of images available and the ease with which they may be and are reproduced, copied, parodied, and reconstructed. Also new is the aggressive nature of the image. Unless we purposefully isolate ourselves from the industrial world, it is difficult to avoid a continuous onslaught of visual communication.

Advertisers depend on people automatically recognizing the message-laden images that they see as they speed down the highway, surf through TV channels, or flip through a magazine. Some images are effective simply because they have been around for so long. A full-color photo of a cowboy silhouetted on a horse at sunset is likely going to call to mind the Marlboro Man, whether or not it is in an ad for cigarettes. These images can almost speak for themselves, and advertisers do not need many words to convey the accompanying message—the Marlboro ad often includes only the product's name and the obligatory FDA warning.

If the advertiser hasn't succeeded in linking the image directly to a product, however, the image is ineffective. For example several years ago, the Whirlpool company ran a commercial featuring a bald eagle. The camera tracked the eagle in slow motion as it flew down toward impossibly still water, reached out, and snatched up a trout with a movement that was sure and elegant and surprising. The image was so appealing that even the advertisers couldn't resist showing it again. And so viewers watched the eagle's catch once more—this time closer up and slightly slower—as the video looped back to the opening sequence. The image of the eagle is, in this country, one laden with the notions of patriotism, freedom, strength, and independence. The ad was beautiful to watch, but it gave no clear message. Because this image had so little obvious connection to the product—Whirlpool appliances—viewers often could remember the ad but not the product. To be effective, an ad image (such as Maytag's lonely repairman) successfully carries a double burden: It catches the viewers' attention, and it links the image it uses to a particular product so that those watching it think of the product the next time they are in a buying mood.

As you read this chapter, you will be asked to look at and read such messages—messages that rely on pictures or graphics more than on words to carry meaning. Many of the images we will discuss here are taken from print ads so that you have easy access to images you can study carefully for long periods of time. However, the power of the image to convey messages is not at all limited to print advertising. Television, film, photographs, music videos, Web pages, even the very layout of the page all signal an increased demand for all of us to become active readers and producers of visual text.

The language of images is much like verbal language. To relay meaning, visual language depends on familiarity, patterns of use, composition, references to other images, and the context in which the image appears. Like verbal language, visual language does not convey simply one stable message to everyone who reads it. Meaning depends on the reader as well as the text. Still, the most quickly read messages are often those that carry with them expressions of common cultural ideas or ideals—images that act as a kind of cultural shorthand.

We begin our discussion, then, with an illustration of that cultural shorthand. The graphic shown on the next page uses a simple design depicting the U.S. flag with shopping bag handles attached to the top and the title, "America: Open for Business."

Even without the words, most readers are likely to understand that this as a statement about what the United States stands for. The flag, as a common symbol for America, sends that message. Many readers will also recognize this as a shopping bag with an American flag motif. The text works to anchor a meaning for the shopping bag handles on the flag, but that meaning is not entirely a stable one. In other words, not everyone will read this graphic in the same way. However, if you know about the

events leading to the creation of this graphic, you are likely to read in it a more complex message than if you see it without knowing that context.

"America: Open for Business" was created in the aftermath of the September 11, 2001, attacks on the World Trade Center. Here is how Craig Frazier, the graphic designer who created this image, explains what he was trying to say with it:

> As I sat in sunny California so insulated from the disaster, feeling its national impact, I wondered what I could do. Unfortunately, the American economy is directly connected to our emotional state of mind, and the national gloom of this attack threatens to be far-reaching and long-lasting. I wanted to create an image that says, "We aren't shutting down because we are American." I am not in any way denying the grief of so many, and the fact that many businesses are not open any more. I am trying to create a sense of community in an effort to lift our heads and carry on. This poster stands to unite the local coffee shop on the corner with the national chain on the opposite corner, and the patrons of both. Ultimately, everyone can do something.

Frazier is relying on the reader's ability to read this poster by using a cultural shorthand that combines the flag with the reference to shopping in the context of 9/11.

What the cultural shorthand cannot control is the additional meaning that readers are able to generate with an image such as this one. Though Frazier clearly wanted to make a positive statement about American strength in the face of tragedy, a reader who is not persuaded that shopping is a positive virtue is likely to see something very different in the graphic. Both the reader Frazier is aiming at and the reader he is not aiming at are likely to understand the intended message, but their response to that message would vary depending on differences in gender, politics, social status, ethnicity, or economic background. Visual meaning, like all meaning, is dependent on both the message being sent and the receiver of that message.

Focusing on the importance of the visual does not mean ignoring the written text. Many images, such as the "America: Open for Business" poster, rely on pictures combined with words to carry meaning, even when the words are few. In Frazier's design or the following ad for Coach bags, words serve to anchor the image to a particular message. Frazier's asks readers to support American business. The Coach ad, not as directly but just as assuredly, asks readers to buy Coach bags. And yet, words can also complicate readers' responses.

On its own, the visual image in the Coach ad is simple and commonplace: The attractive young woman posed in a rugged yet beautiful setting with her dog and her Coach bag is likely meant to associate the product with those things that are appealing in the image. At the same time, the **ad copy** (what is written in the ad about the product) asks the reader to associate the product with more than natural beauty or rugged independence. The copy identifies the young woman as Jacqueline Brown-Smith, the great-great-great-granddaughter of Sitting Bull, the famous Hunkpapa Sioux who resisted being placed on a reservation and whose name continues to call forth the image of Indian people as profoundly independent.

Such identification gives this image a cultural significance. That is, once the woman is identified as the direct descendant of Sitting Bull, the reader is no longer looking at her but through her to her great-great-great-grandfather. Jacqueline Brown-Smith is thereby assigned special significance because of her relation to Sitting Bull. After discovering who she is, the reader is likely to look again at the image, which has now taken on a different meaning. Naturally, the Coach bag is likely to pick up some of that meaning. In this ad, the bag is called "An American Legacy" like, the reader must assume, Sitting Bull's legacy represented here in the image of his great-great-great-granddaughter.

This particular campaign includes ads using the descendants of other luminaries such as Albert Einstein, Jesse Owens, Gene Kelly, and George Washington to suggest that Coach represents intelligence, endurance, priceless quality, good taste, and status. The bag Brown-Smith is carrying is a binocular case, which links her (and, by extension, her great-great-great-grandfather) to the natural world—to a rugged existence with an uptown taste.

Of course, readers might also find meanings in this ad, as in any ad, that the advertiser did not intend. They might question the appropriateness of using Sitting Bull—a man who clearly stood in opposition to U.S. government policies—to sell an expensive bag to what has become a consumer culture. Advertisers are aware of that possibility, which is why they carefully control where they place their ads so that they can pitch ads differently to different groups of people.

Advertisers take advantage of cultural meanings every time they present an image as if it were representative of what everyone desires or understands.

Take, for example, the Jeep ad reprinted on p. 178.

This ad uses a very simple design—the placement of one image above the other—to convey a complex message. By placing the peace symbol ("International

Symbol for Peace") above the word Jeep ("International Symbol for Freedom"), the advertiser is asking us to connect one with the other. When we talk about the arrangement of images in relation to one another, we are describing the **visual syntax** of the ad. In other words, the images are arranged in such a way as to convey meaning. Cartoons, for example, use a sequencing of images to suggest an event unfolding over time. This ad simply juxtaposes one image with the other so that we might see a connection between the two images.

This particular ad has the potential to reach several kinds of readers because of the cultural meanings the two images already carry. The peace symbol and the word *Jeep* are each depicted as if they could be worn on leather laces around the neck, so the retro look of the peace symbol might appeal to current fashion. The peace symbol continues to evoke a strong emotional response from those who were young

during the Vietnam War, so the message is one that could elicit memories of youth and freedom from that generation. In addition, the Jeep is a vehicle that was made popular particularly during World War II, the war Studs Terkel and others have called the last "good war." The Jeep name as an "international symbol for freedom" can, then, even appeal to a generation not entirely in sympathy with the peace movement of the sixties or the retro look of the nineties.

In fact, the fewer words an ad such as this uses, the more likely it will allow for several different readings—many of which will be positive and all of which will call up something of the reader's memories or desires or associations. Finally, with the statement "There's only one Jeep," the ad seems to acknowledge the possibility that there may be many responses to this juxtapositioning, but that there is only one product that can evoke all of those responses. Advertisers naturally hope that those associations eventually will lead readers to think of and then purchase the product after they have seen the ad.

On their own and depending on the person, readers might still question the association of the peace symbol with the Jeep or wonder how the peace symbol could

have changed from a political statement of the sixties to a fashion statement of the nineties. Such a reading, though, would threaten to interrupt the primary purpose of the ad, which is to sell Jeep cars and trucks. That kind of reading is certainly possible, but it must be done consciously. Most ads function at a subconscious, even visceral level. They call on feelings and loyalties and fears and desires—responses most people do not take much time to question.

Other kinds of visual images do the same: logos for sports teams, poster campaigns, graffiti, news photos, and family albums, for example. Some images are purely functional and wholly visual; many of them are multinational signs that tell a great deal in a simple design: the icons that instruct viewers to buckle their seat belts on planes, not to smoke in public places, and which restroom door to walk through.

As you look at and consider the visual messages around you, remember that you don't have to be mindless consumers of visual culture. You are a producer as well, and you can make your own visual messages. One thing that bothers many people when they look at ads is the assuredness with which advertisers sell lifestyles and attempt to create new interests. Knowing that most people let ads go by without reading them closely, some activists write over ads to attract the public's attention to the alternative or oppositional readings possible in an ad campaign.

Designer Tibor Kalman, whose work shaped the earliest issues of the magazine *Colors* used his designs to overturn many of the attitudes taken for granted. In the image reproduced above, "what if…? e se…?" he asks his readers to imagine Queen Elizabeth as a black person. Kalman used a computer photo-manipulation program to make a very simple change, but the resulting image is a powerful statement about race and power and expectations. What would change in the reader's response to the image? Would racial relations change if the person in power were not white? What does the picture tell readers about their own expectations or about stereotypes?

Writing and rewriting, in the hands of designers such as Kalman or groups such as Adbusters or the many unnamed graffitists who carry on similar campaigns in small towns and major cities, have become forceful tools of resistance to the messages that normally go unquestioned and often unnoticed in the public sector. Later in this chapter you will have the opportunity to rewrite and create images of your own, but first, you need to understand how an image conveys meaning.

Reading Images

In this chapter, you will be reading articles by writers who have thought a great deal about the importance of the image, especially, though not exclusively, the advertising image. Stuart and Elizabeth Ewen dramatize just how much our lives are affected by a nearly unbroken stream of popular images. As you read the Ewens' article, begin to gather and think about images from your surroundings. The Visual Essays that follow—"Selling Magic" (pp. 187–189) and "It's a Woman Thing" (pp. 190–194)— provide images to examine and a set of questions designed to help you with visual analysis. As a companion piece to "It's a Woman Thing," we follow with bell hooks's "Facing Difference: The Black Female Body," an essay about African American photographer and artist Lorna Simpson who, hooks believes, subverts the traditional image of women by turning her back on those old representations.

The chapter then shifts to two Visual Essays that further complicate the work of reading the image and of creating visual messages of your own. The first, "Rewriting the Image," encourages you to think about your own role as a producer of cultural meaning. The power of the image is something you can use to your advantage. The image doesn't have to be just another thing that works on you. You can use images to say what you want to say, to talk back to the images surrounding you and the corporations or institutions that create and distribute them. Kalle Lasn, founder of *Adbusters Magazine,* helps set one context for rewriting the image with an excerpt from *Culture Jam.* The second Visual Essay, "Public Health Messages," examines the multiple meanings embedded in such messages as public service announcements, posters, and health campaigns. These are the kinds of visual messages that often go unquestioned because they are government or health service or nonprofit campaigns offering instruction on how people should live their lives, protect their bodies, and treat each other.

The Classic Reading selection extends the discussion of images into the world of documentary photography. In an excerpt from his introduction to *A Way of Seeing. Photographs by Helen Levitt*, James Agee raises crucial questions about what it means to represent the world through pictures. The camera that records only what is in front of it is, Agee writes, a slippery liar.

Throughout this chapter, you will be asked to read images in the same way you read any text—for meaning and for how those images connect to the world around you. As well, you will be given the chance to create visual messages of your own. The first step is to notice and collect examples of the visual messages that are a routine part of your day. Use the list that follows as a starting point for that work. As you begin to develop projects of your own, your collection should become more focused

Some Suggestions for Collecting Images

As you work through this chapter, you will need a good selection of images to draw on for class discussions and writing projects, so begin collecting those images right away. Don't limit yourself only to ad images. The more you pay attention, the more diverse images you are likely to find, so make your collection a rich and varied one. Here are a few suggestions:

- Clip ads from magazines.
- Videotape television programs and commercials.
- Buy postcards of all sorts.
- Pay attention to the posters and other wall hangings you see at home, in dorm rooms, in apartments, and in offices.
- Take note of the kinds of visuals that appear in classrooms, churches, government offices, and all sorts of public institutions.
- Photograph billboards, public murals, shop windows, road signs, and shop and restaurant logos.
- Collect CD, audio, and video tape covers.
- Notice T-shirt images.
- Collect images from cereal boxes and other products with interesting designs or pictures.
- Capture images from the Web.
- Collect news and entertainment magazine covers and front pages of newspapers.
- Collect book covers.
- Carry a small notebook with you so that you can describe the images you see but are unable to reproduce visually.

CHOOSING IMAGES

Until you have clearly defined your projects, collect those images that catch your eye, make you laugh or ask questions, and seem typical of attitudes or fashions or values surrounding you. Don't worry if you cannot always explain why an image appeals to you. If it attracts you for any reason, find a way to add it to your collection.

and purposeful, but you should always have as many choices to draw from as possible, so don't limit yourself too soon. Look for patterns, similarities, and images that surprise you. You could find that you have already been doing much of this work automatically, just by looking at the world around you.

IN THE SHADOW OF THE IMAGE

Stuart and Elizabeth Ewen

Stuart and Elizabeth Ewen have each written several books and articles on the history and meaning of popular culture. Cultural scholar Stuart Ewen's work includes *All Consuming Images: The Politics of Style in Contemporary Culture* and *Captains of Consciousness.* Historian Elizabeth Ewen's work includes *Immigrant Women in the Land of Dollars* (1985). *Channels of Desire* (1982), from which the following selection is taken, is their first full-length collaboration. The Ewens argue that much of what Americans understand about self-image is actually a reflection of mass-media images. As this essay illustrates, today's culture is one living "in the shadow of the image," whether the image is present in advertising, news reporting, or popular television and film. Everywhere people go, they see images created for mass consumption but aimed at individuals. Sometimes consciously but mostly not, people measure their looks, their moods, their success or lack of it against the appearances that surround them daily.

SUGGESTION FOR READING   This series of vignettes describes the daily, often unconscious encounters Americans have with popular culture and especially with commercial images. As you read each vignette, take note of the effects these encounters seem to have on the characters the Ewens have created. If you begin to lose track of what is going on in this selection, skip to the final four paragraphs where the point of the vignettes is explained, then go back and reread individual sections.

1   Maria Aguilar was born twenty-seven years ago near Mayagüez, on the island of Puerto Rico. Her family had lived off the land for generations. Today she sits in a rattling IRT subway car, speeding through the iron-and-rock guts of Manhattan. She sits on the train, her ears dazed by the loud outcry of wheels against tracks. Surrounded by a galaxy of unknown fellow strangers, she looks up at a long strip of colorful signboards placed high above the bobbing heads of the others. All the posters call for her attention.

Looking down at her, a blond-haired lady cabdriver leans out of her driver's side window. Here is the famed philosopher of this strange urban world, and a woman she can talk to. The tough-wise eyes of the cabby combine with a youthful beauty, speaking to Maria Aguilar directly:

Estoy sentada 12 horas al dia.
Lo último que necesito son hemorroides.
(I sit for twelve hours a day. The last thing I need are hemorrhoids.)

Under this candid testimonial lies a package of Preparation H ointment, and the promise

"Alivia dolores y picasonas. Y ayuda a reducir la hinchazón." (Relieves pain and itching. And helps reduce swelling.) As her mind's eye takes it all in, the train sweeps into Maria's stop. She gets out; climbs the stairs to the street; walks to work where she will spend her day sitting on a stool in a small garment factory, sewing hems on pretty dresses.

Every day, while Benny Doyle drives his Mustang to work along State Road Number 20, he passes a giant billboard along the shoulder. The billboard is selling whisky and features a woman in a black velvet dress stretching across its brilliant canvas.

5   As Benny Doyle downshifts by, the lounging beauty looks out to him. Day after day he sees her here. The first time he wasn't sure, but now he's convinced that her eyes are following him.

The morning sun shines on the red-tan forehead of Bill O'Conner as he drinks espresso on his sun deck, alongside the ocean cliffs of La Jolla, California. Turning through the daily paper, he reads a story about Zimbabwe.

"Rhodesia," he thinks to himself.

The story argues that a large number of Africans in Zimbabwe are fearful about black majority rule, and are concerned over a white exodus. Two black hotel workers are quoted by the article. Bill puts this, as a fact, into his mind.

Later that day, over a business lunch, he repeats the story to five white business associates, sitting at the restaurant table. They share a superior laugh over the ineptitude of black African political rule. Three more tellings, children of the first, take place over the next four days. These are spoken by two of Bill O'Conner's luncheon companions; passed on to still others in the supposed voice of political wisdom.

10   Barbara and John Marsh get into their seven-year-old Dodge pickup and drive twenty-three miles to the nearest Sears in Cedar Rapids. After years of breakdowns and months of hesitation they've decided to buy a new washing machine. They come to Sears because it is there, and because they believe that their new Sears machine will be steady and reliable. The Marshes will pay for their purchase for the next year or so.

Barbara's great-grandfather, Elijah Simmons, had purchased a cream-separator from Sears, Roebuck in 1897 and he swore by it.

When the clock-radio sprang the morning affront upon him, Archie Bishop rolled resentfully out of his crumpled bed and trudged slowly to the john. A few moments later he was unconsciously squeezing toothpaste out of a mess of red and white Colgate packaging. A dozen scrubs of the mouth and he expectorated a white, minty glob into the basin.

Still groggy, he turned on the hot water, slapping occasional palmfuls onto his gray face.

A can of Noxzema shave cream sat on the edge of the sink, a film of crud and whiskers across its once neat label. Archie reached for the bomb and filled his left hand with a white creamy mound, then spread it over his beard. He shaved, then looked with resignation at the regular collection of cuts on his neck.

Stepping into a shower, he soaped up with a soap that promised to wake him up. Groggily, he then grabbed a bottle of Clairol Herbal Essence Shampoo. He turned the tablet-shaped bottle to its back label, carefully reading the "Directions."

15   "Wet hair."

He wet his hair.

"Lather."

He lathered.

"Rinse."

20   He rinsed.

"Repeat if necessary."

Not sure whether it was altogether necessary, he repeated the process according to directions.

Late in the evening, Maria Aguilar stepped back in the subway train, heading home to the Bronx after a long and tiring day. This time, a poster told her that "The Pain Stops Here!"

She barely noticed, but later she would swallow two New Extra Strength Bufferin tablets with a glass of water from a rusty tap.

25   Two cockroaches in cartoon form leer out onto the street from a wall advertisement. The man cockroach is drawn like a hipster, wearing shades and a cockroach zoot-suit. He strolls hand-in-hand with a lady cockroach, who is dressed like a floozy and blushing beet-red. Caught in the midst of their cockroach-rendezvous, they step sinfully into a Black Flag Roach Motel. Beneath them, in Spanish, the words:

Las Cucarachas entran…pero non pueden salir.
(In the English version: Cockroaches check in…but they don't check out.)

The roaches are trapped; sin is punished. Salvation is gauged by one's ability to live roach-free. The sinners of the earth shall be inundated by roaches. Moral tales and insects encourage passersby to rid their houses of sin. In their homes, sometimes, people wonder whether God has forsaken them.

Beverly Jackson sits at a metal and tan Formica table and looks through the *New York Post*. She is bombarded by a catalog of horror.

Children are mutilated…subway riders attacked…. Fanatics are marauding and noble despots lie in bloody heaps. Occasionally someone steps off the crime-infested streets to claim a million dollars in lottery winnings.

Beverly Jackson's skin crawls; she feels a knot encircling her lungs. She is beset by immobility, hopelessness, depression.

Slowly she walks over to her sixth-floor window, gazing out into the sooty afternoon. From the empty street below, Beverly Jackson imagines a crowd yelling "Jump!…Jump!"

30   Between 1957 and 1966 Frank Miller saw a dozen John Wayne movies, countless other westerns and war dramas. In 1969 he led a charge up a hill without a name in Southeast Asia. No one followed; he took a bullet in the chest.

Today he sits in a chair and doesn't get up. He feels that images betrayed him, and now he camps out across from the White House while another movie star cuts benefits for veterans. In the morning newspaper he reads of a massive weapons buildup taking place.

Gina Concepcion now comes to school wearing the Jordache look. All this has been made possible by weeks and weeks of afterschool employment at a supermarket checkout counter. Now, each morning, she tugs the decorative denim over her young legs, sucking in her lean belly to close the snaps.

These pants are expensive compared to the "no-name" brands, but they're worth it, she reasons. They fit better, and she fits better.

The theater marquee, stretching out over a crumbling, garbage-strewn sidewalk, announced "The Decline of Western Civilization." At the ticket window a smaller sign read "All seats $5.00."

35   It was ten in the morning and Joyce Hopkins stood before a mirror next to her bed. Her interview at General Public Utilities, Nuclear Division, was only four hours away and all she could think was "What to wear?"

A half hour later Joyce stood again before the mirror, wearing a slip and stockings. On the bed, next to her, lay a two-foot-high mountain of discarded options. Mocking the title of a recent bestseller, which she hadn't read, she said aloud to herself, "Dress for Success….What do they like?"

At one o'clock she walked out the door wearing a brownish tweed jacket; a cream-colored Qiana blouse, full-cut with a tied collar; a dark beige skirt, fairly straight and hemmed (by Maria Aguilar) two inches below the knee; shear fawn stockings, and simple but elegant reddish-brown pumps on her feet. Her hair was to the shoulder, her look tawny.

When she got the job she thanked her friend Millie, a middle manager, for the tip not to wear pants.

Joe Davis stood at the endless conveyor, placing caps on a round-the-clock parade of automobile radiators. His nose and eyes burned. His ears buzzed in the din. In a furtive moment he looked up and to the right. On the plant wall was a large yellow sign with THINK! printed on it in bold type. Joe turned back quickly to the radiator caps.

40   Fifty years earlier, in another factory, in another state, Joe's grandfather, Nat Davis, had looked up and seen another sign:

A Clean Machine Runs Better.
Your Body Is a Machine.
KEEP IT CLEAN.

Though he tried and tried, Joe Davis' grandfather was never able to get the dirt out from under his nails. Neither could his great-grandfather, who couldn't read.

In 1952 Mary Bird left her family in Charleston to earn money as a maid in a Philadelphia suburb. She earned thirty-five dollars a week, plus room and board, in a dingy retreat of a ranch-style tract house.

Twenty-eight years later she sits on a bus, heading toward her small room in North Philly. Across from her, on an advertising poster, a sumptuous meal is displayed. Golden fried chicken, green beans glistening with butter and flecked by pimento, and a fluffy cloud of rice fill the greater part of a calico-patterned dinner plate. Next to the plate sit a steaming boat of gravy, and an icy drink in an amber tumbler. The plate is on a quilted blue placemat, flanked by a thick linen napkin and colonial silverware.

As Mary Bird's hungers are aroused, the wording on the placard instructs her: "Come Home to Carolina."

Shopping List

paper towels
milk
eggs
rice crispies
chicken
snacks for kids (twinkies, chips, etc.)
potatoes
coke, ginger ale, plain soda
cheer
brillo
peanut butter
bread
ragu (2 jars)
spaghetti
saran wrap
salad
get cleaning, bank, must pay electric!!!

45   On his way to Nina's house, Sidney passed an ad for Smirnoff vodka. A sultry beauty with wet hair and beads of moisture on her smooth, tanned face looked out at him. "Try a Main Squeeze." For a teenage boy the invitation transcended the arena of drink; he felt a quick throb-pulse at the base of his belly and his step quickened.

In October of 1957, at the age of two and a half, Aaron Stone was watching television. Suddenly, from the black screen, there leaped a circus clown, selling children's vitamins, and yelling "Hi! boys and girls!" He ran, terrified, from the room, screaming.

For years after, Aaron watched television in perpetual fear that the vitamin clown would reappear. Slowly his family assured him that the television was just a mechanical box and couldn't really hurt him, that the vitamin clown was harmless.

Today, as an adult, Aaron Stone takes vitamins, is ambivalent about clowns, and watches television, although there are occasional moments of anxiety.

These are some of the facts of our lives; disparate moments, disconnected, dissociated. Meaningless moments. Random incidents. Memory traces. Each is an unplanned encounter, part of day-to-day existence. Viewed alone, each by itself, such spaces of our lives seem insignificant, trivial. They are the decisions and reveries of survival; the stuff of small talk; the chance preoccupations of our eyes and minds in a world of images—soon forgotten.

50   Viewed together, however, as an ensemble, an integrated panorama of social life, human activity, hope and despair, images and information, another tale unfolds from these vignettes. They reveal a pattern of life, the structures of perception.

As familiar moments in American life, all of these events bear the footprints of a history that weighs upon us, but is largely untold. We live and breathe an atmosphere where mass images are everywhere in evidence; mass produced, mass distributed. In the streets, in our homes, among a crowd, or alone, they speak to us, overwhelm our vision. Their presence, their messages are given; unavoidable. Though their history is still relatively short, their prehistory is, for the most part, forgotten, unimaginable.

The history that unites the seemingly random routines of daily life is one that embraces the rise of an industrial consumer society. It involves explosive interactions between modernity and old ways of life. It includes the proliferation, over days and decades, of a wide, repeatable vernacular of commercial images and ideas. This history spells new patterns of social, productive, and political life.

SUGGESTIONS FOR DISCUSSION

1. Although many of the vignettes describe the effects of ad images on so much of the public, others, such as the story of Bill O'Conner, the story of the roach motel, and the story of Joe Davis, suggest something about the way information and even cultural attitudes are passed along or processed. Reread those sections and others like them and discuss what kind of information you unconsciously process in your daily life. In your discussion, take into account such things as the choices you make in what to wear, what to take when you have a cold, how to act around others, what to believe about political issues, and the like.

2. The grocery list intersperses generic items such as paper towels with name brands that represent generics (such as brillo for scouring pads). Consider the products you buy that are brand name. How would you say your own or your family's buying habits are influenced by what appears in newspapers, on television, on billboards, or on bus-stop ads? To what extent do you think those habits are influenced by loyalty or habit, like the Marshes' purchase of a new Sears washing machine?

3. Near the end of this selection, the Ewens write, "As familiar moments in American life, all of these events bear the footprints of a history that weighs upon us, but is largely untold." After rereading this series of events, discuss what the authors mean by such a sweeping statement. Do you see that statement illustrated or not in the observations you have made about the way you and the people you know respond to living "in the shadow of the image"?

SUGGESTIONS FOR WRITING

1. Write a series of vignettes about the daily encounters that you, your friends, and your family have with ad images. Pay attention to how the Ewens structure their piece. The vignettes lead to a summary statement in which the Ewens briefly explain what such a sequence of encounters might mean for them. Include a statement that draws your reader away from the vignettes and sums up the stories with a commentary on your daily encounters with visual messages of all sorts.

2. Make a list of images that you see on most days. The list might include posters, billboards, commercials, magazine and newspaper ads, cartoons, road signs, family and news photos, and shop-window displays. Write an essay in which you describe the kinds of images you encounter daily and what those images seem to be asking of you or telling you about the way people should look or act or feel.

3. Near the end of this selection, the Ewens write, "The history that unites the seemingly random routines of daily life is one that embraces the rise of an industrial consumer society. It involves explosive interactions between modernity and old ways of life. It includes the proliferation, over days and decades, of a wide, repeatable vernacular of commercial images and ideas. This history spells new patterns of social, productive, and political life." Write an explanation of what you understand the authors to be saying in that statement. Provide examples from your own experience or reading that help make the meaning clear for your readers.

Selling Magic

Most of us know what advertising images are all about. They sell desire—the desire to look different or be popular or have something more or better or newer or bigger or faster. The trick for the ad designer is to get the public to pay attention to the ad, remember it, and associate it with the product being advertised. That is especially hard for products that have little more than their image to distinguish them from one another. Products such as cosmetics, alcohol, tobacco, and automobiles sell themselves on their image—on what the public associates them with. Much advertising relies on selling the impossible—products that keep people from aging or that melt off unwanted pounds or turn fine, dull hair into a thick, luxurious mane—just like magic. Personal care products, especially, sell magic with just a touch of science.

As you look through the images on the next two pages, begin your analysis by asking fairly simple questions:

1. What is the product being sold, and what is that product used for?

2. What does the ad promise? What claim does the ad make about the product?

3. What visuals are used in the ad? Do they illustrate the product claim or promise? Or do they associate the product with something else—for example, a lifestyle or a celebrity?

4. Who is the target audience? Who is likely to buy the product? Is age or gender an important issue for the ad or the product? Is cost an issue? How can you tell?

5. Where does the ad appear? If it is a magazine or newspaper ad, who reads that publication? If it is a billboard, where is it placed? Who is likely to be the target audience for that publication or location?

6. How are people depicted in the ad image? Do they conform to or break with stereotypes, for example?

7. Can you identify the cultural significance of this product? For example, is it a product that has been around for several generations? Is it associated with a particular idea or ideal about American culture or family life? Is it new to the market and suddenly popular with teens or young children? Does the ad refer to current events in the news or to popular films or media events?

8. Is this ad more text than image or more image than text? In other words, does the advertiser think the audience wants more information about the product, or is the audience one that will more likely be persuaded by the visual appeal of the ad? Typically, ads in electronics equipment magazines will give readers quite a bit of text—the details of the equipment—suggesting that advertisers are assuming the readers are an audience that knows something about the product and are looking for specific features. Ads for clothing, cosmetics, soap products, cigarettes, and the like rarely provide much information beyond the product name, the product claim—"softer, younger-looking skin"—and the advertising image.

9. Does the ad look familiar to you? Does it remind you of other ads or other media? If it does, what is that association?

SUGGESTIONS FOR DISCUSSION

1. Choose one of the ads reprinted here and list words that connect the product with advanced scientific research or with a promise or claim being made for the product. How does the ad you chose promise results through this scientific advancement?

2. Compare the Crest whitening and Olay ads. In what ways do they differ? In what ways are they selling the same thing?

3. The Zoloft ad depends much more on written text than pictoral elements to sell the product. With a group of your classmates, redesign that ad or one like it so that the pictoral outweighs the verbal elements. How does the ad change?

SUGGESTIONS FOR WRITING

1. Choose several ads from recent magazines or newspapers that, like the Zoloft ad, are designed using more text than image. Examine these ads, and choose two or three for a brief essay in which you provide an argument for why these advertisers decided not to

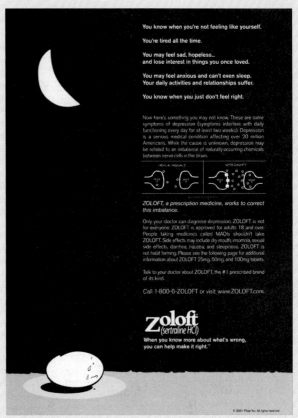

depend primarily on image to sell the product. What do they gain with the choice? What is possibly lost? Who do they assume is their target audience? What about the product might suggest using more words than image?

2. Pick up two or three current fashion magazines and look through them to get an idea of what cosmetics are being sold and how they are being sold today. Then, look carefully at each of the cosmetics ads in this Visual Essay—both published since 2001. Write an essay in which you discuss these ads in relation to the ads you find in those magazines. How are they similar? To what extent are they different? Judging from what you see here and from what you are familiar with in the magazines you can pick up on newsstands today, what is the primary claim in cosmetics ads? What are they actually selling in addition to the product?

3. This Visual Essay suggests that advertisers sell magic using many different kinds of products beyond cosmetics or fashion. Using this Visual Essay or one you put together from ads that you have collected, write an essay on "selling magic." Use these ads or your own to illustrate the essay.

It's a Woman Thing

Much discussion over the years has drawn the public's attention to the image of women in advertising. This Visual Essay, "It's a Woman Thing," illustrates some of the ways women appear in ads today. The ads reprinted below offer a good illustration of how sophisticated advertisers can be as they draw on and challenge gender stereotypes. Notice that, over a period of time, women have been portrayed in very different and yet somehow similar ways.

Of course, not all images of women are the same. You can easily extend and change this Visual Essay by collecting your own images from popular magazines.

As you examine images of people, notice that the way you as a viewer are being asked to relate to the person in the picture is often signaled by whether the person in the image is looking at or away from the camera (or you, as the imaginary viewer).

When the person in the image looks at you directly and at close range, a different message is sent than when the person is depicted looking down, away from, or beyond your gaze. Some images show the model only from behind, as if an imaginary viewer is looking at the model but the model is unaware of that intrusion (as in a lingerie ad). But if the person pictured from behind is clearly looking at and perhaps pointing to something else that the viewer can see in the distance (like the Grand Canyon or a new car), the suggestion is that the viewer can also see that object and be delighted by it or desire it. In other words, you can put yourself in the place of the person in the ad.

In *Reading Images: The Grammar of Visual Design* (Routledge, 1996), Gunther Kress and Theo van Leeuwen describe the position of the subject in an image as portraying either an **offer** or a **demand**. They explain the difference between the two in this way (pp. 122–124):

There is, then, a fundamental difference between pictures from which represented participants look directly at the viewer's eyes and pictures in which this is not the case. When represented participants look at the viewer, vectors, formed by participants' eyelines, connect the participants with the viewer. Contact is established, even if it is only on an imaginary level....[This representation] creates a visual form of direct address. It acknowledges the viewers explicitly, addressing them with a visual "you."...It is for this reason we have called this kind of image a "**demand**": the participant's gaze (and the gesture, if present) demands something from the viewer, demands that the viewer enter into some kind of imaginary relation with him or her. Exactly what kind of relation is then signified by other means, for instance by the facial expression of the represented participants. They may smile, in which case the viewer is asked to enter into a relation of social affinity with them; they may stare at the viewer with cold disdain, in which case the viewer is asked to relate to them, perhaps, as an inferior relates to a superior; they may seductively pout at the viewer, in which case the viewer is asked to desire them. The same applies to gestures. A hand can point at the viewer, in a visual "Hey, you there, I mean you", or invite the viewer to come closer, or hold the viewer at bay with a defensive gesture as if to say: stay away from me. In each case the image wants something from the viewers—wants them to do something (come closer, stay at a distance) or to form a pseudo-social bond of a particular kind with the represented participant....

Other pictures address us indirectly. Here the viewer is not object but subject of the look, and the represented participant is the object of the viewer's dispassionate scrutiny. No contact is made. The viewer's role is that of the invisible onlooker....we have called this kind of image an "**offer**"—it "offers" the represented participants to the viewer as items of information, objects of contemplation, impersonally, as though they were specimens in a display case.

As you examine the following collection of images, keep in mind how the woman in each image looks at or away from the viewer. Use this close attention to detail when you read an image for how it is representing the people being depicted or how stereotypes are conveyed through images. Use it also when you make your own images.

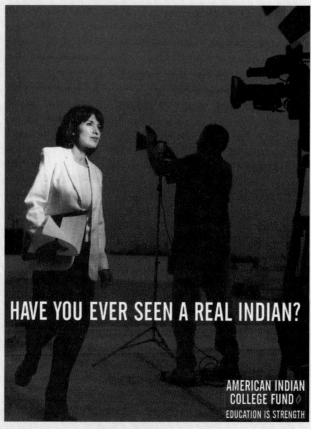

SUGGESTIONS FOR DISCUSSION

1. With a group of your classmates, look carefully at the ads reproduced here, paying particular attention to the manner in which each model is posed looking at or away from the viewer. Which women seem to be individuals? Which seem to be types? What kind of relationship, as Kress and van Leeuwen describe it, is each image setting up with the viewer? How is that relationship likely to change if the viewer is a man or a woman? What else, besides the viewer's gender, might determine the viewer's relationship to these images?

2. The ad for the American Indian College Fund offers an alternative image of women as well as an alternative image of American Indians. It originally appeared as a full-page ad in *Harpers Magazine* in February 2003. In your group, discuss how this ad attempts to challenge the way we see both women and American Indians. How might the message of this ad change depending on who reads it and where it appears?

3. How does the ad "Make Ours Doubles" both break with and conform to typical stereotypes of women in advertising?

Ripe Oregon strawberries are
especially selected as we

feel
it

best complements the rich cream
flavour of Häagen-Dazs.

Häagen-Dazs

Dedicated to Pleasure

SUGGESTIONS FOR WRITING

1. With a group of your classmates, examine this set of advertisements as a visual essay. Determine what the grouping and the sequence of the ads suggests or argues about the depiction of women in advertising today. What does the title refer to? How does the title influence the way a reader might understand this essay? Once you have completed your examination, write a group report in which you explain the argument of this Visual Essay.

2. After examining this Visual Essay, consider what it is saying about female stereotypes and think about what is left out or what you would want to say if you were asked to create a visual essay depicting the image of women in advertising.

   Once you have decided what you would add or change, revise this Visual Essay with images you find in several different sources. You might, for example, discover that the image of women changes in career women's magazines or in ads for different kinds of products.

   Or you might want to consider how the message changes depending on who is reading them or how the camera "treats" the woman being represented. Is there a distancing between the viewer and the model? Does the model look at you straight on? What is the effect of that look? Does the model do anything in the ad, or is she just an object to be looked at? Look for advertising that breaks with the common stereotype.

   Once you have created your revision of the book's Visual Essay, write a one-page explanation for what you found and why you revised the essay in the way you did.

3. Media analyst Jean Kilbourne has written, "The aspect of advertising most in need of analysis and change is the portrayal of women." Some readers think that claim is much too narrow. For this essay, begin collecting ads that focus on other stereotypes. Consider images of men, race, ethnicity, success, poverty, age, family, athletes, and so on. Once you have chosen a topic, collect as many as ten to twenty images. Collecting will be easier if, after you have scanned several magazines or watched commercials, you decide on a focus. For example, you might focus on the changing image of men in advertising. Or you might decide that, though there appears to be a change in the way men are depicted, that change is superficial and not much of a change at all. Sometimes it is easier to write about the stereotype when you find an image that breaks with that stereotype, so don't ignore images that at first do not seem to fit your argument. As you explain the stereotype of the group you have chosen, refer to the ads you have collected as examples of the points you want to make. Your position will be stronger if you can also refer to other places where the stereotype is common—in television sitcoms or Hollywood films, for example. You do not need to argue that women are not stereotyped or that there is no longer any need to pay attention to female stereotyping. Point to other groups that are in as much need of examination as the group chosen for this essay.

FACING DIFFERENCE: THE BLACK FEMALE BODY

bell hooks

A Distinguished Professor of English at City University of New York and leading cultural critic, bell hooks is the author of more than a dozen books on the politics of race, class, and gender. Her most recent work includes the books *Killing Rage (1995)*, *Outlaw Culture (1994)*, and *Art on My Mind (1995)*, from which the following selection has been taken. In it, hooks writes about the work of artist Lorna Simpson, whose compositions, hooks says, are very different from the images of women and particularly of black women in today's culture.

SUGGESTION FOR READING   In this article, hooks argues that Lorna Simpson provides a revolutionary image of black women, one that allows the reader to question traditional representations of women. Before you read, take time to look back at the Visual Essay "It's a Woman Thing." Write a brief summary of how the women in these images are represented.

1 Lorna Simpson's photograph *Waterbearer* was reproduced in 1987 in one of the early issues of *B Culture*, a progressive black newspaper of arts and culture that was fresh beyond all belief. For a brief moment in time *B Culture* was the expressive space for everything radical and black—it was on the edge. Of course, it disappeared. But not before publishing a full-page reproduction of *Waterbearer*.

After carefully pressing my newspaper copy with a hot iron, to remove all creases, I taped this page on the wall in my study, awed by the grace and profound simplicity of the image: a black woman with disheveled hair, seen from the back, pouring water from a jug and a plastic bottle, one in either hand. Underneath the photograph were the subversive phrases.

She saw him disappear by the river
They asked her to tell what happened
Only to discount her memory.

Subversive because it undoes its own seeming innocence, Simpson's portrait is reminiscent of Vermeer's paintings of working women—

She saw him disappear by the river
They asked her to tell what happened
Only to discount her memory.

Water Bearer by Lorna Simpson, 1986. Silver gelatin print, 45 × 77 × 1½ inches. Courtesy Sean Kelly Gallery, New York

maids standing silently by basins of water in still poses that carry no hint of emotional threat. Yet Simpson's language brings a threat to the fore. It invites us to consider the production of history as a cultural text, a narrative uncovering repressed or forgotten memory. And it declares the existence of subjugated knowledge.

Here in this image the keeper of history, the griot, the one who bears water as life and blessing, is a black woman. Her knowledge threatens, cannot be heard. She cannot bear witness. She is refused that place of authority and voice that would allow her to be a subject in history. Or so the phrases suggest. Yet this refusal is interrogated by the intensity of the image, and by the woman's defiant stance. By turning her back on those who cannot hear her subjugated knowledge speak, she creates by her own gaze an alter-native space where she is both self-defining and self-determining.

5   The two containers are reminders of the way history is held and shaped, yet the water that flows from each is constant, undifferentiated, a sign of transcendent possibility, a reminder that it is always possible to transform the self, to remake history. The water flows like a blessing. Despite changes, distortions, misinformation symbolized by its containers, the water will continue to sustain and nurture life. It will redeem. It is the water that allows the black woman figure to reclaim a place in history, to connect with ancestors past and present.

The black woman in the photograph understands that memory has healing power. She is not undone, not in any way torn apart by those dominating gazes that refuse her recognition.

Able to affirm the reality of her presence—of the absent him whose voice, unlike hers, might be listened to—she bears witness to the sound of the water and its meaning for her life. Hers is a portrait of serenity, of being, of making peace with oppositional history.

Few contemporary American artists have worked with images of the black female body in ways that are counterhegemonic. Since most black folks in the United States are colonized—that is think about "blackness" in much the same ways as racist white mainstream culture—simply being a black female artist does not mean one possesses the vision and insight to create groundbreaking revolutionary images of black females. Simpson's reimagining of the black female body not only presents these images in a new way, she does so in a manner that interrogates and intervenes on art practices in general. To do this, she turns her back, in a manner not unlike that of the figure in *Waterbearer*, on art practices that have been traditionally informed by racist and sexist ways of thinking about both the female image and blackness.

Living in white-supremacist culture, we mostly see images of black folks that reinforce and perpetuate the accepted, desired subjugation and subordination of black bodies by white bodies. Resisting these images, some black folks learn early in life to divert our gaze, much in the same way that we might shield a blow to the body. We shield our minds and imaginations by changing positions, by blocking the path, by simply turning away, by closing our eyes.

We learn to look at the images of blackness that abound in the popular cultural imagination with suspicion and mistrust, with the understanding that there may be nothing present in those images that is familiar to us, complex, or profound. Our eyes grow accustomed to images that reflect nothing of ourselves worth seeing close-up. As a survival strategy, aware black folks often cultivate a constructive disregard for the power of the image. Some of us just dismiss it.

10   Given this cultural context, we are often startled, stunned even, by representations of black images that engage and enchant. Creating counterhegemonic images of blackness that resist the stereotypes and challenge the artistic imagination is not a simple task. To begin with, artists have to engage in a process of education that encourages critical consciousness and enables them as individuals to break the hold of colonizing representations. Once that process is completed, they then have a space to map a new terrain—one that can emerge only from an imaginative inventiveness since there is no body of images, no tradition to draw on. Concurrently, even after the images are in place the art world may lack a critical language to speak to the complexities these images evoke. To see new and different images of blackness is to some extent shocking. Since images that are counterhegemonic are necessarily provocative, their seductiveness, their allure lie in the freshness of insight and vision. They fulfill longings that are oftentimes not yet articulated in words: the longing to look at blackness in ways that resist and go beyond the stereotype. Despite the tenacity of white supremacy as a worldview that overdetermines the production of images in this society, no power is absolute to the imagination. The practice of freedom in daily life, and that includes artistic freedom, is always a liberatory act that begins with the will to imagine.

Lorna Simpson's images of black female bodies are provocative and progressive precisely because she calls attention to aspects of black female identity that tend to be erased or overlooked in a racist sexist culture. Her work counters the stereotype. In the accepted version of black female reality that predominates in mainstream images there is no subtlety to our experience. We are always portrayed as lacking in complexity, as transparent. We are all surface, lacking in depth. Within mainstream art photography the vast majority of images representing black females are full frontal views of face or body. These images reaffirm the insistence on transparency, on the kind of surface understanding that says to the viewer, "What you see is what you get." Simpson's images interrogate this assumption, demanding that the viewer take another look, a closer look.

When I look at images of the black female body in Simpson's work, I see recorded an understanding of black female presence that counters racist/sexist stereotypes through the pronounced rejection of the fixed static vision of our identity that exists in the popular imagination. Yet Simpson's concern is not to simply interrogate, set the record straight. She wants us all to look again, to see what has never been seen, to bear witness.

Beginning with the understanding that common racist and sexist stereotypes of black female identity insist that our reality can be easily understood, that we are not mysterious, we confront images, in Simpson's work, that defy this norm. In general, in this culture, black women are seen and depicted as down to earth, practical, creatures of the mundane. Within sexist racist iconography, black females are most often represented as mammies, whores, or sluts. Caretakers whose bodies and beings are empty vessels to be filled with the needs of others. This imagery tells the world that the black female is born to serve—a servant—maid—made to order. She is not herself but always what someone else wants her to be. Against this backdrop of fixed colonizing images, Simpson constructs a world of black female bodies that resist and revolt, that intervene and transform, that rescue and recover.

Her images of black female bodies are initially striking because so many of them are not frontal images. Backs are turned, the bodies are sideways, specific body parts are highlighted—repositioned from the start in a manner that disrupts conventional ways of seeing and understanding black womanhood. This shift in focus is not simplistically calculated. The intent is that viewers look beyond the surface, ponder what lies beyond the gender and race of these subjects. Inviting us to think critically about the black female subject, Simpson positions her camera to document and convey a cultural genealogy based not on hard but on emotional realities, landscapes of the heart—a technology

of the sacred. Whereas female bodies in this culture depict us as hard, low down, mean, nasty, bitchified, Simpson creates images that give poetic expression to the ethereal, the prophetic dimensions of visionary souls shrouded in flesh. Evoking traditions that honor the goddess, she depicts black women in everyday life as if our being brings elegance and grace to whatever world we inhabit. Black female bodies are black madonnas in Simpson's work. In union with the earth, in touch with ancient properties, they embody the sacred. Charlene Spretnak contends in *States of Grace: The Recovery of Meaning in the Postmodern Age* that "When we experience consciousness of the unity in which are embedded, the sacred whole that is in and around, we exist in a state of grace. At such moments our consciousness perceives not only our individual self, but also our larger self, the self of the cosmos." This perfect union of body and spirit is there in the photograph *You're Fine*, where the black female body is surrounded by medical terminology and labels that define her as subordinate, that reduce her to disembodied parts as though she were subhuman. Yet the image that accompanies this text shows a black female reclining with an aura of serenity and repose in the midst of dehumanization. This flesh transcends the limits of domination and oppression which would confine and contain it.

15   Often Simpson playfully and ritualistically juxtaposes images of black females that interrogate the stereotypes by overtly naming them, imagistically, while conveying more radical disruptions at the same time. While series like *Five Day Forecast* and *Three Seated Figures* overtly articulate the mundane terrorism of racist objectification, images like the one presented in *Necklines* contextualize this dehumanization by addressing the history of slavery—a continuum of domination that moves.

Though commemorating and re-membering the past, reconstructing a useful legacy for the present, many of Simpson's photographs articulate the convergence of public and private reality. In *Time Piece* a black woman dressed in black is framed from behind, her story suppressed by the omnipresence of death. The litany that stands alongside this image tells us that death continues, that it is inevitable, that the specifics of black female death matter to few, that the details are not important. The recovery of meaning to black female death is enacted by the photographer, by she who wills recognition.

This abiding sense of memory and sustained grief is present in the series of photographs *Magdalena*. Here it is an empty shoe box, an image of shoes that bear witness. They are the everyday artifacts, left behind, that trace the dead back to the living. These artifacts converge and overlap with the reality of death and dying recorded in the text that bears witness: "at her burial I stood under the tree next to her grave." Yet this memory is juxtaposed with a second narrative that records a different reality: "when I returned the tree was a distance from her marker." In trying to gather the evidence to name black female experience, the reality and

diversity of lives, the facts are muddled, our memories unclear. How to name accurately that which has been distorted, erased, altered to suit the needs of other?

Simpson's photographs name that which is rarely articulated—a technology of the sacred that rejoins body, mind, and spirit. The plain white shifts worn by various black female figures in Simpson's work, like the simple garments worn by monks, are a repudiation of materiality. It is the spirit that matters, the soul flesh shrouds and hides. Beyond the realm of socially imposed identity, the limitations of race and gender, one encounters the metaphysical. Transcendent experiences, like death and dying, put into perspective the finite nature of human activity, the limits of human will and power. Despite all that is imposed on black female flesh, no coercive domination is powerful enough to alter that state of grace wherein the soul finds sanctuary, recovers itself. Simpson's work offers us bodies that bear witness. Through these images subjugated knowledge speaks—remakes history.

SUGGESTIONS FOR DISCUSSION

1. How does hooks's discussion of Lorna Simpson's representation of black females compare with the ways you have noticed women are usually depicted in art or advertising?

2. What is the typical image of black male bodies? How might an artist confront and overturn those representations?

3. Why does hooks begin with the story of her finding the Simpson photo and ironing it out to place on the wall of her study? What is she saying about the photo?

SUGGESTIONS FOR WRITING

1. Simpson's *The Waterbearer* is displayed with the following words running beneath it:

    She saw him disappear by the river

    They asked her to tell what happened

    Only to discount her memory

    Write an essay in which you explain how those words change the way a viewer "reads" this photograph. How does the photo change if the words are not included?

2. In her analysis of Simpson's work, hooks argues that it is very difficult to overturn stereotypes. She writes, "When I look at images of the black female body in Simpson's work, I see recorded an understanding of black female presence that counters racist/sexist stereotypes through the pronounced rejection of the fixed static vision of

our identity that exists in the popular imagination." Write a letter to a friend or trusted adult you would like to explain this message to. Look for images that you can photocopy and include for your point to be clear. Make hooks's arguments in a language your reader will best understand.

3. Collect a series of images of black male bodies and write an analysis of the traditional way black men are represented in art or advertising. You can use bell hooks as a starting point for your analysis, and then extend her discussion of black female representations to black male representations.

HYPE

Kalle Lasn

In the following excerpt from *Culture Jam: How to Reverse America's Suicidal Consumer Binge—and Why We Must (2000)*, Kalle Lasn advocates action meant to subvert the advertising industry. Lasn is the founder of *Adbusters Magazine*. Along with his colleagues at Adbusters Media Foundation, he helped popularize the notion of "culture jamming," which includes rewriting ads to create spoof ads and "uncommercials." His hard talk about advertising today indicates that he doesn't consider rewriting ads to be just something to do but rather to be something that is a necessary reaction to what he calls mental pollution.

SUGGESTION FOR READING   Notice that Lasn is direct about his criticism of advertising. Underline and annotate those places where Lasn's remarks seem especially direct, even angry toward advertising today.

1 Advertisements are the most prevalent and toxic of the mental pollutants. From the moment your radio alarm sounds in the morning to the wee hours of late-night TV, microjolts of commercial pollution flood into your brain at the rate of about three thousand marketing messages per day. Every day, an estimated 12 billion display ads, 3 million radio commercials, and more than 200,000 TV commercials are dumped into North America's collective pollution flood into your brain at the rate of about three thousand marketing messages per day. Every day, an estimated 12 billion display ads, 3 million radio commercials, and more than 200,000 TV commercials are dumped into North America's collective unconscious.

Corporate advertising (or is it the commercial media?) is the largest single psychological project ever undertaken by the human race. Yet for all of that, its impact on us remains unknown and largely ignored. When I think of the media's

influence over years, over decades, I think of those brainwashing experiments conducted by Dr. Ewen Cameron in a Montreal psychiatric hospital in the 1950s (Grierson). The idea of the CIA-sponsored "depatterning" experiments was to outfit conscious, unconscious, or semiconscious subjects with headphones, and flood their brains with thousands of repetitive "driving" messages that would alter their behavior over time. Sound familiar? Advertising aims to do the same thing. Dr. Cameron's guinea pigs emerged from the Montreal trials with serious psychological damage. It was a great scandal. But no one is saying boo about the ongoing experiment of mass media advertising. In fact, new guinea pigs voluntarily come on board every day.

The proliferation of commercial messages has happened so steadily and relentlessly that we haven't quite woken up to the absurdity of it all. No longer are ads confined to the usual places: buses, billboards, stadiums. Anywhere your eyes can possibly come to rest is now a place that, in corporate America's view, can and ought to be filled with a logo or product message.

You reach down to pull your golf ball out of the hole and there, at the bottom of the cup, is an ad for a brokerage firm. You fill your car with gas, there's an ad on the nozzle. You wait for your bank machine to spit out money and an ad pushing GICs scrolls by in the little window. You drive through the heartland and the view of the wheatfields is broken at intervals by enormous billboards. Your kids watch Pepsi and Snickers ads in the classroom. (The school has made the devil's bargain of accepting free audiovisual equipment in exchange for airing these ads on "Channel One.") You think you've seen it all, but you haven't. An Atlanta-based marketing firm announces plans to send an inflatable billboard filled with corporate logos into geostationary orbit viewable every night like a second moon. British sprinter Linford Christie appears at a press conference with little panthers replacing the pupils of his eyes, where his sponsor's logo has been imprinted on specially made contact lenses. New York software engineers demonstrate a program that turns your cursor into a corporate icon whenever you visit a commercial site. A Japanese schoolboy becomes a neon sign during his daily two-hour subway commute by wearing a battery-powered vest promoting an electronics giant. Administrators in a Texas school district announce plans to boost revenues by selling ad space on the roofs of the district's seventeen schools—arresting the attention of the fifty-eight million commercial jet passengers who fly into Dallas each year. Kids tattoo their calves with swooshes. Other kids, at raves, begin wearing actual bar codes that other kids can scan, revealing messages such as "I'd like to sleep with you." A boy named David Bentley in Sydney, Australia, literally rents his head to corporate clients, shaving a new ad into his hair every few weeks. ("I know

for sure that at least two thousand teenagers at my high school will read my head every day to see what it says," says the young entrepreneur. "I just wish I had a bigger head.") You pick up a banana at a supermarket and there, on a little sticker, is an ad for the new summer blockbuster at the multiplex. ("It's interactive because you have to peel them off", says one ad executive of this new delivery system. "And people look at ten pieces of fruit before they pick one, so we get multiple impressions.") Boy Scouts in the U.K. sell corporate ad space on their merit badges. An Australian radio station dyes its logo on two million eggs. IBM beams its logo onto clouds above San Francisco with a scanning electron microscope and a laser—the millennial equivalent of Commissioner Gordon summoning Batman to the Batcave. (The image is visible from ten miles away.) Bestfoods unveils plans to stamp its Skippy brand of peanut butter onto the crisp tabula rasa of a New Jersey beach each morning at low tide, where it will push peanut butter for a few hours before being washed away by the waves. (The company is widely commended for its environmental responsibility.) Coca-Cola strikes a six-month deal with the Australian postal service for the right to cancel stamps with a Coke ad. A company called VideoCarte installs interactive screens on supermarket carts so that you can see ads while you shop. (A company executive calls the little monitors "the most powerful micromarketing medium available today.")

5   A few years ago, marketers began installing ad boards in men's washrooms on college campuses, at eye level above the urinals. From their perspective, it was a brilliant coup: Where else is a guy going to look? But when I first heard this was being done, I was incensed. One of the last private acts was being co-opted. "What's been the reaction on campus?" I asked the reporter who told me the story. "Not much reaction," he said. It became apparent, as these ad boards began springing up in bars and restaurants, and

just about anywhere men stand to pee, that not only did guys not share my outrage, they actually welcomed a little diversion while nature took its course.

This flood of psycho-effluent is spreading all around us, and we love every minute of it. The adspeak means nothing. It means worse than nothing. It is "anti-language" (Dee) that, whenever it runs into truth and meaning, annihilates it.

There is nowhere to run. No one is exempt and no one will be spared. In the silent moments of my life, I often used to hear the opening movement of Beethoven's Ninth Symphony playing in my head. Now I hear that kid singing the Oscar Meyer Wiener song.

NOTES

Dee, Jonathan, "But Is it Advertising?" *Harper's*, January 1999, page 66.

Grierson, Bruce, "Soul Shock," *Adbusters*, Winter 1998, page 18.

SUGGESTIONS FOR DISCUSSION

1. What does Lasn mean by "mental pollution"?

2. At the end of this selection, Lasn tells the story of ad boards being placed in men's washrooms on college campuses. Check out your own campus. Where do ads appear that make it nearly impossible to avoid them?

3. Watch an episode of a popular television sitcom and count the number of product placement ads (products with actual product names showing on camera) in the episode. With a group of your classmates, compare the results you each got as you watched television for placement ads. How effective are product placement ads as what Lasn calls "mental pollution"?

SUGGESTIONS FOR WRITING

1. Make an ad survey of one part of your campus. Note where the ads appear, what they advertise, and whether or not you can avoid seeing or reading them. Write a report on your findings to present to your classmates. If you have access to a camera, use photos to illustrate your findings.

2. Advertisers work very hard to create logos (such as MacDonalds' arches or Nike's swish) and product labels (Captain Krunch or Cheerios) that serve as a sort of shorthand so that people recognize the product every time they see the logo or the label. In fact, most Americans can probably name a product they remember as a child, still recognize today, and perhaps are still loyal to today because of childhood associations and the familiar label. Write a personal essay on product loyalty. What product do you continue to use today because of commercials or familiar logos? How have ads, logos, labels, and childhood associations helped build that product loyalty for you?

3. Write an essay as a response to or an imitation of Lasn's "Hype" about an advertising campaign that you find troublesome or just plain irritating. It might be the way the advertiser represents women or hip clothing or the Christmas season or it could even be the jingle (like that Oscar Mayer wiener song) that you can't get out of your head once you've heard it.

VISUAL ESSAY

Rewriting the Image

Advertising doesn't just create "images," it constructs differences between men and women, which operate under the assumption that they reflect a universal timeless truth. And so it is never merely a case of a good image versus a bad image. Looking itself has to be rewritten....

It is time for some interventions in the belly of the beast.

There are many methods for upsetting the echelons of imagery. There is no one perfect way to intervene, not when the gospel of perfection is the very text being tampered with. From critiques to billboard activism, the creation of alternative imagery to boycotts and protests, strategic intervention is needed on all fronts. Humor and the unexpected are always good tools for deconstructing the codes the advertising world operates under.

—Katherine Dodds, writing in *Adbusters Magazine*

Writing over, remaking or talking back to an image is a tactic that has been around for a long time. Look, for example, at Marcel Duchamp's remake of Leonardo's *Mona Lisa*. The DaVinci portrait had been held up for so long as a masterpiece of Renaissance art that Duchamp, trying to change the way people see the classics, did the unthinkable: He painted a mustache on the *Mona Lisa* (well, actually, on a reproduction of the *Mona Lisa*). It was, it could be argued, one of the most effective acts of graffiti ever created. It shocked many in the art world and those who considered the masterpieces sacred, and it made the public laugh. At the same time, it also made a statement about how art had to change, new voices had to be heard, and new images had to be accepted.

In the same way, the Canadian-based organization Adbusters advocates rewriting ads that represent unhealthy products, products that promote stereotypes, and products that exploit workers. In the article from which Katherine Dodds's statement is taken, she writes of the importance of this act of taking control of advertising images, many of which you have read and written about in this chapter.

Sometimes, though, a rewrite isn't meant to change attitudes or attack stereotypes at all. Sometimes a rewrite is simply necessary, in a world so thick with images, if anyone is ever to say something new, or to revise the ways people see each other, or even to laugh at themselves. Rewriting the image can be activism, as Dodds suggests, but it can also be a way of understanding how images function so that people aren't simply consumers but are also producers of the image.

Of course, if people are going to complain about what's produced out there, then the best way to change it is to change it.

SUGGESTION FOR READING

Because parody depends on knowledge of the original to make its point, the message that results from the parody or rewriting threatens to change one's response to the original. Duchamp, for example, certainly wanted to change the way viewers saw the *Mona Lisa*. As you look at the images here, make notes for yourself on how the rewrite makes you rethink the original image.

Mona Lisa by Leonardo da Vinci, 1503–1506.

L.H.O.O.Q. by Marcel Duchamp, 1930.

The Grand Odalisque by Jean Auguste Dominique Ingres, 1814

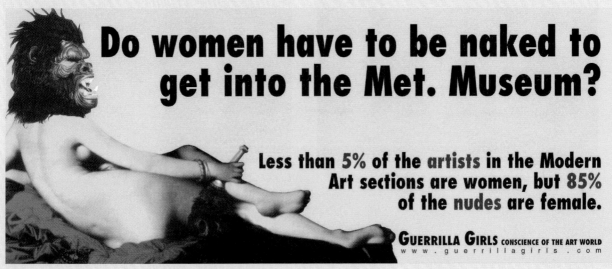

Guerilla Girls' poster displayed on New York City buses

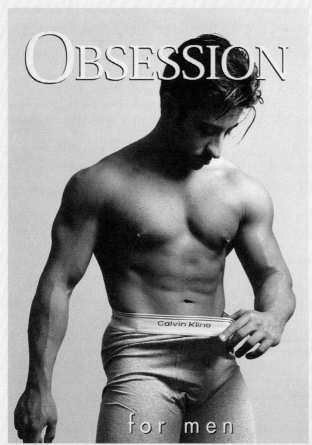

Adbusters spoof Ad

Adbusters spoof Ad

SUGGESTIONS FOR DISCUSSION

1. Like Elizabeth and Stuart Ewens, Lasn describes a contemporary world surrounded by images that work on our unconscious mind all of the time. Quickly review the Ewens' article. In what ways is their argument similar to Lasn's? In what ways are their positions on advertising very different?

2. Some people are offended by the images that are the result of writing over classic paintings. Others find the rewrites to be funny or powerful statements about the originals. What is your response to the Guerrilla Girls' rewrite of Ingres' *Odalisque*? How would you account for your response?

3. With a group of your classmates, choose a popular image to rewrite or parody. Present your rewrite to the class, and explain what your group wanted to accomplish with the image that you created.

SUGGESTIONS FOR WRITING

1. Choose an advertisement or series of ads that illustrates Dodds's statement that advertising "constructs differences between men and women, which operate under the assumption that they reflect a universal timeless truth." Write a brief explanation of what Dodds means, then use your ad or ads to explain how, as Dodds suggests, "Looking itself has to be rewritten." To do that, write over the ads, creating a parody, or explain what a reader needs to understand to look at these images differently.

2. When you rewrite an advertisement as Adbusters suggests, your purpose usually is to bring to the surface the oppositional readings that are possible in any ad image. In the Adbuster ad, for example, the word *Obsession* is taken literally and applied to consumers of Calvin Klein ads. In that way, the ad takes on a powerful new meaning. Find an ad image that you would like to rewrite, and redo the image in a way that clearly draws on the original yet brings to the surface a new and oppositional reading of the original.

3. Choose any kind of image—T-shirts, posters, cereal boxes, magazine covers, commercials, famous paintings, covers from textbooks or novels. Rewrite the image so that you bring an alternate reading of that image to the surface or so that you create an entirely new meaning. One T-shirt rewrite that has become a popular tourist souvenir, for example, is the shirt that reads, "My parents went to Paris and all I got was this lousy T-shirt." It's a rewrite because it acknowledges the habit of buying souvenir T-shirts as gifts to placate family and friends left at home. As well, Duchamp's rewrite of *Mona Lisa* only makes its point if you think *Mona Lisa* is a great work of art that shouldn't be changed. To make your own rewrite, you will have to understand the original message, so pay attention to how the image conveys the meaning it carries at this time, and use the original to create your own image. The image you choose and the meaning you make with that image depends on your interests and on the interests of your intended audience. For whom are you making this image? Classmates? Parents? A "general audience" of readers in a particular age group?

Public Health Messages

Public health campaigns take several forms, with messages that appear everywhere from billboards and subway posters to newspaper and magazine ads to public service announcements on radio and television. Like advertising, public health messages are intended to persuade readers, viewers, and listeners to do something. In the case of public health publicity, however, the pitch is not to buy a product but to live a healthy lifestyle—to eat a balanced diet, stop smoking, drink in moderation, avoid drugs, exercise regularly, use a condom, immunize your kids, or have annual checkups.

Like advertising, public health publicity uses images that readers and viewers will recognize immediately to get its message across. The "be sexy" Candie's Foundation ad, for example, uses a male model who looks like he could just as easily be in a fashion advertisement. This message ran in the magazine *Elle Girl*, the teen version of the upscale fashion magazine *Elle,* and obviously assumes that young people want to be sexy. It's an ad that argues for teen abstinence rather than safe sex while it draws from all of the codes of sultriness and sexuality these readers would be familiar with from ads in the same magazine.

As is true in all advertising, agencies designing public health messages face decisions about how to sell the message: Should the publicity emphasize the negative consequences of unhealthy behavior or the positive benefits of a healthy lifestyle? Some of the most interesting cases of how public health messages use images can be found in publicity concerning sexually transmitted diseases (STDs). The following Visual Essay includes four examples:

- The first two posters were directed at men in the military during World War II.
- The third example is the cover of a recent pamphlet for teens on STDs.
- The final message is a bus-stop bench that was painted by the cartoonist Mike McNeilly in an "Art Attacks AIDS" program.

SUGGESTION FOR READING

As you look at these public health messages, consider how each uses a familiar image or images and whether it emphasizes negative consequences or positive benefits.

SUGGESTIONS FOR DISCUSSION

1. The first two posters were part of a World War II campaign to stem the spread of syphilis and gonorrhea—the most widespread STDs, or venereal diseases (VD)—among allied forces. Notice how each poster portrays women. In the first, a female death figure representing VD is accompanied by Hitler of Nazi Germany and Hirohito of Japan. What assumptions do these posters seem to make about the role of women in spreading STDs? What assumptions do they seem to make about male sexual behavior?

2. Consider the cover of the pamphlet on STDs. It uses a familiar image of romantic love, the rose. How do the public health messages use these familiar images to get their point across? To what extent do the messages emphasize negative consequences or positive benefits?

3. The final example—the bus-stop bench by cartoonist Mike McNeilly—is different from the other public health messages. How would you describe McNeilly's approach? How is it different from or similar to the other examples? Why do you think he has chosen this approach? Do you think it is effective? Why or why not?

SUGGESTIONS FOR WRITING

1. Work with two other classmates. Assemble several public health messages on STDs. (Your campus health center is a good resource, but also notice messages posted around campus or in other public places.) Analyze the kinds of images that appear in the public health publicity. Do your examples use familiar images? If so, are they used in expected or unexpected ways? Do the images seem to transmit messages about negative consequences or positive benefits (or some combination of the two)? How effective do you think the publicity is, given its intended audience? Prepare a report that explains your findings.

2. Design your own public health publicity. Choose any topic you find to be interesting and important (e.g., smoking, drugs, diet, exercise, STDs, alcohol). Decide on your intended audience—college students, teenagers, pregnant women, new mothers. Fashion your message so that it speaks to the particular audience you have in mind. Choose carefully the image or images that can best convey your message.

3. Examine the public health images reprinted here. Each is designed to appeal to a specific audience at a specific time. Choose one of these images for an analysis of how the ad targets that audience and what images, ideals, or ideas the ad takes advantage of from popular culture to create that message.

A WAY OF SEEING: AN INTRODUCTION TO THE PHOTOGRAPHS OF HELEN LEVITT

James Agee

American writer James Agee (1909–1953) worked as a journalist, a playwright, and a novelist, but he is perhaps best remembered today for his collaboration with Walker Evans in the 1941 publication *Let Us Now Praise Famous Men,* which combined Evans's photos of southern sharecroppers with Agee's observations on the lives of the people he and Evans met and lived with in the summer of 1936. In 1946, Agee teamed up with photographer Helen Levitt, who had, since the mid-1930s, been photographing the street life in New York City, and especially in Spanish Harlem. Together, they planned the collection of photos they called *A Way of Seeing,* from which the photos here are reprinted. Levitt continued to be active throughout her life. In 2002, she published *Crosstown: Photographs by Helen Levitt,* a major retrospective of her documentary work.

SUGGESTION FOR READING   As you read, keep in mind that Agee is both introducing Levitt as a photographer and artist and developing an argument for photography as an uncompromising visual record and as a fine art form. Keep track, by underlining and annotating this passage, of how Agee makes that argument.

1   The mind and the spirit are constantly formed by, and as constantly form, the senses, and misuse or neglect the senses only at grave peril to every possibility of wisdom and well-being. The busiest and most abundant of the senses is that of sight. The sense of sight has been served and illuminated by the visual arts for as long, almost, as we have been human. For a little over a hundred years, it has also been served by the camera. Well used, the camera is unique in its power to develop and to delight our ability to see. Ill or indifferently used, it is unique in its power to defile and to destroy that ability. It is clear enough by now to most people that "the camera never lies" is a foolish saying. Yet it is doubtful whether most people realize how extraordinarily slippery a liar the camera is. The camera is just a machine, which records with impressive and as a rule very cruel faithfulness, precisely what is in the eye, mind, spirit, and skill of its operator to make it record. Since relatively few of its operators are notably well endowed in any of these respects, save perhaps in technical skill, the results are, generally, disheartening. It is probably well on the conservative side to estimate that during the past ten to fifteen years the camera has destroyed a thousand pairs of eyes, corrupted ten thousand, and seriously deceived a hundred thousand, for every one pair that it has opened, and taught.

It is in fact hard to get the camera to tell the truth; yet it can be made to, in many ways and on many levels. Some of the best photographs we are ever likely to see are innocent domestic snapshots, city postcards, and news and scientific photographs. If we know how, moreover, we can enjoy and learn a great deal from essentially untrue photographs, such as studio portraits, movie romances, or the national and class types apotheosized in ads for life insurance and feminine hygiene. It is a good deal harder to tell the truth, in this medium, as in all others, at the level of perception and discipline on which an artist works, and the attempt to be "artistic" or, just as bad, to combine "artistry" with something that pays better, has harmed countless photographs

New York, c. 1942. © Helen Levitt. Courtesy Laurence Miller Gallery, New York

for every one it has helped, and is harming more all the time. During the century that the camera has been available, relatively few people have tried to use it at all consistently as an artist might, and of these very few indeed could by any stretch of courtesy be called good artists. Among these few, Helen Levitt is one of a handful who have to be described as good artists, not loosely, or arrogantly, or promotively, but simply because no other description will do.

In every other art which draws directly on the actual world, the actual is transformed by the artist's creative intelligence, into a new and different kind of reality: aesthetic reality. In the kind of photography we are talking about here, the actual is not at all transformed; it is reflected and recorded, within the limits of the camera, with all possible accuracy. The artist's task is not to alter the world as the eye sees it into a world of aesthetic reality, but to perceive the aesthetic

New York, c. 1942. © Helen Levitt. Courtesy Laurence Miller Gallery, New York

reality within the actual world, and to make an undisturbed and faithful record of the instant in which this movement of creativeness achieves its most expressive crystallization. Through his eye and through his instrument the artist has, thus, a leverage upon the materials of existence which is unique, opening to him a universe which has never before been so directly or so purely available to artists, and requiring of his creative intelligence and of his skill, perceptions and dis-

ciplines no less deep than those required in any other act of aesthetic creation, though very differently deprived, and enriched.

The kind of beauty he records may be so monumentally static, as it is in much of the work of Mathew Brady, Eugène Atget, and Walker Evans, that the undeveloped eye is too casual and wandering to recognize it. Or it may be so filled with movement, so fluid and so transient, as it is in much of the work of Henri Cartier-Bresson and

New York, c. 1940. © Helen Levitt. Courtesy Laurence Miller Gallery, New York

of Miss Levitt, that the undeveloped eye is too slow and too generalized to foresee and to isolate the most illuminating moment. It would be mistaken to suppose that any of the best photography is come at by intellection; it is, like all art, essentially the result of an intuitive process, drawing on all that the artist *is* rather than on anything he thinks, far less theorizes about. But it seems quite natural, though none of the artists can have made any choice in the matter, that the static work is generally the richest in meditativeness, in mentality, in attentiveness to the wonder of materials and of objects, and in complex multiplicity of attitudes of perception, whereas the volatile work is richest in emotion; and that, though both kinds, at their best, are poetic in a very high degree, the static work has a kind of Homeric or Tolstoyan nobility, as in Brady's photographs, or a kind of Joycean denseness, insight and complexity resolved in its bitter purity, as in the work of Evans; whereas the best of the volatile work is nearly always lyrical.

5   It is remarkable, I think, that so little of this lyrical work has been done; it is perhaps no less remarkable that, like nearly all good photographic art, the little that has been done has been so narrowly distributed and so little appreciated. For it is, after all, the simplest and most direct way of seeing the everyday world, the most nearly related to the elastic, casual and subjective way in which we ordinarily look around us. One would accordingly suppose that, better than any other kind of photography, it could bring pleasure, could illuminate and enhance our ability to see what is before us and to enjoy what we see, and could relate all that we see to the purification and healing of our emotions and of our spirit, which in our time are beguiled with such

unprecedented dangerousness towards sickness and atrophy.

I do not at all well understand the reasons for the failure, but a few possibilities may be worth mentioning in passing. For a long time the camera was too slow, large, and conspicuous to work in the fleeting and half-secret world which is most abundant in lyrical qualities. More recently it has become all but impossible, even for those who had it in the first place, to maintain intact and uncomplicated the simple liveliness of soul and of talent without which true lyrical work cannot be done. As small, quick, foolproof cameras became generally available, moreover, the camera has been used so much and so flabbily by so many people that it has acted as a sort of contraceptive on the ability to see. And more recently, as the appetite for looking at photographs has grown, and has linked itself with the worship of "facts," and as a prodigious apparatus has been developed for feeding this appetite, the camera has been used professionally, a hundred times to one, in ways which could only condition and freeze the visual standards of a great majority of people at a relatively low grade.

As a further effect of this freezing and standardization, photographers who really have eyes, and who dare to call their eyes their own, and who do not care to modify them towards this standardized, acceptable style, have found it virtually impossible to get their work before most of those who might enjoy it; or to earn, through such work, the food, clothing, shelter, leisure, and equipment which would make the continuance of that work possible. Almost no photographer whose work is preeminently worth looking at has managed to produce more than a small fraction of the work he was capable of, and the work, as a rule, has remained virtually unknown except to a few friends and fellow artists. This is true to a great extent, of course, of artists who work in any field. Yet distinctions, standards, and assumptions exist and have existed for centuries which guarantee a good poet or painter or composer an audience, if generally a small one; and these are not yet formed in relation to photographs. In its broad design, however, this is a familiar predicament, as old as art itself, and as tiresome at least, one may assume, to the artists who suffer the consequences as to the nonartists to whom it is just a weary cliché. I don't propose to discuss who, if anyone, is to blame, being all the less interested in such discussion because I don't think anyone is to blame. I mention it at all only because I presume that the distinction between faithfulness to one's own perceptions and a readiness to modify them for the sake of popularity and self-support is still to be taken seriously among civilized human beings; and because it helps, in its way, to place and evaluate Miss Levitt's work.

At least a dozen of Helen Levitt's photographs seem to me as beautiful, perceptive, satisfying, and enduring as any lyrical work that I know. In their general quality and coherence, moreover, the photographs as a whole body, as a book, seem to me to combine into a unified view of the world, an uninsistent but irrefutable manifesto of a way of seeing, and in a gentle and wholly unpretentious way, a major poetic work. Most of these photographs are about as near the pure spontaneity of true folk art as the artist, aware of himself as such, can come; and an absolute minimum of intellection, of technical finesse, or of any kind of direction or interference on the part of the artist as artist stands between the substance and the emotion and their communication.

It is of absolute importance, of course, that all of these photographs are "real" records; that the photographer did not in any way prepare, meddle with, or try to improve on any one of them. But this is not so important of itself as, in so many of them, unretouched reality is shown transcending itself. Some, to be sure, are so perfectly simple, warm and direct in their understanding of a face or of an emotion that they are likely to mean a great deal to anyone who cares much for human beings: it would be hard to imagine anyone who would not be touched by all that is shown—by all that so beautifully took place in the unimagined world.

SUGGESTIONS FOR DISCUSSION

1. What does Agee mean when he says that the camera is a "slippery liar" and that it "is in fact hard to get the camera to tell the truth"?

2. Agee writes that most art transforms the real world into a new kind of reality. Helen Levitt's photography does not transform. Instead, the actual "is reflected and recorded, within the limits of the camera, with all possible accuracy. The artist's task is not to alter the world...but to perceive the aesthetic reality within the actual world." What does he mean by that? In what ways do the photos reproduced here not transform the actual but find the beauty in what is already there?

3. Choose one of the photographs reproduced here and, with a group of your classmates, discuss what the photo shows. What are the relationships between the people in the photo, for example? How do you know? What is the position of the viewer? What do you think is happening in the photograph?

SUGGESTIONS FOR WRITING

1. Agee writes, "In their general quality and coherence, moreover, the photographs as a whole body, as a book, seem to me to combine into a unified view of the world, an uninsistent but irrefutable manifesto of a way of seeing." In preparation for this writing, reread the selection excerpted here and spend some time looking at the photographs reproduced from this collection. In a brief (two to three page) response, explain what that "way of seeing" is. How would you describe the world Helen Levitt depicts here? What other choices might a documentary photographer make that would change the view of the world that Levitt gives here?

2. In *Camera Lucida,* Roland Barthes' book-length study of how photographs convey meaning, he writes that there is always some detail, something special in a good photograph that makes us take notice, that arouses our curiosity, and that gives the photograph its power over us. He called that detail the "punctum" and said it might be as simple as a missing shoe or as complicated as the way the subject of the photograph looks at the camera or the association a viewer has with the subject of the photo. Whatever the detail, it is what makes us wonder or laugh or cry or simply want to keep looking at the image.

    Choose one of Levitt's photographs or a photo that has always captured your imagination, and in a brief analysis, explain what detail makes this a powerful or interesting photograph for you.

3. As Agee says, the camera can be brutal and it can be kind. It is a technology that depends very much on who is looking through the lens when the picture is taken. For this assignment, you need a camera—even a single-use disposable camera will do. Choose a place, a group of people, or an event and make a series of photographs that conveys your own "way of seeing" that subject.

    Arrange your photographs in a notebook and write an introduction to the photos. You will have to make choices. Not every photo you take will be worth putting in your book. Use the introduction to examine the nature of amateur photography today or to explain the challenge of using the camera to present what you want others to know about a place or group of people, for example. What you say is up to you and will be deter-

CHECKING OUT THE WEB

1. The Library of Congress currently maintains a Web site for the American Memory Project: Historical Collections for the National Digital Library. The American Memory Project boasts more than seven million digital items in its collections. Primary among these is a vast collection of photographs from the Farm Security Administration and other historical photographs relating to the cultural and social history of the United States. The collection has anything from Civil War-era photos to historical and contemporary posters.

    The current URL for the American Memory Project is http://lcweb2.loc.gov. From here, you can search the collections for prints and photographs related to U.S. cultural history. For example, linked to the page titled "America from the Great Depression to World War II: Black and White Photographs from the FSA–OWI 1935–1945" (http://lcweb2.loc.gov/ammem/fsahtml/fahome.html), is the special presentation "Documenting America: Photographers on Assignment." Here is a list of the work of several Depression-era photographers including Walker Evans. You might, for example, choose to compare his collection "New York City Block," taken in 1938, with Helen Levitt's scenes of New York street life taken around the same time. How do the two collections embody what Agee called a "manifesto for a way of seeing" the world?

2. After browsing several of the collections from the American Memory Project, write a report on how the Library of Congress is shaping a view of America—a "way of seeing" America. Is there a prevailing theme in this collection? It is obviously an immense collection of materials, but is there a point of view that you can't readily find in the collection?

3. The magazine *Adbusters* has been mentioned several times throughout this chapter. Like many organizations and corporations these days, *Adbusters* also maintains a Web site where you can find examples of current spoof ads and can submit a spoof ad of your own. Go to the site, find out how you can submit an ad, and create a spoof ad for submission to the site.

mined by the subject you choose and the pictures you get, so wait until you have compiled your collection before you write your introduction.

This is an assignment that will take time. You will have to choose a subject, take the pictures, get the pictures developed, and write your introductory essay. Don't count on one-hour photo services because they are not always reliable and don't develop all types of film in one hour. If you have access to a digital camera, you can get your images immediately, but make sure you have access to a computer and printer that is compatible with your equipment before you commit yourself to digital work.

Advertising Through the Ages

Locate old copies of any popular magazine. *Good Housekeeping*, for example, began publication in January 1900, so it represents a full century of magazine design. You'll see a dramatic change, especially in advertising design over these years.

How do the claims of older ads compare with claims in today's advertisements for the same products? For example, how do they sell magic?

Once you have found several ads ranging from the early to the mid to the late twentieth century, write a report on your findings, comparing the ad copy (written text) of older ads with current advertising. What role do pictoral elements play in those older ads?

How would you describe the change in design over the years? This kind of report is easier to write if you choose one type of product for a focus—for example, cosmetics, bath soaps, laundry detergent, cigarettes.

If you don't have access to a good library, you can find a stockpile of ads from newspapers and magazines between 1911 and 1955 at Duke University *Ad*Access Project*. This project is housed in the Rare Book, Manuscript, and Special Collections room at the Duke University Library and can be accessed on the Internet at http://scriptorium.lib.duke.edu/adaccess. The site also includes useful information about copyright and fair use policies for using images for your class projects.

CHAPTER 5 Style

Diana George

Americans live in a style-conscious culture—even elementary school children know the difference between Air Jordans and the cheaper imitations. By the time they enter junior high school, most American adolescents are already highly skilled at distinguishing between brand names. They are learning to recognize the difference, say, between the Gap and Wal-Mart, between the Pottery Barn and Sears, between a Ford Taurus and a BMW. And, of course, they are also learning that these differences *make a difference*.

The point is more than the importance of being able to recognize brand names, though this is certainly of great interest to consumers and manufacturers alike. The real lesson young Americans learn is that they live in a world where it matters what brand of clothes or furniture or car they buy. It matters what style of music they listen to, how they wear their hair, whether they're tatooed or pierced, and what kind of food they like to eat. Even mundane personal belongings—everyday use-objects from staplers to toothbrushes to laptop computers—matter too.

All of these things matter because the styles we follow and products we use send messages about who we are. They're part of the identity kits we all put together to make up a self.

In many ways, it seems that such a concern for personal style and the appearance of objects is shallow and trivial. After all, what does it really matter whether or not someone's clothes or music or CD player or computer is at the cutting edge of style? Why should anyone care? One reason is that style is a guide to economic and social class in America. Style identifies. Whether consciously or unconsciously, we make judgments about people based on their appearance and their style. Simply by growing up in American culture, we acquire a sense of the style appropriate to different walks of life—how, for example, a high school teacher, a business executive, a truck driver, or a rock star ought to look.

Style communicates messages about economic and social class precisely because we share with others cultural codes that define what's normal and expected. For example, we expect wealthy professionals in metropolitan areas to be museum members, go to the opera, and enjoy gourmet food and fine wine. On the other hand, we are likely to expect that working-class men in the Midwest drink beer, listen to classic rock or country & western, and support their local pro football team. This doesn't mean that everyone in a particular social group conforms to these cultural codes. What it does indicate, however, is that style carries cultural meanings that go far beyond individual likes and dislikes.

Style, in other words, is linked to the way of life that identifies groups of people, cultures, and subcultures. If the styles we adopt seem to be freely taken personal choices, they are contained nonetheless in a larger system of cultural codes that organize the way we think about identity, social status, prestige, good (and bad) taste, tradition, and innovation. The role of food is a good example. On the one hand, the style of food people eat can reaffirm their ties to the ethnicity and traditions of their ancestors, as has been the case for generations of Italian Americans, Chinese Americans, Mexican Americans, and others in the United States. On the other hand, food may serve as the basis for a break with the lifestyle of one's upbringing and a new identification with a different group of people, as may be the case when people become vegetarians or convert to Islam and stop eating pork. Think of it this way: It would be nearly unimaginable to have the countercultural styles of hippies, punks, grunge, and goths without also having a recognized mainstream cultural code that can be rejected, parodied, violated, or otherwise rebelled against.

Fashion designers, graphic designers, and product designers understand this intimate connection between style and identity. They design everything from corporate logos and brand trademarks to the latest style of jeans and athletic shoes to computers and cars. Their job is to match styles to people's identities and, at the same time, to create styles that offer people new identities. But in spite of all these outside influences, people still make choices about what they wear, the products they use, the music they listen to, the way they decorate their living space, and so on, that matches their own personal style of life.

This chapter will be looking at both rebel designers, such as the punks of the 1970s and 1980s who created a whole new style and cultural identity out of mainstream objects, and the professional designers whose work floods the contemporary marketplace.

Reading Style

This chapter opens with Dick Hebdige's "Style in Revolt: Revolting Style," which explores the role style played in the punk movement's defiance of mainstream cultural codes and introduces the Visual Essay "Graphic Design in Rock Culture."

The next set of readings offers several perspectives on analyzing style in product design. Richard Porch considers the message sent by the design style in "Digital

Watches: Tribal Bracelets of Consumer Society," and Judith Williamson, in "Urban Spaceman," looks at the effects on urban lifestyles of the Walkman cassette or CD player. The final reading in this cluster pairs Steven Skov Holt's consideration of recent trends in product design, "Beauty and Blob: Product Culture Now," with the Visual Essay "The Age of Blobjects."

The chapter next turns to the controversy over branding, bringing together the perspective of the anticorporate activist Naomi Klein in "No Logo," the probusiness views of *The Economist* in "Who's Wearing the Trousers," and an enlightening exchange, "No Sweat, No Slang" between Jonah Peretti and Nike. This section closes with a Visual Essay, "Sweet-Talking Spaghetti Sauce: How to Read a Label" by the late and great graphic designer Tibor Kalman.

The reading selections are wrapped up with a Classic Reading, "Wine and Milk," from Roland Barthes' collection of essays *Mythologies*.

As in the chapter "Images," you will be asked to pay particular attention to visual detail—the visual elements that combine to make up a style and how designers, whether professionals or ordinary people, link style to identity.

STYLE IN REVOLT: REVOLTING STYLE

Dick Hebdige

Dick Hebdige is a lecturer in communication at Goldsmith College, University of London. The following selection comes from *Subculture: The Meaning of Style* (1979), in which he examines the political and cultural importance of postwar British youth cultures, including the punk movement. In this excerpt, Hebdige looks at how the punks used style as a tool of disruption and revolt. This selection is also an introduction to the Visual Essay that follows, "Graphic Design in Rock Culture."

SUGGESTION FOR READING   As you read, notice the range of evidence Hebdige brings forward to characterize the style of punk culture. Underline as many different examples of punk style as you can find. Notice too how the final paragraph on graphic design and typography serves as an introduction to the graphic style of the rock posters and T-shirts in the Visual Essay.

Nothing was holy to us. Our movement was neither mystical, communistic nor anarchistic. All of these movements had some sort of programme, but ours was completely nihilistic. We spat on everything, including ourselves. Our symbol was nothingness, a vacuum, a void.

George Grosz on Dada

We're so pretty, oh so pretty...vac-unt.

The Sex Pistols

1   Although it was often directly offensive (T-shirts covered in swear words) and threatening (terrorist/guerilla outfits) punk style was defined principally through the violence of its cut ups. Like

Duchamp's ready mades—manufactured objects which qualified as art because he chose to call them such, the most unremarkable and inappropriate items—a pin, a plastic clothes peg, a television component, a razor blade, a tampon—could be brought within the province of punk (un)fashion. Anything within or without reason could be turned into part of what Vivien Westwood called "confrontation dressing" so long as the rupture between "natural" and constructed context was clearly visible (i.e., the rule would seem to be: if the cap doesn't fit, wear it).

Objects borrowed from the most sordid of contexts found a place in the punks' ensembles:

lavatory chains were draped in graceful arcs across chests encased in plastic bin-liners. Safety pins were taken out of their domestic "utility" context and worn as gruesome ornaments through the cheek, ear or lip. "Cheap" trashy fabrics (PVC, plastic, lurex, etc.) in vulgar designs (e.g., mock leopard skin) and "nasty" colours, long discarded by the quality end of the fashion industry as obsolete kitsch, were salvaged by the punks and turned into garments (fly boy drainpipes, "common" mini-skirts) which offered self-conscious commentaries on the notions of modernity and taste. Conventional ideas of prettiness were jettisoned along with the traditional feminine lore of cosmetics. Contrary to the advice of every woman's magazine, make-up for both boys and girls was worn to be seen. Faces became abstract portraits: sharply observed and meticulously executed studies in alienation. Hair was obviously dyed (hay yellow, jet black, or bright orange with tufts of green or bleached in question marks), and T-shirts and trousers told the story of their own construction with multiple zips and outside seams clearly displayed. Similarly, fragments of school uniform (white brinylon shirts, school ties) were symbolically defiled (the shirts covered in graffiti, or fake blood; the ties left undone) and juxtaposed against leather drains or shocking pink mohair tops. The perverse and the abnormal were valued intrinsically. In particular, the illicit iconography of sexual fetishism was used to predictable effect. Rapist masks and rubber wear, leather bodices and fishnet stockings, implausibly pointed stiletto heeled shoes, the whole paraphernalia of bondage—the belts, straps and chains—were exhumed from the boudoir, closet and the pornographic film and placed on the street where they retained their forbidden connotations. Some young punks even donned the dirty raincoat—that most prosaic symbol of sexual "kinkiness"—and hence expressed their deviance in suitably proletarian terms.

Of course, punk did more than upset the wardrobe. It undermined every relevant discourse. Thus dancing, usually an involving and expressive medium in British rock and mainstream pop cultures, was turned into a dumb-

show of blank robotics. Punk dances bore absolutely no relation to the desultory frugs and clinches which Geoff Mungham describes as intrinsic to the respectable working-class ritual of Saturday night at the Top Rank or Mecca.[1] Indeed, overt displays of heterosexual interest were generally regarded with contempt and suspicion (who let the BOF/wimp[2] in?) and conventional courtship patterns found no place on the floor in dances like the pogo, the pose and the robot. Though the pose did allow for a minimum sociability (i.e., it could involve two people) the "couple" were generally of the same sex and physical contact was ruled out of court as the relationship depicted in the dance was a "professional" one. One participant would strike a suitable cliché fashion pose while the other would fall into a classic "Bailey" crouch to snap an imaginary picture. The pogo forebade even this much interaction, though admittedly there was always a good deal of masculine jostling in front of the stage. In fact the pogo was a caricature—a reductio ad absurdum of all the solo dance styles associated with rock music. It resembled the "anti dancing" of the "Leapniks" which Melly describes in connection with the trad boom (Melly, 1972). The same abbreviated gestures—leaping into the air, hands clenched to the sides, to head an imaginary ball—were repeated without variation in time to the strict mechanical rhythms of the music. In contrast to the hippies' languid, free-form dancing, and the "idiot dancing" of the heavy metal rockers, the pogo made improvisation redundant: the only variations were imposed by changes in the tempo of the music—fast numbers being "interpreted" with manic abandon in the form of frantic on-the-spots, while the slower ones were pogoed with a detachment bordering on the catatonic.

The robot, a refinement witnessed only at the most exclusive punk gatherings, was both more "expressive" and less "spontaneous" within the very narrow range such terms acquired in punk usage. It consisted of barely perceptible twitches of the head and hands or more extravagant lurches (Frankenstein's first steps?) which were abruptly halted at random points. The resulting pose was held for several moments, even minutes, and the whole sequence was as suddenly, as unaccountably, resumed and re-enacted. Some zealous punks carried things one step further and choreographed whole evenings, turning themselves for a matter of hours, like Gilbert and George,[3] into automata, living sculptures.

5   The music was similarly distinguished from mainstream rock and pop. It was uniformly basic and direct in its appeal, whether through intention or lack of expertise. If the latter, then the punks certainly made a virtue of necessity ("We want to be amateurs"—Johnny Rotten). Typically, a barrage of guitars with the volume and treble turned to maximum accompanied by the occasional saxophone would pursue relentless (un)melodic lines against a turbulent background of cacophonous drumming and screamed vocals. Johnny Rotten succinctly defined punk's position on harmonics: "We're into chaos not music."

The names of the groups (the Unwanted, the Rejects, the Sex Pistols, the Clash, the Worst, etc.) and the titles of the songs: "Belsen was a Gas," "If You Don't Want to Fuck Me, Fuck Off," "I Wanna Be Sick on You," reflected the tendency towards willful desecration and the voluntary assumption of outcast status which characterized the whole punk movement. Such tactics were, to adapt Levi-Strauss's famous phrase, "things to whiten mother's hair with." In the early days at least, these "garage bands" could dispense with musical pretensions and substitute, in the traditional romantic terminology, "passion" for "technique," the language of the common man for the arcane posturings of the existing élite, the now familiar armoury of frontal attacks for the bourgeois notion of entertainment or the classical concept of "high art."

It was in the performance arena that punk groups posed the clearest threat to law and order. Certainly, they succeeded in subverting the conventions of concert and nightclub entertainment. Most significantly, they attempted both physically and in terms of lyrics and life-style to move closer to their audiences. This in itself is by no means unique: the boundary between artist and audience has often stood as a metaphor in revolutionary aesthetics (Brecht, the surrealists, Dada, Marcuse, etc.) for that larger and more intransigent barrier which separates art and the dream from reality and life under capitalism.[4] The stages of those venues secure enough to host "new wave" acts were regularly invaded by hordes of punks, and if the management refused to tolerate such blatant disregard for ballroom etiquette, then the groups and their followers could be drawn closer together in a communion of spittle and mutual abuse. At the Rainbow Theatre in May 1977 as the Clash played "White Riot," chairs were ripped out and thrown at the stage. Meanwhile, every performance, however apocalyptic, offered palpable evidence that things could change, indeed were changing: that performance itself was a possibility no authentic punk should discount. Examples abounded in the music press of "ordinary fans" (Siouxsie of Siouxsie and the Banshees, Sid Vicious of the Sex Pistols, Mark P of Sniffin Glue, Jordan of the Ants) who had made the symbolic crossing from the dance floor to the stage. Even the humbler positions in the rock hierarchy could provide an attractive alternative to the drudgery of manual labour, office work or a youth on the dole. The Finchley Boys, for instance, were reputedly taken off the football terraces by the Stranglers and employed as roadies.

If these "success stories" were, as we have seen, subject to a certain amount of "skewed" interpretation in the press, then there were innovations in other areas which made opposition to dominant definitions possible. Most notably, there was an attempt, the first by a predominantly working-class youth culture, to provide an alternative critical space within the subculture itself to counteract the hostile or at least ideologically inflected coverage which punk was receiving in the media. The existence of an alternative punk press demonstrated that it was not only clothes or music that could be immediately and cheaply produced from the limited resources at hand. The fanzines (*Sniffin Glue, Ripped and Torn,* etc.) were journals edited by an individual or a group, consisting of reviews, editorials and interviews with prominent punks, produced on a small scale as cheaply as possible, stapled together and distributed through a small number of sympathetic retail outlets.

The language in which the various manifestoes were framed was determinedly "working class" (i.e., it was liberally peppered with swear words) and typing errors and grammatical mistakes, misspellings and jumbled pagination were left uncorrected in the final proof. Those corrections and crossings out that were made before publication were left to be deciphered by the reader. The overwhelming impression was one of urgency and immediacy, of a paper produced in indecent haste, of memos from the front line.

10   This inevitably made for a strident buttonholing type of prose which, like the music it described, was difficult to "take in" in any quantity. Occasionally a written, more abstract item—what Harvey Garfinkel (the American ethnomethodologist) might call an "aid to sluggish imaginations"—might creep in. For instance, *Sniffin Glue,* the first fanzine and the one which achieved the highest circulation, contained perhaps the single most inspired item of propaganda produced by the subculture—the definitive statement of punk's do-it-yourself philosophy—a diagram showing three finger positions on the neck of a guitar over the caption: "Here's one chord, here's two more, now form your own band."

Even the graphics and typography used on record covers and fanzines were homologous with punk's subterranean and anarchic style. The two typographic models were graffiti which was translated into a flowing "spray can" script, and the ransom note in which individual letters cut up from a variety of sources (newspapers, etc.) in different type faces were pasted together to form an anonymous message. The Sex Pistols' "God Save the Queen" sleeve (later turned into T-shirts, posters, etc.) for instance incorporated both styles: the roughly assembled legend was pasted across the Queen's eyes and mouth which were further disfigured by those black bars used in pulp detective magazines to conceal identity (i.e., they connote crime or scandal). Finally, the process of ironic self abasement which charac-

terized the subculture was extended to the name "punk" itself which, with its derisory connotations of "mean and petty villainy," "rotten," "worthless," etc. was generally preferred by hardcore members of the subculture to the more neutral "new wave."[5]

NOTES

1. In his P.O. account of the Saturday night dance in an industrial town, Mungham (1976) shows how the constricted quality of working-class life is carried over into the ballroom in the form of courtship rituals, masculine paranoia and an atmosphere of sullenly repressed sexuality. He paints a gloomy picture of joyless evenings spent in the desperate pursuit of "booze and birds" (or "blokes and a romantic bus-ride home") in a controlled setting where "spontaneity is regarded by managers and their staff—principally the bouncers—as the potential hand-maiden of rebellion".

2. BOF = Boring Old Fart.

3. Wimp = "wet."

4. Gilbert and George mounted their first exhibition in 1970 when, clad in identical conservative suits, with metallized hands and faces, a glove, a stick and a tape recorder, they won critical acclaim by performing a series of carefully controlled and endlessly repeated movements on a dais while miming to Flanagan and Allen's "Underneath the Arches." Other pieces with titles like "Lost Day" and "Normal Boredom" have since been performed at a variety of major art galleries throughout the world.

5. Of course, rock music had always threatened to dissolve these categories, and rock performances were popularly associated with all forms of riot and disorder—from the slashing of cinema seats by teddy boys through Beatlemania to the hippy happenings and festivals where freedom was expressed less aggressively in nudity, drug taking and general "spontaneity." However, punk represented a new departure.

    The word "punk," like the black American "funk" and "superbad" would seem to form part of that "special language of fantasy and alienation" which Charles Winick describes (1959), "in which values are reversed and in which 'terrible' is a description of excellence." See also Wolfe (1969) where he describes the "cruising" scene in Los Angeles in the mid-60s—a subculture of custom-built cars, sweatshirts and "high-piled, perfect coiffure" where "rank" was a term of approval: Rank! Rank is just the natural outgrowth of Rotten...Roth and Schorsch grew up in the Rotten Era of Los Angeles

teenagers. The idea was to have a completely rotten attitude towards the adult world, meaning, in the long run,
the whole established status structure, the whole system
of people organizing their lives around a job, fitting into
the social structure embracing the whole community.
The idea in Rotten was to drop out of conventional status competition into the smaller netherworld of Rotten
Teenagers and start one's own league.

WORKS CITED

Melly, G. (1972), *Revolt into Style,* Penguin.
Mungham, G. (1976), "Youth in Pursuit of Itself," in G.
  Mungham and G. Pearson (eds.), *Working Class Youth
  Culture,* Routledge & Kegan Paul.
Winick, C. (1959), "The Uses of Drugs by Jazz Musicians,"
  Social Problems, vol. 7, no. 3, Winter.
Wolfe, T. (1969), *The Pump House Gang,* Bantam.

VISUAL ESSAY   Graphic Design in Rock Culture

This Visual Essay gathers artifacts from rock culture—two posters, an AC/DC T-shirt,
and a Nirvana decal. (See also the Sex Pistol T-shirt at the beginning of the chapter).
We have tried to choose examples of distinctive styles, including the psychedelic
'60s, punk, heavy metal, grunge, and rave. As you look through the various visual
artifacts, consider the defining graphic style of each example. What does the graphic
style seem to express about a particular style or movement in rock culture? What
visual elements does it use?

SUGGESTIONS FOR DISCUSSION

1. Compile the examples of punk style you've underlined in a list. Work with others in class to construct a table that starts with general categories (clothes, music,
   dancing, etc.) and then fill in the first column with examples from the punk movement. Add further columns on youth styles and subcultures since the punks.
   Name the subcultural style and give examples.

	Punks	Grunge	Hip hop, etc.
Clothes			
Dancing			
Music			

2. Hebdige's work is primarily about British punks in the late 1970s, though punk
   style still has an influence on fashion, music, and graphics. If Hebdige were writing a book on American and/or British youth subcultures in the late 1990s and
   2000s that are in revolt against the dominant culture, what groups and styles
   might he focus on (or would he find any at all)? What is the nature of the revolt?
   How is it expressed stylistically?

3. It is possible to present here only a few examples of "Graphic Design in Rock
   Culture." To add to the Visual Essay, bring your own examples of posters,
   fanzines, T-shirts, and album covers to class. Be prepared to explain what your

examples signify about a particular style in rock culture. Consider the visual elements—the style of font, the layout, images, and whether any aspects of the design are borrowed and recycled.

SUGGESTIONS FOR WRITING

1. Use the table you constructed to identify an example of subcultural or group style that interests you. Pick a particular example—whether clothes, music, dancing, graphics, and so on—to serve as the topic of an essay. In the essay, explain who the group or subculture is and then show how the example you've chosen illustrates some central meaning about the group's style.

2. As Hebdige explains, punks used common objects and forms of dress in ways that departed from their originally intended uses to create new meanings. This

kind of cultural recycling, however, is by no means limited to the punks. Others have recycled old styles to produce retro looks that are often both ironic and nostalgic. Write an essay about a group or style that recycles fashions and objects. Explain how the recycling creates new meanings for older styles.

3. Use Hebdige's analysis of punk graphics and typography as a model to analyze the graphic design of a visual artifact from rock culture. Use any of the examples in the Visual Essay or others you've brought to class or found on your own.

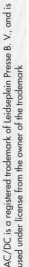

AC/DC is a registered trademark of Leidseplein Presse B. V., and is used under license from the owner of the trademark

Design: Michael Szabo
Art Direction: DB + Scotto

Critical analysis of the design of industrial products began with nineteenth-century writers such as John Ruskin and William Morris, who lamented the loss of craftmanship, the coarse style, and the poor quality of the mass-produced consumer goods that replaced the more durable and esthetically pleasing handmade items of an earlier, preindustrial age. In contrast, twentieth-century modernist designers and design theorists such as Walter Gropius at the Bauhaus in Germany and Buckminster Fuller in the United States reevaluated the possibilities of the machine age, arguing that mass-produced consumer goods, if properly designed, could be functional and stylish use-objects that meet genuine human needs and enrich everyday life. The debate has continued now for more than fifty years about whether such a mass market of consumer goods can actually contribute to the modernist designers' goal of a more democratic and humane society or whether, through advertising and planned obsolescence, the mass market inevitably creates spurious needs, feelings of inadequacy, and longings for possessions and new styles that can never be satisfied.

As you can see from these two readings, contemporary analysts of product design such as Richard Porch and Judith Williamson raise specific questions about the functions that ordinary mass-produced consumer goods, such as digital wrist watches and Walkman cassette or CD players, perform in people's lives. Notice how the writers are both interested in what these use-objects represent as a "consumer icon" (Porch) or a "vivid symbol of our time" (Williamson) and yet bring different perspectives to bear in their analyses. Porch is particularly concerned with the style of the digital watch as a matter of visual design, whereas Williamson focuses more on how the design of the Walkman influences a style of life.

THE DIGITAL WATCH: TRIBAL BRACELET OF THE CONSUMER SOCIETY

Richard Porch

Richard Porch is a British designer who writes about retail planning, shopping mall design, and the use of historic sites. He publishes frequently on design in the British press. "The Digital Watch: Tribal Bracelet of the Consumer Society" appeared originally in *Design Issues: History, Theory, Criticism* in 1985.

SUGGESTION FOR READING   As you read, notice how Richard Porch compares the features of the digital watch with the older fly-wheel mechanism watch. Consider how he uses the style and design of the older watch (which he clearly prefers) as evaluative measures that the digital watch lacks.

1 The digital watch is a perfect example of the reductivist esthetic of modernism: We now look at the time instead of reading it. The early method, internalized in childhood, of reading the time from a clockface has been supplanted by a sidelong glance at a liquid-crystal display (L.C.D.). This economy of intellectually learned skills has come about with the change in technology, from flywheel to liquid-crystal microelectronics. Along with that change in technology has come a vastly

higher level of timepiece accuracy and efficiency. Do we really need such split-second accuracy in our daily activities? Or do we think so, simply because the technology makes it available and advertising tells us we do? Does the advent of the digital watch mean that unpunctuality has been abolished? Now that people have apparently infallible timekeeping machines on their wrists, are they somehow more scrupulous about keeping to life's schedules?

The first wave of the new mode in timekeeping manifested itself in the early 1970s with the arrival of the light-up, light-emitting diode (L.E.D.) watch. If one wanted to read the time one had to press an uncomfortably small button, to make the time light up in miniature, neon-like numerals. With this kind of watch one could read the time at the bottom of a well, but virtually nowhere else. Liquid-crystal technology got around this by developing a permanent time read-out which used black digital numbers on a gray background. It was with the arrival of the L.C.D. watch that modern technology supplanted the idea of the wristwatch as jewelry and replaced it with the timepiece as functional instrument.

The widespread ownership of digital watches and the technology that created them are of cultural significance. Worn either as subliminal badges of efficiency, or as "tribal bracelets," digital watches seem to declare an unspoken allegiance to some sort of ethic of modernism. The old flywheel-movement watches were eminently more pleasing esthetically. They had an aural signature (ticking), required minor attention (winding), and were vaguely anthropomorphic (two *hands* on a clock*face*). The digital watch is a silent affair that requires no attention and has the visual appeal of an instrument more suited to the cockpit of a 747 than to something for your wrist. Such watches are now, to paraphrase Le Corbusier's description of a house as "a machine for living" merely machines for telling the time. And, like many other products in our society, they now also carry many enticing and entire irrelevant extras

with which to titillate and amuse the potent buyer, for example, day, date, bleep alarm, musical alarm, "space invader" game, calculator/file function, compass, and of court jogging odometers. There are children growing up today have never owned a watch that simply tells the time.

I still miss the old Swiss timepiece that I stopped wearing when it became erratic (fatal in a consumer culture, as it spells superfluity for the object concerned), and I was too lazy to get serviced. The trend was then fully underway for digital watches so I thought it was a good opportunity to buy a new watch—a digital one. Who would have thought that I would missed idiosyncracies of my old slim, 18-jewel Swiss timepiece? I was reminded of the late Charles Eames's lament over the advent of the styrofoam cup, how he missed the sensations of heat and cold that the new cup eliminated. As he perceptively pointed out, the "neutral" feel of the new material in the hand had a dulling effect (like the dentist's injection of novocaine into the gum), removing the tactile qualities of glass, china, or pottery. Of course, the plastic cup is both non-breakable and disposable, not to say inevitable cheaper. But for Eames, durability was also an infringement on sensation: The bounce of the plastic cup supplanted the heart-rending crack of china when dropped.

5   I miss the old Swiss timepieces because they were not universal in appearance. They looked by turn expensive, macho, kitsch, or just plain cheap. What they almost never looked like were futuristic identification bracelets, imposed on us by an alien race who wanted cruelly to remind us with split-second accuracy just how much time humans really waste.

If *you* are wearing a digital watch, can you remember exactly how you came by it? Was it an expensive birthday or Christmas present? A cheap holiday impulse buy? Or was it simply that you found it impossible to buy anything else? Perhaps we are all striving subconsciously to subscribe to the latest technological advances, and the arrival of the digital watch dovetailed nicely with acquisitive urges related to consusmerism. In his book *Design for the Real World*, Victor Papanek pointed out that the "Reynolds Pen" (the world's first ball-point pen in 1945) was emblematic of a commitment to a product-future based on principles of functionality and performance, rather than on any innate decorative appeal.

In the digital watch, the modern world has found a product that signifies in its own machine-produced blandness, the world of mass-production, silent efficiency, "functional appeal," and universality. Digital watches, chunky, rectangular, and unattractive are neutral and depersonalized, and are always finished off in some sort of stainless steel case with matching strap. It is interesting to note that coating them in gold never seems to confer any greater sense of luxury or status on them, as it did with the flywheel model. (You know, like gold-plating a machine-gun—it's a bit pointless.) The all stainless-steel finish is entirely consistent with its function in product design, in the same way that the evocation of glass, concrete, and steel as "honest" and functionally appropriate materials are for their extensive use in modern architecture. It is in late twentieth century product design, with its emphasis on formal purity and form following function, that the early-modern notion of a machine esthetic has probably found the truest expression of its ideal. Thus we have in products like the digital watch the promise of high levels of performance and no romantic notions of user appeal or tactile quality.

At the turn of the century, Austrian architect Adolf Loos said in his influential essay "Ornament and Crime," "The evolution of culture is synonymous with the disappearance of ornament from architecture." That essay and its ideas had a seminal impact on esthetics in western culture. That essay, and the people who built on its themes (those of the Bauhaus and modern movements, for example), provided much of the moral and esthetic justification for everything we now see around us that is streamlined, smooth, reductivist, and starkly functional in visual impact—everything that is "modern."

But, unlike the esthetic purists of the Bauhaus and their strictly limited production runs of tubular furniture, it was never likely that late twentieth century marketing people would be content with a product that simply out-performed the opposition technically. In a uniquely modern way, their urge was to trivialize. Once the digital watch had captured the public's imagination and become a consumer icon, it was inevitable that the marketing people would want to reach as many user markets as demographically possible. To achieve this they started to ornament the watches, not with superfluous decoration but with a host of largely useless extra functions. The question of whether the individual actually requires anything of a watch other than its capacity to give the time, date, and (arguably) an alarm signal, was never addressed. Victor Papanek had a picturesque way of describing this marketing process: "sexing the product up." The eighteenth-century French philosopher Rousseau would have appreciated the thinking behind this ornamentation. As he well knew, once the basic needs of the individual have been satisfied, a whole universe of fresh ones would be opened up, requiring further satisfaction.

10   Perhaps I am too much a purist though, since digital watches are statistically more numerous than any other kind of timepiece; they must be what people want. People also seem to want the whole gamut of consumer gadgets, from "talking cars," with synthesized warning voices buried in the dashboard, to domestic robots, and, ultimately, powerful home computers of great capacity. Ironically, the latter development was largely underwritten by the sale of combat and fantasy video games, sold to the young and impressionable so they might live out absurd, vicarious fantasies (via high technology) that serve as an outlet for aggression, competitiveness, and thwarted achievement.

The eventual outcome is a manufacturer's utopia, arrived at via a technologic-economic system advancing continuously on all fronts. The whole edifice is sustained by consumers who feel obliged to purchase, discard, and re-purchase all manner of meaningless products to define themselves as both individuals and peer group members; in other words, to be in on the latest trend you have to buy the latest product. Individual product character counts for naught. How well does it perform? Better than last year's model? But above all, does it have a day, date, alarm, calculator function with a heart-rate analyzer built in? The human capacity to take highly complex technological advances and reduce them to banal, marketable consumer devices continues apace (encouraged by the economic system), and produces, as it does so efficiently, an apparently endless stream of high-tech pacifiers for an increasingly acquisitive and undiscriminating consumer audience.

A backlash against modernism, which is what the digital watch symbolizes, has arisen in recent years. Postmodernism has had an impact in architecture through the work of the "born-again" modernists, such as Philip Johnson (the AT&T Building and others). Michael Graves (since 1974), and James Stirling (museum at Harvard), on both sides of the Atlantic. It has also spread to product design, as seen in the subversive antics of the Italian avant-garde design groups Memphis and Studio Alchymia. Postmodernism still uses modern technology, but puts a witty "mannerist" face on it, acknowledging, often in a startling way, that our obsession with formal purism is only an optional, not a mandatory, esthetic. So let's have digital watches in baroque cases, classical housings, or, alternatively, in Dali-esque, formless pouches. Better still, how about a digital watch whose read-out shows two liquid crystal "hands" circling 'round a dial covered with "digitized" Roman numerals and a synthesized "tick" instead of an alarm. In other words, use the technology to humanize, not de-humanize.

URBAN SPACEMAN

Judith Williamson

Judith Williamson is a cultural critic; her book *Decoding Advertisements: Ideology and Meaning in Advertising* (1979) was a groundbreaking work that combined feminist and Marxist analysis. "Urban Spaceman" comes from her book *Consuming Passions: The Dynamics of Popular Culture* (1986).

SUGGESTION FOR READING Notice that Judith Williamson does not begin with a comparison, as Porch does in the previous selection. Instead, she extends her interpretation of the Walkman by comparing it with the ghetto-blaster. As you read, consider how this comparison helps Williamson clarify and consolidate her main line of analysis.

1 A vodka advertisement in the London underground shows a cartoon man and woman with little headphones over their ears and little cassette-players over their shoulders. One of them holds up a card which asks, "Your place or mine?"—so incapable are they of communicating in any other way. The walkman has become a familiar image of modern urban life, creating troops of sleep-walking space-creatures, who seem to feel themselves invisible because they imagine that what they're listening to is inaudible. It rarely is: nothing is more irritating than the gnats' orchestra which so frequently assails the fellow-passenger of an oblivious walk-person—sounding, literally, like a flea in your ear. Although disconcertingly insubstantial, this phantom music has all the piercing insistency of a digital watch alarm; it is your request to the headphoned one to turn it down that cannot be heard. The argument that the walkman protects the *public* from

hearing one person's sounds, is back-to-front: it is the walk-person who is protected from the outside world, for whether or not their music is audible they are shut off as if by a spell.

The walkman is a vivid symbol of our time. It provides a concrete image of alienation, suggesting an implicit hostility to, and isolation from, the environment in which it is worn. Yet it also embodies the underlying values of precisely the society which produces that alienation—those principles which are the lynch-pin of Thatcherite Britain: individualism, privatization and "choice." The walkman is primarily a way of escaping from a *shared* experience or environment. It produces a privatized sound, in the public domain; a weapon of the individual against the communal. It attempts to negate *chance:* you never know what you are going to hear on a bus or in the streets, but the walk-person is buffered against the unexpected—an apparent triumph of individual control over social spontaneity. Of course, *what* the walk-person controls is very limited; they can only affect their *own* environment, and although this may make the individual *feel* active (or even rebellious) in social terms they are absolutely passive. The wearer of a walkman states that they expect to make no input into the social arena, no speech, no reaction, no intervention. Their own body is the extent of their domain. The turning of desire for control inward toward the body has been a much more general phenomenon of recent years; as if one's muscles or jogging record were all that one *could* improve in this world. But while everyone listens to whatever they want within their "private" domestic space, the peculiarity of the walkman is that it turns the inside of the head into a mobile home—rather like the building society image of the couple who, instead of an umbrella, carry a tiled roof over their heads (to protect them against hazards created by the same system that provides their mortgage).

This interpretation of the walkman may seem extreme, but only because first, we have become accustomed to the privatization of social space, and second, we have come to regard sound as secondary to sight—a sort of accompaniment to a life which appears as essentially visual. Imagine people walking round the streets with little TVs strapped in front of their eyes, because they would rather watch a favourite film or programme than see where they were going, and what was going on around them. (It could be argued that this would be too dangerous—but how about the thousands of suicidal cyclists who prefer taped music to their own safety?) This bizarre idea is no more extreme in principle than the walkman. In the visual media there has already been a move from the social setting of the cinema, to the privacy of the TV set in the living-room, and personalized mobile viewing would be the logical next step. In all media, the technology of this century has been directed toward a shift, first from the social to the private—from concert to record-player—and then of the private *into* the social—exemplified by the walkman, which, paradoxically, allows someone to listen to a recording of a public concert, in public, completely privately.

The contemporary antithesis to the walkman is perhaps the appropriately named ghetto-blaster. Music in the street or played too loud indoors *can* be extremely anti-social—although at least its perpetrators can hear you when you come and tell them to shut up. Yet in its current use, the ghetto-blaster stands for a shared experience, a communal event. Outdoors, ghetto-blasters are seldom used by only their individual owners, but rather act as the focal point for a group, something to gather around. In urban life "the streets" stand for shared existence, a common understanding, a place that is owned by no-one and used by everyone. The traditional custom of giving people the "freedom of the city" has a meaning which can be appropriated for ourselves today. There *is* a kind of freedom about *chance* encounters, which is why conversations and arguments in buses and bus-queues are often so much livelier than those of the wittiest dinner party. Help is also easy to come by on urban streets, whether with a burst shopping bag or a road accident.

5   It would be a great romanticization not to admit that all these social places can also hold danger, abuse, violence. But, in both its good and bad aspects, urban space is like the physical medium of society itself. The prevailing ideology sees society as simply a mathematical sum of its individual parts, a collection of private interests. Yet social life demonstrates the transformation of quantity into quality: it has something extra, over and above the characteristics of its members in isolation. That "something extra" is unpredictable, unfixed, and resides in interaction. It would be a victory for the same forces that have slashed public transport and privatized British Telecom, if the day were to come when everyone walked the street in headphones.

SUGGESTIONS FOR DISCUSSION

1. Richard Porch says that the digital watch is a "perfect example of the reductivist esthetic of modernism." What does Porch mean by "reductivist esthetic"? What examples of this style of design does he give or can you supply? Why is such an esthetic a problem for Porch? Consider here how he believes both that something valuable is missing from the style of modernist design and that the modernist style as illustrated by the digital watch signifies something he finds troubling. What is missing? What is troubling? Do you find his analysis persuasive? Could you apply it to the style and design of other everyday use-objects?

2. Judith Williamson sees the Walkman as a "vivid symbol of our time." What does it symbolize for her? Think here in terms of how the design and use of the product affect the way people experience life in public and their interactions with each other. You've no doubt seen or used a Walkman. Compare your experience with what Williamson writes. In what sense does your experience fit with her analysis? To what extent does it differ? What do you make of such differences?

3. Perhaps even more ubiquitous than the Walkman was in 1986 when Williamson published her essay, the cell phone seems to share some of the same characteristics in terms of design and use today. Work up an analysis of the cell phone that uses the perspective Williamson applies to the Walkman. What do you think Porch might say about the design and style of cell phones? How would his strategy of comparison apply to cell phones in relation to older land lines?

SUGGESTIONS FOR WRITING

1. Digital technologies are pervasive today, not only in the design of watches and clocks but also in a range of items such as computers, pagers, palm pilots, movies, and musical recordings. Household and office appliances such as stoves, washing machines, dryers, blenders, telephones, answering machines, and so on are no longer operated so much as they are programmed to perform. Pick a contemporary example of digital technology in the design and style of a particular product that you can compare with an earlier predigital style. (You might compare computers with typewriters or CDs with phonograph records or palm pilots with notebooks.) Use Richard Porch's essay as a model to consider what, if anything, is lost and gained. You do not need to agree with his point of view, but his essay can be helpful in suggesting what to look at and what criteria of comparison to use.

2. Extend the analysis Judith Williamson does in "Urban Spaceman" to the design of another everyday use-object that affects the way people communicate and interact. Cell phones come to mind immediately, as do pagers, remote controls, VCRs, e-mail, call waiting, and answering machines. Draw on your own experience, but keep in mind that the point of

Williamson's essay is to explore how the design and use of the Walkman affects the every-day life of cities, not just individuals.

3. Richard Porch suggests that the emphasis in modern design on function and high levels of performance ignores decoration, ornamentation, and "romantic notions of user appeal and tactile quality." Certainly he is right that people respond imaginatively to the decorative side of everyday objects as well as to their functional aspects. Pick an everyday object that has captured your imagination because of its style and write an essay that explains your attachment to the object and the kind of pleasure you experience from it. Try to locate the source of the pleasure in its cultural meanings. Is the object a machine that gives you a sense of mastery and power? Is it an old shirt you wore to camp or a pair of cowboy boots that connect you to images of the outdoors or the Wild West? If it's a baby-blue dress, explain how it elicits fantasies of being a princess.

BEAUTY AND THE BLOB: Product Culture Now

Steven Skov Holt

Steven Skov Holt is chair of the industrial design program at the California College of Arts and Crafts and the director of strategy at frogdesign in San Francisco. Along with Donald Albrecht and Ellen Lupton, he was curator of the National Design Triennial in 2000 at the Cooper-Hewitt, National Design Museum of the Smithsonian Institution. His essay "Beauty and the Blob: Product Culture Now" appeared in *Design Culture Now (2000),* the catalog that accompanied the exhibition

SUGGESTION FOR READING Steven Skov Holt's essay elucidates some of the recent ideas and trends in product design. We present it here as a concise overview of the current situation in design and as an introduction to the Visual Essay, "Age of the Blobject." Before you read Holt's essay, take a quick look at the Visual Essay. When you have finished reading, go through the Visual Essay more slowly to see examples of what Holt calls the "free-flowing, retro-futuristic product aesthetics that have emerged over the past few years."

1 We inhabit a time when objects, and even images of objects, hold great sway. We have come to apotheosize all manner of consumer goods, and in the process we have created a society in which anything and everything is a product. The active consumption of products has itself become almost religious, part considered ritual and part spontaneous spectacle of existence. At the same time, those very products with the longest histories—the solid things considered the economic bedrock of the most powerful nation of the twentieth century—have evolved, mutated, shrunk,

and even vanished into thin air. The need to physically travel by car, for example, has given way to the virtual presence provided by products ranging from the ubiquitous fax machines, pagers, and cell phones of today to the ascendent video conferencing systems, electronic agents, and personal digital assistants of the near future. Whole new species of products have appeared, the result of pop culture's mainline connection to a re-energized material sense of well-being.

Not surprisingly, our definition of what constitutes a product has expanded as well. In fact, products have changed more rapidly during the last three years than at any other time in American history. Did you have e-mail or a Web site at the end of 1996? Perhaps. Were you downloading MP-3 digital music three years ago? Almost certainly not. Products have become more than mere commercial goods. Today, we not only understand products tangibly, but experience them systemically.

It is an appropriate time, therefore, to look back on the "productized" output of American culture during the final years of the twentieth century—not just to draw out exemplars of creativity, but to consider the messages products deliver about our society and this particular cultural moment. We know, for example, that media-constructed, product-centric versions of the good life command an ever-increasing portion of our conscious mind. Over time, they accrete. They come to exert a psychic, unspoken level of pressure and expectation on all of us. The quest for material gain is the foundation upon which the American economy is now being built, and the troubling cycle of manufactured desire and requisite consumption driven by this reality has given product designers the greatest creative challenge in the profession's history.

That challenge is to balance competing demands in a way that they have never been balanced before. The commercial must be weighed against the ecological. The needs of the client must be weighed against the needs of the consumer. The urge for self-expression must be weighed against the possibility of communicating to a mass audience. Truth be told, it is not enough for the new generation of designers to weigh these options one against another, for that is already old thinking. Instead, the challenge is to bring all of these previously competing elements together into a larger, more synergistic whole. Designers have bigger, more complex problems to solve than ever before, and to solve them practitioners will have to be bolder, more courageous, and less willing to accept business-as-usual in any of its myriad guises.

5   Enormous opportunities for the design profession are being driven by the possibility to meaningfully combine features, objects, materials, technologies, and ideas previously considered to be separate. There are more new unions of content and commerce than at any other point in history. E-commerce is driving a whole new generation of design, and e-design is changing the world of products as we know it. As combinatory thinking becomes the new norm, design—an intrinsically hybrid practice merging the conflicting needs of art, business, and engineering—will be on its way toward total infiltration of human environments.

We are at a point in history where we can not comfortably define ourselves without the presence of products. Products help us feel more like who we believe we are, who we would like to be, and who we would like other people to think that we already are. To a large degree, we are that certain, unique combination of car, watch, sunglasses, shoes, jewelry, and whatever else we choose. On one level, such products represent the manifestation of our personal brand. On another level, they help us feel special, as if we matter. And on yet another level, they attempt to compensate for what in fact can never be compensated for—enduring feelings of inadequacy, inferiority, and an insatiable desire to belong. Designers must realize that they are complicit in this highly considered cult of consumerist experience. Perhaps the most significant challenge for today's designers is to create an atmosphere that is less about the rampant acquisition of objects and more about the possibilities that those objects present.

By creating things that people touch, and are touched by, every day, the industrial designer is becoming a new kind of hero for our time. When I became editor of *I.D.* magazine in 1983, we could barely give away ad space. But that same year the economy began to pick up, cable TV started to take hold, and graphically challenging networks such as ESPN and MTV started to assume prominence. Soon enough design was a matter of national interest, and industrial design was seen as a potential curative for a host of problems—aesthetic, financial, functional, and otherwise.

Coverage of design began to appear in the papers of record, most notably in a "Form and Function" column in the *Wall Street Journal* and in the Home and Style sections of the *New York Times*. By the late 1980s, the Industrial Designers Society of America was annually highlighting its achievements in *BusinessWeek* in an effort to create new ways of thinking about the intersection of design and commerce. Design is also becoming ever more entwined with the electronic media. By this metric, one of 1999's pinnacle moments occurred when IDEO, a design firm represented in the Triennial, was featured as the subject of an episode of ABC's *Nightline* news program.

Despite its success, industrial design has largely failed to reach out beyond its base audience of white, middle-class males. Women, minorities, children, and the elderly have been overlooked. The profession is dominated by white male practitioners, a fact that reflects the failure of the educational system to recognize design as an area of cultural inquiry. This failure is evident both in our elementary schools and in our most ivy-clad halls. Only a handful of institutions offer classes in design—how inappropriate and ill-considered this seems at the end of the most product-intensive century in history!

10   There is, nonetheless, great cause for optimism. Driven by the possibilities presented by the computer, designers are in a period of unprecedented opportunity. Products have been liberated by flexible, ever-shrinking, and ever-more-powerful system-on-a-chip solutions. Materials and shapes that were inconceivable only a few years ago have become routine. Advances in tooling, manufacturing, and computer-aided software have given the designer new ways to create organic forms. Even those products that remain impossible to physically model can be virtually realized in the digital world.

Product design has been further vitalized by the astonishing development of the Internet—a participatory ecosystem replete with its own rapidly evolving digital flora and fauna. The Internet is built on the overlapping promises of near-instant communication, relationship building, pattern-based thinking, and interactive experience. The implication is clear: the Internet is first and foremost a design event. The American nation—physically fragmented into a series of micro-cultures and macro-factions—has reunited in cyberspace in the form of buddy lists, chat rooms, special interest groups, instant messages, and portal communities. The new generation of simple, smart products just emerging is symbolic of design's new frontier. Design has moved past the mere making of objects into the realm of collaboration and intellectual creativity. The Web now serves as the twentieth century's most potent symbol of how the world might yet come together willingly and peacefully in a shared realm.

Meanwhile, the old model of the designer as the singular creator of discrete objects has been supplanted by a new vision of the design professional as orchestrator of complex systems in which information, materials, sensation, and technology are in a state of flux. Design is now best understood as a team sport. What was a rarity just a few years ago—a multitasked, multidisciplinary project bringing together print, virtual, and environmental aspects of brand, media, and product—is fast becoming the norm. If anything, the need for innovation is pushing designers into the next evolution of the profession, one likely to involve trans- or extra-disciplinary creativity.

Products have become containers for stories, and designers have correspondingly become storytellers and even mythmakers. This focus on the narrative component of design has itself led to a search through both design history and material culture for elements of our physical vocabulary that can be called upon anew. Even as we have been bombarded by news, information, and an ascending cascade of consumer goods, we have seen a corresponding rise in our collective penchant for nostalgia. This has manifested itself in a surge of retro-futuristic solutions that manage to look familiar at the same time that they appear different. The exuberant forms of the 1950s, for example, have been mined for their symbolic riches. Strange time loops keep bringing back long-abandoned images, objects, and celebrities. The result is a hybrid moment where it appears easier to edit and recombine what already exists than it does to create something completely new. The sampling strategy so evident in hip-hop music provides a powerful model for all forms of design creativity, especially in consumer goods, where positive historical associations are cherished.

The free-flowing, retro-futuristic product aesthetics that have emerged over the past few years reflect both the fluidity of the design profession and the liquidity of our particular cultural moment. We are, after all, a nation of dynamists, always off somewhere in search of ourselves. Americans move about constantly—and so do the best shapes that our designers create. We are in the closing years of the Age of the Blobject, a period that began in the 1980s, when everything from the Ford Taurus to the Sony Walkman to the Tylenol caplet was designed with curved contours and swoopy silhouettes.

15   Since then, blobjects, along with accepted standards for good design, have become more visually evolved. In the same way that the first generation of professional industrial design pioneers, in the 1930s, focused on streamlining objects ranging from pencil sharpeners to cruise boats, the designers represented in this book are hyper-streamlining everything from motorcycles and hairbrushes to sunglasses and computers. Everything looks fast, organic, and momentary. A new-found beauty is emerging. Even as we have become a culture of products, we have found that products no longer need to be physical. Technological components will continue to shrink and become more transparent, and will soon entirely recede from view. The relevance of time, place, and space have shifted.

A cascade of goods overflows our imaginations with choices and pseudochoices. Products flood our stores and our landfills, and overwhelm our sense of what is possible. Our economy of excess simultaneously attracts and repulses. Increasingly, designers are expanding their roles to accommodate the contradictions of this economy, becoming anthropologists, psychologists, philosophers, and clairvoyants. Product designers have the ability to peer into the souls of both physical objects and the consumers that use them. Can we survive our success at consumerizing our culture and productizing our profession? Strangely, and yet somehow appropriately, the answer lies most directly in the hands of this generation's practitioners—those who will be generating this culture will be in the best position to ameliorate it.

VISUAL ESSAY   The Age of Blobjects

The Age of Blobjects, as Steven Skov Holt says, began in the 1980s when product designers started borrowing the curvilinear outlines and swooping silhouettes of 1930s streamline design. (For more on streamlining in product design, see Checking Out the Web.) The resulting products—everything from computers, office furniture, and motorcycles to hair brushes, sunglasses, and staplers—took on a sleek organic look that both recalled the past and seemed totally contemporary. Blobjects, as you can see in the following examples, merge the sense of speed and efficiency in older streamlining styles with colorful and translucent surfaces.

SUGGESTIONS FOR DISCUSSION

1. Steven Skov Holt says that products "have become containers for stories, and designers correspondingly have become storytellers and mythmakers." What does he mean by this? In what sense can product design tell a story? What examples can you think of to illustrate Holt's point? What stories do products tell?

2. The iMac was a great success story in computer design—and a considerable financial success for Apple as well. With its egg-shaped design, use of color, and prominent handle, the iMac radically changed the visual style of computers. By the time you read this, given the speed of change in the computer industry, there may well be new designs and new styles of computers. Consider the messages that various designs send to computer users. To what extent do they highlight the technical performance of the computers? To what extent do they highlight user friendliness, humor, and imagination?

3. The motorcycle shown on the following page uses a mix of stock and custom parts to create a bike that, in the words of its designer, Cory Ness, "flows from one end to the other." Arlen and Cory Ness are a father-and-son team who made their reputation customizing Harley-Davidsons in San Leandro, California. Consider how this concept motorcycle accentuates basic design features in motorcycles. What is the visual appeal of motorcycles to begin with? What gives them their particular style?   What cultural meanings do you associate with motorcycles? How does Ness work with these meanings?

SUGGESTIONS FOR WRITING

1. Holt says that "products have changed more rapidly during the last three years [since the end of 1996] than at any other time in American history." He cites e-mail, Web sites,

Swingline Staplers

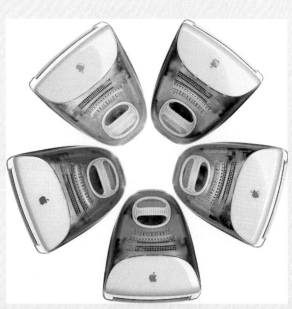

iMac Computer

and MP-3 digital music as examples. Assuming Holt is right about the rate of product change, you are likely to have experienced the emergence of several new products. If this is true, write an essay about a new product that you incorporated into your life. Identify the product, how you became aware of it, and what your initial feelings were. Then explain what happened as you started to use the product. What was new? What changed? What did it make possible? Are there things you stopped doing once you started using the product? Are you still using it? Put your use of the product in a context that considers its overall effect on you and others.

2. Write an essay about the design of computers. For example, compare the style of the iMac, iBook, G4, or more recent Apple computers with other brands and styles. Consider the messages that the various styles send about computers. To what extent do the styles emphasize the technical performance of the computer? To what extent do they emphasize other factors, such as user friendliness, humor, and playfulness?

3. Write an essay about what Holt calls "retro-futuristic solutions" to design. Pick an example of a product whose design style recalls an earlier style. Select a use-object for this assignment, but also consider the graphic design of posters, signs, books, CD covers, or magazines or the architectural style of buildings. How does the "sampling strategy" result in something that looks both familiar and different at the same time?

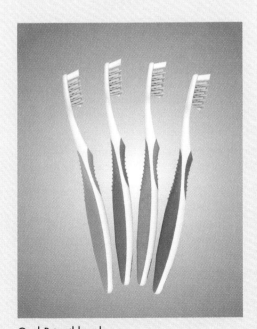

Oral-B toothbrushes

Customized motorcycle

Arlen and Cory Ness, designers

PERSPECTIVES Branding

Branding has become one of the pervasive features of the contemporary cultural landscape. Nowadays, brand names don't just appear in the places they always have, such as packages, labels, stores, billboards, and advertisements. The world in which we live appears to be branded. Stadiums and arenas no longer have names such as Candlestick Park or the Boston Garden. Now they're called 3Com Park and the Fleet Center. The uniforms of college and professional athletes not only identify the players by displaying their numbers but they identify which company—for example, Nike or Reebok—has the team franchise by displaying its brand. And people who once simply wore brand-name clothes are now walking advertisements for several companies, branded by the name and logo on their shirts, shoes, sweaters, caps, and other clothing.

All of this branding has caused a good deal of controversy. We present three selections to explore the terms of the controversy—an excerpt from the opening chapter of Naomi Klein's *No Logo*, a response to Klein that appeared in the British magazine *The Economist*, and an exchange between Jonah Peretti and Nike.

NO LOGO

Naomi Klein

Naomi Klein is a journalist and anticorporate activist. She is a regular columnist for the *Globe and Mail*, Canada's national newspaper; the British *Guardian*; and the weekly U.S. magazine *In These Times*. *No Logo* (2002), the book in which this selection appeared, connects the branding phenomenon to the way multinational corporations operate in a global economy and to the anticorporate activism that has emerged in recent years.

SUGGESTION FOR READING Notice how Naomi Klein develops the idea of branding as a corporate strategy. When you've finished reading the selection, write a short explanation of what Klein means by the term *branding*.

As a private person, I have a passion for landscape, and I have never seen one improved by a billboard. Where every prospect pleases, man is at his vilest when he erects a billboard. When I retire from Madison Avenue, I am going to start a secret society of masked vigilantes who will travel around the world on silent motor bicycles, chopping down posters at the dark of the moon. How many juries will convict us when we are caught in these acts of beneficent citizenship?

—David Ogilvy, founder of the
Ogilvy&Mather advertising agency, in
Confessions of an Advertising Man, 1963

1   The astronomical growth in the wealth and cultural influence of multinational corporations over the last fifteen years can arguably be traced back to a single, seemingly innocuous idea developed by management theorists in the mid-1980s: that successful corporations must primarily produce brands, as opposed to products.

Until that time, although it was understood in the corporate world that bolstering one's brand name was important, the primary concern of every solid manufacturer was the production of goods. This idea was the very gospel of the machine age. An editorial that appeared in *Fortune* magazine in 1938, for instance, argued that the reason the American economy had yet to recover from the Depression was that America had lost sight of the importance of making *things*:

This is the proposition that the basic and irreversible function of an industrial economy is *the making of things*; that the more things it makes the bigger will be the income, whether dollar or real; and hence that the key to those lost recuperative powers lies…in the factory where the lathes and the drills and the fires and the hammers are. It is in the factory and on the land and under the land that purchasing power *originates* [italics theirs].

And for the longest time, the making of things remained, at least in principle, the heart of all industrialized economies. But by the eighties, pushed along by that decade's recession, some of the most powerful manufacturers in the world had begun to falter. A consensus emerged that corporations were bloated, oversized; they owned too much, employed too many people, and were weighed down with *too many things*. The very process of producing—running one's own factories, being responsible for tens of thousands of full-time, permanent employees—began to look less like the route to success and more like a clunky liability.

At around this same time a new kind of corporation began to rival the traditional all-American manufacturers for market share; these were the Nikes and Microsofts, and later, the Tommy Hilfigers and Intels. These pioneers made the bold claim that producing goods was only an incidental part of their operations, and that thanks to recent victories in trade liberalization and labor-law reform, they were able to have their products made for them by contractors, many of them overseas. What these companies produced primarily were not things, they said, but *images* of their brands. Their real work lay not in manufacturing but in marketing. This formula, needless to say, has proved enormously profitable, and its success has companies competing in a race toward weightlessness: whoever owns the least, has the fewest employees on the payroll and produces the most powerful images, as opposed to products, wins the race.

5   And so the wave of mergers in the corporate world over the last few years is a deceptive phenomenon: it only *looks* as if the giants, by joining forces, are getting bigger and bigger. The true key to understanding these shifts is to realize that in several crucial ways—not their profits, of course—these merged companies are actually shrinking. Their apparent bigness is simply the most effective route toward their real goal: divestment of the world of things.

Since many of today's best-known manufacturers no longer produce products and advertise them, but rather buy products and "brand" them, these companies are forever on the prowl for creative new ways to build and strengthen their brand images. Manufacturing products may require drills, furnaces, hammers and the like, but creating a brand calls for a completely different set of tools and materials. It requires an endless parade of brand extensions, continuously renewed imagery for marketing and, most of all, fresh new spaces to disseminate the brand's idea of itself. In this section of the book, I'll look at how, in ways both insidious and overt, this corporate obsession with brand identity is waging a war on public and individual space: on public institutions such as schools, on youthful identities, on the concept of nationality and on the possibilities for unmarketed space.

THE BEGINNING OF THE BRAND

It's helpful to go back briefly and look at where the idea of branding first began. Though the words are often used interchangeably, branding and advertising are not the same process. Advertising any given product is only one part of branding's grand plan, as are sponsorship and logo licensing. Think of the brand as the core meaning of the modern corporation, and of the advertisement as one vehicle used to convey that meaning to the world.

The first mass-marketing campaigns, starting in the second half of the nineteenth century, had more to do with advertising than with branding as we understand it today. Faced with a range of recently invented products—the radio, phonograph, car, light bulb and so on—advertisers had more pressing tasks than creating a brand identity for any given corporation; first, they had to change the way people lived their lives. Ads had to inform consumers about the existence of some new invention, then convince them that their lives would be better if they used, for example, cars instead of wagons, telephones instead of mail and electric light instead of oil lamps. Many of these new products bore brand names—some of which are still around today—but these were almost incidental. These products were themselves news; that was almost advertisement enough.

The first brand-based products appeared at around the same time as the invention-based ads, largely because of another relatively recent innovation: the factory. When goods began to be produced in factories, not only were entirely new products being introduced but old products—even basic staples—were appearing in strikingly new forms. What made early branding efforts different from more straightforward salesmanship was that the market was now being flooded with uniform mass-produced products that were virtually indistinguishable from one another. Competitive branding became a necessity of the machine age—within a context of manufactured sameness, image based difference had to be manufactured along with the product.

10   So the role of advertising changed from delivering product news bulletins to building an image around a particular brand-name version of a product. The first task of branding was to bestow proper names on generic goods such as sugar, flour, soap and cereal, which had previously been scooped out of barrels by local shopkeepers. In the 1880s, corporate logos were introduced to mass-produced products like Campbell's Soup, H.J. Heinz pickles and Quaker Oats cereal. As design historians and theorists Ellen Lupton and J. Abbott Miller note, logos were tailored to evoke familiarity and folksiness, in an effort to counter-

act the new and unsettling anonymity of packaged goods. "Familiar personalities such as Dr. Brown, Uncle Ben, Aunt Jemima, and Old Grand-Dad came to replace the shopkeeper, who was traditionally responsible for measuring bulk foods for customers and acting as an advocate for products...a nationwide vocabulary of brand names replaced the small local shopkeeper as the interface between consumer and product." After the product names and characters had been established, advertising gave them a venue to speak directly to would-be consumers. The corporate "personality," uniquely named, packaged and advertised, had arrived.

For the most part, the ad campaigns at the end of the nineteenth century and the start of the twentieth used a set of rigid, pseudoscientific formulas: rivals were never mentioned, ad copy used declarative statements only and headlines had to be large, with lots of white space—according to one turn-of-the-century adman, "an advertisement should be big enough to make an impression but not any bigger than the thing advertised."

But there were those in the industry who understood that advertising wasn't just scientific; it was also spiritual. Brands could conjure a feeling—think of Aunt Jemima's comforting presence—but not only that, entire corporations could themselves embody a meaning of their own. In the early twenties, legendary adman Bruce Barton turned General Motors into a metaphor for the American family, "something personal, warm and human," while GE was not so much the name of the faceless General Electric Company as, in Barton's words, "the initials of a friend." In 1923 Barton said that the role of advertising was to help corporations find their soul. The son of a preacher, he drew on his religious upbringing for uplifting messages: "I like to think of advertising as something big, something splendid, something which goes deep down into an institution and gets hold of the soul of it....Institutions have souls, just as men and nations have souls," he told GM president Pierre du Pont. General Motors ads began to tell stories about the people who drove its cars—the preacher, the pharmacist or the country doctor who, thanks to his trusty GM, arrived "at the bedside of a dying child" just in time "to bring it back to life."

By the end of the 1940s, there was a burgeoning awareness that a brand wasn't just a mascot or a catchphrase or a picture printed on the label of a company's product; the company as a whole could have a brand identity or a "corporate consciousness," as this ephemeral quality was termed at the time. As this idea evolved, the adman ceased to see himself as a pitchman and instead saw himself as "the philosopher-king of commercial culture," in the words of ad critic Randall Rothberg. The search for the true meaning of brands—or the "brand essence," as it is often called—gradually took the agencies away from individual products and their attributes and toward a psychological/anthropological examination of what brands mean to the culture and to people's lives. This was seen to be of crucial importance, since corporations may manufacture products, but what consumers buy are brands.

It took several decades for the manufacturing world to adjust to this shift. It clung to the idea that its core business was still production and that branding was an important add-on. Then came the brand equity mania of the eighties, the defining moment of which arrived in 1988 when Philip Morris purchased Kraft for $12.6 billion—six times what the company was worth on paper. The price difference, apparently, was the cost of the word "Kraft." Of course Wall Street was aware that decades of marketing and brand bolstering added value to a company over and above its assets and total annual sales. But with the Kraft purchase, a huge dollar value had been assigned to something that had previously been abstract and unquantifiable—a brand name. This was spectacular news for the ad world, which was now able to make the claim that advertising spending was more than just a sales strategy: it was an investment in cold hard equity. The more you spend, the more your company is worth. Not surprisingly, this led to a considerable increase in spending on advertising.

More important, it sparked a renewed interest in puffing up brand identities, a project that involved far more than a few billboards and TV spots. It was about pushing the envelope in sponsorship deals, dreaming up new areas in which to "extend" the brand, as well as perpetually probing the zeitgeist to ensure that the "essence" selected for one's brand would resonate karmically with its target market. For reasons that will be explored in the rest of this chapter, this radical shift in corporate philosophy has sent manufacturers on a cultural feeding frenzy as they seize upon every corner of unmarketed landscape in search of the oxygen needed to inflate their brands. In the process, virtually nothing has been left unbranded. That's quite an impressive feat, considering that as recently as 1993 Wall Street had pronounced the brand dead, or as good as dead.

THE BRAND'S DEATH (RUMORS OF WHICH HAD BEEN GREATLY EXAGGERATED)

15   On April 2, 1993, advertising itself was called into question by the very brands the industry had been building, in some cases, for over two centuries. That day is known in marketing circles as "Marlboro Friday," and it refers to a sudden announcement from Philip Morris that it would slash the price of Marlboro cigarettes by 20 percent in an attempt to compete with bargain brands that were eating into its market. The pundits went nuts, announcing in frenzied unison that not only was Marlboro dead, all brand names were dead. The reasoning was that if a "prestige" brand like Marlboro, whose image had been carefully groomed, preened and enhanced with more than a billion advertising dollars, was desperate enough to compete with no-names, then clearly the whole concept of branding had lost its currency. The public had seen the advertising, and the public didn't care. The Marlboro Man, after all, was not any old campaign; launched in 1954, it was the longest-running ad campaign in history. It was a legend. If the Marlboro Man had crashed, well, then, brand equity had crashed as well. The

implication that Americans were suddenly thinking for themselves en masse reverberated through Wall Street. The same day Philip Morris announced its price cut, stock prices nose-dived for all the household brands: Heinz, Quaker Oats, Coca-Cola, PepsiCo, Procter and Gamble and RJR Nabisco. Philip Morris's own stock took the worst beating.

Bob Stanojev, national director of consumer products marketing for Ernst and Young, explained the logic behind Wall Street's panic: "If one or two powerhouse consumer products companies start to cut prices for good, there's going to be an avalanche. Welcome to the value generation."

Yes, it was one of those moments of overstated instant consensus, but it was not entirely without cause. Marlboro had always sold itself on the strength of its iconic image marketing, not on anything so prosaic as its price. As we now know, the Marlboro Man survived the price wars without sustaining too much damage. At the time, however, Wall Street saw Philip Morris's decision as symbolic of a sea change. The price cut was an admission that Marlboro's name was no longer sufficient to sustain the flagship position, which in a context where image is equity meant that Marlboro had blinked. And when Marlboro—one of the quintessential global brands—blinks, it raises questions about branding that reach beyond Wall Street, and way beyond Philip Morris.

The panic of Marlboro Friday was not a reaction to a single incident. Rather, it was the culmination of years of escalating anxiety in the face of some rather dramatic shifts in consumer habits that were seen to be eroding the market share of household-name brands, from Tide to Kraft. Bargain-conscious shoppers, hit hard by the recession, were starting to pay more attention to price than to the prestige bestowed on their products by the yuppie ad campaigns of the 1980s. The public was suffering from a bad case of what is known in the industry as "brand blindness."

Study after study showed that baby boomers, blind to the alluring images of advertising and deaf to the empty promises of celebrity spokespersons, were breaking their lifelong brand loyalties and choosing to feed their families with private-label brands from the supermarket—claiming, heretically, that they couldn't tell the difference. From the beginning of the recession to 1993, Loblaw's President's Choice line, Wal-Mart's Great Value and Marks and Spencer's St. Michael prepared foods had nearly doubled their market share in North America and Europe. The computer market, meanwhile, was flooded by inexpensive clones, causing IBM to slash its prices and otherwise impale itself. It appeared to be a return to the proverbial shopkeeper dishing out generic goods from the barrel in a prebranded era.

THE BRANDS BOUNCE BACK

20   There were some brands that were watching from the sidelines as Wall Street declared the death of the brand. Funny, they must have thought, we don't feel dead.

Just as the admen had predicted at the beginning of the recession, the companies that exited the downturn running were the ones who opted for marketing over value every time: Nike, Apple, the Body Shop, Calvin Klein, Disney, Levi's and Starbucks. Not only were these brands doing just fine, thank you very much, but the act of branding was becoming a larger and larger focus of their businesses. For these companies, the ostensible product was mere filler for the real production: the brand. They integrated the idea of branding into the very fabric of their companies. Their corporate cultures were so tight and cloistered that to outsiders they appeared to be a cross between fraternity house, religious cult and sanitarium. Everything was an ad for the brand: bizarre lexicons for describing employees (partners, baristas, team players, crew members), company chants, superstar CEOs, fanatical attention to design consistency, a propensity for monument-building, and New Age mission statements. Unlike classic household brand names, such as Tide and Marlboro, these logos weren't losing their currency, they were in the midst of breaking every barrier in the marketing world—becoming cultural accessories and lifestyle philosophers. These companies didn't wear their image like a cheap shirt—their image was so integrated with their business that other people wore it as *their* shirt. And when the brands crashed, these companies didn't even notice—they were branded to the bone.

So the real legacy of Marlboro Friday is that it simultaneously brought the two most significant developments in nineties marketing and consumerism into sharp focus: the deeply unhip big-box bargain stores that provide the essentials of life and monopolize a disproportionate share of the market (Wal-Mart *et al.*) and the extra-premium "attitude" brands that provide the essentials of lifestyle and monopolize ever-expanding stretches of cultural space (Nike *et al.*). The way these two tiers of consumerism developed would have a profound impact on the economy in the years to come. When overall ad expenditures took a nosedive in 1991, Nike and Reebok were busy playing advertising chicken, with each company increasing its budget to outspend the other. In 1991 alone, Reebok upped its ad spending by 71.9 percent, while Nike pumped an extra 24.6 percent into its already soaring ad budget, bringing the company's total spending on marketing to a staggering $250 million annually. Far from worrying about competing on price, the sneaker pimps were designing ever more intricate and pseudoscientific air pockets, and driving up prices by signing star athletes to colossal sponsorship deals. The fetish strategy seemed to be working fine: in the six years prior to 1993, Nike had gone from a $750 million company to a $4 billion one and Phil Knight's Beaverton, Oregon, company emerged from the recession with profits 900 percent higher than when it began.

Benetton and Calvin Klein, meanwhile, were also upping their spending on lifestyle marketing, using ads to associate their lines with risqué art and progressive politics. Clothes barely appeared in these high-concept advertisements, let alone prices. Even more abstract was Absolut Vodka, which for some years now had been developing a marketing strategy in which its product disappeared and its brand was nothing but a blank bottle-shaped space that could be filled with whatever content a particular audience most wanted from its brands: intellectual in *Harper's*, futuristic in *Wired*, alternative in *Spin*, loud and proud in *Out* and "Absolut Centerfold" in *Playboy*. The brand reinvented itself as a cultural sponge, soaking up and morphing to its surroundings.

Saturn, too, came out of nowhere in October 1990 when GM launched a car built not out of steel and rubber but out of New Age spirituality and seventies feminism. After the car had been on the market a few years, the company held a "homecoming" weekend for Saturn owners, during which they could visit the auto plant and have a cookout with the people who made their cars. As the Saturn ads boasted at the time, "44,000 people spent their vacations with us, at a car plant." It was as if Aunt Jemima had come to life and invited you over to her house for dinner.

25   In 1993, the year the Marlboro Man was temporarily hobbled by "brand-blind" consumers, Microsoft made its striking debut on *Advertising Age*'s list of the top 200 ad spenders—the very same year that Apple computer increased its marketing budget by 30 percent after already making branding history with its Orwellian takeoff ad launch during the 1984 Super Bowl (see image on page 86). Like Saturn, both companies were selling a hip new relationship to the machine that left Big Blue IBM looking as clunky and menacing as the now-dead Cold War.

And then there were the companies that had always understood that they were selling brands before product. Coke, Pepsi, McDonald's, Burger King and Disney weren't fazed by the brand crisis, opting instead to escalate the brand war, especially since they had their eyes firmly fixed on global expansion. They were joined in this project by a wave of sophisticated producer/retailers who hit full stride in the late eighties and early nineties. The Gap, Ikea and the Body Shop were spreading like wildfire during this period, masterfully transforming the generic into the brand-specific, largely through bold, carefully branded packaging and the promotion of an "experiential" shopping environment. The Body Shop had been a presence in

Britain since the seventies, but it wasn't until 1988 that it began sprouting like a green weed on every street corner in the U.S. Even during the darkest years of the recession, the company opened between forty and fifty American stores a year. Most baffling of all to Wall Street, it pulled off the expansion without spending a dime on advertising. Who needed billboards and magazine ads when retail outlets were three-dimensional advertisements for an ethical and ecological approach to cosmetics? The Body Shop was all brand.

The Starbucks coffee chain, meanwhile, was also expanding during this period without laying out much in advertising; instead, it was spinning off its name into a wide range of branded projects: Starbucks airline coffee, office coffee, coffee ice cream, coffee beer. Starbucks seemed to understand brand names at a level even deeper than Madison Avenue, incorporating marketing into every fiber of its corporate concept—from the chain's strategic association with books, blues and jazz to its Euro-latte lingo. What the success of both the Body Shop and Starbucks showed was how far the branding project had come in moving beyond splashing one's logo on a billboard. Here were two companies that had fostered powerful identities by making their brand concept into a virus and sending it out into the culture via a variety of channels: cultural sponsorship, political controversy, the consumer experience and brand extensions. Direct advertising, in this context, was viewed as a rather clumsy intrusion into a much more organic approach to image building.

Scott Bedbury, Starbucks' vice president of marketing, openly recognized that "consumers don't truly believe there's a huge difference between products," which is why brands must "establish emotional ties" with their customers through "the Starbucks Experience." The people who line up for Starbucks, writes CEO Howard Shultz, aren't just there for the coffee. "It's the romance of the coffee experience, the feeling of warmth and community people get in Starbucks stores."

Interestingly, before moving to Starbucks, Bedbury was head of marketing at Nike, where he oversaw the launch of the "Just Do It!" slogan, among other watershed branding moments. In the following passage, he explains the common techniques used to infuse the two very different brands with meaning:

> Nike, for example, is leveraging the deep emotional connection that people have with sports and fitness. With Starbucks, we see how coffee has woven itself into the fabric of people's lives, and that's our opportunity for emotional leverage....A great brand raises the bar—it adds a greater sense of purpose to the experience, whether it's the challenge to do your best in sports and fitness or the affirmation that the cup of coffee you're drinking really matters.

30   This was the secret, it seemed, of all the success stories of the late eighties and early nineties. The lesson of Marlboro Friday was that there never really was a brand crisis—only brands that had crises of confidence. The brands would be okay, Wall Street concluded, so long as they believed fervently in the principles of branding and never, ever blinked. Overnight, "Brands, not products!" became the rallying cry for a marketing renaissance led by a new breed of companies that saw themselves as "meaning brokers" instead of product producers. What was changing was the idea of what—in both advertising and branding—was being sold. The old paradigm had it that all marketing was selling a product. In the new model, however, the product always takes a back seat to the real product, the brand, and the selling of the brand acquired an extra component that can only be described as spiritual. Advertising is about hawking product. Branding, in its truest and most advanced incarnations, is about corporate transcendence.

It may sound flaky, but that's precisely the point. On Marlboro Friday, a line was drawn in the sand between the lowly price slashers and the high-concept brand builders. The brand builders conquered and a new consensus was born: the products that will flourish in the future will be the ones presented not as "commodities" but as concepts: the brand as experience, as lifestyle.

Ever since, a select group of corporations has been attempting to free itself from the corporeal world of commodities, manufacturing and products to exist on another plane. Anyone can manufacture a product, they reason (and as the success of private-label brands during the recession proved, anyone did). Such menial tasks, therefore, can and should be farmed out to contractors and subcontractors whose only concern is filling the order on time and under budget (ideally in the Third World, where labor is dirt cheap, laws are lax and tax breaks come by the bushel). Headquarters, meanwhile, is free to focus on the real business at hand—creating a corporate mythology powerful enough to infuse meaning into these raw objects just by signing its name.

The corporate world has always had a deep New Age streak, fed—it has become clear—by a profound need that could not be met simply by trading widgets for cash. But when branding captured the corporate imagination, New Age vision quests took center stage. As Nike CEO Phil Knight explains, "For years we thought of ourselves as a production-oriented company, meaning we put all our emphasis on designing and manufacturing the product. But now we understand that the most important thing we do is market the product. We've come around to saying that Nike is a marketing-oriented company, and the product is our most important marketing tool." This project has since been taken to an even more advanced level with the emergence of on-line corporate giants such as Amazon.com. It is on-line that the purest brands are being built: liberated from the real-world burdens of stores and product manufacturing, these brands are free to soar, less as the disseminators of goods or services than as collective hallucinations.

Tom Peters, who has long coddled the inner flake in many a hard-nosed CEO, latched on to the branding craze as the secret to financial success, separating the transcendental logos and the earthbound products into two distinct categories of companies. "The top half—Coca-Cola, Microsoft, Disney, and so on—are pure 'players' in brainware. The bottom half [Ford and GM] are still lumpy-object purveyors, though automobiles are much 'smarter' than they used to be," Peters writes in *The Circle of Innovation* (1997), an ode to the power of marketing over production.

35   When Levi's began to lose market share in the late nineties, the trend was widely attributed to the company's failure—despite lavish ad spending—to transcend its products and become a free-standing meaning. "Maybe one of Levi's problems is that it has no Cola," speculated Jennifer Steinhauer in *The New York Times*. "It has no denim-toned house paint. Levi makes what is essentially a commodity: blue jeans. Its ads may evoke rugged outdoorsmanship, but Levi hasn't promoted any particular life style to sell other products."

In this high-stakes new context, the cutting-edge ad agencies no longer sold companies on individual campaigns but on their ability to act as "brand stewards": identifying, articulating and protecting the corporate soul. Not surprisingly, this spelled good news for the U.S. advertising industry, which in 1994 saw a spending increase of 8.6 percent over the previous year. In one year, the ad industry went from a near crisis to another "best year yet." And that was only the beginning of triumphs to come. By 1997, corporate advertising, defined as "ads that position a corporation, its values, its personality and character" were up 18 percent from the year before.

With this wave of brand mania has come a new breed of businessman, one who will proudly inform you that Brand X is not a product but a way of life, an attitude, a set of values, a look, an idea. And it sounds really great—way better than that Brand X is a screwdriver, or a hamburger chain, or a pair of jeans, or even a very successful line of running shoes. Nike, Phil Knight announced in the late eighties, is "a sports company"; its mission is not to sell shoes but to "enhance people's lives through sports and fitness" and to keep "the magic of sports alive." Company president-cum-sneaker-shaman Tom Clark explains that "the inspiration of sports allows us to rebirth ourselves constantly."

Reports of such "brand vision" epiphanies began surfacing from all corners. "Polaroid's problem," diagnosed the chairman of its advertising agency, John Hegarty, "was that they kept thinking of themselves as a camera. But the '[brand] vision' process taught us something: Polaroid is not a camera—it's a social lubricant." IBM isn't selling computers, it's selling business "solutions." Swatch is not about watches, it is about the idea of time. At Diesel Jeans, owner Renzo Rosso told *Paper* magazine, "We don't sell a product, we sell a style of life. I think we have created a movement....The Diesel concept is everything. It's the way to live, it's the way to wear, it's the way to do something." And as Body Shop founder Anita Roddick explained to me, her stores aren't about what they sell, they are the conveyers of a grand idea—a political philosophy about women, the environment and ethical business. "I just use the company that I surprisingly created as a success—it shouldn't have been like this, it wasn't meant to be like this—to stand on the products to shout out on these issues," Roddick says.

The famous late graphic designer Tibor Kalman summed up the shifting role of the brand this way: "The original notion of the brand was quality, but now brand is a stylistic badge of courage."

40   The idea of selling the courageous message of a brand, as opposed to a product, intoxicated these CEOs, providing as it did an opportunity for seemingly limitless expansion. After all, if a brand was not a product, it could be anything! And nobody embraced branding theory with more evangelical zeal than Richard Branson, whose Virgin Group has branded joint ventures in everything from music to bridal gowns to airlines to cola to financial services. Branson refers derisively to the "stilted Anglo-Saxon view of consumers," which holds that a name should be associated with a product like sneakers or soft drinks, and opts instead for "the Asian 'trick'" of the *keiretsus* (a Japanese term meaning a network of linked corporations). The idea, he explains, is to "build brands not around products but around reputation. The great Asian names imply quality, price and innovation rather than a specific item.

I call these 'attribute' brands: They do not relate directly to one product—such as a Mars bar or a Coca-Cola—but instead to a set of values."

Tommy Hilfiger, meanwhile, is less in the business of manufacturing clothes than he is in the business of signing his name. The company is run entirely through licensing agreements, with Hilfiger commissioning all its products from a group of other companies: Jockey International makes Hilfiger underwear, Pepe Jeans London makes Hilfiger jeans, Oxford Industries make Tommy shirts, the Stride. Rite Corporation makes its footwear. What does Tommy Hilfiger manufacture? Nothing at all.

So passé had products become in the age of lifestyle branding that by the late nineties, newer companies like Lush cosmetics and Old Navy clothing began playing with the idea of old-style commodities as a source of retro marketing imagery. The Lush chain serves up its face masks and moisturizers out of refrigerated stainless-steel bowls, spooned into plastic containers with grocery-store labels. Old Navy showcases its shrink-wrapped T-shirts and sweatshirts in deli-style chrome refrigerators, as if they were meat or cheese. When you are a pure, concept-driven brand, the aesthetics of raw product can prove as "authentic" as loft living.

And lest the branding business be dismissed as the playground of trendy consumer items such as sneakers, jeans and New Age beverages, think again. Caterpillar, best known for building tractors and busting unions, has barreled into the branding business, launching the Cat accessories line: boots, back-packs, hats and anything else calling out for a postindustrial *je ne sais quoi*. Intel Corp., which makes computer parts no one sees and few understand, transformed its processors into a fetish brand with TV ads featuring line workers in funky metallic space suits dancing to "Shake Your Groove Thing." The Intel mascots proved so popular that the company has sold hundreds of thousands of bean-filled dolls modeled on the shimmery dancing technicians. Little wonder, then, that when asked about the company's decision to diversify its products, the senior vice president for sales and marketing, Paul S. Otellini, replied that Intel is "like Coke. One brand, many different products."

And if Caterpillar and Intel can brand, surely anyone can.

45   There is, in fact, a new strain in marketing theory that holds that even the lowliest natural resources, barely processed, can develop brand identities, thus giving way to hefty premium-price markups. In an essay appropriately titled "How to Brand Sand," advertising executives Sam Hill, Jack McGrath and Sandeep Dayal team up to tell the corporate world that with the right marketing plan, nobody has to stay stuck in the stuff business. "Based on extensive research, we would argue that you can indeed brand not only sand, but also wheat, beef, brick, metals, concrete, chemicals, corn grits and an endless variety of commodities traditionally considered immune to the process."

Over the past six years, spooked by the near-death experience of Marlboro Friday, global corporations have leaped on the brand-wagon with what can only be described as a religious fervor. Never again would the corporate world stoop to praying at the altar of the commodity market. From now on they would worship only graven media images. Or to quote Tom Peters, the brand man himself: "Brand! Brand!! Brand!!! That's the message...for the late '90s and beyond."

WHO'S WEARING THE TROUSERS?

The Economist

The Economist is a leading weekly business and news magazine in the United Kingdom. This "Special Report" on brands appeared in the September 8, 2002, issue, not long after Naomi Klein's *No Logo* was published.

SUGGESTION FOR READING   As you read, notice first how *The Economist* characterizes the "antibranding" argument in Klein's *No Logo*. Then consider how the magazine responds to the criticism of branding.

1   Brands are in the dock, accused of all sorts of mischief, from threatening our health and destroying our environment to corrupting our children. Brands are so powerful, it is alleged, that they seduce us to look alike, eat alike and be alike. At the same time, they are spiritually empty, gradually (and almost subliminally) undermining our moral values.

This grim picture has been popularised by a glut of anti-branding books, ranging from Eric Schlosser's "Fast Food Nation" and Robert Frank's "Luxury Fever" to "The World is Not for Sale" by François Dufour and José Bové—a French farmer who is best known for vandalising a McDonald's restaurant. The argument has, however, been most forcefully articulated in Naomi Klein's book "No Logo: Taking Aim at the Brand Bullies".

Not since Vance Packard's 1957 classic "The Hidden Persuaders" has one book stirred up so much antipathy to marketing. Its author has become the spokesman for a worldwide movement against multinationals and their insidious brands. Britain's *Times* newspaper rated her one of the world's most influential people under 35. Published in at least seven languages, "No Logo" has touched a universal nerve.

Its argument runs something like this. In the new global economy, brands represent a huge portion of the value of a company and, increasingly, its biggest source of profits. So companies are switching from producing products to marketing aspirations, images and lifestyles. They are trying to become weightless, shedding physical assets by shifting production from their own factories in the first world to other people's in the third.

5   These image mongers offer "a Barbie world for adults" says Ms Klein, integrating their brands so fully into our lives that they cocoon us in a "brandscape". No space is untouched: schools, sports stars and even youth identity are all being co-opted by brands. "Powerful brands no longer just advertise in a magazine, they control its content," says Ms Klein.

Now they are the target of a backlash. A new generation of activists is rising up and attacking, not governments or ideologies but brands, directly and often violently. Coca-Cola, Wal-Mart and McDonald's have been rounded on over issues ranging from racism to child labour to advertising in schools.

LESS A PRODUCT, MORE A WAY OF LIFE

In one sense it is easy to understand why Ms Klein and her camp feel as they do. The word "brand" is everywhere, to the point where Disney chairman Michael Eisner calls the term "overused, sterile and unimaginative". Products, people, countries and companies are all racing to turn themselves into brands—to make their image more likeable and understandable. British Airways did it. Target and Tesco are doing it, while people from Martha Stewart to Madonna are branding themselves. Britain tried to become a brand with its "Cool Britannia" slogan, and Wally Olins, a corporate-identity consultant and co-founder of Wolff Olins, a consultancy, even wants to have a crack at branding the European Union.

At the very least, Ms Klein overstates the case. Brands are not as powerful as their opponents allege, nor is the public as easily manipulated. The reality is more complicated. Indeed, many of the established brands that top the league tables are in trouble, losing customer loyalty and value. Annual tables of the world's top ten brands used to change very little from year to year. Names such as Kellogg's, Kodak, Marlboro and Nescafé appeared with almost monotonous regularity. Now, none of these names is in the top ten. Kellogg's, second less than a decade ago, languishes at 39th in the latest league table produced by Interbrand, a brand consultancy.

Of the 74 brands that appear in the top 100 rankings in both of the past two years, 41 declined in value between 2000 and 2001, while the combined value of the 74 fell by $49 billion—to an estimated $852 billion, a drop of more than 5%. Brands fall from grace and newer, nimbler ones replace them.

10   Meanwhile, consumers have become more fickle. A study of American lifestyles by DDB, an advertising agency, found that the percentage of consumers between the ages of 20 and 29 who said that they stuck to well-known brands fell from 66% in 1975 to 59% in 2000. The bigger surprise, though, was that the percentage in the 60—69 age bracket who said that they remained loyal to well-known brands fell over the same period, from 86% to 59%. It is not only the young who flit from brand to brand. Every age group, it seems, is more or less equally disloyal. The result is that many of the world's biggest brands are struggling. If they are making more and more noise, it is out of desperation.

As they move from merely validating products to encapsulating whole lifestyles, brands are evolving a growing social dimension. In the developed world, they are seen by some to have expanded into the vacuum left by the decline of organised religion. But this has made brands—and the multinationals that are increasingly identified with them—not more powerful, but more vulnerable. Consumers will tolerate a lousy product for far longer than they will tolerate a lousy lifestyle.

BRANDS PAST

Historically, building a brand was rather simple. A logo was a straightforward guarantee of quality and consistency, or it was a signal that a product was something new. For that, consumers were, quite rationally, prepared to pay a premium. "Brands were the first piece of consumer protection," says Jeremy Bullmore, a long-time director of J. Walter Thompson, an advertising agency. "You knew where to go if you had a complaint." Even the central planners in the old Soviet Union had to establish "production marks" to stop manufacturers cutting corners on quality.

Brands also helped consumers to buy efficiently. As Unilever's chairman Niall FitzGerald points out: "A brand is a storehouse of trust. That matters more and more as choices multiply. People want to simplify their lives."

This implicit trade-off was efficient and profitable for companies too. Building a brand nationally required little more than an occasional advertisement on a handful of television or radio stations showing how the product tasted better or drove faster. There was little regulation. It was easy for brands such as Coca-Cola, Kodak and Marlboro to become hugely powerful. Because shopping was still a local business and competition limited, a successful brand could maintain its lead and high prices for years. A strong brand acted as an effective barrier to entry for others.

15   In western markets, over time, brand building became much trickier. As standards of manufacturing rose, it became harder for firms to differentiate on quality alone and so to charge a premium price. This was particularly true of packaged goods like food: branded manufacturers lost market share to retailers' own brands, which consumers learned to trust.

Nor were traditional branded products any longer the only choice in town. As shoppers became more mobile and discovered more places to buy, including online websites, they switched products more often. Brands now face competition from the most unexpected quarters, says Rita Clifton, chief executive of Interbrand: "If you were a soap-powder company years ago, your competition would come from the same industry and probably the same country. Now it could be anyone. Who'd have thought that Virgin would sell mobile phones, Versace run hotels or Tesco sell banking services?"

Even truly innovative products can no longer expect to keep the market to themselves for long. Gillette spent $750m and seven years developing its three-bladed Mach 3 men's razor, for which it charged a fat premium. But only months later it was trumped by Asda, a British supermarket that came out with its own version for a fraction of the price.

Consumers are now bombarded with choices. They are "commercials veterans", inundated with up to 1,500 pitches a day. Far from being gullible and easily manipulated, they are cynical about marketing and less responsive to entreaties to buy. "Consumers are like roaches," say Jonathan Bond and Richard Kirshenbaum in their book "Under the Radar—Talking to Today's Cynical Consumer". "We spray them with marketing, and for a time it works. Then, inevitably, they develop an immunity, a resistance."

Some of the most cynical consumers, say the authors, are the young. Nearly half of all American college students have taken marketing courses and "know the enemy". For them, "shooting down advertising has become a kind of sport."

20   Consumers are also harder to reach. They are busier, more distracted and have more media to choose from. And they lead lives that are more complicated and less predictable. A detergent can no longer count on its core consumer being a white housewife. Against this background, it has never been harder to develop or even just sustain a brand. Coca-Cola, Gillette and Nike are prominent examples of the many that are struggling to increase volumes, raise prices and boost margins.

MARKETING MISTAKES

Marketers have to take some of the blame. While consumers have changed beyond recognition, marketing has not. Elliott Ettenberg, author of a forthcoming book on the decline of marketing says: "Everything else has been reinvented—distribution, new product development, the supply chain. But marketing is stuck in the past." Even in America, home to nine of the world's ten most valuable brands, it can be a shockingly old-fashioned business. Marketing theory is still largely based on the days when Procter & Gamble's brands dominated America, and its advertising agencies wrote the rules. Those rules focused on the product and where to sell it, not the customer.

The new marketing approach is to build a brand not a product—to sell a lifestyle or a personality, to appeal to emotions. But this requires a far greater understanding of human psychology. It is a much harder task than describing the virtues of a product.

Sweden's Absolut Vodka, one of the world's biggest spirits brands, demonstrates this well. Its clever, simple ads featuring its now famous clear bottle were dreamt up long before the vodka was fermented. Goran Lundqvist, the company's president, says that Absolut's wit, rather than its taste, is the reason for the spirit's success: "Absolut is a personality," he claims. "We like certain people, but some people are just more fun and interesting." Other products have also succeeded in touching the emotions. Fans of Ben & Jerry's ice cream, for example, think that it is hip for its ethical stance, while many Harley Davidson owners are literally in love with their machines.

The trouble is that most marketers have to struggle to create such feelings for their brands. Many firms, most notably banks, mistake inertia for liking. Others, such as Coca-Cola and McDonald's, complacent from past success, find it difficult to admit that their customers are drifting away to newer offerings. Yet others, panicking that they need to do something, reinvent themselves and unwittingly lose the essence of their appeal. Old-fashioned market-research methods help explain such mistakes. Focus groups, for example, are poor at rooting out the real reasons why people like brands, but they are still heavily used.

25   The attempt by brands to adopt a social component—to embrace a lifestyle—is giving consumers a lever to influence the behaviour of the companies that stand behind them. The "No Logo" proponents are correct that brands are a conduit through which influence flows between companies and consumers. But far more often, it is consumers that dictate to companies and ultimately decide their fate, rather than the other way round. Think of the failure of such high-profile product launches as "New Coke"; the disastrous effect on Hoover of a badly-designed sales promotion in Britain a few years ago; or the boycott of genetically modified foods by Europe's consumers.

The Internet also provides some telling examples. Dotcoms such as Webvan and Kozmo were lauded for the speed with which they built their brands. Unconstrained by the need to make profits, however, such companies built customer loyalty artificially. Once business reality returned, they were revealed as unsustainable promises. Consumers, it turned out, were not gullible. As Mr Olins says: "Is the brand immoral, can it get us to do things we don't want to? No. When we like a brand we manifest our loyalty in cash. If we don't like it, we walk away. Customers are in charge."

LEVERS FOR LIFTING STANDARDS

The truth is that people like brands. They not only simplify choices and guarantee quality, but they add fun and interest. "In technocratic and colourless times, brands bring warmth, familiarity and trust," says Peter Brabeck, boss of Nestlé. They also have a cultish quality that creates a sense of belonging. "In an irreligious world, brands provide us with beliefs," says Mr Olins. "They define who we are and signal our affiliations."

Jim McDowell, head of marketing at BMW North America, says that when young people visit a 3Com-sponsored baseball stadium or a Continental Airlines' hockey arena, they realise that "some of the best things they have ever experienced have come through brands."

Since brands and their corporate parents are becoming ever more entwined—both in the public perception and commercial reality—it follows that consumers can increasingly influence the behaviour of companies. Arrogance, greed and hypocrisy are swiftly punished. Popular outrage forced Shell to retreat over the scrapping of its Brent Spar oil platform and its activities in Nigeria. Nike has had to revamp its whole supply chain after being accused of running sweatshops.

30   Even mighty Coca-Cola has been humbled. Told of a contamination incident in Belgium, its then-boss, Doug Ivester, is said to have dismissed it with the comment: "Where the fuck is Belgium?" A few months later, after a mishandled

public-relations exercise that cost Coke sales across Europe, he was fired. "It is absurd to say that brands can be too powerful," concludes Interbrand's Ms Clifton. "Brands are the ultimate accountable institution. If people fall out of love with your brand, you go out of business."

This ultimately makes brands highly effective tools through which to bring about change. Rafael Gomez, professor of marketing at the London School of Economics, points out that companies like Nike have been forced to invest heavily in improving their manufacturing standards in order to protect their brands. World Bank studies show that brands have been a boon for developing economies, because it is the branded multinationals that pay the best wages and have the best working conditions. Those countries that are more open to trade and foreign investment, such as the Asian tigers, have shown faster increases in living standards than relatively closed countries such as much of Africa.

Brands of the future will have to stand not only for product quality and a desirable image. They will also have to signal something wholesome about the company behind the brand. "The next big thing in brands is social responsibility," says Mr Olins, "It will be clever to say there is nothing different about our product or price, but we behave well." Far from being evil, brands are becoming an effective weapon for holding even the largest global corporations to account. If we do not use them for that purpose, as Mr Olins puts it, "we are lazy and indifferent and we deserve what we get."

Fittingly, brands will then have come full circle. The founders of some of the world's oldest— Hershey, Disney, Cadbury and Boots, for example—devoted their lives and company profits to social improvements, to building spacious towns, better schools and bigger hospitals. The difference in the future will be that it will be consumers, not philanthropists, who will dictate the social agenda.

NO SWEAT, NO SLANG

Jonah Peretti

Jonah Peretti, an MIT student and antisweatshop activist, responded in January 2001 to Nike's offer to personalize shoes for its customers by stitching a word or phrase on their shoes. Peretti filled out the form for this service and sent Nike $50 to stitch "sweatshop" on his shoes. Here is the correspondence between Peretti and Nike that followed.

SUGGESTION FOR READING   As you read the exchange between Nike and Peretti, notice differences in the tone of the correspondence. Consider how Nike presents itself and how Peretti responds.

From: "Personalize, NIKE iD"
To: "Jonah H. Peretti"
Subject: RE: Your NIKE iD order #16468000
Your Nike iD order was cancelled for one or more of the following reasons:

1. Your Personal iD contains another party's trademark or other intellectual property.
2. Your Personal iD contains the name of an athlete or team we do not have the legal right to use.
3. Your Personal iD was left blank. Did you not want any personalization?
4. Your Personal iD contains profanity or inappropriate slang, and besides, your mother would slap us.

If you wish to reorder your NIKE iD product with a new personalization please visit us again at www.nike.com
   Thank you,
   NIKE iD

From: "Jonah H. Peretti"
To: "Personalize, NIKE iD"
Subject: RE: Your NIKE iD order #16468000
Greetings,

My order was canceled but my personal NIKE iD does not violate any of the criteria outlined in your message. The Personal iD on my custom ZOOM XC USA running shoes was the word "sweatshop."

Sweatshop is not: 1) another's party's trademark, 2) the name of any athlete, 3) blank, or 4) profanity.

I chose the iD because I wanted to remember the toil and labor of the children that made my shoes. Could you please ship them to me immediately.

Thanks and Happy New Year,
Jonah Peretti

From: "Personalize, NIKE iD"
To: "Jonah H. Peretti"
Subject: RE: Your NIKE iD order #16468000
Dear NIKE iD Customer,

Your NIKE iD order was canceled because the iD you have chosen contains, as stated in the previous e-mail correspondence, "inappropriate slang."

If you wish to reorder your NIKE iD product with a new personalization please visit us again at www.nike.com

Thank you,
NIKE iD

From: "Jonah H. Peretti"
To: "Personalize, NIKE iD"
Subject: RE: Your NIKE iD order #16468000
Dear NIKE iD,

Thank you for your quick response to my inquiry about my custom ZOOM XC USA running shoes.

Although I commend you for your prompt customer service, I disagree with the claim that my personal iD was inappropriate slang.

After consulting Webster's Dictionary, I discovered that "sweatshop" is in fact part of standard English, and not slang.

The word means: "a shop or factory in which workers are employed for long hours at low wages and under unhealthy conditions" and its origin dates from 1892.

So my personal iD does meet the criteria detailed in your first email.

Your web site advertises that the NIKE iD program is "about freedom to choose and freedom to express who you are." I share Nike's love of freedom and personal statement. The site also says that "If you want it done right... build it yourself."

I was thrilled to be able to build my own shoes, and my personal iD was offered as a small token of appreciation for the sweatshop workers poised to help me realize my vision.

I hope that you will value my freedom of statement and reconsider your decision to reject my order.

Thank you,
Jonah Peretti

From: "Personalize, NIKE iD"
To: "Jonah H. Peretti"
Subject: RE: Your NIKE iD order #16468000
Dear NIKE iD Customer,

Regarding the rules for personalization it also states on the NIKE iD web site that "Nike reserves the right to cancel any Personal iD up to 24 hours after it has been submitted".

In addition it further explains:

"While we honor most personal iDs, we cannot honor every one. Some may be (or contain) others trademarks, or the names of certain professional sports teams, athletes or celebrities that Nike does not have the right to use. Others may contain material that we consider inappropriate or simply do not want to place on our products. Unfortunately, at times this obliges us to decline personal iDs that may otherwise seem unobjectionable. In any event, we will let you know if we decline your personal iD, and we will offer you the chance to submit another."

With these rules in mind we cannot accept your order as submitted.

If you wish to reorder your NIKE iD product with a new personalization please visit us again at www.nike.com

Thank you,
NIKE iD

From: "Jonah H. Peretti"
To: "Personalize, NIKE iD"

Subject: RE: Your NIKE iD order #16468000
Dear NIKE iD,

Thank you for the time and energy you have spent on my request.

I have decided to order the shoes with a different iD, but I would like to make one small request.

Could you please send me a color snapshot of the ten-year-old Vietnamese girl who makes my shoes?

Thanks,
Jonah Peretti

SUGGESTIONS FOR DISCUSSION

1. Compare the explanations of the term *branding* that you and your classmates wrote in response to the excerpt from Naomi Klein's *No Logo*. What exactly does Klein mean? What examples and evidence does she provide to illustrate her meaning? What assumptions does she seem to be making?

2. Consider how *The Economist* article characterizes Klein's "antibranding" point of view. Do you think it's a fair and comprehensive explanation? What, if anything, does it leave out? What are the main points of difference *The Economist* presents to distinguish its view from Klein's? What assumptions does the magazine seem to be making?

3. What do you think Klein and *The Economist* might say about the correspondence between Jonah Peretti and Nike?

SUGGESTIONS FOR WRITING

1. Write an essay about your personal relationship to brands. Pick a particular brand to focus your writing. Take seriously the point that Klein and marketing people make about the way brands identify not just a product but, as Klein puts it, a "way of life, an attitude, a set of values, a look, an idea." How does a particular brand of goods you wear, use, or otherwise consume project a lifestyle? How does the brand influence your own sense of identity? What attitudes does it have for you?

2. There are clearly significant differences in the way Naomi Klein and *The Economist* think about brands. Write an essay that locates your own thinking in relation to what they have written. First, summarize the two points of view. Then analyze what you see as the main differences and the assumptions behind these differences. Finally, explain what you think.

3. Write a news story that might appear in your campus or local newspaper about the correspondence between Jonah Peretti and Nike. Report on what happened to inform your readers but also indicate what you think is at stake in the correspondence. What does it mean? Why does it matter?

Tibor Kalman

Tibor Kalman (1949–1999) was an important and influential graphic designer who worked on everything from the redevelopment of Times Square in New York to Talking Heads' record jackets. The following Visual Essay on the design of labels on spaghetti sauce jars appeared in a special edition of the *New York Times Magazine*, "The Shock of the Familiar," about design in contemporary society. As the *New York Times Magazine* says, "We asked the

Message: Sweet-Talking Spaghetti Sauce

How to really read a label. By Tibor Kalman

Photographs by Davies + Starr

SUPER A

"Good morning, gents. I am interested in conveying the favorable price-quantity ratio of Super A meatless sauce. Our serving-suggestion photo (a pound of spaghetti, a pound of sauce, a fork and a knife) represents an inexpensive, nutritious meal for a very, very large, very, very hungry individual."

MARKET: Thrifty, large, hungry people, all ages.

AUNT MILLIE'S

"Just look at this picture of Aunt Millie. Can you imagine anyone sweeter, purer, more Italian? And we got 'Little Italy,' 'homemade' and '1946' right on the label. What else could you want?"

MARKET: Mama's boys: proud, older Italian-Americans.

CLASSICO

"The Classico typeface is right here. We antiqued it to make sure it looks really old. We have the antique tomato drawing, the Amish jar engineer-made The jar is square, to suggest that people used to put up their own tomatoes in them. And it only took 175 focus groups to get us to this label design."

MARKET: Upscale types 25 to 49 who enjoy fake antique furniture.

designer Tibor Kalman…to pretend he was pitching these labels to various manufacturers. We wanted to know how he thought they would have tried to sell the designs, as well as to get a view of the messages the labels are trying to communicate."

As you read, notice that Tibor Kalman looks first at the message that the label sends and then at the market that the messages address. Consider how the design of the labels sets up a relationship between message and market.

hen you think about it, sauce is mostly sauce. It's the label that makes the difference. A multimillion-dollar business, packaging is the most lucrative form of design work in the United States. We asked the designer Tibor Kalman (shown below the jars) to pretend he was pitching these labels to various manufacturers. We wanted to know how he thought they would have tried to sell the designs, as well as to get a view of the messages the labels are trying to communicate.

VICTORIA
"Mama mia! What do we have here? We have the typeface from the old grocery in Palermo. The gondola picture from the wall of an old bar in Calabria. Traditionalist, but Venetian. Very romantic."
MARKET: 65-plus Sicilian-born Italian-Americans.

MILLINA'S FINEST
"We got Mama, fields, a nice basket of tomatoes, fat free, sun-dried tomatoes, organic. The whole shebang. Perfect for people who want the best but have no idea what the best is."
MARKET: Collegiate 18- to 49-ers who need a lot of "benefits" in their sauce.

NEWMAN'S OWN
"Paul Newman, Paul Newman, Paul Newman. Blue eyes. All the money goes to charity. It's humanitarian, natural, funny and sexy. Selling this is like falling off a log."
MARKET: How could any woman resist?

HUNT'S OLD COUNTRY
"Guys. We gotta make a sauce for guys. So I got some good old Picket Fence Gothic type, with cracked paint and all. Very barbecue. Thought the guys would appreciate these bodacious tomatoes."
MARKET: West of New York, east of Los Angeles, 50-plus guys, weighing 250-plus pounds.

SUGGESTIONS FOR DISCUSSION

1. Tibor Kalman first uses the voice of an advertising pitchman to describe the message in the label. (The pitch appears in quotes.) What visual features of the labels does he seem to notice? He then identifies the market targeted by the message—but without explicitly explaining how the connection works. Fill in that connection. Why would particular labels appeal to particular segments of the spaghetti sauce market?

2. The market in the United States is saturated with similar products. Spaghetti sauce is just one example. Notice that Kalman is interested in how the visual styles of labels differ, but he doesn't mention anything about whether there are consequential differences among the products themselves. In your experience, when there are a range of competing products, do the products themselves differ, or are the differences mainly in the labeling?

3. Work in a group with three or four other students and pick a product you're familiar with that has competing brands. Bring at least four examples of the product to class to make a presentation. Follow Kalman's example, and explain the message on the label and the market that is targeted.

SUGGESTIONS FOR WRITING

1. Using Tibor Kalman's Visual Essay as a guide, write your own essay on the visual design of spaghetti sauce jars. Make explicit how the pitch of the adman connects to the targeted audience. Pick two or three jar labels, and explain how the visual design is related to a particular part of the market.

2. Follow Kalman's example and do a visual essay on the labels of several similar products. Use at least three or four examples. Give the adman's pitch in quotes, and then indicate the targeted audience.

3. Design a label for a product. Accompany the design with a written explanation or an oral presentation (depending on what your teacher asks for) of the message on the label and the market you've targeted. Think here in terms of how to distinguish what is basically the same product from other products of the same type.

CLASSIC READING

WINE AND MILK

Roland Barthes

Roland Barthes (1915–1980) was a professor at the College de France in Paris and one of the most influential cultural and literary critics of the twentieth century. The following selection, "Wine and Milk," comes from *Mythologies*, a collection of essays Barthes wrote and published in French periodicals in the 1950s. "The starting point" of these essays, as Barthes says, was "a feeling of impatience at the sight of 'naturalness' with which newspapers, art, and common sense constantly dress up a reality which, even though it is the one we live in, is undoubtedly determined by history." Barthes was interested in analyzing such common objects and events as toys, food, wrestling, striptease, detergents, and cruises to reveal how their taken-for-granted presence in everyday life shapes the style and sensibility of French culture.

SUGGESTION FOR READING Roland Barthes uses the terms *myth* and *mythology* to refer to words and things that appear to be "natural" and part of common sense. As Barthes puts it, he wants to identify "*what-goes-without-saying*, the ideological abuse" that is hidden in seeing elements of culture as a second nature. Notice how Barthes is seeking to make ordinary things such as wine and milk speak of their hidden meanings.

1 Wine is felt by the French nation to be a possession which is its very own, just like its three hundred and sixty types of cheese and its culture. It is a totem-drink, corresponding to the milk of the Dutch cow or the tea ceremonially taken by the British Royal Family. Bachelard has already given the 'substantial psycho-analysis' of this fluid, at the end of his essay on the reveries on the theme of the will, and shown that wine is the sap of the sun and the earth, that its basic state is not the moist but the dry, and that on such grounds the substance which is most contrary to it is water.

Actually, like all resilient totems, wine supports a varied mythology which does not trouble about contradictions. This galvanic substance is always considered, for instance, as the most efficient of thirst-quenchers, or at least this serves as the major alibi for its consumption ('It's thirsty weather'). In its red form, it has blood, the dense and vital fluid, as a very old hypostasis. This is because in fact its humoral form matters little; it is above all a converting substance, capable of reversing situations and states, and of extracting from objects their opposites—for instance, making a weak man strong or a silent one talkative. Hence its old alchemical heredity, its philosophical power to transmute and create *ex nihilo*.

Being essentially a function whose terms can change, wine has at its disposal apparently plastic powers: it can serve as an alibi to dream as well as reality, it depends on the users of the myth. For the worker, wine means enabling him to do his task with demiurgic ease ('heart for the work'). For the intellectual, wine has the reverse function: the local white wine or the beaujolais of the writer is meant to cut him off from the all too expected environment of cocktails and expensive drinks (the only ones which snobbishness leads one to offer him). Wine will deliver him from myths, will remove some of his intellectualism, will make him the equal of the proletarian; through wine, the intellectual comes nearer to a natural virility, and believes he can thus escape the curse that a century and a half of romanticism still brings to bear on the purely cerebral (it is well known that one of the myths peculiar to the modern intellectual is the obsession to 'have it where it matters').

But what is characteristic of France is that the converting power of wine is never openly presented as an end. Other countries drink to get drunk, and this is accepted by everyone; in France, drunkenness is a consequence, never an intention. A drink is felt as the spinning out of a pleasure, not as the necessary cause of an effect which is sought: wine is not only a philtre, it is also the leisurely act of drinking. The *gesture* has here a decorative value, and the power of wine is never separated from its modes of existence (unlike whisky, for example, which is drunk for its type of drunkenness—'the most agreeable, with the least painful after-effects'—which one gulps down repeatedly, and the drinking of which is reduced to a causal act).

5   All this is well known and has been said a thousand times in folklore, proverbs, conversations and Literature. But this very universality implies a kind of conformism: to believe in wine is a coercive collective act. A Frenchman who kept this myth at arm's length would expose himself to minor but definite problems of integration, the first of which, precisely, would be that of having to explain his attitude. The universality principle fully applies here, inasmuch as society calls anyone who does not believe in wine by *names* such as sick, disabled or depraved: it does not *comprehend* him (in both senses, intellectual and spatial, of the word). Conversely, an award of good integration is given to whoever is a practising wine-drinker: knowing *how* to drink is a national technique which serves to qualify the Frenchman, to demonstrate at once his performance, his control and his sociability. Wine gives thus a foundation for a collective morality, within which everything is redeemed: true, excesses, misfortunes and crimes are possible with wine, but never viciousness, treachery or baseness; the evil it can generate is in the nature of fate and therefore escapes penalization, it evokes the theatre rather than a basic temperament.

Wine is a part of society because it provides a basis not only for a morality but also for an environment; it is an ornament in the slightest ceremonials of French daily life, from the snack (plonk and camembert) to the feast, from the conversation at the local café to the speech at a formal dinner. It exalts all climates, of whatever kind: in cold weather, it is associated with all the myths of becoming warm, and at the height of summer, with all the images of shade, with all things cool and sparkling. There is no situation involving some physical constraint (temperature, hunger, boredom, compulsion, disorientation) which does not give rise to dreams of wine. Combined as a basic substance with other alimentary figures, it can cover all the aspects of space and time for the Frenchman. As soon as one gets to know someone's daily life fairly well, the absence of wine gives a sense of shock, like something exotic: M. Coty, having allowed himself to be photographed, at the beginning of his seven years' presidency, sitting at home before a table on which a bottle of beer seemed to replace, by an extraordinary exception, the familiar litre of red wine, the whole nation was in a flutter; it was as intolerable as having a bachelor king. Wine is here a part of the reason of state.

Bachelard was probably right in seeing water as the opposite of wine: mythically, this is true; sociologically, today at least, less so; economic and historical circumstances have given this part to milk. The latter is now the true anti-wine: and not only because of M. Mendès-France's popularizing efforts (which had a purposely mythological look as when he used to drink milk during his speeches in the Chamber, as Popeye eats spinach), but also because in the basic morphology of substances milk is the opposite of fire by all the denseness of its molecules, by the creamy, and therefore soothing, nature of its spreading. Wine is mutilating, surgical, it transmutes and delivers; milk is cosmetic, it joins, covers, restores. Moreover, its purity, associated with the innocence of the child, is a token of strength, of a strength which is not revulsive, not congestive, but calm, white, lucid, the equal of reality. Some American films, in which the hero, strong and uncompromising, did not shrink from having a glass of milk before drawing his avenging Colt, have paved the way for this new Parsifalian myth. A strange mixture of milk and pomegranate, originating in America, is to this day sometimes drunk in Paris, among gangsters and hoodlums. But milk remains an exotic substance; it is wine which is part of the nation.

The mythology of wine can in fact help us to understand the usual ambiguity of our daily life. For it is true that wine is a good and fine substance, but it is no less true that its production is deeply involved in French capitalism, whether it is that of the private distillers or that of the big settlers in Algeria who impose on the Muslims, on the very land of which they have been dispossessed, a crop of which they have no need, while they lack even bread. There are thus very engaging myths which are however not innocent. And the characteristic of our current alienation is precisely that wine cannot be an unalloyedly blissful substance, except if we wrongfully forget that it is also the product of an expropriation.

SUGGESTIONS FOR DISCUSSION

1. According to Barthes, wine and wine-drinking are intimately connected to what it means to be French. Still, the connection between wine and French culture and identity is not a simple one. Wine seems to have multiple meanings in this essay—"a varied mythology which does not trouble about contradictions." Identify the multiple meanings in the essay. How do these multiple meanings relate to each other? What web of associations do they establish about wine in France? Why do you think Barthes titled his essay "Wine and Milk" and not simply "Wine"?

2. Barthes says that wine is an "ornament in the slightest ceremonials of French daily life." Explain what he means here. Then consider what beverages, whether alcoholic or non-alcoholic, are "ornaments" in American daily life. Don't assume there is necessarily one culturally dominant drink, as Barthes does about France. What do these drinks signify? How do they shape the style of daily life?

3. In the final paragraph, Barthes ties the cultural meaning of wine to its mode of production. How does this alter or amplify the meanings of wine in the essay? Notice in a more general sense that the production of food and drink is largely hidden or suppressed in contemporary culture. We see images of food and drink in newspapers and magazines and on television, but they seem disconnected from the fields and factories and the labor that produced them. What do you see as the meaning of this disconnection?

SUGGESTIONS FOR WRITING

1. Use Roland Barthes' essay on wine as a model to write an essay on the cultural meanings of a food or drink. Pick something that can generate multiple meanings, as wine does for Barthes. Explain what the food or drink signifies and how it connects to and helps shape the style of ordinary life.

2. Find an image of food or drink (or both) in a newspaper or magazine. Pick an advertisement or an article in the food section. Write an essay on how the image presents food. What style of life and what cultural meanings does the image associate with the food?

3. Barthes says that in France, "drunkeness is consequence, never an intention" of drinking wine. This differs, Barthes says, from the way people in other countries drink. Write an essay that considers how drinking takes place among an identifiable group of people. It could be students your age, your parents, or some other group with which you're familiar.

CHECKING OUT THE WEB

1. For a glimpse of some current styles, check out Web sites on tattooing and body piercing. Pay attention to how people are designing their own bodies. According to some, tatooing and body piercing amounts to self-mutilation. For others, it is an expressive style. What sense do you get of these two current styles of body art?

2. The contemporary "blobject" look draws on the streamline style of the 1930s and 1940s. To find about more about the streamline style, check out the work of Raymond Loewy, one of the most influential industrial and graphic designers of his day. Go to http://www.designboom.com and click on Raymond Loewy under the Portraits section. You'll find information about him and examples of his work for Coca-Cola, Shell, and Exxon, among other companies. After you've checked out the site, consider the basic principles of streamline style and how contemporary designers are using it.

3. Do a Web search on the history of a clothing style—costumes, everyday clothing, work clothes, uniforms, or high fashion. You can find sites by entering "fashion history" into your search engine or by narrowing the search to fashion in a particular historical period. Check out Kent State University Museum at www. kent.edu/museum and the Costume Institute at the Metropolitan Museum of Art at http://www.metmuseum.org for on-line collections. After you have examined the collection, write a report on style in history. Focus, for example, on how the ideal shape of women has changed through the ages or how fashion reflects the times (the freedom of the "Roaring Twenties," for example, or how rationing affected fashion during World War II).

Race and Branding

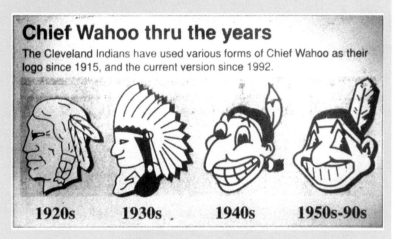

Chief Wahoo thru the years

The Cleveland Indians have used various forms of Chief Wahoo as their logo since 1915, and the current version since 1992.

1920s   1930s   1940s   1950s-90s

The history of branding by companies and sports teams in the United States is deeply implicated in the racial politics of the nation. Companies have for years used images of African Americans such as Aunt Jemima and Uncle Ben as familiar and reassuring symbols of product quality, and critics have argued that these representations perpetuate racial stereotypes of blacks as cooks and servants to whites. A similar issue has arisen about the use of Native American nicknames and logos of professional baseball and football teams—the Cleveland Indians, the Atlanta Braves, the Washington Redskins, and the Kansas City Chiefs. Do these images invoke a powerful identity for their teams as warriors, or do they contribute to the myth of Native Americans as a savage, vanishing race? In recent years, several high schools and colleges have changed their nicknames and logos. There are several archival sources you can consult. To find out more about the representation of African Americans in branding, check out *Aunt Jemima, Uncle Ben, and Rastus: Blacks in Advertising, Yesterday, Today, and Tomorrow* by Marilyn Kern-Foxworth; on Aunt Jemima, see *Slave in a Box* by M. M. Manring. It is possible that your own college or high school or one nearby has a Native American nickname and logo. If that is the case, research the original decision to name the school teams and any stylistic changes that occur over time, as you can see here in the evolution of the Cleveland Indians' "mascot," Chief Wahoo.

Public Space CHAPTER 6

©The Walker Evans Archive, The Metropolitan Museum of Art

In wildness, is the preservation of the world.

—Henry David Thoreau

When you go up to the city, you better have some cash, 'cause the people in the city don't mess around with trash.

—Traditional blues lyric

One way of examining how a culture lives and what it values is to look at its public spaces—its streets, parks, sports arenas, shopping malls, museums—all those places where people gather to do business and play and loiter. Such spaces are abundant in countrysides and suburbs as well as in cities. Megamalls and fast food restaurants line the highway system as a result of urban sprawl, and in small towns and rural areas, the fairgrounds, town halls, county arenas, and churches still function as public gathering spots. In fact, even America's wilderness areas have become places where the public gathers, where tourists travel to catch a glimpse of the Grand Canyon, to picnic in Yellowstone, and to hike in the Adirondacks.

Most public spaces are designed simply to be functional, which is why much of what you see every day is remarkable only for its similarity to nearly everything else you see. Office buildings that seem to pop up from the pavement overnight look like every other office building in the city. The new wing of a local hospital looks tacked on to the old wing as a high-rise box of rooms and corridors. One grocery store looks like all the others, schools look like schools, and doctors' offices look like doctors' offices. A popular motel chain even tried for a while to capitalize on its across-the-continent sameness—Holiday Inn ads promised "no surprises," apparently assuming that most Americans are uncomfortable with anything too different. Perhaps that is why it is so easy to take most public spaces for granted. It is only when a place looks distinctive—newer, flashier, stranger—that most visitors stop to look. In a world crowded with so much to look at, it takes an effort, a real spectacle, to get the public's attention.

It is easy to think of the most famous or infamous public spaces in contemporary America as constituting spectacle above all else. From the Mall of America to Epcot Center, each new public space seems to be vying to be the biggest and most expensive. Such spaces compete for attention, inviting visitors to look, to linger, and to buy. These public spaces turned spectacle characterize at least one impulse in a consumer economy—the impulse to sell.

In America, perhaps the purest example of public space as spectacle is the Las Vegas casino strip. Writer Tom Wolfe once described Vegas as "the only town in the world whose skyline is made up of neither buildings, like New York, nor of trees, like Wilbraham, Massachusetts, but of signs....But such signs! They tower. They revolve, they oscillate, they soar in shapes before which the existing vocabulary of art history is helpless." As a place of spectacle, Las Vegas is pure flash, pure appearance—spectacle for its own sake.

Even that description is misleading, however, for the spectacle that is Las Vegas hardly exists for its own sake; it is there for the sake of the sale. In an era when advertising is one of the most prolific forms of communication, spectacle emerges as a natural manifestation of the sales pitch. Moreover, in this age of the automobile and the highway system, spectacle caters to a moving public, a public that hasn't time for a lengthy meal or a complex ad. Bright lights, motion, glitter, surprise—this is the landscape that modern Americans drive past in their cars and motor homes.

Of course, our interest in public space has to do with more than appearance. To say a space is public is to suggest it is there for the use of the population at large—a space for a community, not simply for private use. Yet more and more spaces that at first seem to be open to the public aren't at all public in the strictest sense. Malls, for example, are often credited with becoming the new "town square," but a town square is clearly a public space where people in the community do have certain rights, such as the right to free speech. Malls are private property. You cannot distribute campaign literature or any other kinds of materials without the permission of mall owners, and those owners are probably going to be very careful about letting anyone into their space who seems to threaten business. So even though a mall might invite a Senior Mall Walker's Club to come and exercise before stores open for business, that is not the same as walking out your door and taking your morning jog through the neighborhood. The mall owners can rescind the invitation at any time and bar from the property anyone they feel interferes with business.

Even public streets are not so free to the public as we might imagine. Demonstrators at the 1996 Democratic National Convention in Chicago found themselves segregated into small groups, some far from the convention site, through the use of a "lottery system," as the city attempted to keep control of potential disturbances. Officials of the St. Patrick's Day Parade in New York City have fought for years to ban gays from having a visible presence in that event. Throughout the United States, town squares, plazas, and shop fronts are purposely designed to keep people from being able to sit and chat or rest comfortably, so that loiterers, street people, groups of teenagers, and anyone without a "purpose" to be there won't be tempted to hang around.

What's more, the tension between public use of public space and private land ownership is a serious one, especially when it comes to wilderness land holdings. In the West, cattle ranchers fight all attempts to limit their access to or increase usage fees on grazing land within national parks. The debate over whether or not to open the Black Hills to more gold mining is ongoing. Throughout the country, the national park system has moved forward with privatizing many of its services. Consequently, parks have been changing in response to revenue generated by those new businesses. In other words, it is a contradiction: Americans want public spaces but value private use. It is a conflict that is not easily resolved.

That conflict has never been more apparent than in the current debate over what to do with Ground Zero, the site of the former World Trade Center in New York City. As a site of tragedy for thousands of Americans, any new construction must memorialize the events of September 11, 2001. However, that spot is also what has been come to be called "prime commercial real estate" that is owned, not by the city or the nation, but by people who want to capitalize on its value. What will eventually come of that space is not likely to be resolved any time soon, but any plan for construction will remain the center of conflict for many years—very likely even after a memorial is built.

The very design of our cities, towns, subdivisions, and planned communities can reflect the concerns and struggles of the culture at large. For example, the gap between rich and poor is apparent not only in people's income (or lack of income) but also in the breakdown of public services and the disrepair of buildings and roads in poorer parts of town. If you live in the city, the suburbs, or the country; have visited historical monuments; spent time in New York or Los Angeles; attended a ball game; watched a parade; shopped in a mall; eaten in a fast food restaurant; or simply attended a church bazaar or school dance, you already know a good deal about how public space is organized in contemporary America, and you probably make more judgments about public spaces than you think.

Reading Public Space

As you read and talk about the public spaces that constitute the "look" of the United States today, you will be asked to write your own impressions of and draw your own meanings from those spaces. The selections and assignments in this chapter move from consideration of wilderness areas to the malls of the suburbs to the world of the city. One way to look at public space is to recall the first impressions you had of places you have seen. As you explore these memories, you may begin to understand how you form your own judgments of places. For many people across the United States, public space means open land, wilderness holdings, national parks, and other lands held by the government in the public trust. This chapter opens with an essay by Barry Lopez, whose experience trying to locate an invisible border between the United States and Canada off the eastern Arctic coast of Alaska leads him both to lyric description and to the realization that land is never simply there to enjoy. It comes with responsibility, especially as people use their votes in zoning referendums or the annexation of rural lands.

John Fiske's analysis of mall culture raises questions about how space is designed, who needs it, and how it is used. Fiske's work suggests that you look at these spaces as emerging from the meanings and values of the culture in which they were created. Fiske is insistent that, though malls might exert a powerful pull on the senses, most consumers are not duped by the hype. Instead, most people are able to use these spaces to meet their own needs, even when those uses directly contradict the carefully planned-for use of the developers. Thus, teenagers become mall rats, hanging out but rarely shopping in those megamalls that seem so seductive.

The next selections—Mike Davis's "Fortress Los Angeles," Murphy Davis's "Woodruff Park and the Search for Common Ground," and Eva Cockroft and Holly Barnet-Sánchez's introduction to the Chicano mural movement ("Signs from the Heart")—offer ways to examine how space is ordered, controlled, and claimed in major cities. Mike Davis describes how city planners have attempted to control who uses city spaces and how they are used. Murphy Davis writes of the renovation of a park in downtown Atlanta and planners' attempts to keep the homeless away. Cockroft and Barnet-Sánchez relate how the mural movement reclaimed a city that many Chicano youth felt had been closed off to them.

In a Perspectives pairing of two articles that address the question of how or whether to rebuild the World Trade Center, Herbert Muschamp and Larry Silverstein offer different views of what Ground Zero now means to the public and on how pressures to rebuild this as a center of commerce will shape the way the city decides to design any memorial to the victims of that event.

The Classic Reading selection, from Jane Jacobs's *The Death and Life of Great American Cities*, offers an explanation of how the most ordinary feature in cities—in this case, sidewalks and how they are used—makes a difference in how people treat one another in public spaces.

Though the work in this chapter begins with observation and memory, you will have the opportunity to do Fieldwork, collect and examine images of public space, and offer your own assessments of the way people use the spaces they inhabit. What you write depends on what you have already experienced and what you already think about the topic. Take time, then, at the beginning of your reading to mine your memory about public spaces.

BORDERS

Barry Lopez

Barry Lopez is a contributing editor for *Harper's* and a regular writer for many publications, including the *New York Times, Paris Review,* and *North American Review.* He has been the recipient of such honors as the National Book Award (for *Arctic Dreams* [1986]), a Guggenheim Fellowship, and the Pushcart prize. The following essay from *Crossing Open Ground* (1989) originally appeared in 1981 in the magazine *Country Journal.* It was written during one of Lopez's trips to the Arctic north. Throughout his career, Lopez's essays and fiction have drawn readers' attention to the kinds of spaces most of us never see or even think much about—from the desert landscapes of the Southwest to the wilderness areas of Alaska and the Arctic.

SUGGESTION FOR READING Lopez's story of his trip to locate the international line that separates Alaska and the Yukon Territory offers him an opportunity to write about the artificial nature of such borders discernible only by the markers set in place to claim territory. As you read, note in the margins where Lopez shifts from his story of the border excursion to his commentary on borders.

1   In early September, the eastern Arctic coast of Alaska shows several faces, most of them harsh. But there are days when the wind drops and the sky is clear, and for reasons too fragile to explain—the overflight of thousands of migrating ducks, the bright, silent austerity of the Romanzof Mountains under fresh snow, the glassy stillness of the ocean—these days have an edge like no others. The dawn of such a clear and windless day is cherished against memories of late August snow squalls and days of work in rough water under leaden skies.

One such morning, a few of us on a biological survey in the Beaufort Sea set that work aside with hardly a word and headed east over the water for the international border, where the state of Alaska abuts the Yukon Territory. The fine weather encouraged this bit of adventure.

There are no settlements along this part of the arctic coast. We did not in fact know if the border we were headed to was even marked. A northeast wind that had been driving loose pack ice close to the shore for several days forced us to run near the beach in a narrow band of open water. In the lee of larger pieces of sea ice, the ocean had begun to freeze, in spite of the strong sunlight and a benign feeling in the air. Signs of winter.

As we drove toward Canada, banking the open, twenty-foot boat in graceful arcs to avoid pieces of drift ice, we hung our heads far back to watch migrating Canada geese and black brant pass over. Rifling past us and headed west at fifty miles an hour a foot off the water were flocks of oldsquaw, twenty and thirty ducks at a time. Occasionally, at the edge of the seaward ice, the charcoal-gray snout of a ringed seal would break the calm surface of the ocean for breath.

We drew nearer the border, wondering aloud how we would know it. I remembered a conversation of years before, with a man who had escaped from Czechoslovakia to come to America and had later paddled a canoe the length of the Yukon. He described the border where the river crossed into Alaska as marked by a great swath cut through the spruce forest. In the middle of nowhere, I said ruefully; what a waste of trees, how ugly it must have seemed. He looked silently across the restaurant table at me and said it was the easiest border crossing of his life.

5   I thought, as we drove on east, the ice closing in more now, forcing us to run yet closer to the beach, of the geographer Carl Sauer and his concept of biologically distinct regions. The idea of bioregionalism, as it has been developed by his followers, is a political concept that would reshape human life. It would decentralize residents of an area into smaller, more self-sufficient, environmentally responsible units, occupying lands the borders of which would be identical with the borders of natural regions—watersheds, for example. I thought of Sauer because we were headed that day for a great, invisible political dividing line: 141 degrees western longitude. Unlike the border between Utah and Colorado, this one is arbitrary. If it were not actually marked—staked—it would not be discernible. Sauer's borders are noticeable. Even the birds find them.

On the shore to our right, as we neared the mouth of Demarcation Bay, we saw the fallen remains of an Eskimo sod house, its meat-drying racks, made of driftwood, leaning askew. Someone who had once come this far to hunt had built the house. The house eventually became a dot on U.S. Coast and Geodetic Survey maps. Now its location is vital to the Inuit, for it establishes a politically important right of prior use, predating the establishment of the Arctic National Wildlife Refuge, within whose borders it has been included. I recall all this as we pass, from poring over our detailed maps the night before. Now, with the warmth of sunlight on the side of my face, with boyhood thoughts of the Yukon Territory welling up inside, the nearness of friends, with whom work has been such keen satisfaction these past few weeks, I have no desire to see maps.

Ahead, it is becoming clear that the closing ice is going to force us right up on the beach before long. The wedge of open water is narrowing. What there is is very still, skimmed with fresh slush ice. I think suddenly of my brother, who lives in a house on Block Island, off the coast of Rhode Island. When I visit we walk and drive around the island. Each time I mean to ask him, does he feel any more ordered in his life for being able to see so clearly the boundary between the ocean and the land in every direction? But I am never able to phrase the question right. And the old and dour faces of the resident islanders discourage it.

Far ahead, through a pair of ten-power binoculars, I finally see what appears to be a rampart of logs, weathered gray-white and standing on a bluff where the tundra falls off fifteen or twenty feet to the beach. Is this the border?

We are breaking ice now with the boat. At five miles an hour, the bow wave skitters across the frozen surface of the ocean to either side in a hundred broken fragments. The rumbling that accompanies this shattering of solid ice is like the low-throttled voice of the outboard engines. Three or four hundred yards of this and we stop. The pack ice is within twenty feet of the beach. We cannot go any farther. That we are only a hundred feet from our destination seems a part of the day, divinely fortuitous.

10   We climb up the bluff. Arctic-fox tracks in the patchy snow are fresh. Here and there on the tundra are bird feathers, remnants of the summer molt of hundreds of thousands of birds that have come this far north to nest, whose feathers blow inland and out to sea for weeks. Although we see no animals but a flock of snow geese in the distance, evidence of their residence and passage is everywhere. Within a few hundred feet I find caribou droppings. On a mossy tundra mound, like one a jaeger might use, I find two small bones that I know to be a ptarmigan's.

We examine the upright, weathered logs and decide on the basis of these and several pieces of carved wood that this is, indeed, the border. No one, we reason, would erect something like this on a coast so unfrequented by humans if it were not. (This coast is ice-free only eight or ten weeks in the year.) Yet we are not sure. The bluff has a certain natural prominence, though the marker's placement seems arbitrary. But the romance of it—this foot in Canada, that one in Alaska—is fetching. The delightful weather and the presence of undisturbed animals has made us almost euphoric. It is, after days of bottom trawls in thirty-one-degree water, of cold hours of patient searching for seals, so clearly a holiday for us.

I will fly over this same spot a week later, under a heavy overcast, forced down to two hundred feet above the water in a search for migrating bowhead whales. That trip, from the small settlement of Inuvik on the East Channel of the Mackenzie River in the Northwest Territories to Deadhorse, Alaska, will make this border both more real and more peculiar than it now appears. We will delay our arrival by circling over Inuvik until a Canadian customs officer can get there from the village of Tuktoyaktuk on the coast, though all we intend to do is to drop off an American scientist and buy gas. On our return trip we are required by law to land at the tiny village of Kaktovik to check through U.S. Customs. The entry through Kaktovik is so tenuous as to not exist at all. One might land, walk the mile to town, and find or not find the customs officer around. Should he not be there, the law requires we fly 250 miles south to Fort Yukon. If no one is there we are to fly on to Fairbanks before returning to Deadhorse on the coast, in order to reenter the country legally. These distances are immense. We could hardly carry the fuel for such a trip. And to fly inland would mean not flying the coast to look for whales, the very purpose of being airborne. We fly straight to Deadhorse, looking for whales. When we land we fill out forms to explain our actions and file them with the government.

Here, standing on the ground, the border seems nearly whimsical. The view over tens of square miles of white, frozen ocean and a vast expanse of tundra which rolls to the foot of snow-covered mountains is unimpeded. Such open space, on such a calm and innocent day as this, gives extraordinary release to the imagination. At such a remove—from horrible images of human death on borders ten thousand miles away, form the press of human anxiety one feels in a crowded city—at such a remove one is lulled nearly to foundering by the simple peace engendered, even at the border between two nations, by a single day of good weather.

As we turn to leave the monument, we see two swans coming toward us. They are immature tundra swans, in steel-gray plumage. Something odd is in their shape. Primary feathers. They have no primary feathers yet. Too young. And their parents, who should be with them, are nowhere to be seen. They are coming from the east, from Canada, paddling in a strip of water a few inches deep right at the edge of the beach. They show no fear of us, although they slow and are cautious. They extend their necks and open their pink bills to make gentle, rattling sounds. As they near the boat they stand up in the water and step ashore. They walk past us and on up the beach. Against the gritty coarseness of beach sand and the tundra-stained ice, their smooth gray feathers and the deep lucidity of their eyes vibrate with beauty. I watch them until they disappear from view. The chance they will be alive in two weeks is very slim. Perhaps it doesn't exist at all.

15   In two weeks I am thousands of miles south. In among the letters and magazines in six weeks of mail sitting on the table is a thick voter-registration pamphlet. One afternoon I sit down and read it. I try to read it with the conscientiousness of one who wishes to vote wisely. I think of Carl Sauer, whose ideas I admire. And of Wendell Berry, whose integrity and sense of land come to mind when I ponder any vote and the effect it might have. I think of the invisible borders of rural landscapes. Of Frost pondering the value of fences. I read in the pamphlet of referendums on statewide zoning and of the annexation of rural lands, on which I am expected to vote. I read of federal legislative reapportionment and the realignment of my county's border with that of an Indian reservation, though these will not require my vote. I must review, again, how the districts of my state representative and state senator overlap and determine if I am included now within the bounds of a newly created county commissioner's territory.

These lines blur and I feel a choking coming up in my neck and my face flushing. I set the pamphlet on the arm of the chair and get up and walk outside. It is going to take weeks, again, to get home.

SUGGESTIONS FOR DISCUSSION

1. Early in his essay, Lopez relates a conversation with a refugee from Czechoslovakia, who tells him that he remembers the border Lopez is looking for because, when he crossed it, it was marked by "a great swath cut through the spruce forest." Lopez, the naturalist, is appalled by the clear-cut, while the Czech man tells him it was "the easiest border crossing of his life." Later, Lopez directs his readers' attention to a sod house that once served as a makeshift fishing and hunting shack but now serves another more far-reaching function both for map makers and for the Inuit of the area. Why does Lopez tell these stories? How do the stories position Lopez for his readers?

2. Lopez recalls the work of Carl Sauer, who argues that borders should not be defined by politics or nationalism but by the natural biological regions of the earth. Lopez writes, "Sauer's borders are noticeable. Even the birds find them." Recount Lopez's brief description of Sauer's argument. Discuss with a group of your classmates your response to Sauer's proposal as Lopez explains it. How does your position compare with the position of your classmates? How do individual experiences contribute to the ways we people might respond to a proposal such as Sauer's?

3. At the end of this essay, Lopez returns home to a pile of mail and, particularly, to a voter registration packet. He writes here of his own role, as a voter, in creating borders and feels himself choking at the thoughts of zoning and reapportionment and more. What, if any, decisions can you make as a voter in your local area or in decisions about nationally held lands?

SUGGESTIONS FOR WRITING

1. Write an exploratory response to the Lopez essay in which you work out your own reactions to Lopez's comments on borders. An exploratory response (see Chapter 1) should allow you to find your voice and bring your thoughts on the essay into focus. This is an informal kind of writing in that it represents the beginnings of your thinking on the topic. However, it isn't private writing. You should be able to share what you have written with others as you and your classmates discuss Lopez. Your explanatory writing should also allow you to begin to shape your own, more formal position on this topic.

2. Near the end of his essay, Lopez writes that he is reminded of "the invisible borders of rural landscapes. Of Frost pondering the value of fences." Locate Robert Frost's poem "Mending Wall." You will find it in most college or public libraries in a volume of Frost's collected works. (You can also find it on the Internet by entering the poem's title into your computer's search engine.) The poem opens with the line, "Something there is that doesn't love a wall," and ends "Good fences make good neighbors." After rereading Lopez and Frost, write a brief explanation of Lopez's reference to the Frost poem.

3. Lopez sets his serious deliberations within narrative (in this case, the story of a side trip to locate an invisible border) and description (images of the land—its textures, its animals, and its expanse of sea and frozen shoreline). In setting his discussion up this way, Lopez attempts to carry his reader with him. In essence, Lopez is giving the reader a reason to question the nature of borders in places where they seem to make little sense. As well, he is knowledgeable about the geographical features of the land, the weather patterns of the place, and the animals and plants that thrive there. Lopez establishes his authority through the use of such detail. Write an essay about a place you know well that you have seen change. Describe the change. Use the nature of that change (good or bad, healthy or unhealthy, beautiful or garish, etc.) to explain your own position on the uses of that area—by developers or the city or private individuals. Like Lopez, establish your authority through what you know of the place, the detail that allows your reader to see and understand this place and its importance to you and to the community that uses or surrounds it.

SHOPPING FOR PLEASURE: Malls, Power, and Resistance

John Fiske

John Fiske is a professor of communication at the University of Wisconsin–Madison. He is among the many scholars today who make use of the artifacts of daily life to interpret modern culture. For Fiske, as well as others engaging in cultural studies, the analysis of popular culture can help reveal how a society produces meaning from its social experience. The following selection, taken from *Reading the Popular* and written in 1989, demonstrates how phenomena we take for granted in our everyday lives, such as shopping malls, are a part of that cultural production of meaning.

SUGGESTION Notice as you read that Fiske makes reference to other studies from which he has drawn ideas,
FOR READING interpretations, and information. He uses those references to give scholarly weight to his argument and to acknowledge his use of others' work in building his own interpretation. If you are
not familiar with the names (he usually uses last names only), don't let that stop your reading.
The context in which the name is used can usually give you enough information to allow you
to continue. As you read, underline passages in which Fiske distinguishes his own view from
that of those other scholars.

1 Shopping malls are cathedrals of consumption—
a glib phrase that I regret the instant it slides off
my pen. The metaphor of consumerism as a religion, in which commodities become the icons of
worship and the rituals of exchanging money for
goods become a secular equivalent of holy communion, is simply too glib to be helpful, and too
attractive to those whose intentions, whether they
be moral or political, are to expose the evils and
limitations of bourgeois materialism. And yet the
metaphor is both attractive and common precisely because it does convey and construct a
knowledge of consumerism; it does point to one
set of "truths," however carefully selected a set.

Truths compete in a political arena, and the
truths that the consumerism-as-contemporary-
religion strives to suppress are those that deny
the difference between the tenor and vehicle of
the metaphor. Metaphor always works within
that tense area within which the forces of similarity and difference collide, and aligns itself with
those of similarity. Metaphor constructs similarity out of difference, and when a metaphor
becomes a cliché, as the shopping mall-cathedral
one has, then a resisting reading must align itself
with the differences rather than the similarities,
for clichés become clichés only because of their
centrality to common sense: the cliché helps to
construct the commonality of common sense.

So, the differences: the religious congregation is powerless, led like sheep through the rituals and meanings, forced to "buy" the truth on
offer, all the truth, not selective bits of it. Where
the interests of the Authority on High differ from
those of the Congregation down Low, the congregation has no power to negotiate, to discriminate: all accommodations are made by the
powerless, subjugated to the great truth. In the
U.S. marketplace, 90 percent of new products fail

to find sufficient buyers to survive (Schudson
1984), despite advertising, promotions, and all
the persuasive techniques of the priests of consumption. In Australia, Sinclair (1987) puts the
new product failure rate at 80 percent—such statistics are obviously best-guesstimates: what
matters is that the failure rate is high. The power
of consumer discrimination evidenced here has
no equivalent in the congregation: no religion
could tolerate a rejection rate of 80 or 90 percent
of what it has to offer.

Religion may act as a helpful metaphor
when our aim is to investigate the power of
consumerism; when, however, our focus shifts
to the power of the consumer, it is counter-
productive....Shopping is the crisis of consumerism: it is where the art and tricks of the
weak can inflict most damage on, and exert most
power over, the strategic interests of the powerful. The shopping mall that is seen as the terrain
of guerrilla warfare looks quite different from the
one constructed by the metaphor of religion.

5   Pressdee (1986), in his study of unemployed
youth in the South Australian town of Elizabeth,
paints a clear picture of both sides in this war. The
ideological practices that serve the interests of the
powerful are exposed in his analysis of the local
mall's promotional slogan, which appears in the
form of a free ticket: "Your ticket to a better shopping world: ADMITS EVERYONE." He comments:

> The words "your" and "everyone" are working to
> socially level out class distinction and, in doing
> so, overlook the city's two working class groups,
> those who have work and those who do not. The
> word "admits" with a connotation of having to
> have or be someone to gain admittance is
> cancelled out by the word "everyone"—there are
> no conditions of admittance; everyone is equal
> and can come in.

This pseudoticket to consumerism denies the basic function of a ticket—to discriminate between those who possess one and those who do not—in a precise moment of the ideological work of bourgeois capitalism with its denial of class difference, and therefore of the inevitability of class struggle. The equality of "everyone" is, of course, an equality attainable only by those with purchasing power: those without are defined out of existence, as working-class interests (derived from class *difference*) are defined out of existence by bourgeois ideology. "The ticket to a better shopping world does not say 'Admits everyone with at least some money to spend'...; money and the problems associated with getting it conveniently disappear in the official discourse" (Pressdee 1986:10–11).

Pressdee then uses a variation of the religious metaphor to sum up the "official" messages of the mall:

> The images presented in the personal invitation to all in Elizabeth is then that of the cargo cult. Before us a lightshaft beams down from space, which contains the signs of the "future"; "Target", "Venture"—gifts wrapped; a table set for two. But beamed down from space they may as well be, because...this imagery can be viewed as reinforcing denial of the production process—goods are merely beamed to earth. The politics of their production and consumption disappear.

Yet his study showed that 80 percent of unemployed young people visited the mall at least once a week, and nearly 100 percent of young unemployed women were regular visitors. He comments on these uninvited guests:

> For young people, especially the unemployed, there has been a congregating within these cathedrals of capitalism, where desires are created and fulfilled and the production of commodities, the very activity that they are barred from, is itself celebrated on the altar of consumerism. Young people, cut off from normal consumer power, are invading the space of those with consumer power. (p. 13)

Pressdee's shift from the religious metaphor to one of warfare signals his shift of focus from the powerful to the disempowered.

10   Thursday nights, which in Australia are the only ones on which stores stay open late, have become the high points of shopping, when the malls are at their most crowded and the cash registers ring up their profits most busily, and it is on Thursday nights that the youth "invasion" of consumer territory is most aggressive. Pressdee (1986) describes this invasion vividly:

> Thursday nights vibrate with youth, eager to show themselves:—it belongs to them, they have possessed it. This cultural response is neither spectacular nor based upon consumerism itself. Nor does it revolve around artifacts or dress, but rather around the possession of space, or to be more precise the possession of consumer space where their very presence challenges, offends and resists.
>
> Hundreds of young people pour into the centre every Thursday night, with three or four hundred being present at any one time. They parade for several hours, not buying, but presenting, visually, all the contradictions of employment and unemployment, taking up their natural public space that brings both life and yet confronts the market place. Security men patrol all night aided by several police patrols, hip guns visible and radios in use, bringing a new understanding to law and order.
>
> Groups of young people are continually evicted from this opulent and warm environment, fights appear, drugs seem plentiful, alcohol is brought in, in various guises and packages. The police close in on a group of young women, their drink is tested. Satisfied that it is only coca-cola they are moved on and out. Not wanted. Shopkeepers and shoppers complain. The security guards become agitated and begin to question all those seen drinking out of cans or bottles who are under 20, in the belief that they must contain alcohol. They appear frightened, totally outnumbered by young people as they continue their job in keeping the tills ringing and the passage to the altar both free and safe. (p. 14)

Pressdee coins the term "proletarian shopping" (p. 16) to describe this window shopping with no intention to buy. The youths consumed images and space instead of commodities, a kind of sensuous consumption that did not create profits. The positive pleasure of parading up and down, of offending "real" consumers and the agents of law and order, of asserting their difference within, and different use of, the cathedral of consumerism became an oppositional cultural practice.

The youths were "tricksters" in de Certeau's terms—they pleasurably exploited their knowledge of the official "rules of the game" in order to identify where these rules could be mocked, inverted, and thus used to free those they were designed to discipline. De Certeau (1984) points to the central importance of the "trickster" and the "guileful ruse" throughout peasant and folk cultures. Tricks and ruses are the art of the weak that enables them to exploit their understanding of the rules of the system, and to turn it to their advantage. They are a refusal to be subjugated:

> The actual order of things is precisely what "popular" tactics turn to their own ends, without any illusion that it will change any time soon. Though elsewhere it is exploited by a dominant power...here order is tricked by an art. (de Certeau 1984: 26)

This trickery is evidence of "an ethics of tenacity (countless ways of refusing to accord the established order the status of a law, a meaning or a fatality)" (p. 26).

Shopping malls are open invitations to trickery and tenacity. The youths who turn them into their meeting places, or who trick the security guards by putting alcohol into some, but only some, soda cans, are not actually behaving any differently from lunch hour window shoppers who browse through the stores, trying on goods, consuming and playing with images, with no intention to buy. In extreme weather people exploit the controlled climate of the malls for their own pleasure—mothers take children to play in their air-conditioned comfort in hot summers, and in winter older people use their concourses for daily walks. Indeed, some malls now have notices welcoming "mall walkers," and a few have even provided exercise areas set up with equipment and instructions so that the walkers can exercise more than their legs.

15 Of course, the mall owners are not entirely disinterested or altruistic here—they hope that some of the "tricky" users of the mall will become real economic consumers, but they have no control over who will, how many will, how often, or how profitably. One boutique owner told me that she estimated that 1 in 30 browsers actually bought something. Shopping malls are where the strategy of the powerful is most vulnerable to the tactical raids of the weak.

REFERENCES

De Certeau, M. (1984). *The Practice of Everyday Life*. Berkeley: University of California Press.

Pressdee, M. (1986). "Agony or Ecstasy: Broken Transitions and the New Social State of Working-Class Youth in Australia." Occasional Papers, S. Australian Centre for Youth Studies, S.A. College of A.E., Magill, S. Australia.

Schudson, M. (1984). *Advertising: The Uneasy Persuasion*. New York: Basic Books.

Sinclair, J. (1987). *Images Incorporated: Advertising as Industry and Ideology*. London: Croom Helm.

SUGGESTIONS FOR DISCUSSION

1. Why does Fiske challenge the cathedral metaphor as a useful one for analyzing the place of malls in today's culture? How is the mall of today like the great cathedrals of the past? How does the metaphor of the mall as a place of warfare work in Fiske's analysis?

2. What do you think Fiske means when he says, "The equality of 'everyone' is, of course, an equality attainable only by those with purchasing power; those without are defined out of existence"?

3. Fiske has based most of what he says on his observations of malls in Australia. How would you describe mall culture in America?

SUGGESTIONS FOR WRITING

1. As we mentioned in the Suggestion for Reading in this selection, the Fiske essay could be difficult to follow because he relies heavily on others' writing as well as his own observations. Begin your work with Fiske by making sure that you know what he is arguing. To get at his argument, write a one-page summary of Fiske's interpretation of mall culture. Share your summary with a group of your classmates. As you read others' summaries, take note of ideas or details they noticed that you did not notice. Once you have finished your discussion, come to a consensus on what your group considers Fiske's most important assertions.

2. Review the opening two paragraphs of Fiske's essay. In that passage, he offers his readers a metaphor and then suggests that there are always problems with any metaphor. It can be a tough passage because it takes in more than just the metaphor of the mall, but it also suggests the problem with that metaphor and the problems with metaphors in general. Still, these early paragraphs contain important information for a reader to understand. Write a one-paragraph paraphrase of those opening paragraphs. (In a paraphrase, you restate using your own words from a portion of a text. This kind of exercise can be useful in helping you to make sure that you understand what you are reading and can apply it to other things, like examining the usefulness of the metaphors that Fiske offers. If you were to use your paraphrase in an essay, you would have to make sure that you acknowledge your source and give information about where you found the material. However, you would not use quotation marks around a paraphrase because you are using your language, not the language of the writer.)

3. Fiske's analysis of mall culture focuses attention away from the store owners and mall managers who make the rules and hope to profit from their investments. Instead, Fiske pays attention to how people use the mall. He writes, "Shopping malls are open invitations to trickery and tenacity. The youths who turn them into their meeting places, or who trick the security guards by putting alcohol into some, but only some, soda cans, are not actually behaving any differently from lunch hour shoppers who browse through the stores, trying on goods, consuming and playing with images, with no intention to buy." Choose another public space that people use for their own purposes rather than or in addition to the purpose for which it was designed, and write an essay that explains what it is about the place that lends itself to "trickery and tenacity," as Fiske says malls do. For this essay, rely on your own recollection of and experience with the place for your analysis. Remember to bring in events you have witnessed or things you and your friends or family have done in that place. You can also draw on Fiske's analysis of the way the public uses mall space to help you understand and explain the way the public uses the place you have chosen. If you wrote summaries and the paraphrase suggested above, you will find those helpful as resources for your own use of Fiske.

FORTRESS LOS ANGELES: The Militarization of Urban Space

Mike Davis

Mike Davis teaches urban planning and political economy at the Southern California Institute of Architecture and at UCLA. He is the author of the 1992 book *City of Quartz*, nominated for the National Book Critics Circle Award, and *Prisoners of the American Dream* (1986). The selection that follows, from *City of Quartz*, is an analysis of the way urban planning reflects cultural change and cultural biases. In it, Davis argues that downtown Los Angeles has become a kind of domestic militarized zone and a place where races and classes are separated visibly and purposefully.

SUGGESTION FOR READING   Mike Davis opens this selection with the following statement: "In Los Angeles—once a paradise of free beaches, luxurious parks, and 'cruising strips'—genuinely democratic space is virtually extinct." As you read, underline and annotate those parts of this selection where Davis explains specifically what he means in that opening statement.

1   In Los Angeles—once a paradise of free beaches, luxurious parks, and "cruising strips"—genuinely democratic space is virtually extinct. The pleasure domes of the elite Westside rely upon the social imprisonment of a third-world service proletariat in increasingly repressive ghettos and barrios. In a city of several million aspiring immigrants (where Spanish-surname children are now almost two-thirds of the school-age population), public amenities are shrinking radically, libraries and playgrounds are closing, parks are falling derelict, and streets are growing ever more desolate and dangerous.

Here, as in other American cities, municipal policy has taken its lead from the security offensive and the middle-class demand for increased spatial and social insulation. Taxes previously targeted for traditional public spaces and recreational facilities have been redirected to support corporate redevelopment projects. A pliant city government—in the case of Los Angeles, one ironically professing to represent a liberal biracial coalition—has collaborated in privatizing public space and subsidizing new exclusive enclaves (benignly called "urban villages"). The celebratory language used to describe contemporary Los Angeles—"urban renaissance," "city of the future," and so on—is only a triumphal gloss laid over the brutalization of its inner-city neighborhoods and the stark divisions of class and race represented in its built environment. Urban form obediently follows repressive function. Los Angeles, as always in the vanguard, offers an especially disturbing guide to the emerging liaisons between urban architecture and the police state.

FORBIDDEN CITY

Los Angeles's first spatial militarist was the legendary General Harrison Gray Otis, proprietor of the *Times* and implacable foe of organized labor. In the 1890s, after locking out his union printers and announcing a crusade for "industrial freedom," Otis retreated into a new *Times* building designed as a fortress with grim turrets and battlements crowned by a bellicose bronze eagle. To emphasize his truculence, he later had a small, functional cannon installed on the hood of his Packard touring car. Not surprisingly, this display of aggression produced a response in kind. On October 1, 1910, the heavily fortified *Times* headquarters—the command-post of the open shop on the West Coast—was destroyed in a catastrophic explosion, blamed on union saboteurs.

Eighty years later, the martial spirit of General Otis pervades the design of Los Angeles's new Downtown, whose skyscrapers march from Bunker Hill down the Figueroa corridor. Two billion dollars of public tax subsidies have enticed big banks and corporate headquarters back to a central city they almost abandoned in the 1960s. Into a waiting grid, cleared of tenement housing by the city's powerful and largely unaccountable redevelopment agency, local developers and offshore investors (increasingly Japanese) have planted a series of block-square complexes: Crocker Center, the Bonaventure Hotel and Shopping Mall, the World Trade Center, California Plaza, Arco Center, and so on. With an increasingly dense and self-contained circulation system linking these superblocks, the new financial district is best conceived as a single, self-referential hyperstructure, a Miesian skyscape of fantastic proportions.

5   Like similar megalomaniacal complexes teth-ered to fragmented and desolate downtowns—such as the Renaissance Center in Detroit and the Peachtree and Omni centers in Atlanta—Bunker Hill and the Figueroa corridor have provoked a storm of objections to their abuse of scale and composition, their denigration of street life, and their confiscation of the vital energy of the cen-ter, now sequestered within their subterranean concourses or privatized plazas. Sam Hall Kaplan, the former design critic of the *Times*, has vocifer-ously denounced the antistreet bias of redevel-opment; in his view, the superimposition of "hermetically sealed fortresses" and random "pieces of suburbia" onto Downtown has "killed the street" and "dammed the rivers of life."[1]

Yet Kaplan's vigorous defense of pedestrian democracy remains grounded in liberal com-plaints about "bland design" and "elitist planning practices." Like most architectural critics, he rails against the oversights of urban design without conceding a dimension of foresight, and even of deliberate repressive intent. For when Down-town's new "Gold Coast" is seen in relation to other social landscapes in the central city, the "fortress effect" emerges, not as an inadvertent failure of design, but as an explicit—and, in its own terms, successful—socio-spatial strategy.

The goals of this strategy may be summa-rized as a double repression: to obliterate all con-nection with Downtown's past and to prevent any dynamic association with the non-Anglo urbanism of its future. Los Angeles is unusual among major urban centers in having preserved, however negligently, most of its Beaux Arts com-mercial core. Yet the city chose to transplant—at immense public cost—the entire corporate and financial district from around Broadway and Spring Street to Bunker Hill, a half-dozen blocks further west.

Photographs of the old Downtown in its 1940s prime show crowds of Anglo, black, and Mexican shoppers of all ages and classes. The contemporary Downtown "renaissance" renders such heterogeneity virtually impossible. It is intended not just to "kill the street" as Kaplan feared, but to "kill the crowd," to eliminate that democratic mixture that Olmsted believed was America's antidote to European class polariza-tion. The new Downtown is designed to ensure a seamless continuum of middle-class work, con-sumption, and recreation, insulated from the city's "unsavory" streets. Ramparts and battle-ments, reflective glass and elevated pedways, are tropes in an architectural language warning off the underclass Other. Although architectural crit-ics are usually blind to this militarized syntax, urban pariah groups—whether young black men, poor Latino immigrants, or elderly homeless white females—read the signs immediately.

MEAN STREETS

This strategic armoring of the city against the poor is especially obvious at street level. In his famous study of the "social life of small urban spaces," William Whyte points out that the qual-ity of any urban environment can be measured, first of all, by whether there are convenient, com-fortable places for pedestrians to sit. This maxim has been warmly taken to heart by designers of the high corporate precincts of Bunker Hill and its adjacent "urban villages." As part of the city's policy of subsidizing the white-collar residential colonization of Downtown, tens of millions of dollars of tax revenue have been invested in the creation of attractive, "soft" environments in favored areas. Planners envision a succession of opulent piazzas, fountains, public art, exotic shrubbery, and comfortable street furniture along a ten-block pedestrian corridor from Bunker Hill to South Park. Brochures sell Downtown's "liv-ability" with idyllic representations of office workers and affluent tourists sipping cappuccino and listening to free jazz concerts in the terraced gardens of California Plaza and Grand Hope Park.

10   In stark contrast, a few blocks away, the city is engaged in a relentless struggle to make the streets as unlivable as possible for the homeless and the poor. The persistence of thousands of street people on the fringes of Bunker Hill and

the Civic Center tarnishes the image of designer living Downtown and betrays the laboriously constructed illusion of an urban "renaissance." City Hall has retaliated with its own version of low-intensity warfare.

Although city leaders periodically propose schemes for removing indigents *en masse*— deporting them to a poor farm on the edge of the desert, confining them in camps in the mountains, or interning them on derelict ferries in the harbor—such "final solutions" have been blocked by council members' fears of the displacement of the homeless into their districts. Instead the city, self-consciously adopting the idiom of cold war, has promoted the "containment" (the official term) of the homeless in Skid Row, along Fifth Street, systematically transforming the neighborhood into an outdoor poorhouse. But this containment strategy breeds its own vicious cycle of contradiction. By condensing the mass of the desperate and helpless together in such a small space, and denying adequate housing, official policy has transformed Skid Row into probably the most dangerous ten square blocks in the world. Every night on Skid Row is Friday the 13th, and, unsurprisingly, many of the homeless seek to escape the area during the night at all costs, searching safer niches in other parts of Downtown. The city in turn tightens the noose with increased police harassment and ingenious design deterrents.

One of the simplest but most mean-spirited of these deterrents is the Rapid Transit District's new barrel-shaped bus bench, which offers a minimal surface for uncomfortable sitting while making sleeping impossible. Such "bumproof" benches are being widely introduced on the periphery of Skid Row. Another invention is the aggressive deployment of outdoor sprinklers. Several years ago the city opened a Skid Row Park; to ensure that the park could not be used for overnight camping, overhead sprinklers were programmed to drench unsuspecting sleepers at random times during the night. The system was immediately copied by local merchants to drive the homeless away from (public) storefront sidewalks. Meanwhile Downtown restaurants and

markets have built baroque enclosures to protect their refuse from the homeless. Although no one in Los Angeles has yet proposed adding cyanide to the garbage, as was suggested in Phoenix a few years back, one popular seafood restaurant has spent $12,000 to build the ultimate bag-lady-proof trash cage: three-quarter-inch steel rod with alloy locks and vicious out-turned spikes to safeguard moldering fishheads and stale french fries.

Public toilets, however, have become the real frontline of the city's war on the homeless. Los Angeles, as a matter of deliberate policy, has fewer public lavatories than any other major North American city. On the advice of the Los Angeles police, who now sit on the "design board" of at least one major Downtown project, the redevelopment agency bulldozed the few remaining public toilets on Skid Row. Agency planners then considered whether to include a "free-standing public toilet" in their design for the upscale South Park residential development; agency chairman Jim Wood later admitted that the decision not to build the toilet was a "policy decision and not a design decision." The agency preferred the alternative of "quasi-public restrooms"—toilets in restaurants, art galleries, and office buildings—which can be made available selectively to tourists and white-collar workers while being denied to vagrants and other unsuitables. The same logic has inspired the city's transportation planners to exclude toilets from their designs for Los Angeles's new subway system.[2]

Bereft of toilets, the Downtown badlands east of Hill Street also lack outside water sources for drinking or washing. A common and troubling sight these days is the homeless men— many of them young refugees from El Salvador—washing, swimming, even drinking from the sewer effluent that flows down the concrete channel of the Los Angeles River on the eastern edge of Downtown. The city's public health department has made no effort to post warning signs in Spanish or to mobilize alternative clean-water sources.

15   In those areas where Downtown professionals must cross paths with the homeless or the working poor—such as the zone of gentrification

along Broadway just south of the Civic Center—extraordinary precautions have been taken to ensure the physical separation of the different classes. The redevelopment agency, for example, again brought in the police to help design "twenty-four-hour, state-of-the-art security" for the two new parking structures that serve the *Los Angeles Times* headquarters and the Ronald Reagan State Office Building. In contrast to the mean streets outside, both parking structures incorporate beautifully landscaped microparks, and one even boasts a food court, picnic area, and historical exhibit. Both structures are intended to function as "confidence-building" circulation systems that allow white-collar workers to walk from car to office, or from car to boutique, with minimum exposure to the public street. The Broadway-Spring Center, in particular, which links the two local hubs of gentrification (the Reagan Building and the proposed Grand Central Square) has been warmly praised by architectural critics for adding greenery and art to parking. It also adds a considerable dose of menace—armed guards, locked gates, and ubiquitous security cameras—to scare away the homeless and the poor.

The cold war on the streets of Downtown is ever escalating. The police, lobbied by Downtown merchants and developers, have broken up every attempt by the homeless and their allies to create safe havens or self-governed encampments. "Justiceville," founded by homeless activist Ted Hayes, was roughly dispersed; when its inhabitants attempted to find refuge at Venice Beach, they were arrested at the behest of the local council member (a renowned environmentalist) and sent back to Skid Row. The city's own brief experiment with legalized camping—a grudging response to a series of deaths from exposure during the cold winter of 1987—was abruptly terminated after only four months to make way for the construction of a transit maintenance yard. Current policy seems to involve perverse play upon the famous irony about the equal rights of the rich and poor to sleep in the rough. As the former head of the city planning commission explained, in the City of the Angels it is not against the law to sleep on the street per

se—"only to erect any sort of protective shelter."[3] To enforce this proscription against "cardboard condos," the police periodically sweep the Nickel, tearing down shelters, confiscating possessions, and arresting resisters. Such cynical repression has turned the majority of the homeless into urban bedouins. They are visible all over Downtown, pushing their few pathetic possessions in stolen shopping carts, always fugitive, always in motion, pressed between the official policy of containment and the inhumanity of Downtown streets.

SEQUESTERING THE POOR

An insidious spatial logic also regulates the lives of Los Angeles's working poor. Just across the moat of the Harbor Freeway, west of Bunker Hill, lies the MacArthur Park district—once upon a time the city's wealthiest neighborhood. Although frequently characterized as a no-man's-land awaiting resurrection by developers, the district is, in fact, home to the largest Central American community in the United States. In the congested streets bordering the park, a hundred thousand Salvadorans and Guatemalans, including a large community of Mayan-speakers, crowd into tenements and boarding houses barely adequate for a fourth as many people. Every morning at 6 A.M. this Latino Bantustan dispatches armies of sewing *operadoras*, dishwashers, and janitors to turn the wheels of the Downtown economy. But because MacArthur Park is midway between Downtown and the famous Miracle Mile, it too will soon fall to redevelopment's bulldozers.

Hungry to exploit the lower land prices in the district, a powerful coterie of developers, represented by a famous ex-councilman and the former president of the planning commission, has won official approval for their vision of "Central City West": literally, a second Downtown comprising 25 million square feet of new office and retail space. Although local politicians have insisted upon a significant quota of low-income replacement housing, such a palliative will hardly compensate for the large-scale population displacement sure to follow the construction of the new skyscrapers and yuppified "urban villages." In the meantime, Korean capital, seeking *lebensraum* for Los Angeles's burgeoning Koreatown, is also pushing into the MacArthur Park area, uprooting tenements to construct heavily fortified condominiums and office complexes. Other Asian and European speculators are counting on the new Metrorail station, across from the park, to become a magnet for new investment in the district.

The recent intrusion of so many powerful interests into the area has put increasing pressure upon the police to "take back the streets" from what is usually represented as an occupying army of drug-dealers, illegal immigrants, and homicidal homeboys. Thus in the summer of 1990 the LAPD announced a massive operation to "retake crime-plagued MacArthur Park" and surrounding neighborhoods "street by street, alley by alley." While the area is undoubtedly a major drug market, principally for drive-in Anglo commuters, the police have focused not only on addict-dealers and gang members, but also on the industrious sidewalk vendors who have made the circumference of the park an exuberant swap meet. Thus Mayan women selling such local staples as tropical fruit, baby clothes, and roach spray have been rounded up in the same sweeps as alleged "narcoterrorists."[4] (Similar dragnets in other Southern California communities have focused on Latino day-laborers congregated at streetcorner "slave markets.")

20   By criminalizing every attempt by the poor—whether the Skid Row homeless or MacArthur Park venders—to use public space for survival purposes, law-enforcement agencies have abolished the last informal safety-net separating misery from catastrophe. (Few third-world cities are so pitiless.) At the same time, the police, encouraged by local businessmen and property owners, are taking the first, tentative steps toward criminalizing entire inner-city communities. The "war" on drugs and gangs again has been the pretext for the LAPD's novel, and disturbing, experiments with community blockades. A large section of the Pico-Union neighborhood, just south of MacArthur Park, has been quarantined since the summer of 1989; "Narcotics Enforcement Area" barriers restrict entry to residents "on legitimate business only." Inspired by the positive response of older residents and local politicians, the police have subsequently franchised "Operation Cul-de-Sac" to other low-income Latino and black neighborhoods.

Thus in November 1989 (as the Berlin Wall was being demolished), the Devonshire Division of the LAPD closed off a "drug-ridden" twelve-block section of the northern San Fernando Valley. To control circulation within this largely Latino neighborhood, the police convinced apartment owners to finance the construction of a permanent guard station. Twenty miles to the south, a square mile of the mixed black and Latino Central-Avalon community has also been converted into Narcotic Enforcement turf with concrete roadblocks. Given the popularity of these quarantines—save amongst the ghetto youth against whom they are directed—it is possible that a majority of the inner city may eventually be partitioned into police-regulated "no-go" areas.

The official rhetoric of the contemporary war against the urban underclasses resounds with comparisons to the War in Vietnam a generation ago. The LAPD's community blockades evoke the infamous policy of quarantining suspect populations in "strategic hamlets." But an even more ominous emulation is the reconstruction of Los Angeles's public housing projects as "defensible spaces." Deep in the Mekong Delta of the Watts-Willowbrook ghetto, for example, the Imperial Courts Housing Project has been fortified with chain-link fencing, restricted entry signs, obligatory identity passes—and a substation of the LAPD. Visitors are stopped and frisked, the police routinely order residents back into their apartments at night, and domestic life is subjected to constant police scrutiny. For public-housing tenants and inhabitants of narcotic-enforcement zones, the loss of freedom is the price of "security."

NOTES

1. *Los Angeles Times,* Nov. 4, 1978.
2. Tom Chorneau, "Quandary Over a Park Restroom," *Downtown News,* Aug. 25, 1986.
3. See "Cold Snap's Toll at 5 as Its Iciest Night Arrives," *Los Angeles Times,* Dec. 29, 1988.
4. *Los Angeles Times,* June 17, 1990.

SUGGESTIONS FOR DISCUSSION

1. From what you have read, what does Davis mean by "genuinely democratic space"?

2. Mike Davis makes it clear that one of the defining features of Los Angeles is the city planners' attempts to destroy public spaces, those places where people can congregate freely or just hang out. What problems do you see with the destruction or the preservation of public space?

3. Davis writes in his essay, "The American city is being systematically turned inward. The 'public' spaces of the new megastructures and supermalls have supplanted traditional streets and disciplined their spontaneity." This statement represents a judgment about what American cities once were and what they should be. With a group of your classmates, examine what that judgment is and respond with your own understanding of what American cities should be like and what they are like currently.

SUGGESTIONS FOR WRITING

1. Read over your annotations for this selection in preparation for writing a summary of Davis's argument. What are Davis's primary reasons for arguing that "The pleasure domes of the elite Westside rely upon the social imprisonment of a third-world service proletariat in increasingly repressive ghettos and barrios"?

2. Davis makes strong charges against city planners, corporate interests, the city council, and other official agencies that have anything to do with how Los Angeles is divided, how public services are distributed and repaired, and where "urban renewal" programs will be sited. His analysis is based partially but not solely on his familiarity with this place. He also has spent time finding out the history of Los Angeles's urban developments, where funding is directed, what areas of the city are in most serious disrepair, and what the ethnic and racial demographics are in each section of the city. You likely will not be able to do all of that, but you can map out the areas you think ought to be of most concern in the place where you grew up or the place with which you are most familiar or in which you are most interested. Choose a place (small town, city, subdivision, etc.), sketch a map of it, and explain what you consider the most important issues to emerge from examining how the place is planned and where most funding or development seems to be occurring. Is there a "genuinely democratic space" available in this place? Does one section of the place seem to be segregated economically from other sections? What else do you notice?

3. In a different chapter of *City of Quartz,* Davis mentions several films—*Bladerunner, Die Hard, Escape from New York*—that show the modern city as a dystopia, a place the opposite of a utopia. Watch one of these films and write an essay in which you compare the dystopian setting of that film with your own experience of or impression of large U.S. cities such as Los Angeles, Chicago, or New York. Your focus in this essay should be on images that you see in popular culture and how they compare with the overall impression that you have of cities. That impression can come from firsthand experience or through news programs, magazine articles and ads, and television shows such as *COPS, Law & Order,* or even *Seinfeld.*

WOODRUFF PARK AND THE SEARCH
FOR COMMON GROUND

Murphy Davis

Murphy Davis is cofounder of the Open Door Community, a group of men and women living in community to work with Atlanta's homeless and with prison inmates in Georgia. Along with providing meals, showers, clothing, and a safe space to gather and sleep, the Open Door also participates in political action and advocacy meant to address city projects and local legislation that unfairly targets people living in the streets. The article reprinted here originally appeared in 1996 in *Hospitality*, the Open Door newspaper. In it, Davis argues that the city's multimillion dollar attempts to keep homeless people out of a downtown park has actually made the park unfriendly to everyone and eliminated one more common ground in Atlanta.

SUGGESTION
FOR READING   Murphy Davis's analysis of the Woodruff Park project argues that a space designed to keep some people out is a space that will keep everyone out. As you read, underline and annotate those passages where she makes that argument clear.

1   Woodruff Park is a 1.7-acre tract of land in the center of downtown Atlanta. Like many other valuable pieces of real estate in American history, it has become the subject of hot debate, quiet deals, great expenditure of funds—both public and private—and has seemed to require, along the way, a military presence to secure its function for those who hold the power and intend to define the park's use.

The park, formerly known as Central City Park, most recently emerged from behind a curtain of chain link with a five-million-dollar facelift. This new park is, more than anything else, a spot to look at. It is not a public gathering place: indeed, there is no area of the park that encourages gathering, conversation, play, human exchange, or interrelatedness of any kind.

While the old park never seemed like a spectacular place to me, its walkways were wide and spacious, lined with benches and grass. People walked to and through, stopped and talked together, waved to, and even hassled, one another. But it was at least somewhat inviting, friendly, and spacious.

The new park is mostly an expanse of concrete, stone, and some grass. The walkway is narrow and has a greatly reduced number of benches (all of these face in the same direc-

tion). The benches, of course, are a crucial symbol of reality.

5   In 1993 we won one of the only (narrowly defined) major political victories in the history of our political action and advocacy. We tested the city ordinance that prohibited lying on a city park bench (or against a tree). In two actions in September and October of 1993, twelve of our number were arrested and went to jail for "slouching" or lying on the benches of Woodruff Park. The city council rescinded the law. Amazing.

Exactly one year later, the park was closed for a five-million-dollar renovation. Nimrod Long, whose firm was paid three hundred thousand dollars for a new design, was frank. He said that they were charged with the mission of creating a park that would be inhospitable to homeless people. This, of course, must include park benches with armrests spaced so that it is impossible to lie down.

Well, we can be proud of the fact that they darn well did their job. This park clearly does not invite homeless people to gather. Trouble is, if we mandate a public space inhospitable to any one group of people, we end with a public space that is inhospitable to everybody.

Woodruff Park is unfriendly space. This is not, for instance, a place you would think to bring children to play. There is no play equipment, no bathroom, no drinking fountain, no convivial space for parents to gather while the children play, and it simply is not clear whether or not the grass is an inviting space to run and tumble.

Gone are the wraparound-bench tree planters that invited long chess games and spontaneous lunch gatherings. What is left is a narrow walkway, a relocated *Phoenix* statue (the post–Civil War image of Atlanta rising out of the ashes), a huge, very expensive thirty-foot cascading waterfall, and a stretch of grass. The grass will be nice if people are allowed to sit for picnics, naps, and conversation. But it will not do to replace the benches, especially for the elderly, the disabled, people in business attire, or for anybody when the weather is wet or cold. Neither will it do if the powers that be decide, as they did with the old park, that people cannot sit or play or walk or lie down on the grass. In fact, in the old park they installed what our street friends call "pneumonia grass"—sprinklers buried invisibly that come on without warning, drenching anyone who might be unwittingly sitting or sleeping.

10   The park is intended to be, as Mayor Campbell proudly proclaimed at the opening ceremony, "a beautiful place to look at," which seems a gross concession to the suburban mentality that controls our city. Downtown Atlanta is designed more to entertain tourists and suburbanites who want to drive through, with doors locked and windows rolled up, than to foster an urban life and culture. In addition, you might be led to question Mayor Campbell's sense of beauty.

Perhaps the opening ceremony was somewhat premature, and more trees, shrubs, and plantings are yet to come. But for now there is much less greenery. From the northeast corner the park looks like a fortress. And when the water is turned off, the "cascading waterfall" actually resembles the exposed, barnacle-encrusted, pocked, and rusted hull of an aging battleship. Beautiful this place is not.

It could be that this "battleship," this lifeless wall, is indeed a fitting monument for the center of Atlanta. The city government and controlling business interests have pursued a course of destruction in the central city for several generations now, displacing people seen as undesirable. When these policies of removal began in the 1950s, it was clear that race was the motivating factor. The powers in Atlanta did not want African American people in the downtown business district. So neighborhoods were broken up and gave way to interstate highways; housing was destroyed, little shops and businesses were forced out, and a stadium, a civic center, and countless parking lots rolled over the poor. These practices, which began thirty years ago, resulted in much of the poverty and homelessness in the African American population we see in our city today.

This pattern of destruction has been repeated, and there is little beauty, culture, or humanity left. What we have instead is precisely what the powers say they want: a "sanitized zone," "vagrant-free," and deserted enough to appear safe, devoid of the color of a rich, urban culture whose life has never been antiseptic, colorless, cold, and heartless.

Eight years ago, the rebirth of Underground Atlanta brought a similar enthusiasm for displacement and destruction to this current renovation of Woodruff Park.

15   Plaza Park, once a lively place filled with street vendors, preachers, homeless folks, and pedestrians on their way to the Five Points MARTA station, was razed to make way for the cement, light tower, glitz, and security guards at Underground. A large number of people made homeless by the destruction of their neighborhoods were once again displaced from Plaza Park.

Within a stone's throw of Woodruff Park, thousands of units of single-room occupancy housing have been demolished since the late 1970s. These SROs were places where many who would now like to rest in the park could have lived, and where some of them probably did at one time. Where was the outcry when the Avon and Capital Hotels were destroyed and replaced with parking decks? Where were the protests when the Francis Hotel was closed, mysteriously burned, and replaced with John Portman's latest gleaming tower? Where now is the outcry from any Atlanta government or business leader for housing for Atlanta's homeless? Their silence is deafening. Instead, editorials and columns whine, "City Doesn't Belong Just to Bums and Winos"; countless city laws have been thrown in place to empower police to hound the homeless and to move them from one corner to the next, and the next.

Now we see this same forced removal in Atlanta's Olympic zeal. Hundreds of public housing units were lost as Techwood Homes was torn down to make room for dormitories for Olympic athletes. Where did all those people go? Why is housing for transient Olympic visitors more important than homes for the people of Atlanta?

Additional examples abound. Seventy-two acres of a low-income, mixed-use area (with shelters, labor pools, day-care centers, small businesses, and ware-houses) are now being plowed under to make way for Centennial Olympic Park and to clear this space of undesirable elements. The area, so that no one would question its removal, was labeled a "cancer" by the former head of the Atlanta Chamber of Commerce. But the lost housing has not been replaced, businesses have folded, and shops and restaurants have nowhere to relocate. Of the seventy-two acres, twenty-five will remain after the Olympics as space for a park, at an estimated cost of fifty million dollars. The space will be given, not to the city, but to the state of Georgia for management and control. Why? Could the reason be to up the ante and to make any infraction there a state offense rather than a violation of municipal laws? The rest of the acreage will be developed as commercial property, and if past patterns remain the same, African American people and businesses that were displaced will not find a welcome. The park and surroundings are being redeveloped, not because Atlanta wants to cultivate public space, but because the world is coming to town, and Atlanta wants a clean façade; the "garbage" will be swept under a rug temporarily.

How do these decisions about public space and policy get made? As a citizen of Atlanta, I have no recollection of being asked for my opinion. Whose park is Woodruff Park? Like most of the important decisions about Atlanta's life and future, this was one more deal cut by the powers in a back room. There was never any public discussion, debate, conversation, or exchange about the park. Why does this autocratic method of decision making exist in a democratic society? The answer seems clear: including everyone in a discussion about the use and regulation of public space might not bring the desired results for those who already have so much and who stand to gain much more. Atlanta is in fact one of the poorest cities in the United States, but the super glitz we put forward is a thin, often convincing, veneer for the rest of the world. If the real poverty were known, would the world come to Atlanta to fill Billy Payne's pockets? Could the world of Coke continue to deceive the world, or would we all realize that the veneer covers an ugly, rat-infested, festering bleakness?

20   How can we have a truly beautiful, friendly city that welcomes all people, without regard for race or economic status? We can all agree that nobody likes to be assailed by an "aggressive panhandler." But why do we like to be, or allow ourselves to be, assailed by the pages of a respectable newspaper, which refers to the poor in epithets laced with strong racist implications? While the columnists complain bitterly about their loathing for the poor and homeless, where is the public outrage and protest that people in Atlanta do not have the food, medical care, housing, and good work they need to sustain life? Instead, we dismiss these poor folk as mere trash to be moved around and pushed out of sight and mind.

The task for those of us who love the city is to transform Woodruff Park into a beautiful, friendly space. Welcoming hospitality cannot be found through another design firm, or with an army of bulldozers. We need to move in with play equipment, music, chairs and benches, picnic tables and blankets, and then all the people of the world can come to celebrate the true urban culture of Atlanta. We need to put up bathrooms and drinking fountains right away. Woodruff Park could yet become a welcoming space for the women and men and boys and girls of the city. Can't you see the rich and poor, the Black and white, the homeless and well-housed, dancing and laughing and clapping their hands to the music of Blind Willie McTell, while the smell of smoked ribs wafts on the breeze, and children swing high enough to touch the sky, as the old folks play a hand of dominoes? Who knows? Such a party could inspire us to build a city with housing, justice, and care for all of its people.

SUGGESTIONS FOR DISCUSSION

1. Murphy Davis provides several examples of "urban renewal" meant to spruce up the city for business and prepare for visitors. Make a list of those examples. What arguments does she make for her claim that the real effect of these changes is to eliminate public space?

2. Basic to Murphy Davis's argument is her belief that the homeless have as much right to gather in public spaces as anyone in a city. How do you respond to that? Why should anyone care if a public space is unfriendly to homeless people?

3. In her argument, Davis writes, "Trouble is, if we mandate a public space inhospitable to any one group of people, we end with a public space that is inhospitable to everybody." What public spaces do you know about that seem to be natural gathering places for people? What are they like? What would make them unfriendly to everybody?

SUGGESTIONS FOR WRITING

1. City planners apparently believe that any place that has a lot of homeless people is going to keep others away. Create a "mental" map of your home town, your campus, or any place you have lived long enough to know pretty well. Start with a real map of the place and identify four kinds of areas: areas where you will not go, areas you consider to be "ethnic," areas of conflict, and areas you would call "normal." After you have completed that map, write a key for it and explain what identifies each of these areas as safe or not safe, comfortable or uncomfortable, foreign or familiar.

2. Once you have completed your mental map and key, examine what you have written and write a response to your mental map and key that explores how others might read your map. What in your background or experience makes some places seem normal to you and others out of bounds? How might the people who live in those areas describe your "normal" spaces?

3. Write a descriptive analysis of a public space you consider friendly to all kinds of people. Who hangs out there? What do they do? Are there structures in place to keep the homeless away? If so, what are those structures like?

SIGNS FROM THE HEART: California Chicano Murals

Eva Sperling Cockcroft and Holly Barnet-Sánchez

In his full-length work on Chicano culture in Los Angeles (*Anything but Mexican: Chicanos in Contemporary Los Angeles*), Rodolfo Acuña writes that "no space in East Lost Angeles is left unused or unmarked." For Acuña, Chicano or Latino culture has claimed, if not always the physical space that Mike Davis writes of, at least interpretive space—signs and images that mark a place as belonging to a certain group or person. Interpretive space is claimed in East

Los Angeles primarily through the Los Angeles mural movement, which was begun in the 1960s, carried on today under the direction of the Social and Public Arts Resource Center (SPARC), and headed by artist and activist Judy Baca. In the following selection, artists Eva Cockcroft and Holly Barnet-Sánchez write of the origins of the mural movement in Los Angeles. Their essay appeared in 1993 in the book *Signs from the Heart: California Chicano Murals*.

SUGGESTION FOR READING   This selection consists of portions of an introduction to a collection of essays about California Chicano murals. The authors set the mural movement in the larger context of public art throughout history as a way of explaining what murals have meant in the past and what they have come to mean today. After you read this selection, write a brief outline that traces the rise and fall of murals from high art to popular statement as described by Cockcroft and Barnet-Sánchez.

1   A truly "public" art provides society with the symbolic representation of collective beliefs as well as a continuing re-affirmation of the collective sense of self. Paintings on walls, or "murals" as they are commonly called, are perhaps the quintessential public art in this regard. Since before the cave paintings at Altamira some 15,000 years before Christ, wall paintings have served as a way of communicating collective visions within a community of people. During the Renaissance in Italy, considered by many to be the golden age of Western Art, murals were regarded as the highest form in the hierarchy of painting. They served to illustrate the religious lessons of the church and to embody the new Humanism of the period through artistic innovations like perspective and naturalistic anatomy.

After the Mexican Revolution of 1910–1917, murals again served as the artistic vehicle for educating a largely illiterate populace about the ideals of the new society and the virtues and evils of the past. As part of a re-evaluation of their cultural identity by Mexican-Americans during the Chicano movement for civil rights and social justice that began in the mid–1960s, murals again provided an important organizing tool and a means for the reclamation of their specific cultural heritage.

The desire by people for beauty and meaning in their lives is fundamental to their identity as human beings. Some form of art, therefore, has existed in every society throughout history. Before the development of a significant private picture market in Seventeenth Century Holland, most art was public, commissioned by royalty, clergy, or powerful citizens for the greater glory of their country, church, or city and placed in public spaces. However, after the Industrial Revolution and the development of modern capitalism with its stress on financial rather than social values, the art world system as we know it today with galleries, critics, and museums gradually developed. More and more, art became a luxury object to be enjoyed and traded like any other commodity. The break-up of the stable structures of feudal society and the fluidity and dynamism of post-Industrial society was reflected symbolically in art by the disruption of naturalistic space and the experimentation characteristic of Modernism.

Modernism has been a mixed blessing for art and artists. Along with a new freedom for innovation and the opportunity to express an individual vision that resulted from the loss of direct control by patrons of artistic production, artists experienced a sense of alienation from the materialistic values of capitalism, loss of a feeling of clearly defined social utility, and the freedom to starve. This unstable class situation and perception of isolation from society was expressed in the attitude of the bohemian *avant garde* artist who scorns both the crass commercialism of the bourgeoisie and the unsophisticated tastes of the working class, creating work exclusively for the appreciation of a new aristocracy of taste. Especially in the United States of the 1960s, for most people art had become an irrelevant and mysterious thing enjoyed only by a small educated elite.

La Familia detail from *Chicano Time Trip* by East Los Streetscapers (Wayne Alaniz Healy & David Rivas Botello), 1977. 18′ × 26′ panel (total mural is 18′ × 90′). Lincoln Heights, East Los Angeles. City Wide Mural Project.

5   When muralism emerged again as an important art movement in Mexico during the 1920s, the murals served as a way of creating a new national consciousness—a role quite similar to that of the religious murals of the Renaissance although directed toward a different form of social cohesion. Unlike the murals of the Italian Renaissance which expressed the commonly held beliefs of both rulers and masses, the Mexican murals portrayed the ideology of a worker, peasant and middle class revolution against the former ruling class: capitalists, clergy, and foreign interests. Since that time in the eyes of many, contemporary muralism has been identified with poor people, revolution, and communism. This association has been a major factor in changing muralism's rank within the hierarchy of the "fine arts" from the highest to the lowest. Once the favored art of popes and potentates, murals, especially Mexican-style narrative murals, now considered a "poor people's art," have fallen to a level of only marginal acceptance within the art world.

The three great Mexican artists whose names have become almost synonymous with that mural renaissance, Diego Rivera, Jose Clemente Orozco, and David Alfaro Siqueiros, were all influenced by stylistic currents in European modernism—Cubism, Expressionism, and Futurism—but they used these stylistic innovations to create a new socially motivated realism. Rather than continuing to use the naturalistic pictorial space of Renaissance murals, the Mexicans explored new forms of composition. Rivera used a collage-like discontinuous space which juxtaposed elements of different sizes; Orozco employed non-naturalistic brushwork, distorted forms, and exaggerated light and dark, while Siqueiros added expressive uses of perspective with extreme foreshortening that made forms burst right out of the wall. The stylistic innovations of the Mexicans have provided the basis for a modern mural language and most contemporary muralism is based to some extent or another on the Mexican model. The Mexican precedent has been especially important in the United States for the social realist muralists of the Works Progress Administration (WPA) and Treasury Section programs of the New Deal period and the contemporary mural movement that began in the late 1960s.

More than 2500 murals were painted with government sponsorship during the New Deal period in the United States. By the beginning of World War II however, support for social realist painting and muralism in general, had ended. During the Cold War period that followed, realistic painting became identified with totalitarian systems like that of the Soviet Union, while abstraction, especially New York-style Abstract Expressionism, was seen as symbolizing individual freedom in *avant garde* art circles. By the early 1960s, only the various kinds of abstract art from the geometric to the bio-morphic were even considered to really be art. Endorsed by critics and the New York museums, abstraction was promulgated abroad as the International Style and considered to be "universal"—in much the same way as straight-nosed, straight-haired, blondes were considered to be the "universal" ideal of beauty. Those who differed or complained were dismissed as ignorant, uncultured, or anti-American.

The concept of a "universal" ideal of beauty was closely related to the "melting pot" theory, then taught in schools, which held that all the different immigrants, races and national groups which composed the population of the United States could be assimilated into a single homogeneous "American." This theory ignored the existence of separate cultural enclaves within the United States as well as blatant discrimination and racism. It also ignored the complex dialectic between isolation and assimilation and the problem of identity for people like the Mexican-Americans of California who were neither wholly "American" nor "Mexican" but a new, unique, and constantly changing composite variously called "American of Mexican descent," "Mexican-American," Latino or Hispanic. In the 1960s the term "Chicano" with its populist origins was adopted by socially-conscious youth as a form of positive self-identification for Mexican-Americans. Its use became a form of political statement in and of itself.[1]

The dialectic between assimilation and separatism can be seen in the history of Los Angeles, for example, first founded in 1781 as a part of New Spain. In spite of constant pressure for assimilation including job discrimination and compulsory use of English in the schools, the Mexican-American population was able to maintain a culture sufficiently distinct so that, as historian Juan Gómez-Quiñones has frequently argued, a city within a city can be defined. This separate culture continues to exist as a distinct entity within the dominant culture, even though it is now approximately 150 years since Los Angeles was acquired by the United States. This situation, by itself, tends to discredit the melting pot concept.

The Civil Rights Movement, known among Mexican-Americans as the Chicano Movement or *el movimiento,* fought against the idea of a "universal" culture, a single ideal of beauty and order. It re-examined the common assumption that European or Western ideas represented the pinnacle of "civilization," while everything else, from the thought of Confucius to Peruvian portrait vases, was second-rate, too exotic, or "primitive." The emphasis placed by Civil Rights leaders on self-definition and cultural pride sparked a revision of standard histories to include the previously unrecognized accomplishments of women and minorities as well as a re-examination of the standard school curriculum. Along with the demonstrations, strikes, and marches of the political movement came an explosion of cultural expression.

As was the case after the Mexican Revolution, the Civil Rights Movement inspired a revival of muralism. However, this new mural movement differed in many important ways from the Mexican one. It was not sponsored by a successful revolutionary government, but came out of the struggle by the people themselves against the *status quo.* Instead of well-funded projects in government buildings, these new murals were located in the *barrios* and ghettos of the inner cities, where oppressed people lived. They served as an inspiration for struggle, a way of reclaiming a cultural heritage, or even as a means of developing self-pride. Perhaps most significantly, these murals were not the expression of an individual vision. Artists encouraged local residents to join them in discussing the content, and often, in doing the actual painting. For the first time, techniques were developed that would allow non-artists working with a professional to design and paint their own murals. This element of community participation, the placement of murals on exterior walls in the community itself, and the philosophy of community input, that is, the right of a community to decide on what kind of art it wants, characterized the new muralism.

Nowhere did the community-based mural movement take firmer root than in the Chicano communities of California. With the Mexican mural tradition as part of their heritage, murals were a particularly congenial form for Chicano artists to express the collective vision of their community. The mild climate and low, stuccoed buildings provided favorable physical conditions, and, within a few years, California had more murals than any other region of the country. As home to the largest concentration of Mexicans and people of Mexican ancestry anywhere outside of Mexico City, Los Angeles became the site of the largest concentration of Chicano murals in the United States. Estimates range from one thousand to fifteen hundred separate works painted between 1969 and the present. The Social and Public Art Resource Center's "California Chicano Mural Archive" compiled in 1984 documents close to 1000 mural projects throughout the state in slide form.

Because Chicano artists were consciously searching to identify the images that represented their shared experience they were continually led back to the *barrio*. It became the site for "finding" the symbols, forms, colors, and narratives that would assist them in the redefinition of their communities. Not interested in perpetuating the Hollywood notion that art was primarily an avenue of escape from reality, Chicano artists sought to use their art to create a dialogue of demystification through which the Chicano community could evolve toward cultural liberation. To this end, murals and posters became an ubiquitous element of the *barrioscape*. According to Ybarra-Frausto, they publicly represented the reclamation of individual Chicano minds and hearts through the acknowledgement and cele-

bration of their community's identity through the creation of an art of resistance.

Prior to the Chicano movement, U.S. Mexicans were defined externally through a series of derogatory stereotypes with total assimilation as the only way to break out of the situation of social marginalization. Art that integrated elements of U.S. Mexican or *barrio* culture was also denigrated as "folk" art and not considered seriously. The explosion of Chicano culture and murals as a result of the political movement, provided new recognition and value for Chicano art which weakened the old barriers. According to S´nchez-Tranquilino, this experience allowed artists to figuratively break through the wall that confined artists either to the *barrio* or to unqualified assimilation. It gave them the confidence to explore new artistic forms and a new relationship to the dominant society.

NOTE

1. Throughout this book several terms are used to identify Americans of Mexican descent: "Mexican-Americans," "U.S. Mexicans," and "Chicanos." Each carries specific meanings and they are not used interchangeably. "Mexican-American" is primarily a post World War II development in regular use until the politicization of *el movimiento,* the Chicano civil rights movement of the 1960s and 1970s. Its use acknowledges with pride the Mexican heritage which was hidden by an earlier, less appropriate term, "Spanish-American." However, its hyphenated construction implies a level of equality in status between the Mexican and the American which in actuality belies the unequal treatment of Americans of Mexican descent within United States society.

   U.S. Mexican is a term developed by essayist Marcos Sánchez-Tranquilino to replace the term Mexican-American with one that represents both more generally and clearly all Mexicans within the United States whether their families were here prior to annexation in 1848, have been here for generations, or for only two days. In other words, it represents all Mexicans living within U.S. borders regardless of residence or citizenship status.

   The most basic definition of the term Chicano was made by journalist Ruben Salazar in 1970: "A Chicano is a Mexican-American who does not have an Anglo image of himself." It is a term of self-definition that denotes politicization.

SUGGESTIONS FOR DISCUSSION

1. Throughout this selection, Cockcroft and Barnet-Sánchez remind their readers that, though mural painting might have been considered high art in earlier periods when it was funded by church or state, by the time the Chicano mural movement had come to California, these highly realistic, working-class, public wall paintings were no longer valued by the art world. Instead, the mural movement became a part of the *barrioscape*—a sign of Chicano culture and a statement about Chicano politics. How do Cockcroft and Barnet-Sánchez explain the fall of murals from high to low in the art world? Why do you think artists or art collectors care whether or not such public art is considered "high culture"? How would you differentiate "art" from "wall paintings"?

2. One of the roles that the Chicano mural movement has played, according to this selection, has been to challenge universal standards of beauty. How do Cockcroft and Barnet-Sánchez define this "universal" standard? What do they see as its relation to the "melting pot"? With a group of your classmantes, look at the mural reprinted in this selection, and explain how it offers a challenge to that standard.

3. The introduction to this selection notes that Chicano murals have claimed an "interpretive space" in Los Angeles. As Cockcroft and Barnet-Sánchez write, these murals "publicly represented the reclamation of individual Chicano minds and hearts through the acknowledgment and celebration of their community's identity through the creation of an art of resistance." Why do you think it might be important for a group such as the one described here to claim a space through art or signs or language or music (i.e., interpretive space)? In what ways do other groups or people that you know claim interpretive space?

SUGGESTIONS FOR WRITING

1. Write an essay in which you discuss how a knowledge of the mural movement, as it is described in the selection above, either changes or reinforces the impression that you got of Los Angeles from reading Mike Davis's analysis of that city.

2. Write an essay that examines why it might be important for marginalized groups to claim interpretive space through images or signs such as the mural movement. Do you know of any similar strategies to the mural movement that other groups use to claim interpretive space? Draw on your reading on Los Angeles and the mural movement to help you with this writing. You might also have experience in your own town, city, or school to explain the need for those who feel like outsiders to claim interpretive space with images or signs.

3. Cockcroft and Barnet-Sánchez write, "Prior to the Chicano movement, U.S. Mexicans were defined externally through a series of derogatory stereotypes." Watch a film that includes or deals with Latinos in the United States (for example, *Selena*, *Mi Familia*, *The Bronze Screen*, or *A Walk in the Clouds*) and write an essay in which you address that comment. In what ways do the characters and their situations break with the familiar stereotypes? In what ways are those stereotypes perpetuated? Before you begin your essay (and even before you begin watching one of these films), make a list of familiar stereotypes. If you are unsure of the common Latino stereotypes, ask classmates, friends, and family to help you.

PERSPECTIVES Ground Zero—Commerce and Commemoration

Even as workers were clearing away the wreckage of the World Trade Center, it became clear to everyone that this place, now called Ground Zero, would never be the same. Many of those killed in the attack remained buried in the wreckage, so for those who survived, those who lost friends and family, and even for those millions of Americans who watched the attack on their television screens, Ground Zero was as sacred as any cemetery. How to memorialize those lost lives quickly became the subject of heated debates about what this space had now become and what should replace the Trade Center towers.

At the center of this controversy was the conflict between private commercial rights and public needs. Before the attack, the World Trade Center was a multimillion dollar commercial property housing dozens of businesses. Developers who held a ninety-nine-year lease on the property expected to continue using that site as a commercial enterprise for a long time. For many, those commercial pressures stand in conflict with commemorating a national tragedy.

The next two readings, which address this conflict, were written almost a year apart and yet wrestle with many of the same issues: What is the nature of this space? What is the appropriate response to tragedy? Is it more appropriate to rebuild—to insist on business as usual—or should the site become a public memorial with little attention to commerce?

THE COMMEMORATIVE BEAUTY
OF TRAGIC WRECKAGE

Herbert Muschamp

Herbert Muschamp is the architecture critic for the *New York Times*. He has also served as architecture critic for the *New Republic* and *Artforum*. Muschamp is past director of the Graduate Program in Architecture and Design Criticism at the Parsons School of Design, where he has been a member of the faculty since 1983. The following article appeared in the *New York Times* on November 11, 2001, only two months after the attack on the World Trade Center. In it, Muschamp examines some of the difficulties of designing a memorial on the site of so much pain and still-raw emotion.

SUGGESTION FOR READING In his article, Muschamp brings together several issues and concerns. The first is embodied in a news story about a clash between New York's police department and firefighters. A second is on the nature of memorial architecture. A third line of concern has to do with something Muschamp calls "the architectural fragment," those pieces of a building or structure that seem to be junk but that also carry historical, emotional, or artistic importance. As you read, keep track of these three lines of discussion and take note of how Muschamp connects them to a central argument.

1   A piece of architecture was created in Lower Manhattan last week, and architects had nothing to do with it. This major new work materialized during the scuffle that broke out between police officers and firefighters over access to ground zero. The firefighters believed, with the emotional logic that has helped prevent the terrorist attack from unraveling the soul of New York, that removal of the wreckage should not proceed without their participation. Their objective, which should be everyone's, is that all efforts should be made to retrieve and identify the remains of their fallen brethren before the wreckage is carted off to the dump.

The conflict between these two groups affirmed a perception that has been taking shape in public consciousness since Sept. 11: a memorial to those lost in the terrorist attack already exists. We will probably see no more eloquent reminder of that day than the twisted steel walls that at present rise from the wreckage of the World Trade Center.

The "potato chip," some have taken to calling these ribbed fragments, because they vaguely resemble a brand of snack food. It's human nature to domesticate such a horrific image. "Wailing wall" is another term in circulation. It's a polemical term, intended to limit attachment to the wreckage and thus pave the way for its removal. The term means, "Do we really want to dedicate this place to feeling sorry for ourselves for all time?"

Most people just call it the Walls. The term is powerful in its purely descriptive neutrality. It doesn't spin the forms into a limited framework of meaning. Rather, like the void left by the collapse of the twin towers, the Walls invites an infinite number of projected associations. It has the classically stoic understatement of the titles Virginia Woolf gave her books. "The Waves." "The Years." "Between the Acts."

5   Logically, an architecture critic's associations begin with the family of forms. For instance, there were reports that after Sept. 11, some architecture fans were unsettled by the resemblance between the wreckage at ground zero and some Frank Gehry projects. Actually, no one was more painfully conscious of the resemblance than the architect himself. By a twist of fate, a Gehry project was scheduled to open in New York a few days after the disaster: a new Issey Miyake shop in TriBeCa, 10 blocks north of ground zero.

Miyake had asked Gehry to create "a tornado." Working with Gordon Kipping, a young New York architect, Gehry obliged by fashioning a sculptural installation of long titanium strips that twist and curl, animating the space with a sense of barely controlled imagination. (The project, which has since opened, is at the corner of Hudson and Harrison Streets.) It pleased Gehry that this was the first publicly accessible work he had designed expressly for New York.

I first saw the space on the night of Sept. 10, a few days before the scheduled opening. Later, I accompanied Gehry, Miyake, Kipping and Gehry's son, Alejandro, an artist responsible for the murals that ornament the shop's interiors, to a restaurant a few doors down the street. It was raining heavily, but during dinner the downpour stopped. When we left the restaurant, a little before midnight, the twin towers reared up to infinity through tumbling, gray Wagnerian clouds. It was a good last look.

If you believe that beauty begins in terror, then it is not sacrilege to speak of the beauty of the remaining walls. Nor is Gehry's architecture the only work that has constructed an aesthetic context for them. A substantial body of literature has been dedicated to the contemplation of ruins. The Neoclassical tradition sprang from within the imaginations of those who meditated on stone fragments of the ancient world. That is why 19th-century architects went to Rome. Piranesi's engraved visions of fantastic classicism should be required study for those now gazing on ground zero.

More recently, the idea of the architectural fragment has surfaced in buildings that attempt a more integrated relationship between architecture and site, landscape or urban context. The bending, folding, curving shapes of the World Trade Center wreckage echo the neo-Baroque contortions of blob architecture as practiced by Greg Lynn, Ben van Berkel and others. As a result of my experience, the Walls remind me of Miyake's pleated clothes, and of peaceful times.

10   Ultimately, however, the Walls are walls, or, rather, the blasted skeletons of walls. It's hard to imagine a more potent architectural symbol, particularly as we confront a high-security future in which walls, borders, boundaries and other varieties of exclusion and restricted access are likely to play a prominent role. Do we know what we will be giving up to inhabit this future? Will any boundaries be placed around efforts to control access in the public realm, or to restrict invasion in the private? By what measure can we count ourselves Americans if freedom is negotiated down to a matter of consumer choices? Add to shopping cart. Free bonus gift. This week only.

Such speculations gained immediate substance from last week's clash between the firefighters and the police. The conflict was as much over meaning as it was over access. The police represented the view that the wreckage is now cartage. To the firefighters, it is sacred space, at least until they have fulfulled their duty to recover the victims' remains. The discrepancy shifted the meaning of the 16-acre site from the future to the present. How we act now assumed priority over what we build later. A tactical maneuver—hey, not so fast—took on philosophical and even spiritual meaning.

Something more important was at stake than the construction of new towers and the design of an "appropriate" memorial. The momentum behind site-clearing was brought to a temporary halt. Its inevitability was questioned. This shift did not emerge from any artificially engineered consensus but from the conflict between two points of view. Both sides became the front-line cultural workers the city has been awaiting. Without the police, the conflict would not have been dramatized.

This column is not an appeal for the permanent preservation of the Walls. My concern is that we not overlook the meaning of events as they unfold. Clearly, the walls have become a landmark, whether or not we choose to preserve them. Even if the decision is made to remove them, they can no longer be treated as junk. This is a major piece of our own place and time. And it does seem weird that a city now thought to be so deeply protective of its history should look the other way as a big chunk of history disappears.

The public does not have to accept, without question, the view that the walls cannot be stabilized. Indeed we should regard that opinion with the deepest suspicion. We have the right, in fact, to insist that an independent study be made of the feasibility of preserving them. The demolition schedule, supervised by the city's Department of Design and Construction, should be reconsidered pending the outcome of that study.

15   With all the talk we are hearing about unity of purpose and unanimity of voice, it is good to be reminded that conflict is essential to the democratic process. If it took a street fight to rearrange the priorities of those contemplating the future of Lower Manhattan, then we should rejoice that cities are places where street fighting can occur. In asserting their right to access, the firefighters claimed it for everyone. The sky did not fall, Broadway didn't go dark, Seventh Avenue wasn't immediately mothballed. Though the firefighters acted emotionally, theirs was the voice of reason—one of the few that have been heard thus far.

REBUILD AT GROUND ZERO

Larry Silverstein

Larry Silverstein is president of Silverstein Properties, a real estate firm whose affiliates hold ninety-nine-year leases on the World Trade Center site. This article appeared in September of 2002 in the *Wall Street Journal*. In it, Silverstein makes his argument for why the Trade Center ought to be rebuilt as a commercial site and a site that commemorates those lives lost.

SUGGESTION FOR READING In many ways, Silverstein is making a difficult argument. After a tragedy of this magnitude witnessed by so many, most people would agree that a memorial is needed at Ground Zero. Silverstein must make his argument within that first position. In other words, he must take care not to dismiss the desire to commemorate those who lost their lives while convincing readers that the space must maintain its viability as commercial property. As you read, keep track of how he makes that argument.

1   Earlier this month, we New Yorkers observed the solemn anniversary of the horrific events that befell our city on Sept. 11, 2001. All of those who perished must never be forgotten. The footprints of the fallen Twin Towers and a portion of the 16-acre site must be dedicated to a memorial and civic amenities that recall the sacrifices that were made there and the anguish that those senseless acts of terror created for the victims' families and, indeed, for all of us.

But for the good of the city and the region, the 10-million-plus square feet of commercial and retail space that was destroyed with the Twin Towers must be replaced on the site.

About 50,000 people worked in the World Trade Center. Those jobs are lost, along with those of another 50,000 people who worked in the vicinity. Together, those jobs in lower Manhattan, for which the Trade Center was the economic stimulus, produced annual gross wages of about $47 billion, or 15% of the annual gross wages earned in the entire state. Some of the firms have relocated elsewhere in the city and region, but many have not. New York City is facing a budget deficit. Without additional jobs, the deficit may become permanent. This is one reason for the importance of rebuilding.

If we do not replace the lost space, lower Manhattan never will regain the vibrancy it had as the world's financial center. Love them or hate them, and there were lots of New Yorkers on both sides of the issue, the Towers made a powerful statement to the world that said, "This is New York, a symbol of our free economy and of our way of life." That is why they were destroyed. This is a second reason why the towers must be replaced, and with buildings that make a potent architectural statement.

5   In recent weeks, redevelopment proposals have been circulated from many sources. Most of these focus not on the Trade Center site, however, but on all of lower Manhattan. Further, many believe that the 10 million square feet either could be located elsewhere, scattered in several sites, or simply never rebuilt.

These proposals miss the point. What was destroyed, and what must be recovered, was the Trade Center, not all of lower Manhattan. Except over the towers' footprints, where there must be no commercial development, the office and retail space lost has to be rebuilt on or close to where it was.

Access to mass transit makes the site ideal for office space of this size. That was a major reason why the Twin Towers were leased to 97% occupancy before 9/11. None of the other sites proposed for office development has remotely equal transportation access. With the reconstruction of the subway and PATH stations, plus an additional $4.5 billion in transit improvements planned, such as the new Fulton Transit Center and the direct "Train-to-the-

Plane" Long Island Rail Road connection, the site becomes even more the logical locus of office development.

And New York will need the space. Before 9/11, the Group of 35, a task force of civic leaders led by Sen. Charles Schumer and former Treasury Secretary Robert Rubin, concluded that the city would need an additional 60 million square feet of new office space by 2020 to accommodate the anticipated addition of 300,000 new jobs. The loss of the Twin Towers only heightens the need.

As for those who say that 10 million square feet of office space downtown cannot be absorbed by the real estate market, I would simply point out that history shows them wrong. New York now has about 400 million square feet of office space. All new construction underway already is substantially leased up. New York had 48 million square feet of vacant office space at the beginning of the recession in 1990. By 1998, this space had been absorbed, at an annual rate of about 6 million square feet.

10   We are seeking to rebuild 10 million square feet on the Trade Center site over a period of about 10 years, with the first buildings not coming on line until 2008 and the project reaching completion in 2012. This is an annual absorption rate of about a million feet, much lower than the 1990s' rate.

Those who argue that New York cannot reabsorb office space that it previously had are saying that the city has had its day and is entering an extended period of stagnation and decline. I will not accept this view, nor will most New Yorkers.

Mayor Michael Bloomberg said in a recent interview with the New York Times that the city "has to do two things: memorialize, but also build for the future." I believe that the Twin Towers site can gracefully accommodate—and that downtown requires—office and retail space of architectural significance, a dignified memorial that both witnesses and recalls what happened, and cultural amenities that would benefit workers as well as residents of the area.

The challenge to accomplish this is enormous. But our city is up to the task.

SUGGESTIONS FOR DISCUSSION

1. Muschamp begins his article by saying that "a piece of architecture was created" by the scuffle between police and firefighters over access to what came to be known as Ground Zero. If the wreckage was there before the scuffle, in what way did that clash "create" a piece of architecture? How is Muschamp distinguishing "wreckage" from "architecture"? How might Silverstein see that same piece of wreckage?

2. Muschamp writes that certain terms used for the remains of the World Trade Center indicate the position different groups take on the issue. Those who call it "potato chip" or the "Wailing Wall" advocate its removal, suggesting that it looks tacky or pitiful rather than dignified or strong. Examine the positions Muschamp outlines in his article for and against the removal of the wreckage. To what extent are you convinced that the wreckage itself can be an appropriate memorial?

3. Silverstein and Muschamp do not necessarily take opposing positions. Instead, they see the meaning of Ground Zero in different ways. Summarize the ways these two writers represent the importance of Ground Zero. Silverstein is a lease holder for the property in question. Muschamp is an architectural design scholar. What is at stake for each of these authors?

SUGGESTIONS FOR WRITING

1. To make sure you know Muschamp's argument, write a summary of his article. Track the different areas of conflict that he raises and make sure to include his use of both contemporary and classic references to architecture. Conclude your summary with a brief statement, in your words, of his central argument.

2. Muschamp writes, "Ultimately, however, the Walls are walls, or, rather, the blasted skeletons of walls. It's hard to imagine a more potent architectural symbol, particularly as we confront a high-security future in which walls, borders, boundaries and other varieties of exclusion and restricted access are likely to play a prominent role. Do we know what we will be giving up to inhabit this future? Will any boundaries be placed around efforts to control access in the public realm, or to restrict invasion in the private? By what measure can we count ourselves Americans if freedom is negotiated down to a matter of consumer choices?" Write a response to Muschamp's concerns about what is done with these walls, especially as the decision depends very much on whether this site is treated as a public or a private space—a commercial or a memorial site.

   You might find it useful to draw on other readings from this chapter. Lopez and Fiske both, for example, offer ways of thinking about the use of space or one's responsibilities to space that you could draw on in your response to Muschamp.

3. Today, many public spaces serve double roles—as commemorative or memorial sites as well as commercial enterprises. The national monuments, for example, do just that. Vendors line the Washington, D.C., mall, for example, to sell T-shirts and other souvenirs. You walk through a gift shop to get to Mount Rushmore. Choose a commemorative space that you know well. Write an opinion piece on that space in terms of its relation to commerce. How are commerce and commemoration balanced at the site? Does one detract from the other? Do they clash?

CLASSIC READING

THE USES OF SIDEWALKS—SAFETY

Jane Jacobs

Jane Jacobs had no formal training in urban development and completed no college degree. Yet *The Death and Life of Great American Cities*, her classic 1961 study of how people live in cities from which this selection is taken, has become a catalyst for many organizations opposed to suburban sprawl and what is known as the gentrification of older, lower income neighborhoods.

SUGGESTION FOR READING Jacobs writes of city streets people feel safe on and those people don't feel safe on. Before you read, write a description of the kind of street you think is a safe one and the kind of street that seems less safe when you are in a city you don't know well.

1 Streets in cities serve many purposes besides carrying vehicles, and city sidewalks—the pedestrian parts of the streets—serve many purposes besides carrying pedestrians. These uses are bound up with circulation but are not identical with it and in their own right they are at least as basic as circulation to the proper workings of cities.

A city sidewalk by itself is nothing. It is an abstraction. It means something only in conjunction with the buildings and other uses that border it, or border other sidewalks very near it. The same might be said of streets, in the sense that they serve other purposes besides carrying wheeled traffic in their middles. Streets and their sidewalks, the main public places of a city, are its most vital organs. Think of a city and what comes to mind? Its streets. If a city's streets look interesting, the city looks interesting; if they look dull, the city looks dull.

More than that, and here we get down to the first problem, if a city's streets are safe from barbarism and fear, the city is thereby tolerably safe from barbarism and fear. When people say that a city, or a part of it, is dangerous or is a jungle what they mean primarily is that they do not feel safe on the sidewalks.

But sidewalks and those who use them are not passive beneficiaries of safety or helpless victims of danger. Sidewalks, their bordering uses, and their users, are active participants in the drama of civilization versus barbarism in cities. To keep the city safe is a fundamental task of a city's streets and its sidewalks.

5   This task is totally unlike any service that sidewalks and streets in little towns or true suburbs are called upon to do. Great cities are not like towns, only larger. They are not like suburbs, only denser. They differ from towns and suburbs in basic ways, and one of these is that cities are, by definition, full of strangers. To any one person, strangers are far more common in big cities than acquaintances. More common not just in places of public assembly, but more common at a man's own doorstep. Even residents who live near each other are strangers, and must be, because of the sheer number of people in small geographical compass.

The bedrock attribute of a successful city district is that a person must feel personally safe and secure on the street among all these strangers. He must not feel automatically menaced by them. A city district that fails in this respect also does badly in other ways and lays up for itself, and for its city at large, mountain on mountain of trouble.

Today barbarism has taken over many city streets, or people fear it has, which comes to much the same thing in the end. "I live in a lovely, quiet residential area," says a friend of mine who is hunting another place to live. "The only disturbing sound at night is the occasional scream of someone being mugged." It does not take many incidents of violence on a city street, or in a city district, to make people fear the streets. And as they fear them, they use them less, which makes the streets still more unsafe.

To be sure, there are people with hobgoblins in their heads, and such people will never feel safe no matter what the objective circumstances are. But this is a different matter from the fear that besets normally prudent, tolerant and cheerful people who show nothing more than common sense in refusing to venture after dark—or in a few places, by day—into streets where they may well be assaulted, unseen or unrescued until too late.

The barbarism and the real, not imagined, insecurity that gives rise to such fears cannot be tagged a problem of the slums. The problem is most serious, in fact, in genteel-looking "quiet residential areas" like that my friend was leaving.

10   It cannot be tagged as a problem of older parts of cities. The problem reaches its most baffling dimensions in some examples of rebuilt parts of cities, including supposedly the best examples of rebuilding, such as middle-income projects. The police precinct captain of a nationally admired project of this kind (admired by planners and lenders) has recently admonished residents not only about hanging around outdoors after dark but has urged them never to answer their doors without knowing the caller. Life here has much in common with life for the three little pigs or the seven little kids of the nursery thrillers. The problem of sidewalk and doorstep insecurity is as serious in cities which have made conscientious efforts at rebuilding as it is in those cities that have lagged. Nor is it illuminating to tag minority groups, or the poor, or the outcast with responsibility for city danger. There are immense variations in the degree of civilization and safety found among such groups and among the city areas where they live. Some of the safest sidewalks in New York City, for example, at any time of day or night, are those along which poor people or minority groups live. And some of the most dangerous are in streets occupied by the same kinds of people. All this can also be said of other cities.

Deep and complicated social ills must lie behind delinquency and crime, in suburbs and towns as well as in great cities. This book will not go into speculation on the deeper reasons. It is sufficient, at this point, to say that if we are to maintain a city society that can diagnose and keep abreast of deeper social problems, the starting point must be, in any case, to strengthen whatever workable forces for maintaining safety and civilization do exist—in the cities we do have. To build city districts that are custom made for easy crime is idiotic. Yet that is what we do.

The first thing to understand is that the public peace—the sidewalk and street peace—of cities is not kept primarily by the police, necessary as police are. It is kept primarily by an intricate, almost unconscious, network of voluntary controls and standards among the people themselves, and enforced by the people themselves. In some city areas—older public housing projects and streets with very high population turnover are often conspicuous examples—the keeping of public sidewalk law and order is left almost entirely to the police and special guards. Such places are jungles. No amount of police can enforce civilization where the normal, casual enforcement of it has broken down.

The second thing to understand is that the problem of insecurity cannot be solved by spreading people out more thinly, trading the characteristics of cities for the characteristics of suburbs. If this could solve danger on the city streets, then Los Angeles should be a safe city because superficially Los Angeles is almost all suburban. It has virtually no districts compact enough to qualify as dense city areas. Yet Los Angeles cannot, any more than any other great city, evade the truth that, being a city, it *is* composed of strangers not all of whom are nice. Los Angeles' crime figures are flabbergasting. Among the seventeen standard metropolitan areas with populations over a million, Los Angeles stands so pre-eminent in crime that it is in a category by itself. And this is markedly true of crimes associated with personal attack, the crimes that make people fear the streets.

Los Angeles, for example, has a forcible rape rate (1958 figures) of 31.9 per 100,000 population, more than twice as high as either of the next two cities, which happen to be St. Louis and Philadelphia; three times as high as the rate of 10.1 for Chicago, and more than four times as high as the rate of 7.4 for New York.

15   In aggravated assault, Los Angeles has a rate of 185, compared with 149.5 for Baltimore and 139.2 for St. Louis (the two next highest), and with 90.9 for New York and 79 for Chicago.

The overall Los Angeles rate for major crimes is 2,507.6 per 100,000 people, far ahead of St. Louis and Houston, which come next with 1,634.5 and 1,541.1, and of New York and Chicago, which have rates of 1,145.3 and 943.5.

The reasons for Los Angeles' high crime rates are undoubtedly complex, and at least in part obscure. But of this we can be sure: thinning out a city does not insure safety from crime and fear of crime. This is one of the conclusions that can be drawn within individual cities too, where pseudosuburbs or superannuated suburbs are ideally suited to rape, muggings, beatings, holdups and the like.

Here we come up against an all-important question about any city street: How much easy opportunity does it offer to crime? It may be that there is some absolute amount of crime in a given city, which will find an outlet somehow (I do not believe this). Whether this is so or not, different kinds of city streets garner radically different shares of barbarism and fear of barbarism.

Some city streets afford no opportunity to street barbarism. The streets of the North End of Boston are outstanding examples. They are probably as safe as any place on earth in this respect. Although most of the North End's residents are Italian or of Italian descent, the district's streets are also heavily and constantly used by people of every race and background. Some of the strangers from outside work in or close to the district; some come to shop and stroll; many, including members of minority groups who have inherited dangerous districts previously abandoned by others, make a point of cashing their paychecks in North

End stores and immediately making their big weekly purchases in streets where they know they will not be parted from their money between the getting and the spending.

20   Frank Havey, director of the North End Union, the local settlement house, says, "I have been here in the North End twenty-eight years, and in all that time I have never heard of a single case of rape, mugging, molestation of a child or other street crime of that sort in the district. And if there had been any, I would have heard of it even if it did not reach the papers." Half a dozen times or so in the past three decades, says Havey, would-be molesters have made an attempt at luring a child or, late at night, attacking a woman. In every such case the try was thwarted by passers-by, by kibitzers from windows, or shopkeepers.

Meantime, in the Elm Hill Avenue section of Roxbury, a part of inner Boston that is suburban in superficial character, street assaults and the ever present possibility of more street assaults with no kibitzers to protect the victims, induce prudent people to stay off the sidewalks at night. Not surprisingly, for this and other reasons that are related (dispiritedness and dullness), most of Roxbury has run down. It has become a place to leave.

I do not wish to single out Roxbury or its once fine Elm Hill Avenue section especially as a vulnerable area; its disabilities, and especially its Great Blight of Dullness, are all too common in other cities too. But differences like these in public safety within the same city are worth noting. The Elm Hill Avenue section's basic troubles are not owing to a criminal or a discriminated against or a poverty-stricken population. Its troubles stem from the fact that it is physically quite unable to function safely and with related vitality as a city district.

Even within supposedly similar parts of supposedly similar places, drastic differences in public safety exist. An incident at Washington Houses, a public housing project in New York, illustrates this point. A tenants' group at this project, struggling to establish itself, held some outdoor ceremonies in mid-December 1958, and put up three Christmas trees. The chief tree, so cumbersome it was a problem to transport, erect, and trim, went into the project's inner "street," a landscaped central mall and promenade. The other two trees, each less than six feet tall and easy to carry, went on two small fringe plots at the outer corners of the project where it abuts a busy avenue and lively cross streets of the old city. The first night, the large tree and all its trimmings were stolen. The two smaller trees remained intact, lights, ornaments and all, until they were taken down at New Year's. "The place where the tree was stolen, which is *theoretically* the most safe and sheltered place in the project, is the same place that is unsafe for people too, especially children," says a social workers who had been helping the tenants' group. "People are no safer in that mall than the Christmas tree. On the other hand, the place where the other trees were safe, where the project is just one corner out of four, happens to be safe for people."

This is something everyone already knows: A well-used city street is apt to be a safe street. A deserted city street is apt to be unsafe. But how does this work, really? And what makes a city street well used or shunned? Why is the sidewalk mall in Washington Houses, which is supposed to be an attraction, shunned? Why are the sidewalks of the old city just to its west not shunned? What about streets that are busy part of the time and then empty abruptly?

25   A city street equipped to handle strangers, and to make a safety asset, in itself, out of the presence of strangers, as the streets of successful city neighborhoods always do, must have three main qualities:

First, there must be a clear demarcation between what is public space and what is private space. Public and private spaces cannot ooze into each other as they do typically in suburban settings or in projects.

Second, there must be eyes upon the street, eyes belonging to those we might call the natural proprietors of the street. The buildings on a street equipped to handle strangers and to insure the safety of both residents and strangers, must be oriented to the street. They cannot turn their backs or blank sides on it and leave it blind.

And third, the sidewalk must have users on it fairly continuously, both to add to the number of effective eyes on the street and to induce the people in buildings along the street to watch the sidewalks in sufficient numbers. Nobody enjoys sitting on a stoop or looking out a window at an empty street. Almost nobody does such a thing. Large numbers of people entertain themselves, off and on, by watching street activity.

In settlements that are smaller and simpler than big cities, controls on acceptable public behavior, if not on crime, seem to operate with greater or lesser success through a web of reputation, gossip, approval, disapproval and sanctions, all of which are powerful if people know each other and word travels. But a city's streets, which must control not only the behavior of the people of the city but also of visitors from suburbs and towns who want to have a big time away from the gossip and sanctions at home, have to operate by more direct, straightforward methods. It is a wonder cities have solved such an inherently difficult problem at all. And yet in many streets they do it magnificently.

30   It is futile to try to evade the issue of unsafe city streets by attempting to make some other features of a locality, say interior courtyards, or sheltered play spaces, safe instead. By definition again, the streets of a city must do most of the job of handling strangers for this is where strangers come and go. The streets must not only defend the city against predatory strangers, they must protect the many, many peaceable and well-meaning strangers who use them, insuring their safety too as they pass through. Moreover, no normal person can spend his life in some artificial haven, and this includes children. Everyone must use the streets.

On the surface, we seem to have here some simple aims: To try to secure streets where the public space is unequivocally public, physically unmixed with private or with nothing-at-all space, so that the area needing surveillance has clear and practicable limits; and to see that these public street spaces have eyes on them as continuously as possible.

But it is not so simple to achieve these objects, especially the latter. You can't make people use streets they have no reason to use. You can't make people watch streets they do not want to watch. Safety on the streets by surveillance and mutual policing of one another sounds grim, but in real life it is not grim. The safety of the street works best, most casually, and with least frequent taint of hostility or suspicion precisely where people are using and most enjoying the city streets voluntarily and are least conscious, normally, that they are policing.

The basic requisite for such surveillance is a substantial quantity of stores and other public places sprinkled along the sidewalks of a district; enterprises and public places that are used by evening and night must be among them especially. Stores, bars and restaurants, as the chief examples, work in several different and complex ways to abet sidewalk safety.

First, they give people—both residents and strangers—concrete reasons for using the sidewalks on which these enterprises face.

35   Second, they draw people along the sidewalks past places which have no attractions to public use in themselves but which become traveled and peopled as routes to somewhere else; this influence does not carry very far geographically, so enterprises must be frequent in a city district if they are to populate with walkers those other stretches of street that lack public places along the sidewalk. Moreover, there should be many different kinds of enterprises, to give people reasons for crisscrossing paths.

Third, storekeepers and other small businessmen are typically strong proponents of peace and order themselves; they hate broken windows and holdups; they hate having customers made nervous about safety. They are great street watchers and sidewalk guardians if present in sufficient numbers.

Fourth, the activity generated by people on errands, or people aiming for food or drink, is itself an attraction to still other people.

This last point, that the sight of people attracts still other people, is something that city planners and city architectural designers seem to find incomprehensible. They operate on the premise that city people seek the sight of emptiness, obvious order and quiet. Nothing could be less true. People's love of watching activity and other people is constantly evident in cities everywhere. This trait reaches an almost ludicrous extreme on upper Broadway in New York, where the street is divided by a narrow central mall, right in the middle of traffic. At the cross-street intersections of this long north-south mall, benches have been placed behind big concrete buffers and on any day when the weather is even barely tolerable these benches are filled with people at block after block after block, watching the pedestrians who cross the mall in front of them, watching the traffic, watching the people on the busy sidewalks, watching each other. Eventually Broadway reaches Columbia University and Barnard College, one to the right, the other to the left. Here all is obvious order and quiet. No more stores, no more activity generated by the stores, almost no more pedestrians crossing—and no more watchers. The benches are there but they go empty in even the finest weather. I have tried them and can see why. No place could be more boring. Even the students of these institutions shun the solitude. They are doing their outdoor loitering, outdoor homework and general street watching on the steps overlooking the busiest campus crossing.

It is just so on city streets elsewhere. A lively street always has both its users and pure watchers. Last year I was on such a street in the Lower East Side of Manhattan, waiting for a bus. I had not been there longer than a minute, barely long enough to begin taking in the street's activity of errand goers, children playing, and loiterers on the stoops, when my attention was attracted by a woman who opened a window on the third floor of a tenement across the street and vigorously yoo-hooed at me. When I caught on that she wanted my attention and responded, she shouted down, "The bus doesn't run here on Saturdays!" Then by a combination of shouts and pantomime she directed me around the corner. This woman was one of thousands upon thousands of people in New York who casually take care of the streets. They notice strangers. They observe everything going on. If they need to take action, whether to direct a stranger waiting in the wrong place or to call the police, they do so. Action usually requires, to be sure, a certain self-assurance about the actor's proprietorship of the street and the support he will get if necessary, matters which will be gone into later in this book. But even more fundamental than the action and necessary to the action, is the watching itself.

40   Not everyone in cities helps to take care of the streets, and many a city resident or city worker is unaware of why his neighborhood is safe. The other day an incident occurred on the street where I live, and it interested me because of this point.

My block of the street, I must explain, is a small one, but it contains a remarkable range of buildings, varying from several vintages of tenements to three- and four-story houses that have been converted into low-rent flats with stores on the ground floor, or returned to single-family use like ours. Across the street there used to be mostly four-story brick tenements with stores below. But twelve years ago several buildings, from the corner to the middle of the block, were converted into one building with elevator apartments of small size and high rents.

The incident that attracted my attention was a suppressed struggle going on between a man and a little girl of eight or nine years old. The man seemed to be trying to get the girl to go with him. By turns he was directing a cajoling attention to her, and then assuming an air of nonchalance. The girl was making herself rigid, as children do when they resist, against the wall of one of the tenements across the street.

As I watched from our second-floor window, making up my mind how to intervene if it seemed advisable, I saw it was not going to be necessary. From the butcher shop beneath the tenement had emerged the woman who, with her husband, runs the shop; she was standing within earshot of the man, her arms folded and a look of determination on her face. Joe Cornacchia, who with his sons-in-law keeps the delicatessen, emerged about the same moment and stood solidly to the other side. Several heads poked out of the tenement windows above, one was withdrawn quickly and its owner reappeared a moment later in the doorway behind the man. Two men from the bar next to the butcher shop came to the doorway and waited. On my side of the street, I saw that the locksmith, the fruit man and the laundry proprietor had all come out of their shops and that the scene was also being surveyed from a number of windows besides ours. That man did not know it, but he was surrounded. Nobody was going to allow a little girl to be dragged off, even if nobody knew who she was.

I am sorry—sorry purely for dramatic purposes—to have to report that the little girl turned out to be the man's daughter.

45   Throughout the duration of the little drama, perhaps five minutes in all, no eyes appeared in the windows of the high-rent, small-apartment building. It was the only building of which this was true. When we first moved to our block, I used to anticipate happily that perhaps soon all the buildings would be rehabilitated like that one. I know better now, and can only anticipate with gloom and foreboding the recent news that exactly this transformation is scheduled for the rest of the block frontage adjoining the high-rent building. The high-rent tenants, most of whom are so transient we cannot even keep track of their faces (some, according to the storekeepers, live on beans and bread and spend their sojourn looking for a place to live where all their money will not go for rent) have not the remotest idea of who takes care of their street, or how. A city neighborhood can absorb and protect a substantial number of these birds of passage, as our neighborhood does. But if and when the neighborhood finally *becomes* them, they will gradually find the streets less secure, they will be vaguely mystified about it, and if things get bad enough they will drift away to another neighborhood which is mysteriously safer.

In some rich city neighborhoods, where there is little do-it-yourself surveillance, such as

residential Park Avenue or upper Fifth Avenue in New York, street watchers are hired. The monotonous sidewalks of residential Park Avenue, for example, are surprisingly little used; their putative users are populating, instead, the interesting store-, bar- and restaurant-filled sidewalks of Lexington Avenue and Madison Avenue to east and west, and the cross streets leading to these. A network of doormen and superintendents, of delivery boys and nursemaids, a form of hired neighborhood, keeps residential Park Avenue supplied with eyes. At night, with the security of the doormen as a bulwark, dog walkers safely venture forth and supplement the doormen. But this street is so blank of built-in eyes, so devoid of concrete reasons for using or watching it instead of turning the first corner off of it, that if its rents were to slip below the point where they could support a plentiful hired neighborhood of doormen and elevator men, it would undoubtedly become a woefully dangerous street.

Once a street is well equipped to handle strangers, once it has both a good, effective demarcation between private and public spaces and has a basic supply of activity and eyes, the more strangers the merrier.

Strangers become an enormous asset on the street on which I live, and the spurs off it, particularly at night when safety assets are most needed. We are fortunate enough, on the street, to be gifted not only with a locally supported bar and another around the corner, but also with a famous bar that draws continuous troops of strangers from adjoining neighborhoods and even from out of town. It is famous because the poet Dylan Thomas used to go there, and mentioned it in his writing. This bar, indeed, works two distinct shifts. In the morning and early afternoon it is a social gathering place for the old community of Irish longshoremen and other craftsmen in the area, as it always was. But beginning in midafternoon it takes on a different life, more like a college bull session with beer, combined with a literary cocktail party, and this continues until the early hours of the morning. On a cold winter's night, as you pass the White Horse, and the doors open, a solid wave of conversation and animation surges out and hits you; very warming. The comings and goings from this bar do much to keep our street reasonably populated until three in the morning, and it is a street always safe to come home to. The only instance I know of a beating in our street occurred in the dead hours between the closing of the bar and dawn. The beating was halted by one of our neighbors who saw it from his window and, unconsciously certain that even at night he was part of a web of strong street law and order, intervened.

A friend of mine lives on a street uptown where a church youth and community center, with many night dances and other activities, performs the same service for his street that the White Horse bar does for ours. Orthodox planning is much imbued with puritanical and Utopian conceptions of how people should spend their free time, and in planning, these moralisms on people's private lives are deeply confused with concepts about the workings of cities. In maintaining city street civilization, the White Horse bar and the church-sponsored youth center, different as they undoubtedly are, perform much the same public street civilizing service. There is not only room in cities for such differences and many more in taste, purpose and interest of occupation; cities also have a need for people with all these differences in taste and proclivity. The preferences of Utopians, and of other compulsive managers of other people's leisure, for one kind of legal enterprise over others is worse than irrelevant for cities. It is harmful. The greater and more plentiful the range of all legitimate interests (in the strictly legal sense) that city streets and their enterprises can satisfy, the better for the streets and for the safety and civilization of the city.

50 Bars, and indeed all commerce, have a bad name in many city districts precisely because they do draw strangers, and the strangers do not work out as an asset at all.

This sad circumstance is especially true in the dispirited gray belts of great cities and in once fashionable or at least once solid inner residential areas gone into decline. Because these neighborhoods are so dangerous, and the streets typically so dark, it is commonly believed that their trouble may be insufficient street lighting. Good lighting is important, but darkness alone does not account for the gray areas' deep, functional sickness, the Great Blight of Dullness.

SUGGESTIONS FOR DISCUSSION

1. Jacobs writes that most urban designers think that an empty space—one in which there is nowhere to sit or gather in groups—is a place that looks safe to the people in a city. Her argument is that people feel safe in spaces where others gather, where shopkeepers and neighbors pay attention to what goes on in the streets. How does her description of safe streets compare with the description you wrote before you read? Would you revise your description after reading Jacobs?

2. What does Jacobs mean when she writes, "A city sidewalk by itself is nothing. It is an abstraction. It means something only in conjunction with the buildings and other uses that border it, or border other sidewalks near it."

3. What point is Jacobs making with her story of the "suppressed struggle going on between a man and a little girl of eight or nine years old" that she witnesses on the street below her window?

SUGGESTIONS FOR WRITING

1. One of the features that distinguishes country from city is the sidewalk. The countryside does not have sidewalks. Small towns have sidewalks, but suburbs often do not, or the sidewalks are limited to small areas in subdivisions or at the front of malls, schools, and other public buildings. Write an essay in which you discuss your own experience of sidewalks as a gathering place. Did they function for you, your family, and your friends in the same way Jacobs noticed that they functioned in cities in the early 1960s?

2. Jacobs writes that cities are distinguished from towns and suburbs because "they are, by definition, full of strangers." Moreover, a sidewalk should be a place where all of these strangers feel safe with one another. Write of a time when you found yourself in a place surrounded by strangers—a large campus, a city, a mall, for example. Explain what made that place feel safe, or not. Draw on Jacobs's discussion of safety in public places where it is useful.

3. In "Shopping for Pleasure: Malls, Power, and Resistance," in "Fortress Los Angeles," and in "Woodruff Park and the Search for Common Ground," John Fiske, Mike Davis, and Murphy Davis write of spaces that have been strictly regulated and ordered to keep some people away from others and to make sure that the users of these public spaces behave themselves or keep to themselves. Jacobs's discussion of "natural proprietors of the street" who keep an eye on things would suggest that one of the problems with trying to police people's use of space, as mall owners and L.A. city planners have tried to do, is that it simply does not work. Instead, it discourages community use of a place, and encourages illegal uses of the place. Jacobs also points out that a successful neighborhood has a "clear demarcation between what is public space and what is private space." The two cannot "ooze into one another."

Choose a space on your campus or in your town or city that you consider unattractive, uncomfortable, even dangerous to some extent. What gives it that feeling? What measures have been taken to make it a safer or more comfortable place? Write a letter to local or school officials recommending changes that you believe will improve the space for people to use it. Draw on the work of Jane Jacobs, Mike Davis, Murphy Davis, and John Fiske where it seems helpful in your recommendation.

VISUAL CULTURE   Reading Interpretive Space

As we suggested earlier in this chapter, there are many ways a space can be claimed. Graffiti artists, for example, claim the spaces on walls, sidewalks, the sides of subway cars or even, as illustrated here, the final resting place of a pop icon. In doing so, these artists are saying they have a right to be there. This place belongs to them as well as to the city or whatever corporation might actually own it. The Chicano mural movement has become one powerful way for a group to claim interpretive space, but there are many other ways such space is claimed. The images people use to decorate office or dorm-room doors so that the doors look personal rather than institutional, the signs officials put up to tell people how to use a space—all of these signs and symbols make attempts to claim space.

The images reprinted here are some examples of the way signs and images can mark and even change a space entirely. Notice that ads in a ballpark, for example, make one kind of claim on a space—a claim about commerce—whereas graffiti on a subway or on a rock star's grave makes a statement about the person's relationship to that space. A mural such as the one telling the story of the Pullman strike and labor organizing is yet another kind of claim on space. In this case, it is a history lesson on the walls of the Pullman library. As you read these images, think of your own interpretive claims on public space or the claims you see daily—such as billboards in a cornfield or a banner stretched across a city plaza or park to claim it as the site of a protest rally, for example. These signs change the place, at least briefly, and as surely as astronauts planting a flag on the moon, the creators of these signs are saying that, if only for the moment, this space belongs to them.

SUGGESTIONS FOR DISCUSSION

1. With a group of your classmates, examine the images reprinted here and discuss what each of these signs or images says about who is attempting to control the space and for what purpose.

2. Although they are both public and populist forms, some people would argue that graffiti, unlike murals, is not an art form. Others would argue that murals are simply more graffiti. What do you think distinguishes what people call graffiti from what they consider art?

3. Collect several images or signs that mark or claim a public space for a group or an individual. Bring your images to class for a discussion of how signs claim interpretive space.

SUGGESTED ASSIGNMENT

Use the images you collected for class discussion to create a poster illustrating how signs and images claim interpretive space. Make sure that your poster can be easily read. It isn't enough simply to put a lot of pictures together. If you want to illustrate or argue a point, create a title for your visual piece. Consider what words or phrases summarize the point you are trying to make. Present your poster argument to your classmates when it is completed.

Mets Stadium Scoreboard

Forces of Pullman Labor by Bernard Williams, 1995. Acrylic on canvas, 10' by 11'6". Commissioned by the Chicago Department of Cultural Affairs, Percent for Art Program. Courtesy of the Chicago Public Art Program.

Greg, 1977. New York City subway art

Graffitti on the grave of rock star Jim Morrison.
Paris, France

FIELDWORK   Observing the Uses of Public Space

Choose a space that offers some possibility for the kind of observation, description, and analysis that you have been reading about throughout this chapter. To some extent, all of the writers focus on the use of public space and what certain spaces are designed for. John Fiske, for example, suggests that even though a mall might be designed to bring more people to stores to buy more goods, people go to malls for different reasons. Some are not at all interested in buying, but they are interested in the space. Mike Davis and Murphy Davis each suggest that urban planning (the design of public space) can reflect the extent to which race, class, and income level inform public policy decisions about urban space. Jane Jacobs uses her observations of sidewalk culture to discover that when city planners try to "clear out" a public space, they also change the way people use that space, often making it more dangerous or less friendly.

To find out more about how a space is used, spend time watching to see who goes there and what they do once they are there. Make several visits to the same place and get as much information as possible.

Mapping the Space

When you begin your observation, sketch a map of the space. Note the layout of the place. Where do groups of people gather? Do different groups (teens, senior citizens, serious shoppers, etc.) tend to congregate in certain places? Make a note of that on your map.

Taking Notes

As you begin this project, you probably will not have a clear focus for your notes. Look back at the notebook entry you wrote as a starting point for your observations; however, your questions and concerns will likely change as you watch. Your notes may seem random at first. It takes practice to get used to noting the kinds of things that happen daily that you don't notice or take for granted, so make several visits. Comparing your notes with others will help you to get distance on what you are recording. However, even at the beginning, you can focus on simple things: What does the space look like? Who uses it? What are they doing there?

Watching People

Record who comes to the space. Note age, gender, ethnicity, appearance, and whether they are alone or with others.

Note how people seem to be using this space. In a mall, for example, are teens actually the "tricksters" who know the rules only to invert or mock them, as Fiske claims? How else might their activity be described? Fast food restaurants are designed so that people get their food and, presumably, eat it quickly and get out. Is that how everyone uses this kind of space? How else might these spaces function for people in ways other than those for which they are designed by developers?

Asking Questions

Although your primary job will be to watch and to take notes, you will find out even more if you ask questions. Ask people how often they come to the space, when, and why. Ask owners, business people, or caretakers what they think the space is meant for and how many of them actually use it for that purpose.

Writing Up Your Findings

When you have completed your observations, you will discover that what you write will depend on what you would like to emphasize from your findings. Your paper might look more like an interpretation of space and the way it is used (in the way Fiske or Davis or Jacobs write), or it might look more like a report on what you have found. If you write your findings as an interpretive essay, review several of the essays in this chapter. Each gives both a strong sense of place and a reflection on what the place means to the people who live there or use it. Many include first-person impressions or feelings but ground those impressions in information about the way the place is used, developed, or designed. It is easy, in this type of essay, to forget about the observation notes that you have taken and to fall back on your own impressions. However, your impressions will be more convincing when they are tied to the field-work that you have done for this project.

If you are writing a report, review instructions on writing a report in the field-work assignment in Chapter 3, Schooling. A report should fall into the typical report pattern: Introduction, Methods, Observations.

1. When most people think about shopping malls, they naturally think of the kind of place John Fiske writes about—an enclosed space containing department stores and several smaller stores where they go to shop or to hang out or to get out of the weather. However, with increased use of Internet technology, virtual malls are now being created. Explore the Web for one of those virtual malls and consider how the entire concept of "mall" changes when the space it occupies is electronic. Use a search engine such as Yahoo or Lycos—entering the words "virtual" + "mall" yielded 538 sites, proving that there are many sites that consider themselves virtual malls. What would you say constitutes a "mall" space, virtual or not?

2. Since the publication of the two articles in the Perspectives section, discussion has continued about what to do with the space left behind by the World Trade Center attack. Using a search engine in one of the major newspapers or magazines such as the *New York Times*, the *Washington Post*, the *Nation*, or *Time Magazine*, for example, search for stories on the Ground Zero memorial. Write

Take a Walking Tour

An archive is usually thought of as a collection of papers or documents. Yet a city, town, or national park area can also function as a kind of archive—a place where you will find sites of historic, political, or cultural importance.

Certainly one of the best ways to learn about a public space and its archival potential is to take a walking tour. Cities, towns, local and national parks, botanical gardens, museums, campuses, cemeteries, and historical buildings across this country have walking tours designed to show visitors the history of the place; the best places to shop; popular restaurants; homes of poets, artists, and politicians; little-known places of historic interest; and more. These tours usually include a step-by-step guide to the places on the tour, an easy-to-follow map, and a thumbnail description of the importance of each stop.

Begin this project by locating several sample walking tours. Most travel guides in local bookstores and public libraries will include walking tours. For example, Frommer's guide to San Francisco includes a walking tour of Chinatown. *The Eyewitness Travel Guide to New York* includes walking tours of Greenwich Village, Lower Manhattan, and the Upper East Side. There are even alternative walking tours such as Bruce Kayton's *Radical Walking Tours of New York City*, whose maps include the homes of leftists, anarchists, and radicals who are

13 Finnish American Heritage Center

In 1990, Suomi College renovated the former St. Joseph's Catholic Church as a Finnish cultural center. The renovation reflects traditional Finnish architectural styles including the clipped gable roof, the stucco finish and the extensive use of trim moldings painted white. The fixed upper sash with mullions of the narrow casement windows form a cross. Vertical trim casing extends down past the horizontal apron. The blue roof and white walls not only reflect Finnish colors (the same as those in the flag of Finland), but also introduce bright colors to the mostly dark red block of the downtown.

The building currently houses a gallery, a performing arts center and the Finnish archives.

---

a report updating your class on the decisions that have been made for the space or on the designs that have been proposed or decided on for the space.

3. One role of public space in this country has been to provide a site for free speech. On city sidewalks, in parks, on campuses, and in small town plazas, people frequently hand out pamphlets, make speeches, or rally support for one cause or another. Malls are not literally public spaces, and so mall owners can ban the distribution of literature or the gathering of protests from their spaces. In fact, many people are concerned that the space given over to true free speech has been limited more and more by city planning and the privatizing of public spaces. Some, in fact, argue that the last real place for free speech is the Internet and that even the Web is beginning to limit the free use of this public space.

Make your own search on the Internet for discussions of freedom of speech and free access to conversations, information, and more. Try entering key words such as "Internet free access" into a search engine.

often left out of the commercial guides or chamber of commerce maps designed for most tourists.

Bring the walking tours you have located to class for a general discussion of what walking tours include, what they leave out, and how they identify public space.

A good walking tour should have the following:

- A focus or theme
- A clear map
- A brief description of each stop on the tour
- Information about how to get there, how long the tour will take, and what difficulties a walker might encounter.

Displayed here are portions of a walking tour of historic Hancock, Michigan. Study the map and entries we have selected from the guide's description of each stop. When you have a good sense of what a walking tour entails, make a walking tour of a place you know well. Be sure to draw a clear map and time the walk. Give your tour a theme or focus. Michigan Tech's School of Forestry and Wood Products, for example, has published a botanical walking tour—"Tech Tree Walk—which locates and identifies the different trees on campus. Your tour can focus on people, places, events, whatever ties the place together and might be of interest to visitors. You can even create an underground tour—of campus dorms or the library or the place where you grew up—that, like Bruce Kayton's Radical Walking Tours of New York City, highlights the people, places, and events not considered mainstream or not usually shown to visitors.

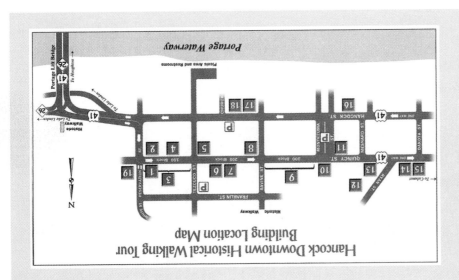

Hancock Downtown Historical Walking Tour
Building Location Map

Richard Hutchings/PhotoEdit, Inc.

*Experience which is passed on from mouth to mouth is the
source from which all storytellers have drawn. And among
those who have written down the tales, it is the great ones whose
written version differs least from the speech of the many
nameless storytellers.*

—Walter Benjamin, *The Storyteller*

CHAPTER 7

Storytelling

One of the pleasures of listening to stories is suspending disbelief and entering into the imaginary world that storytelling creates. It doesn't matter so much whether the story is true or if it could have happened. What matters is that listeners know their feelings and their responses to a story are real. When people hear the words "Once upon a time…" at the beginning of a fairy tale (or Jason's footsteps in the *Friday the 13th* horror movies), they know they are entering a world that could never happen, yet this knowledge does not stop them from trying on, at least temporarily, the version of reality (or unreality) that the story offers.

Storytelling is a persistent form of popular entertainment, whether people tell ghost stories around a campfire or watch the electronic glow of a television set. Every culture has its own storytelling tradition of myths, legends, epics, fables, animal stories, fairy tales, and romances. Listeners take delight in the mythic powers of their heroes, laugh at the comic predicaments clowns and tricksters get themselves into, and feel awe—and sometimes terror—when they hear stories of unseen worlds and the supernatural. In every storytelling tradition, there is a repertoire of stock characters and plots that listeners recognize immediately—and know how to respond to through laughter, tears, excitement, fear, and grief.

But the fact that people everywhere, in all known cultures, tell stories only raises a series of questions we will ask you to explore in this chapter. We will be asking you to recall stories from the past and present to think about the functions storytelling performs, the occasions on which stories are told, and the people who tell stories. The reading and writing assignments in this chapter will ask you to look at some of the stories circulating in contemporary America. We will be asking you to explore the familiar stories that you hear from family and friends, read in novels and comic books, or watch in the movies to see what these stories can tell you about the culture that you are living in and the kinds of knowledge the imaginary worlds of storytelling transmit.

One of the key functions of storytelling, aside from entertaining listeners, is a pedagogical one. Storytelling is one of the oldest forms of human communication, and stories are important ways young people learn about the world and what their culture values. In traditional societies, stories were passed along from generation to generation orally. The elders were responsible for initiating young people into the lore of the tribe. In many respects, the same is true today, in the mass-mediated world of contemporary America. To be an adult and a full member of society means knowing the stories a particular culture tells about the world and about itself.

What's more, the kinds of stories people tell teach them as much about who they want to be and how they want to live as about who they are now. The stories uncover fears and desires. They comfort and disturb. Even the fantasy worlds people create look amazingly like the real world they live in—only much better—with heroes who know what to do and villains so evil it's impossible not to know they are the bad guys. Storytelling is, then, as much about understanding and reordering the world as it is about entertaining.

In addition to the stories you read and watch, we will be asking you to recall the stories that you tell in the course of casual conversation, when you explain what happened over the weekend or pass along the latest gossip, political controversy, or scandal. People love to tell and listen to stories about politicians, celebrities, and professional athletes—who is dating whom, who is getting divorced, who is checking into a drug or alcohol abuse clinic, who is under investigation for what. These kinds of stories—personal anecdotes, gossip, bits and pieces of the evening news—may seem so trivial that they don't really merit the title of storytelling. But although telling and listening to these stories may appear to be no more than a way to pass the time with family, neighbors, coworkers, and friends, in fact this type of story-telling performs a useful social function within local communities. As people tell and listen to stories, perhaps without fully recognizing it, they are working out their own attitudes and evaluations of a wide range of social realities, from relations between the sexes to politics.

If you have seen such popular television and film genres as family sitcoms, hospital dramas, soap operas, action adventure stories, science fiction, mysteries, Westerns, and slasher flicks, you already know about many of the conventions of storytelling. In each, the cast of characters is a familiar one: interracial cop teams, superheroes, cyberpunks, urban vigilantes, gangsters, android terminators, martial arts masters, hard-boiled private eyes, cowboys, swinging singles, career women, men behaving badly, dumb parents and precocious kids. These popular figures inhabit fictional worlds—the Western frontier, the criminal underworld, interstellar space, the mean streets of the city, the middle-class homes of the suburbs—where they are working out the aspirations and anxieties of average people while dealing with whichever conflict threatens to overturn their/our world.

Reading Storytelling

Reading and writing about stories and storytelling requires you to listen again to the stories that surround you and to look for patterns in their familiar plots and characters.

The opening selections explore contemporary folk stories—rumors and contemporary legends—some that are frightening and others that explain social relationships. The first is the folklorist Jan Harold Brunvand's "'The Hook' and Other Teenage Horrors," a part of Brunvand's larger work of collecting what he calls "urban legends." These are stories people tell that are plausible and have realistic settings but are bizarre and sometimes horrifying—the baby-sitter on LSD who put an infant in the oven because she thought it was a chicken, the spiders who laid eggs in the scalp of a woman with a beehive hairdo, the mouse's head in the Dr. Pepper bottle. We follow Brunvand with a selection from folklorist Patricia A. Turner's *I Heard It Through the Grapevine: Rumor in African-American Culture*. Turner keeps track of urban legends and rumors specific to the African American community. They range from the tale of fast-food chicken spiced with a drug that will make African American men sterile to conspiracy stories such as the one rumoring an FBI plot in the mass murder of African American children in Atlanta. Turner argues that these rumors, or "contemporary legends," "do not necessarily reflect pathological preoccupations" but function as "tools of resistance" for the many African Americans who share them.

Next are two selections on storytelling in the movie industry. In his analysis "Why We Crave Horror Movies," the well-known horror story writer Stephen King examines why people seem to like a "good scare" when they go to the movies. For King, horror films are so popular because they offer viewers an experience of violating the normal boundaries of everyday life while at the same time reestablishing a need for normality. The next selection, A.O. Scott's "A Hunger for Fantasy and an Empire to Feed It," also addresses the escapist function of film story but suggests that fantasy stories are especially popular at a time when the audience longs for renewed innocence. In the winter and summer of 2002, writes Scott, the films most popular were those that took viewers into a world where the most unassuming and unlikely young man is suddenly thrust into the hero's role.

Scott is followed by a Perspectives pairing of readings on telling superhero stories. In the first, veteran film critic Roger Ebert reviews the 2002 film *Spider-Man* and raises questions about how comic book superheroes are translated for the movie screen. In the second, an excerpt from Michael Chabon's Pulitzer Prize-winning novel, *The Amazing Adventures of Kavalier & Clay*, the two young protagonists talk about what it takes to create a real superhero. What are the qualities of the superhero? One question at the center of both of these selections is the issue of motivation: What makes characters do the things they do? Why does a superhero go around saving lives and fighting crime? Superheroes all have "origin stories," the stories that explain that motivation, so you will be asked to think about some of the superheroes you are familiar with and to recount their origin stories.

The Classic Reading, Robert Warshow's "The Gangster as Tragic Hero," looks at one of the most familiar characters in American film. Warshow is interested in why the story of the American gangster turns out inevitably to be a tragic one—and what this tragedy says about American culture.

Throughout this chapter, you will be asked to recall and retell stories that you know well. One of the pleasures in such research is that of simply remembering, not just the story but the occasion on which you heard it and the people you were with at the time. Remembering the stories you learned growing up—bringing them back into view to think and write about—can help you reconstruct the imaginary worlds they created and the versions of reality they transmitted. By the same token, looking for patterns in the familiar stories you hear in songs and see on television and at the movies can help you give shape to the larger popular culture and the fears and aspirations it represents.

"THE HOOK" AND OTHER TEENAGE HORRORS

Jan Harold Brunvand

Jan Harold Brunvand is a folklorist and professor emeritus of English at the University of Utah. "'The Hook' and Other Teenage Horrors" is a chapter from Brunvand's book *The Vanishing Hitchhiker: American Urban Legends and Their Meaning* (1981). In *The Vanishing Hitchhiker* and its two sequels, *The Choking Doberman* (1986) and *The Mexican Pet* (1988). Brunvand has gathered examples of contemporary storytelling—strange, scary, funny, macabre, and embarrassing tales storytellers relate as true accounts of real-life experience. Brunvand calls these stories "urban legends" because they are, by and large, set in contemporary America and, like all legends, are alleged to be about real people and real events. These legends, often about someone that the narrator knows or the "friend of a friend," are passed on by word of mouth, forming an oral tradition in the midst of America's print and media culture. As Brunvand says, urban legends "survive by being as lively and 'factual' as the television evening news, and, like the daily newscasts, they tend to concern deaths, injuries, kidnappings, tragedies, and scandals." Stories such as "The Hook" are told and are believed—or at least are believable—as "human interest" stories that capture some of the fears and anxieties of contemporary America.

SUGGESTION FOR READING   As a folklorist, Brunvand is interested in interpreting urban legends as well as in gathering them. As you read through "'The Hook' and Other Teenage Horrors," underline and annotate the passages where Brunvand offers his own interpretations or those of other folklore scholars.

GROWING UP SCARED

1 People of all ages love a good scare. Early child-lore is full of semiserious spooky stories and ghastly threats, while the more sophisticated black humor of Little Willies, Bloody Marys, Dead Babies, and other cycles of sick jokes enters a bit later. Among the favorite readings at school are Edgar Allan Poe's blood-soaked tales, and favorite stories at summer camp tell of maniacal ax-murderers and deformed giants lurking in the dark forest to ambush unwary Scouts. Halloween spook houses and Hollywood horror films cater to the same wish to push the level of tolerable fright as far as possible.

The ingredients of horror fiction change little through time, but the style of such stories does develop, even in oral tradition. In their early teens young Americans apparently reject the overdramatic and unbelievable juvenile "scaries" and adopt a new lore of more plausible tales with realistic settings. That is, they begin to enjoy urban legends, especially those dealing with "folks" like themselves—dating couples, students, and baby-sitters—who are subjected to grueling ordeals and horrible threats.

One consistent theme in these teenage horrors is that as the adolescent moves out from home into the larger world, the world's dangers may close in on him or her. Therefore, although the immediate purpose of many of these legends is to produce a good scare, they also serve to deliver a warning: Watch out! This could happen to you! Furthermore, the horror tales often contain thinly-disguised sexual themes which are, perhaps, implicit in the nature of such plot situations as parking in a lovers' lane or baby-sitting (playing house) in a strange home. These sexual elements furnish both a measure of further entertainment and definite cautionary notices about the world's actual dangers. Thus, from the teenagers' own major fears, concerns, and experiences, spring their favorite "true" oral stories.

The chief current example of this genre of urban legend—one that is even older, more popular, and more widespread than "The Boyfriend's Death"—is the one usually called "The Hook."

"THE HOOK"

5 On Tuesday, November 8, 1960, the day when Americans went to the polls to elect John F. Kennedy as their thirty-fifth president, thousands of people must have read the following letter from a teenager in the popular newspaper column written by Abigail Van Buren:

Dear Abby: If you are interested in teenagers, you will print this story. I don't know whether it's true or not, but it doesn't matter because it served its purpose for me:

A fellow and his date pulled into their favorite "lovers' lane" to listen to the radio and do a little necking. The music was interrupted by an announcer who said there was an escaped convict in the area who had served time for rape and robbery. He was described as having a hook instead of a right hand. The couple became frightened and drove away. When the boy took his girl home, he went around to open the car door for her. Then he saw—a hook on the door handle! I don't think I will ever park to make out as long as I live. I hope this does the same for other kids.

Jeanette

This juicy story seems to have emerged in the late 1950s, sharing some common themes with "The Death Car" and "The Vanishing Hitchhiker" and then...influencing "The Boyfriend's Death" as that legend developed in the early 1960s. The story of "The Hook" (or "The Hookman") really needed no national press report to give it life or credibility, because the teenage oral-tradition underground had done the job well enough long before the election day of 1960. Teenagers all over the country knew about "The Hook" by 1959, and like other modern legends the basic plot was elaborated with details and became highly localized.

One of my own students, originally from Kansas, provided this specific account of where the event supposedly occurred:

Outside of "Mac" [McPherson, Kansas], about seven miles out towards Lindsborg, north on old highway 81 is an old road called "Hookman's Road." It's a curved road, a traditional parking spot for the kids. When I was growing up it [the legend] was popular, and that was back in the '60's, and it was old then.

Another student told a version of the story that she had heard from her baby-sitter in Albuquerque in 1960:

over the radio came an announcement that a crazed killer with a hook in place of a hand had escaped from the local insane asylum. The girl got scared and begged the boy to take her home. He got mad and stepped on the gas and roared off. When they got to her house, he got out and went around to the other side of the car to let her out. There on the door handle was a bloody hook.

But these two students were told, after arriving in Salt Lake City, that it had actually occurred *here* in Memory Grove, a well-wooded city park. "Oh, no," a local student in the class insisted. "This couple was parked outside of Salt Lake City *in a mountain canyon* one night, and…" It turned out that virtually every student in the class knew the story as adapted in some way to their hometowns.

10   Other folklorists have reported collecting "The Hook" in Maryland, Wisconsin, Indiana, Illinois, Kansas, Texas, Arkansas, Oregon, and Canada. Some of the informants' comments echo Dear Abby's correspondent in testifying to the story's effect (to discourage parking) even when its truth was suspect. The student said, "I believe that it *could* happen, and this makes it seem real," or "I don't really [believe it], but it's pretty scary; I sort of hope it didn't happen."

Part of the great appeal of "The Hook"—one of the most popular adolescent scare stories— must lie in the tidiness of the plot. Everything fits. On the other hand, the lack of loose ends would seem to be excellent testimony to the story's near impossibility. After all, what are the odds that a convicted criminal or crazed maniac would be fitted with a hook for a missing hand, that this same threatening figure would show up precisely when a radio warning had been broadcast of his escape, and that the couple would drive away rapidly just at the instant the hook-

man put his hook through the door handle? Besides, why wouldn't he try to open the door with his good hand, and how is it that the boy— furious at the interruption of their lovemaking— is still willing to go around politely to open the girl's door when they get home? Too much, too much—but it makes a great story.

In an adolescent novel titled *Dinky Hocker Shoots Smack!,* M. E. Kerr captured the way teenagers often react to such legends—with cool acceptance that it might have happened, and that's good enough:

She told Tucker this long story about a one-armed man who was hanging around a lovers' lane in Prospect Park [Brooklyn]. There were rumors that he tried to get in the cars and carry off the girls. He banged on the windshields with his hooked wooden arm and frothed at the mouth. He only said two words: *bloody murder;* and his voice was high and hoarse.

Dinky claimed this girl who went to St. Marie's was up in Prospect Park one night with a boyfriend. The girl and her boyfriend began discussing the one-armed man while they were parked. They both got frightened and decided to leave. The boy dropped the girl off at her house, and drove home. When he got out of his car, he found this hook attached to his door handle.

Dinky said, "They must have driven off just as he was about to open the door."

"I thought you weren't interested in the bizarre, anymore," Tucker said.

"It's a true story."

"It's still bizarre."

A key detail lacking in the *Dinky Hocker* version, however, is the boyfriend's frustrated anger resulting in their leaving the scene in a great hurry. Almost invariably the boy guns the motor and roars away: "…so he revs up the car and he goes torquing out of there." Or, "The boy floored the gas pedal and zoomed away," or "Her boyfriend was annoyed and the car screeched off…." While this behavior is essential to explain the sudden sharp force that tears loose the maniac's hook, it is also a reminder of the original sexual purpose of the parking, at least on the boy's part. While Linda Dégh saw "the natural dread of the handicapped," and "the boy's disappointment and suddenly recognized fear as an adequate explanation for the jump start of the car," folklorist Alan Dundes disagreed, mainly because of the curtailed sex quest in the plot.

Dundes, taking a Freudian line, interpreted the hook itself as a phallic symbol which penetrates the girl's door handle (or bumps seductively against her window) but which is torn off (symbolic of castration) when the car starts abruptly. Girls who tell the story, Dundes suggests, "are not afraid of what a man lacks, but of what he has"; a date who is "all hands" may really want to "get his hooks into her." Only the girl's winding up the window or insisting upon going home at once saves her, and the date has to "pull out fast" before he begins to act like a sex maniac himself. The radio—turned on originally for soft, romantic background music—introduces instead "the consciencelike voice from society," a warning that the girl heeds and the boy usually scorns. Dundes concluded that this popular legend "reflects a very real dating practice, one which produces anxiety…particularly for girls."

"THE KILLER IN THE BACKSEAT"

15   A similar urban legend also involves cars and an unseen potential assailant; this time a man threatens a woman who is driving alone at night. The following version of "The Killer in the Backseat" was contributed in 1967 by a University of Utah student who had heard other versions set in Denver and Aurora, Colorado:

A woman living in the city [i.e., Salt Lake City] was visiting some friends in Ogden. When she got into her car in front of this friend's house, she noticed that a car started up right behind her car. It was about 2:00 in the morning, and there weren't any other cars on the road. After she had driven to the highway, she began to think that this car was following her. Some of the time he would drive up real close to her car, but he wouldn't ever pass. She was really scared to death and kept speeding to try to get away from him.

When she got to Salt Lake, she started running stop lights to get away from him, but he would run right through them too. So when she got to her driveway she pulled in really fast, and this guy pulled in right behind her. She just laid on the horn, and her husband came running out. Just then, the guy jumped out of the car, and her husband ran over and said, "What the hell's goin' on here?" So he grabbed the guy, and his wife said, "This man's followed me all the way from Ogden." The man said, "I followed your wife because I was going to work, and as I got into my car, I noticed when I turned my lights on, a man's head bob down in her back seat." So the husband went over to her backseat, opened the door, and pulled this guy from out of the backseat.

This legend first appeared in print in 1968 in another version, also—coincidentally—set in Ogden, Utah, but collected at Indiana University, Bloomington. (This shows how the presence of folklorists in a locality will influence the apparent distribution patterns of folk material.) Twenty further texts have surfaced at Indiana University with, as usual, plenty of variations and localizations. In many instances the pursuing driver keeps flashing his headlights between the high and low beam in order to restrain the assailant who is popping up and threatening to attack the driver. Sometimes the pursuer is a burly truck driver or other tough-looking character, and in several of the stories the supposed would-be attacker (the pursuing rescuer) is specifically said to be a black man. (Both motifs clearly show white middle class fears of minorities or of groups believed to be socially inferior.)

In a more imaginative set of these legends the person who spots the dangerous man in back is a gas station attendant who pretends that a ten dollar bill offered by the woman driver in payment for gas is counterfeit. With this ruse he gets her safely away from her car before calling the police. In another version of the story, a passing motorist sharply warns the woman driver to roll up her window and follow him, driving in exactly the same manner he does. She obeys, speeding and weaving along the highway, until a suspected assailant—usually carrying an ax—is thrown from his perch on the roof of her car.

"THE BABY-SITTER AND THE MAN UPSTAIRS"

Just as a lone woman may unwittingly be endangered by a hidden man while she is driving at night, a younger one may face the same hazard in a strange home. The horror legend of "The Baby-sitter and the Man Upstairs," similar in structure to "The Killer in the Backseat," is possibly a later variation of the same story relocated to fit teenagers' other direct experiences. This standard version is from a fourteen-year-old Canadian boy (1973):

> There was this baby-sitter that was in Montreal baby-sitting for three children in a big house. She was watching TV when suddenly the phone rang. The children were all in bed. She picked up the phone and heard this guy on the other end laughing hysterically. She asked him what it was that he wanted, but he wouldn't answer and then hung up. She worried about it for a while, but then thought nothing more of it and went back to watching the movie.
>
> Everything was fine until about fifteen minutes later when the phone rang again. She picked it up and heard the same voice laughing hysterically at her, and then hung up. At this point she became really worried and phoned the operator to tell her what had been happening. The operator told her to calm down and that if he called again to try and keep him on the line as long as possible and she would try to trace the call.
>
> Again about fifteen minutes later the guy called back and laughed hysterically at her. She asked him why he was doing this, but he just kept laughing at her. He hung up and about five seconds later the operator called. She told the girl to get out of the house at once because the person who was calling was calling from the upstairs extension. She slammed down the phone and just as she was turning to leave she saw the man coming down the stairs laughing hysterically with a bloody butcher knife in his hand and meaning to kill her. She ran out onto the street but he didn't follow. She called the police and they came and caught the man, and discovered that he had murdered all the children.

The storyteller added that he had heard the story from a friend whose brother's girlfriend was the baby-sitter involved.

20   By now it should come as no surprise to learn that the same story had been collected two years earlier (1971) some 1500 miles southwest of Montreal, in Austin, Texas, and also in Bloomington, Indiana, in 1973 in a college dormitory. These three published versions are only samples from the wide distribution of the story in folk tradition. Their similarities and differences provide another classic case of folklore's variation within traditional boundaries. In all three legend texts the hour is late and the baby-sitter is watching television. Two of the callers make threatening statements, while one merely laughs. In all versions the man calls three times at regular intervals before the girl calls the operator, then once more afterwards. In both American texts the operator herself calls the police, and in the Indiana story she commands "Get out of the house immediately; don't go upstairs; don't do anything; just leave the house. When you get out there, there will be policemen outside and they'll take care of it." (One is reminded of the rescuers' orders not to look back at the car in "The Boyfriend's Death.") The Texas telephone operator in common with the Canadian one gives the situation away by adding, "The phone call traces to the upstairs." The murder of the child or children (one, two, or three of them—no pattern) is specified in the American versions: in Texas they are "chopped into little bitty pieces"; in Indiana, "torn to bits." All of the storytellers played up the spookiness of the situation—details that would be familiar to anyone who has ever baby-sat—a strange house, a television show, an unexpected phone call, frightening sounds or threats, the abrupt orders from the operator, and finally the shocking realization at the end that (as in "The Killer in the Backseat") the caller had been there in the house (or behind her) all the time. The technical problems of calling another telephone from an extension of the same number, or the actual procedures of call-tracing, do not seem to worry the storytellers.

Folklorist Sue Samuelson, who examined hundreds of unpublished "Man Upstairs" stories filed in American folklore archives, concluded that the telephone is the most important and emotionally-loaded item in the plot: the assailant is harassing his victim through the device that is her own favorite means of communication. Baby-sitting, Samuelson points out, is an important socializing experience for young women, allowing them to practice their future roles, imposed on them in a male-dominated society, as homemakers and mothers. Significantly, the threatening male figure is upstairs—on top of and in control of the girl—as men have traditionally been in the sexual relationship. In killing the children who were in her care, the man brings on the most catastrophic failure any mother can suffer. Another contributing factor in the story is that the baby-sitter herself is too intent on watching television to realize that the children are being murdered upstairs. Thus, the tale is not just another scary story, but conveys a stern admonition to young women to adhere to society's traditional values.

Occasionally these firmly believed horror legends are transformed from ghastly mysteries to almost comical adventures. The following Arizona version of "The Baby-sitter and the Man Upstairs," collected in 1976, is a good example:

It was August 8, 1969. She was going to baby-sit at the Smiths who had two children, ages five and seven. She had just put the children to bed and went back to the living room to watch TV.

The phone began to ring; she went to answer it; the man on the other end said, "I'm upstairs with the children; you'd better come up."

She hung the phone up immediately, scared to death. She decided that it must be a prank phone call; again she went to watch TV. The phone rang again; she went to answer it, this time more scared than last.

The man said, "I'm upstairs with the children," and described them in detail. So she hung up the phone, not knowing what to do. Should I call the police? Instead she decided, "I'll call the operator. They can trace these phone calls." She called the operator, and the operator said that she would try and do what she could. Approximately ten minutes later the phone rang again; this time she was shaking.

She answered the phone and the man again said, "I'm upstairs with the children; you'd better come quick!" She tried to stay on the phone as long as she could so that the operator could trace the call; this time the man hung up.

She called back, and the operator said, "Run out of the house; the man is on the extension."

She didn't quite know what to do; should she go and get the children? "No," she said, "he's up there; if I go and get the children, I'll be killed too!!" She ran next door to the neighbor's house and called the police. The sirens came—there must have been at least ten police cars. They went inside the house, ran upstairs, and found not a man, but a seven-year-old child who was sitting next to the phone with a tape recorder. Later they found that a boy down the street had told this young boy to do this next time he had a baby-sitter. You see the boy didn't like his parents going out, and he didn't like having baby-sitters. So he felt this was the only way he could get rid of them. The boys [sic] don't have baby-sitters anymore; now they go to the nursery school.

"THE ROOMMATE'S DEATH"

Another especially popular example of the American adolescent shocker story is the widely known legend of "The Roommate's Death." It shares several themes with other urban legends. As in "The Killer in the Backseat" and "The Baby-sitter and the Man Upstairs," it is usually a lone woman in the story who is threatened—or thinks she is—by a strange man. As in "The Hook" and "The Boyfriend's Death," the assailant is often said to be an escaped criminal or a maniac. Finally, as in the latter legend, the actual commission of the crime is never described; only the resulting mutilated corpse is. The scratching sounds outside the girl's place of refuge are an additional element of suspense. Here is a version told by a University of Kansas student in 1965 set in Corbin Hall, a freshman women's dormitory there:

These two girls in Corbin had stayed late over Christmas vacation. One of them had to wait for a later train, and the other wanted to go to a fraternity party given that night of vacation. The dorm assistant was in her room—sacked out. They waited and waited for the intercom, and then they heard this knocking and knocking outside in front of the dorm. So the girl thought it was her date and she went down. But she didn't come back and she didn't come back. So real late that night this other girl heard a scratching and gasping down the hall. She couldn't lock the door, so she locked herself in the closet. In the morning she let herself out and her roommate had had her throat cut, and if the other girl had opened the door earlier, she [the dead roommate] would have been saved.

At all the campuses where the story is told the reasons for the girls' remaining alone in the dorm vary, but they are always realistic and plausible. The girls' homes may be too far away for them to visit during vacation, such as in Hawaii or a foreign country. In some cases they wanted to avoid a campus meeting or other obligation. What separates the two roommates may be either that one goes out for food, or to answer the door, or to use the rest room. The girl who is left behind may hear the scratching noise either at her room door or at the closet door, if she hides there. Sometimes her hair turns white or gray overnight from the shock of the experience (an old folk motif). The implication in the story is that some maniac is after her (as is suspected about the pursuer in "The Killer in the Backseat"); but the truth is that her own roommate needs help, and she might have supplied it had she only acted more decisively when the noises were first heard. Usually some special emphasis is put on the victim's fingernails, scratched to bloody stumps by her desperate efforts to signal for help.

25   A story told by a California teenager, remembered from about 1964, seems to combine motifs of "The Baby-sitter and the Man Upstairs" with "The Roommate's Death." The text is unusually detailed with names and the circumstances of the crime:

Linda accepted a baby-sitting job for a wealthy family who lived in a two-story home up in the hills for whom she had never baby-sat for before.

Linda was rather hesitant as the house was rather isolated and so she asked a girlfriend, Sharon, to go along with her, promising Sharon half of the baby-sitting fee she would earn. Sharon accepted Linda's offer and the two girls went up to the big two-storey house.

The night was an especially dark and windy one and rain was threatening. All went well for the girls as they read stories aloud to the three little boys they were sitting for and they had no problem putting the boys to bed in the upstairs part of the house. When this was done, the girls settled down to watching television.

It was not long before the telephone rang. Linda answered the telephone, only to hear the heavy breathing of the caller on the other end. She attempted to elicit a response from the caller but he merely hung up. Thinking little of it and not wanting to panic Sharon, Linda went back to watching her television program, remarking that the caller had dialed a wrong number. Upon receiving the second call at which time the caller first engaged in a bit of heavy breathing and then instructed them to check on the children, the two girls became frightened and decided to call the operator for assistance. The operator instructed the girls to keep the caller on the line as long as possible should he call again so that she might be able to trace the call. The operator would check back with them.

The two girls then decided between themselves that one should stay downstairs to answer the phone. It was Sharon who volunteered to go upstairs. Shortly, the telephone rang again and Linda did as the operator had instructed her. Within a few minutes, the operator called back telling Linda to leave the house immediately with her friend because she had traced the calls to the upstairs phone.

Linda immediately hung up the telephone and proceeded to run to the stairway to call Sharon. She then heard a thumping sound coming from the stairway and when she approached the stairs she saw her friend dragging herself down the stairs by her chin, all of her limbs severed from her body. The three boys also lay dead upstairs in their beds.

Once again, the Indiana University Folklore Archive has provided the best published report on variants of "The Roommate's Death," Linda Dégh's summary of thirty-one texts and several subtypes and related plots collected since 1961. The most significant feature, according to her report, is the frequent appearance of a male rescuer at the end of the story. In one version, for example, two girls are left behind alone in the dorm by their roommate when she goes downstairs for food; they hear noises, and so stay in their room all night without opening the door. Finally the mailman comes around the next morning, and they call him from the window:

> The mailman came in the front door and went up the stairs, and told the girls to stay in their room, that everything was all right but that they were to stay in their rooms [sic]. But the girls didn't listen to him cause he had said it was all right, so they came out into the hall. When they opened the door, they saw the girlfriend on the floor with a hatchet in her head.

In other Indiana texts the helpful male is a handyman, a milkman, or the brother of one of the roommates.

According to folklorist Beverly Crane, the male-female characters are only one pair of a series of significant opposites, which also includes home and away, intellectual versus emotional behavior, life and death, and several others. A male is needed to resolve the female's uncertainty—motivated by her emotional fear—about how to act in a new situation. Another male has mutilated and killed her roommate with a blow to her head, "the one part of the body with which women are not supposed to compete." The girls, Crane suggested, are doubly out of place in the beginning, having left the haven of home to engage in intellectual pursuits, and having remained alone in the campus dormitory instead of rejoining the family on a holi-day. Ironically, the injured girl must use her fingernails, intended to be long, lovely, feminine adornments, in order to scratch for help. But because her roommate fails to investigate the sound, the victim dies, her once pretty nails now bloody stumps. Crane concluded this ingenious interpretation with these generalizations:

> The points of value implicit in this narrative are then twofold. If women wish to depend on traditional attitudes and responses they had best stay in a place where these attitudes and responses are best able to protect them. If, however, women do choose to venture into the realm of equality with men, they must become less dependent, more self-sufficient, more confident in their own abilities, and, above all, more willing to assume responsibility for themselves and others.

One might not expect to find women's liberation messages embedded in the spooky stories told by teenagers, but Beverly Crane's case is plausible and well argued. Furthermore, it is not at all unusual to find up-to-date social commentary in other modern folklore—witness the many religious and sexual jokes and legends circulated by people who would not openly criticize a church or the traditional social mores. Folklore does not just purvey the old codes of morality and behavior; it can also absorb newer ideas. What needs to be done to analyze this is to collect what Alan Dundes calls "oral-literary criticism," the informants' own comments about their lore. How clearly would the girls who tell these stories perceive—or even accept—the messages extrapolated by scholars? And a related question: Have any stories with clear liberationist themes replaced older ones cautioning young women to stay home, be good, and—next best—be careful, and call a man if they need help?

SUGGESTIONS FOR DISCUSSION

1. Brunvand suggests that teenagers tell horror stories not only "to produce a good scare" but also "to deliver a warning" about the "world's actual dangers." To what extent do you think the stories in "'The Hook'" serve as cautionary tales? Do you think they would be heard and understood in different ways by male and female listeners?

2. Do you find Beverly Crane's interpretation of "The Roommate's Death" persuasive? How would you answer the question Brunvand poses at the end of this selection?

3. Work together with classmates to create your own collection of urban legends. Which of the stories in this selection or similar types of stories have you heard before? Where, when, and from whom did you hear a particular story? How were the details of the story adapted to local conditions? Did the narrator and the listeners seem to believe the story? What did the narrator and the listeners seem to feel were the most important meanings of the story? What fears, concerns, or experiences does the story seem to reflect?

SUGGESTIONS FOR WRITING

1. Jan Harold Brunvand begins this selection with the statement, "People of all ages love a good scare." Write an essay that explains why people enjoy being scared by ghost stories, horror films, and thrillers. Compare the horror story with another kind of storytelling, such as fairy tales or adventure stories. Or begin with the kinds of stories that scare you but that you read or watch anyway. What is it that draws you to them? What kinds of stories did you and your friends tell to scare each other as you were growing up? What did you like about the experience of sharing scary stories?

2. Reread "'The Hook' and Other Teenage Horrors," and notice the interpretations of the stories you have marked. Pick one of the interpretations that you find particularly interesting or striking. Write an essay in which you summarize the interpretation and explain why it seems adequate or inadequate. Are there alternative interpretations that you would offer?

3. Use the individual stories and commentaries in this selection ("The Hook," "The Killer in the Backseat," "The Baby-Sitter and the Man Upstairs," and "The Roommate's Death") as a model to recreate and comment on an urban legend you have heard. Set the scene of the storytelling—where, when, and who told it—and then give an account of the story. Follow this with a commentary of your own that interprets the dominant theme of the story.

I HEARD IT THROUGH THE GRAPEVINE

Patricia A. Turner

Patricia A. Turner is currently vice-provost of undergraduate studies and professor of folklore in the Department of African-American and African Studies at the University of California-Davis. Her work includes the book-length study of images of African Americans, *Ceramic Uncles and Celluloid Mammies: Black Images and their Influence on Culture* (1994), *Whispers on the Color Line: Rumor and Race in America* (2001) with Gary Alan Fine, and *I Heard It Through the Grapevine: Rumor in African-American Culture* (1993), from which the following selection has been excerpted. Turner's work takes its start from Brunvand's claim in his introduction to *The Vanishing Hitchhiker* that urban legends are "an integral part of white Anglo-American culture." Turner traces African American contemporary legends and rumors to the earliest slave ships and argues that the stories emerging from that experience, and from periods of racial discord since, function as a tool of resistance for the African Americans who tell them.

SUGGESTION FOR READING Like Brunvand, Turner recounts rumors and contemporary legends that are horrifying but somehow believable. Where Brunvand would emphasize the role of urban legends to keep sexually active teens aware of potential dangers surrounding their activities, Turner argues that African American rumors are linked to racial strife and arise from actual horrors that African

Americans have faced since the beginnings of the slave trade. After you have read this selection, write a short response in which you compare the kinds of stories popular in African American traditions with the urban legends Brunvand collects. In what ways are they similar? In what ways are they specific to the African American experience in this country?

1 I was teaching Introduction to Black Literature at the University of Massachusetts at Boston in February 1986. Like most folklorists, I rely on folk material for examples in even my nonfolklore courses. After telling the students about the popular contemporary legend known as the Kentucky Fried Rat, Wayne, an intelligent young African-American, raised his hand to say, "Oh well, I guess that's like what they say about eating at Church's Chicken—you know the Klan owns it and they do something to the chicken so that when black men eat there they become sterile. Except that I guess it isn't really like the one about the Kentucky Fried Rat because it is true about Church's. I know because a friend of mine saw the story on '60 Minutes.'" Several other black students nodded in silent agreement; the white students looked at them in rapt disbelief, while the remaining black students seemed to be making a mental note not to eat at Church's. After class I sprinted to my office and began calling folklore colleagues. No professional folklorists (all white) had heard any version of the Church's text, but throughout the remainder of the day I was able to collect several variations from black students and black members of the university staff.

Several months later, as I was finishing an article on the Church's cycle, I found myself discussing it with another class. An African-American student raised her hand and said, "Well, if you don't believe that one, you probably don't believe that the FBI was responsible for the deaths of all those children in Atlanta. I heard that they were taking the bodies to the Centers for Disease Control in Atlanta to perform interferon experiments on them." As I began research on *that* story, also unknown to my white colleagues, I confirmed my earlier suspicions that these contemporary texts were not mere ephemera lacking in historical antecedents. Indeed, a provocative corpus of related material

can be traced back to the early sixteenth century, when white Europeans began to have regular contact with sub-Saharan Africa. I realized that this discourse was sufficiently rich to explore in book-length form.

A white colleague familiar with my work on the Church's and Atlanta Child Killer stories then pointed out that the increasingly common claim that the AIDS virus was the product of an anti-black conspiracy fit the pattern of my research. And in early 1989 I was querying a black studies class about the Church's item when one student raised her hand and said, "I don't know about the Klan owning Church's, but I do know that they are supposed to own Troop clothing." Other African-American students expressed agreement, while white students sat perplexed by this unfamiliar news. With this text the students had a real advantage over me because I had never even heard of the popular line of clothing apparently marketed quite aggressively to young black consumers.

I was convinced that these items fit into the category dubbed by folklorists as "urban" or "contemporary legend." Interestingly enough, Jan Harold Brunvand, a prolific writer on urban legend, referred to such stories as "an integral part of *white* [emphasis added] Anglo-American culture and are told and believed by some of the most sophisticated 'folk' of modern society— young people, urbanites, and the well-educated." The fact that no in-depth investigation of the texts that circulate among African-Americans has been conducted is not surprising. Most folklorists are white, and they have not discovered the black urban legend tradition.

5   The following is a representative sampling of rumors known to many African-Americans from all over the United States during this era:

Text #1: Church's [fast food chicken franchise] is owned by the Ku Klux Klan [KKK], and they put something in it to make black men sterile.

Text #2: I remember hearing that the killings [of twenty-eight African-Americans] in Atlanta were related to genocide of the black race. The FBI [Federal Bureau of Investigation] was responsible and using the bodies for interferon research.

Text #3: I have heard that U.S. scientists created AIDS in a laboratory (possibly as a weapon to use against enemy in the event of war), and they needed to test the virus, so they go to Africa, as they [Africans] are expendable, introduce the disease, and then are unable to control its spread to Europeans and Americans.

Text #4: Troop [a popular brand of athletic wear] is owned by the Ku Klux Klan. They are using the money they make from the products to finance the lawsuit that they lost to the black woman whose son was killed by the Klan.

10   Text #5: Reebok is made in South Africa. All of the money they make off of those shoes goes to support whites in South Africa.

Text #6: The production and mass distribution of drugs is an attempt by the white man to keep blacks who are striving to better themselves from making it in the world. So many blacks take drugs in order to find release and escape from the problems they face in life. By taking drugs, blacks are killing themselves, and by selling them they are bringing about the imminent destruction of their race. Overall, the white man has conspired to wipe out the black population by using them [blacks] to destroy themselves.

Text #7: Tropical Fantasy [a fruit-flavored soft drink] is made by the KKK. There is a special ingredient in it that makes black men sterile.

CONTAMINATION

Let us now look at texts in which the conspiracy in question is intended specifically to contaminate blacks in a physical way, either directly or indirectly. The majority of people who spoke with me about the Church's rumor, for example, allege much more than a simple KKK plot to capitalize monetarily on a product preferred by African-Americans. The first informant who shared the item told me, "They're doing something to the chicken so that when black men eat it, they become sterile," and this comment accusing the KKK of imposing a sinister form of ethnic birth control pervades my fieldwork. The same motif dominates the Tropical Fantasy cycle. Many informants who claim that the FBI was responsible for the Atlanta child murders elaborate by reporting that the bodies were taken to the Centers for Disease Control in Atlanta for biological experiments. A college-aged African-American female said, "I remember hearing that the killings in Atlanta were related to the genocide of the black race. The FBI was responsible and using the bodies for interferon during research." (Interferon is an antiviral glycoprotein produced by human cells exposed to a virus; according to certain research reports of the late 1970s and early 1980s, the scientific community was well on its way to testing it so that it could be marketed as a genuine "miracle drug.")

In some folk items, contamination is a much more prominent motif than conspiracy. Growing public awareness of the threat implicit in the acquired immune deficiency syndrome (AIDS) epidemic caused various contemporary legends to arise connecting this fatal, sexually transmitted disease with an ethnically based contamination plot. Some informants, for instance, claimed that AIDS was developed from experiments having to do with disease, chemical, or germ warfare. These experiments were supposedly conducted in Haiti or West Africa, populations that the experimenters (usually identified as some group affiliated with "the government") perceived to be expendable. As one informant reported, "The United States government was developing germ warfare when it got out of control. AIDS was the project, and they tried it out in Africa first to see if it would work. It did." Others claim even more heinous motives, saying that the disease was developed for the express purpose of limiting the growth of third world populations. A New England–born thirty-nine-year-old African-American female offered this succinct version: "AIDS originated in Africa by the [U.S.] government in that it was a conspiracy to kill off a lot of black people."

Dangerous Chicken

15   Approximately half of my informants claimed that the Klan's goal in its ownership of Church's was to put something (spices, drugs) into the chicken (either into the batter or flour coating, or, by injections, directly into the chicken) that would cause sterility in black male eaters. Similar aims and tactics were true of the Tropical Fantasy conspiracy. This motif contains the specificity and narrative closure that folklorists often find in contemporary legend texts. However, the other texts I collected lacked any such closure. Most informants used the present tense and described the contamination as an ongoing, relatively unfocused conspiracy. Typical of the comments I collected was, "I heard that the Klan owns Church's chicken and has been lacing the batter with a spermicide." Several people suggested that the KKK's goal was to "make blacks infertile." Thus both men and women have something to fear. One black female informant claimed that eating the chicken "makes something go wrong with pregnant black women so that their children come out retarded."

Typically, food contamination rumors and contemporary legends are associated either with instances of accidental, incidental contamination (the Kentucky Fried Rat, the mouse in the Coke bottle) or with premeditated food substitution, ostensibly for the purpose of increasing the company's profit ("wormburgers," the use of dog food on fast food pizzas). In the latter case, the company is not trying to hurt its customers, but rather to decrease costs through the use of socially distasteful but essentially safe ingredients. In the Church's rumor, by contrast, greed is not stated as a strong motive for the Klan. Although a few informants contributed versions that lacked any contamination motif, maintaining merely that the KKK owned the company, not a single informant speculated on how much money the Klan could make by selling fast food fried chicken to African-Americans. The white supremacist organization's goal, simply put, was to implement domestic genocide.

To those outside the rumor's public, the mechanism of contamination makes the accusa-tion seem highly implausible. I encountered very few white informants who were familiar with the rumor. Upon hearing a summary, most responded by asking, "How is this mysterious substance supposed to distinguish between white male eaters and black male eaters?" When this question is posed to blacks, a common explanation is that most Church's franchises are located in black neighborhoods. Similarly, those who believe the Tropical Fantasy rumors note that the beverage is sold in inner-city ma-and-pa grocery stores, not at downtown soda counters. Hence, the KKK runs very little risk of sterilizing white male consumers. Other informants suggest that a substance has been discovered that impedes the production of sperm in black males but is harmless when consumed by whites.

When the Church's rumor surfaced in San Diego in 1984, Congressman Jim Bates arranged to have the Food and Drug Administration test the chicken using gas chromatography and mass spectrometry. After finding no evidence of foreign materials, an assistant of Bates together with two West Coast Church's officials held a press conference to share their findings with the public. Tropical Fantasy was tested in 1991. A female informant told me that the Klan had probably "fixed things up with the FDA" so that the test on Church's would come out negative. Although I performed no scientific investigation of the chicken myself, I queried University of Massachusetts biologists and chemists about the possibility of such tampering. They maintained that there is no known tasteless, odorless substance that could be disguised in the chicken that would result in sterilization with no discernible side effects. I asked a black male student who overheard one of these conversations if he still believed the rumor. He said he did not. I asked him if he would patronize the nearby Church's. He said he would not.

To better understand the appeal of the contamination motif in the Church's and Tropical Fantasy rumors, it is useful to look at a very similar rumor. In speculating on just how the alleged sterilization agent in the chicken could function, none of my informants made any specific reference to the "ethnic weapon." This is the label that the U.S. intelligence community applied to rumors alleging that government scientists had developed a substance that could kill blacks but leave whites unharmed. These rumors, which appeared in leftist publications in the mid-1980s, caused great concern for the United States Information Agency (USIA). However, officials charged with exploring the reports drew no connections between them and other items of folk belief concerning people of color; rather, they claimed that the Soviet Union had designed and disseminated the rumors. In a publication familiarizing members of Congress with the scope of communist propaganda activity, the agency introduced the segment on the ethnic weapon thus:

Since at least 1980, the Soviet press has been circulating claims that the United States is conducting research on or has developed a so-called "ethnic weapon," which would kill only non-whites. The Soviet media typically also charges that the South Africans—or less frequently the Israelis—are supposedly collaborating with the United States in this research. The Soviet goal in this campaign seems clear: to make it appear as if the United States and its alleged collaborators are pursuing racist, genocidal policies.

    The Soviet charge is absurd on the face of it. Even if the U.S. government wanted to produce such a weapon, it would make no sense to do so, given the multi-ethnic composition of the American population and the armed forces. The only plausible group that would want to produce such a weapon would be unregenerate white supremacists—a portrait of the U.S. government that Soviet disinformation specialists apparently want their audiences to believe.

20   These comments are followed by various statements by scientific authorities explaining why such a substance could not be developed, as well as forty-five references in left-wing and communist publications to the U.S. government's role in the development of such a weapon.

    Because none of my over two hundred Church's and Tropical Fantasy informants mentioned the "ethnic weapon" by name, I can only conclude that this rumor was not embraced by the African-American population. Whether communist-inspired journalists actually planted the rumor or simply reported one that was gaining popularity is less relevant, in my view, than the fact that the item did not capture the African-American imagination. Why did a rumor alleging the KKK's malevolent involvement in a fast food company find more acceptance than one claiming the government was manufacturing a weapon for racial genocide?

    In the various left-wing print references cited in the USIA pamphlet, the so-called ethnic weapon is either a perfected substance or one still under development. Except in one item linking it to the AIDS virus, there are no hints that the weapon has been deployed. Nor are there any real indications of how, when, or why it would be used. The threat is in its mere existence—in the possibility that the U.S. government might want to have such a weapon, in the fact that it could not be used in a clandestine manner, and in the fact that the potential victims have no control over its implementation. In the Church's and Tropical Fantasy texts, by contrast, a form of random deployment is at work. Any African-American who chances to eat at Church's or sip a Tropical Fantasy soft drink is a potential victim. Yet in these cases, people can avoid victimization by refusing to purchase the product. The Church's and Tropical Fantasy rumors, in short, give people some control over their fate, whereas the ethnic weapon texts do not.

    The other primary difference between the Church's rumor—as well as the other contamination rumors—and the ethnic weapon item resides in the mode of contamination. With the ethnic weapon, there is no clue as to how the victims will be infected with the deadly substance or what modus operandi will govern the weapon's use. In the other items, however, the contamination is more specifically rendered: poisoned food or soft drinks, postmortem intrusions, and sexual intercourse are concrete threats. In short, rumors that contain specific physical consequences are more likely to seize the interest of a public than ambiguous, unspecific ones.

With motifs pinpointing a particular company, a known antiblack conspiratorial group, a familiar prepared food, and a detrimental outcome, the Church's rumor contains all of the nuances the ethnic weapon rumor lacks. Because a person can do something about the threat contained in the Church's item simply by not patronizing the restaurant, it is ultimately a much less ominous rumor. No informants who professed belief in the Church's story believed themselves to have been sterilized permanently because they consumed the chicken before they heard the item. No one said anything like, "It's too late for me now." Instead they merely observed, "So I haven't eaten any since."

25   Like other folk groups, African-Americans assign food and its preparation symbolic importance; food choice is part of the ordering process by which humans endow the environment with meaning and feeling. At first glance, a fast food chain that provides decent, familiar foods at a friendly price is offering a fair service and product. But by removing the preparation of an ethnic food from the home kitchens most strongly identified with it, the Church's corporation unwittingly intruded on sacred territory.

Ethnic foods, as a rule, are prepared and consumed by the very people who have created the dishes or by descendants who have had the recipes handed down to them. On special occasions or in special settings, these foods are shared with outsiders eager to participate in "equal opportunity eating." Church's created a new, public context for the sharing of what had thus far been considered communal foods—and foods, moreover, that carried with them strong symbolic associations. Nor are these associations necessarily positive. American popular culture has long perpetuated a stereotype in which blacks are portrayed as inordinately fond of foods that can be eaten without utensils, such as fried chicken and watermelon. Given this background, it is not surprising that blacks wish to approach these foods, particularly when offered outside the home, cautiously. The anthropologist Mary Douglas has pointed out that people with a minority status in their society are often suspicious of cooked foods as well as protective of the body's orifices: "If we treat ritual protection of bodily orifices as a symbol of social preoccupations about exits and entrances," she writes, "the purity of cooked food becomes important. I suggest that food is not likely to be polluting at all unless the external boundaries of the social system are under pressure."

The popularity of the Church's rumor indicates that the black community perceives itself as vulnerable to the hostile desires of the majority population, which, it seems, will stop at nothing to inhibit the growth of the minority population—including the use of polluted food to weaken individual sexual capacity. In this case, indeed, the threat to fertility comes from a source that employs the name of the very religious structure presumed by the black community to offer the most safety: the church.

The key to understanding the item's popularity, however, resides in the power it bestowed upon its public to seize control over a perceived threat to all African-American people. In the spring of 1990, an African-American female Californian discussed it as if it were ancient history. She recalled first hearing it "a long time ago," and concluded her commentary by stating, with obvious satisfaction, "A lot of these Church's have closed up now." Like many other informants who used similar closing motifs, she believed that a battle had been "won."

SUGGESTIONS FOR DISCUSSION

1. With a group of your classmates, compare the responses you each wrote to this selection. As a group, discuss how the rumors Turner recounts compare with the urban legends Brunvand collects. In what ways are they similar? How do they differ?

2. Examine the list of "Texts" Turner provides. Which of these stories have you heard before? Are there versions of the stories circulating today outside the African American community? Why might these remain within African American rumor circles? How might they change for a different audience?

3. Why does one of Turner's informants believe that the "battle" against Church's Chicken "has been won"? What is the battle? How was it won?

SUGGESTIONS FOR WRITING

1. In her introduction to *I Heard It Through the Grapevine*, Turner argues that African American contemporary legends and rumors go beyond teenage scare stories to function as "tools of resistance" in the African American community. Once a conspiracy story is circulated widely, the conspiracy can no longer be carried out because too many people know about it. Write an essay in which you examine how stories of contamination or KKK conspiracy function as tools of resistance. In your discussion, consider how the power shifts to the teller of the story as it is circulated through a community.

2. Turner makes it clear that African American rumors, like all urban legends, begin with a seed of truth. In Brunvand's stories, you can see how adult worries over teenage sexuality, for example, can feed into the perpetuation of stories such as "The Hook" or all of those baby-sitter stories. Turner's stories, however, connect with fears of genocide and racism. Write an essay in which you compare the kinds of stories Brunvand tells with the stories Turner tells. Is one more believable than another? More serious? More likely to be taken as fact by only some groups and not others? Why? What makes a rumor or legend believable to some and not to others?

3. Retell a contamination story—either a food story or a disease story (like AIDS or the ebola virus, for example). If you don't know one, ask friends, family members, or adults in your life. Write the story with as much detail as you can, including any variations you have heard or are able to find. Note down where you heard the story, who told it, and how much of the story you find believable. After reviewing both Brunvand and Turner, explain the function the story seems to have either to warn hearers or to blame someone or a part of the population for the contamination. How would you explain the popularity of the story?

WHY WE CRAVE HORROR MOVIES

Stephen King

Stephen King is a writer whose best-selling novels and short stories have taken the genre of horror fiction to new heights of popularity. Several of his works have been turned into successful Hollywood films, such as *Carrie* and *The Shining*. In the following essay, originally published in *Playboy* (December 1981), King seeks to identify the reasons horror films have such a grip on the popular imagination. Before you read the essay, think about your own experience as a moviegoer and television viewer. Are there particular forms of storytelling—thrillers, soap operas, romances, science fiction, action-adventure, cops and robbers, Westerns, and so on—to which you are particularly drawn? The question he asks—Why do we crave horror movies?—could be applied as well to other forms of popular storytelling.

SUGGESTION Notice how Stephen King presents his assumptions about people in the opening paragraph.
FOR READING As you read, follow King's argument by underlining the reasons he gives. Consider how his initial assumptions have shaped the reasons he offers as answers to the question: Why do we crave horror movies?

1   I think that we're all mentally ill; those of us outside the asylums only hide it a little better—and maybe not all that much better, after all. We've all known people who talk to themselves, people who sometimes squinch their faces into horrible grimaces when they believe no one is watching, people who have some hysterical fear—of snakes, the dark, the tight place, the long drop...and, of course, those final worms and grubs that are waiting so patiently underground.

When we pay our four or five bucks and seat ourselves at tenth-row center in a theater showing a horror movie, we are daring the nightmare.

Why? Some of the reasons are simple and obvious. To show that we can, that we are not afraid, that we can ride this roller coaster. Which is not to say that a really good horror movie may not surprise a scream out of us at some point, the way we may scream when the roller coaster twists through a complete 360 or plows through a lake at the bottom of the drop. And horror movies, like roller coasters, have always been the special province of the young; by the time one turns 40 or 50, one's appetite for double twists or 360-degree loops may be considerably depleted.

We also go to re-establish our feelings of essential normality; the horror movie is innately conservative, even reactionary. Freda Jackson as the horrible melting woman in *Die, Monster, Die!* confirms for us that no matter how far we may be removed from the beauty of a Robert Redford or a Diana Ross, we are still light-years from true ugliness.

5   And we go to have fun.

Ah, but this is where the ground starts to slope away, isn't it? Because this is a very peculiar sort of fun, indeed. The fun comes from seeing others menaced—sometimes killed. One critic has suggested that if pro football has become the voyeur's version of combat, then the horror film has become the modern version of the public lynching.

It is true that the mythic, "fairy-tale" horror film intends to take away the shades of gray.... It urges us to put away our more civilized and adult penchant for analysis and to become children again, seeing things in pure blacks and whites. It may be that horror movies provide psychic relief on this level because this invitation to lapse into simplicity, irrationality and even outright madness is extended so rarely. We are told we may allow our emotions a free rein...or no rein at all.

If we are all insane, then sanity becomes a matter of degree. If your insanity leads you to carve up women like Jack the Ripper or the Cleveland Torso Murderer, we clap you away in the funny farm (but neither of those two amateur-night surgeons was ever caught, heh-heh-heh); if, on the other hand, your insanity leads you only to talk to yourself when you're under stress or to pick your nose on your morning bus, then you are left alone to go about your business...though it is doubtful that you will ever be invited to the best parties.

The potential lyncher is in almost all of us (excluding saints, past and present; but then, most saints have been crazy in their own ways), and every now and then, he has to be let loose to scream and roll around in the grass. Our emotions and our fears form their own body, and we recognize that it demands its own exercise to maintain proper muscle tone. Certain of these emotional muscles are accepted—even exalted—in civilized society; they are, of course, the emotions that tend to maintain the status quo of civilization itself. Love, friendship, loyalty, kindness—these are all the emotions that we applaud, emotions that have been immortalized in the couplets of Hallmark cards and in the verses (I don't dare call it poetry) of Leonard Nimoy.

10   When we exhibit these emotions, society showers us with positive reinforcement; we learn this even before we get out of diapers. When, as children, we hug our rotten little puke of a sister and give her a kiss, all the aunts and uncles smile and twit and cry "Isn't he the sweetest little thing?" Such coveted treats as chocolate-covered graham crackers often follow. But if we deliberately slam the rotten little puke of a sister's fingers in the door, sanctions follow—angry remonstrance from parents, aunts and uncles; instead of a chocolate-covered graham cracker, a spanking.

But anticivilization emotions don't go away, and they demand periodic exercise. We have such "sick" jokes as, "What's the difference between a truckload of bowling balls and a truckload of dead babies?" (You can't unload a truckload of bowling balls with a pitchfork...a joke, by the way, that I heard originally from a ten-year-old). Such a joke may surprise a laugh or a grin out of us even as we recoil, a possibility that confirms the thesis: If we share a brotherhood of man, then we also share an insanity of man.

None of which is intended as a defense of either the sick joke or insanity but merely as an explanation of why the best horror films, like the best fairy tales, manage to be reactionary, anarchistic, and revolutionary all at the same time.

The mythic horror movie, like the sick joke, has a dirty job to do. It deliberately appeals to all that is worst in us. It is morbidity unchained, our most base instincts let free, our nastiest fantasies realized...and it all happens, fittingly enough, in the dark. For those reasons, good liberals often shy away from horror films. For myself, I like to see the most aggressive of them—*Dawn of the Dead,* for instance—as lifting a trap door in the civilized forebrain and throwing a basket of raw meat to the hungry alligators swimming around in that subterranean river beneath.

Why bother? Because it keeps them from getting out, man. It keeps them down there and me up here. It was Lennon and McCartney who said that all you need is love, and I would agree with that.

As long as you keep the gators fed.

SUGGESTIONS FOR DISCUSSION

1. Look over the reasons that you underlined. Do you find some of the reasons King offers to explain why people "crave" horror movies more persuasive than others? Explain why his reasons are or are not persuasive to you. Are there reasons you can think of that King leaves out?

2. King begins his essay with a powerful assertion: "I think that we're all mentally ill." How does this assumption guide the development of the rest of the essay? What other assumptions might you begin with to explain the appeal of horror movies?

3. King suggests that horror movies perform a social function that is "innately conservative." To what extent do horror movies allow readers, in King's words, "to re-establish our feelings of essential normality"? Give specific examples of how particular horror movies do this. Can you make a similar argument about other kinds of movies, such as thrillers, romances, action-adventure, Westerns, and so on?

SUGGESTIONS FOR WRITING

1. Begin with King's suggestion that one of the social functions of the horror movie is first to violate and then to "re-establish our feelings of essential normality." Write an essay on a particular book, movie, or television show that uses this notion of violating and reestablishing social norms to analyze the story it tells and the appeal it has for readers or viewers.

2. Pick a genre of popular fiction, movies, or television shows that you know well (such as soap operas, situation comedies, police shows, science fiction, fantasy, Westerns, and so on). Use King's essay as a model to write your own explanation of why the public craves that form of storytelling.

3. Choose a genre of storytelling with which you are not familiar or do not care for. Find someone—a friend, classmate, relative, or acquaintance—who really likes that particular form of storytelling, whether in the novels he or she reads or in the movies and television shows he or she watches. Write an essay to explain the person's attraction to the genre and also to generalize about the larger popular appeal of the genre.

A HUNGER FOR FANTASY, AN EMPIRE TO FEED IT

A.O. Scott

A.O. Scott is a film critic at the *New York Times* and the former Sunday book critic for *Newsday*. His writing has appeared in such publications as the *New York Review of Books* and *Slate*. In the following article, which appeared in the *New York Times* on June 16, 2002, Scott seeks to explain the continuing popularity for moviegoers of fantasy stories such as J.R.R. Tolkien's *The Lord of the Rings*, J.K. Rowling's *Harry Potter and the Sorcerer's Stone*, and comic book superhero *Spider-Man*.

SUGGESTION FOR READING Keep the title of this article in mind as you read. After you have completed your reading, write a brief explanation for the title. Who has the "hunger" for fantasy? What "empire" feeds that hunger?

1 So far, this year's two most lucrative summer movies concern the perilous adventures of male teenagers, one in contemporary New York and the other long ago in a galaxy far away, struggling with the moral and physical burdens of their special powers. Over the winter, the box office was dominated by two rather similar young men, one at an English boarding school, the other in the meticulously mapped Anglo-Saxon dreamworld of Middle Earth. Together, these four movies, "Spider-Man," 'Star Wars: Episode II —Attack of the Clones," "Harry Potter and the Sorcerer's Stone" and "The Lord of the Rings: The Fellowship of the Ring," have earned more than $1 billion in domestic ticket sales.

This is, needless to say, only a partial accounting. It leaves out overseas box office, DVD and video revenues, and the all-important merchandising of action figures, light sabers and round, black-framed eye-glasses. And, of course, none of these movies stands alone: "Attack of the Clones" is the fifth installment in a double trilogy that has been unfolding for 25 years; "Fellowship" is the first episode in a three-film sequence, the second part of which, "The Two Towers," is to appear in December; and the Harry Potter and Spider-Man pictures have inaugurated franchises likely to carry their juvenile heroes at least to the brink of adulthood.

Perhaps more than ever before, Hollywood is an empire of fantasy. But despite the popularity of these movies—and despite the unmatched power of the studios to blanket the real world with publicity, advertising and media hype—Hollywood is not the center of this empire. It is, rather a colonial outpost whose conquest has been recent and remains incomplete.

The rapid evolution of digital technology has made it possible for filmmakers like Peter Jackson and George Lucas to summon up ever more plausible and richly imagined counterfeit worlds, free of clunky mechanical props and stagy costumes. But the origins of these worlds is, for the most part, to be found not on the screen but on the page. Of the four films mentioned, only "Star Wars" belongs solely to the world of movies. The rest are adapted from comic books and novels.

5   Twenty-five years ago, the first "Star Wars" helped to transform moviemaking and moviegoing. It gave birth to the current era of blockbuster serials, intensive special effects and wide-release, critic-resistant summer popcorn extravaganzas. But the true genius of that picture was the way it opened mainstream cinema to a vital strain in American popular culture that Hollywood had until then largely ignored or treated with condescension. "Star Wars" tapped into an impulse that had been flourishing at least since the end of the Second World War in the pages of comic books and pulp novels, on television and in the nascent subculture of role-playing games like Dungeons and Dragons. (Even today, the primary locus for fantasy scenarios in which lone heroes do battle with demons and bad guys in archaic or futuristic landscapes is not movies but video and computer games, which are open-ended and participatory in ways that even a boxed-set DVD version of a movie can never be.)

The film versions of "Lord of the Rings" and "Harry Potter" undoubtedly follow in the footsteps of Luke Skywalker. It's also evident that the pop explosion that "Star Wars" set off in 1977 would not have occurred without the equally explosive success, a decade earlier, of the one-volume American paperback edition of J. R. R. Tolkien's "Lord of the Rings," and that the Harry Potter publishing phenomenon seized the fancies of late-90's American schoolchildren much as "The Lord of the Rings" and "Star Wars" had captivated their parents.

The juggernaut grows with each generation. Unlike virtually everything else in the irony-saturated, ready-to-recycle cosmos of postmodern pop culture, stories of this kind don't seem to date. Yes, the hairstyles in the original "Star Wars" are a little shaggy, and the FX are a little rickety by current standards, but 10-year-olds watching it today experience the same freshness and sublimity their parents discovered in the 70's. Yes, the copies of "The Lord of the Rings" found in used bookstores may be perfumed with the marijuana smoke of ancient dorm rooms and suburban basements, but the story surely transcends the era of its first great American vogue.

The appeal is perennial because it fulfills the widespread and ever-renewing desire for a restoration of innocence. The major texts of modern fantasy have all been pointedly, even deliberately regressive. Tolkien, in inventing Middle Earth, was motivated by an extreme nostalgia, a desire to restore, at least in imagination, the language and folkways of an England uncorrupted by modernity. (Modernity, for him, began with the Norman conquest of 1066, which ruined everything.)

"Star Wars" arrived not only in the midst of the malaise that followed Vietnam and Watergate, but also at a time when the stalwart heroic movie genres, the war movie and the western, could no longer in good faith sustain narratives of simple virtue. The moral universe of "Star Wars" was and remains, despite the growing political complications of the last two episodes, reassuringly simple because it is fundamentally allegorical. Turning his back on the dark, dystopian visions of the era's science fiction, which extrapolated a stark future from the confusion of the present, Mr. Lucas situated his epic in an ancient, distant world intended to recapture the gee whiz spirit of Buck Rogers and the 1939 World's Fair.

10   Fantasy literature, which in the broadest sense includes modes of storytelling from novels to movies to video games, depends on patterns, motifs and archetypes. It is therefore hardly surprising that the most visible modern variants of the ancient genres of saga, romance and quest narrative are so richly crosspollinated and resemble one another. The central characters show an especially close kinship. They are, following a convention so deep it seems to be encoded in the human storytelling gene, orphans, summoned

out of obscurity to undertake a journey into the heart of evil that will also be a voyage of self-discovery. Frodo Baggins lives quietly in an obscure corner of the Shire, oblivious to the metaphysical storm brewing in distant Mordor. Luke Skywalker dwells, like Dorothy in Kansas, in a dusty hinterland far removed from the imperial center of things. Harry Potter, in his suburban Muggle exile, bides his time shut up in a closet under the stairs, a prisoner of his beastly aunt and uncle. Peter Parker (Spidey), meanwhile, occupies a more benign and familiar modern environment in Wood-haven, Queens, and is cared for by much nicer relatives.

All of these young men—and fantasy heroes are, overwhelmingly, men—discover themselves to be in possession of extraordinary gifts, and become, unexpectedly and sometimes reluctantly, the central figures in a struggle against absolute evil. Destiny has selected them for great things. Their episodic adventures lead them forward, toward a climactic confrontation with the enemy (foreshadowed in a series of battles with subsidiary forms of evil) and also backward into the mysteries of their own past and parentage.

For all their ancient and futuristic trappings, fantasy stories speak directly to the condition of contemporary male adolescence, and they offer a Utopian solution to the anxiety and dislocation that are part of the pyschic landscape of youth. Freaks become heroes. The confusing issue of sex is kept at a safe distance; romantic considerations are ancillary to the fight against evil, and to the cameraderie of warriors. But ultimately, whatever fellowship he may have found along the way, the hero's quest is solitary, his triumph an allegory of the personal fulfillment that is, in the real world, both a birthright and a mirage.

The structure of fantasy calls for episodes of increasingly perilous action connected by passages of exposition, in which the necessary facts of history, geography and genealogy are revealed to the hero and, over his shoulder, to the audience.

These moments, which often feature secondary characters in outlandish costumes delivering earnest, learned speeches—the Jedi elders in "Attack of the Clones"; the war council over at

Cate Blanchett's (Galadriel's) place in "Fellowship of the Rings"—are routinely mocked by critics (not excluding this one) for their tedium and portentousness. Such derision, however, is precisely what separates the casual fan from the true adept (the latter being one who uses his esoteric powers to vanquish the former by means of angry e-mail).

15   Any Muggle can thrill to a sword fight or a computer-generated aerial battle, but true wizardry lies in the mastery of arcane detail. It is obvious that much of the appeal of these chronicles lies in the possibility of vicarious heroism, of identifying with the unprepossessing, marginal, nerdy guys who turn out to be indispensable to the survival of the universe. The way that identification is sealed is not through imitation of their feats of cunning or physical courage, but by mimicking their progress from innocence to mastery, by acquiring a body of esoteric knowledge for which the books and movies themselves provide the raw material.

In the United States today there are hundred of thousands, perhaps millions of people whose grasp of the history, politics and mythological traditions of entirely imaginary places could surely qualify them for an advanced degree. This learning is fed by quasi-official concordances, encyclopedias and other reference works, but these exist mainly to exploit a spontaneous process that takes place in classrooms and chat rooms around the world. The drive and discipline that leads 9-year-olds to school themselves in the institutional history of Hogwarts and college sophomores to analyze the diplomatic crises of the intergalactic empire might, it could be argued, be more profitably spent in learning something about the real world, but this criticism misses the point.

Like all knowledge, fantasy lore is acquired partly for its own sake and partly for the social privilege it confers, which in this case is membership in a select order, like the Wizards or the Jedi or the Fellowship of the Ring, of which the rest of the world is only dimly aware and whose codes and protocols it will never know.

The history of postwar American popular culture is to some degree a history of subcultures—communities of enthusiasts walking the fine line between ardor and obsession. These have come in all varieties: hot rodders, Barbie collectors, followers of the Grateful Dead. But the fantasy genres have been especially fertile breeding grounds for such communities of enthusiasm, from Trekkies to D&D players to the intrepid souls who camp out in front of the cineplexes where the next "Star Wars" movie will be showing. These fans see themselves not only as consumers of popular culture, but as participants in its making, which may be why the exemplary form of fantasy culture is not reading or moviegoing but gaming, in which each player can be the hero of his own saga.

Similarly, both long-running and short-lived fantasy series on television—from "Star Trek" to "Beauty and the Beast" to "Buffy the Vampire Slayer"—have inspired fans to create and circulate their own stories in fanzines, self-published novels and now on the Internet. The convertibility of entire movies into digital files creates further opportunities for fan participation (and also for intellectual property litigation), a specter raised by the circulation of a fan-edited (and, in some respects, improved) version of "Star Wars: Episode One" over the Internet last year.

20   The appeal of fantasy has been especially powerful among those who find themselves marginalized by the brutal social universe of American secondary education—geeks, losers, nerds. You remember them from high school—or you remember being one of them—the guys who filled their notebooks with meticulous line drawings of broad-sword-wielding berserkers and their large-breasted consorts, who staffed the tech crew for the spring theatricals and dominated the computer club, who used words like "grok" in ordinary conversation. Their devotion to sci-fi and sword-and-sorcery arcana invited ridicule, but was also a defense against it. But such mockery is, by now, obsolete. The triumph of fantasy culture, like the transformation of the cult of the computer into mainstream religion, is their revenge. We are all nerds now. And we had better do our homework.

SUGGESTIONS FOR DISCUSSION

1. Scott writes that, although the rapid evolution of digital technology may have made it possible to create the worlds of these fantasy films, it isn't digital technology that has made them so popular. What does account for their popularity?

2. According to Scott, "fantasy stories speak directly to the condition of contemporary male adolescence, and they offer a Utopian solution to the anxiety and dislocation that are part of the psychic landscape of youth." Which of the fantasy stories that you are familiar with seem to conform to that description? In what ways do they depart from that description? Is there anything in these stories that speaks to the condition of contemporary female adolescence?

3. Scott calls these films the revenge of the nerds. What does he mean by that?

SUGGESTIONS FOR WRITING

1. Early in this selection, Scott points out that, except for *Star Wars*, the films most popular in 2002—*Spider-Man, Harry Potter and the Sorcerer's Stone,* and *The Lord of the Rings: Fellowship of the Rings*—were all popular stories from comic books and novels. In other words, they already had loyal reading audiences long before film technology made their fantasy worlds so vivid on-screen. Write an essay about a story you would like to see filmed. It might come from comic books, video games, or novels. What is the setting? Who are the characters? What is the central conflict? Who would the story appeal to? Why? Explain why you think this story would be popular with today's film audience or why it might only appeal to a very specialized audience. Does it conform, as Scott says fantasy literature does, to certain storytelling patterns—such as the young hero on a quest or on a mission to save something or someone?

2. Scott writes that fantasy appeals to viewers because it expresses "the widespread and ever-renewing desire for a restoration of innocence." Watch one of the films Scott writes about in this article. (They are all available for rent in video or on DVD.) In an essay in which you address the claim that fantasy is, in essence, nostalgia—a desire to return to an innocent world—explain how or if the film you watched accomplishes that. In *Spider-Man*, for example, the film ends with Peter Parker rejecting the girl he has wanted to be with for the entire film. *The Fellowship of the Ring* ends with Frodo and Sam separated from the group and off on a fearsome journey. How, then, does the audience experience the nostalgia that Scott writes of, even if the characters themselves have not reached that world of innocence?

3. By the time you read this chapter, many of the films that A.O. Scott wrote about—*The Lord of the Rings*, *Harry Potter*, and *Spider-Man*, in particular—will have sequels that follow the characters and story lines of the originals. Watch one or more of these sequels and write an assessment of it in terms of what Scott says is the role of fantasy stories for audiences today. To what extent does the film retain much of what made the original popular? What is new or different in the sequel?

PERSPECTIVES   Writing Superheroes

In the pair of readings selected here, Roger Ebert and Michael Chabon tackle the question of how to create a superhero that the audience will believe. By its very nature, the superhero is larger than life, but the best superhero is still one the audience can relate to—even feel a little sorry for now and then. The trick for a writer is to make that formula work.

As A.O. Scott explains, the hero in so much fantasy fiction is the outsider, the orphan, the marginalized. Superheroes fall into that category quite easily. And many, such as Spider-Man, find out about their super powers only by accident. Others, such as Batman, don't really have super powers at all. They are simply very good at what they do, or as in Batman's case, are wealthy enough to finance slick new inventions such as the Batmobile to help them fight crime.

The real question, still, is why they do what they do. Is it just that some people are more obsessed with justice and right than others? What drives the superhero, and how does a good novelist or screenwriter tell that story?

As you read, notice how Ebert characterizes the film adaptation of Spider-Man's life and how the comic book writers in Chabon's novel explain what they have to do to create a credible superhero. Keep in mind the superhero stories you already know—Superman, Batman, Wonder Woman, and others who remain popular in comic books, cartoons, and movies.

SPIDER-MAN

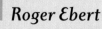
Roger Ebert

Roger Ebert has served as film critic for the *Chicago Sun Times* since 1967. He was the first recipient of the Pulitzer Prize for film criticism (1975) and for several years appeared with cohost Gene Siskel on PBS's *At the Movies*. He is the author of several books on cinema, including *A Kiss is Still a Kiss* (1984).

SUGGESTION Before you read, find out what Spider-Man's "origin story" is. Go to the Marvel Comics Web
FOR READING site to find his origin story.

1 Imagine *Superman* with a Clark Kent more charismatic than the Man of Steel, and you'll understand how *Spider-Man* goes wrong. Tobey Maguire is pitch-perfect as the socially retarded Peter Parker, but when he becomes Spider-Man, the film turns to action sequences that zip along like perfunctory cartoons. Not even during Spidey's first experimental outings do we feel that flesh and blood are contending with gravity. Spidey soars too quickly through the skies of Manhattan; he's as convincing as Mighty Mouse.

The appeal of the best sequences in the Superman and Batman movies is that they lend weight and importance to comic-book images. Within the ground rules set by each movie, they even have plausibility. As a reader of the Spider-Man comics, I admired the vertiginous frames showing Spidey dangling from terrifying heights. He had the powers of a spider and the instincts of a human being, but the movie is split between a plausible Peter Parker and an inconsequential superhero.

Consider a sequence early in the film, after Peter Parker is bitten by a mutant spider and discovers his new powers. His hand is sticky. He doesn't need glasses anymore. He was scrawny yesterday, but today he's got muscles. The movie shows him becoming aware of these facts, but insufficiently amazed (or frightened) by them. He learns how to spin and toss webbing, and finds that he can make enormous leaps. And then there's a scene where he's like a kid with a new toy, jumping from one rooftop to another, making giant leaps, whooping with joy.

Remember the first time you saw the characters defy gravity in *Crouching Tiger, Hidden Dragon*? They transcended gravity, but they didn't dismiss it: They seemed to possess weight, dimension and presence. Spider-Man as he leaps across the rooftops is landing too lightly, rebounding too much like a bouncing ball. He looks like a video game figure, not like a person having an amazing experience.

5 The other super-being in the movie is the Green Goblin, who surfs the skies in jet-shoes. He, too, looks like a drawing being moved quickly around a frame, instead of like a character who has mastered a daring form of locomotion. He's handicapped, too, by his face, which looks like a high-tech action figure with a mouth that doesn't move. I understand why it's immobile (we're looking at a mask), but I'm not persuaded; the movie could simply ordain that the Green Goblin's exterior shell has a face that's mobile, and the character would become more interesting. (True, Spider-Man has no mouth, and Peter Parker barely opens his—the words slip out through a reluctant slit.)

The film tells Spidey's origin story—who Peter Parker is, who Aunt May (Rosemary Harris) and Uncle Ben (Cliff Robertson) are, how Peter's an outcast at school, how he burns with unrequited love for Mary Jane Watson (Kirsten Dunst), how he peddles photos of Spider-Man to cigar-chomping editor J. Jonah Jameson (J.K. Simmons).

Peter Parker was crucial in the evolution of Marvel comics because he was fallible and had recognizable human traits. He was a nerd, a loner, socially inept, insecure, a poor kid being raised by relatives. Maguire gets all of that just right, and I enjoyed the way Dunst is able to modulate her gradually increasing interest in this loser who begins to seem attractive to her. I also liked the complexity of the villain, who in his Dr. Jekyll manifestation is brilliant tycoon Norman Osborn (Willem Dafoe) and in his Mr. Hyde persona is a cackling psychopath. Osborn's son Harry (James Franco) is a rich kid, embarrassed by his dad's wealth, who is Peter's best and only friend, and Norman is affectionate toward Peter even while their alter-egos are deadly enemies. That works, and there's an effective scene where Osborn has a conversation with his invisible dark side.

The origin story is well told, and the characters will not disappoint anyone who values the original comic books. It's in the action scenes that things fall apart. Consider the scene where Spider-Man is given a cruel choice between saving Mary Jane or a cable car full of school kids. He tries to save both, so that everyone dangles from webbing that seems about to pull loose. The visuals here could have given an impression of the enormous weights and tensions involved, but instead the scene seems more like a bloodless storyboard of the idea. In other CGI scenes, Spidey swoops from great heights to street level and soars back up among the skyscrapers again with such dizzying speed that it seems less like a stunt than like a fast-forward version of a stunt.

I have one question about the Peter Parker character: Does the movie go too far with his extreme social paralysis? Peter tells Mary Jane he just wants to be friends. "Only a friend?"she repeats. "That's all I have to give," he says. How so? Impotent? Spidey-sense has skewed his sexual instincts? Afraid his hands will get stuck?

THE AMAZING ADVENTURES OF KAVALIER & CLAY

Michael Chabon

Michael Chabon's *Amazing Adventures of Kavalier & Clay*, from which this selection is taken, won the 2001 Pulitzer Prize for fiction. In it, Chabon tells the tale of two young men breaking into the comic book business just as superheroes such as Superman, Batman, Aquaman, and others are coming on the scene. Chabon's novel opens in 1939 with the story of Josef Kavalier's escape from Nazi-occupied Prague. He makes it to New York, where he meets his cousin Sammy Klayman, a would-be comic book writer working for a novelty company that sells items such as fart cushions and fake vomit. Together, Sammy and Joe create the Escapist, a superhero to rival Superman.

SUGGESTION FOR READING   The chapter excerpted here begins immediately after Sammy has convinced his boss to let him and Joe create their own comic book superhero. As you read, pay attention to what Sammy and Joe say must be the qualities of their superhero.

1   The first official meeting of their partnership was convened outside the Kramler Building, in a nimbus compounded of the boys' exhalations and of subterranean steam purling up from a grate in the pavement.

"This is good," Joe said.

"I know."

"He said *yes*," Joe reminded his cousin, who stood patting idly with one hand at the front of his overcoat and a panicked expression on his face, as though worried that he had left something important behind in Anapol's office.

5   "Yes, he did. He said yes."

"Sammy." Joe reached out and grabbed Sammy's wandering hand, arresting it in its search of his pockets and collar and tie. "This is *good*."

"Yes, this is good, god damn it. I just hope to God we can *do* it."

Joe let go of Sammy's hand, shocked by this expression of sudden doubt. He had been completely taken in by Sammy's bold application of the Science of Opportunity. The whole morning, the rattling ride through the flickering darkness under the East River, the updraft of Klaxons and rising office blocks that had carried them out of the subway station, the ten thousand men and

women who immediately surrounded them, the ringing telephones and gum-snapping chitchat of the clerks and secretaries in Sheldon Anapol's office, the sly and harried bulk of Anapol himself, the talk of sales figures and competition and cashing in big, all this had conformed so closely to Joe's movie-derived notions of life in America that if an airplane were now to land on Twenty-fifth Street and disgorge a dozen bathing-suit-clad Fairies of Democracy come to award him the presidency of General Motors, a contract with Warner Bros., and a penthouse on Fifth Avenue with a swimming pool in the living room, he would have greeted this, too, with the same dreamlike unsurprise. It had not occurred to him until now to consider that his cousin's display of bold entrepreneurial confidence might have been entirely bluff, that it was 8°C and he had neither hat nor gloves, that his stomach was as empty as his billfold, and that he and Sammy were nothing more than a couple of callow young men in thrall to a rash and dubious promise.

"But I have belief in you," Joe said. "I trust you."

10   "That's good to hear."

"I mean it."

"I wish I knew why."

"Because," said Joe. "I don't have any choice."

"Oh ho."

15   "I need money," Joe said, and then tried adding, "god *damn* it."

"Money." The word seemed to have a restorative effect on Sammy, snapping him out of his daze. "Right. Okay. First of all, we need horses."

"Horses?"

"Arms. Guys."

"Artists."

20   "How about we just call them 'guys' for right now?"

"Do you know where we can find some?"

Sammy thought for a moment. "I believe I do," he said. "Come on."

They set off in a direction that Joe decided was probably west. As they walked Sammy

seemed to get lost quickly in his own reflections. Joe tried to imagine the train of his cousin's thoughts, but the particulars of the task at hand were not clear to him, and after a while he gave up and just kept pace. Sammy's gait was deliberate and crooked, and Joe found it a challenge to keep from getting ahead. There was a humming sound everywhere that he attributed first to the circulation of his own blood in his ears before he realized that it was the sound produced by Twenty-fifth Street itself, by a hundred sewing machines in a sweat-shop overhead, exhaust grilles at the back of a warehouse, the trains rolling deep beneath the black surface of the street. Joe gave up trying to think like, trust, or believe in his cousin and just walked, head abuzz, toward the Hudson River, stunned by the novelty of exile.

"Who is he?" Sammy said at last, as they were crossing a broad street which a sign identified, improbably somehow, as Sixth Avenue. Sixth Avenue! The Hudson River!

25   "Who is he," Joe said.

"Who is he, and what does he do?"

"He flies."

Sammy shook his head. "Superman flies."

"So ours does not?"

30   "I just think I'd..."

"To be original."

"If we can. Try to do it without flying, at least. No flying, no strength of a hundred men, no bulletproof skin."

"Okay," Joe said. The humming seemed to recede a little. "And some others, they do what?"

"Well, Batman—"

35   "He flies, like a bat."

"No, he doesn't fly."

"But he is blind."

"No, he only dresses like a bat. He has no batlike qualities at all. He uses his fists."

"That sounds dull."

40   "Actually, it's spooky. You'd like it."

"Maybe another animal."

"Uh, well, yeah. Okay. A hawk. Hawkman."

"Hawk, yes, okay. But that one must fly."

"Yeah, you're right. Scratch the bird family. The, uh, the Fox. The Shark."

45 "A swimming one."

"Maybe a swimming one. Actually, no, I know a guy works in the Chesler shop, he said they're already doing a guy who swims. For Timely."

"A lion?"

"Lion. The Lion. Lionman."

"He could be strong. He roars very loud."

50 "He has a super roar."

"It strikes fear."

"It breaks dishes."

"The bad guys go deaf."

They laughed. Joe stopped laughing.

55 "I think we have to be serious," he said.

"You're right," said Sammy. "The Lion, I don't know. Lions are lazy. How about the Tiger. Tigerman. No, no. Tigers are killers. Shit. Let's see."

They began to go through the rolls of the animal kingdom, concentrating naturally on the predators: Catman, Wolfman, the Owl, the Panther, the Black Bear. They considered the primates: the Monkey, Gorillaman, the Gibbon, the Ape, the Mandrill with his multicolored wonder ass that he used to bedazzle opponents.

"Be serious," Joe chided again.

"I'm sorry, I'm sorry. Look, forget animals. Everybody's going to be thinking of animals. In two months, I'm telling you, by the time our guy hits the stands, there's going to be guys running around dressed like every damn animal in the zoo. Birds. Bugs. Underwater guys. And I'll bet you anything there's going to be five guys who are really strong, and invulnerable, and can fly."

60 "If he goes as fast as the light," Joe suggested.

"Yeah, I guess it's good to be fast."

"Or if he can make a thing burn up. If he can—listen! If he can, you know. Shoot the fire, with his eyes!"

"His eyeballs would melt."

"Then with his hands. Or, yes, he turns into a fire!"

65 "Timely's doing that already, too. They got the fire guy and the water guy."

"He turns into *ice*. He makes the ice everywhere."

"Crushed or cubes?"

"Not good?"

Sammy shook his head. "Ice," he said. "I don't see a lot of stories in ice."

70 "He turns into electricity?" Joe tried. "He turns into acid?"

"He turns into gravy. He turns into an enormous hat. Look, stop. Stop. Just stop."

They stopped in the middle of the sidewalk, between Sixth and Seventh avenues, and that was when Sam Clay experienced a moment of global vision, one which he would afterward come to view as the one undeniable brush against the diaphanous, dollar-colored hem of the Angel of New York to be vouchsafed to him in his lifetime.

"This is not the question," he said. "If he's like a cat or a spider or a fucking wolverine, if he's huge, if he's tiny, if he can shoot flames or ice or death rays or Vat 69, if he turns into fire or water or stone or India rubber. He could be a Martian, he could be a ghost, he could be a god or a demon or a wizard or monster. Okay? It doesn't *matter*, because right now, see, at this very moment, we have a bandwagon rolling, I'm telling you. Every little skinny guy like me in New York who believes there's life on Alpha Centauri and got the shit kicked out of him in school and can smell a dollar is out there right this minute trying to jump onto it, walking around with a pencil in his shirt pocket, saying, 'He's like a falcon, no, he's like a tornado, no, he's like a goddamned wiener dog.' Okay?"

"Okay."

75 "And no matter what we come up with, and how we dress him, some other character with the same shtick, with the same style of boots and the same little doodad on his chest, is already out there, or is coming out tomorrow, or is going to be knocked off from our guy inside a week and a half."

Joe listened patiently, awaiting the point of this peroration, but Sammy seemed to have lost the thread. Joe followed his cousin's gaze along the sidewalk but saw only a pair of what looked to be British sailors lighting their cigarettes off a single shielded match.

"So…" Sammy said. "So…"

"So that is not the question," Joe prompted.

"That's what I'm saying."

80 "Continue."

They kept walking.

"How? is not the question. What? is not the question," Sammy said.

"The question is why."

"The question is *why*."

85 "Why," Joe repeated.

"Why is he doing it?"

"Doing what?"

"Dressing up like a monkey or an ice cube or a can of fucking corn."

"To fight the crime, isn't it?"

90 "Well, yes, to fight crime. To fight evil. But that's all any of these guys are doing. That's as far as they ever go. They just…you know, it's the right thing to do, so they do it. How interesting is that?"

"I see."

"Only Batman, you know…see, yeah, that's good. That's what makes Batman good, and not dull at all, even though he's just a guy who dresses up like a bat and beats people up."

"What is the reason for Batman? The why?"

"His parents were killed, see? In cold blood. Right in front of his eyes, when he was a kid. By a robber."

95 "It's revenge."

"That's *interesting*," Sammy said. "See?"

"And he was driven mad."

"Well…"

"And that's why he puts on the bat's clothes."

100 "Actually, they don't go so far as to say that," Sammy said. "But I guess it's there between the lines."

"So, we need to figure out what is the why."

" 'What is the why,' " Sammy agreed.

"Flattop."

Joe looked up and saw a young man standing in front of them. He was short-waisted and plump, and his face, except for a pair of big black spectacles, was swaddled and all but invisible in an elaborate confection of scarf and hat and earflaps.

105 "Julius," Sammy said. "This is Joe. Joe, this is a friend from the neighborhood, Julie Glovsky."

Joe held out his hand. Julie studied it a moment, then extended his own small hand. He had on a black woolen greatcoat, a fur-lined leather cap with mammoth earflaps, and too-short green corduroy trousers.

"This guy's brother is the one I told you about," Sammy told Joe. "Making good money in comics. What are you doing here?"

Somewhere deep within his wrappings, Julie Glovsky shrugged. "I need to see my brother."

"Isn't that remarkable, we need to see him, too."

110 "Yeah? Why's that?" Julie Glovsky shuddered. "Only tell me fast before my nuts fall off."

"Would that be from cold or, you know, atrophy?"

"Funny."

"I am funny."

"Unfortunately not in the sense of 'humorous.'"

115 "Funny," Sammy said.

"I am funny. What's your idea?"

"Why don't you come to work for me?"

"For you? Doing what? Selling shoestrings? We still got a box of them at my house. My mom uses them to sew up chickens."

"Not shoelaces. My boss, you know, Sheldon Anapol?"

120 "How would I know him?"

"Nevertheless, he is my boss. He's going into business with his brother-in-law, Jack Ashkenazy, who you also do not know, but who publishes *Racy Science, Racy Combat*, et cetera. They're going to do comic books, see, and they're looking for talent."

"What?" Julie poked his tortoise face out from the shadows of its woolen shell. "Do you think they might hire *me*?"

"They will if I tell them to," said Sammy. "Seeing as how I'm the art director in chief."

Joe looked at Sammy and raised an eyebrow. Sammy shrugged.

125 "Joe and I, here, we're putting together the first title right now. It's going to be all adventure heroes. All in costumes," he said, extemporizing

now. "You know, like Superman. Batman. The Blue Beetle. That type of thing."

"Tights, like."

"That's it. Tights. Masks. Big muscles. It's going to be called *Masked Man Comics*," he continued. "Joe and I've got the lead feature all taken care of, but we need backup stuff. Think you could come up with something?"

"Shit, Flattop, yes. You bet."

"What about your brother?"

130   "Sure, he's always looking for more work. They got him doing *Romeo Rabbit* for thirty dollars a week."

"Okay, then, he's hired, too. You're both hired, on one condition."

"What's that?"

"We need a place to work," said Sammy.

"Come on then," said Julie. "I guess we can work at the Rathole." He leaned toward Sammy as they started off, lowering his voice. The tall skinny kid with the big nose had fallen a few steps behind them to light a cigarette. "Who the hell *is* that guy?"

135   "This?" Sammy said. He took hold of the kid's elbow and tugged him forward as though bringing him out onstage to take a deserved bow. He reached up to grab a handful of the kid's hair and gave it a tug, just kind of rocking his head from side to side while holding on to his hair, grinning at him. Had Joe been a young woman, Julie Glovsky might almost have been inclined to think that Sammy was sweet on her. "This is my *partner*."

SUGGESTIONS FOR DISCUSSION

1. Make a list of the superheroes you know about. What are their special powers? What are their attributes? How do they dress? What is their motivation?

2. What problems do Sammy and Joe encounter as they try to create their own original superhero?

3. Roger Ebert begins by saying, "Imagine Superman with a Clark Kent more charismatic than the Man of Steel and you'll understand how *Spider-Man* goes wrong." What is he saying about the choices the screenwriters have made as they created this character for film? Why is it a problem to have a Clark Kent more charismatic than the Man of Steel?

SUGGESTIONS FOR WRITING

1. As they walk and talk, Sammy tells Joe, "How? is not the question. What? is not the question. The question is *why*." To make a superhero that people will care about, Sammy and Joe have to find his motivation. From the list of superheroes you have generated, choose one and write about his motivation. Why does he do what he does? Does his motivation match the motivation of other superheroes you know about? Why might readers or viewers respond to that motivation?

2. In his article about fantasy stories, A.O. Scott writes that the central characters are archetypal, "following a convention so deep it seems to be encoded in the human storytelling gene, orphans summoned out of obscurity to undertake a journey into the heart of evil that will also be a voyage of self-discovery." As *The Amazing Adventures of Kavalier & Clay* continues, Sammy and Joe too create an orphan hero—to fight Hitler and the Nazis. Create a superhero for today. What would he or she look like? What would be the "why?"

3. Choose a film currently popular and write your own review. Pay attention to the story, the characters, and how convincing the acting and the action sequences (if there are action sequences) are. Can you identify what makes this a popular film? Is it the way the story is told? The way it looks? The acting? Does the subject of the movie appeal to a specific audience or age group, or does it have a broader audience appeal? Does the film draw on interests, concerns, fears, or desires that seem current to you? What is your recommendation to classmates? Should they see this movie or pass this one up?

CLASSIC READING

THE GANGSTER AS TRAGIC HERO

Robert Warshow

Robert Warshow was a film critic and one of the first American intellectuals to write seriously about popular culture. The following essay, "The Gangster as Tragic Hero" is taken from his book *The Immediate Experience*, published posthumously in 1962. (Warshow died in 1955.) The essay, though brief, is considered by many to be a classic example of film criticism and cultural analysis. Since the 1950s, when Warshow was writing, any number of gangster films have appeared—*Bonnie and Clyde*, the famous *Godfather* trilogy, *Goodfellas*, a remake of *Scarface* (starring Al Pacino this time), a film version of the TV show *The Untouchables*, black gangster films such as *New Jack City*, and, on television, HBO's series *The Sopranos* continues to draw large and loyal audiences.

SUGGESTION   As you read, keep the title of the essay "The Gangster as Tragic Hero" in mind. Underline and
FOR READING   annotate passages in the essay where Warshow explains what makes gangsters tragic figures.

1   America, as a social and political organization, is committed to a cheerful view of life. It could not be otherwise. The sense of tragedy is a luxury of aristocratic societies, where the fate of the individual is not conceived of as having a direct and legitimate political importance, being determined by a fixed and supra-political—that is, non-controversial—moral order or fate. Modern equalitarian societies, however, whether democratic or authoritarian in their political forms, always base themselves on the claim that they are making life happier; the avowed function of the modern state, at least in its ultimate terms, is not only to regulate social relations, but also to determine the quality and the possibilities of human life in general. Happiness thus becomes the chief political issue—in a sense, the only political issue—and for that reason it can never be treated as an issue at all. If an American or a Russian is unhappy, it implies a certain reprobation of his society, and therefore, by a logic of which we can all recognize the necessity, it becomes an obligation of citizenship to be cheerful; if the authorities find it necessary, the citizen may even be compelled to make a public display of his cheerfulness on important occasions, just as he may be conscripted into the army in time of war.

Naturally, this civic responsibility rests more strongly upon the organs of mass culture. The individual citizen may still be permitted his private unhappiness so long as it does not take on political significance, the extent of this tolerance being determined by how large an area of private life the society can accommodate. But every production of mass culture is a public act and must conform with accepted notions of the public good. Nobody seriously questions the principle that it is the function of mass culture to maintain public morale, and certainly nobody in the mass audience objects to having his morale maintained.[1] At a time when the normal condition of the citizen is a state of anxiety, euphoria spreads over our culture like the broad smile of an idiot. In terms of attitudes towards life, there is very little difference between a "happy" movie like *Good News*, which ignores death and suffering, and a "sad" movie like *A Tree Grows in Brooklyn*, which uses death and suffering as incidents in the service of a higher optimism.

But, whatever its effectiveness as a source of consolation and a means of pressure for maintaining "positive" social attitudes, this optimism is fundamentally satisfying to no one, not even to those who would be most disoriented without its support. Even within the area of mass culture, there always exists a current of opposition, seeking to express by whatever means are available to it that sense of desperation and inevitable failure which optimism itself helps to create. Most often, this opposition is confined to rudimentary or semiliterate forms: in mob politics and journalism, for example, or in certain kinds of religious enthusiasm. When it does enter the field of art, it is likely to be disguised or attenuated: in an unspecific form of expression like jazz, in the basically harmless nihilism of the Marx Brothers, in the continually reasserted strain of hopelessness that often seems to be the real meaning of the soap opera. The gangster film is remarkable in that it fills the need for disguise (though not sufficiently to avoid arousing uneasiness) without requiring any serious distortion. From its beginnings, it has been a consistent and astonishingly complete presentation of the modern sense of tragedy.[2]

In its initial character, the gangster film is simply one example of the movies' constant tendency to create fixed dramatic patterns that can be repeated indefinitely with a reasonable expectation of profit. One gangster film follows another as one musical or one Western follows another. But this rigidity is not necessarily opposed to the requirements of art. There have been very successful types of art in the past which developed such specific and detailed conventions as almost to make individual examples of the type interchangeable. This is true, for example, of Elizabethan revenge tragedy and Restoration comedy.

5   For such a type to be successful means that its conventions have imposed themselves upon the general consciousness and become the accepted vehicles of a particular set of attitudes and a particular aesthetic effect. One goes to any individual example of the type with very definite expectations, and originality is to be welcomed only in the degree that it intensifies the expected experience without fundamentally altering it. Moreover, the relationship between the conventions which go to make up such a type and the real experience of its audience or the real facts

of whatever situation it pretends to describe is of only secondary importance and does not determine its aesthetic force. It is only in an ultimate sense that the type appeals to its audience's experience of reality; much more immediately, it appeals to previous experience of the type itself: it creates its own field of reference.

Thus the importance of the gangster film, and the nature and intensity of its emotional and aesthetic impact, cannot be measured in terms of the place of the gangster himself or the importance of the problem of crime in American life. Those European movie-goers who think there is a gangster on every corner in New York are certainly deceived, but defenders of the "positive" side of American culture are equally deceived if they think it relevant to point out that most Americans have never seen a gangster. What matters is that the experience of the gangster *as an experience of art* is universal to Americans. There is almost nothing we understand better or react to more readily or with quicker intelligence. The Western film, though it seems never to diminish in popularity, is for most of us no more than the folklore of the past, familiar and understandable only because it has been repeated so often. The gangster film comes much closer. In ways that we do not easily or willingly define, the gangster speaks for us, expressing that part of the American psyche which rejects the qualities and the demands of modern life, which rejects "Americanism" itself.

The gangster is the man of the city, with the city's language and knowledge, with its queer and dishonest skills and its terrible daring, carrying his life in his hands like a placard, like a club. For everyone else, there is at least the theoretical possibility of another world—in that happier American culture which the gangster denies, the city does not really exist; it is only a more crowded and more brightly lit country—but for the gangster there is only the city; he must inhabit it in order to personify it: not the real city, but that dangerous and sad city of the imagination which is so much more important, which is the modern world. And the gangster—

though there are real gangsters—is also, and primarily, a creature of the imagination. The real city, one might say, produces only criminals; the imaginary city produces the gangster: he is what we want to be and what we are afraid we may become.

Thrown into the crowd without background or advantages, with only those ambiguous skills which the rest of us—the real people of the real city—can only pretend to have, the gangster is required to make his way, to make his life and impose it on others. Usually, when we come upon him, he has already made his choice or the choice has already been made for him, it doesn't matter which: we are not permitted to ask whether at some point he could have chosen to be something else than what he is.

The gangster's activity is actually a form of rational enterprise, involving fairly definite goals and various techniques for achieving them. But this rationality is usually no more than a vague background; we know, perhaps, that the gangster sells liquor or that he operates a numbers racket; often we are not given even that much information. So his activity becomes a kind of pure criminality: he hurts people. Certainly our response to the gangster film is most consistently and most universally a response to sadism; we gain the double satisfaction of participating vicariously in the gangster's sadism and then seeing it turned against the gangster himself.

10   But on another level the quality of irrational brutality and the quality of rational enterprise become one. Since we do not see the rational and routine aspects of the gangster's behavior, the practice of brutality—the quality of unmixed criminality—becomes the totality of his career. At the same time, we are always conscious that the whole meaning of this career is a drive for success: the typical gangster film presents a steady upward progress followed by a very precipitate fall. Thus brutality itself becomes at once the means to success and the content of success—a success that is defined in its most general terms, not as accomplishment or specific gain, but simply as the unlimited possibility of aggression. (In the same way, film presentations of businessmen tend to make it appear that they achieve their success by talking on the telephone and holding conferences and that success *is* talking on the telephone and holding conferences.)

From this point of view, the initial contact between the film and its audience is an agreed conception of human life: that man is a being with the possibilities of success or failure. This principal, too, belongs to the city; one must emerge from the crowd or else one is nothing. On that basis, the necessity of the action is established, and it progresses by inalterable paths to the point where the gangster lies dead and the principal has been modified: there is really only one possibility—failure. The final meaning of the city is anonymity and death.

In the opening scene of *Scarface,* we are shown a successful man; we know he is successful because he has just given a party of opulent proportions and because he is called Big Louie. Through some monstrous lack of caution, he permits himself to be alone for a few moments. We understand from this immediately that he is about to be killed. No convention of the gangster film is more strongly established than this: it is dangerous to be alone. And yet the very conditions of success make it impossible not to be alone, for success is always the establishment of an *individual* preeminence that must be imposed on others, in whom it automatically arouses hatred; the successful man is an outlaw. The gangster's whole life is an effort to assert himself as an individual, to draw himself out of the crowd, and he always dies *because* he is an individual; the final bullet thrusts him back, makes him, after all, a failure. "Mother of God," says the dying Little Caesar, "Is this the end of Rico?"—speaking of himself thus in the third person because what has been brought low is not the undifferentiated *man,* but the individual with a name, the gangster, the success; even to himself he is a creature of the imagination. (T. S. Eliot has pointed out that a number of Shakespeare's tragic heroes have this trick of looking at themselves dramatically; their true identify, the thing that is destroyed when they die, is something outside themselves—not a man, but a style of life, a kind of meaning.)

At bottom, the gangster is doomed because he is under the obligation to succeed, not because the means he employs are unlawful. In the deeper layers of the modern consciousness, *all* means are unlawful, every attempt to succeed is an act of aggression, leaving one alone and guilty and defenseless among enemies: one is *punished* for success. This is our intolerable dilemma: that failure is a kind of death and success is evil and dangerous, is—ultimately—impossible. The effect of the gangster film is to embody this dilemma in the person of the gangster and resolve it by his death. The dilemma is resolved because it is *his* death, not ours. We are safe; for the moment, we can acquiesce in our failure, we can choose to fail.

NOTES

1. In her testimony before the House Committee on Un-American Activities, Mrs. Leila Rogers said that the movie *None But the Lonely Heart* was un-American because it was gloomy. Like so much else that was said during the unhappy investigation of Hollywood, this statement was at once stupid and illuminating. One knew immediately what Mrs. Rogers was talking about; she had simply been insensitive enough to carry her philistinism to its conclusion.

2. Efforts have been made from time to time to bring the gangster film into line with the prevailing optimism and social constructiveness of our culture; *Kiss of Death* is a recent example. These efforts are usually unsuccessful; the reasons for their lack of success are interesting in themselves, but I shall not be able to discuss them here.

SUGGESTIONS FOR DISCUSSION

1. Warshow says that the gangster film is "a consistent and astonishingly complete presentation of the modern sense of tragedy." What does Warshow mean by tragedy here? In what sense are gangster films tragic? Pick a gangster film or two that you are familiar with and see if they fit Warshow's definition of tragedy. Does Warshow's definition hold? How might it be updated?

2. Warshow says that for the gangster, "the whole meaning of [his] career is a drive for success." What does he mean by this statement? What does "success" mean in this context? What do gangster films have to tell about the American dream of success?

3. Warshow begins the essay by saying that "it is the function of mass culture to maintain public morale" and to "conform with accepted notions of public good." Think about some of the movies you have seen recently. To what extent does Warshow's statement seem valid? Consider the benefits and limits of America's commitment to what Warshow calls "a cheerful view of life."

SUGGESTIONS FOR WRITING

1. According to Warshow, gangsters are more attractive figures than the "good guys." Why is this so? Write an essay that explains why the gangster—or any other hero who lives outside the law—is such a popular figure in the American imagination.

2. Use Warshow's definition of tragedy to analyze a film or TV show featuring the gangster as a tragic hero.

3. Think of other films besides gangster movies that have a tragic ending for the main character or characters (such as *Titanic, American Beauty, Vanilla Sky,* or *American History X*). Pick one whose tragic end represents something interesting and important about the limits of American culture. Write an essay that explains the tragedy in the film. What were the main character or characters striving to do? Why was their tragic end inevitable? What does this tragic end tell about American culture?

Composing a Visual Narrative

Although storytelling is usually considered to be an oral or written form, people have been telling stories with pictures—making visual narratives—since ancient times. Prehistoric cave paintings tell hunting stories or detail rituals. Medieval church murals narrate the lives of saints. Even today, many modes of telling stories are visual ones. Obviously, television and film carry much of the story through pictures. But still pictures arranged in sequence—cartoons, comic books, children's books, and much print advertisement—depend on visual sequence and arrangement to move the narrative (the story) along.

In this section, pay attention to how a story can be told using pictures in sequence so that you can make a visual narrative of your own. As a starting point, look closely at these scenes from Jacob Lawrence's visual biography of Harriet Tubman.

Jacob Lawrence and the Harriet Tubman Series

Between 1938 and 1940, Jacob Lawrence (1917–2000) told the biographies of anti-slavery activists Frederick Douglass and Harriet Tubman in a series of paintings. By arranging key scenes of his subjects' lives in sequence, Lawrence was able to tell entire stories using individual paintings with brief captions. Today, Lawrence's series paintings are considered great works of American art and crucial stories that preserve the history of African American struggles for freedom.

Pages 348–349 show four of the thirty-one prints from the Tubman series to give you an indication of how story painting in a series works. The entire series is available both in print (Ellen Harkins West, *Jacob Lawrence: The Frederick Douglass and Harriet Tubman Series of 1938–40*) and at several Web sites, including the Whitney Museum site (http://www.whitney.org) and the Jacob Lawrence virtual archive (http://www.jacoblawrence.org).

In the thirty-one paintings and captions that make up the Tubman series, Lawrence told the story of Harriet Tubman's slavery, her escape to the North, her role as a conductor in the Underground Railroad, and her influence as a powerful abolitionist speaker.

Notice that this visual narrative does not entirely exclude words, but the words are set in short captions meant to give a viewer a quick way of telling what part of the story the scene is about. Captions can play more roles than one in a visual narrative. Frequently, as in the scenes reproduced here, the captions describe what is in the image. Sometimes, however, the captions are more general to set up the story's theme.

Jacob Lawrence's Harriet Tubman series uses both kinds of captions. The captions that accompany the first three paintings of the series tell the viewer what Harriet Tubman's life story meant to the antislavery movement. They include remarks about the slave trade made by statesmen and abolitionists of Tubman's time. For example, the caption for the third painting is Abraham Lincoln's statement, "A house divided against itself cannot stand." By opening his series with these core statements about slavery, Lawrence reminds viewers that this story is about more than Harriet Tubman. It is about a battle to abolish slavery and to establish equality in this country.

Remember, though, that most captions simply help a viewer follow the events of a story by identifying what is going on in the image, as is the case in the captions that accompany the paintings reproduced here.

The scenes reproduced here represent four moments in Tubman's life and career.

10. "Harriet Tubman was between twenty and twenty-five years of age at the time of her escape. She was now alone. She turned her face toward the North, and fixing her eyes on the guiding star, she started on her long, lonely journey."

The Life of Harriet Tubman, no. 10 by Jacob Lawrence. Artwork copyright 2003 Gwendolyn Knight Lawrence, courtesy of the Jacob and Gwendolyn Lawrence Foundation. Hampton University Museum, Hampton, Virginia.

12. "Night after night, Harriet Tubman traveled, occasionally stopping to buy bread. She crouched behind trees or lay concealed in swamps by day until she reached the North."

The Life of Harriet Tubman, no. 12 by Jacob Lawrence. Artwork copyright 2003 Gwendolyn Knight Lawrence, courtesy of the Jacob and Gwendolyn Lawrence Foundation. Hampton University Museum, Hampton, Virginia.

19. "Such a terror did she become to the slaveholders that a reward of $40,000 was offered for her head, she was so bold, daring, and elusive."

The Life of Harriet Tubman, no. 19 by Jacob Lawrence. Artwork copyright 2003 Gwendolyn Knight Lawrence, courtesy of the Jacob and Gwendolyn Lawrence Foundation. Hampton University Museum, Hampton, Virginia.

21. "Every antislavery convention held within 500 miles of Harriet Tubman found her at the meeting. She spoke in words that brought tears to the eyes and sorrow to the hearts of all who heard her speak of the suffering of her people."

The Life of Harriet Tubman, no. 21 by Jacob Lawrence. Artwork copyright 2003 Gwendolyn Knight Lawrence, courtesy of the Jacob and Gwendolyn Lawrence Foundation. Hampton University Museum, Hampton, Virginia.

SUGGESTIONS FOR DISCUSSION

1. The basis of all visual sequencing is the reader's ability to connect the actions or characters of one image to the actions or characters of the image that follows it. That is how comics tell stories. If a character is shown in one panel with his hand on a doorknob and in the next greeting someone at an open door, we assume the character opened the door to find this visitor on the other side. We don't see the door open, but the logic of the sequence tells us what the action is.

   Look carefully at the sequence of paintings reproduced from Lawrence's *Tubman* series. Discuss with a group of your classmates what part of Harriet Tubman's story this visual sequence narrates. What in the visuals and their captions helps you read the story? Would the story read the same if you began, say, with the painting of Tubman speaking to an abolitionist convention? Does the size of the Tubman figure in the painting tell you anything about this woman? When is she smallest? What might it suggest when she takes up most of the picture?

2. How much of the story of Harriet Tubman do you already know? How does that previous knowledge help you read this visual narrative? How do these paintings of Harriet Tubman change or add to your knowledge of Harriet Tubman, the Underground Railroad, or the abolitionist movement?

3. What is the relationship between the captions and the images? How much of a story would you get if you just had the captions? How much of the story would you understand if you had no captions? What do the pictures add to the information in the captions?

SUGGESTED ASSIGNMENT

Create your own visual narrative. You do not have to be an artist to make a visual narrative. Use computer programs such as PowerPoint to arrange clip art, use photographs arranged in a sequence, cut images from magazines, or make your own drawings or paintings that you arrange in a sequence to tell a story.

To get started on your visual narrative, try following these steps:

- **Choose a story** that you can tell in pictures. Remember that, for this story, your classmates are your audience, so choose a story they know. It can be from history, of a famous person, a familiar story or poem—such as something from Edgar Allan Poe. It could even be one of the Urban Legends you read about earlier in this chapter. ("The Killer in the Backseat" would make a good visual narrative, for example.) The story can be funny or serious.

- **Write your story down.** Write down the basics of your story. Make sure you write out the parts of the story that interest you the most and that you believe will interest others.

- **Make a list of the key scenes in your story**. Your visual narrative cannot tell every detail in the story, so you have to decide which parts of the story make for good visual narration. What can you show? Decide on the number of scenes (Lawrence often painted more than thirty). Choose scenes that are crucial for telling the story and that have good potential for visual impact.

- **Arrange your scenes**. On a piece of paper (or in a computer program with storyboard capabilities), make a storyboard such as the storyboard reproduced on page 351. Fill your storyboard in with general sketches or notes on what scenes must go in each space. Sequencing is important in the way you tell your story, so pay attention the order of your scenes.

Lawrence arranged his images so that his series has a beginning, a middle, and an end. He also repeated certain colors, shapes, textures, and patterns that hold the series together so that they are clearly all a part of the same story. Make sure that your sequence makes sense and the images relate to one another.

Linear Storyboard

- **Complete your story and present it to classmates**. Lawrence used both words and images to tell his story. Do the same by using titles or captions. Just make sure that whatever words you use help your readers follow the story but don't take the story over.

FIELDWORK   Writing a Questionnaire

Everyone has strong preferences when it comes to what they like to read, what they hate, what they think is too sappy or gory or outright boring. And, since everyone knows what they like and why they like it, it's often difficult to imagine other people's preferences. Who reads those romance novels? What is the audience for cyberfiction? Does anybody, outside of English teachers and the students they force to, really still read *Silas Marner*? For pleasure?

One way to find out what people like to read is, quite simply, to ask them. For this assignment, you will be doing just that by designing and distributing a questionnaire that asks people what they read for pleasure and how their reading tastes have changed over the years.

Design this questionnaire on your own, with a small group of classmates, or as an entire class. If you do it on your own, try to get fifteen to twenty-five responses. If you work with a small group, each person should get ten responses to compile a fairly large sampling. If the entire class uses the same questionnaire, each person can get ten responses and have a substantial amount of information to sort through.

Even if you have only twenty-five responses to your questionnaire, you will have more than your own and your classmates' impressions from which to draw. That kind of information can help you broaden your own response and begin to account for the differences as well as the similarities that you see around you.

SUGGESTIONS FOR DESIGNING A QUESTIONNAIRE

1. *Make it brief and readable.* It is best to put your questionnaire on one side of a page. The simpler it seems to your audience members, the more likely they will be to it. Make it readable as well. Don't try to crowd too many questions on the page or make instructions complicated. There should be plenty of white space, and the language should be simple and direct.

2. *Write different kinds of questions to get different kinds of answers.* The kind of questions that you ask will determine the kind of information that you receive. If you ask questions that can be answered with a yes or a no, then you will likely get more responses but less specific information. If you ask people to write quite a bit, you won't get as many participants and might have trouble summarizing your findings.

3. *Decide who will answer your questionnaire.* If you want to know what a certain age group is reading—middle school or high school or college age students, for example, target that audience.

   You might, however, want to know what older adults are reading and how their reading interests have changed over the years.

   Or you might want to know what women read or what men read.

   You could also ask about a certain kind of reading. Stephen King says that people love a good scare, but not everyone does, just as not everyone is fond of romance novels or stories about superheroes or fantasy and science fiction. You can create one kind of questionnaire to focus on a particular kind of story—such as science fiction—and try to get at what it is in those stories that appeals to the audience.

It's probably best that you decide as a class or as a group what information you hope to get from your questionnaire. The sample questionnaire below is adapted from Janice Radway's *Reading the Romance*, a study of women whose favorite reading for pleasure is the romance novel.

Sample Questionnaire

1. At what age did you begin reading for pleasure?
   a. ____ 5–10
   b. ____ 11–20
   c. ____ 21–30
   d. ____ 30 or above

2. Age today:
   a. ____ 18–21
   b. ____ 22–30
   c. ____ 30–45
   d. ____ 45–55
   e. ____ over 55

3. What kinds of books did you read for pleasure when you were a teenager?
   a. ____ biography
   b. ____ historical fiction
   c. ____ romances
   d. ____ westerns
   e. ____ mysteries
   f. ____ comic books
   g. ____ sports stories
   h. ____ other (specify)

4. What kind of book do you read for pleasure now?
   a. ____ biography
   b. ____ historical fiction
   c. ____ romances
   d. ____ westerns
   e. ____ mysteries
   f. ____ comic books
   g. ____ sports stories
   h. ____ other (specify)

5. What kinds of books do you never read for pleasure?
   a. ____ biography
   b. ____ historical fiction
   c. ____ romances
   d. ____ westerns
   e. ____ mysteries
   f. ____ comic books
   g. ____ sports stories
   h. ____ other (specify)

6. What book or story have you read most recently for pleasure?

Remember that your questionnaire should be designed to answer the questions you and your classmates have about reading for pleasure. Some or all of these questions might be useful, but be sure to target your audience, decide on what you want to know, and ask questions that can get at that information.

Report on Your Findings

Once you have completed your questionnaire, report your findings to the rest of the class. Write a report, give a presentation, or design a chart or graph that visually illustrates your findings.

1. Urban legends are no longer simply a matter of word of mouth. New technologies—cellular phones, fax machines, and the World Wide Web—are providing people with new means to circulate stories. In his book *The Baby Train* (1993), Jan Harold Brunvand traces the twists added by the new technologies to an urban legend about someone waking up in a hotel room only to discover that one of his or her kidneys has been carved out to be sold on the black market for transplant. The setting and characters change in the various accounts. In one version, a female tourist wakes up in a tub of ice in a third-rate hotel in Mexico to find one kidney missing. In another, a fraternity boy vacationing in Manhattan awakens from a night of debauchery with a fresh surgical wound on his back. In still another, a salesman is drugged in a New Orleans bar and wakes up minus one kidney.

   The "Urban Legends Reference Page" at http://www.snopes.com has become a prime source of such tales. It has not only urban legends such as the kidney-snatching one but also testimonials to their validity that claim the story really happened to a friend or friend of a friend. It also has a link to 9/11 rumors, some of which you may have heard. Visit the "Urban Legends Reference Page," choose a story that you recognize, and report back to your class on how it has been modified as it continues to circulate.

2. Television has been, from its earliest days, a source of popular stories. Soap operas and continuing dramas such as *The Sopranos*, *Six Feet Under*, and *24* keep their audiences because viewers want to know what will happen next to their favorite characters. Sometimes audiences actually want to participate in shaping these stories. Search on the Web for a television show and find any fan sites that allow fans either to comment on the events in the story or to suggest plots of their own. Most soap operas such as *All My Children* and *Days of Our Lives* have inspired such sites. Report back to your classmates on what fans say. What do they object to in current story lines? What do they want to happen? If they have an opportunity to retell the story themselves, what changes do they make?

3. As Janet Murray writes in *Hamlet on the Holodeck: The Future of Narrative in Cyber Space*, access to spaces for participating in storytelling has changed considerably with digital technology. Today you will find several sites devoted to interactive storytelling—sites where you help create a story begun by others or begin a story for others to help you create. Just enter "storytelling" into your search engine. Sites such as http://www.storycenter.org or http://www.storynet.org also lead you to interactive storytelling sites. Go to one of these sites to participate in shaping characters or developing the narrative and bring the narrative back to your classmates to get their responses. How would they have added to the story? What characters might they add? Use this activity as the core of a discussion about the nature of interactive storytelling.

Comic Strips and Comic Books

Comic strips started to appear in daily newspapers and the Sunday papers in the late 1890s and early 1900s, establishing a new medium of storytelling that brings together three key ingredients: a narrative sequence of pictures, speech balloons, and a regular cast of characters. The Yellow Kid (1895)—a bald, gap-toothed street urchin dressed in a yellow nightshirt—became the first comic-strip celebrity, followed by the Katzenjammer Kids (1897), Happy Hooligan (1900), Mutt and Jeff (1907), and Krazy Kat (1910).

Examples of these early joke-a-day gag strips that anticipate Pogo (1949), Peanuts (1950), Doonesbury (1970), Cathy (1976), and Dilbert (1989) are in Robert C. Harvey's books, *The Art of the Funnies: An Aesthetic History* (1994) and *Children of the Yellow Kid: The Evolution of the American Comic Strip* (1998). The Web site Krazy Kat Daily Strips at rrnet.com/-nakamura/soba/kat/day/ contains thirty enlargements of Krazy Kat strips. As you look at old comic strips, consider how the narrative sequencing from panel to panel sets up the humor and how cartooning styles give the characters their particular identities.

You can also find examples in Harvey's two books of detective and adventure themes in comic strips such as Dick Tracy (1931), Terry and the Pirates (1934), Prince Valiant (1937), and Steve Canyon (1947), as well as domestic sitcoms such as Bringing Up Father (1913), Gasoline Alley (1918), Little Orphan Annie (1924), and Blondie (1930).

In the 1930s, the narrative techniques of the comic strip found a new outlet in comic books. In 1938, Superman—the first of the great comic-book heroes—made his appearance, followed quickly by Batman, Green Lantern, Wonder Woman, Captain America, and Plastic Man. You can find examples of these superheroes in Jules Feiffer's *The Great Comic Book Heroes* (1965) and Robert C. Harvey's *The Art of the Comic Book: An Aesthetic History* (1996). Comic books offer opportunities to think about how the integration of the visual and the verbal has created new narrative possibilities in graphic storytelling.

Superman and all related elements are trademarks of DC Comics. ©1939 DC Comics. All Rights Reserved. Used with Permission.

CHAPTER 8 Work

Never leave that to tomorrow, which you can do today.
>   —Benjamin Franklin, *Poor Richard's Almanac*

I'm goin'...where they hung the jerk who invented work on the Big Rock Candy Mountain.
>   —Harry McClintock

Lewis W. Hine, Courtesy George Eastman House

Historically, Americans have had a love/hate relationship with their jobs. That may be due partially to something typically called the "Protestant work ethic," a philosophy of living that has formed a part of this nation's character from the first European settlements. According to this ethic, "Idle hands are the devil's workshop." The contrast between fruitful labor and wasteful leisure is one the Puritans brought with them as they traveled to the New World to explore and to settle in this country. Its message is a simple (and simplistic) one: Success is the reward for diligence. Failure is the consequence of idleness.

Of course, success and failure are never so easily explained away, but a cultural myth—even one as readily dispelled as this one—is difficult to ignore. For many American workers, getting a good job and keeping it is a measure of success. Losing it, for whatever reason, means failure. Workers who lose their jobs might well have been fired through no fault of their own, but the suspicion often remains that those let go somehow deserved dismissal.

Our identities are formed, in many respects, by the jobs that we hold or want to hold. From the time children start school, parents and teachers ask them what they want to be when they grow up. By adulthood, we are expected to have a "career"— a job that will support a family, provide opportunities for professional advancement, buy leisure time, perhaps contribute to community well-being, signal status, and be fulfilling, all at once.

Even though many workers know that their jobs are subject to the whims of the marketplace, researchers are finding that the workplace has become a sanctuary from the tensions of home life, or a second neighborhood where friendships are forged, jokes are traded, and identities are formed. Work as a home away from home continues to be a popular theme for television series that place sitcoms and dramas— shows such as *ER, NYPD Blue,* or *Scrubs*—in what has been called the "work–family" setting. On television, the work–family is a group of people in the workplace who substitute for the home family. When, for example, *NYPD Blue*'s perpetually cranky cop Sippowitz lost his original partner because the actor playing the role wanted to move from television to film, audiences were much more concerned than when Sippowitz's on-screen wife suddenly disappeared from the storyline. At least in part, that reaction indicates that while Sippowitz's work–family involves intense drama and ongoing action, his home life is pretty boring. The work–family setting is a formula that began with the old *Mary Tyler Moore Show* and has grown in popularity ever since. That these work–family shows are so popular might indicate some of the public's fascination with and hopes for the world of work.

Work has historically been a site of struggle as well as a home away from home. Management and labor have often been at odds over such issues as the forty-hour week, the minimum wage, child labor regulations, health and safety issues, and the rights of workers to organize. Disputes that may have been settled for American workers in the first half of the twentieth century have now reemerged as global struggles, with companies outsourcing their labor to countries where sweatshop conditions are commonplace. In the past decade, consumers have begun to demand more information about where their clothing is made and under what conditions it was produced. That may be why Students United Against Sweatshops has become the fastest growing, most powerful campus movement since sixties protests. This grassroots opposition to sweatshops indicates that American students care very much about working conditions both inside and outside their country's borders.

Reading Work

As you read, talk, and write about work, you will be asked to pay attention to how the writers excerpted here voice their concerns about the state of their own workplace or the fairness of wages, working conditions, and advancement. The selections in this chapter represent the good and bad experiences of working and the ongoing battles for a living wage for all workers.

The chapter opens with Sandra Cisneros's "The First Job," a story about a young woman experiencing the work world for the first time. Cisneros's story might prompt you to think about your own first expectations of the workplace and the times that you did not understand interactions with others or even the basic routine of the job you had been assigned. It is followed by an excerpt from Scott Adams's satire on office work, *The Dilbert Principle*. Adams's humor suggests that much of the world of work is a daily encounter with the absurd. In his piece, Adams explains how he created the cartoon character Dilbert, who continues to be one of the most popular commentators on the bureaucracy of office life.

The next selection asks you to reconsider what work and the workplace have come to mean in a high-technology, work-oriented culture. In fact, many workers choose to spend more and more time at work because they simply feel more "at home" there than they do in their own homes. At least that is what Arlie Russell Hochschild discovered when she interviewed workers for her article "Work: The Great Escape."

The next set of articles moves away from individual stories to broader discussions of economic politics. Barbara Ehrenreich's "Nickel-and-Dimed: On (Not) Getting By in America" recounts her experiment living on the wages of a minimum-wage job, throwing into question the reported success of welfare reform policies. Then a Perspectives feature on sweatshops pairs Nicholas Kristof and Sheryl WuDunn's "Two Cheers for Sweatshops" and Tom Hayden and Charles Kernaghan's "Pennies an Hour and No Way Up." Kristof and WuDunn argue that to boycott clothing made at sweatshops is to eliminate much needed jobs in developing countries. Hayden and Kernaghan counter by attacking the assumption that extremely low wages are not a problem in developing countries.

The Classic Reading is Tillie Olsen's short story "I Stand Here Ironing." In it, Olsen writes powerfully of the dilemma so many mothers—especially single mothers—face when hard economic times force them to work any job that can support their family even though that might mean neglecting the emotional needs of children left to be tended by others.

Throughout this chapter, you will be asked to think and write about the role that work plays in this culture. You will need to think about your own work experiences, how work has been represented in this culture, how workers have interpreted their own work environments, and what can be learned by researching current labor and marketplace issues.

Work, as you will see, is rarely just as simple as a place to go to earn a paycheck. Workers' identities are often tied to the work that they do or the work that they would like to do. We may not continue to believe in the simple logic of the Protestant work ethic, but this is a culture concerned at some level with the dignity of work. It is that concern for dignity and fair play that comes into nearly every discussion about work.

THE FIRST JOB

Sandra Cisneros

Sanda Cisneros was born in Chicago, the daughter of a Mexican father and a Mexican American mother. She has been a poet in the schools, a teacher for high school dropouts, and an arts administrator. Cisneros is the author of *My Wicked Ways* (1987), a volume of poetry; two collections of short stories: *The House on Mango Street* (1985), from which the following selection has been excerpted; *Woman Hollering Creek* (1991); and the novel *Caramelo* (2002).

SUGGESTION FOR READING   Write a brief description of a time when you found yourself in a situation that was uncomfortable—a place where you did not know what to expect. After you have read Cisneros's story, use your own memory piece to help you focus on what the event that she writes of means to you.

1   It wasn't as if I didn't want to work. I did. I had even gone to the social security office the month before to get my social security number. I needed money. The Catholic high school cost a lot, and Papa said nobody went to public school unless you wanted to turn out bad. I thought I'd find an easy job, the kind other kids had, working in the dime store or maybe a hotdog stand. And though I hadn't started looking yet, I thought I might the week after next. But when I came home that afternoon, all wet because Tito had pushed me into the open water hydrant—only I had sort of let him—Mama called me in the kitchen before I could even go and change, and Aunt Lala was sitting there drinking her coffee with a spoon. Aunt Lala said she had found a job for me at the Peter Pan Photo Finishers on North Broadway where she worked and how old was I and to show up tomorrow saying I was one year older and that was that.

So the next morning I put on the navy blue dress that made me look older and borrowed money for lunch and bus fare because Aunt Lala said I wouldn't get paid 'til the next Friday and I went in and saw the boss of the Peter Pan Photo Finishers on North Broadway where Aunt Lala worked and lied about my age like she told me to and sure enough I started that same day.

In my job I had to wear white gloves. I was supposed to match negatives with their prints, just look at the picture and look for the same one on the negative strip, put it in the envelope, and do the next one. That's all. I didn't know where these envelopes were coming from or where they were going. I just did what I was told.

It was real easy and I guess I wouldn't have minded it except that you got tired after a while and I didn't know if I could sit down or not, and then I started sitting down only when the two ladies next to me did. After a while they started to laugh and came up to me and said I could sit when I wanted to and I said I knew.

5   When lunch time came I was scared to eat alone in the company lunchroom with all those men and ladies looking, so I ate real fast standing in one of the washroom stalls and had lots of time left over so I went back to work early. But then break time came and not knowing where else to go I went into the coatroom because there was a bench there.

I guess it was time for the night shift or middle shift to arrive because a few people came in and punched the time clock and an older Oriental man said hello and we talked for a while about my just starting and he said we could be friends and next time to go in the lunchroom and sit with him and I felt better. He had nice eyes and I didn't feel so nervous anymore. Then he asked if I knew what day it was and when I said I didn't he said it was his birthday and would I please give him a birthday kiss. I thought I would because he was so old and just as I was about to put my lips on his cheek, he grabs my face with both hands and kisses me hard on the mouth and doesn't let go.

SUGGESTIONS FOR DISCUSSION

1. Why does the narrator say, "It wasn't as if I didn't want to work"? How would you describe her motivations for getting a job, and how would you explain the situation in which she finds herself?

2. Compare the event that you wrote about before you read this story with the events that your classmates wrote about. Do they have anything in common with what the narrator experienced? How typical do you think an experience like hers is?

3. Why do you think the older man thought he could get away with his actions? Would anything comparable to this have happened to her had she been a young man?

SUGGESTIONS FOR WRITING

1. As a reader, you may understand or relate to stories because they touch upon something that you already have experienced or an emotion that you have felt. Cisneros's story about a young woman's first day on a new job describes a brief and confusing encounter with an adult world of which she had no prior knowledge. In an exploratory piece of writing, examine the narrator's response to this world of work and human interaction using your own experiences in the working world or in situations that seemed out of your control. Even if you have experienced nothing like this, you probably have a reaction to or an understanding of how the young woman in this story felt. Use this writing to explain that reaction and how you think it is evoked in the story.

2. Reread Cisneros and notice how abruptly Cisneros's story ends and especially how the attitude of the narrator shifts so suddenly in that last paragraph. Write an explanation of how that sudden shift changes the story. How does that ending affect the way that you understand what this story is about?

3. Tell a story about one of the first jobs you ever held (whether it was a paying job or just some new responsibility that you were asked to take on in the family, the community, your peer group, an organization, or for school or church). Try to convey what the job meant to you and how you did or didn't fit into this new world. Choose a moment that sticks with you because it seemed to represent your entire experience with the world of work or the world of adults. In preparation for this writing, spend some time listing jobs you did and jotting memories of people, places, and events connected to those jobs. Notice how Cisneros manages to tell a great deal about why she began working, about the workplace, and about the event that concludes this story in a short piece of writing. Before you begin composing your story, reread Cisneros to see how the form of her narrative might help you to plan your own.

THE DILBERT PRINCIPLE

Scott Adams

Scott Adams received his MBA from the University of California at Berkeley and worked for several years in a cubicle in the offices of Pacific Bell in northern California before he quit to devote all his time to the Dilbert comic strip. The article included here originally appeared in the *Wall Street Journal* on May 22, 1995. It got a huge response, which led to the publication of Adams's book of the same title. In August 1996, *Newsweek* published a cover story on Adams and his newly published book, *The Dilbert Principle,* reporting that the comic character had moved "from cult status to mass phenomenon," as *The Dilbert Principle* moved to number one on the *New York Times* bestseller list shortly after it was published. Office workers all over the United States were clipping Dilbert strips because Dilbert's office life seemed so much like their own. That closeness to reality is partially due to the fact that Adams gets many of his ideas from readers who send him stories of their workplaces via e-mail.

SUGGESTION FOR READING   When you read this piece, you may have to remind yourself that, though there is much in it that strikes office workers as real, its purpose is to be humorous. Some might call it serious humor, but it is humor nonetheless. Humor (especially satire) historically has been one way to comment on the shortcomings of modern society. Take note of places that strike you as funny but painfully true.

1   I use a lot of "bad boss" themes in my syndicated cartoon strip "Dilbert." I'll never run out of material. I get at least two hundred e-mail messages a day, mostly from people who are complaining about their own clueless managers. Here are some of my favorite stories, all allegedly true:

- A vice president insists that the company's new battery-powered product be equipped with a light that comes on to tell you when the power is off.
- An employee suggests setting priorities so the company will know how to apply its limited resources. The manager's response: "Why can't we concentrate our resources across the board?"
- A manager wants to find and fix software bugs more quickly. He offers an incentive plan: $20 for each bug the Quality Assurance people find and $20 for each bug the programmers fix. (These are the same programmers who create the bugs.) Result: An underground economy in "bugs" springs up instantly. The plan is rethought after one employee nets $1,700 the first week.

Stories like these prompted me to do the first annual Dilbert Survey to find out what management practices were most annoying to employees. The choices included the usual suspects: Quality, Empowerment, Reengineering, and the like. But the number-one vote-getter in this highly unscientific survey was "Idiots Promoted to Management."

This seemed like a subtle change from the old concept by which capable workers were promoted until they reached their level of incompetence—best described as the "Peter Principle." Now, apparently, the incompetent workers are promoted directly to management without ever passing through the temporary competence stage.

When I entered the workforce in 1979, the Peter Principle described management pretty well. Now I think we'd all like to return to those Golden Years when you had a boss who was once good at something.

5   I get all nostalgic when I think about it. Back then, we all had hopes of being promoted beyond our levels of competence. Every worker had a shot at someday personally navigating the company into the tar pits while reaping large bonuses and stock options. It was a time when inflation meant everybody got an annual raise; a time when we freely admitted that the customers didn't matter. It was a time of joy.

We didn't appreciate it then, but the much underrated Peter Principle always provided us with a boss who understood what we did for a living. Granted, he made consistently bad decisions—after all he had no management skills. But at least they were the informed decisions of a seasoned veteran from the trenches.

EXAMPLE

Boss: "When I had your job I could drive a three-inch rod through a metal casing with one motion. If you're late again I'll do the same thing to your head."

Nitpickers found lots of problems with the Peter Principle, but on the whole it worked. Lately, however, the Peter Principle has given way to the "Dilbert Principle." The basic concept of the Dilbert Principle is that the most ineffective workers are systematically moved to the place where they can do the least damage: management.

This has not proved to be the winning strategy that you might think.

10   Maybe we should learn something from nature. In the wild, the weakest moose is hunted down and killed by dingo dogs, thus ensuring survival of the fittest. This is a harsh system—especially for the dingo dogs who have to fly all the way from Australia. But nature's process is a good one; everybody agrees, except perhaps for the dingo dogs and the moose in question…and the flight attendants. But the point is that we'd

all be better off if the least competent managers were being eaten by dingo dogs instead of writing Mission Statements.

It seems as if we've turned nature's rules upside down. We systematically identify and promote the people who have the least skills. The usual business rationalization for promoting idiots (the Dilbert Principle in a nutshell) is something along the lines of "Well, he can't write code, he can't design a network, and he doesn't have any sales skill. But he has very good hair..."

If nature started organizing itself like a modern business, you'd see, for example, a band of mountain gorillas led by an "alpha" squirrel. And it wouldn't be the most skilled squirrel; it would be the squirrel nobody wanted to hang around with.

I can see the other squirrels gathered around an old stump saying stuff like "If I hear him say, 'I like nuts' one more time, I'm going to kill him."

The gorillas, overhearing this conversation, lumber down from the mist and promote the unpopular squirrel. The remaining squirrels are assigned to Quality Teams as punishment.

You may be wondering if you fit the description of a Dilbert Principle manager. Here's a little test:

1. Do you believe that anything you don't understand must be easy to do?
2. Do you feel the need to explain in great detail why "profit" is the difference between income and expense?
3. Do you think employees should schedule funerals only during holidays?
4. Are the following words a form of communication or gibberish:

The Business Services Leadership Team will enhance the organization in order to continue

on the journey toward a Market Facing Organization (MFO) model. To that end, we are consolidating the Object Management for Business Services into a cross strata team.

5. When people stare at you in disbelief do you repeat what you just said, only louder and more slowly?

15   Now give yourself one point for each question you answered with the letter "B." If your score is greater than zero, congratulations—there are stock options in your future.

(The language in question four is from an actual company memo.)

SUGGESTIONS FOR DISCUSSION

1. How would you explain the popularity of Dilbert? Does it appeal to people who have never done office work? Why? Why not?

2. Scott Adams gets many of his ideas from office workers who e-mail him real situations and real memos. With two or three of your classmates, make a list of absurdities from your own experience with bureaucracy that you would send to Adams.

3. Scott Adams's humor is much like the humor in Matt Groening (his Hell series) or Gary Larson's Far Side. Bring to class a comic strip that uses satire or dark humor to make you laugh. What is it about these strips that makes you laugh even when they make you cringe?

SUGGESTIONS FOR WRITING

1. In his introduction to *Working*, Studs Terkel writes that his book, as it is about work, "is, by its very nature, about violence—to the spirit as well as to the body. It is about ulcers as well as accidents, about shouting matches as well as fistfights…To survive the day is triumph enough for the walking wounded among the great many of us." In the years it took Terkel to assemble the stories of the men and women in his collection, he had reached the conclusion that the real drive of most workers was for a job that gave them "daily meaning as well as daily bread." No matter the work people do, they want to believe that it is for something more than the paycheck. That doesn't mean that the paycheck is inconsequential, but it does mean that it matters to most folks how they spend their time making that pay. Write an essay in which you explain how Dilbert addresses the question of what the workplace ought to be about as opposed to what it actually is about.

2. Write about a time when you found yourself caught up in the sort of bureaucracy that Scott Adams uses as the basis for his satire of the workplace—perhaps a situation where none of the employees quite knew what the job they were assigned was supposed to be. How did you handle it? In what ways was it typical of that workplace or that organization?

3. In a *Newsweek* cover story on *The Dilbert Principle, Newsweek* reporters write of "the suppressed rage of workers who tolerate abuses and absurdities in a marketplace leaned-and-meaned to Wall Street's specifications. Reading Dilbert allows them, in some small way, to strike back, or at least to experience a pleasant catharsis by identifying the nature of the beast: a general yet pervasive sense of idiocy in corporate America that is seldom dealt with by the captains of industry who have great hair and offices with doors." Write an essay in which you offer a possible explanation for how reading Dilbert helps abused workers strike back or how humor, graffiti, or any underground type of activity can help people in what seems like a repressive system feel as if they have some control.

WORK: THE GREAT ESCAPE

Arlie Russell Hochschild

Arlie Russell Hochschild is a professor of sociology at the University of California at Berkeley. For more than three years, Hochschild interviewed workers about their jobs and their daily routines in preparation for her book *The Time Bind: When Work Becomes Home and Home Becomes Work* (1997). The selection reprinted here has been adapted from that book and originally appeared in the *New York Times Magazine* (April 20, 1997). In it, Hochschild describes the workplace as a haven from the tensions of home. Hers is a departure from more recent discussions of Americans who spend too much time at work with no time left in their lives for leisure or family activities. According to Hochschild's research, Americans are spending more time at work not because they must but because they want to.

SUGGESTION FOR READING Hochschild alternates her argument about work as refuge with stories of workers who choose to spend more time at work than they might have to. As you read, pay attention to each of these stories as individual examples of the larger argument that Hochschild wants to make.

1 Over three years, I interviewed 130 respondents for a book. They spoke freely and allowed me to follow them through "typical" days, on the understanding that I would protect their anonymity. I have changed the names of the company and of those I interviewed, and altered certain identifying details. Their words appear here as they were spoken.—A. R. H.

It's 7:40 A.M. when Cassie Bell, 4, arrives at the Spotted Deer Child-Care Center, her hair half-combed, a blanket in one hand, a fudge bar in the other. "I'm late," her mother, Gwen, a sturdy young woman whose short-cropped hair frames a pleasant face, explains to the child-care worker in charge. "Cassie wanted the fudge bar so bad, I gave it to her," she adds apologetically.

"*Pleeese*, can't you take me with you?" Cassie pleads.

"You know I can't take you to work," Gwen replies in a tone that suggests that she has been expecting this request. Cassie's shoulders droop. But she has struck a hard bargain—the morning fudge bar—aware of her mother's anxiety about the long day that lies ahead at the center. As Gwen explains later, she continually feels that she owes Cassie more time than she gives her— she has a "time debt."

5 Arriving at her office just before 8, Gwen finds on her desk a cup of coffee in her personal mug, milk no sugar (exactly as she likes it), pre-pared by a co-worker who managed to get in ahead of her. As the assistant to the head of public relations at a company I will call Amerco, Gwen has to handle responses to any reports that may appear about the company in the press—a challenging job, but one that gives her satisfaction. As she prepares for her first meeting of the day, she misses her daughter, but she also feels relief; there's a lot to get done at Amerco.

Gwen used to work a straight eight-hour day. But over the last three years, her workday has gradually stretched to eight and a half or nine hours, not counting the E-mail messages and faxes she answers from home. She complains about her hours to her co-workers and listens to their complaints—but she loves her job. Gwen picks up Cassie at 5:45 and gives her a long, affectionate hug.

At home, Gwen's husband, John, a computer programmer, plays with their daughter while Gwen prepares dinner. To protect the dinner "hour"—8:00–8:30—Gwen checks that the phone machine is on, hears the phone ring during dinner but resists the urge to answer. After Cassie's bath, Gwen and Cassie have "quality time," or "Q.T.," as John affectionately calls it. Half an hour later, at 9:30, Gwen tucks Cassie into bed.

There are, in a sense, two Bell households: the rushed family they actually are and the relaxed family they imagine they might be if only they had time. Gwen and John complain that they are in a time bind. What they say they want seems so modest—time to throw a ball, to read to Cassie, to witness the small dramas of her development, not to speak of having a little fun and romance themselves. Yet even these modest wishes seem strangely out of reach. Before going to bed, Gwen has to E-mail messages to her colleagues in preparation for the next day's meeting; John goes to bed early, exhausted—he's out the door by 7 every morning.

Nationwide, many working parents are in the same boat. More mothers of small children than ever now work outside the home. In 1993, 56 percent of women with children between 6 and 17 worked outside the home full time year round; 43 percent of women with children 6 and under did the same. Meanwhile, fathers of small children are not cutting back hours of work to help out at home. If anything, they have increased their hours at work. According to a 1993 national survey conducted by the Families and Work Institute in New York, American men average 48.8 hours of work a week, and women 41.7 hours, including overtime and commuting. All in all, more women are on the economic train, and for many—men and women alike— that train is going faster.

10   But Amerco has "family friendly" policies. If your division head and supervisor agree, you can work part time, share a job with another worker, work some hours at home, take parental leave or use "flex time." But hardly anyone uses these policies. In seven years, only two Amerco fathers have taken formal parental leave. Fewer than 1 percent have taken advantage of the opportunity to work part time. Of all such policies, only flex time— which rearranges but does not shorten work time—has had a significant number of takers (perhaps a third of working parents at Amerco).

Forgoing family-friendly policies is not exclusive to Amerco workers. A 1991 study of 188 companies conducted by the Families and Work Institute found that while a majority offered part-time shifts, fewer than 5 percent of employees made use of them. Thirty-five percent offered "flex place"—work from home—and fewer than 3 percent of their employees took advantage of it. And an earlier Bureau of Labor Statistics survey asked workers whether they preferred a shorter workweek, a longer one or their present schedule. About 62 percent preferred their present schedule; 28 percent would have preferred longer hours. Fewer than 10 percent said they wanted a cut in hours.

Still, I found it hard to believe that people didn't protest their long hours at work. So I contacted Bright Horizons, a company that runs 136 company-based child-care centers associated with corporations, hospitals and Federal agencies in 25 states. Bright Horizons allowed me to add questions to a questionnaire they sent out to 3,000 parents whose children attended the centers. The respondents, mainly middle-class parents in their early 30's, largely confirmed the picture I'd found at Amerco. A third of fathers and a fifth of mothers described themselves as "workaholic," and 1 out of 3 said their partners were.

To be sure, some parents have tried to shorten their hours. Twenty-one percent of the nation's women voluntarily work part time, as do 7 percent of men. A number of others make under-the-table arrangements that don't show up on surveys. But while working parents say they need more time at home, the main story of their lives does not center on a struggle to get it. Why? Given the hours parents are working these days, why aren't they taking advantage of an opportunity to reduce their time at work?

The most widely held explanation is that Working Parents cannot afford to work shorter hours. Certainly this is true for many. But if money is the whole explanation, why would it be that at places like Amerco, the best-paid employees—upper-level managers and professionals— were the least interested in part-time work or job sharing, while clerical workers who earned less were more interested?

15   Similarly, if money were the answer, we would expect poorer new mothers to return to work more quickly after giving birth than rich

mothers. But among working women nation-wide, well-to-do new mothers are not much more likely to stay home after 13 weeks with a new baby than low-income new mothers. When asked what they look for in a job, only a third of respondents in a recent study said salary came first. Money is important, but by itself, money does not explain why many people don't want to cut back hours at work.

A second explanation goes that workers don't dare ask for time off because they are afraid it would make them vulnerable to layoffs. With recent downsizings at many large corporations, and with well-paying, secure jobs being replaced by lower-paying, insecure ones, it occurred to me that perhaps employees are "working scared." But when I asked Amerco employees whether they worked long hours for fear of getting on a layoff list, virtually everyone said no. Even among a particularly vulnerable group—factory workers who were laid off in the downturn of the early 1980's and were later rehired—most did not cite fear for their jobs as the only, or main, reason they worked overtime. For unionized workers, layoffs are assigned by seniority, and for nonunionized workers, layoffs are usually related to the profitability of the division a person works in, not to an individual work schedule.

Were workers uninformed about the company's family-friendly policies? No. Some even mentioned that they were proud to work for a company that offered such enlightened policies. Were rigid middle managers standing in the way of workers using these policies? Sometimes. But when I compared Amerco employees who worked for flexible managers with those who worked for rigid managers, I found that the flexible managers reported only a few more applicants than the rigid ones. The evidence, however counterintuitive, pointed to a paradox: workers at the company I studied weren't protesting the time bind. They were accommodating to it.

Why? I did not anticipate the conclusion I found myself coming to: namely, that work has become a form of "home" and home has become "work." The worlds of home and work have not begun to blur, as the conventional wisdom goes, but to reverse places. We are used to thinking that home is where most people feel the most appreciated, the most truly "themselves," the most secure, the most relaxed. We are used to thinking that work is where most people feel like "just a number" or "a cog in a machine." It is where they have to be "on," have to "act," where they are least secure and most harried.

But new management techniques so pervasive in corporate life have helped transform the workplace into a more appreciative, personal sort of social world. Meanwhile, at home the divorce rate has risen, and the emotional demands have become more baffling and complex. In addition to teething, tantrums and the normal developments of growing children, the needs of elderly parents are creating more tasks for the modern family—as are the blending, unblending, reblending of new stepparents, stepchildren, exes and former in-laws.

20   This idea began to dawn on me during one of my first interviews with an Amerco worker. Linda Avery, a friendly, 38-year-old mother, is a shift supervisor at an Amerco plant. When I meet her in the factory's coffee-break room over a couple of Cokes, she is wearing blue jeans and a pink jersey, her hair pulled back in a long, blond ponytail. Linda's husband, Bill, is a technician in the same plant. By working different shifts, they manage to share the care of their 2-year-old son and Linda's 16-year-old daughter from a previous marriage. "Bill works the 7 A.M. to 3 P.M. shift while I watch the baby," she explains. "Then I work the 3 P.M. to 11 P.M. shift and he watches the baby. My daughter works at Walgreen's after school."

Linda is working overtime, and so I begin by asking whether Amerco required the overtime, or whether she volunteered for it. "Oh, I put in for it," she replies. I ask her whether, if finances and company policy permitted, she'd be interested in cutting back on the overtime. She takes off her safety glasses, rubs her face and, without answering my question, explains: "I get home, and the minute I turn the key, my daughter is right there. Granted, she needs somebody to talk to about her day....The baby is still up. He should have been in bed two hours ago, and that upsets me. The dishes are piled in the sink. My daughter comes right up to the door and complains about anything her stepfather said or did, and she wants to talk about her job. My husband is in the other room hollering to my daughter, 'Tracy, I don't ever get any time to talk to your mother, because you're always monopolizing her time before I even get a chance!' They all come at me at once."

Linda's description of the urgency of demands and the unarbitrated quarrels that await her homecoming contrast with her account of arriving at her job as a shift supervisor: "I usually come to work early, just to get away from the house. When I arrive, people are there waiting. We sit, we talk, we joke. I let them know what's going on, who has to be where, what changes I've made for the shift that day. We sit and chitchat for 5 or 10 minutes. There's laughing, joking, fun."

For Linda, home has come to feel like work and work has come to feel a bit like home. Indeed, she feels she can get relief from the "work" of being at home only by going to the "home" of work. Why has her life at home come to seem like this? Linda explains it this way: "My husband's a great help watching our baby. But as far as doing housework or even taking the baby when I'm at home, no. He figures he works five days a week; he's not going to come home and clean. But he doesn't stop to think that I work seven days a week. Why should I have to come home and do the housework without help from anybody else? My husband and I have been through this over and over again. Even if he would just pick up from the kitchen table and stack the dishes for me, that would make a big difference. He does nothing. On his weekends off, he goes fishing. If I want any time off, I have to get a sitter. He'll help out if I'm not here, but the minute I am, all the work at home is mine."

With a light laugh, she continues: "So I take a lot of overtime. The more I get out of the house,

the better I am. It's a terrible thing to say, but that's the way I feel."

25   When Bill feels the need for time off, to relax, to have fun, to feel free, he climbs in his truck and takes his free time without his family. Largely in response, Linda grabs what she also calls "free time"—at work. Neither Linda nor Bill Avery wants more time together at home, not as things are arranged now.

How do Linda and Bill Avery fit into the broader picture of American family and work life? Current research suggests that however hectic their lives, women who do paid work feel less depressed, think better of themselves and are more satisfied than women who stay at home. One study reported that women who work outside the home feel more valued at home than housewives do. Meanwhile, work is where many women feel like "good mothers." As Linda reflects: "I'm a good mom at home, but I'm a better mom at work. At home, I get into fights with Tracy. I want her to apply to a junior college, but she's not interested. At work, I think I'm better at seeing the other person's point of view."

Many workers feel more confident they could "get the job done" at work than at home. One study found that only 59 percent of workers feel their "performance" in the family is "good or unusually good," while 86 percent rank their performance on the job this way.

Forces at work and at home are simultaneously reinforcing this "reversal." The lure of work has been enhanced in recent years by the rise of company cultural engineering—in particular, the shift from Frederick Taylor's principles of scientific management to the Total Quality principles originally set out by W. Edwards Deming. Under the influence of a Taylorist world view, the manager's job was to coerce the worker's mind and body, not to appeal to the worker's heart. The Taylorized worker was de-skilled, replaceable and cheap, and as a consequence felt bored, demeaned and unappreciated.

Using modern participative management techniques, many companies now train workers to make their own work decisions, and then set before their newly "empowered" employees moral as well as financial incentives. At Amerco, the Total Quality worker is invited to feel recognized for job accomplishments. Amerco regularly strengthens the familylike ties of co-workers by holding "recognition ceremonies" honoring particular workers or self-managed production teams. Amerco employees speak of "belonging to the Amerco family," and proudly wear their "Total Quality" pins or "High Performance Team" T-shirts, symbols of their loyalty to the company and of its loyalty to them.

30   The company occasionally decorates a section of the factory and serves refreshments. The production teams, too, have regular get-togethers. In a New Age recasting of an old business slogan—"The Customer Is Always Right"—Amerco proposes that its workers "Value the Internal Customer." This means: Be as polite and considerate to co-workers inside the company as you would be to customers outside it. How many recognition ceremonies for competent performance are being offered at home? Who is valuing the internal customer there?

Amerco also tries to take on the role of a helpful relative with regard to employee problems at work and at home. The education-and-training division offers employees free courses (on company time) in "Dealing With Anger," "How to Give and Accept Criticism," "How to Cope With Difficult People."

At home, of course, people seldom receive anything like this much help on issues basic to family life. There, no courses are being offered on "Dealing With Your Child's Disappointment in You" or "How to Treat Your Spouse Like an Internal Customer."

If Total Quality calls for "re-skilling" the worker in an "enriched" job environment, technological developments have long been de-skilling parents at home. Over the centuries, store-bought goods have replaced homespun cloth, homemade soap and home-baked foods. Day care for children, retirement homes for the elderly, even psychotherapy are, in a way, commercial substitutes for jobs that a mother once

did at home. Even family-generated entertainment has, to some extent, been replaced by television, video games and the VCR. I sometimes watched Amerco families sitting together after their dinners, mute but cozy, watching sitcoms in which television mothers, fathers and children related in an animated way to one another while the viewing family engaged in relational loafing.

The one "skill" still required of family members is the hardest one of all—the emotional work of forging, deepening or repairing family relationships. It takes time to develop this skill, and even then things can go awry. Family ties are complicated. People get hurt. Yet as broken homes become more common—and as the sense of belonging to a geographical community grows less and less secure in an age of mobility—the corporate world has created a sense of "neighborhood," of "feminine culture," of family at work. Life at work can be insecure; the company can fire workers. But workers aren't so secure at home, either. Many employees have been working for Amerco for 20 years but are on their second or third marriages or relationships. The shifting balance between these two "divorce rates" may be the most powerful reason why tired parents flee a world of unresolved quarrels and unwashed laundry harmony and managed cheer of work. People are getting their "pink slips" at home.

35   Amerco workers have not only turned their offices into "home" and their homes into workplaces; many have also begun to "Taylorize" time at home, where families are succumbing to a cult of efficiency previously associated mainly with the office and factory. Meanwhile, work time, with its ever longer hours, has become more hospitable to sociability—periods of talking with friends on E-mail, patching up quarrels, gossiping. Within the long workday of many Amerco employees are great hidden pockets of inefficiency while, in the far smaller number of waking weekday hours at home, they are, despite themselves, forced to act increasingly time-conscious and efficient.

The Averys respond to their time bind at home by trying to value and protect "quality time." A concept unknown to their parents and grandparents, "quality time" has become a powerful symbol of the struggle against the growing pressures at home. It reflects the extent to which modern parents feel the flow of time to be running against them. The premise behind "quality time" is that the time we devote to relationships can somehow be separated from ordinary time. Relationships go on during quantity time, of course, but then we are only passively, not actively, wholeheartedly, specializing in our emotional ties. We aren't "on." Quality time at home becomes like an office appointment. You don't want to be caught "goofing off around the water cooler" when you are "at work."

Quality time holds out the hope that scheduling intense periods of togetherness can compensate for an overall loss of time in such a way that a relationship will suffer no loss of quality. But this is just another way of transferring the cult of efficiency from office to home. We must now get our relationships in good repair in less time. Instead of nine hours a day with a child, we declare ourselves capable of getting "the same result" with one intensely focused hour.

Parents now more commonly speak of time as if it is a threatened form of personal capital they have no choice but to manage and invest. What's new here is the spread into the home of a financial manager's attitude toward time. Working parents at Amerco owe what they think of as time debts at home. This is because they are, in a sense, inadvertently "Taylorizing" the house—speeding up the pace of home life as Taylor once tried to "scientifically" speed up the pace of factory life.

Advertisers of products aimed at women have recognized that this new reality provides an opportunity to sell products, and have turned the very pressure that threatens to explode the home into a positive attribute. Take, for example, an ad promoting Instant Quaker Oatmeal: it shows a smiling mother ready for the office in her square-shouldered suit, hugging her happy son. A caption reads: "Nicky is a very picky eater. With Instant Quaker Oatmeal, I can give him a terrific hot breakfast in just 90 seconds. And I don't have to spend any time coaxing him to eat it!" Here, the modern mother seems to have absorbed the lessons of Frederick Taylor as she presses for efficiency at home because she is in a hurry to get to work.

40   Part of modern parenthood seems to include coping with the resistance of real children who are not so eager to get their cereal so fast. Some parents try desperately not to appease their children with special gifts or smooth-talking promises about the future. But when time is scarce, even the best parents find themselves passing a system-wide familial speed-up along to the most vulnerable workers on the line. Parents are then obliged to try to control the damage done by a reversal of worlds. They monitor mealtime, homework time, bedtime, trying to cut out "wasted" time.

In response, children often protest the pace, the deadlines, the grand irrationality of "efficient" family life. Children dawdle. They refuse to leave places when it's time to leave. They insist on leaving places when it's not time to leave. Surely, this is part of the usual stop-and-go of childhood itself, but perhaps, too, it is the plea of children for more family time, and more control over what time there is. This only adds to the feeling that life at home has become hard work.

Instead of trying to arrange shorter or more flexible work schedules, Amerco parents often avoid confronting the reality of the time bind. Some minimize their ideas about how much care a child, a partner or they themselves "really need." They make do with less time, less attention, less understanding and less support at home than they once imagined possible. They *emotionally downsize* life. In essence, they deny the needs of family members, and they themselves become emotional ascetics. If they once "needed" time with each other, they are now increasingly "fine" without it.

Another way that working parents try to evade the time bind is to buy themselves out of it—an approach that puts women in particular at the heart of a contradiction. Like men, women absorb the work-family speed-up far more than they resist it; but unlike men, they still shoulder most of the workload at home. And women still represent in people's minds the heart and soul of family life. They're the ones—especially women of the urban middle and upper-middle classes—who feel most acutely the need to save time, who are the most tempted by the new "time saving" goods and services—and who wind up feeling the most guilty about it. For example, Playgroup Connections, a Washington-area business started by a former executive recruiter, matches playmates to one another. One mother hired the service to find her child a French-speaking playmate.

In several cities, children home alone can call a number for "Grandma, Please!" and reach an adult who has the time to talk with them, sing to them or help them with their homework. An ad for Kindercare Learning Centers, a for profit child-care chain, pitches its appeal this way: "You want your child to be active, tolerant, smart, loved, emotionally stable, self-aware, artistic and get a two-hour nap. Anything else?" It goes on to note that Kindercare accepts children 6 weeks to 12 years old and provides a number to call for the Kindercare nearest you. Another typical service organizes children's birthday parties, making out invitations ("sure hope you can come") and providing party favors, entertainment, a decorated cake and balloons. Creative Memories is a service that puts ancestral photos into family albums for you.

45   An overwhelming majority of the working mothers I spoke with recoiled from the idea of buying themselves out of parental duties. A bought birthday party was "too impersonal," a 90-second breakfast "too fast." Yet a surprising amount of lunchtime conversation between female friends at Amerco was devoted to expressing complex, conflicting feelings about the lure of trading time for one service or another. The temptation to order flash-frozen dinners or to call a local number for a homework helper did not come up because such services had not yet appeared at Spotted Deer Child-Care Center. But many women dwelled on the question of how to decide where a mother's job

began and ended, especially with regard to baby sitters and television. One mother said to another in the breakroom of an Amerco plant: "Damon doesn't settle down until 10 at night, so he hates me to wake him up in the morning and I hate to do it. He's cranky. He pulls the covers up. I put on cartoons. That way, I can dress him and he doesn't object. I don't like to use TV that way. It's like a drug. But I do it."

The other mother countered: "Well, Todd is up before we are, so that's not a problem. It's after dinner, when I feel like watching a little television, that I feel guilty, because he gets too much TV at the sitter's."

As task after task falls into the realm of time-saving goods and services, questions arise about the moral meanings attached to doing or not doing such tasks. Is it being a good mother to bake a child's birthday cake (alone or together with one's partner)? Or can we gratefully save time by ordering it, and be good mothers by planning the party? Can we save more time by hiring a planning service, and be good mothers simply by watching our children have a good time? "Wouldn't that be nice!" one Amerco mother exclaimed. As the idea of the "good mother" retreats before the pressures of work and the expansion of motherly services, mothers are in fact continually reinventing themselves.

The final way working parents tried to evade the time bind was to develop what I call "potential selves." The potential selves that I discovered in my Amerco interviews were fantasy creations of time-poor parents who dreamed of living as time millionaires.

One man, a gifted 55-year-old engineer in research and development at Amerco, told how he had dreamed of taking his daughters on a camping trip in the Sierra Mountains: "I bought all the gear three years ago when they were 5 and 7, the tent, the sleeping bags, the air mattresses, the backpacks, the ponchos. I got a map of the area. I even got the freeze-dried food. Since then the kids and I have talked about it a lot, and gone over what we're going to do. They've been on me to do it for a long time. I feel bad about it. I keep putting it off, but we'll do it, I just don't know when."

50   Banished to garages and attics of many Amerco workers were expensive electric saws, cameras, skis and musical instruments, all bought with wages it took time to earn. These items were to their owners what Cassie's fudge bar was to her—a substitute for time, a talisman, a reminder of the potential self.

Obviously, not everyone, not even a majority of Americans, is making a home out of work and a work-place out of home. But in the working world, it is a growing reality, and one we need to face. Increasing numbers of women are discovering a great male secret—that work can be an escape from the pressures of home, pressures that the changing nature of work itself are only intensifying. Neither men nor women are going to take up "family friendly" policies, whether corporate or governmental, as long as the current realities of work and home remain as they are. For a substantial number of time-bound parents, the stripped-down home and the neighborhood devoid of community are simply losing out to the pull of the workplace.

There are several broader, historical causes of this reversal of realms. The last 30 years have witnessed the rapid rise of women in the workplace. At the same time, job mobility has taken families farther from relatives who might lend a hand, and made it harder to make close friends of neighbors who could help out. Moreover, as women have acquired more education and have joined men at work, they have absorbed the views of an older, male-oriented work world, its views of a "real career," far more than men have taken up their share of the work at home. One reason women have changed more than men is that the world of "male" work seems more honorable and valuable than the "female" world of home and children.

So where do we go from here? There is surely no going back to the mythical 1950's family that confined women to the home. Most women don't wish to return to a full-time role at home—and couldn't afford it even if they did. But equally troubling is a workaholic culture that strands both men and women outside the home.

For a while now, scholars on work-family issues have pointed to Sweden, Norway and Denmark as better models of work-family balance. Today, for example, almost all Swedish fathers take two paid weeks off from work at the birth of their children, and about half of fathers and most mothers take additional "parental leave" during the child's first or second year. Research shows that men who take family leave when their children are very young are more likely to be involved with their children as they grow older. When I mentioned this Swedish record of paternity leave to a focus group of American male managers, one of them replied, "Right, we've already heard about Sweden." To this executive, paternity leave was a good idea not for the U.S. today, but for some "potential society" in another place and time.

55   Meanwhile, children are paying the price. In her book *When the Bough Breaks: The Cost of Neglecting Our Children,* the economist Sylvia Hewlett claims that "compared with the previous generation, young people today are more likely to "underperform at school; commit suicide; need psychiatric help; suffer a severe eating disorder; bear a child out of wedlock; take drugs, be the victim of a violent crime." But we needn't dwell on sledgehammer problems like heroin or suicide to realize that children like those at Spotted Deer need more of our time. If other advanced nations with two-job families can give children the time they need, why can't we?

SUGGESTIONS FOR DISCUSSION

1. Although Hochschild says she is writing about all workers, most of her information seems to focus on women in the workplace. Identify the main argument of her article and explain why women's stories of finding a haven at work might be more useful for that argument than would men's stories.

2. What are the overall impressions of work vs. home that Hochschild leaves you with? To what extent do you accept her representation of home and work? What of that representation does not seem entirely convincing to you?

3. Hochschild writes that salary is not the most important reason for working long hours because, according to her research, some of the best-paid employees are least willing to cut back their hours while the lower-paid workers seem to be willing to choose time away from work for home. Are there other reasons, besides finding more pleasure at work than at home, that you can think of for employees to make these choices?

SUGGESTIONS FOR WRITING

1. Write an exploratory essay that addresses Hochschild's discussion of women in the workplace. To begin planning your writing, consider asking questions such as the following: How representative are Hochschild's descriptions of working women's lives? Do you know any woman who holds a job and is raising a family at the same time? Is her story like the stories in Hochschild's article, or do you find something different in the choices she makes? What is your overall impression of what Hochschild expects from women in the workplace?

2. Hochschild writes that even though many companies have "family friendly" policies that offer flex-time or part-time work to give parents a chance to spend more time at home, very few employees take advantage of those benefits. It is possible that part of the reason some employees don't take advantage of these policies is the way that the company presents them. Imagine that you have to write a memo convincing employees to take advantage of family friendly policies. You will have to address many different kinds of employees, all with the same memo. You cannot assume they are all in the same situation. You will have to make the policy seem attractive, but you can't promise too much because, after all, the company does need its employees on the job—it is a rare company that would be willing to lose money on such a benefit. You will also have to convey the sense that, as a manager, you value both the work and the home environments. Because it is a memo, and you'll want everyone to read it, it should be direct and brief—no more than one single-spaced page.

3. The introduction to this chapter suggested that television dramas and sitcoms often use the work–family as a setting for their stories. Choose a current television show with a workplace environment and write an essay in which you examine the characters and setting as the work–family. In what ways does this setting take precedence over any home setting for the characters? In what ways does the work–family spill over into the home setting? How might Hochschild's analysis of the ways people feel about their jobs, as opposed to their obligations at home, help you to explain the appeal or popularity of the work–family on television?

NICKEL-AND-DIMED: On (Not) Getting By in America

Barbara Ehrenreich

Barbara Ehrenreich is a contributing editor of *Harper's Magazine,* a regular contributor to the *Nation,* and the author of a dozen books, including *Fear of Falling: The Inner Life of the Middle Class* (1989), which was nominated for a National Book Critics Award. The following excerpts, taken from a longer essay detailing Ehrenreich's experiment living the life of a minimum-wage laborer, originally appeared in *Harper's* (January 1999) and appeared as a book-length study under the same title in 2001.

SUGGESTION FOR READING   Throughout her narrative, Ehrenreich uses figures from such sources as the Department of Housing and Urban Development, the Economic Policy Institute, and the National Coalition for the Homeless to support her discussion of how difficult it is for anyone to live on the wages paid in most service jobs. It will help you keep track of Ehrenreich's argument if you keep those reports in mind as you read.

1   At the beginning of June 1998 I leave behind everything that normally soothes the ego and sustains the body—home, career, companion, reputation, ATM card—for a plunge into the low-wage workforce. There, I become another, occupationally much diminished "Barbara Ehrenreich"—depicted on job-application forms as a divorced homemaker whole sole work experience consists of housekeeping in a few private homes. I am terrified, at the beginning, of being unmasked for what I am: a middle-class journalist setting out to explore the world that welfare mothers are entering, at the rate of approximately 50,000 a month, as welfare reform kicks in. Happily, though, my fears turn out to be entirely unwarranted: during a month of poverty and toil, my name goes unnoticed and for the most part unuttered. In this parallel universe where my father never got out of the mines and I never got through college, I am "baby," "honey," "blondie," and, most commonly, "girl."

My first task is to find a place to live. I figure that if I can earn $7 an hour—which, from the want ads, seems doable—I can afford to spend $500 on rent, or maybe, with severe economies, $600. In the Key West area, where I live, this pretty much confines me to flophouses and trailer homes—like the one, a pleasing fifteen-minute drive from town, that has no air-conditioning, no screens, no fans, no television, and, by way of diversion, only the challenge of evading the landlord's Doberman pinscher. The big problem with this place, though, is the rent, which at $675 a month is well beyond my reach. All right, Key West is expensive. But so is New York City, or the Bay Area, or Jackson Hole, or Telluride, or Boston, or any other place where tourists and the wealthy compete for living space with the people who clean their toilets and fry their hash browns.[1] Still, it is a shock to realize that "trailer trash" has become, for me, a demographic category to aspire to.

So I decide to make the common trade-off between affordability and convenience, and go for a $500-a-month efficiency thirty miles up a two-lane highway from the employment opportunities of Key West, meaning forty-five minutes if there's no road construction and I don't get caught behind some sun-dazed Canadian tourists. I hate the drive, along a roadside studded with white crosses commemorating the more effective head-on collisions, but it's a sweet little place—a cabin, more or less, set in the swampy back yard of the converted mobile home where my landlord, an affable TV repairman, lives with his bartender girlfriend. Anthropologically speaking, a bustling trailer park would be preferable, but here I have a gleaming white floor and a firm mattress, and the few resident bugs are easily vanquished.

Besides, I am not doing this for the anthropology. My aim is nothing so mistily subjective as to "experience poverty" or find out how it "really feels" to be a long-term low-wage worker. I've had enough unchosen encounters with poverty and the world of low-wage work to know it's not a place you want to visit for touristic purposes; it just smells too much like fear. And with all my real-life assets—bank account, IRA, health insurance, multiroom home—waiting indulgently in the background, I am, of course, thoroughly insulated from the terrors that afflict the genuinely poor.

5   No, this is a purely objective, scientific sort of mission. The humanitarian rationale for welfare reform—as opposed to the more punitive and stingy impulses that may actually have

motivated it—is that work will lift poor women out of poverty while simultaneously inflating their self-esteem and hence their future value in the labor market. Thus, whatever the hassles involved in finding child care, transportation, etc., the transition from welfare to work will end happily, in greater prosperity for all. Now there are many problems with this comforting prediction, such as the fact that the economy will inevitably undergo a downturn, eliminating many jobs. Even without a downturn, the influx of a million former welfare recipients into the low-wage labor market could depress wages by as much as 11.9 percent, according to the Economic Policy Institute (EPI) in Washington, D.C.

But is it really possible to make a living on the kinds of jobs currently available to unskilled people? Mathematically, the answer is no, as can be shown by taking $6 to $7 an hour, perhaps subtracting a dollar or two an hour for child care, multiplying by 160 hours a month, and comparing the result to the prevailing rents. According to the National Coalition for the Homeless, for example, in 1998 it took, on average nationwide, an hourly wage of $8.89 to afford a one-bedroom apartment, and the Preamble Center for Public Policy estimates that the odds against a typical welfare recipient's landing a job at such a "living wage" are about 97 to 1. If these numbers are right, low-wage work is not a solution to poverty and possibly not even to homelessness.

It may seem excessive to put this proposition to an experimental test. As certain family members keep unhelpfully reminding me, the viability of low-wage work could be tested, after a fashion, without ever leaving my study. I could just pay myself $7 an hour for eight hours a day, charge myself for room and board, and total up the numbers after a month. Why leave the people and work that I love? But I am an experimental scientist by training. In that business, you don't just sit at a desk and theorize; you plunge into the everyday chaos of nature, where surprises lurk in the most mundane measurements. Maybe, when I got into it, I would discover some hidden economies in the world of the low-wage

worker. After all, if 30 percent of the workforce toils for less than $8 an hour, according to the EPI, they may have found some tricks as yet unknown to me. Maybe—who knows?—I would even be able to detect in myself the bracing psychological effects of getting out of the house, as promised by the welfare wonks at places like the Heritage Foundation. Or, on the other hand, maybe there would be unexpected costs—physical, mental, or financial—to throw off all my calculations. Ideally, I should do this with two small children in tow, that being the welfare average, but mine are grown and no one is willing to lend me theirs for a month-long vacation in penury. So this is not the perfect experiment, just a test of the best possible case: an unencumbered woman, smart and even strong, attempting to live more or less off the land.

On the morning of my first full day of job searching, I take a red pen to the want ads, which are auspiciously numerous. Everyone in Key West's booming "hospitality industry" seems to be looking for someone like me—trainable, flexible, and with suitably humble expectations as to pay. I know I possess certain traits that might be advantageous—I'm white and, I like to think, well-spoken and poised—but I decide on two rules: One, I cannot use any skills derived from my education or usual work—not that there are a lot of want ads for satirical essayists anyway. Two, I have to take the best-paid job that is offered me and of course do my best to hold it; no Marxist rants or sneaking off to read novels in the ladies' room. In addition, I rule out various occupations for one reason or another: Hotel front-desk clerk, for example, which to my surprise is regarded as unskilled and pays around $7 an hour, gets eliminated because it involves standing in one spot for eight hours a day. Waitressing is similarly something I'd like to avoid, because I remember it leaving me bone tired when I was eighteen, and I'm decades of varicosities and back pain beyond that now. Telemarketing, one of the first refuges of the suddenly indigent, can be dismissed on grounds of personality. This leaves certain supermarket jobs, such as deli clerk, or housekeeping in Key West's thousands of hotel and guest rooms. Housekeeping is especially appealing, for reasons both atavistic and practical: it's what my mother did before I came along, and it can't be too different from what I've been doing part-time, in my own home, all my life.

So I put on what I take to be a respectful-looking outfit of ironed Bermuda shorts and scooped-neck T-shirt and set out for a tour of the local hotels and supermarkets. Best Western, Econo Lodge, and Ho Jo's all let me fill out application forms, and these are, to my relief, interested in little more than whether I am a legal resident of the United States and have committed any felonies. My next stop is Winn-Dixie, the supermarket, which turns out to have a particularly onerous application process, featuring a fifteen-minute "interview" by computer since, apparently, no human on the premises is deemed capable of representing the corporate point of view. I am conducted to a large room decorated with posters illustrating how to look "professional" (it helps to be white and, if female, permed) and warning of the slick promises that union organizers might try to tempt me with. The interview is multiple choice: Do I have anything, such as child-care problems, that might make it hard for me to get to work on time? Do I think safety on the job is the responsibility of management? Then, popping up cunningly out of the blue: How many dollars' worth of stolen goods have I purchased in the last year? Would I turn in a fellow employee if I caught him stealing? Finally, "Are you an honest person?"

10   Apparently, I ace the interview, because I am told that all I have to do is show up in some doctor's office tomorrow for a urine test. This seems to be a fairly general rule: if you want to stack Cheerio boxes or vacuum hotel rooms in chemically fascist America, you have to be willing to squat down and pee in front of some health worker (who has no doubt had to do the same thing herself). The wages Winn-Dixie is offering—$6 and a couple of dimes to start

with—are not enough, I decide, to compensate for this indignity.[2]

I lunch at Wendy's, where $4.99 gets you unlimited refills at the Mexican part of the Super-bar, a comforting surfeit of refried beans and "cheese sauce." A teenage employee, seeing me studying the want ads, kindly offers me an application form, which I fill out, though here, too, the pay is just $6 and change an hour. Then it's off for a round of the locally owned inns and guest-houses. At "The Palms," let's call it, a bouncy manager actually takes me around to see the rooms and meet the existing housekeepers, who, I note with satisfaction, look pretty much like me—faded ex-hippie types in shorts with long hair pulled back in braids. Mostly, though, no one speaks to me or even looks at me except to proffer an application form. At my last stop, a palatial B&B, I wait twenty minutes to meet "Max," only to be told that there are no jobs now but there should be one soon, since "nobody lasts more than a couple of week." (Because none of the people I talked to knew I was a reporter, I have changed their names to protect their privacy and, in some cases perhaps, their jobs.)

Three days go by like this, and, to my chagrin, no one out of the approximately twenty places I've applied calls me for an interview. I had been vain enough to worry about coming across as too educated for the jobs I sought, but no one even seems interested in finding out how overqualified I am. Only later will I realize that the want ads are not a reliable measure of the actual jobs available at any particular time. They are, as I should have guessed from Max's comment, the employers' insurance policy against the relentless turnover of the low-wage workforce. Most of the big hotels run ads almost continually, just to build a supply of applicants to replace the current workers as they drift away or are fired, so finding a job is just a matter of being at the right place at the right time and flexible enough to take whatever is being offered that day. This finally happens to me at one of the big discount hotel chains, where I go, as usual, for housekeeping and am sent, instead, to try out as a waitress at the attached "family restaurant," a dismal spot with a counter and about thirty tables that looks out on a parking garage and features such tempting fare as "Pollish [sic] sausage and BBQ sauce" on 95-degree days. Philip, the dapper young West Indian who introduces himself as the manager, interviews me with about as much enthusiasm as if he were a clerk processing me for Medicare, the principal questions being what shifts can I work and when can I start. I mutter something about being woefully out of practice as a waitress, but he's already on to the uniform: I'm to show up tomorrow wearing black slacks and black shoes; he'll provide the rust-colored polo shirt with HEARTHSIDE embroidered on it, though I might want to wear my own shirt to get to work, ha ha. At the word "tomorrow," something between fear and indignation rises in my chest. I want to say, "Thank you for your time, sir, but this is just an experiment, you know, not my actual life."

So begins my career at the Hearthside, I shall call it, one small profit center within a global discount hotel chain, where for two weeks I work from 2:00 till 10:00 P.M. for $2.43 an hour plus tips.[3] In some futile bid for gentility, the management has barred employees from using the front door, so my first day I enter through the kitchen, where a red-faced man with shoulder-length blond hair is throwing frozen steaks against the wall and yelling, "Fuck this shit!" "That's just Jack," explains Gail, the wiry middle-aged waitress who is assigned to train me. "He's on the rag again"—a condition occasioned, in this instance, by the fact that the cook on the morning shift had forgotten to thaw out the steaks. For the next eight hours, I run after the agile Gail, absorbing bits of instruction along with fragments of personal tragedy. All food must be trayed, and the reason she's so tired today is that she woke up in a cold sweat thinking of her boyfriend, who killed himself recently in an upstate prison. No refills on lemonade. And the reason he was in prison is that a few DUIs caught up with him, that's all, could have happened to anyone. Carry the creamers to the table in a

monkey bowl, never in your hand. And after he was gone she spent several months living in her truck, peeing in a plastic pee bottle and reading by candlelight at night, but you can't live in a truck in the summer, since you need to have the windows down, which means anything can get in, from mosquitoes on up.

At least Gail put to rest any fears I had of appearing overqualified. From the first day on, I find that of all the things I have left behind, such as home and identity, what I miss the most is competence. Not that I have ever felt utterly competent in the writing business, in which one day's success augurs nothing at all for the next. But in my writing life, I at least have some notion of procedure: do the research, make the outline, rough out a draft, etc. As a server, though, I am beset by requests like bees: more iced tea here, ketchup over there, a to-go box for table fourteen, and where are the high chairs, anyway? Of the twenty-seven tables, up to six are usually mine at any time, though on slow afternoons or if Gail is off, I sometimes have the whole place to myself. There is the touch-screen computer-ordering system to master, which is, I suppose, meant to minimize server-cook contact, but in practice requires constant verbal fine-tuning: "That's gravy on the mashed, okay? None on the meatloaf," and so forth—while the cook scowls as if I were inventing these refinements just to torment him. Plus, something I had forgotten in the years since I was eighteen: about a third of a server's job is "side work" that's invisible to customers—sweeping, scrubbing, slicing, refilling, and restocking. If it isn't all done, every little bit of it, you're going to face the 6:00 P.M. dinner rush defenseless and probably go down in flames. I screw up dozens of times at the beginning, sustained in my shame entirely by Gail's support—"It's okay, baby, everyone does that sometime"—because, to my total surprise and despite the scientific detachment I am doing my best to maintain, I care.

15   You might imagine, from a comfortable distance, that people who live, year in and year out, on $6 to $10 an hour have discovered some sur-

vival stratagems unknown to the middle class. But no. It's not hard to get my co-workers to talk about their living situations, because housing, in almost every case, is the principal source of disruption in their lives, the first thing they fill you in on when they arrive for their shifts. After a week, I have compiled the following survey:

- Gail is sharing a room in a well-known downtown flophouse for which she and a roommate pay about $250 a week. Her roommate, a male friend, has begun hitting on her, driving her nuts, but the rent would be impossible alone.

- Claude, the Haitian cook, is desperate to get out of the two-room apartment he shares with his girlfriend and two other, unrelated, people. As far as I can determine, the other Haitian men (most of whom only speak Creole) live in similarly crowded situations.

- Annette, a twenty-year-old server who is six months pregnant and has been abandoned by her boyfriend, lives with her mother, a postal clerk.

- Marianne and her boyfriend are paying $170 a week for a one-person trailer.

- Jack, who is, at $10 an hour, the wealthiest of us, lives in the trailer he owns, paying only the $400-a-month lot fee.

- The other white cook, Andy, lives on his dry-docked boat, which, as far as I can tell from his loving descriptions, can't be more than twenty feet long. He offers to take me out on it, once it's repaired, but the offer comes with inquiries as to my marital status, so I do not follow up on it.

- Tina and her husband are paying $60 a night for a double room in a Days Inn. This is because they have no car and the Days Inn is within walking distance of the Hearthside. When Marianne, one of the breakfast servers, is tossed out of her trailer for subletting (which is against the trailer-park rules), she leaves her boyfriend and moves in with Tina and her husband.

- Joan, who had fooled me with her numerous and tasteful outfits (hostesses wear their own clothes), lives in a van she parks behind a shopping center at night and showers in Tina's motel room. The clothes are from thrift shops.[4]

When I moved out of the trailer park, I gave the key to number 46 to Gail and arranged for my deposit to be transferred to her. She told me that Joan is still living in her van and that Stu had been fired from the Hearthside. I never found out what happened to George.

In one month, I had earned approximately $1,040 and spent $517 on food, gas, toiletries, laundry, phone, and utilities. If I had remained in my $500 efficiency, I would have been able to pay the rent and have $22 left over (which is $78 less than the cash I had in my pocket at the start of one month). During this time I bought no clothing except for the required slacks and no prescription drugs or medical care (I did finally buy some vitamin B to compensate for the lack of vegetables in my diet). Perhaps I could have saved a little on food if I had gotten to a supermarket more often, instead of convenience stores, but it should be noted that I lost almost four pounds in four weeks, on a diet weighted heavily toward burgers and fries.

How former welfare recipients and single mothers will (and do) survive in the low-wage workforce, I cannot imagine. Maybe they will figure out how to condense their lives—including child-raising, laundry, romance, and meals—into the couple of hours between full-time jobs. Maybe they will take up residence in their vehicles, if they have one. All I know is that I couldn't hold two jobs and I couldn't make enough money to live on with one. And I had advantages unthinkable to many of the long-term poor—health, stamina, a working car, and no children to care for and support. Certainly nothing in my experience contradicts the conclusion of Kathryn Edin and Laura Lein, in their recent book *Making Ends Meet: How Single Mothers Survive Welfare and Low-Wage Work*, that low-wage work actually involves more hardship and deprivation than life at the mercy of the welfare state. In the coming months and years, economic conditions for the working poor are bound to worsen, even without the almost inevitable recession. As mentioned earlier, the influx of former welfare recipients into the low-skilled workforce will have a depressing effect on both wages and the number of jobs available. A general economic downturn will only enhance these effects, and the working poor will of course be facing it without the slight, but nonetheless often saving, protection of welfare as a backup.

The thinking behind welfare reform was that even the humblest jobs are morally uplifting and psychologically buoying. In reality they are likely to be fraught with insult and stress. But I did discover one redeeming feature of the most abject low-wage work—the camaraderie of people who are, in almost all cases, far too smart and funny and caring for the work they do and the wages they're paid. The hope, of course, is that someday these people will come to know what they're worth, and take appropriate action.

NOTES

1. According to the Department of Housing and Urban Development, the "fair-market rent" for an efficiency is $551 here in Monroe County, Florida. A comparable rent in the five boroughs of New York City is $704; in San Francisco, $713; and in the heart of Silicon Valley, $808. The fair-market rent for an area is defined as the amount that would be needed to pay rent plus utilities for "privately owned, decent, safe, and sanitary rental housing of a modest (non-luxury) nature with suitable amenities."

2. According to the *Monthly Labor Review* (November 1996), 28 percent of work sites surveyed in the service industry conduct drug tests (corporate workplaces have much higher rates), and the incidence of testing has risen markedly since the Eighties. The rate of testing is highest in the South (56 percent of work sites polled), with the Midwest in second place (50 percent). The drug most likely to be detected—marijuana, which can be detected in urine for weeks—is also the most innocuous, while heroin and cocaine are generally undetectable three days after use. Prospective employees sometimes try to cheat the tests by consuming excessive amounts of liquids and taking diuretics and even masking substances available through the Internet.

3. According to the Fair Labor Standards Act, employers are not required to pay "tipped employees," such as restaurant servers, more than $2.13 an hour in direct wages. However, if the sum of tips plus $2.13 an hour falls below the minimum wage, or $5.15 an hour, the employer is required to make up the difference. This fact was not mentioned by managers or otherwise publicized at either of the restaurants where I worked.

4. I could find no statistics on the number of employed people living in cars or vans, but according to the National Coalition for the Homeless's 1997 report, "Myths and Facts About Homelessness," nearly one in five homeless people (in twenty-nine cities across the nation) is employed in a full- or part-time job.

SUGGESTIONS FOR DISCUSSION

1. Ehrenreich tells the story of her own experience and of the lives of people she encountered during her experiment. She also makes an argument using both her story and the studies and reports she cites. With a group of your classmates, summarize Ehrenreich's argument. What in the argument depends on her stories of individuals and what depends on the broader reports and studies?

2. Recently one fast-food chain ran advertisements that depicted jobs at its restaurants as "starter jobs." In these commercials, employees are shown making shakes, handing food out the drive-up window, or ringing up an order while the voice-over says that one is a future aerospace engineer, and another is a future CEO of a multimillion-dollar corporation. Why might a successful fast-food chain bother to make what is clearly an image-building advertisement? Why focus on the future of its employees?

3. How does Ehrenreich's discussion of the workplace touch on the descriptions of work in Dilbert's world? How does it compare with Hochschild's findings?

SUGGESTIONS FOR WRITING

1. Make a list of service-sector jobs you are familiar with—because you have held them or have frequented a business that depends on them (fast-food restaurants, motels, bars, for example). Write an essay in which you examine to what extent Ehrenreich's experience

working in the service sector rings true for you. How does your own experience (or lack of experience) with these kinds of jobs influence your reading?

2. Ehrenreich writes that she does not expect to "experience poverty" because she is aware that she can always go back to her middle-class lifestyle when things get tough or when she tires of this life. In addition, she admits that friends have pointed out that if she just wants to prove that it is extremely difficult to live on minimum-wage work, she can do that easily enough on paper. Given that Ehrenreich knows she does not have to do the experiment, write an assessment of what she accomplished by posing as an out-of-work, down-on-her-luck single woman.

3. Throughout this chapter, several of the writers have suggested that work has to be about more than just bringing home a paycheck. Ehrenreich's experience trying to live on low pay for long hours suggests that the pay takes priority when there is so little of it. Write an essay in which you consider the conditions that must be in place for a job to mean more than the paycheck. Whether the paycheck is large or small might not be the most important element for some workers. What makes a job feel like "the great escape" that Arlie Hochschild writes of? If necessary, go back and reread several of the selections that precede Erhenreich's to get a feel for what people seem to value in their working lives.

PERSPECTIVES Sweatshop Economy

It has become a commonplace today to talk of a global marketplace and to express concern over what some call "outsourcing" and others call "exporting jobs" to countries where wages are low and unionization difficult. No industry has been criticized more for this practice than the fashion industry. Organizations such as the National Labor Committee, Students United Against Sweatshops, Global Exchange, and UNITE have organized boycotts and demonstrations against companies that profit on sweatshop labor. United Students Against Sweatshop Labor has been a particularly powerful voice in its efforts to force colleges and universities to stop buying school logo clothing that has been produced in sweatshops.

For some critics, the answer to sweatshop economy is simple: Boycott sweatshop goods. Others, however, argue that sweatshops have become a crucial part of the economy base in developing countries. They say that $1 a day might not seem like much to Americans, but it is a good wage to workers in East Asia.

The two articles that follow do not see the issue as such a simple dichotomy. Both acknowledge that all workers deserve a decent wage. They do, however, differ markedly in how they would define decent wages and in what to do about companies that rely on sweatshop labor.

TWO CHEERS FOR SWEATSHOPS

Nicholas D. Kristof and Sheryl WuDunn

Nicholas Kristof and Sheryl WuDunn won the 1990 Pulitzer Prize for international reporting for their *New York Times* stories on the Tiananmen democracy movement in China. Kristof has been the *Times* bureau chief in Hong Kong, Beijing, and Tokyo. WuDunn has served as a foreign correspondent in Beijing and Tokyo. The following article was excerpted in the *New York Times Sunday Magazine* (September 24, 2000) from their book *Thunder from the East: Portrait of a Rising Asia.*

SUGGESTION FOR READING   In their article, Kristof and WuDunn are careful to explain that they came to their position on sweatshops after many years of living in Asia and interviewing Asian workers. As you read, take note of how they make their argument for not boycotting sweatshops despite the low wages and bad conditions that they do acknowledge.

1   It was breakfast time, and the food stand in the village in northeastern Thailand was crowded. Maesubin Sisoipha, the middle-aged woman cooking the food, was friendly, her portions large and the price right. For the equivalent of about 5 cents, she offered a huge green mango leaf filled with rice, fish paste and fried beetles. It was a hearty breakfast, if one didn't mind the odd antenna left sticking in one's teeth.

One of the half-dozen men and women sitting on a bench eating was a sinewy, bare-chested laborer in his late 30's named Mongkol Latlakorn. It was a hot, lazy day, and so we started chatting idly about the food and, eventually, our families. Mongkol mentioned that his daughter, Darin, was 15, and his voice softened as he spoke of her. She was beautiful and smart, and her father's hopes rested on her.

"Is she in school?" we asked.

"Oh, no," Mongkol said, his eyes sparkling with amusement. "She's working in a factory in Bangkok. She's making clothing for export to America." He explained that she was paid $2 a day for a nine-hour shift, six days a week.

5   "It's dangerous work," Mongkol added. "Twice the needles went right through her hands. But the managers bandaged up her hands, and both times she got better again and went back to work."

"How terrible," we murmured sympathetically.

Mongkol looked up, puzzled. "It's good pay," he said. "I hope she can keep that job. There's all this talk about factories closing now, and she said there are rumors that her factory might close. I hope that doesn't happen. I don't know what she would do then."

He was not, of course, indifferent to his daughter's suffering; he simply had a different perspective from ours—not only when it came to

food but also when it came to what constituted desirable work.

Nothing captures the difference in mind-set between East and West more than attitudes toward sweatshops. Nike and other American companies have been hammered in the Western press over the last decade for producing shoes, toys and other products in grim little factories with dismal conditions. Protests against sweatshops and the dark forces of globalization that they seem to represent have become common at meetings of the World Bank and the World Trade Organization and, this month, at a World Economic Forum in Australia, livening up the scene for Olympic athletes arriving for the competition. Yet sweatshops that seem brutal from the vantage point of an American sitting in his living room can appear tantalizing to a Thai laborer getting by on beetles.

10   Fourteen years ago, we moved to Asia and began reporting there. Like most Westerners, we arrived in the region outraged at sweatshops. In time, though, we came to accept the view supported by most Asians: that the campaign against sweatshops risks harming the very people it is intended to help. For beneath their grime, sweatshops are a clear sign of the industrial revolution that is beginning to reshape Asia.

This is not to praise sweatshops. Some managers are brutal in the way they house workers in firetraps, expose children to dangerous chemicals, deny bathroom breaks, demand sexual favors, force people to work double shifts or dismiss anyone who tries to organize a union. Agitation for improved safety conditions can be helpful, just as it was in 19th-century Europe. But Asian workers would be aghast at the idea of American consumers boycotting certain toys or clothing in protest. The simplest way to help the poorest Asians would be to buy more from sweatshops, not less.

On our first extended trip to China, in 1987, we traveled to the Pearl River delta in the south of the country. There we visited several factories, including one in the boomtown of Dongguan, where about 100 female workers sat at workbenches stitching together bits of leather to make purses for a Hong Kong company. We chatted with several women as their fingers flew over their work and asked about their hours.

"I start at about 6:30, after breakfast, and go until about 7 p.m.," explained one shy teenage girl. "We break for lunch, and I take half an hour off then."

"You do this six days a week?"

15   "Oh, no. Every day."

"Seven days a week?"

"Yes." She laughed at our surprise. "But then I take a week or two off at Chinese New Year to go back to my village."

The others we talked to all seemed to regard it as a plus that the factory allowed them to work long hours. Indeed, some had sought out this factory precisely because it offered them the chance to earn more.

"It's actually pretty annoying how hard they want to work," said the factory manager, a Hong Kong man. "It means we have to worry about security and have a supervisor around almost constantly."

20   It sounded pretty dreadful, and it was. We and other journalists wrote about the problems of child labor and oppressive conditions in both China and South Korea. But, looking back, our worries were excessive. Those sweatshops tended to generate the wealth to solve the problems they created. If Americans had reacted to the horror stories in the 1980's by curbing imports of those sweatshop products, then neither southern China nor South Korea would have registered as much progress as they have today.

The truth is, those grim factories in Dongguan and the rest of southern China contributed to a remarkable explosion of wealth. In the years since our first conversations there, we've returned many times to Dongguan and the surrounding towns and seen the transformation. Wages have risen from about $50 a month to $250 a month or more today. Factory conditions have improved as businesses have scrambled to attract and keep the best laborers. A private housing market has emerged, and video arcades and computer schools have opened to cater to workers with rising incomes. A hint of a middle class has appeared—as has China's closest thing to a Western-style independent newspaper, Southern Weekend.

Partly because of these tens of thousands of sweatshops, China's economy has become one of the hottest in the world. Indeed, if China's 30 provinces were counted as individual countries, then the 20 fastest-growing countries in the world between 1978 and 1995 would all have been Chinese. When Britain launched the Industrial Revolution in the late 18th century, it took 58 years for per capita output to double. In China, per capita output has been doubling every 10 years.

In fact, the most vibrant parts of Asia are nearly all in what might be called the Sweatshop Belt, from China and South Korea to Malaysia, Indonesia and even Bangladesh and India. Today these sweatshop countries control about one-quarter of the global economy. As the industrial revolution spreads through China and India, there are good reasons to think that Asia will continue to pick up speed. Some World Bank forecasts show Asia's share of global gross domestic product rising to 55 to 60 percent by about 2025—roughly the West's share at its peak half a century ago. The sweatshops have helped lay the groundwork for a historic economic realignment that is putting Asia back on its feet. Countries are rebounding from the economic crisis of 1997–98 and the sweatshops—seen by Westerners as evidence of moribund economies—actually reflect an industrial revolution that is raising living standards in the East.

Of course, it may sound silly to say that sweatshops offer a route to prosperity, when wages in the poorest countries are sometimes less than $1 a day. Still, for an impoverished Indonesian or Bangladeshi woman with a handful of kids who would otherwise drop out of school and risk dying of mundane diseases like diarrhea, $1 or $2 a day can be a life-transforming wage.

25   This was made abundantly clear in Cambodia, when we met a 40-year-old woman named Nhem Yen, who told us why she moved to an area with particularly lethal malaria. "We needed to eat," she said. "And here there is wood, so we thought we could cut it and sell it."

But then Nhem Yen's daughter and son-in-law both died of malaria, leaving her with two grandchildren and five children of her own. With just one mosquito net, she had to choose which children would sleep protected and which would sleep exposed.

In Cambodia, a large mosquito net costs $5. If there had been a sweatshop in the area, however harsh or dangerous, Nhem Yen would have leapt at the chance to work in it, to earn enough to buy a net big enough to cover all her children.

For all the misery they can engender, sweatshops at least offer a precarious escape from the poverty that is the developing world's greatest problem. Over the past 50 years, countries like India resisted foreign exploitation, while countries that started at a similar economic level—like Taiwan and South Korea—accepted sweatshops as the price of development. Today there can be no doubt about which approach worked better. Taiwan and South Korea are modern countries with low rates of infant mortality and high levels of education; in contrast, every year 3.1 million Indian children die before the age of 5, mostly from diseases of poverty like diarrhea.

The effect of American pressure on sweatshops is complicated. While it clearly improves conditions at factories that produce branded merchandise for companies like Nike, it also raises labor costs across the board. That encourages less well established companies to mechanize and to reduce the number of employees needed. The upshot is to help people who currently have jobs in Nike plants but to risk jobs for others. The only thing a country like Cambodia has to offer is terribly cheap wages; if companies are scolded for paying those wages, they will shift their manufacturing to marginally richer areas like Malaysia or Mexico.

30   Sweatshop monitors do have a useful role. They can compel factories to improve safety. They can also call attention to the impact of sweatshops on the environment. The greatest downside of industrialization is not exploitation of workers but toxic air and water. In Asia each year, three million people die from the effects of pollution. The factories springing up throughout the region are far more likely to kill people through the chemicals they expel than through terrible working conditions.

By focusing on these issues, by working closely with organizations and news media in foreign countries, sweatshops can be improved. But refusing to buy sweatshop products risks making Americans feel good while harming those we are trying to help. As a Chinese proverb goes, "First comes the bitterness, then there is sweetness and wealth and honor for 10,000 years."

PENNIES AN HOUR AND NO WAY UP

Tom Hayden and Charles Kernaghan

Tom Hayden is a writer, former California state senator, and long-time activist. Charles Kernaghan is director of the National Labor Committee (NLC) in New York City. The NLC is an independent, nonprofit human-rights organization focused on the protection of worker rights.

Kernaghan has led fact-finding missions to Central America and the Caribbean—most recently bringing a delegation of U.S. university students to investigate working condition in the free-trade zones. He and the NLC have also hosted U.S. tours of workers from Honduras, El Salvador, Haiti, and China. This article first appeared on the *New York Times* op-ed page on July 6, 2002.

SUGGESTION FOR READING As you read, note those places in their argument where Hayden and Kernaghan touch upon the same issues Kristof and WuDunn use in their discussion of sweatshop economy. Notice where they seem to agree and where their positions differ.

1 In last week's meeting in Canada, the Group of Eight industrial nations grappled with the question of how to better economic conditions in poor nations. One powerful means would be to improve the conditions of workers in sweatshops. Two billion people in the world make less than two American dollars a day. As voters and consumers of sweatshop products, Americans can make a difference in ending the miserable conditions under which these people work.

Some argue that sweatshops are simply a step up a ladder toward the next generation's success: the garment worker at her loom is carrying out some objective law of development, or the young girl making toys for our children is breaking out of male-dominated feudalism. This line of thinking recalls the mythic rise of our immigrant ancestors to the middle class and beyond.

But the real story of those white ethnic ancestors was hardly a smooth ride up the escalator. Life in New York was better than oppression abroad, but people worked 16 hours a day for paltry wages, lived in cellars with raw sewage, died of starvation and fever and were crowded into tenements. Their misery shocked reformers like Jacob Riis and Charles Dickens. They fought their way out — marched for economic justice, built unions, voted and finally forced the Gilded Age to become the New Deal.

Today young, mostly female workers in Bangladesh, a Muslim country that is the fourth-largest garment producer for the United States market, are paid an average of 1.6 cents for each baseball cap with a Harvard logo that they sew. The caps retail at the Harvard bookstore for $17, which means the garment workers, who often are younger than the Harvard students, are being paid a tenth of 1 percent of the cap's price in the market. Also in Bangladesh, women receive 5 cents for each $17.99 Disney shirt they sew. Wages like these are not enough to climb the ladder with.

5 There are similar conditions in China. Three million young Chinese women working for wages as low as 12 cents an hour make 80 percent of the sporting goods and toys sold in the United States each year. Companies like Mattel spend 30 times more to advertise a toy than they pay the workers in China to make it.

Each year Americans buy 924 million garments and other textile items made in Bangladesh and $23.5 billion worth of toys and sporting goods from China. Don't we have the consumer and political power to pressure our corporations to end sweatshop wages paid to the people who make these goods? These workers are not demanding stock options and Jazzercise studios. Women in Bangladesh say they could care for their children if their wages rose to 34 cents an hour, two-tenths of 1 percent of the retail price of the Harvard hat.

Some economists argue that even the most exploited and impoverished workers are better off than those who are unemployed or trapped in slave labor. But that argument is not about offering anyone a ladder up, but about which ring of Dante's inferno people in developing nations are consigned to. We don't want Disney, Mattel, Wal-Mart or other major American companies to leave the developing world. We simply want to end the race to the bottom in which companies force countries to compete in offering the lowest wages for their people's labor. There should be a floor beneath which no one has to live.

Our elected officials should end their subservience to corporate donors and begin asking some big questions: Aren't we entitled to know the addresses of corporate sweatshops in developing countries so they can be open to monitoring by local advocates? Why should our tax dollars subsidize government purchases from companies that operate sweatshops?

Under our customs laws, we ban imports made with inmate and indentured labor, so why not extend the ban to include those made with sweatshop and child labor? And if we insist on enforcement of laws against pirate labels and CD's, why not protect 16-year-olds who make CD's for American companies? We should be helping these workers elbow and push their way up from squalor just as American progressives once helped our immigrant forebears.

SUGGESTIONS FOR DISCUSSION

1. With a group of your classmates, make a list of areas where these writers agree. To what extent is it total agreement? Where do their arguments depart?

2. Why do Kristof and WuDunn make it a point to tell their readers that they lived in Asia for fourteen years and began their investigations firmly opposed to sweatshops? How does that information shape the way a reader is likely to receive their argument?

3. Explain why Hayden and Kernaghan compare sweatshop wages and conditions today to the wages and conditions prevalent in the United States at the turn of the twentieth century? What do they hope to accomplish with that comparison?

SUGGESTIONS FOR WRITING

1. Make a survey of the clothes in your closet, the clothes for sale at any local clothing store, or the clothes most popular with your friends. How many of these items are made in countries named in the articles reproduced here and identified with sweatshop labor? How many have union labels? How easy is it to locate union-made clothing? Can you tell if an item that is made in the United States is a sweatshop-free item? After you have completed your investigations, write a brief report in which you indicate your findings and their implications. For example, if you and your friends only want to wear what are called "Sweat Free" clothes, how could you do that, based on what you were able to discover?

2. Reread the two essays, taking care to note where the authors of each article would agree and where they would disagree. Write an essay in which you position yourself within this discussion. What of each or either of these articles is convincing? What is missing in their arguments?

3. United Students Against Sweatshops has organized on campuses across the country such as Yale, Harvard, the University of Michigan, Johns Hopkins, and the University of Pennsylvania to convince their schools not to buy college logo clothes made in sweatshops. Write an editorial for your school paper addressing the issue of sweatshop-made clothing for colleges and universities. Make it clear why you believe your school should stop dealing with or be allowed to deal with companies that rely on sweatshop labor.

I STAND HERE IRONING

Tillie Olson

Tillie Olsen was born in 1912, began writing in the 1930s, and is considered a major voice for women in twentieth-century American literature. Olsen stopped writing for twenty years to raise four children and to work at a series of low-paying jobs to help support the family. She didn't return to writing as a profession until she was in her mid-forties and her last child had started school. The title story in the collection *Tell Me a Riddle* (1961), from which the following selection has been taken, won an O'Henry Prize for short fiction. "I Stand Here Ironing" has become a classic statement of the tensions women face between motherhood and the need to make a living outside the home.

SUGGESTION FOR READING   This story has little or no real "action." The woman telling it remains at the ironing board throughout as she recalls the story of her daughter's life. Keep track of that story as you read.

1   I stand here ironing, and what you asked me moves tormented back and forth with the iron.

"I wish you would manage the time to come and talk with me about your daughter. I'm sure you can help me understand her. She's a youngster who needs help and whom I'm deeply interested in helping."

"Who needs help." …Even if I came, what good would it do? You think because I am her mother I have a key, or that in some way you could use me as a key? She has lived for nineteen years. There is all that life that has happened outside of me, beyond me.

And when is there time to remember, to sift, to weigh, to estimate, to total? I will start and there will be an interruption and I will have to gather it all together again. Or I will become engulfed with all I did or did not do, with what should have been and what cannot be helped.

5   She was a beautiful baby. The first and only one of our five that was beautiful at birth. You do not guess how new and uneasy her tenancy in her now-loveliness. You did not know her all those years she was thought homely, or see her poring over her baby pictures, making me tell her over and over how beautiful she had been— and would be, I would tell her—and was now, to the seeing eye. But the seeing eyes were few or nonexistent. Including mine.

I nursed her. They feel that's important nowadays. I nursed all the children, but with her, with all the fierce rigidity of first motherhood, I did like the books then said. Though her cries battered me to trembling and my breasts ached with swollenness, I waited till the clock decreed.

Why do I put that first? I do not even know if it matters, or if it explains anything.

She was a beautiful baby. She blew shining bubbles of sound. She loved motion, loved light, loved color and music and textures. She would lie on the floor in her blue overalls patting the surface so hard in ecstasy her hands and feet would blur. She was a miracle to me, but when she was eight months old I had to leave her daytimes with the woman downstairs to whom she was no miracle at all, for I worked or looked for work and for Emily's father, who "could no longer endure" (he wrote in his good-bye note) "sharing want with us."

I was nineteen. It was the pre-relief, pre-WPA world of the depression. I would start running as soon as I got off the streetcar, running up the stairs, the place smelling sour, and awake or asleep to startle awake, when she saw me she would break into a clogged weeping that could not be comforted, a weeping I can hear yet.

10   After a while I found a job hashing at night so I could be with her days, and it was better. But it came to where I had to bring her to his family and leave her.

It took a long time to raise the money for her fare back. Then she got chicken pox and I had to wait longer. When she finally came, I hardly knew her, walking quick and nervous like her father, looking like her father, thin, and dressed in a shoddy red that yellowed her skin and glared at the pockmarks. All the baby loveliness gone.

She was two. Old enough for nursery school they said, and I did not know then what I know now—the fatigue of the long day, and the lacerations of group life in the kinds of nurseries that are only parking places for children.

Except that it would have made no difference if I had known. It was the only place there was. It was the only way we could be together, the only way I could hold a job.

And even without knowing, I knew. I knew the teacher that was evil because all these years it has curdled into my memory, the little boy hunched in the corner, her rasp, "why aren't you outside, because Alvin hits you? that's no reason, go out, scaredy." I knew Emily hated it even if she did not clutch and implore "don't go Mommy" like the other children, mornings.

15   She always had a reason why we should stay home. Momma, you look sick. Momma, I feel sick. Momma, the teachers aren't there today, they're sick. Momma, we can't go, there was a fire there last night. Momma, it's a holiday today, no school, they told me.

But never a direct protest, never rebellion. I think of our others in their three-, four-year-oldness—the explosions, the tempers, the denunciations, the demands—and I feel suddenly ill. I put the iron down. What in me demanded that goodness in her? And what was the cost, the cost to her of such goodness?

The old man living in the back once said in his gentle way: "You should smile at Emily more when you look at her." What *was* in my face when I looked at her? I loved her. There were all the acts of love.

It was only with the others I remembered what he said, and it was the face of joy, and not of care or tightness or worry I turned to them— too late for Emily. She does not smile easily, let alone almost always as her brothers and sisters do. Her face is closed and sombre, but when she wants, how fluid. You must have seen it in her pantomimes, you spoke of her rare gift for comedy on the stage that rouses laughter out of the audience so dear they applaud and applaud and do not want to let her go.

Where does it come from, that comedy? There was none of it in her when she came back to me that second time, after I had had to send her away again. She had a new daddy now to learn to love, and I think perhaps it was a better time.

20   Except when we left her alone nights, telling ourselves she was old enough.

"Can't you go some other time, Mommy, like tomorrow?" she would ask. "Will it be just a little while you'll be gone? Do you promise?"

The time we came back, the front door open, the clock on the floor in the hall. She rigid awake. "It wasn't just a little while. I didn't cry. Three times I called you, just three times, and then I ran downstairs to open the door so you could come faster. The clock talked loud. I threw it away, it scared me what it talked."

She said the clock talked loud again that night I went to the hospital to have Susan. She was delirious with the fever that comes before red measles, but she was fully conscious all the week I was gone and the week after we were home when she could not come near the new baby or me.

She did not get well. She stayed skeleton thin, not wanting to eat, and night after night she had nightmares. She would call for me, and I would rouse from exhaustion to sleepily call back: "You're all right, darling, go to sleep, it's just a dream," and if she still called, in a sterner voice, "now go to sleep, Emily, there's nothing to hurt you." Twice, only twice, when I had to get up for Susan anyhow, I went in to sit with her.

25   Now when it is too late (as if she would let me hold and comfort her like I do the others) I get up and go to her at once at her moan or restless stirring. "Are you awake, Emily? Can I get you something?" And the answer is always the same: "No, I'm all right, go back to sleep, Mother."

They persuaded me at the clinic to send her away to a convalescent home in the country where "she can have the kind of food and care you can't manage for her, and you'll be free to concentrate on the new baby." They still send children to that place. I see pictures on the society page of sleek young women planning affairs to raise money for it, or dancing at the affairs, or decorating Easter eggs or filling Christmas stockings for the children.

They never have a picture of the children so I do not know if the girls still wear those gigantic red bows and the ravaged looks on the every other Sunday when parents can come to visit "unless otherwise notified"—as we were notified the first six weeks.

Oh it is a handsome place, green lawns and tall trees and fluted flower beds. High up on the balconies of each cottage the children stand, the girls in their red bows and white dresses, the boys in white suits and giant red ties. The parents stand below shrieking up to be heard and the children shriek down to be heard, and between them the invisible wall: "Not to Be Contaminated by Parental Germs or Physical Affection."

There was a tiny girl who always stood hand in hand with Emily. Her parents never came. One visit she was gone. "They moved her to Rose Cottage," Emily shouted in explanation. "They don't like you to love anybody here."

30   She wrote once a week, the labored writing of a seven-year-old. "I am fine. How is the baby. If I write my leter nicly I will have a star. Love." There never was a star. We wrote every other day, letters she could never hold or keep but only hear read—once. "We simply do not have room for children to keep any personal possessions," they patiently explained when we pieced one Sunday's shrieking together to plead how much it would mean to Emily, who loved so to keep things, to be allowed to keep her letters and cards.

Each visit she looked frailer. "She isn't eating," they told us.

(They had runny eggs for breakfast or mush with lumps, Emily said later, I'd hold it in my mouth and not swallow. Nothing ever tasted good, just when they had chicken.)

It took us eight months to get her released home, and only the fact that she gained back so little of her seven lost pounds convinced the social worker.

I used to try to hold and love her after she came back, but her body would stay stiff, and after a while she'd push away. She ate little. Food sickened her, and I think much of life too. Oh she had physical lightness and brightness, twinkling by on skates, bouncing like a ball up and down up and down over the jump rope, skimming over the hill; but these were momentary.

35   She fretted about her appearance, thin and dark and foreign-looking at a time when every little girl was supposed to look or thought she should look a chubby blonde replica of Shirley Temple. The doorbell sometimes rang for her, but no one seemed to come and play in the house or be a best friend. Maybe because we moved so much.

There was a boy she loved painfully through two school semesters. Months later she told me how she had taken pennies from my purse to buy him candy. "Licorice was his favorite and I brought him some every day, but he still liked Jennifer better'n me. Why, Mommy?" The kind of question for which there is no answer.

School was a worry to her. She was not glib or quick in a world where glibness and quickness were easily confused with ability to learn. To her overworked and exasperated teachers she was an overconscientious "slow learner" who kept trying to catch up and was absent entirely too often.

I let her be absent, though sometimes the illness was imaginary. How different from my now-strictness about attendance with the others. I wasn't working. We had a new baby, I was home anyhow. Sometimes, after Susan grew old enough, I would keep her home from school, too, to have them all together.

Mostly Emily had asthma, and her breathing, harsh and labored, would fill the house with a curiously tranquil sound. I would bring the two old dresser mirrors and her boxes of collections to her bed. She would select beads and single earrings, bottle tops and shells, dried flowers and pebbles, old postcards and scraps, all sorts of oddments; then she and Susan would play Kingdom, setting up landscapes and furniture, peopling them with action.

40   Those were the only times of peaceful companionship between her and Susan. I have edged away from it, that poisonous feeling between them, that terrible balancing of hurts and needs I had to do between the two, and did so badly, those earlier years.

Oh there are conflicts between the others too, each one human, needing, demanding, hurting, taking—but only between Emily and Susan, no, Emily toward Susan that corroding resentment. It seems so obvious on the surface, yet it is not obvious. Susan, the second child, Susan, golden- and curly-haired and chubby, quick and articulate and assured, everything in appearance and manner Emily was not; Susan, not able to resist Emily's precious things, losing or sometimes clumsily breaking them; Susan telling jokes and riddles to company for applause while Emily sat silent (to say to me later: that was *my* riddle, Mother, I told it to Susan); Susan, who for all the five years' difference in age was just a year behind Emily in developing physically.

I am glad for that slow physical development that widened the difference between her and her contemporaries, though she suffered over it. She was too vulnerable for that terrible world of youthful competition, of preening and parading, of constant measuring of yourself against every other, of envy, "If I had that copper hair," "If I had that skin...." She tormented herself enough about not looking like the others, there was enough of the unsureness, the having to be conscious of words before you speak, the constant caring—

what are they thinking of me? without having it all magnified by the merciless physical drives.

Ronnie is calling. He is wet and I change him. It is rare there is such a cry now. That time of motherhood is almost behind me when the ear is not one's own but must always be racked and listening for the child cry, the child call. We sit for a while and I hold him, looking out over the city spread in charcoal with its soft aisles of light. "*Shoogily*," he breathes and curls closer. I carry him back to bed, asleep. *Shoogily*. A funny word, a family word, inherited from Emily, invented by her to say: *comfort*.

In this and other ways she leaves her seal, I say aloud. And startle at my saying it. What do I mean? What did I start to gather together, to try and make coherent? I was at the terrible, growing years. War years. I do not remember them well. I was working, there were four smaller ones now, there was not time for her. She had to help be a mother, and housekeeper, and shopper. She had to set her seal. Mornings of crisis and near hysteria trying to get lunches packed, hair combed, coats and shoes found, everyone to school or Child Care on time, the baby ready for transportation. And always the paper scribbled on by a smaller one, the book looked at by Susan then mislaid, the homework not done. Running out to that huge school where she was one, she was lost, she was a drop; suffering over the unpreparedness, stammering and unsure in her classes.

45   There was so little time left at night after the kids were bedded down. She would struggle over books, always eating (it was in those years she developed her enormous appetite that is legendary in our family) and I would be ironing, or preparing food for the next day, or writing V-mail to Bill, or tending the baby. Sometimes, to make me laugh, or out of her despair, she would imitate happenings or types at school.

I think I said once: "Why don't you do something like this in the school amateur show?" One morning she phoned me at work, hardly understandable through the weeping: "Mother, I did it. I won, I won; they gave me first prize; they clapped and clapped and wouldn't let me go."

Now suddenly she was Somebody, and as imprisoned in her difference as she had been in anonymity.

She began to be asked to perform at other high schools, even in colleges, then at city and statewide affairs. The first one we went to, I only recognized her that first moment when thin, shy, she almost drowned herself into the curtains. Then: Was this Emily? The control, the command, the convulsing and deadly clowning, the spell, then the roaring, stamping audience, unwilling to let this rare and precious laughter out of their lives.

Afterwards: You ought to do something about her with a gift like that—but without money or knowing how, what does one do? We have left it all to her, and the gift has as often eddied inside, clogged and clotted, as been used and growing.

50   She is coming. She runs up the stairs two at a time with her light graceful step, and I know she is happy tonight. Whatever it was that occasioned your call did not happen today.

"Aren't you ever going to finish the ironing, Mother? Whistler painted his mother in a rocker. I'd have to paint mine standing over an ironing board." This is one of her communicative nights and she tells me everything and nothing as she fixes herself a plate of food out of the icebox.

She is so lovely. Why did you want me to come in at all? Why were you concerned? She will find her way.

She starts up the stairs to bed. "Don't get me up with the rest in the morning." "But I thought you were having midterms." "Oh, those," she comes back in, kisses me, and says quite lightly, "in a couple of years when we'll all be atom-dead they won't matter a bit."

She has said it before. She *believes* it. But because I have been dredging the past, and all that compounds a human being is so heavy and meaningful in me, I cannot endure it tonight.

55   I will never total it all. I will never come in to say: She was a child seldom smiled at. Her father left me before she was a year old. I had to work her first six years when there was work, or I sent her home and to his relatives. There were years she had care she hated. She was dark and thin and foreign-looking in a world where the prestige went to blondeness and curly hair and dimples, she was slow where glibness was prized. She was a child of anxious, not proud, love. We were poor and could not afford for her the soil of easy growth. I was a young mother, I was a distracted mother. There were other children pushing up, demanding. Her younger sister seemed all that she was not. There were years she did not want me to touch her. She kept too much in herself, her life was such she had to keep too much in herself. My wisdom came too late. She has much to her and probably little will come of it. She is a child of her age, of depression, of war, of fear.

Let her be. So all that is in her will not bloom—but in how many does it? There is still enough left to live by. Only help her to know—help make it so there is cause for her to know—that she is more than this dress on the ironing board, helpless before the iron.

SUGGESTIONS FOR DISCUSSION

1. Sort out the details of the story. What is the setting? Who is the narrator and who is she talking to? What is the situation? What does the narrator mean when she says, "Even if I came, what good would it do? You think because I am her mother I have a key …? There is all that life that has happened outside of me, beyond me."

2. At the end of the story Emily says, "Whistler painted his mother in a rocker. I'd have to paint mine standing over an ironing board." What does Emily mean by that? Is she joking? Is she criticizing? In terms of how you imagine she spent most of her time, choose a woman in your life and explain how you would "paint" her. What characterizes the way she spends her days?

3. In what ways does the narrator take blame for her daughter's troubles? How much credit does she take for her daughter's successes? What role does Emily's father play in this situation?

SUGGESTIONS FOR WRITING

1. Write a response to this story in which you speculate how Emily might tell the same story. What would she have noticed in her mother's life? What might she miss?

2. Write an analysis of the role that work plays in the narrator's life. How does she use work to explain her daughter? To what extent does she describe herself through work? How does her work or her need to work determine the kind of mother she can be to Emily?

3. This story ends with a plea: "Only help her to know—help make it so there is cause for her to know—that she is more than this dress on the ironing board, helpless before the iron." Write an explanation for that final comment. How does it summarize the dilemma this narrator finds herself in? How might it represent the conflict many mothers have felt over the years as they worked to raise a family and to support that family?

VISUAL CULTURE   Women's Work

When the United States entered the second world war, the country experienced a shortage of working men at the same time that there was a clear need to increase production, especially in the defense industry. To help meet those needs, the government entered into a long campaign to convince women who were traditionally housewives to work outside the home. The campaign called those women "soldiers without guns," and popularized the character Rosie the Riveter as its symbol of the strength of women in the workforce.

Rosie the Riveter has since become an icon for working women, appearing today on T-shirts, coffee mugs, posters for women's organizations, and even on a first-class postage stamp in a series commemorating important events, people, and symbols of the twentieth century. On May 22, 2002, the auction house Sotheby's sold Norman Rockwell's original painting of Rosie the Riveter for $4,959,500. The painting that had originally appeared as the cover illustration on the May 29, 1943, *Saturday Evening Post* has become a multimillion dollar investment, its popularity perhaps spurred on by the events of September 11, 2001.

The aim of the Rosie campaign was to convince women that they could do any job a man could do. It was a campaign that threatened to backfire once the war was over and the government then wanted to convince women that the patriotic thing to do was to quit their outside jobs and get back to women's work—managing the household and raising children.

As you examine the images that follow, think about what "women's work" is and how that concept changes depending on who is using it and why it is being used. Is there anything today that could be called "women's work"?

Post-World War II poster

Rosie the Riveter image reprinted on commemorative postage stamp in 2000

Land's End catalogue cover featuring Norman Rockwell's original rendition of
Rosie the Riveter, June 2002

Artwork printed by permission of the Norman Rockwell Family Agency. Copyright ©1943 The Norman
Rockwell Family Entities. Catalog cover ©2002 Land's End, Inc. Used with permission.

"American Gothic"—Ella Watson with Broom and Mop
by Gordon Parks

Cover of *Nervy Girl!* magazine
Courtesy of *Nervy Girl!* Photography by Leia Windham.

SUGGESTIONS FOR DISCUSSION

1. The first image in this grouping depicts a man telling a woman worker, "We never figured you could do a man-size job." What does that statement and the comment that runs at the bottom of the poster—"America's women have met the test!"—suggest about attitudes toward women in the workforce before and after the war? Does the statement suggest gender equality? If so, why might some men think that women should have stepped aside and quit their jobs after the war?

2. Rosie the Riveter became a familiar and well-liked image of the American woman worker in World War II and has since become an icon for women's movements through the twentieth century.

   Consider three versions of the icon:

   • A "Rosie" in a post–World War II poster.

   • A U.S. stamp printed in the year 2000 to commemorate the decade of the 1940s and issued with a series of stamps commemorating each decade of the twentieth century.

   • A 2002 clothing catalogue cover illustration that reproduces Norman Rockwell's original Rosie the Riveter.

   How does the meaning of that image change depending on where, when, and for what purpose it is reproduced?

3. Look at and think about the final two images in this series. What are Gordon Parks and the editors of *Nervy Girl Magazine* saying about "women's work"? Are the two similar? How does Parks's comment seem to differ from *Nervy Girl*'s?

SUGGESTED ASSIGNMENT

Make your own visual—a poster, an illustration, a brochure, a photograph—illustrating the meaning of "women's work" today. As an introduction to or a reflection on your visual, write a commentary explaining what you tried to illustrate and what, in working conditions for women today or in the political or economic climate, made your choices possible or difficult.

FIELDWORK   Reconstructing the Network of a Workplace

In any job you hold, negotiating the workplace involves more than performing the work you were hired to do. You need to understand your coworkers and how they do their jobs, how they relate to each other and to you, how they have established unspoken rules for daily routines and interactions, and where you fit into all of that. As the narrator in Sandra Cisneros's story "The First Job" discovered, the people who have worked at a place for some time seem to know almost automatically how to act, when to speak, when to sit, and when to make sure they are working diligently.

This is what's known as the "social network" established in any job that involves more than two people. Most of these unspoken rules are unique to each work place and are unknown to those on the outside. If, for example, you entered an office, stood in front of what you thought was the receptionist's desk, and felt frustrated or confused when the person behind the desk pointedly ignored you until you discovered that the receptionist was at the next desk, you probably stumbled onto one of the unspoken rules that has evolved from the social network in that office. Customers often are confused by such networks and, for example, might call the waitress assigned to another area to their table in a restaurant or ask the stocker rather than a sales clerk at a discount store to help them purchase an item. New workers must learn to negotiate these social networks quickly or they are likely to make mistakes in front of the supervisor that veterans in that workplace would never make.

One way that anthropologists have studied the culture of the workplace is to try to understand the social networks established on the job. To do so, they have relied on interviews and on participant-observation studies, such as the one described in the next selection by James Spradley and Brenda Mann.

THE COCKTAIL WAITRESS

James P. Spradley and Brenda J. Mann

James Spradley, a professor of anthropology at MacAlaster College in St. Paul, Minnesota, and Brenda Mann, who has worked as a senior product analyst at Dialog Information Services, spent a year studying the culture of the workplace from the point of view of "cocktail waitresses," as waitresses in bars were still called in 1975 when this study was completed. The selection reprinted below is from *The Cocktail Waitress* and illustrates how workers daily and almost automatically interpret their own workplace so they know who to go to for information, whom to avoid, or what tasks will hang them up.

SUGGESTION FOR READING Spradley and Mann make a clear distinction between the "social structure" that has been established in Brady's bar and the "social network." Underline and annotate those places in the selection where Spradley and Mann provide examples or explanations for each. After you complete your reading, review your annotations and use them to write a short explanation of the difference between the two.

1   Denise moves efficiently through her section, stopping at a few of her tables. "Another round here?" she asks at the first table. They nod their assent and she moves on. "Would you like to order now?" "Two more of the usual here?" She takes orders from four of the tables and heads back to the bar to give them to the bartender. The work is not difficult for her now, but when she first started at Brady's, every night on the job was confusing, frustrating, embarrassing, and exhausting. Now it is just exhausting.

Her first night was chaos. When introduced to the bartender, Mark Brady, he responded with: "Haven't I seen you somewhere before?" Flustered, she shook her head. "He's not going to be one of those kind, is he?" she thought. Then later, following previous instruction, she asked two obviously underaged girls for identification, which they didn't have. As she was asking them to leave Mark called Denise over and told her not to card those two particular girls. Embarrassed, Denise returned to their table, explained they could stay, and took their order. A customer at the bar kept grabbing her every time she came to her station, and tried to engage her in conversation. Not knowing what to do, she just smiled and tried to look busy. She asked one customer what he wanted to drink and he said, "the usual" and she had to ask him what that was. An older man seated at the bar smiled and said, "Hello, Denise," as he put a dollar bill on her tray. Again, she didn't know what to say or do so she just smiled and walked away, wondering what she had done or was supposed to do to make her worth the dollar. Another customer at a table grabbed her by the waist each time she walked past his table and persistently questioned her: "Are you new here?" "What nights do you work?" "What are you doing after work?" And so went the rest of the evening. It wasn't until several nights later and following similar encounters that she began to sort out and make sense of all this. She began to learn who these people were, what special identities they had in the bar culture, and where each one was located in the social structure of Brady's Bar.

The bartender's initial question, albeit a rather standard come-on, had been a sincere and friendly inquiry. The two girls she carded were *friends of the Brady family* and often drank there despite their young age. The grabby and talkative customer at the bar was Jerry, a *regular customer* and harmless drinker. The dollar tip came from *Mr. Brady,* the patriarch of the business. The man with the hands and persistent questions was a *regular* from the University who had a reputation with the other waitresses as a *hustler* to be avoided. These people were more than just customers, as Denise had initially categorized them. Nor could she personalize them and treat each one as a unique individual. They were different *kinds* of people who came into Brady's, and all required different kinds of services and responses from her.

SOCIAL STRUCTURE

Social structure is a universal feature of culture. It consists of an organized set of social identities and the expected behavior associated with them. Given the infinite possibilities for organizing people, anthropologists have found it crucial to discover the particular social structure in each society they study. It is often necessary to begin by asking informants for the social identity of specific individuals. "He is a *big man*." "That's my *mother*." "She is my *co-wife*." "He is my *uncle*." "She is my *sister*." Then one can go on to examine these categories being used to classify people. A fundamental feature of every social

structure is a set of such categories, usually named, for dividing up the social world. In the area of kinship, for example, some societies utilize nearly 100 categories, organizing them in systematic ways for social interaction.

5   When we began our research at Brady's Bar, the various categories of the social structure were not easy to discern. Of course the different activities of waitresses, bartenders, and customers suggested these three groupings, but finer distinctions were often impossible to make without the assistance of informants. At first we thought it would be possible to arrange all the terms for different kinds of people into a single folk taxonomy, much like an anthropologist might do for a set of kinship terms. With this in mind, we began listening, for example, to the way informants talked about customers and asked them specifically, "What are all the different kinds of customers?" This procedure led to a long list of terms, including the following:

girl	regular	cougar
jock	real regular	sweetie
animal	person off street	waitress
bartender	policeman	loner
greaser	party	female
businessman	zoo	drunk
redneck	bore	Johnny
bitch	pig	hands
creep	slob	couple
bastard	hustler	king and
obnoxo	Annie	his court

This list was even more confusing as we checked out the various terms. For example, we asked, "Would a waitress say that a bartender is a kind of customer?" Much to our surprise, the answer was affirmative. Then we discovered that a *regular* could be an *obnoxo* or a *bore,* a *party* could be a *zoo,* a *cougar* was always a *jock,* but a *jock* could also be a *regular* or *person off the street.* Even though it seemed confusing, we knew it was important to the waitresses to make such fine distinctions among types of customers and that they organized all these categories in some way. As our research progressed it became clear that waitresses operated with several different sets of categories. One appeared to be the basis for the formal social structure of the bar, the others could only be understood in terms of the specific social networks of the waitresses. Let us examine each briefly.

The formal social structure included three major categories of people *customers, employees,* and *managers*. When someone first enters the bar and the waitresses look to see who it is, they quickly identify an individual in terms of one or another category in this formal social structure. The terms used form a folk taxonomy shown in Figure 8.1. Waitresses use these categories to identify who people are, anticipate their behavior, and plan strategies for performing their role.

Although waitresses often learn names and individual identities, it is not necessary. What every girl must know is the category to which people belong. It is essential, for example, to distinguish between a real regular and a person off the street. Both are customers, but both do not receive identical service from her. For example, a waitress should not have to ask a real regular what he's drinking, she should expect some friendly bantering as she waits on him, and she won't be offended if he puts his arm around her waist. A person off the street, however, receives only minimal attention from the waitress. Denise will have to inquire what he or she wants to drink, she won't be interested in spending her time talking with him, and she will be offended if he makes physical advances. It is important that Denise recognize these differences and not confuse the two kinds of customers. Being a good waitress means she can make such important distinctions. Although a knowledge of this formal social structure is essential to waitresses, it is not sufficient for the complexities of social interaction in Brady's Bar. In order to understand the other categories for identifying people and also to see how waitresses use the social structure, we need to examine the nature of *social networks*.

SOCIAL NETWORK

Social network analysis shifts our attention from the social structure as a formal system to the way it is seen through the eyes of individual members, in this case, the cocktail waitresses. Each waitress is at the center of several social networks.

FIGURE 8.1

Kinds of people at Brady's Bar	Managers		
	Employees	Bartenders	Night bartenders
			Day bartenders
		Bouncers	
		Waitresses	Day waitresses
			Night waitresses
	Customers	Regulars	Real regulars
			Regulars
		People off the street	Loners
			Couples
			Businessmen
			People off the street
			Drunks
		Female customers	

[See Figure 8.2] Some link her to specific individuals in the bar; other networks have strands that run outside the bar to college professors, roommates, friends, and parents. In addition to the formal social structure, we discovered at least three different sets of identities that make up distinct social networks. Only through an awareness of these networks is it possible to understand the way waitresses view their social world.

10   The first is a social network determined by the behavioral attributes of people. As the girls make their way between the bar and tables each night, identities such as *customer, waitress,* and *bartender* become less significant than ones like *bitch* and *obnoxo* based on specific actions of individuals. Sue returns to a table of four men as she balances a tray of drinks. No sooner has she started placing them on the table than she feels a hand on her leg. In the semidarkness no one knows of this encounter but the customer and the waitress. Should she ignore it or call attention to this violation of her personal space? She quietly steps back and the hand disappears, yet every time she serves the table this regular makes a similar advance. By the middle of the evening Sue is saying repeatedly, "Watch the hands." When Sandy takes over for her break, Sue will point out

hands, a man who has taken on a special social identity in the waitresses' network. The real regular, businessman, loner, person off the street, or almost any kind of male customer can fall into the same network category if his behavior warrants it. A customer who peels paper off the beer bottles and spills wax from the candle becomes a *pig*. The person who slows down the waitress by always engaging her in conversation, perhaps insisting that she sit at his table and talk, becomes a *bore*. As drinking continues during an evening, the behavior of some individuals moves so far outside the bounds of propriety that they become *obnoxos*. *Hustlers* gain their reputation by seeking to engage the waitress in some after-work rendezvous. The bartender who is impatient or rude becomes someone for the waitress to avoid, a real *bastard*. Even another waitress can be a *bitch* by her lack of consideration for the other girls. When a new waitress begins work, she doesn't know what kind of actions to expect nor how to evaluate them. Part of her socialization involves learning the categories and rules for operating within this network.

A second social network is based on social identities from outside the bar itself. Holly's roommate from college often visits the bar and

FIGURE 8.2

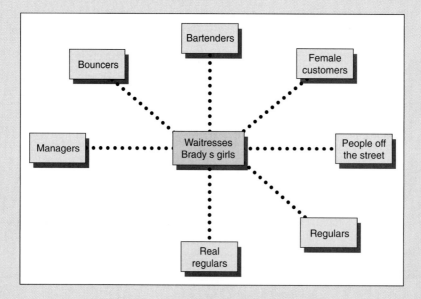

one or another waitress serves her. Although she is a *customer*, they treat her as one of the other girl's *roommates* who has a special place in this social network. Each waitress will reciprocate when the close friends of other waitresses come to the bar, offering special attention to these customers. The colleges attended by customers and employees provide another basis for identifying people. "That's a table of Annie's," Joyce will say about the girls from St. Anne's College. *Cougars* are customers who also play on the university football team. Even *bartenders* and *waitresses* can be terms for kinds of customers when they have these identities from other bars where they work.

Finally, there is a special network of insiders that crosscuts the formal social structure. This is *the Brady family*, made up of managers, employees, and customers—especially real regulars. The new waitress does not know about this select group of people when she first starts work. Sooner or later she will end up hanging around after work to have a drink on the house and talk. In this inner circle she will no longer think of the others as waitresses, bartenders, or customers, but now they are part of the Brady family. This network overarches all the specific categories of people in a dualistic kind of organization, a system not uncommon in non-Western societies. For example, a Nuer tribesman in Africa organizes people primarily on the basis of kinship. He has dozens of kinship terms to sort people into various identities and to anticipate their behavior. But every fellow tribesman, in a general sense, is either *both* or *mar*, distinctions that are important for social interaction. For the waitress, everyone in the bar is either in the Brady family or outside of it.

The social life of Brady's Bar derives its substance and form from the formal social structure as well as the various networks that waitresses and others activate for special purposes. Each waitress finds herself linked in some way to others in the bar with varying degrees of involvement.

SUGGESTIONS FOR DISCUSSION

1. Although this selection opens with a scene of a particular waitress working Brady's Bar, Spradley and Mann are not writing a story of the bar or a description of the shift of one waitress. Why provide this opening scene? How does it help readers to understand the information and analysis provided in the rest of the selection?

2. Recall a place where you have worked or think about the place where you currently work. What are some of the types of people who make up that workplace? Make a "single folk taxonomy" list the way Spradley and Mann do for Brady's Bar. In what way might your list be divided into a more formal social structure as the researchers divided their list of types at Brady's?

3. From what you have read here, explain how the social network at Brady's functions to help waitresses do their job and, at the same time, creates what Spradley and Mann call the "social life" of the bar.

Fieldwork Project

For this assignment, reconstruct the social network in a workplace, much like Spradley and Mann did. Do this assignment whether or not you are currently holding a job. If you currently hold a job (even if it is volunteer work, campus work, or work for an organization that is paid or unpaid), spend some time taking field notes (see Participant Observation Fieldwork in Chapter 3, Schooling) and keep the questions below in mind. If you currently do not hold a job, write about one you have done before and use the questions below to help you recall details of that workplace. Divide your report into three sections: Background, Analysis, and Conclusion.

Background

Begin your report by giving your audience a general background summary of the workplace. The questions below can help you to prepare that summary:

1. What is the nature of this business or organization?

2. When did you begin working there? What was/is your job? What difficulties did you encounter during the initial stages of the job?

3. Who are the people in this workplace, and how many employees typically are on the job at one time?

4. Who supervises the workplace? Is that person always present or only occasionally present?

5. What is the pay, if it is a paying position; if it is not, how many volunteer hours are expected of those who work there?

6. What do people expect from employees in this workplace? (For example, do customers expect to be waited on or are they left to themselves to browse?)

7. What is the work space like? Describe it. How large is it? Is there enough room here for workers to do a job comfortably? Is there anything in particular that is important to mention about the space? (For example, is it exceptionally dark or open or crowded?)

Analysis: Reconstructing the Social Network of the Workplace

Your aim in this central section of your report is to reconstruct the social network of the workplace. Spradley and Mann use both visual diagrams and descriptive analysis to explain how workers and customers interact in the bar to form the social network at Brady's. You can do the same. Begin by visually mapping out relationships and follow that diagram with a description of the social network you have reconstructed. The following questions can help you with your analysis:

1. Who is in charge (either by actually having a position above others or by virtue of less formal or unstated determinations)? Is the boss or supervisor always in control, or do subordinates have their own ways of doing what they want?

2. How do workers spend their time while on the job?

3. How do workers know what to do and when to do it?

4. What kinds of things happen that help or impede the work done in this place? Are there certain people you would identify as interfering with work and others you would say facilitate the work being done?

5. What seems to be the attitude of those working as they are doing their job?

6. How do workers interact with each other? Do they interact with customers or outside people coming into the work space? For example, what are the typical informal as well as formal interactions among employees, employees and customers, staff and supervisors, and so on?

7. Is there a person (supervisor or not) who must be pleased or not crossed? How do workers know that?

8. What are some things that go on in the job that you only learned on your own after working there for a time?

9. What are the unspoken rules of this workplace, and how does the social network that has evolved here seem to convey and sustain those rules?

Conclusion

The concluding paragraph of the Spradley and Mann selection offers a quick summary of their descriptive analysis:

> The social life of Brady's Bar derives its form from the formal social structure as well as the various networks that waitresses and others activate for special purposes. Each waitress finds herself linked in some way to others in the bar with varying degrees of involvement.

Your conclusion ought to do the same. Summarize your analysis quickly in this concluding portion of the report.

CHECKING OUT THE WEB

1. Besides the e-mail address, included in most of the Dilbert strips, Scott Adams with United Feature Syndicate, Inc., maintains an official Web site called "The Dilbert Zone." Locate the Web site and look for unofficial sites to see what difference it makes when fans represent or use this cartoon character and the situational humor of Dilbert. You will also find other sites on "job humor" on the Internet. How does the humor in these compare with Dilbert?

2. As you can see from the Perspectives discussion of sweatshops today, concern over sweatshop economy has returned to the news as a serious social matter. Much of the discussion has to do with working conditions outside the United States, but little attention has been given to sweatshops that investigators continue to find in this country.

   Some of the most interesting and innovative reporting and activism connected with this issue is available through Internet sources. By far the most thorough and interactive site for sweatshop history is the Smithsonian Institution's site devoted to its exhibit *Between a Rock and a Hard Place: A History of American Sweatshops 1820–Present* (http://americanhistory.si.edu/sweatshops/). Begin your work by visiting this site and following the many links that trace sweatshop history from the early part of the nineteenth century to the El Monte, California, sweatshop raid on August 2, 1995. After you have visited this site, extend your searches to sites such as the Cornell WorkNet page.

   Use the information you find in your research to create a public service announcement (video, audio, or print) to make consumers aware of this issue.

3. Visit the site http://www.hardhattedwomen.org, where the organization Hard Hatted Women has set up on-line support for women seeking jobs traditionally designated as jobs for men. The site was begun in 1979 when three women—a steelworker, a truck driver, and a telephone repair technician—decided to make resources available to women looking for jobs in nontraditional professions. Using that site and its related links to such sites as the Women's Labor Bureau as the basis for research on issues relevant to women's labor, what would you say are the primary issues for women in today's workforce? How are they different from men's labor issues?

Lewis Hine and the Social Uses of Photography

"Glass Factory Workers."

American photographer Lewis Hine believed that photography had an educational and social role to play, and he used his photographs to educate Americans about the conditions of working life in the United States in the first part of the twentieth century. For many years, Hine did work for the National Child Labor Committee. Historian Alan Trachtenberg has written that, for Hine, "social photography means that the photography itself performed a social act, made a particular communication." Hine believed that pictures could make a difference in the way people thought about issues, such as those surrounding child labor laws. He saw photography as a means of interpreting and revealing the world of work to the public at large.

In 1907, Hine was invited to participate in what came to be called "The Pittsburgh Survey," an investigation of labor conditions in Pittsburgh at the time. Hine's photos from that project were used in six volumes of the magazine *The Survey*, a new publication that had originally been called *Charities and the Commons*. Hine's work was also a familiar feature of *The Survey Graphic*, a monthly magazine begun in 1921.

Both of these publications are still available in many local and college libraries today. Check your library for that publication, and locate Hine's photographs in the early volumes. If you cannot find copies of *The Survey*, enter "Lewis Hine" into the image search engine on your computer and find representative examples of his work in dozens of Internet locations including sites for the George Eastman House, the Library of Congress, the New York Public Library, the University of Georgia Libraries, and the Chicago Historical Society.

Once you have located photographs by Lewis Hine and information on him and his work, use that material to report on the world of child labor as Hine interpreted it in these photos. In your report, look for what is distinctive about Lewis Hine's vision of child labor in America and speculate about why his photographs remain in the public eye today, even showing up occasionally in labor publicity.

CHAPTER 9

American History

Alfred Stieglitz's "The Steerage," 1907. Library of Congress

One of the marks of a good professional historian is the consistency with which he reminds his readers of the purely provisional nature of his characterization of events, agents, and agencies found in the always incomplete historical record.

—Hayden White, Tropics of Discourse

When asked what history is, most people say that it is the story of what has happened in the past. They might think of the dates they memorized and the events they learned in school—history as a set of facts about the Louisiana Purchase, the Mexican-American War, or the Homestead Act. Accounts of these events can be verified by records and evidence from the past, and based on these facts, these accounts are taken to be true.

But it is precisely because history claims an authority based on fact that it is important to ask a further question, namely, where do the facts come from? It is true that in one sense, the facts are simply there—in historical records, newspapers, government documents, archives, and so forth. The facts, however, cannot come forward on their own to speak for themselves. So although it seems incontestable that

405

Columbus did indeed sail from Spain to the West Indies in 1492, the meanings of the event, depending on how people have presented them, can vary considerably.

Students have to learn by heart many things in school. The alphabet. The multiplication tables. The names of the continents and oceans. But students also learn history by heart—and it is worth examining just what "to learn by heart" means. On the one hand, it means memorizing dates, names, and events—and probably getting tested on them. On the other hand, it also suggests an emotional investment. To learn the history of the American Revolution or the Civil War by heart is not just to acquire the facts but to acquire judgments and attitudes and to form social allegiances and loyalties. History, most students understand, despite the ostensibly objective tone of their textbooks, is a moral drama that contains lessons to teach them about which side they belong to in the unfolding story of the American nation.

The story Americans learn through school and history textbooks is a tale of national destiny—of how hard-working Americans developed a democratic society in the New World and how America prospered and grew bigger and stronger to become an industrial and geopolitical power in the twentieth century. According to this story, the expansion of America's borders and productivity is simply the natural growth and development of the nation, the inevitable unfolding of the country's role in history. This sense of destiny and national purpose is linked closely to Americans' image of themselves and their mission as a people. For many Americans, history is a form of collective memory that joins the country together in a national identity and explains how America became what it is today. American history, in this regard, is not just a matter of the facts. It takes on a mythic dimension by telling of the founding events, heroic acts, and tragic sacrifices that have made this country a powerful nation.

Until fairly recently, there existed a broad consensus about the meaning of American history and its principles of development. Nowadays, however, the version of American history that had prevailed in schools and textbooks has been called into question. Historians have started to reread the historical record to see what voices have been silenced or ignored in the story of America's national development. New perspectives—from women, African Americans, Latinos, Native Americans, Asian Americans, and working-class people—are being added to America's collective history; these alternative accounts complicate the picture of the American past considerably. The westward expansion, for example, from the perspective of Native Americans, looks less like the progressive development of the land and its agricultural and mineral resources and more like the military conquest and occupation of traditional tribal holdings.

The purpose of this chapter is to investigate the writing of history—and why individuals and groups might tell different versions of the past. You will be asked to read, think, and write about the version of American history that you learned in school. You will be asked to recall not only what you learned but also what lessons you were led to draw from the study of the past. You will be asked to think about whose version of the American past you learned, and whose perspectives are included and whose are excluded in the story. You will be asked to consider whether American history needs to be rewritten to include those perspectives that are absent—the voices from the past that have been silent in the history Americans learn in school.

You will be asked to read for the plot in historians' and other writers' accounts of the past—to describe what their perspectives bring into view about the past and how they have selected and arranged the events to tell a story. By looking at how historians and writers construct versions of the past (always from their particular perspective in the present), you can identify not only the techniques that they use to tell a story but also the different versions of the past that they make available to readers today. In contemporary America, to think about history is to think about competing versions of the past, and you will want to consider how the plots differ—and what is thereby at stake—in the various accounts of the past that you read in the following selections. The chapter's readings have been chosen to include contrasting examples of historical writing—official versions of American history taken from textbooks as well as efforts of revisionist historians and writers to retell the story of the American past. What you will see is that the differences in plots and perspectives raise profound questions about who is entitled to write American history and whose voices are heard.

The answers you get to these and to other questions are concerned finally not just with the study of the past but also with how you as a reader and writer align yourself in the present—how you know what the sides are in American history and where your sympathies reside. The purpose of this chapter, therefore, is to cause you to think about the role that history plays in your own and other people's lives and how it defines (or challenges) Americans' sense of identity as a people and as a nation.

Reading History

The opening selection offers perspectives on how learning about history is not simply a matter of learning what happened in the past. As Mary Gordon suggests in "More Than Just a Shrine: Paying Homage to the Ghosts of Ellis Island," visiting historical sites can be more than a history lesson. It can also offer an occasion to honor ancestors, in this case the Irish, Italians, and Lithuanian Jews in Gordon's family who immigrated to the United States around the turn of the century and whose lives show up only as statistics in the official historical record.

In "'Indians': Textualism, Morality, and the Problem of History," Jane Tompkins takes up the question of how historians' differing points of view and underlying assumptions result in conflicting interpretations of the past. Tompkins provides a personal account of her research on the Puritans' relations with Native Americans and how she dealt with the differences she found in a variety of historians' accounts of the past. Her written essay leads to Warren Neidich's Visual Essay on how Native Americans have been represented visually, "Contra Curtis: Early American Cover-Ups," with an introduction, "Necessary Fictions: Warren Neidich's Early American Cover-Ups" by Christopher Phillips.

The next cluster of readings concern the Vietnam War and make up a case study of how the history of this traumatic time is told and interpreted not only by professional historians but also by veterans, the media, and other types of observers. First is the pair included in the Perspective section: "The Tragedy of Vietnam," from George B. Tindall and David E. Shi's textbook *America: A Narrative History,* and "God's Country and American Know-How," several passages from Loren Baritz's book-length study of the cultural causes of the Vietnam War, *Backfire: A History of How American Culture Led Us Into the Vietnam War.* Both selections, as you will see, offers an explanation of American military involvement in Vietnam but differs considerably in scope and emphasis.

The next three readings deal in various ways with how people remember the Vietnam War. "Private First Class Reginald 'Malik' Edwards," an oral history from Wallace Terry's book *Bloods,* offers the recollections of an American soldier. Then Kristin Ann Hass's "Making a Memory of War: Building the Vietnam Veterans Memorial" explores the way memorials, monuments, statues, and other commemorations seek to make sense of war, thereby raising questions about how Americans have come to terms with painful memories and the still unsettled experience of the Vietnam War.

Finally, in "Spectacle of Memory and Amnesia: Remembering the Persian Gulf War," Marita Sturken argues that the Persian Gulf War amounted in many ways to a rewriting of the Vietnam War.

The Classic Reading in this chapter is Margaret Mead's "We Are All Third Generation." Written in 1942, this selection from Mead's book *And Keep Your Powder Dry* echoes the concerns in Mary Gordon's opening essay about how people become Americans.

As you read, think, talk, and write about how American history has been constructed, you will be asked to consider where the meanings Americans ascribe to their history come from and how the meanings they give to the past position them in relation to the social, cultural, and political realities of the present. What do Americans as a people choose to remember and commemorate about their past? How does historical memory influence life in contemporary America?

MORE THAN JUST A SHRINE: Paying Homage to the Ghosts of Ellis Island

Mary Gordon

Mary Gordon is an acclaimed novelist and short-story writer who teaches at Barnard College. Her novels *Final Payments*, *The Company of Women*, and *The Other Side* explore the history and culture of Irish Catholics in America. In the following selection, an essay originally published in the *New York Times* (1987), Gordon offers her personal reflections on the history of immigration that brought her ancestors—Irish, Italian, and Lithuanian Jews—to the United States by way of Ellis Island, the point of entry in New York Harbor for more than sixteen million immigrants between 1892 and 1924. In her essay, Gordon suggests that history is a living relationship to the past, in this case to the "ghosts of Ellis Island" that she wants to honor.

SUGGESTION FOR READING As you read, notice that Mary Gordon provides a good deal of historical information about Ellis Island, and yet her main point is to establish her own personal connection to this American landmark. Mark passages where Gordon locates herself in relation to what took place in the past.

1 I once sat in a hotel in Bloomsbury trying to have breakfast alone. A Russian with a habit of compulsively licking his lips asked if he could join me. I was afraid to say no; I thought it might be bad for détente. He explained to me that he was a linguist and that he always liked to talk to Americans to see if he could make any connection between their speech and their ethnic background. When I told him about my mixed ancestry—my mother is Irish and Italian, my father was a Lithuanian Jew—he began jumping up and down in his seat, rubbing his hands together and licking his lips even more frantically.

"Ah," he said, "so you are really somebody who comes from what is called the boiling pot of America." Yes, I told him; yes, I was; but I quickly rose to leave. I thought it would be too hard to explain to him the relation of the boiling potters to the main course, and I wanted to get to the British Museum. I told him that the only thing I could think of that united people whose backgrounds, histories, and points of view were utterly diverse was that their people had landed at a place called Ellis Island.

I didn't tell him that Ellis Island was the only American landmark I'd ever visited. How could I describe to him the estrangement I'd always felt from the kind of traveler who visits shrines to America's past greatness, those rebuilt forts with muskets behind glass and sabers mounted on the walls and gift shops selling maple sugar candy in the shape of Indian headdresses, those reconstructed villages with tables set for fifty and the Paul Revere silver gleaming? All that Americana—Plymouth Rock, Gettysburg, Mount Vernon, Valley Forge—it all inhabits for me a zone of blurred abstraction with far less hold on my imagination than the Bastille or Hampton Court. I suppose I've always known that my uninterest in it contains a large component of the willed: I am American, and those places purport to be my history. But they are not mine.

Ellis Island is, though; it's the one place I can be sure my people are connected to. And so I made a journey there to find my history, like any Rotarian traveling in his Winnebago to Antietam to find his. I had become part of that humbling democracy of people looking in some site for a past that has grown unreal. The monument I traveled to was not, however, a tribute to some old glory. The minute I set foot upon the island I could feel all that it stood for: insecurity, obedience, anxiety, dehumanization, the terrified and careful deference of the displaced. I hadn't traveled to the Battery and boarded a ferry across from the Statue of Liberty to raise flags or breathe a richer, more triumphant air. I wanted to do homage to the ghosts.

5   I felt them everywhere, from the moment I disembarked and saw the building with its high-minded brick, its hopeful little lawn, its ornamental cornices. The place was derelict when I arrived; it had not functioned for more than thirty years— almost as long as the time it had operated at full capacity as a major immigration center. I was surprised to learn what a small part of history Ellis Island had occupied. The main building was constructed in 1892, then rebuilt between 1898 and 1900 after a fire. Most of the immigrants who arrived during the latter half of the nineteenth century, mainly northern and western Europeans, landed not at Ellis Island but on the western tip of the Battery, at Castle Garden, which had opened as a receiving center for immigrants in 1855.

By the 1880s, the facilities at Castle Garden had grown scandalously inadequate. Officials looked for an island on which to build a new immigration center, because they thought that on an island immigrants could be more easily protected from swindlers and quickly transported to railroad terminals in New Jersey. Bedloe's Island was considered, but New Yorkers were aghast at the idea of a "Babel" ruining their beautiful new treasure, "Liberty Enlightening the World." The statue's sculptor, Frédéric-Auguste Bartholdi, reacted to the prospect of immigrants landing near his masterpiece in horror; he called it a "monstrous plan." So much for Emma Lazarus.

Ellis Island was finally chosen because the citizens of New Jersey petitioned the federal government to remove from the island an old naval powder magazine that they thought dangerously close to the Jersey shore. The explosives were removed; no one wanted the island for anything. It was the perfect place to build an immigration center.

I thought about the island's history as I walked into the building and made my way to the room that was the center in my imagination of the Ellis Island experience: the Great Hall. It had been made real for me in the stark, accusing photographs of Louis Hine and others, who took those pictures to make a point. It was in the Great Hall that everyone had waited—waiting, always, the great vocation of the dispossessed. The room was empty, except for me and a handful of other visitors and the park ranger who showed us around. I felt myself grow insignificant in that room, with its huge semicircular windows, its air, even in dereliction, of solid and official probity.

I walked in the deathlike expansiveness of the room's disuse and tried to think of what it might have been like, filled and swarming. More than sixteen million immigrants came through that room; approximately 250,000 were rejected. Not really a large proportion, but the implications for the rejected were dreadful. For some, there was nothing to go back to, or there was certain death; for others, who left as adventurers, to return would be to adopt in local memory the fool's role, and the failure's. No wonder that the island's history includes reports of three thousand suicides.

10   Sometimes immigrants could pass through Ellis Island in mere hours, though for some the process took days. The particulars of the experience in the Great Hall were often influenced by the political events and attitudes on the mainland. In the 1890s and the first years of the new century, when cheap labor was needed, the newly built receiving center took in its immigrants with comparatively little question. But as the century progressed, the economy worsened, eugenics became both scientifically respectable and popular, and World War I made American xenophobia seem rooted in fact.

Immigration acts were passed; newcomers had to prove, besides moral correctness and financial solvency, their ability to read. Quota laws came into effect, limiting the number of immigrants from southern and eastern Europe to less than 14 percent of the total quota. Intelligence tests were biased against all non-English-speaking persons, and medical examinations became increasingly strict, until the machinery of immigration nearly collapsed under its own weight. The Second Quota Law of 1924 provided that all immigrants be inspected and issued visas at American consular offices in Europe, rendering the center almost obsolete.

On the day of my visit, my mind fastened upon the medical inspections, which had always seemed to me most emblematic of the ignominy and terror the immigrants ensured. The medical inspectors, sometimes dressed in uniforms like soldiers, were particularly obsessed with a disease of the eyes called trachoma, which they checked for by flipping back the immigrants' top eyelids with a hook used for buttoning gloves—a method that sometimes resulted in the transmission of the disease to healthy people. Mothers feared that if their children cried too much, their red eyes would be mistaken for a symptom of the disease and the whole family would be sent home. Those immi-

grants suspected of some physical disability had initials chalked on their coats. I remembered the photographs I'd seen of people standing, dumb-struck and innocent as cattle, with their manifest numbers hung around their necks and initials marked in chalk upon their coats: "E" for eye trouble, "K" for hernia, "L" for lameness, "X" for mental defects, "H" for heart disease.

I thought of my grandparents as I stood in the room: my seventeen-year-old grandmother, coming alone from Ireland in 1896, vouched for by a stranger who had found her a place as a domestic servant to some Irish who had done well. I tried to imagine the assault it all must have been for her; I've been to her hometown, a collection of farms with a main street—smaller than the athletic field of my local public school. She must have watched the New York skyline as the first- and second-class passengers were whisked off the gangplank with the most cursory of inspections while she was made to board a ferry to the new immigration center.

What could she have made of it—this buff-painted wooden structure with its towers and its blue slate roof, a place *Harper's Weekly* described as "a latter-day watering place hotel"? It would have been the first time she had heard people speaking something other than English. She would have mingled with people carrying baskets on their heads and eating foods unlike any she had ever seen—dark-eyed people, like the Sicilian she would marry ten years later, who came over with his family at thirteen, the man of the family, responsible even then for his mother and sister. I don't know what they thought, my grandparents, for they were not expansive people, nor romantic; they didn't like to think of what they called "the hard times," and their trip across the ocean was the single adventurous act of lives devoted after landing to security, respectability, and fitting in.

15   What is the potency of Ellis Island for someone like me—an American, obviously, but one who has always felt that the country really belonged to the early settlers, that, as J. F. Powers wrote in *Morte D'Urban,* it had been "handed

down to them by the Pilgrims, George Washington and others, and that they were taking a risk in letting you live in it." I have never been the victim of overt discrimination; nothing I have wanted has been denied me because of the accidents of blood. But I suppose it is part of being an American to be engaged in a somewhat tiresome but always self-absorbing process of national definition. And in this process, I have found in traveling to Ellis Island an important piece of evidence that could remind me I was right to feel my differentness. Something had happened to my people on that island, a result of the eternal wrongheadedness of American protectionism and the predictabilities of simple greed. I came to the island, too, so I could tell the ghosts that I was one of them, and that I honored them—their stoicism, and their innocence, the fear that turned them inward, and their pride. I wanted to tell them that I liked them better than I did the Americans who made them pass through the Great Hall and stole their names and chalked their weaknesses in public on their clothing. And to tell the ghosts what I have always thought: that American history was a very classy party that was not much fun until they arrived, brought the good food, turned up the music, and taught everyone to dance.

SUGGESTIONS FOR DISCUSSION

1. Mary Gordon describes the "estrangement I'd always felt from the kind of traveler who visits shrines to America's past greatness" and goes on to say that "those places purport to be my history. But they are not mine." Why does Gordon feel this way? What is she suggesting about the way that people experience the history of America? Do some parts belong to you but not others?

2. What historical landmarks have you visited with your family or on class trips in elementary or high school? What were your feelings about those trips? Compare your experience with Gordon's. Did you experience these historical sites as part of your history? Explain.

3. Gordon says that Ellis Island is "the one place I can be sure my people are connected to." Name a place to which your people are connected, where you could, as Gordon puts it, "do homage to the ghosts." To what extent is the place you have named alike or different from the places that your classmates have named?

SUGGESTIONS FOR WRITING

1. Mary Gordon says the one thing that unifies her ancestors—Irish, Italian, and Lithuanian Jews "whose backgrounds, histories, and points of view were utterly diverse"—is that they all landed at Ellis Island. Write an essay that explores the diversity among your ancestors and considers whether there is something—a place such as Ellis Island or a historical event such as immigration—that unites them.

2. Use Gordon's account of her visit to Ellis Island as a model to write an essay that explains your response to visiting a historical site. Explain the historical importance of the place you visited, but also follow Gordon's example to explain your own relation to that history. Did you experience the place as part of a history to which you felt connected, or did you, for some reason, feel estranged?

3. Gordon's essay suggests that history is as much a matter of paying "homage to the ghosts" as it is learning a chronology of events. Pick a historical figure, place, or event in American history with which you feel a strong personal identification. Describe it and then explain the reasons for your identification. Use the essay as an occasion to pay homage—to explain your personal allegiances and why the person, place, or event seems important to you.

"INDIANS": Textualism, Morality, and the Problem of History

Jane Tompkins

Jane Tompkins currently is a professor of English and education at University of Illinois, Chicago. She is well known for her literary criticism, including the two books *Sensational Designs: The Cultural Work of American Fiction, 1790–1860* (1985) and *West of Everything: The Inner Life of Westerns* (1992). The following essay was written for the journal of literary criticism *Critical Inquiry* and originally appeared in 1986. As you will see, the essay reports on how Tompkins dealt with the conflicting historical interpretations that she encountered in her research on the Puritans' relation with Native Americans.

SUGGESTION FOR READING   Notice that Tompkins's essay can be divided into three parts. The first part raises the problem of conflicting interpretations. The second part—the longest part of the essay—reports on her research and the differing assumptions, perspectives, and interpretations that she has found. In the final part, Tompkins explains how she found a "way out" of the difficulties that these "irreconcilable points of view" posed for her. As you read, annotate the essay to help you keep track of what Tompkins is doing.

1   When I was growing up in New York City, my parents used to take me to an event in Inwood Park at which Indians—real American Indians dressed in feathers and blankets—could be seen and touched by children like me. This event was always a disappointment. It was more fun to imagine that you were an Indian in one of the caves in Inwood Park than to shake the hand of an old man in a headdress who was not overwhelmed at the opportunity of meeting you. After staring at the Indians for a while, we would take a walk in the woods where the caves were, and once I asked my mother if the remains of a fire I had seen in one of them might have been left by the original inhabitants. After that, wandering up some stone steps cut into the side of the hill, I imagined I was a princess in a rude castle. My Indians, like my princesses, were creatures totally of the imagination, and I did not care to have any real exemplars interfering with what I already knew.

I already knew about Indians from having read about them in school. Over and over we were told the story of how Peter Minuit had bought Manhattan Island from the Indians for twenty-four dollars' worth of glass beads. And it was a story we didn't mind hearing because it gave us the rare pleasure of having someone to feel superior to, since the poor Indians had not known (as we eight-year-olds did) how valuable a piece of property Manhattan Island would become. Generally, much was made of the Indian presence in Manhattan; a poem in one of our readers began: "Where we walk to school today / Indian children used to play," and we were encouraged to write poetry on this topic ourselves. So I had a fairly rich relationship with Indians before I ever met the unprepossessing people in Inwood Park. I felt that I had a lot in common with them. They, too, liked animals (they were often named after animals); they, too, made mistakes—they liked the brightly colored trinkets of little value that the white men were always offering them; they were handsome, warlike, and brave and had led an exciting, romantic life in the forest long ago, a life such as I dreamed of leading myself. I felt lucky to be living in one of the places where they had definitely been. Never mind where they were or what they were doing now.

My story stands for the relationship most non-Indians have to the people who first populated this continent, a relationship characterized by narcissistic fantasies of freedom and adventure, of a life lived closer to nature and to spirit than the life we lead now. As Vine Deloria Jr. has pointed out, the American Indian Movement in the early seventies couldn't get people to pay attention to what was happening to Indians who were alive in the present, so powerful was this country's infatuation with people who wore loincloths, lived in tepees, and roamed the plains and forests long ago.[1] The present essay, like these fantasies, doesn't have much to do with actual Indians, though its subject matter is the histories of European-Indian relations in seventeenth-century New England. In a sense, my encounter with Indians as an adult doing "research" replicates the childhood one, for while I started out to learn about Indians, I ended up preoccupied with a problem of my own.

This essay enacts a particular instance of the challenge poststructuralism poses to the study of history. In simpler language, it concerns the difference that point of view makes when people are giving accounts of events, whether at first or second hand. The problem is that if all accounts of events are determined through and through by the observer's frame of reference, then one will never know, in any given case, what really happened.

5   I encountered this problem in concrete terms while preparing to teach a course in colonial American literature. I'd set out to learn what I could about the Puritans' relations with American Indians. All I wanted was a general idea of what had happened between the English settlers and the natives in seventeenth-century New England; poststructuralism and its dilemmas were the furthest thing from my mind. I began, more or less automatically, with Perry Miller, who hardly mentions the Indians at all, then proceeded to the work of historians who had dealt exclusively with the European-Indian encounter. At first, it was a question of deciding which of these authors to believe, for it quickly became apparent that there was no unanimity on the subject. As I read on, however, I discovered that the problem was more complicated than deciding whose version of events was correct. Some of the conflicting accounts were not simply contradictory, they were completely incommensurable, in that their assumptions about what counted as a valid approach to the subject, and what the subject itself was, diverged in fundamental ways. Faced with an array of mutually irreconcilable points of view, points of view which determined what was being discussed as well as the terms of the discussion, I decided to turn to primary sources for clarification, only to discover that the primary sources reproduced the problem all over again. I found myself, in other words, in an epistemological quandary, not only unable to decide among conflicting versions of events but also unable to believe that any such decision could, in principle, be made. It was a moral quandary as well. Knowledge of what really happened when the Europeans and the Indians first met seemed particularly important, since the result of that encounter was virtual genocide. This was the kind of past "mistake" which, presumably, we studied history in order to avoid repeating. If studying history couldn't put us in touch with actual events and their causes, then what was to prevent such atrocities from happening again?

For a while, I remained at this impasse. But through analyzing the process by which I had reached it, I eventually arrived at an understanding which seemed to offer a way out. This essay records the concrete experience of meeting and solving the difficulty I have just described (as an abstract problem, I thought I had solved it long ago). My purpose is not to throw new light on antifoundationalist epistemology—the solution I reached is not a new one—but to dramatize and expose the troubles antifoundationalism gets you into when you meet it, so to speak, in the road.

My research began with Perry Miller. Early in the preface to *Errand into the Wilderness,* while explaining how he came to write his history of the New England mind, Miller writes a sentence that stopped me dead. He says that what fascinated him as a young man about his country's history was "the massive narrative of the movement of European culture into the vacant wilderness of America."[2] "Vacant?" Miller, writing in 1956, doesn't pause over the word "vacant," but to people who read his preface thirty years later, the word is shocking. In what circumstances could someone proposing to write a history of colonial New England not take account of the Indian presence there?

The rest of Miller's preface supplies an answer to this question, if one takes the trouble to piece together its details. Miller explains that as a young man, jealous of older compatriots who had had the luck to fight in World War I, he had gone to Africa in search of adventure. "The adventures that Africa afforded," he writes, "were tawdry enough, but it became the setting for a sudden epiphany" (p. vii). "It was given to me," he writes, "disconsolate on the edge of a jungle of central Africa, to have thrust upon me the mission of expounding what I took to be the innermost propulsion of the United States, while supervising, in that barbaric tropic, the unloading of drums of case oil flowing out of the inexhaustible wilderness of America" (p. viii). Miller's picture of himself on the banks of the Congo furnishes a key to the kind of history he will write and to his mental image of a vacant wilderness; it explains why it was just there, under precisely these conditions, that he should have had his epiphany.

The fuel drums stand, in Miller's mind, for the popular misconception of what this country is about. They are "tangible symbols of [America's] appalling power," a power that everyone but Miller takes for the ultimate reality (p. ix). To Miller, "the mind of man is the basic factor in human history," and he will plead, all unaccommodated as he is among the fuel drums, for the intellect—the intellect for which his fellow historians, with their chapters on "stoves or bathtubs, or tax laws," "the Wilmot Proviso" and "the chain store," "have so little respect" (p. viii, ix). His preface seethes with a hatred of the merely physical and mechanical, and this hatred, which is really a form of moral outrage, explains not

only the contempt with which he mentions the stoves and bathtubs but also the nature of his experience in Africa and its relationship to the "massive narrative" he will write.

10   Miller's experiences in Africa are "tawdry," his tropic is barbaric because the jungle he stands on the edge of means nothing to him, no more, indeed something less, than the case oil. It is the nothingness of Africa that precipitates his vision. It is the barbarity of the "dark continent," the obvious (but superficial) parallelism between the jungle at Matadi and America's "vacant wilderness" that releases in Miller the desire to define and vindicate his country's cultural identity. To the young Miller, colonial Africa and colonial America are—but for the history he will bring to light—mirror images of one another. And what he fails to see in the one landscape is the same thing he overlooks in the other: the human beings who people it. As Miller stood with his back to the jungle, thinking about the role of mind in human history, his failure to see that the land into which European culture had moved was not vacant but already occupied by a varied and numerous population, is of a piece with his failure, in his portrait of himself at Matadi, to notice who was carrying the fuel drums he was supervising the unloading of.

The point is crucial because it suggests that what is invisible to the historian in his own historical moment remains invisible when he turns his gaze to the past. It isn't that Miller didn't "see" the black men, in a literal sense, any more than it's the case that when he looked back he didn't "see" the Indians, in the sense of not realizing they were there. Rather, it's that neither the Indians nor the blacks *counted* for him, in a fundamental way. The way in which Indians can be seen but not counted is illustrated by an entry in Governor John Winthrop's journal, three hundred years before, when he recorded that there had been a great storm with high winds "yet through God's great mercy it did no hurt, but only killed one Indian with the fall of a tree."[3] The juxtaposition suggests that Miller shared with Winthrop a certain colonial point of view, a point of view from which Indians, though present, do not finally matter.

A book entitled *New England Frontier: Puritans and Indians, 1620–1675,* written by Alden Vaughan and published in 1965, promised to rectify Miller's omission. In the outpouring of work on the European-Indian encounter that began in the early sixties, this book is the first major landmark, and to a neophyte it seems definitive. Vaughan acknowledges the absence of Indian sources and emphasizes his use of materials which catch the Puritans "off guard."[4] His announced conclusion that "the New England Puritans followed a remarkably humane, considerate, and just policy in their dealings with the Indians" seems supported by the scope, documentation, and methodicalness of his project (NEF, p. vii). The author's fair-mindedness and equanimity seem everywhere apparent, so that when he asserts "the history of interracial relations from the arrival of the Pilgrims to the outbreak of King Philip's War is a credit to the integrity of both peoples," one is positively reassured (NEF, p. viii).

But these impressions do not survive an admission that comes late in the book, when, in the course of explaining why works like Helen Hunt Jackson's *Century of Dishonor* had spread misconceptions about Puritan treatment of the Indians, Vaughan finally lays his own cards on the table.

> The root of the misunderstanding [about Puritans and Indians]…lie[s] in a failure to recognize the nature of the two societies that met in seventeenth century New England. One was unified, visionary, disciplined, and dynamic. The other was divided, self-satisfied, undisciplined, and static. It would be unreasonable to expect that such societies could live side by side indefinitely with no penetration of the more fragmented and passive by the more consolidated and active. What resulted, then, was not—as many have held—a clash of dissimilar ways of life, but rather the expansion of one into the areas in which the other was lacking. (NEF, p. 323)

From our present vantage point, these remarks seem culturally biased to an incredible degree, not to mention inaccurate: was Puritan society unified? If so, how does one account for its internal dissensions and obsessive need to cast out deviants? Is "unity" necessarily a positive culture trait? From what standpoint can one say that American Indians were neither disciplined nor visionary, when both these characteristics loom so large in the ethnographies? Is it an accident that ways of describing cultural strength and weakness coincide with gender stereotypes—active/passive, and so on? Why is one culture said to "penetrate" the other? Why is the "other" described in terms of "lack"?

15 Vaughan's fundamental categories of apprehension and judgment will not withstand even the most cursory inspection. For what looked like evenhandedness when he was writing *New England Frontier* does not look that way anymore. In his introduction to *New Directions in American Intellectual History,* John Higham writes that by the end of the sixties

> the entire conceptual foundation on which [this sort of work] rested [had] crumbled away….Simultaneously, in sociology, anthropology, and history, two working assumptions…came under withering attack: first, the assumption that societies tend to be integrated, and second, that a shared culture maintains that integration….By the late 1960s all claims issued in the name of an "American mind"…were subject to drastic skepticism.[5]

"Clearly," Higham continues, "the sociocultural upheaval of the sixties created the occasion" for this reaction.[6] Vaughan's book, it seemed, could only have been written before the events of the sixties had sensitized scholars to questions of race and ethnicity. It came as no surprise, therefore, that ten years later there appeared a study of European-Indian relations which reflected the new awareness of social issues the sixties had engendered. And it offered an entirely different picture of the European-Indian encounter.

Francis Jennings's *The Invasion of America* (1975) rips wide open the idea that the Puritans were humane and considerate in their dealings with the Indians. In Jennings's account, even more massively documented than Vaughan's, the early settlers lied to the Indians, stole from them, murdered them, scalped them, captured them, tortured them, raped them, sold them into slavery, confiscated their land, destroyed their crops, burned their homes, scattered their possessions, gave them alcohol, undermined their systems of belief, and infected them with diseases that wiped out ninety percent of their numbers within the first hundred years after contact.[7]

Jennings mounts an all-out attack on the essential decency of the Puritan leadership and their apologists in the twentieth century. The Pequot War, which previous historians had described as an attempt on the part of Massachusetts Bay to protect itself from the fiercest of the New England tribes, becomes, in Jennings's painstakingly researched account, a deliberate war of extermination, waged by whites against Indians. It starts with trumped-up charges, is carried on through a series of increasingly bloody reprisals, and ends in the massacre of scores of Indian men, women, and children, all so that Massachusetts Bay could gain political and economic control of the southern Connecticut Valley. When one reads this and then turns over the page and sees a reproduction of the Bay Colony seal, which depicts an Indian from whose mouth issue the words "Come over and help us," the effect is shattering.[8]

But even so powerful an argument as Jennings's did not remain unshaken by subsequent work. Reading on, I discovered that if the events of the sixties had revolutionized the study of European-Indian relations, the events of the seventies produced yet another transformation. The American Indian Movement, and in particular the founding of the Native American Rights Fund in 1971 to finance Indian litigation, and a court decision in 1975 which gave the tribes the right to seek redress for past injustices in federal court, created a climate within which historians began to focus on the Indians themselves. "Almost simultaneously," writes James Axtell, "frontier and colonial historians began to discover the necessity of considering the American natives as real determinants of history and the utility of ethnohistory as a way of ensuring parity of focus and impartiality of judgment."[9] In Miller, Indians had been simply beneath notice; in Vaughan, they belonged to an inferior culture; and in Jennings, they were the more or less innocent prey of power-hungry whites. But in the most original and provocative of the ethnohistories, Calvin Martin's *Keepers of the Game,* Indians became complicated, purposeful human beings, whose lives were spiritually motivated to a high degree.[10] Their relationship to the animals they hunted, to the natural environment, and to the whites with whom they traded became intelligible within a system of beliefs that formed the basis for an entirely new perspective on the European-Indian encounter.

20   Within the broader question of why European contact had such a devastating effect on the Indians, Martin's specific aim is to determine why Indians participated in the fur trade which ultimately led them to the brink of annihilation. The standard answer to this question had always been that once the Indian was introduced to European guns, copper kettles, woolen blankets, and the like, he literally couldn't keep his hands off them. In order to acquire these coveted items, he decimated the animal populations on which his survival depended. In short, the Indian's motivation in participating in the fur trade was assumed to be the same as the white European's—a desire to accumulate material goods. In direct opposition to this thesis, Martin argues that the reason why Indians ruthlessly exploited their own resources had nothing to do with supply and demand, but stemmed rather from a breakdown of the cosmic worldview that tied them to the game they killed in a spiritual relationship of parity and mutual obligation.

The hunt, according to Martin, was conceived not primarily as a physical activity but as a spiritual quest, in which the spirit of the hunter must overmaster the spirit of the game animal before the kill can take place. The animal, in effect, *allows* itself to be found and killed, once the hunter has mastered its spirit. The hunter prepared himself through rituals of fasting, sweating, or dreaming which revealed the identity of his prey and where he can find it. The physical act of killing is the least important element in the process. Once the animal is killed, eaten, and its parts used for clothing or implements, its remains must be disposed of in ritually prescribed fashion, or the game boss, the "keeper" of that species, will not permit more animals to be killed. The relationship between Indians and animals, then, is contractual; each side must hold up its end of the bargain, or no further transactions can occur.

What happened, according to Martin, was that as a result of diseases introduced into the animal population by Europeans, the game suddenly disappeared, began to act in inexplicable ways, or sickened and died in plain view, and communicated their diseases to the Indians. The Indians, consequently, believed that their compact with the animals had been broken and that the keepers of the game, the tutelary spirits of each animal species whom they had been so careful to propitiate, had betrayed them. And when missionization, wars with the Europeans, and displacement from their tribal lands had further weakened Indian society and its belief structure, the Indians, no longer restrained by religious sanctions, in effect, turned on the animals in a holy war of revenge.

Whether or not Martin's specific claim about the "holy war" was correct, his analysis made it clear to me that, given the Indians' understanding of economic, religious, and physical processes, an Indian account of what transpired when the European settlers arrived here would look nothing like our own. Their (potential, unwritten) history of the conflict could bear only a marginal resemblance to Eurocentric views. I began to think that the key to understanding European-Indian relations was to see them as an encounter between wholly disparate cultures, and that therefore either defending or attacking the colonists was beside the point since, given the cultural disparity between the two groups, conflict was inevitable and in large part a product of mutual misunderstanding.

But three years after Martin's book appeared, Shepard Krech III edited a collection of seven essays called *Indians, Animals, and the Fur Trade,* attacking Martin's entire project. Here the authors argued that we don't need an ideological or religious explanation for the fur trade. As Charles Hudson writes,

> The Southeastern Indians slaughtered deer (and were prompted to enslave and kill each other) because of their position on the outer fringes of an expanding modern world-system....In the modern world-system there is a core region which establishes *economic* relations with its colonial periphery....If the Indians could not produce commodities, they were on the road to cultural extinction....To maximize his chances for survival, an eighteenth-century Southeastern Indian had to...live in the interior, out of range of European cattle, forestry, and agriculture....He had to produce a commodity which was valuable enough to earn him some protection from English slavers.[11]

25   Though we are talking here about Southeastern Indians, rather than the subarctic and Northeastern tribes Martin studied, what really accounts for these divergent explanations of why Indians slaughtered the game are the assumptions that underlie them. Martin believes that the Indians acted on the basis of perceptions made available to them by their own cosmology; that is, he explains their behavior as the Indians themselves would have explained it (insofar as he can), using a logic and a set of values that are not Eurocentric but derived from within Amerindian culture. Hudson, on the other hand, insists that the Indians' own beliefs are irrelevant to an explanation of how they acted, which can only be understood, as far as he is concerned, in the terms of a Western materialist economic and political analysis. Martin and Hudson, in short, don't agree on what counts as an explanation,

and this disagreement sheds light on the preceding accounts as well. From this standpoint, we can see that Vaughan, who thought that the Puritans were superior to the Indians, and Jennings, who thought the reverse, are both, like Hudson, using Eurocentric criteria of description and evaluation. While all three critics (Vaughan, Jennings, and Hudson) acknowledge that Indians and Europeans behave differently from one another, the behavior differs, as it were, within the order of the same: all three assume, though only Hudson makes the assumption explicit, that an understanding of relations between the Europeans and the Indians must be elaborated in European terms. In Martin's analysis, however, what we have are not only two different sets of behavior but two incommensurable ways of describing and assigning meaning to events. This difference at the level of explanation calls into question the possibility of obtaining any theory-independent account of interaction between Indians and Europeans.

At this point, dismayed and confused by the wildly divergent views of colonial history the twentieth-century historians had provided, I decided to look at some primary materials. I thought, perhaps, if I looked at some firsthand accounts and at some scholars looking at those accounts, it would be possible to decide which experts were right and which were wrong by comparing their views with the evidence. Captivity narratives seemed a good place to begin, since it was logical to suppose that the records left by whites who had been captured by Indians would furnish the sort of firsthand information I wanted.

I began with two fascinating essays based on these materials written by the ethnohistorian James Axtell, "The White Indians of Colonial America" and "The Scholastic Philosophy of the Wilderness."[12] These essays suggest that it would have been a privilege to be captured by North American Indians and taken off to Canada to dwell in a wigwam for the rest of one's life. Axtell's reconstruction of the process by which Indians taught European captives to feel comfortable in the wilderness, first taking their shoes away and giving them moccasins, carrying the children on their backs, sharing the scanty food supply equally, ceremonially cleansing them of their old identities, giving them Indian clothes and jewelry, assiduously teaching them the Indian language, finally adopting them into their families, and even visiting them after many years if, as sometimes happened, they were restored to white society—all of this creates a compelling portrait of Indian culture and helps to explain the extraordinary attraction that Indian culture apparently exercised over Europeans.

But, as I had by now come to expect, this beguiling portrait of the Indians' superior humanity is called into question by other writings on Indian captivity—for example, Norman Heard's *White into Red,* whose summation of the comparative treatment of captive children east and west of the Mississippi seems to contradict some of Axtell's conclusions:

> The treatment of captive children seems to have been similar in initial stages....Most children were treated brutally at the time of capture. Babies and toddlers usually were killed immediately and other small children would be dispatched during the rapid retreat to the Indian villages if they cried, failed to keep the pace, or otherwise indicated a lack of fortitude needed to become a worthy member of the tribe. Upon reaching the village, the child might face such ordeals as running the gauntlet or dancing in the center of a throng of threatening Indians. The prisoner might be so seriously injured at this time that he would no longer be acceptable for adoption.[13]

One account which Heard reprints is particularly arresting. A young girl captured by the Comanches who had not been adopted into a family but used as a slave had been peculiarly mistreated. When they wanted to wake her up the family she belonged to would take a burning brand from the fire and touch it to her nose. When she was returned to her parents, the flesh of her nose was completely burned away, exposing the bone.[14]

30   Since the pictures drawn by Heard and Axtell were in certain respects irreconcilable, it made sense to turn to a firsthand account to see how the Indians treated their captives in a particular instance. Mary Rowlandson's "The Soveraignty and Goodness of God," published in Boston around 1680, suggested itself because it was so widely read and had set the pattern for later narratives. Rowlandson interprets her captivity as God's punishment on her for failing to keep the Sabbath properly on several occasions. She sees everything that happens to her as a sign from God. When the Indians are kind to her, she attributes her good fortune to divine Providence; when they are cruel, she blames her captors. But beyond the question of how Rowlandson interprets events is the question of what she saw in the first place and what she considered worth reporting. The following passage, with its abrupt shifts of focus and peculiar emphases, makes it hard to see her testimony as evidence of anything other than the Puritan point of view:

> Then my heart began to fail: and I fell weeping, which was the first time to my remembrance, that I wept before them. Although I had met with so much Affliction, and my heart was many times ready to break, yet could I not shed one tear in their sight: but rather had been all this while in a maze, and like one astonished: but not I may say as, Psal. 137.1. *By the Rivers of Babylon, there we sate down; yea, we wept when we remembered Zion.* There one of them asked me, why I wept, I could hardly tell what to say: yet I answered, they would kill me: No, said he, none will hurt you. Then came one of them and gave me two spoon-fulls of Meal to comfort me, and another gave me half a pint of Pease; which was more worth than many Bushels at another time. Then I went to see King Philip, he bade me come in and sit down, and asked me whether I woold smoke it (a usual Complement nowadayes among Saints and Sinners) but this no way suited me. For though I had formerly used Tobacco, yet I had left it ever since I was first taken. It seems to be a Bait, the Devil layes to make men loose their precious time: I remember with shame, how formerly, when I had taken two or three pipes, I was presently ready for another, such a bewitching thing it is: But I thank God, he has now given me power over it; surely there are many who may be better imployed than to ly sucking a stinking Tobacco-pipe.[15]

Anyone who has ever tried to give up smoking has to sympathize with Rowlandson, but it is nonetheless remarkable, first, that a passage which begins with her weeping openly in front of her captors, and comparing herself to Israel in Babylon, should end with her railing against the vice of tobacco; and, second, that it has not a word to say about King Philip, the leader of the Indians who captured her and mastermind of the campaign that devastated the white population of the English colonies. The fact that Rowlandson has just been introduced to the chief of chiefs makes hardly any impression on her at all. What excites her is a moral issue which was being hotly debated in the seventeenth century: to smoke or not to smoke (Puritans frowned on it, apparently, because it wasted time and presented a fire hazard). What seem to us the peculiar emphases in Rowlandson's relation are not the result of her having screened out evidence she couldn't handle, but of her way of constructing the world. She saw what her seventeenth-century English Separatist background made visible. It is when one realizes that the biases of twentieth-century historians like Vaughan or Axtell cannot be corrected for simply by consulting the primary materials, since the primary materials are constructed according to *their* authors' biases, that one begins to envy Miller his vision at Matadi. Not for what he didn't see—the Indian and the black—but for his epistemological confidence.

Since captivity narratives made a poor source of evidence for the nature of European-Indian relations in early New England because they were so relentlessly pietistic, my hope was that a better source of evidence might be writings designed simply to tell Englishmen what the American natives were like. These authors could be presumed to be less severely biased, since they hadn't seen their loved ones killed by Indians or been made to endure the hardships of captivity, and because they weren't writing propaganda calculated to prove that God had delivered his chosen people from the hands of Satan's emissaries.

The problem was that these texts were written with aims no less specific than those of the captivity narratives, though the aims were of a different sort. Here is a passage from William Wood's *New England's Prospect,* published in London in 1634.

> To enter into a serious discourse concerning the natural conditions of these Indians might procure admiration from the people of any civilized nations, in regard of their civility and good natures....These Indians are of affable, courteous and well disposed natures, ready to communicate the best of their wealth to the mutual good of one another;...so...perspicuous is their love...that they are as willing to part with a mite in poverty as treasure in plenty....If it were possible to recount the courtesies they have showed the English, since their first arrival in those parts, it would not only steady belief, that they are a loving people, but also win the love of those that never saw them, and wipe off that needless fear that is too deeply rooted in the conceits of many who think them envious and of such rancorous and inhumane dispositions, that they will one day make an end of their English inmates.[16]

However, in a pamphlet published twenty-one years earlier, Alexander Whitaker of Virginia has this to say of the natives:

> These naked slaves...serve the divell for feare, after a most base manner, sacrificing sometimes (as I have heere heard) their own Children to him....They live naked in bodie, as if their shame of their sinne deserved no covering: Their names are as naked as their bodie: They esteem it a virtue to lie, deceive and steale as their master the divell teacheth to them.[17]

35   According to Robert Berkhofer in *The White Man's Indian,* these divergent reports can be explained by looking at the authors' motives. A favorable report like Wood's, intended to encourage new emigrants to America, naturally represented Indians as loving and courteous, civilized and generous, in order to allay the fears of prospective colonists. Whitaker, on the other hand, a minister who wishes to convince his readers that the Indians are in need of conversion, paints them as benighted agents of the devil. Berkhofer's commentary constantly implies that white men were to blame for having represented the Indians in the image of their own desires and needs.[18] But the evidence supplied by Rowlandson's narrative, and by the accounts left by early reporters such as Wood and Whitaker, suggests something rather different. Though it is probably true that in certain cases Europeans did consciously tamper with the evidence, in most cases there is no reason to suppose that they did not record faithfully what they saw. And what they saw was not an illusion, was not determined by selfish motives in any narrow sense, but was there by virtue of a way of seeing which they could no more consciously manipulate than they could choose not to have been born. At this point, it seemed to me, the ethnocentric bias of the firsthand observers invited an investigation of the cultural situation they spoke from. Karen Kupperman's *Settling with the Indians* (1980) supplied just such an analysis.

Kupperman argues that Englishmen inevitably looked at Indians in exactly the same way that they looked at other Englishmen. For instance, if they looked down on Indians and saw them as people to be exploited, it was not because of racial prejudice or antique notions about savagery, it was because they looked down on ordinary English men and women and saw them as subjects for exploitation as well.[19] According to Kupperman, what concerned these writers most when they described the Indians were the insignia of social class, of rank, and of prestige. Indian faces are virtually never described in the earliest accounts, but clothes and hairstyles, tattoos and jewelry, posture and skin color are. "Early modern Englishmen believed that people can create their own identity, and that therefore one communicates to the world through signals such as dress and other forms of decoration who one is, what group or category one belongs to."[20]

Kupperman's book marks a watershed in writings on European-Indian relations, for it reverses the strategy employed by Martin two years before. Whereas Martin had performed an ethnographic analysis of Indian cosmology in order to explain, from within, the Indians' motives for engaging in the fur trade, Kupperman performs an ethnographic study of seventeenth-century England in order to explain, from within, what motivated Englishmen's behavior. The sympathy and understanding that Martin, Axtell, and others extend to the Indians are extended in Kupperman's work to the English themselves. Rather than giving an account of "what happened" between Indians and Europeans, like Martin, she reconstructs the worldview that gave the experience of one group its content. With her study, scholarship on European-Indian relations comes full circle.

It may well seem to you at this point that, given the tremendous variation among the historical accounts, I had no choice but to end in relativism. If the experience of encountering conflicting versions of the "same" events suggests anything certain it is that the attitude a historian takes up in relation to a given event, the way in which he or she judges and even describes "it"—and the "it" has to go in quotation marks because depending on the perspective, that event either did or did not occur—this stance, these judgments and descriptions are a function of the historian's position in relation to the subject. Miller, standing on the banks of the Congo, couldn't see the black men he was supervising because of his background, his assumptions, values, experiences, goals. Jennings, intent on exposing the distortions introduced into the historical record by Vaughan and his predecessors stretching all the way back to Winthrop, couldn't see that Winthrop and his peers were not racists but only Englishmen who looked at other cultures in the way their own culture had taught them to see one another. The historian can never escape the limitations of his or her own position in history and so inevitably gives an account that is an extension of the circumstances from which it springs. But it seems to me that when one is confronted with this particular succession of stories, cultural and historical rela-

tivism is not a position that one can comfortably assume. The phenomena to which these histories testify—conquest, massacre, and genocide, on the one hand; torture, slavery, and murder on the other—cry out for judgment. When faced with claims and counterclaims of this magnitude one feels obligated to reach an understanding of what actually did occur. The dilemma posed by the study of European-Indian relations in early America is that the highly charged nature of the materials demands a moral decisiveness which the succession of conflicting accounts effectively precludes. That is the dilemma I found myself in at the end of this course of reading, and which I eventually came to resolve as follows.

After a while it began to seem to me that there was something wrong with the way I had formulated the problem. The statement that the materials on European-Indian relations were so highly charged that they demanded moral judgment, but that the judgment couldn't be made because all possible descriptions of what happened were biased, seemed to contain an internal contradiction. The statement implied that in order to make a moral judgment about something, you have to know something else first—namely, the facts of the case you're being called upon to judge. My complaint was that their perspectival nature would disqualify any facts I might encounter and that therefore I couldn't judge. But to say as I did that the materials I had read were "highly charged" and therefore demanded judgment suggests both that I was reacting to something real—to some facts—*and* that I had judged them. Perhaps I wasn't so much in the lurch morally or epistemologically as I had thought. If you—or I—react with horror to the story of the girl captured and enslaved by Comanches who touched a firebrand to her nose every time they wanted to wake her up, it's because we read this as a story about cruelty and suffering, and not as a story about the conventions of prisoner exchange or the economics of Comanche life. The *seeing* of the story as a cause for alarm rather than as a droll anecdote or a piece of curious information is evidence of values we already hold, of judgments already made, of facts already perceived as facts.

40   My problem presupposed that I couldn't judge because I didn't know what the facts were. All I had, or could have, was a series of different perspectives, and so nothing that would count as an authoritative source on which moral judgments could be based. But, as I have just shown, I did judge, and that is because, as I now think, I did have some facts. I seemed to accept as facts that ninety percent of the native American population of New England died after the first hundred years of contact, that tribes in eastern Canada and the northeastern United States had a compact with the game they killed, that Comanches had subjected a captive girl to casual cruelty, that King Philip smoked a pipe, and so on. It was only where different versions of the same event came into conflict that I doubted the text was a record of something real. And even then, there was no question about certain major catastrophes. I believed that four hundred Pequots were killed near Saybrook, that Winthrop was the Governor of the Massachusetts Bay Colony when it happened, and so on. My sense that certain events, such as the Pequot War, did occur in no way reflected the indecisiveness that overtook me when I tried to choose among the various historical versions. In fact, the need I felt to make up my mind was impelled by the conviction that certain things *had* happened that shouldn't have happened. Hence it was never the case that "what happened" was completely unknowable or unavailable. It's rather that in the process of reading so many different approaches to the same phenomenon I became aware of the difference in the attitudes that informed these approaches. This awareness of the interests motivating each version cast suspicion over everything, in retrospect, and I ended by claiming that there was nothing I could know. This, I now see, was never really the case. But how did it happen?

Someone else, confronted with the same materials, could have decided that one of these historical accounts was correct. Still another person might have decided that more evidence was needed in order to decide among them. Why did I conclude that none of the accounts was accurate because they were all produced from some particular angle of vision? Presumably there was something in my background that enabled me to see the problem in this way. That something, very likely, was poststructuralist theory. I let my discovery that Vaughan was a product of the fifties, Jennings of the sixties, Rowlandson of a Puritan worldview, and so on lead me to the conclusion that all facts are theory dependent because that conclusion was already a thinkable one for me. My inability to come up with a true account was not the product of being situated nowhere; it was the product of certitude that existed *somewhere else,* namely, in contemporary literary theory. Hence, the level at which my indecision came into play was a function of particular beliefs I held. I was never in a position of epistemological indeterminacy, I was never *en abyme.* The idea that all accounts are perspectival seemed to me a superior standpoint from which to view all the versions of "what happened," and to regard with sympathetic condescension any person so old-fashioned and benighted as to believe that there really was some way of arriving at the truth. But this skeptical standpoint was just as firm as any other. The fact that it was also seriously disabling—it prevented me from coming to any conclusion about what I had read—did not render it any less definite.

At this point something is beginning to show itself that has up to now been hidden. The notion that all facts are only facts within a perspective has the effect of emptying statements of their content. Once I had Miller and Vaughan and Jennings, Martin and Hudson, Axtell and Heard, Rowlandson and Wood and Whitaker, and Kupperman; I had Europeans and Indians, ships and canoes, wigwams and log cabins, bows and arrows and muskets, wigs and tattoos, whiskey and corn, rivers and forts, treaties and battles, fire and blood—and then suddenly all I had was a metastatement about perspectives. The effect of bringing perspectivism to bear on history was to wipe out completely the subject matter of history. And it follows that bringing perspectivism to bear in this way on any subject matter would have a similar effect; everything is wiped out and you are left with nothing but a single idea—perspectivism itself.

But—and it is a crucial but—all this is true only if you believe that there is an alternative. As long as you think that there are or should be facts that exist outside of any perspective, then the notion that facts are perspectival will have this disappearing effect on whatever it touches. But if you are convinced that the alternative does not exist, that there really are no facts except as they are embedded in some particular way of seeing the world, then the argument that a set of facts derives from some particular worldview is no longer an argument against that set of facts. If all facts share this characteristic, to say that any one fact is perspectival doesn't change its factual nature in the slightest. It merely reiterates it.

This doesn't mean that you have to accept just anybody's facts. You can show that what someone else asserts to be a fact is false. But it does mean that you can't argue that someone else's facts are not facts *because they are only the product of a perspective,* since this will be true of the facts that you perceive as well. What this means then is that arguments about "what happened" have to proceed much as they did before poststructuralism broke in with all its talk about language-based reality and culturally produced knowledge. Reasons must be given, evidence adduced, authorities cited, analogies drawn. Being aware that all facts are motivated, believing that people are always operating inside some particular interpretive framework or other is a pertinent argument when what is under discussion is the way beliefs are grounded. But it doesn't give one any leverage on the facts of a particular case.[21]

45   What this means for the problem I've been addressing is that I must piece together the story of European-Indian relations as best I can, believing this version up to a point, that version not at all, another almost entirely, according to what seems reasonable and plausible, given everything else that I know. And this, as I've shown, is what I was already doing in the back of my mind without realizing it, because there was nothing else I *could* do. If the accounts don't fit together neatly, that is not a reason for rejecting them all in favor of a metadiscourse about epistemology; on the contrary, one encounters contradictory facts and divergent points of view in practically every phase of life, from deciding whom to marry to choosing the right brand of cat food, and one decides as best one can given the evidence available. It is only the nature of the academic situation which makes it appear that one can linger on the threshold of decision in the name of an epistemological principle. What has really happened in such a case is that the subject of debate has changed from the question of what happened in a particular instance to the question of how knowledge is arrived at. The absence of pressure to decide what happened creates the possibility for this change of venue.

The change of venue, however, is itself an action taken. In diverting attention from the original problem and placing it where Miller did, on "the mind of man," it once again ignores what happened and still is happening to American Indians. The moral problem that confronts me now is not that I can never have any facts to go on, but that the work I do is not directed toward solving the kinds of problems that studying the history of European-Indian relations has awakened me to.

NOTES

1. See Vine Deloria Jr., *God Is Red* (New York, 1973), pp. 39–56.
2. Perry Miller, *Errand into the Wilderness* (Cambridge, Mass., 1964), p. vii; all further references will be included in the text.
3. This passage from John Winthrop's *Journal* is excerpted by Perry Miller in his anthology *The American Puritans: Their Prose and Poetry* (Garden City, N.Y., 1956), p. 43. In his headnote to the selections from the *Journal,* Miller speaks of Winthrop's "characteristic objectivity" (p. 37).
4. Alden T. Vaughan, *New England Frontier: Puritans and Indians, 1620–1675* (Boston, 1965), pp. vi–vii; all further references to this work, abbreviated NEF, will be included in the text.

5. John Higham, intro. to *New Directions in American Intellectual History,* ed. Higham and Paul K. Conkin (Baltimore, 1979), p. xii.

6. Ibid.

7. See Francis Jennings, *The Invasion of America: Indians, Colonialism, and the Cant of Conquest* (New York, 1975), pp. 3–31. Jennings writes: "The so-called settlement of America was a resettlement, reoccupation of a land made waste by the diseases and demoralization introduced by the newcomers. Although the source data pertaining to populations have never been compiled, one careful scholar, Henry F. Dobyns, has provided a relatively conservative and meticulously reasoned estimate conforming to the known effects of conquest catastrophe. Dobyns has calculated a total aboriginal population for the western hemisphere within the range of 90 to 112 million, of which 10 to 12 million lived north of the Rio Grande" (p. 30).

8. Jennings, fig. 7, p. 229; and see pp. 186–229.

9. James Axtell, *The European and the Indian: Essays in the Ethnohistory of Colonial North America* (Oxford, 1981), p. viii.

10. See Calvin Martin, *Keepers of the Game: Indian-Animal Relationships and the Fur Trade* (Berkeley and Los Angeles, 1978).

11. See the essay by Charles Hudson in *Indians, Animals, and the Fur Trade: A Critique of "Keepers of the Game,"* ed. Shepard Krech III (Athens, Ga., 1981), pp. 167–69.

12. See Axtell, "The White Indians of Colonial America" and "The Scholastic Philosophy of the Wilderness," *The European and the Indian,* pp. 168–206 and 131–67.

13. J. Norman Heard, *White into Red: A Study of the Assimilation of White Persons Captured by Indians* (Metuchen, N.J., 1973), p. 97.

14. See ibid., p. 98.

15. Mary Rowlandson, "The Sovereignty and Goodness of God, Together with the Faithfulness of His Promises Displayed; Being a Narrative of the Captivity and Restauration of Mrs. Mary Rowlandson (1676)," in *Held Captive by Indians: Selected Narratives, 1642–1836,* ed. Richard VanDerBeets (Knoxville, Tenn., 1973), pp. 57–58.

16. William Wood, *New England's Prospect,* ed. Vaughan (Amherst, Mass., 1977), pp. 88–89.

17. Alexander Whitaker, *Goode Newes from Virginia* (1613), quoted in Robert F. Berkhofer Jr., *The White Man's Indian: Images of the American Indian from Columbus to the Present* (New York, 1978), p. 19.

18. See, for example, Berkhofer's discussion of the passages he quotes from Whitaker (*The White Man's Indian,* pp. 19, 20).

19. See Karen Ordahl Kupperman, *Settling with the Indians: The Meeting of English and Indian Cultures in America, 1580–1640* (Totowa, N.J., 1980), pp. 3, 4.

20. Ibid., p. 35.

21. The position I've been outlining is a version of neopragmatism. For an exposition, see *Against Theory: Literary Studies and the New Pragmatism,* ed. W. J. T. Mitchell (Chicago, 1985).

SUGGESTIONS FOR DISCUSSION

1. What exactly is the problem that Tompkins poses in the opening section of the essay? What does she mean when she says that conflicting historical interpretations posed an "epistemological" and a "moral quandary" for her? According to Tompkins, what is at stake when research turns up "an array of mutually irreconcilable points of view"?

2. Return to Tompkins's essay and notate each of the historians or first-person witnesses discussed in the long middle section. What interpretation of European-Indian relations in colonial New England does each offer? What differing assumptions does each make? It may help to create a chart that notes each historian or eyewitness and the interpretations and assumptions.

3. Think of an occasion or two when you encountered conflicting and irreconcilable interpretations of an event. The event could be one that you studied in a history class or one from personal experience. What differing perspectives and points of view produced the conflicting interpretations? How did you deal with these conflicting interpretations? Explain how Tompkins deals with conflicting interpretations in the final section of the essay. In what sense has she found the "way out" that she describes in the opening section? Compare her resolution of the issue with the way that you handled conflicting interpretations. What do you see as the main similarities and differences? How do you account for them?

SUGGESTIONS FOR WRITING

1. Write an essay that uses Jane Tompkins's account of her research as a model. Choose a research project that you did for a class in school—for example, a term paper, a report, or a history fair exhibit. Following Tompkins's style, explain the connections between the topic that you researched and your personal experience. Then take readers behind the scenes to explain how you did the research and how you dealt with any differing points of view or conflicting interpretations that you encountered. Use your account as a way to pose the problem of historical research and working with other people's accounts of the past.

2. Write a critical review of the historians' points of view and the interpretations that Tompkins presents in her essay. Provide an introduction that generally explains the problems and issues that the historians as a group are addressing. Assess the perspective that each historian brings to his or her research—what it helps you to see and what it obscures—and compare the strengths and weaknesses of the historians' various interpretations. As you review the historians' accounts, explain how you might piece them together and what view of Indian-settler relations in colonial New England ultimately emerges for you.

3. Consult American history textbooks that are used in high school and college and compare their treatment of European-Indian relations in seventeenth-century New England with the perspectives of the various historians in Tompkins's essay. (You can focus on just one textbook or extend your research to several texts.) What point of view and what assumptions seem to determine the treatment of Indians and Europeans in the textbook? How is this treatment similar to or different from the interpretations that you have read in Tompkins's essay? What perspectives seem to dominate? The textbook may well present this material as a factual account. If so, read between the lines to identify the perspective that the textbook author or authors bring to Indian-settler relations in colonial New England.

NECESSARY FICTIONS: Warren Neidich's Early American Cover-Ups

Christopher Phillips

Christopher Phillips is a photography critic who has published in *October, Art in America,* and elsewhere. "Necessary Fictions" introduces the Visual Essay that follows—Warren Neidich's "Contra Curtis: Early American Cover-Ups."

SUGGESTION FOR READING   Edward Sheriff Curtis's images, as Christopher Phillips notes, are "elegiac" depictions of a "vanishing race" of American Indians, seemingly caught in a timeless, aboriginal past. As you read this selection and Neidich's photographic essay, keep in mind Phillips's comments on how images can enable people to forget as well as to remember.

STRATAGEMS FOR FORGETTING

1 "They from the beginning announced that they wanted to maintain their way of life....And we set up these reservations so they could, and have a Bureau of Indian Affairs to help take care of them.... Maybe we made a mistake. Maybe we should not have humored them in wanting to stay in that kind of primitive lifestyle. Maybe we should have said, 'No, come join us.'...You'd be surprised. Some of them became very wealthy, because some of those reservations were overlaying great pools of oil. And so I don't know what their complaint might be." (Ronald Reagan, in response to a question at Moscow University

about the condition of Native Americans, quoted in *Time*, June 13, 1988.)

A CHILDHOOD MEMORY

Only a few days after Reagan provided students in Moscow with this hallucinatory account of the winning of the West, an item in the *New York Times* (June 5, 1988) reported that the designer Oleg Cassini planned a vast "Navajo Nation" complex in Arizona to repackage for the tourist industry the history, art, and culture of that apparently willing tribe. This odd conjunction of events sent me back in thought to the several summers, long ago, when our family paid regular visits to the Appalachian resort town of Cherokee, North Carolina. We were usually accompanied by a friend of my parents…a woman whose interest in the trip sprang principally from the fact that one of her own friends, a New York dancer, migrated to Cherokee every summer to earn a few dollars performing in a popular "outdoor historical drama." Minus the feathers and war paint that went with his role as a leaping Cherokee warrior, Louis proved unremarkable, aside from a rasping Brooklyn accent and the purple sports car in which he raced around the mountain roads. I remember, though, being puzzled when I was taken backstage before one evening's performance, and discovered there an assortment of equally improbable characters donning their costumes and makeup. Very interesting, I thought, but where were the real Indians?

The play itself proposed a relatively bland answer to that question. Situated in a past so hazy as to be utterly remote from the concerns of the present day, it unfolded in a series of melodramatic incidents the tale of the Cherokees' encounter with the homespun agents of Manifest Destiny, their expulsion from their mountain homeland, and their arduous trek to a new, ostensibly happier home on the plains of Oklahoma. Nevertheless another, more ominous possibility was planted in my already suspicious ten-year-old mind each time we passed a crowded burger drive-in situated in the heart of Cherokee. It announced its specialty in brazenly flashing red letters that I can still see: Squawburgers.

CONTRA CURTIS

It's from a similar unmarked crossroads of historical representation and popular memory that Warren Neidich's "Contra Curtis" photographs begin. Disinterred from the vast necropolis of American culture comprised of late-night TV's reruns of the pulp entertainment of earlier decades, Neidich's images are at once perfectly innocuous and painfully provoking. All-too-typical examples of the estimated 17,000 acts of mediated mayhem witnessed by all of us who have grown up in the television era, these achingly familiar specimens focus on moments of ritualized violence directed against "Indians." Of course we know that these aren't real Indians being burned, shot, knifed, or burst asunder, but actors, actresses, and stuntmen dressed up for the part. These figures serve as stand-ins or surrogates for a "historical actor" long pushed off the main stage of American life, but preserved in cultural memory in the long line of phantasmic Others against whom any violence is permitted.

5   It's the way that such phantasms weave in and out of our culture's interlocking networks of personal memory, popular memory, and archival memory that furnishes the real subject of much of Neidich's work. But aside from this general predilection, "Contra Curtis" has a more specific target in mind. Neidich seems clearly to wish that these photographs be attached as permanently as a shadow to the famous body of work produced around the turn of the century by the celebrated photographer Edward Sheriff Curtis. Curtis's elegiac images of Native American tribes turned a benign paternal gaze upon the "picturesque" tribespeople whom he singled out, costumed, and directed for his camera. Printed (like Neidich's) on platinum paper, Curtis's photographs were circulated in lavish volumes and portfolios to such discerning patrons as J. P. Morgan and Teddy Roosevelt. Neidich, using images drawn from a later, less discreet cultural sector, suggests the bloody historical preliminaries that were genteelly elided in Curtis's nostalgic account of a "vanishing race." Indeed, like that flashing red sign in Cherokee,

his images disclose, behind Curtis's veil of tasteful exoticism, an oblique vision of the return of the historically repressed.

COGITO INTERRUPTUS

Once the very embodiment of the qualities of objectivity, precision, and fidelity, the photographic image occupies an increasingly unstable place in the systems which today generate cultural memory. Certainly the photograph's partaking of the prestige of the indexical sign seemed until very recently to exempt it from the so-called referential illusion that had mired so many other sign-systems in the Slough of Undecidability. Only a decade ago reputable philosophers of history still argued that observing a Brady photograph of the Civil War was, for all practical purposes, equivalent to observing the historical scene itself.

But too often photographs convey a dangerously weak sense of the past …substituting a mute and fleeting commemoration for the more active, critical processes of remembering, interrogating, and understanding. Nearly three decades ago Alain Resnais in "Last Year at Marienbad" shared his suspicion that personal memory and photographic images might well lead in different, equally untrustworthy directions. By the 1980s, with the film "Blade Runner" (based on Philip K. Dick's novel) we find android "replicants" conspicuously outfitted with ersatz family snapshots, which provide them with prepackaged "memories" of a human past that blocks their discovery of their real mechanical origin. This film's implicit allusion to the human condition …still camped in Plato's cave…is hardly inappropriate as we move into the age of the digitally edited, electronically generated photocomposite: an image indistinguishable from a "real" photograph, an image which renders superfluous the remaining distinctions between photographic fact and fiction.

THE PACIFICATION OF THE PAST

If the camera's images no longer compel unflinching conviction, they nonetheless retain their currency as the standard visual language of the spectacle. Where Warren Neidich's previous work evidenced a fascination with the possibility of fabricating ersatz historical photographs, "Contra Curtis" points not only to the structuring absences of the historical archive but to the historical residue that can be gleaned from spectacle itself. Taking a cue from Duchamp and Breton, these photographs could perhaps be considered "compensation documents," provisional stand-ins for images too often erased from the official picture of the American past.

In regard to the contending claims of the image and the historical sense, Guy Debord's recent "Commentaries on the Society of the Spectacle" affords considerable insight, if small consolation. Writing twenty years after he identified the "spectacle" as the succession of images that provides the contemporary world with its distorting mirror, Debord points out that during the past two decades the discrediting of the historical sense has been increasingly adopted as a tactic of power. He notes that such recently fashionable slogans as "the ruins of post-history" can only bring comfort to those who exercise power now, to all those who can avail themselves of the flagrant historical lie in assurance that no correction will be registered. The self-serving flight of fantasy cited at the head of this essay was dutifully reproduced in Time magazine, after all, without commentary or correction …sign of an extraordinary public prudence in regard to power, or confirmation of a jaded reluctance to bother to point to the chasm between fact and phantasmagoria.

CIRCUIT BREAKERS

10 To interrupt the precipitous succession of mutually canceling images that hurdle past us each day, to replace that rhythm, if only for a moment, with another…such is the recurrent dream of the art of the 1980s. If they were not disguised as art, Neidich's photographs might be described as attempts at visual sedition, or local campaigns of "critical disinformation." It remains to be determined, of course, whether they (or any other artwork today) can break out of that subcircuit of

activity that Debord shrugs off as the "spectacu-lar critique of the spectacle." For the moment, Neidich's photographs modestly propose that the recycled images of popular history available on every channel can be recycled yet again...this time to provide an ironic corrective to at least a few of the more transparent idiocies which today parade as public discourse.

VISUAL ESSAY

Contra Curtis: Early American Cover-Ups

Warren Neidich

Warren Neidich is a photographer living in New York and Los Angeles; his photographs have been exhibited in and collected by museums in Europe and the United States. Neidich is known for his work on the media saturation surrounding the O.J. Simpson murder trial and on Calico, a restored silver mining town in Barstow, California. An ophthalmologist by training, Neidich is interested in cognitive science and sight. Presented here are selections from his photographic essay "Contra Curtis: Early American Cover-Ups" that appear in his book *American History Reinvented* (1989).

As the title of his photographs, "Contra Curtis," indicates, Warren Neidich locates his work in relation to Edward Sheriff Curtis, the well-known photographer of American Indians in the early twentieth century. Neidich uses platinum prints, just as Curtis did, which give the images an antique glow that seems to assign them to a vanished past. At the same time, Neidich wants to make these images relevant to the present. Included here is an example of Curtis's work, "The Three Chiefs—Piegan," to demonstrate the relationship between Neidich's photographs and those of Curtis (and why Neidich's are "contra").

Three Chiefs-Piegan

Photography by Edward Sheriff Curtis

Warren Neidich, "Contra Curtis: Early American Cover-Ups," Number 2

"Contra Curtis," Number 5

"Contra Curtis,"
Number 9

"Contra Curtis,"
Number 14

SUGGESTIONS FOR DISCUSSION

1. Warren Neidich joins together two visual codes — the platinum prints Edward Sheriff Curtis used in his photographs and the conventions of the Hollywood Western. How do these go together? What viewer response do they provoke?

2. Compare Neidich's photographs with those of Curtis. Think here in terms of the monumental character of Curtis's photographs and the action in Neidich's. Do Curtis's photographs prompt historical amnesia, as Chrisopher Phillips suggests? In what sense are Neidich's photographs a critique of Curtis? What is Neidich asking the viewer to remember?

3. Compare Neidich's project to "reinvent" American history with Jane Tompkins's struggle to understand the "Indian" in American history.

SUGGESTIONS FOR WRITING

1. What images come to your mind when you hear the term "American Indian"? How have you learned about American Indians? Write an essay that explains your own understanding of American Indians, drawing on Tompkins and Neidich as you see fit.

2. Christopher Phillips says Neidich's photographs "might be described as an act of visual sedition." What does he mean? Write an essay that explains why and how Neidich's photographs are seditious.

3. Write your own introduction to Neidich's photographs. Explain his purposes and the means he has chosen to carry out these purposes.

PERSPECTIVES: Interpreting the Vietnam War

The Vietnam War was the longest and perhaps most controversial war in American history. From the mid-1950s, when the Eisenhower administration sent CIA advisors and a military cadre to Vietnam, through Lyndon Johnson's escalation of the war in the 1960s, to the eventual withdrawal of American forces in 1972 and 1973 and the ultimate victory of Ho Chi Minh in 1975, the Vietnam War increasingly preoccupied American policy makers and divided the country. Of all the wars fought by the United States, the Vietnam War still seems in some fundamental sense unresolved, a bitter legacy that continues to trouble the nation.

The following two selections are the work of professional historians who have tried to come to grips with the meaning of the Vietnam War. As you will see, they offer different perspectives and, in the process, raise important questions about how historians seek to explain the causes and significance of historical events. George B. Tindall and David E. Shi's "The Tragedy of Vietnam" may appear, at first reading, to be simply a historical narrative of U.S. involvement in Vietnam, and Loren Baritz's "God's Country and American Know-How" is clearly tied to Baritz's thesis that long-standing patterns in American culture led to military intervention in Vietnam. Your task as a reader is to make sense of these two treatments of the Vietnam War and to decide whether Tindall and Shi offer an interpretation as much as Baritz does.

THE TRAGEDY OF VIETNAM

George B. Tindall and David E. Shi

George B. Tindall teaches history at the University of North Carolina, Chapel Hill, and David E. Shi is the president of Furman College. The following selection, "The Tragedy of Vietnam," appeared originally in their textbook *American: A Narrative History* (1999).

SUGGESTION FOR READING Notice how the headings "Escalation" and "Turning Point" lend a dramatic structure to the Vietnam War, with a rising plot line and a crisis. Consider how this way of narrating the Vietnam War fits with the title "The Tragedy of Vietnam."

1 As violence was escalating in America's inner cities, the war in Vietnam also reached new levels of intensity and destruction. At the time of President Kennedy's death there were 16,000 American military advisors in Vietnam. Lyndon Johnson inherited a commitment to prevent a Communist takeover in South Vietnam along with a reluctance to assume the military burden for fighting the war. One president after another had done just enough to avoid being charged with having "lost" Vietnam. Johnson did the same, fearing that any other course would undermine his influence and endanger his Great Society programs in Congress. But this path took him and the United States inexorably deeper into intervention in Asia.

ESCALATION

The official sanction for America's "escalation"—a Defense Department term coined in the Vietnam era—was the Tonkin Gulf Resolution, voted by Congress on August 7, 1964. Johnson reported in a national television address that two American destroyers had been attacked by North Vietnamese vessels on August 2 and 4 in the Gulf of Tonkin off the coast of North Vietnam. Although he described the attacks as unprovoked, in truth the destroyers had been monitoring South Vietnamese raids against two North Vietnamese islands—raids planned by American advisors. The Tonkin Gulf Resolution authorized the president to "take all necessary measures to repel any armed attack against the forces of the United States and to prevent further aggression."

Three months after Johnson's landslide victory over Goldwater, he and his advisors made the crucial decisions that shaped American policy in Vietnam for the next four years. On February 5, 1965, Vietcong guerrillas killed 8 and wounded 126 Americans at Pleiku. Further attacks on Americans later that week led Johnson to order operation "Rolling Thunder," the first sustained American bombings of North Vietnam, which were intended to stop the flow of soldiers and supplies into the south. Six months later a task force concluded that the bombing had little effect on the supplies pouring down the "Ho Chi Minh Trail" from North Vietnam through Laos. Still, the bombing continued.

In March 1965 the new American army commander in Vietnam, Gen. William C. Westmoreland, requested and got the first installment of combat troops, ostensibly to defend American airfields. By the end of 1965 there were 184,000 American troops in Vietnam; in 1966 the troop level reached 385,000. And as combat operations increased, so did the list of American casualties, announced each week on the nightly news along with the "body count" of alleged enemy dead. "Westy's War," although fought with helicopter gunships, chemical defoliants, and napalm, became like the trench warfare of World War I—a grinding war of attrition.

THE CONTEXT FOR POLICY

5   Johnson's decision to "Americanize" the war, so ill-starred in retrospect, was entirely consistent with the foreign policy principles pursued by all American presidents after World War II. The version of the containment theory articulated in the Truman Doctrine, endorsed by Eisenhower and Dulles throughout the 1950s, and reaffirmed by Kennedy, pledged United States opposition to the advance of communism anywhere in the world. "Why are we in Vietnam?" Johnson asked rhetorically at Johns Hopkins University in 1965. "We are there because we have a promise to keep....To leave Vietnam to its fate would shake the confidence of all these people in the value of American commitment." Secretary of State Dean Rusk repeated this rationale before countless congressional committees, warning that Thailand, Burma, and the rest of Southeast Asia would fall to communism if American forces withdrew. American military intervention in Vietnam was thus no aberration, but a logical culmination of the assumptions widely shared by the foreign policy establishment and leaders of both political parties since the early days of the Cold War.

Nor did the United States blindly "stumble into a quagmire" in Vietnam, as some commentators maintained. Johnson insisted from the start that American military involvement must not reach levels that would provoke the Chinese or Soviets into direct intervention. He therefore exercised a tight rein over the bombing campaign, once boasting that "they can't even bomb an outhouse without my approval." Such a restrictive policy meant, in effect, that military victory in any traditional sense of the term was never possible. "It was startling to me to find out," the new secretary of defense, Clark Clifford, recalled in 1968, "that we had no military plan to end the war." America's goal was not to win the war in a conventional sense by capturing enemy territory, but to prevent the North Vietnamese and Vietcong from winning. This meant that America would have to maintain a military presence as long as the enemy retained the will to fight.

As it turned out, American public support for the war eroded faster than the will of the North Vietnamese leaders to tolerate casualties. Opposition to the war broke out on college campuses with the escalation of 1965. And in January 1966 Sen. J. William Fulbright of Arkansas, chairman of the Senate Foreign Relations Committee, began congressional investigations into American policy. George Kennan, the founding father of the containment doctrine, told Fulbright's committee that the doctrine was appropriate for Europe, but not Southeast Asia. By 1967 opposition to the war had become so pronounced that antiwar demonstrations in New York and at the Pentagon attracted massive support. Nightly television accounts of the fighting—Vietnam was the first war to receive extended television coverage, and hence has been dubbed the "living room war"—brought the horrors of guerrilla warfare into American dens. As Secretary of Defense McNamara admitted, "The picture of the world's greatest superpower killing or injuring 1,000 noncombatants a week, while trying to pound a tiny backward nation into submission on an issue whose merits are hotly disputed, is not a pretty one."

In a war of political will, North Vietnam had the advantage. Johnson and his advisors never came to appreciate the tenacity of North Vietnam's commitment to unify Vietnam and expel the United States. Ho Chi Minh had warned the French in the 1940s that "You can kill ten of my men for every one I kill of yours, but even at those odds, you will lose and I will win." He knew that in a battle of attrition, the Vietnamese Communists had the advantage, for they were willing to sacrifice all for their cause. Indeed, just as General Westmoreland was assuring Johnson and the American public that his forces in early 1968 were on the verge of gaining the upper hand, the Communists again displayed their resilience.

THE TURNING POINT

On January 31, 1968, the first day of the Vietnamese New Year (Tet), the Vietcong and North Vietnamese defied a holiday truce to launch a wave of surprise assaults on American and South Vietnamese forces throughout South Vietnam. The old capital city of Hué fell to the Communists, and Vietcong units temporarily occupied the grounds of the American embassy in Saigon. But within a few days American and South Vietnamese forces organized a devastating counterattack. General Westmoreland justifiably proclaimed the Tet offensive a major defeat for the Vietcong. But while Vietcong casualties were enormous, the psychological impact of the offensive on the American public was more telling. *Time* and *Newsweek* soon ran antiwar editorials urging American withdrawal. Walter Cronkite, the dean of American television journalists, confided to his viewers that he no longer believed the war was winnable. "If I've lost Walter," Johnson was reported to say, "then it's over. I've lost Mr. Average Citizen." Polls showed that Johnson's popularity declined to 35 percent, lower than any president since Truman's darkest days. In 1968 the United States was spending $322,000 on every enemy killed in Vietnam; the poverty programs at home received only $53 per person.

10   During 1968 Johnson grew increasingly isolated. The secretary of defense reported that a task force of prominent soldiers and civilians saw no prospect for a military victory. Robert Kennedy was considering a run for the presidency in order to challenge Johnson's Vietnam policy. And Sen. Eugene McCarthy of Minnesota had already decided to oppose Johnson in the Democratic primaries. With antiwar students rallying to his candidacy, McCarthy polled 42 percent of the vote to Johnson's 48 percent in New Hampshire's March primary. Though voters had to write in Johnson's name to vote for the president, it was still a remarkable showing for a little-known senator, and each presidential primary now promised to become a referendum on Johnson's Vietnam policy.

Despite Johnson's troubles in the conduct of foreign policy, he remained a master at reading the political omens. On March 31 he announced a limited halt to the bombing of North Vietnam and fresh initiatives for a negotiated cease-fire. Then he added a dramatic postscript: "I have concluded that I should not permit the Presidency to become involved in the partisan divisions that are developing in this political year. Accordingly, I shall not seek, and I will not accept, the nomination of my party for another term as your President."

Although American troops would remain in Vietnam for five more years and the casualties would mount, the quest for military victory had ended. Now the question was how the most powerful nation in the world could extricate itself from Vietnam with a minimum of damage to its prestige. It would not be easy. When direct negotiations with the North Vietnamese finally began in Paris in May 1968 they immediately bogged down over North Vietnam's demand for an American bombing halt as a precondition for further discussion.

GOD'S COUNTRY AND AMERICAN KNOW-HOW

Loren Baritz

Loren Baritz taught American Studies for many years at the University of Michigan and is now retired. The following selection, "God's Country and American Know-How," is taken from his book *Backfire: A History of How American Culture Led Us into Vietnam* (1985).

SUGGESTION FOR READING   As you read, notice how Loren Baritz develops his idea that America's quest for moral leadership led policymakers to involve the United States in Vietnam. Compare this perspective on American military intervention in Vietnam with the perspective offered by Tindall and Shi in "The Tragedy of Vietnam" and think about what these perspectives have in common and how they differ.

1 Americans were ignorant about the Vietnamese not because we were stupid, but because we believe certain things about ourselves. Those things necessarily distorted our vision and confused our minds in ways that made learning extraordinarily difficult. To understand our failure we must think about what it means to be an American.

The necessary test for understanding the condition of being an American is a single sentence written by Herman Melville in his novel *White Jacket:* "And we Americans are the peculiar, chosen people—the Israel of our time; we bear the ark of the liberties of the world." This was not the last time this idea was expressed by Americans. It was at the center of thought of the men who brought us the Vietnam War. It was at the center of the most characteristic American myth.

This oldest and most important myth about America has an unusually specific origin. More than 350 years ago, while in mid-passage between England and the American wilderness, John Winthrop told the band of Puritans he was leading to a new and dangerous life that they were engaged in a voyage that God Himself not only approved, but in which He participated. The precise way that Brother Winthrop expressed himself echoes throughout the history of American life. He explained to his fellow travelers, "We shall find that the God of Israel is among us, when ten of us shall be able to resist a thousand of our enemies, when he shall make us a praise and glory, that men shall say of succeeding plantations [settlements]: the Lord make it like that of New England: for we must Consider that we shall be as a City upon a Hill, the eyes of all people are upon us." The myth of America as a city on a hill implies that America is a moral example to the rest of the world, a world that will presumably keep its attention riveted on us. It means that we are a Chosen People, each of whom, because of God's favor and presence, can smite one hundred of our heathen enemies hip and thigh.

The society Winthrop meant to establish in New England would do God's work, insofar as sinners could. America would become God's country. The Puritans would have understood this to mean that they were creating a nation of, by, and for the Lord. About two centuries later, the pioneers and the farmers who followed the Puritans translated God's country from civilization to the grandeur and nobility of nature, to virgin land, to the purple mountains' majesty. Relocating the country of God from civilization to nature was significant in many ways, but the conclusion that this New World is specially favored by the Lord not only endured but spread.

5   In countless ways Americans know in their gut—the only place myths can live—that we have been Chosen to lead the world in public morality and to instruct it in political virtue. We believe that our own domestic goodness results in strength adequate to destroy our opponents who, by definition, are enemies of virtue, freedom, and God. Over and over, the founding Puritans described their new settlement as a beacon in the darkness, a light whose radiance could keep Christian voyagers from crashing on the rocks, a light that could brighten the world. In his inaugural address John Kennedy said, "The energy, the faith, the devotion which we bring to this endeavor [defending freedom] will light our country and all who serve it—and the glow from that fire can truly light the world." The city on a hill grew from its first tiny society to encompass the entire nation. As we will see, that is one of the reasons why we compelled ourselves to intervene in Vietnam.

An important part of the myth of America as the city on a hill has been lost as American power increased. John Winthrop intended that his tiny settlement should be only an example of rectitude to the cosmos. It could not have occurred to him that his small and weak band of saints should charge about the world to impose the One Right Way on others who were either too wicked, too stupid, or even too oppressed to follow his example. Because they also had domestic distractions, the early American Puritans could not even consider foreign adventures. In almost no time they had their hands full with a variety of local malefactors: Indians, witches, and, worst of all, shrewd Yankees who were more interested in catching fish than in catching the spirit of the Lord. Nathaniel Hawthorne, brooding about these Puritans, wrote that civilization begins by building a jail and a graveyard, but he was only two-thirds right. Within only two generations, the New England saints discovered that there was a brothel in Boston, the hub of the new and correct Christian order.

The New World settlement was puny, but the great ocean was a defensive moat that virtually prohibited an onslaught by foreign predators. The new Americans could therefore go about perfecting their society without distracting anxiety about alien and corrupting intrusions from Europe. This relative powerlessness coupled with defensive security meant that the city on a hill enjoyed a favorable "peculiar situation." It was peculiarly blessed because the decadent world could not come here, and we did not have to go there. The rest of the world, but especially Europe, with its frippery, pomp, and Catholicism, was thought to be morally leprous. This is what George Washington had in mind when he asked a series of rhetorical questions in his farewell address in 1796:

Why forego the advantages of so peculiar a situation? Why quit our own to stand upon foreign ground? Why, by interweaving our destiny with that of any part of Europe, entangle our peace and prosperity in the toils of European ambition, rivalship, interest, humor, of caprice?

This is also what Thomas Jefferson told his countrymen when he was inaugurated five years later. This enlightened and skeptical philosopher-President announced that this was a "chosen country" which had been "kindly separated by nature and a wide ocean from the exterminating havoc of one quarter of the globe." He said that the young nation could exult in its many blessings if it would only keep clear of foreign evil. His prescription was that America should have "entangling alliances with none."

One final example of the unaggressive, unimperial interpretation of the myth is essential. The entire Adams family had a special affinity for old Winthrop. Perhaps it was that they grew up on the soil in which he was buried. On the Fourth of July, in 1821, John Quincy Adams gave a speech that captured every nuance of the already ancient myth. His speech could have been the text for the Vietnam War critics. He said that America's heart and prayers would always be extended to any free and independent part of the world. "But she goes not abroad in search of monsters to destroy." America, he said, hoped that freedom and independence would spread across the face of the earth. "She will recommend the general cause by the countenance of her voice, and by the benignant sympathy of her example." He said that the new nation understood that it should not actively intervene abroad even if such an adventure would be on the side of freedom because "she would involve herself beyond the power of extrication." It just might be possible for America to try to impose freedom elsewhere, to assist in the liberation of others. "She might," he said, "become the dictatress of the world. She would no longer be the ruler of her own spirit."

10   In 1966, this speech was quoted by George F. Kennan, the thoughtful analyst of Soviet foreign affairs, to the Senate Foreign Relations Committee which was conducting hearings on the Vietnam War. Perhaps not knowing the myth, Mr. Kennan said that he was not sure what Mr. Adams had in mind when he spoke almost a century and a half earlier. But whatever it was, Mr. Kennan told the senators who were then worry-

ing about Vietnam, "He spoke very directly and very pertinently to us here today."

The myth of the city on a hill became the foundation for the ritualistic thinking of later generations of Americans. This myth helped to establish nationalistic orthodoxy in America. It began to set an American dogma, to fix the limits of thought for Americans about themselves and about the rest of the world, and offered a choice about the appropriate relationship between us and them.

The benevolence of our national motives, the absence of material gain in what we seek, the dedication to principle, and our impenetrable ignorance were all related to the original myth of America. It is temptingly easy to dismiss this as some quaint idea that perhaps once had some significance, but lost it in this more sophisticated, toughminded, modern America. Arthur Schlesinger, Jr., a close aide to President Kennedy, thought otherwise. He was concerned about President Johnson's vastly ambitious plans to create a "Great Society for Asia." Whatever the President meant, according to Professor Schlesinger, such an idea

demands the confrontation of an issue deep in the historical consciousness of the United States: whether this country is a chosen people, uniquely righteous and wise, with a moral mission to all mankind…The ultimate choice is between messianism and maturity.

The city myth should have collapsed during the war. The war should have taught us that we could not continue to play the role of moral adviser and moral enforcer to the world. After the shock of the assassinations, after the shock of Tet, after President Johnson gave up the presidency, after the riots, demonstrations, burned neighborhoods, and the rebellion of the young, it should have been difficult to sustain John Winthrop's optimism. It was not difficult for Robert Kennedy who, after Senator Eugene McCarthy had demonstrated LBJ's vulnerability in New Hampshire, finally announced that he would run for the presidency himself. The language he used in his announcement speech

proved that the myth was as alive and as virulent as it had ever been: "At stake," Senator Kennedy said, "is not simply the leadership of our party, and even our own country, it is our right to the moral leadership of this planet." Members of his staff were horrified that he could use such language because they correctly believed that it reflected just the mind-set that had propelled us into Vietnam in the first place. He ignored their protests. This myth could survive in even the toughest of the contemporary, sophisticated, hard-driving politicians. Of course, he may have used this language only to persuade his listeners, to convince the gullible. But, even so, it showed that he believed that the myth was what they wanted to hear. In either case, the city on a hill continued to work its way.

The myth of the city on a hill combined with solipsism in the assumptions about Vietnam made by the American war planners. In other words, we assumed that we had a superior moral claim to be in Vietnam, and because, despite their quite queer ways of doing things, the Vietnamese shared our values, they would applaud our intentions and embrace our physical presence. Thus, Vice President Humphrey later acknowledged that all along we had been ignorant of Vietnam. He said that "to LBJ, the Mekong and the Pedernales were not that far apart." Our claim to virtue was based on the often announced purity of our intentions. It was said, perhaps thousands of times, that all we wanted was freedom for other people, not land, not resources, and not domination.

15   Because we believed that our intentions were virtuous, we could learn nothing from the French experience in Vietnam. After all, they had fought only to maintain their Southeast Asian colonies and as imperialists deserved to lose. We assumed that this was why so mighty a European power lost the important battle of Dien Bien Phu to General Giap's ragged army. America's moral authority was so clear to us that we assumed that it also had to be clear to the Vietnamese. This self-righteousness was the clincher in the debate to intensify the conflict in Vietnam, according to

George W. Ball, an undersecretary of state for Presidents Kennedy and Johnson. Washington's war planners, Mr. Ball said in 1973, had been captives of their own myths. Another State Department official also hoped, after the fact, that Americans "will be knocked out of our grandiosity...[and] will see the self-righteous, illusory quality of that vision of ourselves offered by the high Washington official who said that while other nations have 'interests' the United States has 'a sense of responsibility.'" Our power, according to this mentality, gives us responsibility, even though we may be reluctant to bear the burden. Other peoples' greed or selfishness gives them interests, even though they may not be strong enough to grab all they want.

Our grandiosity will, however, not be diminished so easily. At least since World War II, America's foreign affairs have been the affairs of Pygmalion. We fall in love with what we create. We create a vision of the world made in what we think is our own image. We are proud of what we create because we are certain that our intentions are pure, our motives good, and our behavior virtuous. We know these things to be true because we believe that we are unique among the nations of the world in our collective idealism.

Although the nationalists of the world all share a peoples' pride in who they are, a loyalty to place and language and culture, there are delicate but important differences. Because of its Puritan roots, it is not surprising that America's nationalism is more Protestant than that of other countries. It is more missionary in its impulses, more evangelical. It typically seeks to correct the way other people think rather than to establish its own physical dominion over them. It is, as it were, more committed to the Word, as befits serious Protestants, than other nationalisms.

One of the peculiarities of American Protestant nationalism, especially in its most aggressive mood, is its passion about ideas. What we want is to convert others to the truth as we understand it. We went to war in Vietnam in the name of ideas, of principles, of abstractions. Thus, President Johnson said in his inaugural, "We aspire to nothing that belongs to others." And added in his important address at Johns Hopkins in April 1965: "Because we fight for values and we fight for principles, rather than territory or colonies, our patience and our determination are unending." This is what we mean when we think of ourselves as idealists, magnanimous and moral. It is what cold warriors mean when they say over and over that we are engaged with the Soviet Union "in a competition of ideas."

Tangled up in old myths, fearful of speaking plain English on the subject, the political conscience of many Americans must be troubled. There is bad faith in accepting the city myth of American uniqueness as if the myth can be freed from its integral Protestantism, almost always of a fundamentalist flavor. Conservatives have less need to launder the myth of its religion. Because liberals require a secular version of nationalism, and if they need or want to retain some sense of the unique republic, they are required to rest their case on a secular basis. Wilsonian idealism was the answer in the 1960s, as liberals argued that America was the only society capable of creating social justice and genuine democracy at home and abroad. These ideals merged with the cold war and persuaded the best of American liberals to bring us Vietnam.

In America, as elsewhere, elected officials are especially susceptible to the fundamental myths of nationalism because they must embody them to get elected and act on them to govern. The vision of the world that suffused Mr. Wilson's Fourteen Points and League of Nations was also the vision of John Kennedy and his circle. They were pained by the knowledge that a people anywhere in the world struggled toward freedom but was frustrated by the imposition of force. So it was that John F. Kennedy's inspired inaugural address carried the burden of Woodrow Wilson's idealism, and also carried the deadly implication that America was again ready for war in the name of goodness.

President Kennedy's language must be understood in the light of what was just around the corner in Vietnam. He announced to the world. "We shall pay any price, bear any burden, meet any hardship, support any friend, oppose any foe to assure the survival and the success of liberty." He said that it was the rare destiny of his generation to defend freedom when it was at its greatest risk. "I do not shrink from this responsibility—I welcome it."

The difference between the two sons of the Commonwealth of Massachusetts, John Quincy Adams and John Fitzgerald Kennedy, was the difference between good wishes and war, but also the difference between a tiny and isolated America and the world's most powerful nation. Presidents Wilson and Kennedy both fairly represented American liberalism at its most restless and energetic. This was a liberalism that wanted, as President Wilson put it, to make the world safe for democracy, or as President Kennedy said, to defend "those human rights to which this nation has always been committed, and to which we are committed today at home and around the world." JFK described this as "God's work."

An important part of the reason we marched into Vietnam with our eyes fixed was liberalism's irrepressible need to be helpful to those less fortunate. But the decency of the impulse, as was the case with President Wilson, cannot hide the bloody eagerness to kill in the name of virtue. In 1981, James C. Thomson, an aide in the State Department and a member of the National Security Council under President Johnson, finally concluded that our Vietnamese intervention had been motivated by a national missionary impulse, a "need to do good to others." In a phrase that cannot be improved, he and others called this "sentimental imperialism." The purity of intention and the horror of result is unfortunately the liberal's continuing burden.

American conservatives had it easier, largely because they believed in the actuality of evil. In his first public statement, President Eisenhower informed the American public, "The forces of good and evil are massed and armed and opposed as rarely before in history." For him the world struggle was not merely between conflicting ideologies. "Freedom is pitted against slavery; lightness against the dark."

25   Conservatives in America are closer than liberals to the myth of the city on a hill because they are not embarrassed by public professions of religion. They are therefore somewhat less likely to ascribe American values and behavior to other cultures. This is so because of the conservatives' conviction that America is so much better—more moral, godly, wise, and especially rich—than other nations that they could not possibly resemble us. Thus, President Eisenhower announced that one of America's fixed principles was the refusal to "use our strength to try to impress upon another people our own cherished political and economic institutions." The idea of uniqueness means, after all, that we are alone in the world.

Conservatives shared with liberals the conviction that America could act, and in Vietnam did act, with absolute altruism, as they believed only America could. Thinking of this war, President Nixon, another restless descendent of Mr. Wilson, declared that "never in history have men fought for less selfish motives—not for conquest, not for glory, but only for the right of a people far away to choose the kind of government they want." This was especially attractive because in this case the kind of government presumably sought by this faraway people was opposed to Communism, our own enemy. It was therefore an integral part of the universal struggle between freedom and slavery, lightness and dark. As a result it was relatively easy for conservatives to think of Vietnam as a laboratory to test ways to block the spreading stain of political atheism.

Power is sometimes a problem for liberals and a solution for conservatives. When Senator Goldwater rattled America's many sabers in his presidential campaign of 1964, and when General Curtis LeMay wanted to bomb North Vietnam "back to the stone age," they both made liberals cringe, partly from embarrassment, and partly because the liberals were appalled at the apparent cruelty. In the 1950s, Dr. Kissinger cleverly argued that the liberal embarrassment over power made its use, when necessary, even worse than it had to be. "Our feeling of guilt with respect to power," he wrote, "has caused us to transform all wars into crusades, and then to apply our power in the most absolute ways." Later, when he ran America's foreign policy, his own unambivalent endorsement of the use in Vietnam of enormous power inevitably raised the question of whether bloody crusades are caused only by the squeamishness of liberals or also by the callousness of conservatives.

Implicit in John Winthrop's formulation of the city myth was the idea that the new Americans could, because of their godliness, vanquish their numerically superior enemies. The idea that warriors, because of their virtue, could beat stronger opponents, is very ancient. Pericles spoke of it in his funeral oration to the Athenians. The Christian crusaders counted on it. *Jihad*, Islam's conception of a holy war, is based on it. The Samurai believed it. So did the Nazis.

In time, the history of America proved to Americans that we were militarily invincible. The Vietnam War Presidents naturally cringed at the thought that they could be the first to lose a war. After all, we had already beaten Indians, French, British (twice), Mexicans, Spaniards, Germans (twice), Italians, Japanese, Koreans, and Chinese. Until World War II, the nation necessarily had to rely on the presumed virtue, not the power, of American soldiers to carry the day, and the war. This was also the case in the South during our Civil War.

30   Starting in the eighteenth century, the nation of farmers began to industrialize. As the outcome of war increasingly came to depend on the ability to inject various forms of flying hardware into the enemy's body, victory increasingly depended on technology. The acceleration of industrialization in the late nineteenth century inevitably quickened the pace of technological evolution. By then no other power could match the Americans' ability to get organized, to commit resources to development, and to invent the gadgets that efficiently produced money in the marketplace, and, when necessary, death on the battlefield. The idea of Yankee ingenuity, Ameri-

can know-how, stretches back beyond the nineteenth century. Our admiration for the tinkerer whose new widget forms the basis of new industry is nowhere better shown than in our national reverence of Thomas Edison.

Joining the American sense of its moral superiority with its technological superiority was a marriage made in heaven, at least for American nationalists. We told ourselves that each advantage explained the other, that the success of our standard of living was a result of our virtue, and our virtue was a result of our wealth. Our riches, our technology, provided the strength that had earlier been missing, that once had forced us to rely only on our virtue. Now, as Hiroshima demonstrated conclusively, we could think of ourselves not only as morally superior, but as the most powerful nation in history. The inevitable offspring of this marriage of an idea with a weapon was the conviction that the United States could not be beaten in war—not by any nation, and not by any combination of nations. For that moment we thought that we could fight where, when, and how we wished, without risking failure. For that moment we thought that we could impose our will on the recalcitrant of the earth.

A great many Americans, in the period just before the war in Vietnam got hot, shared a circular belief that for most was probably not very well formed: America's technological supremacy was a symptom of its uniqueness, and technology made the nation militarily invincible. In 1983, the playwright Arthur Miller said, "I'm an American. I believe in technology. Until the mid-60s I never believed we could lose because we had technology."

The memory of World War II concluding in a mushroom cloud was relatively fresh throughout the 1950s. It was unthinkable that America's military could ever fail to establish its supremacy on the battlefield, that the industrial, scientific, and technological strength of the nation would ever be insufficient for the purposes of war. It was almost as if Americans were technology. The American love affair with the automobile was at its most passionate in the 1950s, our well-equipped armies stopped the Chinese in Korea, for a moment our nuclear supremacy was taken for granted, and affluence for many white Americans seemed to be settling in as a way of life.

It is, of course, unfortunate that the forces of evil may be as strong as the forces of virtue. The Soviet Union exploded its first atomic bomb way ahead of what Americans thought was a likely schedule. This technology is not like others because even a weak bomb is devastating. Even if our bombs are better than theirs, they can still do us in. America's freedom of action after 1949 was not complete. President Eisenhower and John Foster Dulles, the Secretary of State, threatened "massive retaliation" against the Soviet Union if it stepped over the line. They knew, and we knew, that this threat was not entirely real, and that it freed the Soviets to engage in peripheral adventures because they correctly believed that we would not destroy the world over Korea, Berlin, Hungary, or Czechoslovakia.

35   Our policy had to become more flexible. We had to invent a theory that would allow us to fight on the edges without nuclear technology. This theory is called "limited war." Its premise is that we and the Soviets can wage little wars, and that each side will refrain from provoking the other to unlock the nuclear armory.

Ike threatened the Chinese, who at the time did not have the bomb, with nuclear war in Korea. JFK similarly threatened the Soviets, who had nuclear capability, over Cuba. But, although some military men thought about using nuclear weapons in Vietnam, the fundamental assumption of that war was to keep it limited, not to

force either the Soviets or the Chinese, who now had their own sloppy bombs, to enter the war. Thus, we could impose our will on the recalcitrant of the earth if they did not have their own nuclear weapons, and if they could not compel the Soviets or the Chinese to force us to quit.

In Vietnam we had to find a technology to win without broadening the war. The nuclear stalemate reemphasized our need to find a more limited ground, to find, so to speak, a way to fight a domesticated war. We had to find a technology that would prevail locally, but not explode internationally. No assignment is too tough for the technological mentality. In fact, it was made to order for the technicians who were coming into their own throughout all of American life. This war gave them the opportunity to show what they could do. This was to be history's most technologically sophisticated war, most carefully analyzed and managed, using all of the latest wonders of managerial procedures and systems. It was made to order for bureaucracy.

James C. Thomson, who served both JFK and LBJ as an East Asia specialist, understood how the myths converged. He wrote of *the rise of a new breed of American ideologues who see Vietnam as the ultimate test of their doctrine.* These new men were the new missionaries and had a trinitarian faith: in military power, technological superiority, and our altruistic idealism. They believed that the reality of American culture "provides us with the opportunity and obligation to ease the nations of the earth toward modernization and stability: toward a full-fledged *Pax Americana Technocratica.*" For these parishioners in the church of the machine, Vietnam was the ideal laboratory.

SUGGESTIONS FOR DISCUSSION

1. How are these two accounts alike and different in the way they explain U.S. involvement in Vietnam? What do the titles that these historians have given to the selections—"The Tragedy of Vietnam" and "God's Country and American Know-How"—indicate about their respective points of view? What advantages and disadvantages do you see in each selection's attempt to explain the origins of the Vietnam War?

2. Recall how and what you have learned about the Vietnam War. What has shaped your understanding—school, friends, relatives, movies, books, television shows? How does

your own sense of the Vietnam War compare with the perspectives presented by the two reading selections?

3. Baritz describes the "trinitarian faith" of American policymakers in "military power, technological superiority, and altruistic idealism" that he believes led the country into the Vietnam War. Is this "faith" still strongly held today? What, if any, relation do you see between this faith and post–Vietnam military interventions in Grenada, Panama, Iraq, Somalia, Kosovo, and Haiti? What problems or issues does such "faith" ignore or suppress?

SUGGESTIONS FOR WRITING

1. Write an essay that compares Tindall and Shi's and Baritz's accounts of the origins of the Vietnam War. End the essay with your own sense of the relative strengths and weaknesses of each way of doing and explaining history.

2. Write an essay on what Baritz calls America's "missionary impulse." What do you see as the problems, if any, with this "altruistic idealism"? Does it invariably lead, as Baritz suggests, to "purity of intention" on the one hand, and "the horror of result" on the other? Look at a particular situation during which the desire to act "in that name of goodness" backfired on the benefactors. Don't limit yourself here to matters of international or military policy. There may be instances closer to home in which some person or some group that seeks to do good actually produces the opposite effect. Your task here is to analyze why and how this is the case.

3. Write an essay that locates your own understanding of the Vietnam War in relation to the accounts of these professional historians. Agree and disagree with them as you see fit, but the main point is to use their versions of the Vietnam War to develop your own. Make sure you explain how you learned about the Vietnam War, through which sources—school, friends, relatives, popular media—and how these sources shaped your understanding.

PRIVATE FIRST CLASS REGINALD "MALIK" EDWARDS

Wallace Terry

The following selection is a chapter from *Bloods: An Oral History of the Vietnam War by Black Veterans* (1984) by the journalist and documentary film producer Wallace Terry. *Bloods* consists of twenty oral histories that Terry gathered from African Americans who served in Vietnam, enlisted men and officers from the U.S. Army, Navy, Marines, and Air Force—what Terry calls "a representative cross-section of the black combat force." As Terry says, these men's "stories are not to be found in the expanding body of Vietnam literature" but "deservedly belong in the forefront because of the unique experience of the black Vietnam veteran." The story told by Malik Edwards is printed here, but all of the stories in Terry's book are equally eloquent, telling of life in combat, racism in the military, relations between Americans and Vietnamese, and the difficulties of returning to civilian life in a racially divided society.

SUGGESTION FOR READING   As you read, notice how Malik Edwards offers both anecdotal accounts of particular incidents in the war and his own commentary on the meaning of the war. Mark those passages where Edwards explains his feelings about the war.

1   Rifleman
9th Regiment
U.S. Marine Corps
Danang

5   June 1965–March 1966

I'm in the Amtrac with Morley Safer, right? The whole thing is getting ready to go down. At Cam Ne. The whole bit that all America will see on the *CBS Evening News,* right? Marines burning down some huts. Brought to you by Morley Safer. Your man on the scene. August 5, 1965.

When we were getting ready for Cam Ne, the helicopters flew in first and told them to get out of the village 'cause the Marines are looking for VC. If you're left there, you're considered VC.

They told us if you receive one round from the village, you level it. So we was coming into the village, crossing over the hedges. It's like a little ditch, then you go through these bushes and jump across, and start kickin' ass, right?

Not only did we receive one round, three Marines got wounded right off. Not only that, but one of the Marines was our favorite Marine, Sergeant Bradford. This brother that everybody loved got shot in the groin. So you know how we felt.

10   The first thing happened to me, I looked out and here's a bamboo snake. That little short snake, the one that bites you and you're through bookin'. What do you do when a bamboo snake comin' at you? You drop your rifle with one hand, and shoot his head off. You don't think you can do this, but you do it. So I'm so rough with this snake, everybody thinks, well, Edwards is shootin' his ass off today.

So then this old man runs by. This other sergeant says, "Get him, Edwards." But I missed the old man. Now I just shot the head off a snake. You dig what I'm sayin'? Damn near with one hand. M-14. But all of a sudden, I missed this old man. 'Cause I really couldn't shoot him.

So Brooks—he's got the grenade launcher— fired. Caught my man as he was comin' through the door. But what happened was it was a room full of children. Like a schoolroom. And he was runnin' back to warn the kids that the Marines were coming. And that's who got hurt. All those little kids and people.

Everybody wanted to see what had happened, 'cause it was so fucked up. But the officers wouldn't let us go up there and look at what shit they were in. I never got the count, but a lot of people got screwed up. I was telling Morley Safer and his crew what was happening, but they thought I was trippin', this Marine acting crazy, just talking shit. 'Cause they didn't want to know what was going on.

So I'm going on through the village. Like the way you go in, you sweep, right? You fire at the top of the hut in case somebody's hangin' in the rafters. And if they hit the ground, you immediately fire along the ground, waist high, to catch them on the run. That's the way I had it worked out, or the way the Marines taught me. That's the process.

15   All of a sudden, this Vietnamese came runnin' after me, telling me not to shoot: "Don't shoot. Don't shoot." See, we didn't go in the village and look. We would just shoot first. Like you didn't go into a room to see who was in there first. You fired and go in. So in case there was somebody there, you want to kill them first. And we was just gonna run in, shoot through the walls. 'Cause it was nothin' to shoot through the walls of a bamboo hut. You could actually set them on fire if you had tracers. That used to be a fun thing to do. Set hootches on fire with tracers.

So he ran out in front of me. I mean he's runnin' into my line of fire. I almost killed him. But I'm thinking, what the hell is wrong? So then we went into the hut, and it was all these women and children huddled together. I was gettin' ready to wipe them off the planet. In this one hut. I tell you, man, my knees got weak. I dropped down, and that's when I cried. First time I cried in the 'Nam. I realized what I would have done. I almost killed all them people. That was the first time I had actually had the experience of weak knees.

Safer didn't tell them to burn the huts down with they lighters. He just photographed it. He could have got a picture of me burning a hut, too. It was just the way they did it. When you say level a village, you don't use torches. It's not like in the 1800s. You use a Zippo. Now you would use a Bic. That's just the way we did it. You went in there with your Zippos. Everybody. That's why people bought Zippos. Everybody had a Zippo. It was for burnin' shit down.

I was a Hollywood Marine. I went to San Diego, but it was worse in Parris Island. Like you've heard the horror stories of Parris Island—people be marchin' into the swamps. So you were happy to be in San Diego. Of course, you're in a lot of sand, but it was always warm.

At San Diego, they had this way of driving you into this base. It's all dark. Back roads. All of a sudden you come to this little adobe-looking place. All of a sudden, the lights are on, and all you see are these guys with these Smokey the Bear hats and big hands on their hips. The light is behind them, shining through at you. You all happy to be with the Marines. And they say, "Better knock that shit off, boy. I don't want to hear a goddamn word out of your mouth." And everybody starts cursing and yelling and screaming at you.

20   My initial instinct was to laugh. But then they get right up in your face. That's when I started getting scared. When you're 117 pounds, 150 look like a monster. He would just come screaming down your back, "What the hell are you looking at, shit turd?" I remembered the time where you cursed, but you didn't let anybody adult hear it. You were usually doing it just to be funny or trying to be bold. But these people were actually serious about cursing your ass out.

Then here it is. Six o'clock in the morning. People come in bangin' on trash cans, hittin' my bed with night sticks. That's when you get really scared, 'cause you realize I'm not at home anymore. It doesn't look like you're in the Marine Corps either. It looks like you're in jail. It's like you woke up in a prison camp somewhere in the South. And the whole process was not to allow you to be yourself.

I grew up in a family that was fair. I was brought up on the Robin Hood ethic, and John

Wayne came to save people. So I could not understand that if these guys were supposed to be the good guys, why were they treating each other like this?

I grew up in Plaquemines Parish. My folks were poor, but I was never hungry. My stepfather worked with steel on buildings. My mother worked wherever she could. In the fields, pickin' beans. In the factories, the shrimp factories, oyster factories. And she was a housekeeper.

I was the first person in my family to finish high school. This was 1963. I knew I couldn't go to college because my folks couldn't afford it. I only weighed 117 pounds, and nobody's gonna hire me to work for them. So the only thing left to do was go into the service. I didn't want to go into the Army, 'cause everybody went into the Army. Plus the Army didn't seem like it did anything. The Navy I did not like 'cause of the uniforms. The Air Force, too. But the Marines was bad. The Marine Corps built men. Plus just before I went in, they had all these John Wayne movies on every night. Plus the Marines went to the Orient.

25   Everybody laughed at me. Little, skinny boy can't work in the field going in the Marine Corps. So I passed the test. My mother, she signed for me 'cause I was seventeen.

There was only two black guys in my platoon in boot camp. So I hung with the Mexicans, too, because in them days we never hang with white people. You didn't have white friends. White people was the aliens to me. This is '63. You don't have integration really in the South. You expected them to treat you bad. But somehow in the Marine Corps you hoping all that's gonna change. Of course, I found out this was not true, because the Marine Corps was the last service to integrate. And I had an Indian for a platoon commander who hated Indians. He used to call Indians blanket ass. And then we had a Southerner from Arkansas that liked to call you chocolate bunny and Brillo head. That kind of shit.

I went to jail in boot camp. What happened was I was afraid to jump this ditch on the obstacle course. Every time I would hit my shin. So a white lieutenant called me a nigger. And, of course, I jumped the ditch farther than I'd ever jumped before. Now I can't run. My leg is really messed up. I'm hoppin'. So it's pretty clear I can't do this. So I tell the drill instructor, "Man, I can't fucking go on." He said, "You said what?" I said it again. He said, "Get out." I said, "Fuck you." This to a drill instructor in 1963. I mean you just don't say that. I did seven days for disrespect. When I got out of the brig, they put me in a recon. The toughest unit.

We trained in guerrilla warfare for two years at Camp Pendleton. When I first got there, they was doing Cuban stuff. Cuba was the aggressor. It was easy to do Cuba because you had a lot of Mexicans. You could always let them be Castro. We even had Cuban targets. Targets you shoot at. So then they changed the silhouettes to Vietnamese. Everything to Vietnam. Getting people ready for the little gooks. And, of course, if there were any Hawaiians and Asian-Americans in the unit, they played the roles of aggressors in the war games.

Then we are going over to Okinawa, thinking we're going on a regular cruise. But the rumors are that we're probably going to the 'Nam. In Okinawa we was trained as raiders. Serious, intense jungle-warfare training. I'm gonna tell you, it was some good training. The best thing about the Marine Corps, I can say for me, is that they teach you personal endurance, how much of it you can stand.

30   The only thing they told us about the Viet Cong was they were gooks. They were to be killed. Nobody sits around and gives you their historical and cultural background. They're the enemy. Kill, kill, kill. That's what we got in practice. Kill, kill, kill. I remember a survey they did in the mess hall where we had to say how we felt about the war. The thing was, get out of Vietnam or fight. What we were hearing was Vietnamese was killing Americans. I felt that if people were killing Americans, we should fight them. As a black person, there wasn't no problem fightin' the enemy. I knew Americans were prejudiced, were racist and all that, but basically, I believed in America 'cause I was an American.

I went over with the original 1st Battalion 9th Marines. When we got there, it was nothing like you expect a war to be. We had seen a little footage of the war on TV. But we was on the ship dreaming about landing on this beach like they did in World War II. Then we pulled into this area like a harbor almost and just walked off the ship.

And the first Vietnamese that spoke to me was a little kid up to my knee. He said, "You give me cigarette. You give me cigarette." That really freaked me out. This little bitty kid smokin' cigarettes. That is my first memory of Vietnam. I thought little kids smokin' was the most horrible thing that you could do. So the first Vietnamese words I learned was *Toi khong hut thuoc lo.* "I don't smoke cigarettes." And *Thuoc la co hai cho suc khoe.* "Cigarettes are bad for your health."

Remember, we were in the beginning of the war. We wasn't dealing with the regular army from the North. We was still fightin' the Viet Cong. The NVA was moving in, but they really hadn't made their super move yet. So we were basically runnin' patrols out of Danang. We were basically with the same orders that the Marines went into Lebanon with. I mean we couldn't even put rounds in the chambers at first.

It was weird. The first person that died in each battalion of the 9th Marines that landed was black. And they were killed by our own people. Comin' back into them lines was the most dangerous thing then. It was more fun sneakin' into Ho Chi Minh's house than comin' back into the lines of Danang. Suppose the idiot is sleeping on watch and he wake up. All of a sudden he sees people. That's all he sees. There was a runnin' joke around Vietnam that we was killing more of our people than the Vietnamese were. Like we were told to kill any Vietnamese in black. We didn't know that the ARVN had some black uniforms, too. And you could have a platoon commander calling the air strikes, and he's actually calling on your position. It was easy to get killed by an American.

35   They called me a shitbird, because I would stay in trouble. Minor shit, really. But they put me on point anyway. I spent most of my time in

Vietnam runnin'. I ran through Vietnam 'cause I was always on point, and points got to run. They can't walk like everybody else. Specially when you hit them open areas. Nobody walked through an open area. After a while, you develop a way to handle it. You learned that the point usually survived. It was the people behind you who got killed.

And another thing. It's none of that shit, well, if they start shootin' at you, now all of a sudden we gonna run in there and outshoot them. The motherfuckers hit, you call in some air. Bring in some heavy artillery, whatever you need to cool them down. You wipe that area up. You soften it up. Then you lay to see if you receive any fire. And *then* you go on in.

I remember the first night we had went out on patrol. About 50 people shot this old guy. Everybody claimed they shot him. He got shot 'cause he started running. It was an old man running to tell his family. See, it wasn't s'posed to be nobody out at night but the Marines. Any Vietnamese out at night was the enemy. And we had guys who were frustrated from Korea with us. Guys who were real gung ho, wanted a name for themselves. So a lot of times they ain't tell us shit about who is who. People get out of line, you could basically kill them. So this old man was running like back towards his crib to warn his family. I think people said "Halt," but we didn't know no Vietnamese words.

It was like shootin' water buffaloes. Somebody didn't tell us to do this. We did it anyway. But they had to stop us from doing that. Well, the water buffaloes would actually attack Americans. I guess maybe we smelled different. You would see these little Vietnamese kids carrying around this huge water buffalo. That buffalo would see some Marines and start wantin' to run 'em down. You see the poor little kids tryin' to hold back the water buffalo, because these Marines will kill him. And Marines, man, was like, like we was always lookin' for shit to go wrong. Shit went wrong. That gave us the opportunity.

I remember we had went into this village and got pinned down with a Australian officer. When we finally went on through, we caught these two women. They smelled like they had weapons. These were all the people we found. So the Australian dude told us to take the women in. So me and my partner, we sittin' up in this Amtrac with these women. Then these guys who was driving the Amtrac come in there and start unzippin' their pants as if they gonna screw the women. So we say, "Man, get outta here. You can't do it to our prisoners." So they get mad with us. Like they gonna fight us. And we had to actually lock and load to protect the women. They said, "We do this all the time."

40   One time we had went into this place we had hit. We was takin' prisoners. So this one guy broke and ran. So I chased him. I ran behind him. Everybody say, "Shoot him. Shoot him." 'Cause they was pissed that I was chasin' him. So I hit him. You know I had to do something to him. I knew I couldn't just grab him and bring him back. And his face just crumbled. Then I brought him back, and they said, "You could have got a kill, Edwards."

The first time we thought we saw the enemy in big numbers was one of these operations by Marble Mountain. We had received fire. All of a sudden we could see people in front of us. Instead of waiting for air, we returned the fire, and you could see people fall. I went over to this dude and said, "Hey, man, I saw one fall." Then everyone started yelling, "We can see 'em fall. We can see 'em fall." And they were fallin'. Come to find out it was Bravo Company. What the VC had done was suck Bravo Company in front of us. 'Cause they attacked us and Bravo Company at the same time. They would move back as Bravo Company was in front of us. It was our own people. That's the bodies we saw falling. They figured out what was happening, and then they ceased fire. But the damage is done real fast. I think we shot up maybe 40 guys in Bravo Company. Like I said, it was easy to get killed by an American.

The first time I killed somebody up close was when we was tailing Charlie on a patrol somewhere around Danang. It was night. I was real tired. At that time you had worked so hard during the day, been on so many different details, you were just bombed out.

I thought I saw this dog running. Because that white pajama top they wore at night just blend into that funny-colored night they had over there. All of a sudden, I realized that somebody's runnin'. And before I could say anything to him, he's almost ran up on me. There's nothing I can do but shoot. Somebody get that close, you can't wait to check their ID. He's gonna run into you or stop to shoot you. It's got to be one or the other. I shot him a bunch of times. I had 20-round clip, and when he hit the ground, I had nothing. I had to reload. That's how many times he was shot.

Then the sergeant came over and took out the flashlight and said, "Goddamn. This is fucking beautiful. This is fucking beautiful."

45   This guy was really out of it. He was like moanin'. I said, "Let me kill him." I couldn't stand the sound he was makin'. So I said, "Back off, man. Let me put this guy out of his misery." So I shot him again. In the head.

He had a grenade in his hand. I guess he was committing suicide. He was just runnin' up to us, pullin' a grenade kind of thing. I caught him just in time.

Everybody was comin' congratulatin' me, saying what a great thing it was. I'm tryin' to be cool, but I'm really freakin' out. So then I start walking away, and they told me I had to carry the body back to base camp. We had a real kill. We had one we could prove. We didn't have to make this one up.

So then I start draggin' this body by the feet. And his arm fell off. So I had to go back and get his arm. I had to stick it down his pants. It was a long haul.

And I started thinkin'. You think about how it feels, the weight. It was rainin'. You think about the mist and the smells the rain brings out. All of a sudden I realize this guy is a person, has got a family. All of a sudden it wasn't like I was carrying a gook. I was actually carrying a human being. I started feeling guilty. I just started feeling really badly.

50   I don't feel like we got beat in Vietnam. We never really fought the war. People saying that America couldn't have won that war is crazy.

The only way we could actually win the war was to fight every day. You couldn't fight only when you felt like it. Or change officers every month. Troops would learn the language, learn the people, learn the areas. If you're gonna be fighting in an area, you get to know everybody in the area and you stay there. You can't go rotate your troops every 12 months. You always got new people coming in. Plus they may not get to learn anything. They may die the first day. If you take a guy on patrol and he gets killed the first day, what good is he? See, if you have seasoned troops, you can move in and out of the bush at will. You get the smell of the country on you. You start to eat the food. You start to smell like it. You don't have that fresh smell so they can smell you when you're comin'. Then you can fight a war. Then you can just start from one tip of South Vietnam and work your way to the top. To China. Of course, if we had used the full might of the military, we'd be there now. We could never give the country back up. Plus we'd have to kill millions of Vietnamese. Do we want to do that? What had they done to us to deserve all that? So to do it would have been wrong. All we did was give our officers the first combat training they had since Korea. It was more like a big training ground. If it was a real war, you either would have come out in a body bag or you would have come out when the war was over.

Sometimes I think we would have done a lot better by getting them hooked on our lifestyle than by trying to do it with guns. Give them credit cards. Make them dependent on television and sugar. Blue jeans works better than bombs. You can take blue jeans and rock 'n' roll records and win over more countries than you can with soldiers.

When I went home, they put me in supply, probably the lowest job you can have in the Marines. But they saw me drawing one day and they said, "Edwards can draw." They sent me over to the training-aids library, and I became an illustrator. I reenlisted and made sergeant.

When I went to Quantico, my being black, they gave me the black squad, the squad with most of the blacks, especially the militant blacks. And they started hippin' me. I mean I was against racism. I didn't even call it racism. I called it prejudice. They hipped me to terms like "exploitation" and "oppression." And by becoming an illustrator, it gave you more time to think. And I was around people who thought. People who read books. I would read black history where the white guys were going off on novels or playing rock music. So then one day, I just told them I was black. I didn't call them *blanco,* they didn't have to call me Negro. That's what started to get me in trouble. I became a target. Somebody to watch.

55   Well, there was this riot on base, and I got busted. It started over some white guys using a bunch of profanity in front of some sisters. I was found guilty of attack on an unidentified Marine. Five months in jail, five months without pay. And a suspended BCD. In jail they didn't want us to read our books, draw any pictures, or do anything intellectually stimulating or what they thought is black. They would come in my cell and harass me. So one day I was just tired of them, and I hit the duty warden. I ended up with a BCD in 1970. After six years, eight months, and eight days, I was kicked out of the Corps. I don't feel it was fair. If I had been white, I would never have went to jail for fighting. That would have been impossible.

With a BCD, nothing was happenin'. I took to dressin' like the Black Panthers, so even blacks wouldn't hire me. So I went to the Panther office in D.C. and joined. I felt the party was the only organization that was fighting the system.

I liked their independence. The fact that they had no fear of the police. Talking about self-determination. Trying to make Malcolm's message reality. This was the first time black people had stood up to the state since Nat Turner. I mean armed. It was obvious they wasn't gonna give us anything unless we stood up and were willing to die. They obviously didn't care anything about us, 'cause they had killed King.

For me the thought of being killed in the Black Panther Party by the police and the thought of being killed by Vietnamese was just a qualitative difference. I had left one war and came back and got into another one. Most of the Panthers

then were veterans. We figured if we had been over in Vietnam fighting for our country, which at that point wasn't serving us properly, it was only proper that we had to go out and fight for our own cause. We had already fought for the white man in Vietnam. It was clearly his war. If it wasn't, you wouldn't have seen as many Confederate flags as you saw. And the Confederate flags was an insult to any person that's of color on this planet.

I rose up into the ranks. I was an artist immediately for the newspaper. Because of my background in the military, obviously I was able to deal with a lot of things of a security nature. And eventually I took over the D.C. chapter.

60   At this time, Huey Newton and Bobby Seale were in jail and people sort of idealized them. The party didn't actually fall apart until those two were released, and then the real leader, David Hilliard, was locked up. Spiro Agnew had a lot to do with the deterioration when he said take the Panthers out of the newspapers and then they will go away. And the FBI was harassing us, and we started turning on each other because of what they were spreading. And the power structure started to build up the poverty programs. Nobody was going to follow the Panthers if they could go down to the poverty program and get a check and say they are going to school.

We just didn't understand the times. All we wanted to do was kick whitey's ass. We didn't think about buying property or gaining economic independence. We were, in the end, just showing off.

I think the big trip America put us on was to convince us that having money was somehow harmful. That building businesses and securing our economic future, and buying and controlling areas for our group, our family, our friends like everybody else does, was wrong. Doing that doesn't make you antiwhite. I think white people would even like us better if we had more money. They like Richard Pryor. And Sammy Davis. And Jabbar.

Economically, black folks in America have more money than Canada or Mexico. It's obvious that we are doing something wrong. When people say we're illiterate, that doesn't bother me as much. Literacy means I can't read these books. Well neither does a Korean or a Vietnamese. But where they're not illiterate is in the area of economics. Sure, we're great artists, great singers, play great basketball. But we're not great managers yet. It's pretty obvious that you don't have to have guns to get power. People get things out of this country and they don't stick up America to do it. Look at the Vietnamese refugees running stores now in the black community where I live.

Right now, I'm an unemployed artist, drawing unemployment. I spent time at a community center helping kids, encouraging kids to draw.

65   I work for the nuclear-freeze movement, trying to convince people nuclear war is insane. Even when I was in the Marine Corps, I was against nuclear war. When I was a child, I was against nuclear weapons, because I thought what they did to Hiroshima and Nagasaki was totally cold. There's nothing any human being is doing on the planet that I could want to destroy the planet for future generations. I think we should confine war to our century and our times. Not to leave the residue around for future generations. The residue of hate is a horrible thing to leave behind. The residue of nuclear holocaust is far worse.

I went to see *Apocalypse Now*, because a friend paid my way. I don't like movies about Vietnam 'cause I don't think that they are prepared to tell the truth. *Apocalypse Now*, didn't tell the truth. It wasn't real. I guess it was a great thing for the country to get off on, but it didn't remind me of anything I saw. I can't understand how you would have a bridge lit up like a Christmas tree. A USO show at night? Guys attacking the women on stage. That made no sense. I never saw us reach the point where nobody is in charge in a unit. That's out of the question. If you don't know anything, you know the chain of command. And the helicopter attack on the village? Fuckin' ridiculous. You couldn't hear music comin' out of a helicopter. And attacking a beach in helicopters was just out of the question. The

planes and the napalm would go in first. Then, the helicopters would have eased in after the fact. That was wild.

By making us look insane, the people who made that movie was somehow relieving themselves of what they asked us to do over there. But we were not insane. We were not insane. We were not ignorant. We knew what we were doing.

I mean we were crazy, but it's built into the culture. It's like institutionalized insanity. When you're in combat, you can do basically what you want as long as you don't get caught. You can get away with murder. And the beautiful thing about the military is there's always somebody that can serve up as a scapegoat. Like Calley. I wondered why they didn't get Delta Company 1–9 because of Cam Ne. We were real scared. But President Johnson came out and defended us. But like that was before My Lai. When they did My Lai, I got nervous again. I said my God, and they have us on film.

I was in Washington during the National Vietnam Veterans Memorial in 1982. But I didn't participate. I saw all these veterans runnin' around there with all these jungle boots on, all these uniforms. I didn't want to do that. It just gave me a bad feeling. Plus some of them were braggin' about the war. Like it was hip. See, I don't think the war was a good thing. And there's no memorial to Cam Ne, to My Lai. To all those children that was napalmed and villages that were burned unnecessarily.

70   I used to think that I wasn't affected by Vietnam, but I been livin' with Vietnam ever since I left. You just can't get rid of it. It's like that painting of what Dali did of melting clocks. It's a persistent memory.

I remember most how hard it was to just shoot people.

I remember one time when three of our people got killed by a sniper from this village. We went over to burn the village down. I was afraid that there was going to be shootin' people that day, so I just kind of dealt with the animals. You know, shoot the chickens. I mean I just couldn't shoot no people.

I don't know how many chickens I shot. But it was a little pig that freaked me out more than the chickens. You think you gonna be shootin' a little pig, it's just gonna fall over and die. Well, no. His little guts be hangin' out. He just be squiggling around and freakin' you out.

See, you got to shoot animals in the head. If we shoot you in your stomach, you may just fall over and die. But an animal, you got to shoot them in the head. They don't understand that they supposed to fall over and die.

SUGGESTIONS FOR DISCUSSION

1. Compare the passages that you marked with the passages that were marked by your classmates. See if you can decide what Edwards's feelings are about the Vietnam War. How would you characterize his understanding of why the war was fought and what it means? If you think his feelings are contradictory or inconsistent, how would you explain this?

2. Edwards says that the "only thing they told us about the Viet Cong was they were gooks. They were to be killed. Nobody sits around and gives you their historical and cultural background. They're the enemy. Kill, kill, kill." Explain the meaning of this passage. How, in wartime, is the "enemy" created? What might have happened if American soldiers knew the historical and cultural background of the Vietnamese people?

3. Edwards says that when he returned to the United States, he "had left one war and came back and got into another one." What does he mean? How are these two "wars" alike and different?

SUGGESTIONS FOR WRITING

1. Write an essay that develops your own personal response to reading the selection by Malik Edwards. How did it make you feel about the Vietnam War? What changes, if any, occurred in your understanding of the war? Why do you think you reacted as you did?

2. Edwards says, "You can take blue jeans and rock 'n' roll records and win over more countries than you can with soldiers." Write an essay that explains what Edwards means by this statement. Use the essay to develop your own position on what it means for the United States to "hook" other countries "on our life-style." How does this (or does it not) differ from "trying to do it with guns"? What are the wider issues—ethical, cultural, and political—that you see involved here?

3. Write an essay that compares Edwards's experience of the Vietnam War with the textbook account in Tindall and Shi's "The Tragedy of Vietnam." Consider the main differences and similarities in these two descriptions of the war. What perspective does Edwards's account offer you that you don't find in the textbook version? Do Tindall and Shi seem to be asking the same questions about the war that Edwards does? What do you see as the values and limits of each account?

MAKING A MEMORY OF WAR: Building the Vietnam Veterans Memorial

Kristin Ann Hass

Kristin Ann Hass teaches in the program in American Culture at the University of Michigan, Ann Arbor. The selection "Making a Memory of War: Building the Vietnam Veterans Memorial" is taken from the first chapter of her book *Carried to the Wall: American Memory and the Vietnam Veterans Memorial.* Hass is interested in how the American public has grappled with the problem of memorializing the 58,000 soldiers killed in the long, unpopular, and controversial Vietnam War. As you will see, Americans' unresolved feelings about the war played a powerful role in debates about Maya Lin's design of the Vietnam Veterans Memorial and the subsequent addition of two other memorials, Frederick Hart's *The Three Fightingmen* and Glenna Goodacre's Vietnam Women's Memorial.

Maya Lin. Vietnam Veterans Memorial

Frederick Hart, *The Three Fightingmen*

Glenna Goodacre. Vietnam Women's Memorial

SUGGESTION FOR READING At the end of Hass's introductory section, she asks why so many Americans have left letters, military medals, beer cans, teddy bears, and other offerings at the Vietnam Veterans Memorial. The purpose of her book *Carried to the Wall* is to provide analysis and interpretation to answer this question. As you read, notice how Hass's discussion of the memorial's design complicates her question and anticipates her answers.

American materialism is…The materialism of action and abstraction.

> *Gertrude Stein, in* Gertrude Stein's America

1   In 1971 angry Vietnam veterans gathered outside the White House gates and on the steps of Capitol Hill. Chanting and jeering, they hurled their Purple Hearts, their Bronze Stars, their awards of valor and bravery, over the White House fence and against the limestone Capitol. In a radical breach of military and social decorum, these highly decorated military men spit back their honors. They had been betrayed, lied to, and abandoned. They had had no chance to be Hollywood heroes; instead they had fought an ugly war, survived, and lost.

In 1982, in the calm of the Constitution Gardens, these medals started to appear at the base of the Vietnam Veterans Memorial. They were set carefully under a name (or a group of names of soldiers who lost their lives together) by the owners of the medals and the fathers of the dead. Chances are good that there was no chanting or jeering as the medals were laid down; the Wall is a startlingly quiet place. And although the medals and ribbons were sometimes accompanied by a photograph or a note hastily written on stationery from a local hotel, the awards were left at the Wall one at a time. At first, they were set down without publicity or organized purpose. Thousands of Americans had the same unanticipated response to the memorial. They came and left their precious things. Why?

Hurling your Purple Heart at the powers that be and setting it at the foot of a memorial to your dead friends are very different acts. The veterans' throwing of their medals is not difficult to interpret as the rejection of an honor, a disdainful public protest against betrayal. However defiant, these veterans were still acting within commonly understood social codes. The things they threw had clearly defined social meanings.

The things offered at the memorial were given new meaning in a much less clear social context. Mainstream funerary and memorial traditions in American culture do not involve the offering of things. Flowers and flags are for memorials. Medals of valor and old cowboy boots are for mantels and attics. This new response to a veterans memorial, then, raises some fascinating questions. Why did so many people have the same unconventional, unanticipated response to the memorial? Where did it come from? What meaning do these things have? Are these offerings left for the dead or the living? Is the medal left as a show of respect? Or of anger?

5   More than 20 million visitors, about one in ten Americans, have visited the Wall, and every day for fifteen years some of these visitors have left offerings. The flowers and flags have been accompanied by long letters to the dead, poems, teddy bears, wedding rings, human remains, photographs, ravaged military uniforms, high school yearbooks, fishing lures, cans of beer, collections of stories, Bibles, and bullets. In November of 1990, eight years after the dedication of the monument, nearly six hundred objects were left, including seventy military medals, one urn containing human ashes, and a large sliding glass door. Why?

THE MEMORIAL

Dear Smitty,

Perhaps, now I can bury you; at least in my soul. Perhaps now I won't again see you night after night when the war reappears and we are once more amidst the myriad hells that Vietnam engulfed us in….I never cried. My chest becomes unbearably painful and my throat tightens so I can't even croak, but I haven't cried. I wanted to, just couldn't. I think I can today. Damm, I'm crying now. Bye Smitty. Get some rest.

Anonymous note left at the Wall

The average age of the soldiers killed in Vietnam was nineteen; most of those who died had been drafted. The Vietnam Veterans Memorial was born out of a clear vision of what was to be represented: the dead, the veterans, and the sense of community that had made the war palatable to some Americans between 1957 and 1975. The problem, however, of what the death, the veterans, and the lost community suggested together and how they might be represented was the subject of many public and private battles. The work of any memorial is to construct the meaning of an event from fragments of experience and memory. A memorial gives shape to and consolidates public memory; it makes history. As historian James Mayo argues, "how the past is commemorated through a country's war memorials mirrors what people want to remember, and lack of attention reflects what they wish to forget." The veterans fighting to shape the meaning of the Vietnam War found that their efforts to commemorate this country's longest war were met with all of the conflicting emotions and ideologies expressed about the war itself. There was no consensus about what the names represented, about what to remember or what to forget.

The deeply controversial nature of the war, its unpopularity, and the reality that it was lost created an enormous void of meaning that compounded the difficult work of memorializing. What it meant to die in this war was as unclear as what it meant to fight in it. Moreover, the duration of the war, the military's system of rotation, and the defeat precluded the ticker-tape parades young boys going to war might have anticipated. Veterans came home to changing ideas about patriotism and heroism; they returned to a society riven by the civil rights movement, Watergate, and the assassinations of the men who had inspired many of them to fight. There was no clear ideology around which a community of grief

could have formed. It was a muddled, lost war waiting to be forgotten even before it was over. People who lost their children, husbands, father, sisters, and their own hearts were without a public community for the expression of grief or rage or pride. This lack of community not only made them deeply crave a remembrance of the experience of Americans in Vietnam but also made the work of remembering especially difficult. Commemorating the war and the deaths required giving new shape to the broken meanings of the war. It required a reimagination of the nation.

In March of 1979 Jan Scruggs, a vet and the son of a rural milkman, went to see *The Deer Hunter*. He came home terrified and inspired. This Hollywood movie, about the horrors of the war, the impossibility of coming home, and the struggles of a small, working-class Pennsylvania community to come to terms with its losses, convinced Scruggs that it was time for the nation to publicly remember the war. In the movie a community shattered by the war regains its bearings in a tentative return to the patriotic ideals that had inspired its boys to fight. It is a troubling response, but it offered Scruggs some hope; the possibility of a community healing itself inspired in him the idea of building a memorial. So with a few of his veteran friends, Scruggs formed the Vietnam Veterans Memorial Fund (VVMF) in April of 1979.

The fund's first attempts to gain public support were not entirely successful. No more than a dozen reporters showed up for the first press conference, on May 28, 1979. Scruggs and his friends tried to launch a national fundraising campaign, but they received a handful of heart-wrenching letters and worn dollar bills instead of the generous checks for which they had hoped. The veterans fighting for a memorial were angry and determined, but they were not socially or politically powerful; and their cause was not easily or quickly embraced. They did, however, attract the attention of a few influential Vietnam veterans. Jack Wheeler, a Harvard- and Yale-educated West Pointer, joined the VVMF and began to draw in Vietnam veterans from high places throughout Washington. And although the founders of the VVMF had wanted to oppose the power structures whose work they were trying to memorialize, they learned that they could not raise public interest—let alone funds—without the aid of a few Washington power brokers. The fund's first major contributions came after a brunch for defense contractors organized by Senator John Warner.

10   The men and women who came to form the core of the VVMF were by no means politically or socially unified. Some had protested after serving in the war, and others continued to believe in the ideals of the conflict; nearly all, however, were white veterans who were keenly aware of their outcast social position as survivors of a deeply unpopular war. They wanted a national monument to help them reclaim a modicum of recognition and social standing.

As the money began to trickle in, the VVMF made several key decisions that determined a great deal about the character of the memorial and the kind of community that it rebuilt. The fund wanted a monument that listed all the names of those killed, missing in action, or still held as prisoners of war in Vietnam. Although the dead became the heart of the project because they were, in an important sense, all these veterans could agree upon, there was no easy agreement about how the memorial should remember the dead. The fund imagined a *veterans* memorial not a *war* memorial; the former would ensure a memory that emphasized the contributions of the soldiers rather than the federal government. The members of the fund did not ask for federal money because they did not want to be perceived as more Vietnam vets looking for a handout and because after Ronald Reagan cut $12 million from the Veterans Administrations budget in 1980, the vets did not trust his administration to give them the kind of memorial they hoped for. Building it with private contributions would also prove that a larger American public wanted to remember, and they wanted the memorial built on the Mall in Washington, D.C., to assure the memory of the veterans a place of national prominence.

The VVMF found itself in a complicated political position. The fund expected strong opposition from the antiwar movement and from the Washington bureaucracy; so it had to negotiate a public memory without either celebrating or explicitly renouncing the war, which would have been politically disastrous for any administration. As a result, strange alliances were formed at every step of the memorializing process. In 1980 the VVMF raised money through letters from Bob Hope calling for a reward for sacrifices made. Gerald Ford, Rosalynn Carter, Nancy Reagan, James Webb, Admiral James Stockdale, General William Westmoreland, and George McGovern made unlikely companions on the fund's letterhead. Few of the alliances were easily made, and not all of them held.

Early on the average donation to the $10 million project was $17.93 and envelopes were sent in with $2 change. Eventually, however, the campaign worked, and the success clearly demonstrated to the VVMF organizers that there was a population that wanted to publicly remember this war. Building this community of supportees and contributors, tenuous though it may have been, was an essential first step in the work of making a public meaning of the war. To memorialize the war, to solidify its shape and meaning, the fund had to bring together diverse experiences and ideologies. The seeming impossibility of the project was not only in facing the "myriad hells that Vietnam engulfed" the country in but also in repairing the social and political understandings that the war had fractured. In the end, the design of the memorial was a response to the problem of making memory in the wake of the Vietnam War; this is the history they made.

THE DESIGN

I came down today to pay respects to the good friends of mine. Go down to visit them sometime. They are on panel 42E, lines 22 and 26. I think that you will like them.
Anonymous note left at the Wall

Most war memorials in America—statues, schools, stadiums, bridges, parks—proudly salute

American triumph. How do you memorialize a painfully mired, drawn-out defeat that called into question the most fundamental tenets of American patriotism?

15   The design of the Vietnam Memorial was bound to be controversial. Its promoters understood that it would be impossible to find a representation of the war that could satisfy a deeply polarized society. The leaders of the VVMF decided to hold an open juried contest because they knew that without the participation of some recognized bearers of cultural capital they would never get a design through Washington's notoriously difficult architectural gatekeepers—The National Planning Commission. Choosing the jury was difficult, though. Who should decide how the war would be represented? There was some noise made about including a Vietnam veteran, an African American, and a woman; but it was feared that jurors might defer too much to the opinions of a vet, and, oddly, they were unable to locate a qualified woman or a qualified African American. So the decision was turned over to the most traditional bearers of culture: early in 1981 a panel of distinguished architects, landscape architects, sculptors, and critics was organized by Washington architect Paul Spreiregen. The unpaid veterans who had worked long hours to bring the memorial to this point were impressed by the prestige of the jury but nervous about turning their project over to men "the same age as the people who sent [them] to 'Nam."

The jury and the contestants were given only a few simple, if wildly ambitious, instructions: the design should "(1) be reflective and contemplative in character; (2) harmonize with its surroundings; (3) contain the names of those who had died in the conflict or who were still missing; and (4) make no political statement about the war." The most important task of the design, however, was the creation of a memorial that would, as Scruggs wrote, "begin a healing process, a reconciliation of the grievous divisions wrought by the war." One of the great ironies of these guidelines is that Vietnam's death toll of fifty-eight thousand is, compared with that of most

other American wars, so low that all of the names could actually be reproduced on one memorial. (The effect is overwhelming, of course, but possible only because so relatively few Americans died.)

By April 26, 1981, more than fourteen hundred designs had been entered. On May 1, 1981, the jurors, after remarkably little deliberation, unanimously selected a simple black granite V, set into a small hill in the Constitution Gardens, carved with the name of every man and woman who never came back from Vietnam. They were impressed with the eloquence and the simplicity of the design. The jurors, one of whom noted of the designer, "he knows what he's doing, all right," were no doubt startled to discover that their winner was a remarkable impossibility: a twenty-one-year-old art student at Yale University—young, intellectual, female, and Chinese American.

In imagining her design, Maya Ying Lin made a clear decision not to study the history of the war, or to enmesh herself in the controversies surrounding it. Her design lists the names of the men and women killed in Vietnam in the order in which they were killed. The names are carved into black granite panels that form a large V at a 125-degree angle and suggest the pages of an open book. The first panel cuts only a few inches into the gently sloping hillside, but each panel is longer than the last and cuts more deeply into the ground, so that you walk down-hill toward the apex, at which point the black panels tower three or four feet above your head. At the center you are half buried in a mass of names; pulled toward the black granite, you see yourself and the open lawns of the mall behind you reflected in the memorial. The center of the monument is a strangely private, buffered public space. Literally six feet into the hillside you are confronted simultaneously with the names and with yourself. The black granite is so highly reflective that even at night visitors see their own faces as they look at the Wall. The Wall manages to capture the unlikely simultaneous experiences of reflection and burial. This brilliant element of the design asks for a personal, thoughtful response. As you exit, the panels diminish in size, releasing you back into the daylight. Lin's design did not initially include the word "Vietnam"; she gave form not to the event that caused the deaths but to the names of the dead, to the fact of the deaths.

The names are carved out of polished granite from Bangalore, India. The carving invites tangible interaction. Each name has a physical presence. It asks to be touched. Lin wanted visitors to be able to feel the names in many different ways, and she wanted people to be able to take something of the Wall away with them—a rubbing of a name.

20   The Wall tries to make a somehow individuated memory of a war. The events in Vietnam are remembered through the names of the dead: these men and women—many of whom, even those drafted against their will, might have imagined, at least in part, that their experience would be like that portrayed in the movie *How I Won the War with John Wayne*—are each remembered as tragically fallen individuals. The power of the design lies in the overwhelming presence of individual names, which represent complicated human lives cut short. This attention to individual lives lost would not, however, be as potent if it were separated from the black expanse of all of the names together, the effect of which is so overwhelming that it both foregrounds the individual names and hides them. Lin's organization of the names also contributes to this tension between particular names and the whole formed by the names together. The dead appear on the Wall not alphabetically but rather in the order in which they died in Vietnam. Soldiers who died together are listed together on the Wall, so that on every line on every panel stories of particular times and places are inscribed with the names. This placement of the names, however, makes finding an individual name in the list impossible without the aid of the phone book–like alphabetical indexes at the entrances to the memorial. Although the index provides information about every name—including hometown, birth date, and death date—it requires a certain amount of participation on the part of any visitor interested in a particular name.

Maya Lin's design earned her a B in her funerary architecture class at Yale, but that was the least of her troubles. She was thrown into a noisy "firestorm of the national heart." Her design was dubbed the "black gash of shame." Its shape was considered an affront to veteran and conservative manhood especially when compared to the shape of the neighboring Washington Monument: the V shape hinted at the peace sign, or a reference to the Vietcong; the black stone was more mournful than heroic. It seemed to many too clear an admission of defeat. The public outcry reflected outrage with Lin's design and with the principles that the VVMF required of all designs: the Wall was too abstract, too intellectual, too reflective. It was, in the minds of many, high art, the art of the class that lost the least in the war. It was not celebratory, heroic, or manly. James Webb, a member of the VVMF's National Sponsoring Committee, called it a "wailing Wall for future anti-draft and anti-nuclear demonstrators." Tom Carhart, a veteran who had been awarded a Purple Heart and had submitted a design of his own, coined a key phrase for those who hated the design when he wrote in a *New York Times* op-ed piece that it was "pointedly insulting to the sacrifices made for their country by all Vietnam veterans...by this we will be remembered: a black gash of shame and sorrow, hacked into the national visage that is the mall."

The popular press offered some support for the design, but the conservative press was enraged by it. In the *Moral Majority Weekly* Phyllis Schlafly called it a "tribute to Jane Fonda." *National Review* described it as an "Orwellian glob." In an open letter to President Reagan, Republican Representative Henry Hyde complained that it was "a political statement of shame and dishonor." And in September of 1981 an editorial in *National Review* demanded that Reagan intervene, arguing: "Okay, we lost the Vietnam war, okay the thing was mismanaged from start to finish. But American soldiers who died in Vietnam fought for their country and for the freedom of others, and they deserve better than the outrage that has been approved as their memorial...the Reagan administration should throw the switch on the project."

Its implicit admission that the war was disastrous, of course, is precisely what others loved about the design. A great many Vietnam veterans reacted with cautious approval. The VVMF and all leading veterans organizations, including the Veterans of Foreign Wars and the American Legion, officially approved of the design. The best evidence of the reaction of the larger community of veterans was their continued effort to support the monument despite the barrage of bitter publicity about the design. Veterans held garage sales, bingo games, and "pass the helmet" campaigns to raise funds for construction. At one of these events in Matoon, Illinois, a vet remarked to Scruggs that "everything Vietnam touches seems to go sour....I may never have the money to get to D.C., but it would make me feel good to know that my buddies' names are up there."

Of course, since the official dedication of the Wall in 1982 volumes of praise have been written for the design and the reflection that it has inspired. The Wall's emphasis on the tragedy of each death has appealed to critics and supporters alike. Strong hopes that this monument will guard against future wars have been expressed: James Kilpatrick, a nationally syndicated columnist, wrote, "this will be the most moving memorial even erected...each of us may remember what he wishes to remember—the cause, the heroism, the blunders, or the waste." One vet carried a sign at the memorial's opening that expressed a commonly held sentiment: "I am a Vietnam Veteran / I like the memorial / And if it makes it difficult to send people to battle again / I like it even more." A *New York Times* editorial reprinted in the Gold Star Mothers Association newsletter argued, "Nowadays, patriotism is a complicated matter. Ideas about heroism, or art, for that matter, are no longer what they were before Vietnam....But perhaps the V-shaped, black granite lines merging gently with the sloping earth make the win-

ning design seem a lasting and appropriate image of dignity and sadness."

25   Understanding the design as an attempt to represent a new, complicated patriotism may have appealed to many veterans and Gold Star Mothers, but to the newly elected leaders of the "Reagan revolution" it was an abomination. The design flew in the face of the recently revived strain of relentlessly nostalgic patriotism that had sent them to the capital. It is not surprising that in this political climate, the czars of American conservatism resented the abstraction and the ambiguity of the proposed war memorial, or that opposition to the design came from high places in Washington. James Watt, then secretary of the interior, was a key figure in the design controversy. It was Watt—with the support of irate VVMF contributor H. Ross Perot—who demanded that Lin's deign be supplemented, if not supplanted, by a more heroic, representational, figural memorial. Watt would not let the Wall be *the* Vietnam War memorial. Sculptor Frederick Hart made himself and his concrete bronze design, *The Three Fightingmen*, readily available to Watt, Perot, and the press. His intense lobbying efforts were well rewarded. Watt took to Hart's figures and threatened to hold up construction indefinitely unless the VVMF agreed to use the sculpture. With their backs against the wall, the VVMF decided that the memorial was worth the compromise.

Ultimately, this compromise reflects the impossibility of finding a single design that could represent the Vietnam War for all Americans. Hart's figural sculpture satisfied powerful voices that required concrete representation, but it did not solve the problem of representation presented by the war. His figures, a white man flanked by an African American man and a third man whose race is unclear, stand a hundred feet away facing the Wall, apparently transfixed by its power. They are strong, highly masculinized, and heroic. The white man holds his hands out slightly to his side as if to warn his companions, in a patrician gesture that mimics the imperial nature of the war, of some impending danger. Although frozen, they, like the human figures who walk the memorial's path, are drawn to the black granite that recedes into the earth and then delivers into the light. Hart had intended the figures to look warily into the distance for the ubiquitous, hidden Vietnamese enemy, but the negotiations involved in the addition of the sculpture turned their gaze on the Wall and opened up a broad range of interpretive possibilities. This ironic fate for Hart's symbolically stable, heroic figures is indicative of the difficulty he faced in trying to divert attention from Lin's design. The sculpture in the end dramatizes the difficulties of representation and the power of the names; the main attraction of the memorial continues to be the Wall.

Even after the addition of the figures in 1984, the official commemoration of the war was not yet finished. In 1993, nearly ten years later, another battle over the memory of the war took shape on the Mall. After years of struggling to raise money and interest, Vietnam veteran Diane Carlson Evans presided over the dedication of the Vietnam Women's Memorial. This memorial is the first national memorial to female veterans. Its four figures—a prone, blindfolded, injured male soldier, a white nurse who holds him in her arms, an African American woman comforting the nurse and looking to the sky, and a third woman kneeling over medical equipment—stand about three hundred feet from the Wall, sheltered in a grove of tall trees. It is a very straightforward figural memorial. And while the sculptor, Glenna Goodacre, was swiftly written off by art critics for whom her pietà is uninspiring, the principal argument against a memorial to the women who served in Vietnam was that it would set a precedent for a whole slew of other "special interest memorials." This complaint, as hollow as it might seem in light of the utter lack of memorials to the sacrifices made by American women at war, held considerable sway with the Park Service and the Fine Arts Commission; it is a reminder of the strength of the ideal that one symbolic gesture should be able to make a memory of this twenty-year war.

Evans wanted a women's memorial because the Wall did not heal the particular, complicated alienation of women veterans she had experienced, and it did not make women visible at the memorial. But her efforts to make the work of women in this war an obvious part of its official memory became a struggle against the firmly held ideal of a singular public memory. This struggle was particularly frustrating because the monument already included two sculptures and because women's war work in the United States has been invisible for so long despite the central role of women in the forging of public memory. The Mount Vernon Ladies' Association of the Union, the Daughters of the Confederacy, the Gold Star Mothers Association, and other women's volunteer associations have been essential to the history of memorializing in America. They have worked to ensure that national memories have been preserved and respected, but their contributions to the history of commemoration have not been recorded. Their roles in the work of making memory have been carefully prescribed—they have nurtured the memories of war as mothers, daughters, wives, and sisters but have not been seen as participants worth remembering. Women were undoubtedly a part of the life of the Vietnam Veterans Memorial in its first ten years, but they were principally visible as grievers, not as veterans. Diane Evans wanted to rewrite the history with the figure of a nurse.

Maya Lin sagely observed about the first statue, "In a funny sense, the compromise brings the memorial closer to the truth. What is also memorialized is that people still cannot resolve the war, nor can they separate the issues, the politics from it." This is true about both of the added statues. Hart's sculpture memorializes a need to remember these veterans as manly and heroic; Goodacre's sculpture, eight years later, memorializes a victory for women veterans over the perceived threat to patriotism posed by the idea of making any memory of war that is not singular and masculine. Hart's and Goodacre's additions to the Wall commemorate the difficulty of making memory in the midst of shifting cultural values. It is, in part, this sense of the impossibility of representation that pulls personal, individual memorials from visitors to the Wall; with their things people are bringing the monument "closer to the truth."

30   In the statement she submitted with her design proposal, Maya Lin wrote, "it is up to each individual to resolve or to come to terms with this loss. For death is in the end a personal and private matter and the area containing this within the memorial is a quiet place, meant for personal reflection and private reckoning." Lin was entirely right. She probably could not have anticipated the extent to which visitors to this memorial would take on the responsibility for the memory of the war, but she did appreciate the constantly unfinished, contested nature of the memory of this war. She understood that memorializing the war necessarily meant undoing the traditional idea of patriotic nationalism in the shape of a singular, heroic memorial. The multiplication of memorials, names, and objects at the Wall has, indeed, replaced the possibility of a singular memory of the war; the single figure of the male citizen embodying the nation has been supplanted by three official memorials and a steady stream of combat boots, bicycle parts, and St. Christophers. People come to this memorial and they make their own memorials.

SUGGESTIONS FOR DISCUSSION

1. In the final line of this selection, Kristin Ann Hass says, "People come to this memorial and they make their own memorials." Consider this statement in light of the questions Hass begins with, about why people leave offerings at the wall. Trace her line of reasoning through the two sections "The Memorial" and "The Design." How does her discussion in these middle sections provide the groundwork for the answer she suggests? What evidence does she provide to link her closing answer to the opening question?

2. Hass notes that in 1984, two years after the wall was built, another memorial—Frederick Hart's heroic, representational *The Three Fightingmen*—was added. Then nearly ten years later, in 1993, a third was completed, the Vietnam Women's Memorial. What does Hass see as the significance of these additions? Consider the designs of the three memorials. What does each seem to signify? What do they signify when taken together as a group? How do they compare with earlier war memorials, such as *The Flag-Raising at Iwo Jima* and its commemoration of World War II?

3. Locate memorials around your college or hometown. You are likely to find several war memorials, but don't limit yourself to just commemorations of the military dead. Americans have also memorialized Holocaust and AIDS victims, those killed or maimed in the Oklahoma City bombing, and students who died or were wounded in the Littleton shootings. A wall was erected in South Central Los Angeles to memorialize those injured in the uprising following the Rodney King trial, and murals in Chicano communities commemorate those who died in gang violence. The memorials you choose could be, like the Vietnam memorials, official monuments as well as schools, bridges, stadiums, parks, or plaques. Consider also more informal or popular memorials that exist outside established institutions. Work together in groups of three or four, with each group preparing a class presentation on one of the memorials. Do research on who sponsored the memorial and why as well as on public attitudes to the war or event. In your presentation, describe the memorial in detail, paying attention to its design and its location. Bring in photographs and other print or visual information available of the memorial . Explain how the memorial commemorates the dead and what cultural meanings it seems to project. What vision of the past does it bring to the present? What sense of national identity, patriotism, or community does it seem to embody?

SUGGESTIONS FOR WRITING

1. Kristin Ann Hass sees the addition of the two memorials—*The Three Fightingmen* and the Vietnam Women's Memorial—as a compromise that reflects "the impossibility of finding a single design that could represent the Vietnam War for all Americans." Write an essay that focuses on the visual design of the three memorials and the lack of consensus they reveal in American memories of the Vietnam War. Consider what each memorial signifies and what they signify as a group.

2. Hass talks about Americans' "restless memory of the Vietnam War," an apparent inability to reach emotional closure about the meaning of the war for individuals and for the country. In the previous reading, Malik Edwards says, "I used to think I wasn't affected by Vietnam, but I been livin' with Vietnam ever since I left. You just can't get rid of it." Interview someone who lived through the Vietnam years—who went to Vietnam, was active in the antiwar movement, whose son or daughter was in the military. How does your subject remember those years? What lasting effects did the war have on the person? What memories does the person carry with him or her? Use the interview to write a character sketch of how history lives in the memory of ordinary people.

3. Monuments and statues are not the only forms of cultural expression that reflect and shape the way Americans remember the Vietnam War. Films are also important repositories of historical memory. Hollywood films have a long history of memorializing war—from the vision of the Civil War contained in *Gone with the Wind* to Stephen Spielberg's tribute to World War II, *Saving Private Ryan*. Some of the best-known and readily available films that treat the Vietnam War are *Coming Home, The Deer Hunter, Platoon, Born on the Fourth of July, Full Metal Jacket,* and the *Rambo* series. Watch one or more of these films. Write an essay that explains the historical memory of the Vietnam War they offer viewers. Keep in mind the issue is not whether the film is historically accurate but the vision of the past it presents.

SPECTACLE OF MEMORY AND AMNESIA:
Remembering the Persian Gulf War

Marita Sturken

Marita Sturken teaches in the Annenberg School of Communication at the University of Southern California. This selection is taken from her book *Tangled Memories: The Vietnam War, the AIDS Epidemic, and the Politics of Remembering* (1992), in which she looks at the way watching "national events" such as the Kennedy assassination, the Vietnam War, the first moon walk, and the Persian Gulf War "enables Americans ...to situate themselves as members of a national culture." As you will see, she compares the televised images of the Persian Gulf War of 1991 with the images from the Vietnam War.

SUGGESTION FOR READING Notice how the opening section locates the Persian Gulf War in relation to World War II, the Korean War, and the Vietnam War. As you read, consider how these references to earlier wars enable Sturken to explain why the "cultural memory" of the Persian Gulf War is so contradictory.

CNN is live and alive as our humanity is about to die.

A Turkish writer

1 The way a nation remembers a war and constructs its history is directly related to how that nation further propagates war. Hence, the rewriting of the Vietnam War in contemporary Ameri-

can films directly affected the manufactured "need" for the United States's involvement in the Persian Gulf War.

The insistent and ongoing memorialization of World War II in American popular culture continues to haunt subsequent wars: The Vietnam War has been memorialized as the war with the difficult memory, and the Korean War has simply been forgotten. Vietnam has been the war that popular culture needed to rewrite and restage in order to remember, yet, as the Vietnam Veterans Memorial has demonstrated, memories of the war continue to disrupt simple narratives. The Persian Gulf War, by contrast, is a war about which Americans, even during the war itself, were perceived to have a collective amnesia—supposedly produced by the war's elaborate staging before an international audience. Yet the Persian Gulf War is not simply a war of empty spectacle and amnesia. It is remembered in complex ways through its effect upon the lives of its veterans; their presence tangles with the sanitized public story of the war.

Attempts to give the Persian Gulf War a neat narrative reinscribing master narratives of World War II—in which the United States liberates a desperate and weak country imperiled by a dangerous tyrant—are intended to chart the lineage of war directly from 1945 to 1991 in order to establish the Vietnam War (and its shadow, the Korean War) as aberrations. The Persian Gulf War will not need to be rescripted like the Vietnam War; it was expressly manufactured for the screen and a global audience, complete with a premiere date (January 15, 1991) and a cast of familiar characters (the evil, dark tyrant; the fearless newsman; the infallible weaponry). In one sense, the history of the Persian Gulf War was written before it began; it was, like the reinscriptions of Hollywood cinema, a spectacular orchestration of a new ending for the Vietnam War.

Indeed, the Persian Gulf War was choreographed as the ending of the "Vietnam Syndrome," the national "malaise" that fueled popular sentiment against interventions with American troops in foreign conflicts. The military perceived the renewed image of a sensational, efficient American war machine as a tool with which to eradicate images of the failure of technology in Vietnam. The image of American helicopters landing Marines on the roof of the U.S. embassy in Kuwait City in January 1991 could wipe out the humiliating image of helicopters evacuating people from the roof of the U.S. embassy in Saigon in 1975.

5   The Vietnam Syndrome was an image of emasculation, a "disease" that prevented the government from displaying strength. Abouali Farmanfarmanian notes that the "travesty of manhood" perpetrated by the Vietnam War was reiterated in the Iran hostage crisis of 1979:

> The 1979 hostage drama left America impotent, unable to wield its might. The small, confused, rather desperate attempt at freeing the hostages led to a humiliating catastrophe in the desert near Tabas, Iran. While the U.S. army was looking pitiful in the sand, white American masculinity—since all African American and white women hostages were released by the Iranian captors—was gagged, tied, and put on display for the world to see.

The hostage crisis also signaled the end of the administration of Jimmy Carter (whom Farmanfarmanian terms "forever the antimacho") and the election of the icon of American rugged masculinity, Ronald Reagan, as president.

Although the term "syndrome" applied to Vietnam before the advent of AIDS, it carried with it all the associations of a diseased condition—a "syndrome" as a weakened state, with a vulnerable immune system (read: military defense). The post–Vietnam War agenda of the Persian Gulf War was clear when a gleeful President George Bush declared, "The Vietnam Syndrome is over!" The Gulf War offered certain symbolic kinds of closure in the public arena for the fragmented narratives of the Vietnam War; yet by their very presence the Gulf War veterans, like the Vietnam veterans, have prevented the history of this war from remaining uncontested.

It is almost a cliché at this point to refer to the collective amnesia that surrounds the Persian Gulf War. This amnesia is fueled by the war's lack of a final outcome (Hussein's continued existence), the rescripting in public discourse of the war as a president's neglect of domestic issues (the public was quick to forget his "victory" and elect Bill Clinton in his place), and the spectacle of television images (which told the story not of war but of weaponry) that constituted the war's representation. The Gulf War was so quickly forgotten in public discourse that it needed to be restaged rather than remembered on its second anniversary, as President Bush bombed Iraq yet again, producing identical images of missiles in the night sky.

What was the purpose of this war, and what should its national memory have been? The government never adequately answered the question of how this six-week war, fought in countries that most Americans had never heard of, defended the national interest. Rather, it became clear that the Gulf War served very specific domestic interests of the U.S. military, which sought to test its weaponry and to establish its continued importance in a post–Cold War era.

10   I would argue that the cultural memory of the Persian Gulf War is particularly contradictory precisely because the military's attempts to regulate its public representation were so stringent. This was no accident but rather a primary legacy of the Vietnam War; one of the lessons the military establishment learned quite well was that its lack of control over media representation of the Vietnam War had had disastrous consequences for its public image. Because representation of the Gulf War was heavily controlled, the cultural memory of this war has been slower to evolve. Yet there are 700,000 veterans of the Gulf War whose stories are increasingly filtering into public discourse and whose struggles with a strange and unidentified disease, Gulf War Syndrome, have been increasingly difficult for the government to ignore. It is through these veterans that the simple narrative of the Gulf War is disrupted and through their bodies that cultural memory of the war is produced.

THE TELEVISION IMAGE: THE IMMEDIATE AND THE VIRTUAL

The American public "experienced" the Persian Gulf War through the medium of television, and television's images are central to its history. Yet television images have a slippery relationship to the making of history. The essence of the television image is transmission. It is relentlessly in the present, immediate, simultaneous, and continuous. Hence, television is defined by its capacity to monitor (in the form of surveillance cameras) and to be monitored, transmitting its image regardless of whether we continue to watch it. Raymond Williams wrote that television is defined by "flow," its capacity to unify fragmentary elements and to incorporate interruption.

Television is coded, like all electronic technology, as immediate and live. It is about the instant present, in which information is more valuable the more quickly we get it, the more immediate it is. Television allows for an immediate participation in the making of history; it produces "instant history." When television images become "historic" images—the lone student halting a tank at Tiananmen Square, the fall of the Berlin Wall, the bombs exploding at night over the city of Baghdad—they retain some of the cultural meaning of electronic technology, connoting the instant and the ephemeral. Their low-resolution, slightly blurred quality allows them to retain a sense of immediacy, as if they were presenting the unfolding of history rather than its image set in the past.

The Persian Gulf War was the first actual television war of the United States. Though the Vietnam War is often termed the first "living room war," its images were shot almost exclusively on film and hence subject to the delays of the developing process. There was always at least a twenty-four-hour delay before images of the Vietnam War reached the United States. The Persian Gulf War, by contrast, took place in the era of satellite technology and highly portable video equipment. It was technologically possible for the world to watch the Persian Gulf War as it happened. This is why military censorship was instituted in such a strict fashion—to make sure that it was *not* seen live. Still, claims of the "immediate" and the "live" reigned. Reporters in the Persian Gulf have noted that many of their stories never aired because they were delayed for a day or two by military censors. Any information that was not "immediate" was considered irrelevant by news producers. The illusion of live coverage given by the twentyfour-hour Cable News Network (CNN) worked in consort with military censorship to mark war news useless unless it was instantaneous.

Thus, one of the ironies of Persian Gulf War is that although it could have been copiously and immediately documented, it was instead depicted in sterile coverage that yielded very few images. Most of what the American audience saw were maps, still photographs of reporters, and live images of reporters in Israel. CNN's round-the-clock television coverage of the war offered only the illusion that viewers could see everything. The few images that were produced did not accumulate in cultural memory but rushed past in a succession of replays. Ernest Larsen writes: "This was the first war in history that everyone could turn off at night in order to sleep…and then switch on again in the morning to know if the world had yet fallen to pieces. The knowledge that such television produces tends not to accumulate, in part because each new moment literally cancels, without a trace, what we have just seen."

15   That the Persian Gulf War was fought in the era of satellite technology affected not only the choice of images that were disseminated in the media but also the surveillance and weapons systems of the war itself. The Gulf War was apparently one of the first in which a computer virus was used as a weapon. Electronic and satellite communications rendered the actual site of the war unclear. As McKenzie Wark writes:

> Did the Gulf War take place in Kuwait, Baghdad or Washington? Was the site the Middle East or the whole globe? This is a particularly vexing point. If Iraqi commanders order a SCUD missile launch via radio-telephone from Baghdad, the signal may be intercepted by orbiting US satellites. Another satellite detects the launch using infra-red sensors. Information from both will be relayed to the Pentagon, then again to US command HQ in Saudi Arabia and to Patriot missile bases in Saudi Arabia and Israel.

Wark describes the common notion that the expanded "theater" of the Gulf War included electronic space. This "virtual war" of satellite technology was above all a war of communication

vectors. This contributed to the illusion that only those watching CNN, like the TV spectators at a sports event, knew what was "really" happening in the war. As reporter Scott Simon has said:

> People around the world often had the sensation of being wired into that war. During the first week, the telephone rang in our workroom in Dhahran. "Get down to the bomb shelter," said an editor on the foreign desk who was watching television. "They've just launched a SCUD at you." And a minute later in eastern Saudi Arabia, the air raid sirens sounded. Weeks later, I stood in line with some soldiers waiting to make phone calls back to the United States. "Calling home before the ground war begins?" I asked. And a paratrooper answered, "Calling to find out what's happening in this war. My folks can really see it."…Sometimes I have to remind myself that when I say, "I was there—I saw that," I saw that only on television, just like the people watching the war in Kansas or Kenosha.

Simon evokes the pervasive conflation during the Gulf War of the television experience with the "real" story. Yet it is too simple to allow the Gulf War to be historicized as a virtual high-tech war. Though the image of the war on CNN may have made it appear that the television screen was the war's primary location, this illusion effaced the war that took place among human bodies and communities. The capacity to render the Gulf War in retrospect as a virtual war eclipses the fact that it was still a conventional war, fought with conventional weaponry, in which the body of the other was obliterated. Implicit in many of these statements is the concept that the "real" war is that which is recorded by a camera.

IMAGE ICONS

In this context of censorship and virtual participation, the few images of the war that did filter through took on tremendous significance in defining its narratives. The two images that have emerged as most iconic of the Persian Gulf War—bombs in the night sky over Baghdad and the point-of-view approach of the "smart" bomb to its target—contrast sharply with the iconic images of the Vietnam War.

Baghdad's fiery night sky is an image of both spectacle and the "unseen." Shot by an ABC cameraman with a special "night sight" heat-sensor lens, it is a surreal, otherworldly image that easily evokes the facile appearance of missiles chasing targets in video games. The "beauty" of war is shown here at its most extreme, formally and aesthetically riveting. One pilot said, "I could see the outline of Baghdad lit up like a giant Christmas tree. The entire city was just sparkling." The Vietnam War never produced such images of war as spectacle, the bombs' destructive power sanitized and erased in the darkness. The image of the Baghdad night has commonly been likened to a Fourth of July scene. Indeed, it was reenacted with fireworks at the 1991 Fourth of July celebration in New York, only a month after the huge "welcome home" parade for veterans of the Gulf War, completing the metaphor.

20   The image of the night sky over Baghdad was initially mythologized in the media as depicting Allied Patriot missiles shooting down Iraqi SCUD missiles headed for Israel and Saudi Arabia. However, since the Gulf War, it has been revealed that the video actually depicted the SCUDS coming apart at the end of their flight and falling into pieces onto the Patriots. Yet these qualifying explanations have not changed the meaning of this image as it achieves historic status: It signifies the myth of the war as one of clean technology.

The other image icons of the Gulf War—the electronic "missile-cam" footage taken from aircraft and bombs—also emphasize the predominating narrative of the war as a battle of technology. These images portray targeted buildings as seen through the crosshairs (and then exploding) and point-of-view perspectives of a bomb's approach to a site, flashing off the instant before impact. They carry power not only because they are the first popular images of their kind but also because they provide the viewer with a particular experience of military hardware voyeurism. In these images, the technologies of media and war merge to the point of inseparability. It can be said, however, that these technologies have always been inseparable, as television technology has always been derived from technology developed through military research. As Wark notes, "Most of the technologies now accessible to television, including the

Night sensor image of Baghdad, Persian Gulf War, 1991

Copyright 2003 ABC Photography Archives. Photography by Leslie Wong.

portable satellite news-gatherers (SNG), are the civilian progeny of equipment developed for military applications."

These missile-cam images are "secret" images, shown to audiences in the camaraderie of the military briefing room, usually on a small screen, with a military spokesman using a pointer to brief the "American public" on the interpretive codes needed to understand "our" weaponry. This approach allowed Gen. Norman Schwarzkopf and other military officials to employ sports metaphors, as if they were football coaches narrating their team's plays. Despite the presence of several woman reporters, the military briefing room for the press during the Gulf War was a male domain deliberately constructed as secretive and exclusive. The good-humored inside jokes and comradeship of word jockeying in these press conferences made clear the clubby relationship between the press and the military, masking the fact that many questions went unasked and unanswered. The shared secrecy implied in the presentation of these images is also the result of their visual coding as images of surveillance. In black and white and framed with crosshairs, these images of bombs exploding on their targets thus

afforded audiences the feeling of having a special kind of sight, a privileged view.

The camera image has a long history in both the propagation of wars and their documentation and memorialization. Since World War I, camera technology has been integral to the battlefield and image surveillance of the enemy, an essential strategic device. As Paul Virilio has written:

> Thus, alongside the "war machine," there has always existed an ocular (and later optical and electro-optical) "watching machine" capable of providing soldiers, and particularly commanders, with a visual perspective on the military action under way. From the original watch-tower, through the anchored balloon to the reconnaissance aircraft and remote-sensing satellites, one and the same function has been indefinitely repeated, the eye's function being the function of a weapon.

These two roles of the camera—as a device for constructing cultural memory and history and as a device for waging warfare—were inseparable in the production of images of the Gulf War. Yet what distinguishes the Gulf War surveillance images from previous ones is not only their technological proficiency but, more important, their use as the primary *public* images of the war;

Missile-cam image,
Persian Gulf War.

indeed, they have become the image icons of the war. As part of a well-orchestrated public relations and censorship campaign, these missile-cam images served to screen out images that were never taken or never shown. Hence, American viewers—and, by extension, the rest of the world, watching CNN—not only were given the illusion that they were welcomed into the military briefing room but also were situated as spectators within the frame of reference of the bomb. The camera's point of view was the bomb's point of view and the viewer's point of view. Watching these images, the viewer can imagine being in the bomber, imagine being the bomb itself, blasting forward and exploding in an orgasmic finale, the spectator and the weapon merged. Ironically, the audience did not seem to be implicated. Rather, the bombs took on agency, absolving viewers as distanced spectators.

25   Metaphors of sight were prevalent during the Gulf War; struggles over who had access to and control over the power to see dominated the war. At press briefings, Gen. Norman Schwartzkopf talked initially of blinding Saddam Hussein—"We took out his eyes"—by destroying his air force, and American weaponry was consistently referred to as having vision. For instance, the "thermal night sight" employed by American tanks was described as allowing them to fight at night or in bad weather, when "Iraqi tanks were virtually blind." Thus, "smart weapons" meant weapons that could "see." This emphasis on sight included a concern with concealment through the use of stealth bombers and other stealth technology.

The preoccupation with establishing American technology's ability to see can be directly traced to the representations of American technology in the Vietnam War. The "inpenetrable" jungle foliage of Vietnam has been consistently blamed for the inability of American military technology to win the war (hence the campaign of massive defoliation by Agent Orange perpetrated by the U.S. in Vietnam Not coincidentally, the desert terrain of the Middle East provided the ideal terrain for sight, enabling the American military to see its own technology at work. These "smart" weapons (only 70 percent of which, it

was revealed after the war, hit their targets) were awarded intelligence, sight, and even memory—they were said to "hold the characteristics of enemy vehicles in their memory."

DIS-REMEMBERING BODIES

The contrast between these images and the iconic images of the Vietnam War—Kim Phue fleeing naked from napalm, the point-blank killing of a Vietcong suspect by General Loan, the victims of the My Lai massacre—is obvious. The image icons of the Gulf War are of weapons and targets, not of human beings. Military censorship kept reporters and their cameras where they often had access only to distant images of bombers taking off and weapons in the sky. Images of the dead, of incinerated bodies on the road to Basra (the scene of the "turkey shoot" by U.S. planes on retreating Iraqis), were shown only selectively by the U.S. media. They clearly did not fit into the script, which cast the weapons as the subject of the war and the bodies of American, Allied, Kuwaiti, and Iraqi soldiers and civilians as extras.

The "bloodless" coverage of the war erased the effects of this weaponry on the sentient bodies of civilians. The iconic images of the Vietnam War gained their power by portraying graphically the damage war inflicts upon the human body—the torn flesh of Kim Phue, the piles of dead at My Lai, the graphic images of wounded American soldiers. Whereas Vietnam War images show terror at the moment of death, the images of the Gulf War depict spectacle at the moment of the bomb's impact. Instead of images of man against man, these are images of weapons against weapons. This is clearly a reaction to the bodies of the Vietnam War, the bodies of the war dead listed relentlessly on the Vietnam Veterans Memorial, and the problematic bodies of the Vietnam veterans, bodies that have resisted simple narratives of history.

In the Gulf War, bodies and weapons were reified in the media. Dead civilians were referred to as "collateral damage" and Iraqi soldiers as "targets" (objects of the "turkey shoot"), whereas weapons were ascribed the human characteristics of sight and memory. The media thus adopted without irony the technospeak of the military.

They depicted the destruction caused by American bombs only once, when an Iraqi bomb shelter was destroyed, killing several hundred people. This image was shown all over the world, but only in very limited and sanitized form in the United States, amid assertions that it had been faked or that Hussein had deliberately placed innocent civilians at a strategic military site. The general absence of images of destruction erased from the screen and the American psyche the spectacle of the war victims bodies, coded already as the dark bodies of the other. Even the graphic images of the "highway of death" of retreating Iraqi forces on the road to Basra concentrated on the mangled and burned corpses of cars and trucks rather than the people who had been killed inside.

30   Ironically, the desert landscape of the Persian Gulf contributed to this absence of bodies; the desert is mythologized in American culture as an uninhabited site. The image of the desert landscape as both postapocalyptic (already inscribed as a site of war) and unpeopled is reinforced by the fact that most of the desert in the United States is occupied by the military; the Nevada desert is even the site of unclear tests.

Instead of images of human beings at war, the media presented images of a war of machines: tanks, bombs, helicopters, and planes. Body counts (a central focus of government and media reports of the Vietnam War) were replaced by weapon counts. The only bodies that counted in the coverage of the war were the bodies of reporters and the single, sanitized body of the American military. The vast majority of the footage from the Gulf War showed reporters standing before the camera on the outskirts of combat zones. A significant amount of the coverage concerned the safety of reporters, some of whom were evacuated by force from Baghdad so that they couldn't witness the war, others of whom were photographed wearing gas masks in Tel Aviv. These reporters were the surrogate bodies under peril, standing in for the American soldiers and Iraqi people, whose moments of danger went unrecorded.

Unlike the fragmented body of the American military during the Vietnam War, the body of the military in the Gulf War was perceived as a whole, moving forward in a single mass. Elaine Scarry writes that the convention of imaging an army as a singular body "assists the disappearance of the human body from accounts of the very event that is the most radically embodying event in which human beings ever participate." Thus, the depiction of the American forces as a singular mass allowed for an effacement of the actual sentient bodies of men and women at risk. Similarly, the bodies of Iraqi soldiers were subsumed into a single unit and obliterated from view by American officials' consistent use of Saddam Hussein as their surrogate. These officials talked of "bombing Saddam," which, Hugh Gusterson notes, "submerged individual Iraqi soldiers into the single unloved figure of Saddam Hussein." Scarry adds that "the disappearance of the injurable bodies of the enemy citizenry has as counterpart, in almost any war, the magnification of the injury that the enemy can inflict." She contends that in the Gulf War, the potential threat of Iraq was exaggerated through "nuclear blackmail"—Bush justified Iris actions on the contention that Iraq was months away from using nuclear weapons—and through a magnification of the television coverage of Iraq's invasion of Kuwait, coverage orchestrated in its entirety by a public relations firm hired by a small group of wealthy Kuwaitis.

The bodies rendered invisible through this process were clearly marked by race and gender. The Arab body was subsumed into the Orientalist portrayals of Saddam Hussein as the quintessential terrorist, Iraqi forces as fanatic followers, and the Middle East as a place of dark chaos. The disruptive issue of gender was also efficiently effaced. The presence of many women among U.S. forces did not offset a reinscription of the American male soldier's masculinity, lost in the Vietnam War. American masculinity was reinscribed through the hypermasculine weaponry, which stood in for the American soldier and for a president fighting his image as a "wimp."

Largely through the media's preoccupation with the service of significant numbers of American women in the Gulf, sexual equality emerged as a redeeming narrative of the war. However, these women were almost exclusively portrayed as mothers and pictured with photographs of their children. Ironically, in the midst of a significant amount of rhetoric about "family values," the military was issuing orders to women who had just given birth and sending both parents of small children to war—a hypocritical policy that the media largely overlooked. At the same time, the media depiction of women soldiers in the Gulf was filled with ambivalence about the upheaval of traditional gender divisions in war. The preoccupation with their motherhood negated their role as soldiers and placed them in the more traditional role of women in wartime—as mothers who send their sons off to war. If the women were mothers, they could be construed as unthreatening to the gendered military status quo; yet they were also depicted as soldiers fighting symbolically for their children. They were, ironically, both figures of power and traditional icons of womanhood.

35   Given the hypermasculine narratives surrounding the American participation in the Gulf War, with President Bush and military leaders swaggering before the cameras and the masculine-coded weaponry proclaimed as victorious, the emergence of women soldiers had to be played down in public discourse by traditional images. Bodies, whether marked by race, gender, or the fragility of flesh, were rendered invisible in the spectacular images of the Gulf War. The pleasures of viewing spectacle necessitate the absence of its consequences. The bodies of the Gulf War needed to be dis-remembered in order for the story of technological prowess to be told.

SUGGESTIONS FOR DISCUSSION

1. Marita Sturken says the Persian Gulf War was "choreographed as the ending of the 'Vietnam Syndrome.'" What is the "Vietnam Syndrome"? How, in her view, did the Gulf War end it?

2. According to Sturken, the images people remember from the Gulf War—the night-sensor image of Baghdad and the missile-cam image—differ from the iconic images that have shaped the collective memory of the Vietnam War. Compare the two Gulf War images with those in the Visual Essay "The Vietnam War" that appears later in the chapter. What does Sturken see as the key differences? What meaning do you think these differences have in the way people remember the two wars?

3. How do representations of the current "war on terrorism" fit into the framework Sturken develops? What images do you remember from the second Persian Gulf War against Saddam Hussein in Iraq in 2003? What role do these images—and other representations of the "war on terrorism"—play in shaping a collective memory?

SUGGESTIONS FOR WRITING

1. Use Sturken's comparison of the iconic images of the Persian Gulf War and the Vietnam War as the basis for an essay about how Americans remember the two wars. There are several ways to approach this essay. For example, extend and deepen Sturken's analysis by looking closely at images of the two wars. Or argue with Sturken or suggest revisions of her analysis. In any case, begin by explaining how she compares the images of war and how she believes they shape historical memory. Then provide your own explanation of these images and their influence on public memory.

2. Sturken says that the iconic images of the Persian Gulf War created a perspective that joined the "smart bombs" and the viewer's point of view. Write an essay that explains the meaning and consequences of such a merger of the spectator and the weapon.

3. What are the powerful, telling images of the second Persian Gulf War of 2003 that you think will or should shape the public memory? Pick an image or two and write an essay that explains what these images represent and how they are likely to be remembered. What meanings about the war do they reveal? How do they compare with images of other wars?

CLASSIC READING

WE ARE ALL THIRD GENERATION

Margaret Mead

Margaret Mead (1901–1978) was an anthropologist interested in the way culture influences the development of individual personality. Curator of ethnology at the American Museum of Natural History in New York City from 1926 to 1969, Mead produced a series of books, including *Coming of Age in Samoa* (1928), *Growing Up in New Guinea* (1930), *Sex and Temperament in Three Primitive Societies* (1935), and *Culture and Commitment* (1970). This selection comes from *And Keep Your Powder Dry: An Anthropologist Looks at America* (1942). As you will see, Mead believed the "American character" could be described and analyzed as "shared habits and view of the world." Such studies of the American character have, subsequently, become a point of contention. The field of American Studies was established after World War II in many respects to elucidate the American national character. More recently, scholars have questioned whether such a monolithic national character really exists.

SUGGESTION FOR READING Notice how Margaret Mead opens "We Are All Third Generation" with a question –what is the American character, "its expression of American institutions and of American attitude"? As you read, pay attention to how Mead answers this question. Keep in mind that the question itself rests on Mead's assumption that there is such a thing as the "American character."

1 What then is this American character, this expression of American institutions and of American attitudes which is embodied in every American, in everyone born in this country and sometimes even in those who have come later to these shores? What is it that makes it possible to say of a group of people glimpsed from a hotel step in Soerabaja or strolling down the streets of Marseilles, 'There go some Americans,' whether they have come from Arkansas or Maine or Pennsylvania, whether they bear German or Swedish or Italian surnames? Not clothes alone, but the way they wear them, the way they walk along the street without awareness that anyone of higher status may be walking there also, the way their eyes rove as if by right over the façade of palaces and the rose windows of cathedrals, interested and unimpressed, referring what they see back to the Empire State building, the Chrysler tower, or a good-sized mountain in Montana. Not the towns they come from—Sioux City, Poughkeepsie, San Diego, Scotsdale—but the tone of voice in which they say, 'Why, I came from right near there. My home town was Evansville. Know anybody in Evansville?' And the apparently meaningless way in which the inhabitant of Uniontown warms to the inhabitant of Evansville as they name over a few names of people whom neither of them know well, about whom neither of them have thought for years, and about whom neither of them care in the least. And yet, the onlooker, taking note of the increased warmth in their voices, of the narrowing of the distance which had separated them when they first spoke, knows that something has happened, that a tie has been established[1] between two people who were lonely before, a tie which every American hopes he may be able to establish as he hopefully asks every stranger: 'What's your home town?'

Americans establish these ties by finding common points on the road that all are expected to have traveled, after their forebears came from Europe one or two or three generations ago, or from one place to another in America, resting for long enough to establish for each generation a 'home town' in which they grew up and which they leave to move on to a new town which will become the home town of their children. Whether they meet on the deck of an Atlantic steamer, in a hotel in Singapore, in New York or in San Francisco, the same expectation underlies their first contact—that both of them have moved on and are moving on and that potential intimacy lies in paths that have crossed. Europeans, even Old Americans whose pride lies not in the circumstance that their ancestors have moved often but rather in the fact that they have not moved for some time, find themselves eternally puzzled by this 'home town business.' Many Europeans fail to find out that in nine cases out of ten the 'home town' is not where one lives but where one did live; they mistake the sentimental tone in which an American invokes Evansville and Centerville and Unionville for a desire to live there again; they miss entirely the symbolic significance of the question and answer which say diagrammatically, 'Are you the same kind of person I am? Good, how about a coke?'

Back of that query lies the remembrance and the purposeful forgetting of European ancestry. For a generation, they cluster together in the Little Italies, in the Czech section or around the Polish Church, new immigrants clinging together so as to be able to chatter in their own tongue and buy their own kind of red peppers, but later there is a scattering to the suburbs and the small towns, to an 'American' way of life, and this is dramatized by an over acceptance of what looks, to any European, as the most meaningless sort of residence—on a numbered street in Chicago or the Bronx. No garden, no fruit trees, no ties to the earth, often no ties to the neighbors, just a number on a street, just a number of a house for which the rent is $10 more than the rent in the old foreign district from which they moved –how can it mean anything? But it does.

For life has ceased to be expressed in static, spatial terms as it was in Europe, where generation after generation tied their security to the same plot of ground, or if they moved to a city, acted as if the house there, with its window plants, was still a plot of ground anchored, by

fruit trees. On a plot of ground a man looks around him, looks at the filled spaces in the corner of the garden. There used to be plum trees there, but father cut them down, when he was a child; now he has planted young peaches—the plot is filled up again. And he can lean over the wall and talk to the neighbor who has planted plums again—they are the same kind of people, with the same origins and the same future. Having the same origins and the same future, they can dwell in the present which is assumed to be part of one continuous way of life.

5   But for two Americans, chance met on a train or at adjacent desks in a big office building, working in a road gang or a munition plant or on the same ground crew at an airport, there are no such common origins or common expectations. It is assumed, and not mentioned, that grandparents likely were of different nationality, different religion, different political faith, may have fought on opposite sides of the same battles—that great-great-grandparents may have burned each other at the stake. 'My name—Sack. Yes, I know that you know that it was likely something else, likely something you couldn't pronounce, but it's Sack now, see? I was born in Waynesboro.' 'Your name—Green. I don't even stop to think whether that is a changed name. Too many Greens. An American name. Maybe it had a second syllable before. Did you say you had an uncle in Waynesboro? Well, I declare! Isn't life full of coincidences!' And the president of a national scientific society in making his inaugural address, takes five minutes to mention that the president of another great national society who made *his* inaugural address last week, actually came from the same county and went to the same high school—many years later, of course. 'Never'—and his voice, which has just been dealing in fulsome phrases with the role of his profession in the war, now breaks for the first time—'never has such a thing happened before in America.' Each and every American has followed a long and winding road; if the roads started in the same spot in Europe, best forget that—that tie leads backwards to the past which is best left behind. But if the roads touched here, in this vast country where everyone

is always moving, that is a miracle which brings men close together.

In our behavior, however many generations we may actually boast of in this country, however real our lack of ties in the old world may be, we are all third generation,[2] our European ancestry tucked away and half forgotten, the recent steps in our wanderings over America immortalized and over-emphasized. When a rising man is given an administrative job and a chance to choose men for other jobs, he does not, if he is an American, fill those jobs with members of his family—such conduct is left to those who have never left their foreign neighborhoods, or to the first generation. He does not fill them exclusively with members of his own class; his own class is an accidental cross-section which wouldn't contain enough skills. He can't depend upon his golfing mates or this year's neighbors to provide him with the men he needs. Instead, he fills the jobs with men from somewhere along the road he has traveled, his home town, his home state, his college, his former company. They give him the same kind of assurance that a first-generation Hollywood producer felt when he put his cousins in charge of the accounts—their past and his past are one—at one spot anyway—just as in a kin-oriented society common blood assures men of each other's allegiance. The secretary, trying to shield her boss from the importunities of the office seeker, knows it's no use trying to turn away a man from that little North Dakota college that the boss went to. The door is always open to them, any one of them, any day. And a newspaper headline screams: 'Rocks of Chickamauga blood still flows in soldiers' veins.'

European social scientists look at this picture of American intimacy and fail to understand it. In the first place, they cannot get inside it. An Englishman, who has never been in America before, arriving in Indianapolis and trying to establish relationships with an American who has never been in England, finds himself up against what seems to be a blank wall. He meets hearty greetings, eager hospitality, an excessive attempt to tie the visitor to the local scene by taking him rapidly over its civic wonders, an equally excessive attempt to tie in Uncle Josiah's trip to India with the fact that the guest was reared in the Punjab—and then blankness. But if the Englishman then takes a tour in the Northwest, spends a week in the town where his Indiana host lived as a boy and then returns to Indianapolis, he will find a very different greeting awaiting him, which he may mistakenly put down to the fact that this is a second meeting. Only if he is a very astute observer will he notice how the path he has taken across the United States has the power to thaw out any number of hosts at any number of dinner parties.

The wife of the European scientist, now living as a faculty wife in a small university town in Colorado, will find herself similarly puzzled. She doesn't seem to get anywhere with the other faculty wives. Their husbands and her husband have the same status, the same salary, perhaps the same degree of world-wide reputation. She has learned their standards of conspicuous consumption; she can make exactly the same kind of appetizers, set a bridge table out with prizes just as they do—and yet, there is no intimacy. Only when both have children can she and some faculty wife really get together. She thinks it is the common interest in the children which forms the tie; actually it is the common experience of the children, who have something in common which the two women will never have in the same way—the same home town, which provides the necessary link, so fragile, and from a European point of view so meaningless and contentless, and yet, for an American, so essential. Later, even if they have lived childlessly beside each other, should they meet again in Alaska or Mississippi, they would be friends—with no real accession of common interests that the European wife could see. For she does not realize that to Americans only the past can give intimacy, nor can she conceive how such an incredibly empty contact in the past can be enough.

A group of people travel together from Australia to San Francisco: a manufacturer from Kansas City; a nurse from Sydney; a missionary from India; a young English stockbroker temporarily resident in New York; and a jobber from

Perth. They form a fair enough table group on the boat, dance together, go ashore together, and separate on the dock without a shadow of regret. Then, to the amazement of the Englishman, he begins to get letters from the Kansas City manufacturer, reporting on the whereabouts and doings of every one of the ill-assorted group. The man actually keeps up with them—these people who shared three uneventful weeks on an ocean liner.

10   But it is impossible for all Americans who must work or play together to have a bit of identical past, to have lived, even in such rapidly shifting lives, within a few miles of the spot where the others have lived, at some different period for some different reason. Thin and empty as is the 'home town' tie, substitutes for it must be found; other still more tenuous symbols must be invoked. And here we find the enthusiastic preferences for the same movie actor, the same brand of peaches, the same way of mixing a drink. Superficially it makes no sense at all that preference for one brand of cigarette over another may call forth the same kind of enthusiasm that one might expect if two people discovered that they had both found poetry through Keats or both nearly committed suicide on account of the same girl. Only by placing these light preferences against a background of idiosyncratic experience—by realizing that every American's life is different from every other American's; that nowhere, except in parts of the Deep South and similar pockets, can one find people whose lives and backgrounds are both identical or even similar—only then do these feverish grabs at a common theme make sense. English or Dutch residents in the colonies will spend hours sighing over the names of the shops or drinks of their respective Bond Streets, creating in their nostalgia a past atmosphere which they miss in the harsh tropical landscape about them. Americans, in a sense colonials in every part of America, but colonials who have come to have no other home, also create a common atmosphere within which to bask in the present as they criticize or approve the same radio program or moving picture actor.

There is also that other American method of forming ties, the association—the lodge, frater-

nity, club which is such a prominent feature of American life. Lloyd Warner[3] has described our societies of veterans of past wars as comparable to a cult of the dead which binds a community together, with the veterans of the most distant war lowest in the social scale. Seen from the point of view which I have been discussing, each war creates a magnificent common past for large numbers of men. It is not surprising that those who have the fewest ties among themselves—those whose poverty-stricken way of life admits of few associations—cling longest to this common experience.

Social scientists have observed with mild wonder that among American Indians, ranging the Great Plains before the coming of the white man, there was the same efflorescence of associations,[4] that Blackfoot and Omaha Indians were also joiners. But Blackfoot and Omaha, like the inhabitants of Kansas City and Fort Worth, were also newcomers. They came from a wooded land where the rituals of their lives were localized and particularized to the great undifferentiated open spaces where men had not lived before. Like the Palefaces who came later, they needed new ties and based them upon new patterns of group relationship; and those new patterns served at least as a bulwark against loneliness, in a land so great that the myths are full of stories of groups of playing children who wandered away and were never found until they were grown. So the white man, having left his brothers—in Sicily and Bohemia, in New York and Boston and Chicago—rapidly creates new patterns of social kinship, trying to compensate by rigidness of the ritual for the extemporized quality of the organization, so that men who have no common past may share symbolic adoption into the same fraternal society.

Social scientists, taking their cues from Eastern colleges or from Sinclair Lewis, have been inclined to sneer at the American habit of 'joining,' at the endless meetings, the clasp of fellowship, the songs, the allegedly pseudo-enthusiasm with which 'brothers' greet each other. Safe on the eminence of available intellectual ties and able to gossip together about the famous names and the scandals of their professions, they have failed to appreciate that these associational ties give not the pseudo-security which some European philosopher feels he would get out of them if he had to share in them, but very real security. Not until he has been marooned—his train missed, no taxi available—and driven sixty miles across bad roads in the middle of the night by someone who belongs to another chapter of the same national organization does he begin to realize that the tie of common membership, flat and without content as it is, bolstered up by sentimental songs which no one really likes to sing but which everyone would miss if they weren't sung, has an intensity of its own; an intensity measured against the loneliness which each member would feel if there were no such society.

If this then, this third-generation American, always moving on, always, in his hopes, moving up, leaving behind him all that was his past and greeting with enthusiasm any echo of that past when he meets it in the life of another, represents one typical theme of the American character structure, how is this theme reflected in the form of the family, in the upbringing of the American child? For to the family we must turn for an understanding of the American character structure. We may describe the adult American, and for descriptive purposes we may refer his behavior to the American scene, to the European past, to the state of American industry, to any other set of events which we wish; but to understand the regularity of this behavior we must investigate the family within which the child is reared. Only so can we learn how the newborn child, at birth potentially a Chinaman or an American, a Pole or an Irishman, becomes an American. By referring his character to the family we do not say that the family is the cause of his character and that the pace of American industry or the distribution of population in America are secondary effects, but merely that all the great configuration of American culture is mediated to the child by his parents, his siblings,[5] his near relatives, and his nurses. He meets American law first in the warning note of his mother's voice: 'Stop digging, here comes a cop.'

He meets American economics when he finds his mother unimpressed by his offer to buy another copy of the wedding gift he has just smashed: 'At the 5 and 10 cent store, can't we?' His first encounter with puritan standards may come through his mother's 'If you don't eat your vegetables you can't have any dessert.' He learns the paramount importance of distinguishing between vice and virtue; that it is only a matter of which comes first, the pleasure or the pain.[6] All his great lessons come through his mother's voice, through his father's laughter, or the tilt of his father's cigar when a business deal goes right. Just as one way of understanding a machine is to understand how it is made, so one way of understanding the typical character structure of a culture is to follow step by step the way in which it is built into the growing child. Our assumption when we look at the American family will be that each experience of early childhood is contributing to make the growing individual 'all of a piece,' is guiding him towards consistent and specifically American inconsistency in his habits and view of the world.

15   What kind of parents are these 'third generation' Americans? These people who are always moving, always readjusting, always hoping to buy a better car and a better radio, and even in the years of Depression orienting their behavior to their 'failure' to buy a better car or a better radio. Present or absent, the better car, the better house, the better radio are key points in family life. In the first place, the American parent expects his child to leave him, leave him physically, go to another town, another state; leave him in terms of occupation, embrace a different calling, learn a different skill; leave him socially, travel if possible with a different crowd. Even where a family has reached the top and actually stayed there for two or three generations, there are, for all but the very, very few, still larger cities or foreign courts to be stormed. Those American families which settle back to maintain a position of having reached the top in most cases moulder there for lack of occupation, ladder-climbers gone stale from sitting too long on the top step, giving a poor imitation of the aristocracy of other

lands. At the bottom, too, there are some with-out hope, but very few. Studies of modern youth dwell with anxiety upon the disproportion between the daydreams of the under-privileged young people and the actuality which confronts them in terms of job opportunities. In that very daydream the break is expressed. The daughter who says to her hard-working mother: 'You don't know. I may be going to be a great writer,' is play-ing upon a note in her mother's mind which accepts the possibility that even if her daughter does not become famous, she will at least go places that she, the mother, has never gone.

In old societies such as those from which their grandparents and great-grandparents came (and it is important to remember that Americans are oriented towards the Europe from which their ancestors emigrated not to the Europe which exists today) parents had performed an act of singular finality when they married, before ever a child was born. They had defined its prob-able place in the sun. If they maintained the same status throughout the child's growing life, kept the necessary bit of ground or inheritance to start him off as befitted him, reared him to act and feel and believe in a way appropriate to 'that state of life to which it has pleased God to call him,' the parents had done their share. Their ser-vice to their child was majorly the maintenance of their own place in the world. His care, his food, his shelter, his education—all of these were by-products of the parents' position. But in America, such an attitude, such a concentration on one's own position make one, in most cases, a bad parent. One is not just restaking the same old claim for one's child, nor can one stake out the child's new claim for him. All one can do is to make him strong and well equipped to go prospecting for himself. For proper behavior *in* that state of life to which it has pleased God to call one, is substituted proper behavior *towards* that state of life to which God, if given enough assistance, may call one's son and daughter. Europeans laugh at the way in which parents pick for their newborn babies colleges which they have never seen. It does, of course, make sense to plan one's affairs so that one's son goes

to the same school one went to oneself; but this fantastic new choice—for a squirming bit of humanity which may after all not have the brains to get through the third grade—is inexplicable. Parenthood in America has become a very spe-cial thing, and parents see themselves not as giv-ing their children final status and place, rooting them firmly for life in a dependable social struc-ture, but merely as training them for a race which they will run alone.

With this orientation towards a different future for the child comes also the expectation that the child will pass beyond his parents and leave their standards behind him. Educators exclaim impatiently over the paradox that Amer-icans believe in change, believe in progress and yet do their best—or so it seems—to retard their children, to bind them to parental ways, to inoc-ulate them against the new ways to which they give lip service. But here is a point where the proof of the pudding lies in the eating. If the par-ents were really behaving as the impatient edu-cators claim they are, really strangling and hobbling their children's attempts to embrace the changing fashions in manners or morals, we would not have the rapid social change which is so characteristic of our modern life. We would not go in twenty years from fig leaves on Greek statues to models of unborn babies in our public museums. It is necessary to distinguish between ritual and ceremonial resistances and real resis-tances. Among primitive peoples, we find those in which generation after generation there is a mock battle between the young men and the old men: generation after generation the old men lose. An observer from our society, with an unre-solved conflict with his father on his mind, might watch that battle in terror, feeling the outcome was in doubt. But the members of the tribe who are fighting the mock battle consciously or unconsciously know the outcome and fight with no less display of zeal for the knowing of it. The mock battle is no less important because the issue is certain.

Similarly, on the island of Bali, it is unthink-able that a father or a brother should plan to give a daughter of the house to some outsider. Only when a marriage is arranged between cousins, both of whose fathers are members of the same paternal line, can consent be appropriately given. Yet there flourishes, and has flourished probably for hundreds of years, a notion among Balinese young people that it is more fun to marry someone who is not a cousin. So, generation after generation, young men carry off the daughters of other men, and these daughters, their consent given in advance, nevertheless shriek and protest noisily if there are witnesses by. It is a staged abduction, in which no one believes, neither the boy nor the girl nor their relatives. Once in a while, some neurotic youth misunderstands and tries to abduct a girl who has not given her consent, and as a result the whole society is plunged into endless confusion, recrimination, and litigation.

So it is in American society. American parents, to the extent that they are Americans, expect their children to live in a different world, to clothe their moral ideas in different trappings, to court in automobiles although their forebears courted, with an equal sense of excitement and moral trepidation, on horsehair sofas. As the parents' course was uncharted when they were young—for they too had gone a step beyond their parents and transgressed every day some boundary which their parents had temporarily accepted as absolute—so also the parents know that their children are sailing uncharted seas. And so it comes about that American parents lack the sure hand on the rudder which parents in other societies display, and that they go in for a great deal of conventional and superficial grumbling. To the traditional attitudes characteristic of all oldsters who find the young a deteriorated version of themselves, Americans add the mixture of hope and envy and anxiety which comes from knowing that their children are not deteriorated versions of themselves, but actually—very actually—manage a car better than father ever did. This is trying; sometimes very trying. The neurotic father, like the neurotic lover in Bali, will misunderstand the license to grumble, and will make such a fuss over his son or daughter when they behave as all of their age are behaving, that the son or daughter has to be very

unneurotic indeed not to take the fuss as something serious, not to believe that he or she is breaking father's heart. Similarly, a neurotic son or daughter will mistake the ceremonial grumbling for the real thing, and break their spirits in a futile attempt to live up to the voiced parental standards. To the average child the parents' resistance is a stimulus.

20 On the east coast, people grumble about the coming of winter, lament over the wild geranium which marks the end of spring, and shudder noisily away from the winter that they would not do without. Occasionally, someone takes this seasonal grumbling seriously and moves to Southern California; but for most people, born and bred in a north temperate climate, the zest and tang of the too cold winter is as essential a part of life as the sultry heat and wilting flowers of the too hot summer. If one were to do a series of interviews among immigrants to Southern California, one would go away convinced that Americans had but one aim, to escape from the dreadful rigors of the north temperate zone into the endless health-giving, but eventless balminess, of a Riviera climate. This would be quite wrong. It would be equally wrong to suppose the Southern Californian insincere in his passionate climatophilism. Just as the flight from the bruising effects of winter to the soothing effects of no winter at all is a part of the American scene, so each generation of Americans produces a certain number of fathers and sons who make personal tragedies out of the changing character of the American scene; tragedies which have their own language, music and folklore, and are an inalienable part of that American scene.

By and large, the American father has an attitude towards his children which may be loosely classified as autumnal. They are his for a brief and passing season, and in a very short while they will be operating gadgets which he does not understand and cockily talking a language to which he has no clue. He does his best to keep ahead of his son, takes a superior tone as long as he can, and knows that in nine cases out of ten he will lose. If the boy goes into his father's profession, of course, it will take him a time to catch up. He finds out that the old man knows a trick or two; that experience counts as over against this new-fangled nonsense. But the American boy solves that one very neatly: he typically does not go into his father's profession, nor take up land next to his father where his father can come over and criticize his plowing. He goes somewhere else, either in space or in occupation. And his father, who did the same thing and expects that his son will, is at heart terrifically disappointed if the son accedes to his ritual request that he docilely follow in his father's footsteps and secretly suspects the imitative son of being a milksop. He knows he is a milksop—so he think—because he himself would have been a milksop if he had wanted to do just what his father did.

This is an attitude which reaches its most complete expression in the third-generation American. His grandfather left home, rebelled against a parent who did not expect final rebellion, left a land where everyone expected him to stay. Come to this country, his rebellious adventuring cooled off by success, he begins to relent a little, to think perhaps the strength of his ardor to leave home was overdone. When his sons grow up, he is torn between his desire to have, them succeed in this new country—which means that they must be more American than he, must lose entirely their foreign names and every trace of allegiance to a foreign way of life—and his own guilt towards the parents and the fatherland which he has denied. So he puts on the heat, alternately punishing the child whose low marks in school suggest that he is not going to be a successful American and berating him for his American ways and his disrespect for his father and his father's friends from the old country. When that son leaves home, he throws himself with an intensity which his children will not know into the American way of life; he eats American, talks American, dresses American, he will be American or nothing. In making his way of life consistent, he inevitably makes it thin; the overtones of the family meal on which strange, delicious, rejected European dishes were set, and

about which low words in a foreign tongue wove the atmosphere of home, must all be dropped out. His speech has a certain emptiness; he rejects the roots of words—roots lead back, and he is going forward—and comes to handle language in terms of surfaces and clichés. He rejects half of his life in order to make the other half self-consistent and complete. And by and large he succeeds. Almost miraculously, the sons of the Polish day laborer and the Italian fruit grower, the Finnish miner and the Russian garment worker become Americans.

Second generation—American-born of foreign-born parents—they set part of the tone of the American eagerness for their children to go onward. They have left their parents; left them in a way which requires more moral compensation than was necessary even for the parent generation who left Europe. The immigrant left his land, his parents, his fruit trees, and the little village street behind him. He cut the ties of military service; he flouted the king or the emperor; he built himself a new life in a new country. The father whom he left behind was strong, a part of something terribly strong, something to be feared and respected and fled from. Something so strong that the bravest man might boast of a successful flight. He left his parents, entrenched representatives of an order which he rejected. But not so his son. He leaves his father not a part of a strong other-way of life, but bewildered on the shores of the new world, having climbed only halfway up the beach. His father's ties to the old world, his mannerisms, his broken accent, his little foreign gestures are not part parcel of something strong and different; they are signs of his failure to embrace this new way of life. Does his mother wear a kerchief over her head? He cannot see the generations of women who have worn such kerchiefs. He sees only the American women who wear hats, and he pities and rejects his mother who has failed to become—an American. And so there enters into the attitude of the second-generation American—an attitude which again is woven through our folkways, our attitude towards other languages, towards anything foreign, towards anything European—a combination of contempt and avoidance, a fear of yielding, and a sense that to yield would be weakness. His father left a father who was the representative of a way of life which had endured for a thousand years. When he leaves his father, he leaves a partial failure; a hybrid, one who represents a step towards freedom, not freedom itself. His first-generation father chose between freedom and what he saw as slavery; but when the second-generation American looks at his European father, and through him, at Europe, he sees a choice between success and failure, between potency and ignominy. He passionately rejects the halting English, the half-measures of the immigrant. He rejects with what seems to him equally good reasons 'European ties and entanglements.' This second-generation attitude which has found enormous expression in our culture especially during the last fifty years, has sometimes come to dominate it—in those parts of the country which we speak of as 'isolationist.' Intolerant of foreign language, foreign ways, vigorously determined on being themselves, they are, in attitude if not in fact, second-generation Americans.

When the third-generation boy grows up, he comes up against a father who found the task of leaving his father a comparatively simple one. The second-generation parent lacks the intensity of the first, and his son in turn fails to reflect the struggles, the first against feared strength and the second against guiltily rejected failure, which have provided the plot for his father and grandfather's maturation. He is expected to succeed; he is expected to go further than his father went; and all this is taken for granted. He is furthermore expected to feel very little respect for the past. Somewhere in his grandfather's day there was an epic struggle for liberty and freedom. His picture of that epic grandfather is a little obscured, however, by the patent fact that his father does not really respect him; he may have been a noble character, but he had a foreign accent. The grandchild is told in school, in the press, over the radio, about the founding fathers, but they were not after all *his* founding fathers;

they are, in ninety-nine cases out of a hundred, somebody else's ancestors. Any time one's own father, who in his own youth had pushed his father aside and made his own way, tries to get in one's way, one can invoke the founding fathers—those ancestors of the real Americans; the Americans who got here earlier—those Americans which father worked so very hard, so slavishly, in fact, to imitate. This is a point which the European observer misses. He hears an endless invocation of Washington and Lincoln, of Jefferson and Franklin. Obviously, Americans go in for ancestor worship, says the European. Obviously, Americans are longing for a strong father, say the psycho-analysts.[7] These observers miss the point that Washington is not the ancestor of the man who is doing the talking; Washington does not represent the past to which one belongs by birth, but the past to which one tries to belong by effort. Washington represents the thing for which grandfather left Europe at the risk of his life, and for which father rejected grandfather at the risk of his integrity. Washington is not that to which Americans passionately cling but that to which they want to belong, and fear, in the bottom of their hearts, that they cannot and do not.

25   This odd blending of the future and the past, in which another man's great-grandfather becomes the symbol of one's grandson's future, is an essential part of American culture. 'Americans are so conservative.' say Europeans. They lack the revolutionary spirit. Why don't they rebel? Why did President Roosevelt's suggestion of altering the structure of the Supreme Court and the Third-Term argument raise such a storm of protest? Because, in education, in attitudes, most Americans are third generation, they have just really arrived. Their attitude towards this country is that of one who has just established membership, just been elected to an exclusive club, just been initiated into the rites of an exacting religion. Almost any one of them who inspects his own ancestry, even though it goes back many more generations than three, will find a gaping hole somewhere in the family tree. Campfire girls give an honor to the

girl who can name all eight great-grandparents, including the maiden names of the four great-grandmothers. Most Americans cannot get this honor. And who was that missing great-grandmother? Probably, oh, most probably, not a grand-niece of Martha Washington.

We have, of course, our compensatory mythology. People who live in a land torn by earthquakes have myths of a time when the land was steady, and those whose harvest are uncertain dream of a golden age when there was no drought. Likewise, people whose lives are humdrum and placid dream of an age of famine and rapine. We have our rituals of belonging, our DAR's and our Descendants of King Philip's Wars, our little blue book of the blue-blooded Hawaiian aristocracy descended from the first missionaries, and our *Mayflower*, which is only equaled in mythological importance by the twelve named canoes which brought the Maoris to New Zealand. The mythology keeps alive the doubt. The impressive president of a patriotic society knows that she is a member by virtue of only one of the some eight routes through which membership is possible. Only one. The other seven? Well, three are lost altogether. Two ancestors were Tories. In some parts of the country she can boast of that; after all, Tories were people of substance, real 'old families.' But it doesn't quite fit. Of two of those possible lines, she has resolutely decided not to think. Tinkers and tailors and candlestick makers blend indistinctly with heaven knows what immigrants! She goes to a meeting and is very insistent about the way in which the Revolutionary War which only one-eighth of her ancestors helped to fight should be represented to the children of those whose eight ancestors were undoubtedly all somewhere else in 1776.

On top of this Old American mythology, another layer has been added, a kind of placatory offering, a gesture towards the Old World which Americans had left behind. As the fifth- and sixth- and seventh-generation Americans lost the zest which came with climbing got to the

top of the pecking order[8] in their own town or city and sat, still uncertain, still knowing their credentials were shaky, on the top of the pile, the habit of wanting to belong—to really belong, to be accepted absolutely as something which one's ancestors had NOT been—became inverted. They turned towards Europe, especially towards England, towards presentation at Court, towards European feudal attitudes. And so we have had in America two reinforcements of the European class attitudes—those hold-overs of feudal caste attitudes, in the newly-come immigrant who carries class consciousness in every turn and bend of his neck, and the new feudalism, the 'old family' who has finally toppled over backwards into the lap of all that their remote ancestors left behind them.

When I say that we are most of us—whatever our origins—third-generation in character structure, I mean that we have been reared in an atmosphere which is most like that which I have described for the third generation. Father is to be outdistanced and outmoded, but not because he is a strong representative of another culture, well entrenched, not because he is a weak and ineffectual attempt to imitate the new culture; he did very well in his way, but he is out of date. He, like us, was moving forwards, moving away from something symbolized by his own ancestors, moving towards something symbolized by other people's ancestors. Father stands for the way things were done, for a direction which on the whole was a pretty good one, in its day. He was all right because he was on the right road. Therefore, we, his children, lack the mainsprings of rebellion. He was out of date; he drove an old model car which couldn't make it on the hills. Therefore it is not necessary to fight him, to knock him out of the race. It is much easier and quicker to pass him. And to pass him it is only necessary to keep on going and to see that one buys a new model every year. Only if one slackens, loses one's interest in the race towards success, does one slip back. Otherwise, it is onward and upward, *towards* the world of Washington and Lincoln; a world in which we don't fully belong, but which we feel, if we work at it, we some time may achieve.

NOTES

1. I owe my understanding of the significance of these chronological ties to discussions with Kurt Lewin and John G. Pilley.
2. Mead, Margaret (1940) Conflict of Cultures in America. *Proceedings, 54th Annual Convention, Middle States Association of Colleges and Secondary Schools* (November) pp. 30–44.
3. Warner, W. L., and P. S. Lunt (1941) *The Social Life of a Modern Community* (Yankee City Series, 1) (New Haven Yale University Press).
4. Lowie, Robert H. 'Plains Indian Age-Societies: Historical and Comparative Summary', *Anthropological Papers*, American Museum of Natural History, 11 (13), pp. 877–984.
5. Sibling is a coined word used by scientists for both brothers and sisters. The English language lacks such a word.
6. Cf. Samuel Butler's definition: That vice is when the pain follows the pleasure and virtue when the pleasure follows the pain.
7. I owe my classification of the American attitude towards the 'founding fathers' to a conversation with Dr. Ernst Kris, in which he was commenting on the way in which Americans, apparently, wanted a strong father, although, in actual fact, they always push their fathers aside.
8. Pecking order is a very convenient piece of jargon which social psychologists use to describe a group in which it is very clear to everybody in it just which bird can peck which, or which cow can butt which other cow away from the water trough. Among many living creatures these 'pecking orders' are fixed and when a newcomer enters the group he has to fight and scramble about until everybody is clear just where he belongs—below No. 8 chick, for instance, and above old No. 9.

SUGGESTIONS FOR DISCUSSION

1. How does Margaret Mead answer the question she begins with—what is "this American character"? How does she use the idea that we are all "third generation"? Why do you think she has chosen to locate the formation of an American "character structure" in the dynamics of the American family?

2. Do you accept Mead's assumption that there is an "American character" that can be described and analyzed? What evidence does she provide to support this assumption? What evidence might contradict the idea?

3. Americans, Mead says, compensate for the lack of a common past by "joining" associations—"the lodge, fraternity, club." To what extent does this habit of "joining" continue to play a role in establishing ties among individuals? What do you see as the function of such associations?

SUGGESTIONS FOR WRITING

1. Use Mead's idea that "We Are All Third Generation" to analyze your own family. She offers a predictable sequence from first to second to third generation. Begin by describing this sequence and then show how it fits or fails to fit the experience of your family. What modifications, if any, would you want to make?

2. Mead wrote this chapter in 1942. Is it possible to update it—to identify a common "American character" today as confidently as Mead did sixty years ago? Is the notion of an "American character" useful at all? Explain your answers to these questions by either proposing an updated version or explaining why the notion doesn't work in contemporary America. (Consider also whether it ever worked.)

3. Write an essay that compares Mary Gordon's sense of what it means to be an American in "More Than Just a Shrine: Paying Homage to the Ghosts of Ellis Island" with Mead's sense in "We Are All Third Generation."

CHECKING OUT THE WEB

1. Jane Tompkins and Warren Neidich raise questions about how Native Americans have been represented in historical writing and photography. For consideration of how Native Americans have been represented in American fiction and in the media, check out the Web site Representations of American Indians at staff.washington.edu/~pshafer/rep~1.htm. It has several links, including "Romancing the Indian," about nineteenth-century fiction and graphics, and several sites about Pocahontas. Take a look at these and then come to class prepared to talk about the ways Native Americans have been represented in fiction and the media.

2. Check out the Vietnam War Internet Project at the University of Texas http://www.lbjlib.utexas.edu/shwv/shwvhome.html and the Vietnam War Pictorial site at dspace.dial.pipex.com/nam/index.shtml. Spend some time browsing through the two sites. What different types of information are available? How would you categorize them? Compare your findings with what others found. How might the results of these searches fit into a writing project on an aspect of the Vietnam War?

3. Do a search for Web sites devoted to oral history. Check out several of the sites. What kinds of issues about oral history are raised? What considerations should you take into account if you are doing an oral history fieldwork project?

VISUAL CULTURE

Photographing History

One of the ways people remember the past is through photographs. Family scrapbooks, photo albums, wedding portraits, high school yearbooks, school pictures exchanged with friends—all record the history of ordinary lives. The same is true of people's collective memory of public history. Single photographic images have taken on the power to contain and represent whole historical events.

From Mathew Brady's photographs of the American Civil War to present-day photojournalism, photographs have created immediately recognizable images of complex historical forces that have been captured in the concrete details of a moment. For example, Alfred Stieglitz's "The Steerage" (1907), which appears at the opening of the chapter, seems to distill the waves of immigration from southern and eastern Europe from 1880 to 1920 in a single frame depicting "huddled masses."

By the same token, the Depression of the 1930s has come to be known and remembered through the photographs of Dorothea Lange, Walker Evans, Arthur Rothstein, and others in the Farm Security Administration (see, for example, Dorothea Lange's famous photograph "Migrant Mother, Florence Thompson and Her Children"). People think of these photos as a reliable source, a documentary account of the life experience of workers, sharecroppers, Dust Bowl migrants, and the unemployed. These photos have taken on the authority to bring the past to life and to show how things really were.

"A Harvest of Death,"
Gettysburg, July 1863,"
T.H. O'Sullivan.

"Migrant Mother, Florence Thompson and Her
Children, 1936,"
Dorothea Lange.

The flag-raising at Iwo Jima,
Joe Rosenthal, 1945

John Carlos and Tommy Smith at the 1968 Olympics

Such photographs not only convey images that stand, in immediately recognizable ways, for larger historical events. They also carry attitudes toward these events. Grounded in the relationship that they have with their subjects, photographers' attitudes become visible in the way that they aim the viewfinder and frame the shot. Photographs convey visual images to viewers, not directly but mediated through a lens, from a perspective or way of seeing.

Photographs offer viewers identities as well as information. When people look at a photograph of the flag raising at Iwo Jima, for example, they are likely to recall the story of World War II as one of national unity to fight the "good war." In a sense, the photo seeks to recruit viewers—to have them join the just cause and commemorate American victory. In other instances, such as the picture of John Carlos and Tommy Smith raising their fists on the victory stand at the 1968 Olympics in Mexico City while the American national anthem was playing, the insurgent force of a photograph can precipitate a crisis of identity, as viewers respond with fear, anxiety, outrage, pleasure, identification, or some combination of mixed feelings to this powerful image of black power and the freedom struggle of the 1960s.

This section investigates how photographs have become such a powerful means to document history and to shape historical memory.

READING AMERICAN PHOTOGRAPHS

Alan Trachtenberg

Alan Trachtenberg is a distinguished professor of English and American Studies at Yale and the author of many articles and books, including *The Incorporation of America: Culture and Society in the Gilded Age* (1982). The following selection is an excerpt from the preface to his book *Reading American Photographs: Images as History Mathew Brady to Walker Evans* (1989). Trachtenberg holds that the historian and photographer share a similar task, namely "how to make the random, fragmentary, and accidental details of everyday existence meaningful without loss of the details themselves."

SUGGESTION FOR READING   As you read, consider what Trachtenberg means when he says that "photographs are not simple depictions but constructions." When you are finished reading, summarize Trachtenberg's argument in three to four sentences.

My argument throughout is that American photographs are not simple depictions but constructions, that the history they show is inseparable from the history they enact: a history of photographers employing their medium to make sense of their society. It is also a history of photographers seeking to define themselves, to create a role for photography as an American art. How might the camera be used for social commentary and cultural interpretation? Consisting of images rather than words, photography places its own constraints on interpretation, requiring that pho-

tographers invent new forms of presentation, of collaboration between image and text, between artist and audience.

For the reader of photographs there is always the danger of overreading, of too facile a conversion of images into words. Speaking of "the camera's affinity for the indeterminate," Kracauer remarks that, "however selective," photographs are still "bound to record nature in the raw. Like the natural objects themselves, they will therefore be surrounded by a fringe of indistinct multiple meanings." All photographs have the effect of making their subjects seem at least momentarily strange, capable of meaning several things at once, or nothing at all. Estrangement allows us to see the subject in new and unexpected ways. Photographs entice viewers by their silence, the mysterious beckoning of another world. It is as enigmas, opaque and inexplicable as the living world itself, that they most resemble the data upon which history is based. Just as the meaning of the past is the prerogative of the present to invent and choose, the meaning of an image does not come intact and whole. Indeed, what empowers an image to represent history is not just what it shows but the struggle for meaning we undergo before it, a struggle analogous to the historian's effort to shape an intelligible and usable past. Representing the past, photographs serve the present's need to understand itself and measure its future. Their history lies finally in the political visions they may help us realize.

Reading Photographs for History

To understand the relation of photographs to historical events, it is necessary to begin with the physical presence of the camera at some precisely datable moment in the past. Unlike writing or painting, which necessarily take place over time, shooting a picture occurs in an instant, and the events that the camera records are thereby unrepeatable. This technical ability to capture such unique and distinct moments gives photographs an authority in documenting the past that no other records or accounts can claim.

But the technical character of the photographic image also poses a problem in terms of historical meaning. The photographic image, after all, is visual. It sends a message but, as Roland Barthes says, an "uncoded message," one that cannot immediately and self-evidently be converted into words. The photographic image simultaneously is filled with information and is opaque. The "meaning of the image," as Trachtenberg puts it, "does not come intact and whole." The reason a photograph can stand in for a larger historical event such as the Civil War or the Depression is not just what it shows but how the image has been made memorable—the "struggle for meaning we undergo before it."

VISUAL ESSAY   The Vietnam War

The "struggle for meaning" that Trachtenberg refers to is strikingly evident in the photographs that are assembled here from the Vietnam War. Alone, each captures a distinct moment that proposes to represent the Vietnam War. Taken together, the images stand in an uneasy relationship to each other, bound by a common event but divided by what they depict and the meanings that they make available. Just as the meaning of the Vietnam War remains volatile and contested in politics, historical interpretation, and popular culture, these images jostle against each other, and call the viewer to different scenes and different ways of seeing the war.

Colonel Nguyen Ngoc
Loan, South Vietnam's
police chief, executing
a Viet-cong suspect
in Saigon

Kent State,
May 4, 1970

Trang Bang,
June 1972

Americans
and South
Vietnamese
fleeing from
American
embassy, 1975

SUGGESTIONS FOR DISCUSSION

1. Look closely at each of the photographs. Read each alone as an icon of the war. How does each image shape America's historical memory of the war? To what extent do they tell the same version or different versions of the war?

2. The images in this Visual Essay have been arranged in chronological order, but that is not the only way they could be organized. Photographers often create sequences of images so that individual photos interact with each other and enable meanings to emerge that are not available through a single photo. Work together in a group with two or three other students to create your own visual essay about the Vietnam War. Use the Vietnam photos presented here or supplement them with photos from Web sites (see the "Checking Out the Web" box for helpful sites). As you assemble your visual essay, take into account what you want your viewers' experience of the photos to be and the story you want the photos to tell. Then compare the visual essay your group composed with those of other groups. Don't argue about whether one set of choices is right or wrong. The issue is how the various visual essays juxtapose photographs and shape the way Americans remember the Vietnam War.

3. The written captions that sometimes accompany photographic images can influence the way that viewers understand photos. Depending on the circumstances, captions can be informative by identifying the date, place, and people depicted in the photo. Other times, captions can be interpretive or argumentative by providing not just information but a point of view. Work with a group of classmates and find three photos of historical events (use any of the photos in this chapter if you wish). Write two captions for each photo—one that is informative, the second interpretive or argumentative. Exchange your photos and captions with those from another group. Ask members of the other group how the captions shape or slant their experience of the photo. In turn, respond to the other group's captions in the same way.

SUGGESTED ASSIGNMENT

Select one of the photographs in this chapter or another historical photo of your own choosing. Write a detailed analysis of how the photo brings to life an historical event and how its composition establishes a vantage point for viewers. Look at the photograph closely and carefully and consider these questions:

- *What is depicted in the photo?* How do the details create an impression on viewers? How is the image able to stand in for a larger historical event? What version of the event does it seem to tell?

- *Does the photo have vectors (or eye lines) that establish relationships among the people (and perhaps things) in the photo?* What story do the vectors enable viewers to fill in? (See the discussion of vectors in the Visual Culture "Picturing Schooldays" section in Chapter 3.)

- *What is the perspective of the camera shot—frontal, oblique, high, low?* How does the use of perspective shape the viewer's attitude toward the event depicted in the photo? (See the discussion of perspective in the Visual Culture "Picturing Schooldays" section in Chapter 3.)

- *How does the camera space frame the event that it records?* How close does the camera take viewers to its subject? Is the photo a wide shot, full shot, medium shot, or close up? How does camera space influence the viewer's experience of the photo? (See the discussion of camera space in Chapter 1, "Reading the News.")

FIELDWORK   Oral History

As you have seen, oral histories, such as the chapter "Private First Class Reginald 'Malik' Edwards" from Wallace Terry's *Bloods: An Oral History of the Vietnam War by Black Veterans,* offer the personal perspectives of people who are caught up in the history of their time. Oral history is a branch of historical studies that draws on the experience and memories of ordinary people to provide new insight into the meaning and texture of historical events. Sometimes referred to as "history from the bottom up," oral history is an organized effort to record the stories of people such as Malik Edwards who traditionally have been ignored by historians. In this sense, oral histories are important correctives to older versions of history that focus on "great men," geopolitics, and institutions of power.

This does not mean, however, that oral histories are any more useful or authoritative than traditional historical work that is based on archives, government documents, or the correspondence of national leaders. Their value depends on how the oral historian handles the material once it is collected.

This fieldwork project asks you to do an oral history. Follow these steps to get started.

1. *Choose a person and an event that will interest readers*—a Vietnam or Gulf War veteran; someone with experience in the antiwar movement or the counterculture of the sixties; an older person who remembers the Great Depression, the bombing of Pearl Harbor, the end of World War II; a trade unionist involved in an important organizing drive or strike. The events listed here are largely on the national or international scene, but you may also find informants to talk about an important and interesting local event.

2. *Prepare for the interview by familiarizing yourself with the event in question.* Do some background reading. Develop a list of leading questions that will elicit detailed and in-depth responses from your informant (but don't be tied rigidly to them in the interview if it takes another, potentially fruitful, direction). Set a time with your informant, bring a tape recorder, and conduct the interview.

3. *Type up a transcript from the interview that you can edit into an oral history.* Review point number three, "Writing the oral history," for advice on editing your interview.

Considerations in Doing an Oral History

1. **Selection.** Not every person will be a good interview subject, even if he or she was intimately involved in an historical event—some people just don't have interesting things to say. Therefore, oral historians usually select an informant who wants to share part of his or her past. Moreover, everyone's memory is selective in some sense. Oral historians expect to get one version of events, though it may be a perspective they didn't foresee.

2. **Interviewing.** The interview is not just a matter of turning on the tape recorder and allowing the informant to speak. The oral historian should let

the informant know the purpose for the interview and encourage the informant to tell his or her history in detail, but in keeping the informant on track, the historian should be careful not to provide too much direction. The informant may skip over what might be key information or tailor his or her recitation to what the historian seems to want to hear.

Once an interview begins, the historian faces many decisions —about, say, whether a rambling account is going somewhere or if it is time to intervene to redirect the informant, or if stopping an informant to clarify a point will risk interrupting the speaker's train of thought.

3. **Writing the oral history**. The transcript of an interview amounts to a kind of raw data that is likely to be filled with pauses, asides, fragmentary remarks, false starts, and undeveloped trains of thought. The oral historian's task is to fashion an account that is faithful to the informant as well as readable. There are several decisions that oral historians typically face at this point:

How much of the original transcript should be used? Oral historians rarely use all of the material in the transcript. In the Introduction to *Portraits in Steel* (1993), a collection of photographs and oral histories of Buffalo steel workers, the oral historian Michael Frisch says he used as little as twenty percent of an original transcript and in no case more than sixty percent. When they decide to omit material from the transcript, oral historians are careful to make sure that their editing does not distort the informant's views or suppress important information.

How should the material in the transcript be arranged? Oral historians often decide to rearrange some of the material in the original transcript so that related points appear together and the final version has a coherence that may be missing from the taped interview. The oral historian is by no means obliged to follow the chronological order of the transcript but needs to make sure that any restructuring is faithful to the informant.

Should the interviewer's questions appear? In many long oral histories, such as in Wallace Terry's *Bloods* and the many oral histories by Studs Terkel (*Working, The Good War, American Dreams*), the oral historian crafts the interview into a narrative that is told through the informant's voice. The oral historian stays out of the way, and readers get the sense that the informant is speaking directly to them. In other cases, however, the oral historian may decide to appear in the final text as an interviewer, and the question-and-answer format gives the oral history more of a conversational character, with a greater sense of dialogue and give-and-take.

How much editing should be done at the sentence level? Oral historians face the task of turning the transcript into readable prose that retains the distinctive qualities of the informant's voice. Notice, for example, how Wallace Terry has edited Malik Edwards's oral history so that it appears in complete, grammatically correct sentences, but uses a few exceptions ("people be marchin' into swamps," "'cause it was nothin' to shoot through the walls"), along with slang and profanity, to suggest Edwards's particular way of speaking.

MINING THE ARCHIVE

Local Museums and Historical Societies

Telling a story of change

The Mount Zion Albany Civil Rights Movement Museum will tell the story of the impact of the southwest Georgia movement on the rest of the world while focusing on the role of the African American church and the freedom music that emerged during this period.

The stories will be told through oral histories from those who were there—those who lived it, those who breathed it, those who walked it, those who went to jail and those who attended the mass meetings and sang about it.

The museum will restore much of Mount Zion Church as it was in the 1960s. The sanctuary will convey the sense of place as a church where visitors will be treated to stirring renditions of freedom songs and other public performances. Restored pews will seat 100.

A portion of the church will house the museum's artifacts. Educational exhibits will detail the civil rights struggle ranging from voter education and registration to nonviolent protest, song, economic boycott and legal action. The museum will also serve as a center for ongoing academic research and provide school tours and other programs and lectures. Through educational programming, the museum will preserve a part of the history of America and south Georgia and challenge today's and tomorrow's youth to learn more about themselves as citizens.

Promoters of the Mount Zion Albany Civil Rights Movement Museum have a vision beyond restoring the church into a museum. Long-range planning, in coordination with the Albany Dougherty Inner-City Authority and the Albany Convention and Visitors Bureau, includes a historic district and walking tours of restored buildings and residences in the Whitney Avenue neighborhood. These tours will depict life in the African American neighborhood before the end of segregation.

MOUNT ZION
ALBANY CIVIL RIGHTS MOVEMENT
MUSEUM INC.

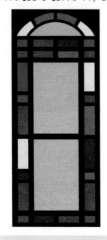

A celebration of courage and freedom

The Mount Zion Albany Civil Rights Movement Museum is a celebration of courage and freedom of ordinary people and their leaders in the Albany and southwest Georgia movements who bore witness to equal rights and helped to spark the national Civil Rights Movement and international struggles for freedom.

The eyes of the nation were on Albany in the early 1960s as thousands of people attended mass meetings and marched in the streets seeking freedom and justice. In December 1961, Dr. Martin Luther King Jr. joined local activists and further inspired overflowing crowds who gathered to hear him at Mount Zion and neighboring Shiloh Baptist Church.

The strength of the Albany Movement gave rise to campaigns in nearby communities:

"Woke up this morning with my mind stayed on freedom..."
Freedom Song

Americus, Moultrie, Dawson, Thomasville, Cordele, Leesburg, Cairo and Newton.

We have in Albany a symbol of that historic struggle in Mount Zion Church. Silent for decades, the boarded-up windows and dust-covered pews of this historic 1906 church, that once echoed with freedom songs and the call for nonviolent social change, soon will give voice to a key part of the 1960s history of Albany and southwest Georgia.

The Albany Movement sprang from the community's grass roots. Young and old, rich and poor—citizens of every class, color and occupation were involved in it.

Many of those who participated in the Movement are members of the community today—our neighbors, co-workers and family members. The museum offers us a chance to hear their stories.

Many towns and cities, as well as colleges and universities, have local museums or historical societies that collect and display historical materials, sponsor research, and put on public programs about local and regional history. There is likely to be one or more in the area near you. Your college library can help you find out where they are and what kind of archival materials they hold.

Visit a local museum or historical society. Sometimes this will require making specific arrangements with its staff. The purpose of your visit should be to acquire an overview of the archival materials and collections. How does the museum or historical society describe its function? What are the nature and scope of the holdings? How were they acquired? What historical periods are represented? What kind of research do they do? Does the archive publish books, pamphlets, or journals? Does it issue an annual report, newsletter, or other informative materials about its holdings and activities? Who uses the collection?

Use your answers to these questions—and other information you picked up during your visit—to prepare a report (either written or oral) on the kinds of historical questions you could answer by drawing on the archive's collection.

CHAPTER 10

Living in a Postcolonial World

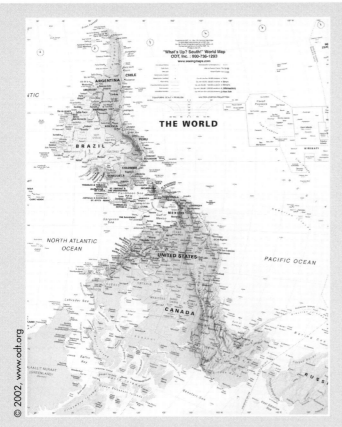

THE WORLD

© 2002, www.odt.org

I, too, know something of this immigrant business. I am an emigrant from one country (India) and a newcomer in two (England, where I live, and Pakistan, to which my family moved against my will). And I have a theory that the resentments we mohajirs engender have something to do with our conquest of the force of gravity. We have performed the act of which all men anciently dream, the thing for which they envy the birds; that is to say, we have flown.

Salman Rushdie

Most of the readings in this book focus on the United States and what has been called throughout the book "American culture." In the discussion questions and writing assignments, you have examined ways of life, modes of expression, and controversies in contemporary United States. This makes sense, because the lived experience of many who use this book is firmly rooted in the history and culture of the United States. At the same time, in this closing chapter, it's worth noting that the very idea of American culture can amount to a systematic forgetting that there are many Americas in this hemisphere—Latin America, Central America, Mexico, Canada, and the Caribbean. There is the risk that in focusing on American culture

491

within U.S. borders, it is possible to ignore the fact that since its origins as an English colony, the United States has always been connected in important ways to the rest of the hemisphere and, more broadly, to the rest of the world.

From Columbus's first contact with the Taino tribe in the West Indies, the exploration and settlement of North America has involved a series of encounters with peoples and cultures outside the dominant white, Protestant, middle-class culture in the United States—not only with Native Americans but also with West Africans who were brought forcibly to America through the slave trade; with Mexicans, when the United States appropriated California, Texas, and the Southwest in the Mexican War; with the Irish and Chinese laborers who were recruited to build the transcontinental railroad; and with Italian Catholics and Eastern European Catholics and Jews who immigrated to the United States between 1880 and 1920 to work in mines, steel mills, garment factories, and other industries of an expanding capitalist economy.

To say that the United States has always been a nation of immigrants is true, but the migration of people has never been one way. Though official histories often suggest immigrants came to the United States with the goal of staying and assimilating into an American melting pot, in fact many went back and forth to Italy, Mexico, the West Indies, Central America, the Arab countries, and elsewhere. If anything, this movement of people has intensified in recent decades, propelled by the disruptions of the Vietnam War, the effects of the North American Free Trade Agreement (NAFTA), and the impact of an increasingly global economy. The result is that the national borders of the United States are more porous and the national identity less stable than ever, with people from all over the world bringing new languages and ways of life to this country and spreading U.S. culture and language to places it has never been before.

As the events of September 11, 2001, reveal so tellingly, the United States is enmeshed in a world system of economics, politics, and culture. *Globalization* is the term often used to describe the rise of multinational corporations and transnational organizations such as the European Union. Automobiles once built in Detroit now have their parts manufactured in Mexico or Taiwan. The software on your computer may be written in Ireland or India. The clothes and shoes you buy with American brands on them are likely to be made in Indonesia, Vietnam, Malaysia, or elsewhere. Signs of globalization are apparent in the appearance of Coca Cola ads in Saudi Arabia or American sitcoms on French television.

For some, the era of globalization is a brave new world of innovation and opportunity, linked together by the immediacy of communication via the Internet. From another perspective, however, it looks more like a continuation of older relations between the rich American and European countries and their former colonies in the Third World—in Asia, Africa, the Caribbean, and Latin America. This chapter is called "Living in a Postcolonial World" to bring attention to these relationships and help you to think about not just American culture but the world system everyone now lives within.

The term *postcolonial* shows the way the world has changed in the half century since the end of World War II. In the 1940s, 1950s, and 1960s, former British and French colonies such as Egypt, Kenya, Nigeria, Ghana, Tanzania, Algeria, and Senegal in Africa; India, Pakistan, and Sri Lanka in South Asia; and Vietnam and Laos in Southeast Asia mounted successful struggles to throw off their colonial status and achieve national independence. In the 1970s, Mozambique, Angola, and Guinea-Bissau became independent of Portugal, and in the 1990s, South Africa threw off the legacy of Dutch and British colonialism and fifty years of apartheid to begin a new era as a democratic nation.

The "post" in "postcolonial" notes these dramatic developments in world history, but, at the same time, leaves open the relation of these countries to their colonial past. In a time of globalization, NAFTA, the International Monetary Fund, and the World Bank, the question remains whether the former colonies in Africa and Asia as well as the countries in Central and South America and in the Middle East that gained national liberation have actually secured self-determination and independence from Europe and the United States. Some describe the present situation as "neocolonialism," where formal independence has not necessarily ended economic and political dependence on the West.

In keeping with the main themes discussed throughout the other chapters of *Reading Culture*, this chapter focuses on investigating culture from a postcolonial perspective. This investigation has gone in two main directions. On the one hand, it looks at the way Western powers represented—and continue to represent—former colonial subjects as Others; as people different from "us"; as those in need of Western guidance, expertise, and technology; and as exotic cultures for sophisticated consumption. On the other hand, it looks at the way formerly colonized people view the West and make sense of their relations to it.

Reading Life in a Postcolonial World

The reading selections in this chapter challenge you to see things in terms of the relationships and cultural encounters between the West and the rest of the world. The first three selections all look at life at the border, where cultures collide. Amitava Kumar's "Passport Photos" goes directly to encounters between immigrants—documented and undocumented—and the United States. Elaine H. Kim's "Home Is Where the 'Han' Is: A Korean American Perspective on the Los Angeles Upheavals," reveals the various pressures on Korean Americans in locating themselves in relation to the United States and Korea. The last selection, Gloria Anzaldúa's "How to Tame a Wild Tongue," examines the dialects of English and Spanish—and the various identities—that take shape at the border.

The following section shifts focus away from the United States to the Case Study: The Politics of World English. First, Alastair Pennycock reviews the claims made for English as an international lingua franca and then shows how his students in Hong Kong make sense of learning English as a second language. Next, in a Perspectives feature, Chinua Achebe and Ngũgĩ wa Thiong'o carry on their argument about whether Africans should write in English.

Excerpts from Edward Said's book *Culture and Imperialism* ask readers to consider relations between the United States and the Arab world. And the Classic Reading is W.E.B. DuBois's "Of Our Spiritual Strivings," from *The Souls of Black Folks*, a powerful statement about the "double consciousness" of colonized people.

PASSPORT PHOTOS

Amitava Kumar

Amitava Kumar teaches English at the University of Florida. This reading consists of excerpts from the introduction "The Shame of Arrival" and the opening chapter "Language" from Kumar's *Passport Photos* (2000), a multigenre book that combines poetry and photography with literary and cultural analysis. As you can see, Kumar is concerned with the transnational movement of people, encounters at the border, and the condition of immigrants in the Western metropolis.

SUGGESTION FOR READING Notice the four photographs that accompany the written text. The photos are not meant, Kumar says, to illustrate an argument. Rather, they "raise the question about how these images are to be seen." As you read, consider how the text and photos offer perspectives to map what Kumar calls "a mixed, postcolonial space."

THE SHAME OF ARRIVAL

A book is a kind of passport.

Salman Rushdie

1 If it can be allowed that the passport is a kind of book, then the immigration officer, holding a passport in his hand, is also a reader. Like someone in a library or even, in the course of a pleasant afternoon, on a bench beneath a tree. Under the fluorescent lights, he reads the entries made in an unfamiliar hand under categories that are all too familiar. He examines the seals, the stamps, and the signatures on them.

He looks up. He reads the immigrant's responses to his questions, the clothes, the accent. The officer's eyes return to the passport. He appears to be reading it more carefully. He frowns. Suddenly he turns around and tries to catch a colleague's eye. It is nothing, he wants more coffee.

You notice all this if you are an immigrant.

Let us for a moment pretend you are not. Imagine you are drinking your coffee in the café close to your place of work. You notice that the woman who is picking up the cups and then stooping to wipe the floor is someone you have never seen before. She is dark but dressed cleanly in the gray and pink uniform of the employees here. You smile at her and ask if you could please have some more cream. She looks at you but doesn't seem to understand you. You realize she doesn't speak English. Oddly, or perhaps not so oddly, the first thought that crosses your mind is that she is an illegal immigrant in your country. But you don't say anything, you get up and ask someone else for the cream. You smile at her, as if to say, See, nothing to be afraid of here. She probably doesn't smile back. It might or might not occur to you that she doesn't know how to read your smile.

Indian taxi driver, New York City, 1997

5   Standing in front of the immigration officer, the new arrival from Somalia, El Salvador, or Bangladesh is also a reader. When looking at the American in the café who addresses her—asking her, perhaps, if she wants to have coffee with him—the immigrant reads an unwelcome threat.

If we allow that the passport is a kind of book, we might see the immigrant as a very different kind of reader than the officer seated at his desk with a gleaming badge on his uniform. The immigrant's reading of that book refers to an outside world that is more real. The officer is paid to make a connection only between the book and the person standing in front of him.

The immigrant has a scar on his forehead at the very place his passport says that he does. For the officer this probably means that the man is not a fraud. For the immigrant, that scar is a reminder of his childhood friend in the village, the one whose younger sister he married last May. Or it is likely he doesn't even notice the officer's glance. He is conscious only of a dark weariness behind his eyes because he has not slept for three days.

The officer reads the name of the new arrival's place of birth. He has never heard of it. The immigrant has spent all of the thirty-one years of his life in that village. This difference in itself is quite ordinary. But for some reason that he does not understand, the immigrant is filled with shame.

My attempt, as an immigrant writer, to describe that shame is a part of a historical process.

10   Part of that process is the history of decolonization and the presence, through migration, of formerly colonized populations in the metropolitan centers of the West. What has accompanied this demographic change is the arrival of writers and intellectuals from, say, India or Pakistan, who are giving voice to experiences and identities that Western readers do not encounter in the writings of Saul Bellow or John Updike.

But a crucial part of this narrative and its self-interrogation is the emergence of the discipline that can loosely be called postcolonial studies. Based most prominently in literary and cultural studies, but often engaged in conversations with older projects in the disciplines of history or anthropology, postcolonial scholars have made their task the study of the politics of representing the Other. This has meant, to put it in very reductive terms, not simply that there are more of those people speaking and writing today who are a part of the populations that were formerly solely the object of study by Europeans; it also has meant that a fundamental questioning of the privilege and politics of knowledge has made any representation problematic. There is now no escaping the questions "who is speaking here, and who is being silenced?"

I need to revisit and revise the scene at the customs desk. The new arrival responds to the questions asked by the immigration officer. The postcolonial writer, male, middle-class, skilled in the uses of English, is standing nearby and wants to follow the exchange between the officer and the immigrant. Perhaps he wants to help, perhaps he is interested in this conversation only for professional reasons (or both). But for some reason that he does not understand, that he *cannot* understand, the writer is filled with shame.

The postcolonial writers who are read in the West are mostly migrants. They have traveled to the cities of the West—often for economic reasons, and sometimes for political ones, though it could be argued, of course, that all economic reasons are political too—and in the books they write they undertake more travels.

In Amitav Ghosh's *In An Antique Land*, the writer is a young Indian student in rural Egypt doing research in social anthropology. The book follows Ghosh's archival search for a twelfth-century relationship between a Middle Eastern Jewish trader in India, Abraham Ben Yiju, and his toddy-drinking Indian slave, Bomma. These details are interwoven with the more contemporary relationship that develops between the Indian intellectual and the friends he makes in the Egyptian villages not too far from the Cairo synagogue where for a very long time the papers of Ben Yiju were housed.

15   Ghosh was only twenty-two when he traveled in 1980 to Egypt. One day, while making tea

for two young men in his rented room in the village, he is caught short by an observation made by one of his visitors, Nabeel: "It must make you think of all the people you left at home ...when you put that kettle on the stove with just enough water for yourself."

This comment, Ghosh notes, stayed in his mind. "I was never able to forget it, for it was the first time that anyone in Lataifa or Nashawy had attempted an enterprise similar to mine—to enter my imagination and look at my situation as it might appear to me." Ghosh, the traveler, appreciates the travel undertaken by his friend, Nabeel, in his imagination. That effort brings Nabeel closer to that place where Ghosh himself has traveled—which is not so much Egypt as much as a place away from home, or from that which could be called the familiar. To be where one is not, or where one is not expected to be, and sometimes not even welcome ...to travel to that place and write about it becomes the credo of the postcolonial writer.

This movement is not always possible. People are held down where they are, or there are intransigent barriers between them. A shared language is an impossibility. In one of the episodes that Ghosh describes with instructive wit, some older Egyptian men at a wedding in the village want to know what is done with the dead in India, whether it is really true that they are cremated, and whether women are "purified" ("you mean you let the clitoris just grow and grow?"), and boys, are they not "purified" either, and you, doctor, are you? Our writer is unable to respond and flees the scene. The trauma of a childhood memory merges with a shared trauma of a public memory and ties his tongue. Ghosh broods over memories of Hindu-Muslim riots in the Indian subcontinent (present in the narrative of his earlier novel *The Shadow Lines*):

The stories of those riots are always the same: tales that grow out of an explosive barrier of symbols—of cities going up in flames because of a cow found dead in a temple or a pig in a mosque; of people killed for wearing a lungi or a dhoti, depending on where they find themselves; of women disembowelled for wearing veils or vermilion, of men dismembered for the state of their foreskins.

But I was never able to explain very much of this to Nabeel or anyone else in Nashawy. The fact was that despite the occasional storms and turbulence their country had seen, despite even the wars that some of them had fought in, theirs was a world that was far gentler, far less violent, very much more humane and innocent than mine.

I could not have expected them to understand an Indian's terror of symbols.

The name that Ghosh gives to the reality—or, at least, the possibility—of travel and historical understanding is "a world of accommodation." When the young writer and a village Imam get into a fight about the West and its advanced status in terms of "guns and tanks and bombs," and then both make claims about India's and Egypt's respective prowess in this regard, Ghosh confesses that he feels crushed because their heated exchange has most indelibly announced an end to that world of accommodation:

[I]t seemed to me that the Imam and I had participated in our own final defeat, in the dissolution of the centuries of dialogue that had linked us: we had demonstrated the irreversible triumph of the language that has usurped all the others in which people once discussed their differences. We had acknowledged that it was no longer possible to speak, as Ben Yiju or his Slave, or any of the thousands of travellers who had crossed the Indian Ocean in the Middle Ages might have done.

But the postcolonial writer need not blame himself here. It is not his debate with the Imam but the might of U.S. armed forces supported by most of the Western nations that rubs out, at the end of Ghosh's narrative, his friend Nabeel—lost among the countless migrant workers in Iraq from countries like Egypt and India, displaced in the desert because of the sudden onset of the Persian Gulf War.

20   In this scenario, the immigrant does not ever appear before the customs officer in the airport of a Western metropolis. As driver, carpenter, servant, or nanny, the immigrant from countries of South and South-East Asia provides service in the

Gulf states of the Middle East and Libya. In some of their cases the passport is a missing book.

Lacking proper documents, and much more vulnerable to exploitation and abuse, those immigrants are given the name "contract labor" in the zones of shifting, global capital. In the 1950s and 1960s U.S. capital first attracted foreign labor in the Middle East and today, benefiting from investments of the rentier oil-rich Arab states, still profits from the labor of migrants. And when Western capital's profits were threatened, it was the lives of such migrants, and not only those who were employed in Iraq, that the Gulf War threw into devastating crisis. The postcolonial writer speaking of the migrant worker during the war is doing something rather simple. He is reminding us that the man who said to the foreign visitor in his room one evening, "It must make you think of all the people you left at home …when you put that kettle on the stove with just enough water for yourself," is alone now in a distant city threatened with destruction. And that man, when not seen in the footage of the epic exodus shown on television, is then assumed to have "vanished into the anonymity of History."

The migrant laborer might have "vanished into the anonymity of History," but the postcolonial writer clearly has not. By presenting those contrasting conditions, I am making a statement here about class, but besides that fairly obvious fact, what do I say about *writing*?

To ask a question about writing, especially postcolonial writing, perhaps we need to reverse our reading of the passport as a book and, instead, examine the formulation put forward by Rushdie, "A book is a kind of passport." Rushdie's point is on surface a fairly general one. For aspiring writers—"would-be migrants from the World to the Book"—certain books provide permission to travel. Recounting the history of his own formation, Rushdie pays homage, among others, to Günter Grass's *Tin Drum*. Grass's great novel, Rushdie writes, served as a passport to the world of writing. But even when writing of the book as a passport in a *metaphorical* sense, Rushdie is writing about a book—*The Tin Drum*—that is in a *specific* way about migrancy and a migrant's sense of place and language.

That is not a universal trait among writers. The trope of migrancy does not exist as a material fact, in either a metaphorical or literal sense, in the writings of Norman Mailer or John Grisham. But it emerges as an obsession in the pages of a writer like Rushdie. For him, in fact, "the very word *metaphor*, with its roots in the Greek words for *bearing across*, describes a sort of migration, the migration of ideas into images." Rather than oppose the metaphorical to the literal, it is the idea of the metaphorical itself that Rushdie renders literal and equates with a universal condition: "Migrants—borne-across humans—are metaphorical beings in their very essence; and migration, seen as a metaphor, is everywhere around us. We all cross frontiers; in that sense, we are all migrant peoples."

25   There is a danger here in migrancy becoming everything and nothing. Aijaz Ahmad points out that exile is a particular fetish of European High Modernism and in Rushdie's case becomes simply ontological rootlessness. And, Ahmad argues, novels like *Shame* display a form of "unbelonging" and an absence of any "existing community of praxis." If we agree with Ahmad and see the obsessive celebration of migrancy in Rushdie as a mere repetition of the desolation experienced by the modernist writer in exile, we might also sense that the inexplicable shame that permeates the postcolonial writer is only that of being taken as a representative by the West but having no one, in any real sense, to represent.

That is a real, hard-to-shake-off, nagging shame. And what complicates it further is that the writer is aware that while the migrant worker has "vanished into the anonymity of History," the writer himself or herself hasn't. But why has the writer escaped that destiny? We can be reductive and attribute the appeal of a writer like Rushdie or Ghosh only to Western tokenism, and indeed much can be said about the subject even without being reductive. But books written by immigrants or writers of immigrant origins are not merely hollow receptacles for the will of the West. This book that you are holding in your hands has been written in the belief that words matter. Words from an alien language. But also words in a familiar language that attest to different realities: words are our defense against invisibility.

I'd like to imagine the immigration officer as a curious reader of my book. But the officer should not assume that this passport doesn't have any missing pages; indeed, he would be wise to be skeptical even of his own interest. I am reminded of the wary response of Mahasweta Devi, an Indian writer who has earned high recognition for her work among the aboriginal or tribal populations in Bihar and Bengal: "Why should American readers want to know from me about Indian tribals, when they have present-day America? How was it built? Only in the names of places the Native American legacy survives." I take Devi's words as a provocation to present in this book, interspersed with my images from India and other places, the photographs that I have also taken in the United States. (The Other shoots back.) In which case, why only quote Devi? In order to go on with this mapping of a mixed, postcolonial space, I would like to frame these images with a line borrowed from the black hip-hop artist Rakim: "It ain't where you're from, it's where you're at."

This is where I'm at: in the spaces claimed or established by these images. These photographs—please see the notes as well as the list of illustrations for more information on them—detail a different kind of immigrant experience. What these images offer cannot be described as "illustrating" any kind of argument; in the image of a woman holding a rubber Miss Liberty, for example, it is for the viewer to construct a story that binds or divides the three female figures in their distinct moments of emergence as objects or subjects. The recording of the difference that I am calling "immigrant experience" also has partly to do with labor and protest. Hence the images of workers and, in some cases, their organized protest, on the streets of New Delhi and New York City. The accompanying narratives, and oftentimes the photographs themselves,

raise the question about how these images are to be seen. And from where. As a way of announcing that difference, let me offer at the beginning of this book a photograph that sets itself against the photo of the White House taken by the visiting tourist. This is the photograph of the First House from the viewpoint of the homeless sleeping outside its walls one Christmas Eve.

LANGUAGE

Everytime I think I have forgotten,
I think I have lost the mother tongue,
it blossoms out of my mouth.
Days I try to think in English:
I look up,
paylo kallo kagdo
oodto oodto jai, huhvay jzaday pohchay
ainee chanchma kaeek chay
the crow has something in his beak.

Sujata Bhatt

Name
Place of Birth
Date of Birth
Profession
Nationality
Sex
Identifying Marks

My passport provides no information about my language. It simply presumes I have one.

30   If the immigration officer asks me a question—his voice, if he's speaking English, deliberately slow, and louder than usual—I do not, of course, expect him to be terribly concerned about the nature of language and its entanglement with the very roots of my being. And yet it is in language that all immigrants are defined and in which we all struggle for an identity. That is how I understand the postcolonial writer's declaration about the use of a language like English that came to us from the colonizer:

Those of us who do use English do so in spite of our ambiguity towards it, or perhaps because of that, perhaps because we can find in that linguistic struggle a reflection of other struggles taking place

Homeless
outside the
White House,
1992

in the real world, struggles between the cultures within ourselves and the influences at work upon our societies. To conquer English may be to complete the process of making ourselves free.

I also do not expect the immigration officer to be very aware of the fact that it is in that country called language that immigrants are reviled. I'd like to know what his thoughts were when he first heard the Guns N' Roses song:

Immigrants
and faggots
They make no sense to me
They come to our country—
And think they'll do as they please
Like start some mini-Iran
Or spread some fuckin' disease.

It is between different words that immigrants must choose to suggest who they are. And if these words, and their meanings, belong to others, then it is in a broken language that we must find refuge. Consider this example.

I took this photograph while standing outside an Arab grocery store in Brooklyn. While pressing the shutter I was aware of another grocery store, in the film *Falling Down*, where the fol-

lowing exchange took place between a white American male, played by Michael Douglas, and a Korean grocer:

MR. LEE: Drink eighty-five cent. You pay or go.
FOSTER: This "fie," I don't understand a "fie." There's a "v" in the word. It's "fie-vah." You don't got "v's" in China?
MR. LEE: Not Chinese. I'm Korean.
FOSTER: Whatever. You come to my country, you take my money, you don't even have the grace to learn my language?

What Foster doesn't realize is that not only is it not his country alone, it is also not his language anymore. (That should be obvious to the ordinary American viewer, except that it *wasn't* obvious to every one. And it isn't.) But what I'm interested in asking is this: what is it that Mr. Lee is saying?

In saying "Not Chinese. I'm Korean," Mr. Lee is talking about difference. He is trying to tell another story. His story. Except that Foster won't listen. He is more interested in taking apart Mr. Lee's store with a baseball bat—the same way that, as Rita Chaudhry Sethi reminds us, others destroyed Japanese cars before Vincent Chin died. Vincent Chin was a young Chinese American who

35

Shop
advertisement,
Brooklyn
grocery, 1992

was murdered, also with a baseball bat, by two white autoworkers in Detroit. Chin was called a "Jap" and told "It's because of you motherfuckers that we're out of work." When I say Mr. Lee is talking about differences, I don't simply mean the difference between someone who is Chinese and someone else who is Korean. Instead, by difference I mean a sense of where it is a person is coming from. Both in terms of a location in place and in history.

Vincent Chin was an American of Chinese origin. The year he was killed marked the hundred-year anniversary of the Chinese Exclusion Act; in the year 1882, lynch mobs had murdered Chinese workers who were working on the West Coast.

Chin's murderers, Ronald Ebens and Michael Nitz, were autoworkers in Detroit, the city that entered the annals of early U.S. industrialism through its success in manufacturing cars. Ebens and Nitz did not know the difference between a worker and a capitalist. They were kept ignorant of the world of transnational capitalism, their very own world in which "General Motors owns 34 percent of Isuzu (which builds the Buick Opel), Ford 25 percent of Mazda (which makes transmissions for the Escort), and Chrysler 15 percent of Mitsubishi (which produces the Colt and the Charger)." Chin's killers did not spend a single night in prison and were fined $3,780 each. A Chinese American protesting the scant sentence is reported to have said, "Three thousand dollars can't even buy a good used car these days."

What does the word "Jap" mean? What is the difference between a Japanese and a Chinese American? What is the difference between a Chinese American and a used car? How does language mean and why does it matter?

As the Swiss linguist Ferdinand de Saussure argued very early in this century, language is a system of signs. And any sign consists of a signifier (the sound or written form) and a signified (the concept). As the two parts of the sign are linked or inseparable (the word "camera," for instance, accompanies the concept "camera" and remains quite distinct in our minds from the concept "car"), what is prompted is the illusion that language is transparent. The relationship between the signifier and the signified, and hence language itself, is assumed to be natural.

40   When we use the word "alien" it seems to stick rather unproblematically and unquestioningly to something or someone, and it is only by a conscious, critical act that we think of something different. Several years ago, in a public speech, Reverend Jesse Jackson seemed to be questioning the fixed and arbitrary assumptions in the dominant ideology when he reminded his audience that undocumented Mexicans were not aliens, they were *migrant workers*.

     E.T., Jackson said emphatically, was an *alien*.

     I took this photograph very close to the U.S.–Mexico border, somewhere between San Diego and Tijuana. There was a tear in the fence; I climbed under it and came up close to the highway to get a better shot. When I went back to the place in the fence, I was startled out of my skin by a Border Patrol van that was very slowly driving past. The officer did not see me, however, and I was soon back in the bar next to my motel.

     While sipping my beer, I imagined a conversation with the border patrol officer who had only narrowly missed catching me.

OFFICER: I saw you photographing that sign. That was good, an excellent idea. What do you think about the sign though?

ME: Mmm. I don't know. It's just that—this is the first time I saw that sign. In my country, we have family-planning signs with figures like that. Father, mother, kid. The Health Ministry has a slogan painted beneath it, One or Two Kids. Then Stop.

OFFICER: That's very interesting. This is what I like about multiculturalism. You get to learn about cultural difference.

ME: You really think so? Yes, that's great. What can I learn from *this* sign?

OFFICER: Well, you've gotta get into the semiotics of it, you know what I'm saying?

ME: Uh-huh.

OFFICER: I'll be damned if language is transparent. That's the bottom line here. Just look at that sign—in English it's Caution, but in Spanish, it's *Prohibido*. You don't think those two words mean the same thing, do you?

ME: I don't know. I don't know Spanish.

California road sign near U.S.-Mexico border, 1994

OFFICER: Okay, well, I'll be patient with you. The sign in English is for folks who drive. They're being cautioned. Now, the sign in Spanish—

ME: Yes, yes, I see what you're driving at! The *Prohibido* sign is for the Spanish speaker—

OFFICER: There you go! Bingo! Bull's eye! They don't have the word *Caución* there. It's plain Prohibited: pure and simple. The picture, the image—it splits, right before your eyes!

ME: The scales have fallen…

OFFICER: Well, but you gotta stay alert. 'Cause culture is a moving thing, meanings change. Or sometimes, just get plain run over. All the time.

ME: Yes, yes.

OFFICER: What work do you do?

ME: I teach English.

OFFICER: No kidding! See, this is America! You teaching *English* to our kids, I love it. Say, did you ever watch *Saturday Night Live* when it first came on?

ME: No, I don't think so.

OFFICER: Michael O'Donoghue played a language instructor. He was teaching this confused immigrant played by John Belushi. You know the sentence that O'Donoghue used to introduce the language?

ME: What was it?

OFFICER: I will feed your fingers to the wolverines.

We could have gone on, the officer and I. If we were swapping stories today, I'd have mentioned the news report that the telephone company Sprint, in its billing letter in Spanish, threatens customers with phone cutoff unless their check is received by the end of the month. According to the news report, the Anti-Defamation League and the National Council of La Raza have filed complaints. Why? Because the billing letter in English is somewhat differently worded: "As a customer you are Sprint's number one priority. We …look forward to serving your communication needs for many years to come."

45   And, if the officer had had more time, we might have arrived at an understanding that language, especially English, has been used as a racial weapon in immigration.

To cite a historical example: in 1896 a colonial official argued against the restrictions imposed on the entry of Indians in South Africa, adding that this would be "most painful" for Queen Victoria to approve. At the same time, he sanctioned a European literacy test that would automatically exclude Indians while preserving the facade of racial equality.

Almost a hundred years later a Texas judge ordered the mother of a five-year-old to stop speaking in Spanish to her child. Judge Samuel Kiser reminded the mother that her daughter was a "full-blooded American." "Now, get this straight. You start speaking English to this child because if she doesn't do good in school, then I can remove her because it's not in her best interest to be ignorant. The child will only hear English."

Who is permitted to proceed beyond the gates into the mansion of full citizenship? And on what terms? These are the questions that the episode in the Texas courthouse raises. Apart from the issue of gross paternalism and an entirely injudicious jingoism, what comes into play here is the class bias in North American society that promotes bilingualism in the upper class but frowns on it when it becomes an aspect of lower-class life.

More revealing of the ties between language and U.S. Immigration is the following newspaper report: "School and city officials expressed outrage this week over the Border Patrol's arrest of three Hispanic students outside an English as Second Language class."

50   For the Chicano poet Alfred Arteaga, the above story about arrest and deportation has a double irony: "irony, not only that 'officials expressed outrage' at so typical an INS action, but irony also, that the story made it into print in the first place." Arteaga knows too well that what Chicanos say and do in their own language is rarely found worthy of printing.

I think it is equally significant to remark on the fact that the officers who conducted the arrest were patrolling the borders of the dominant language to pick up the illegals. They are ably assisted by the likes of the California state assemblyman William J. Knight, who distributed among his fellow legislators a poem, "I Love America." That poem begins with the words "I come for visit, get treated regal, / So I stay, who care illegal." This little ditty makes its way through the slime of a racist fantasy. Its landscape is filled with greedy swindlers and dishonest migrant workers. The breeding subhumans speak in a broken syntax and mispronounce the name Chevy, the heartbeat of America, as (call the National Guard, please!) Chebby. The poem ends with a call that emanates like a howl from the guts of the Ku Klux Klan:

We think America damn good place,
Too damn good for white man's race.
If they no like us, they can go,
Got lots of room in Mexico.

If the immigration officer were to ask me about my language, what would I say? That any precious life-giving sense of language loses all form in this arid landscape of Buchanan-speak? Perhaps. That any answer I could possibly give is nothing more defined than a blur moving on the infrared scopes of those guarding the borders of fixed identity.

Homi Bhabha writes: "The enchantment of art lies in looking in a glass darkly—a wall, stone, a screen, paper, canvas, steel—that turns suddenly into the almost unbearable lightness of being." But where is this buoyancy, the refulgence, the mix of new life and new art? As the case of Fauziya Kasinga reminds us—the young woman who fled Togo to avoid genital mutilation and was held for long in detention by the U.S. Immigration authorities—grim reality so often persists in its unenchanting rudeness.

In such conditions to speak is only to declare any speech a station of loss.

I brought two bags from home, but there was a third that I left behind. In this new country, apart from the struggles that made me a stranger, were your needs, of the ones who bid me goodbye, those I left behind. Among the papers I collected, you had put a small bag of sweets, I left behind.
There were divisions at home, there were other possibilities;
there were communities in my town, there were communities where I came;
I found a job, called it a struggle for survival, everything else I left behind. I didn't want to forget my traditions, the tradition of forgetting I left behind.
Bags, passport, my shoes crossed the yellow lines, something was left behind.
Here I am, a sum of different parts; travel agents everywhere are selling ads for the parts that were left behind.

And yet, while speaking of the patrolling of the borders of dominant identity, I must note the presence of one who is still eluding arrest: a border-artist/poet-performer/hoarder-of-hypehs/warrior-for-Gringostroika. Officer, meet Guillermo Gómez-Peña. You have been looking for him not only because Gómez-Peña declares "I speak in English therefore you listen/I speak in English therefore I hate you." But also because, like a "Pablo Neruda gone punk," this "border brujo" threatens mainstream America with the swaggering banditry of language, demanding as ransom a pure reality-reversal:

What if the U.S. was Mexico?
What if 200,000 Anglo-Saxicans
Were to cross the border each month
to work as gardeners, waiters
3rd chair musicians, movie extras
bouncers, babysitters, chauffeurs
syndicated cartoons, feather-weight boxers, fruit-pickers
and anonymous poets?
What if they were called Waspanos
Waspitos, Wasperos or Waspbacks?
What if literature was life, eh?

SUGGESTIONS FOR DISCUSSION

1. One of the threads running through Amitava Kumar's writing is the idea that a passport is a book that enables different and complex readings. He also uses a line from Salman Rushdie, "A book is a kind of passport," as an epigram to the introduction. What is the relationship between these two ideas? What comes to light if you put the emphasis on the passport (as a kind of book) or on the book (as a kind of passport)?

2. In the excerpt from the introduction Kumar defines the "task" of postcolonial scholars as "the study of the politics of representing the Other." Later in the same paragraph, he says a "fundamental questioning of the privilege and politics of knowledge have made any representation problematic. There is now no escaping the questions 'who is speaking here, and who is being silenced?'" What does Kumar mean here? Put in your own words what you think he is saying about the purposes of a postcolonial perspective and the kinds of questions raised by such a perspective. Draw on the rest of the reading selection to give examples of what a postcolonial perspective looks like as Kumar presents it.

3. In these excerpts and throughout *Passport Photos*, Kumar uses a mixed and episodic style that combines, among other things, photos, poetry, song lyrics, movie dialogue, imagined conversations, reporting, and analysis instead of straightforward exposition. Why do you think Kumar has chosen this writing strategy? In what sense is the writing strategy linked to Kumar's themes of migration, borders, postcolonialism, and globalization? Consider, for example, the imagined conversation with the border patrol officer. To hear how this passage fits into the mosaic of styles Kumar uses, have two people in class take the two parts and read them aloud.

SUGGESTIONS FOR WRITING

1. Write a letter to a friend at another college that explains what the term *postcolonial* means in these excerpts from *Passport Photos*. Assume your friend is curious about the term but hasn't read this selection. Explain how Kumar defines and illustrates the term, but it may help your friend, who hasn't read these excerpts, to use other examples from your shared knowledge and experience as well. Because this is a letter to a friend, describe your own experience working through Kumar's writing and explain what you see as the value and significance of the term *postcolonial*.

2. Many of these excerpts from *Passport Photos* are devoted to the idea of international borders or actually take place at the U.S. border. Here is a passage from an essay by Richard Rodriquez, "Illegal Immigrants: Prophets of a Borderless World."

Before professors in business schools were talking about global economics, illegals knew all about it. Before fax machines punctured the Iron Curtin, coyotes knew the most efficient ways to infiltrate southern California. Before businessmen flew into Mexico City to sign big deals, illegals were picking peaches in the fields of California or flipping pancakes at the roadside diner.

We live in a world in which economies overlap, in which we no longer know where our automobiles are assembled. We are headed for a century in which the great question will be exactly this: What is a border?

The illegal immigrant is the bravest among us. The most modern among us. The prophet. "The border, señor?" the illegal immigrant sighs. The border is an inconvenience surely. A danger in the dark. But the border does not hold. The peasant knows the reality of our world decades before the California suburbanites will ever get the point.

Write an essay that takes seriously Rodriquez's claim that the "great question" of the twenty-first century will be, "What is a border?" Explain Rodriquez's and Kumar's perspectives on the question, noting similarities and differences. Use this discussion to set up your own commentary on what you see as the implications of the question, "What is a border?"

3. Write an essay that imitates Kumar's mixed, episodic style. Draw upon any or all of the genres Kumar does to create your own reflections on life in a postcolonial world.

HOME IS WHERE THE "HAN" IS:
A Korean American Perspective on the Los Angeles Upheavals

Elaine H. Kim

Elaine H. Kim teaches Asian American Studies at the University of California–Berkeley. She has written and edited several books on Asian American writers and artists, and she has been involved in the production of television documentaries on Asian women. The following selection originally appeared as a chapter in a collection of essays, *Reading Rodney King/Reading Urban Uprising* (1993). In her chapter, Kim suggests that the uprising that followed the acquittal of four police officers in the Rodney King beating case was a "baptism into what it really means for a Korean to 'become American' in the 1990s." The failure of the Los Angeles police to respond to the looting and burning of stores and homes in Koreatown revealed to the Korean community, Kim says, the contradiction between the American dream and American reality and what she calls the "interstitial position" of Korean Americans, caught in a racially divided society between "predominantly Anglo and mostly African American and Latino communities."

SUGGESTION FOR READING   As you read, notice how Elaine H. Kim combines commentary on the Los Angeles uprising with the history of the Korean people and an analysis of readers' responses to the "My Turn" column she wrote for *Newsweek* magazine. To help you follow Kim's line of thought, underline and annotate key passages that develop her central ideas. How do the various sections locate Korean Americans as caught in the middle—on the one hand, between the dominant Anglo and the minority African American and Latino communities, and on the other, between the United States and Korea?

1 About half of the estimated $850 million in estimated material losses incurred during the Los Angeles upheavals was sustained by a community no one seems to want to talk much about. Korean Americans in Los Angeles, suddenly at the front lines when violence came to the buffer zone they had been so precariously occupying, suffered profound damage to their means of livelihood.[1] But my concern here is the psychic damage which, unlike material damage, is impossible to quantify.

I want to explore the questions of whether or not recovery is possible for Korean Americans, and what will become of our attempts to "become American" without dying of *han*. *Han* is a Korean word that means, loosely translated, the sorrow and anger that grow from the accumulated experiences of oppression. Although the word is frequently and commonly used by Koreans, the condition it describes is taken quite seriously. When people die of *han*, it is called dying of *hwabyong*, a disease of frustration and rage following misfortune.

Situated as we are on the border between those who have and those who have not, between predominantly Anglo and mostly African American and Latino communities, from our current interstitial position in the American discourse of race, many Korean Americans have trouble calling what happened in Los Angeles an "uprising." At the same time, we cannot quite say it was a "riot." So some of us have taken to calling it *sa-i-ku*, April 29, after the manner of naming other events in Korean history—3.1 (*sam-il*) for March 1, 1919, when massive protests against Japanese colonial rule began in Korea; 6.25 (*yook-i-o*), or June 25, 1950, when the Korean War began; and 4.19 (*sa-il-ku*), or April 19, 1960, when the first student movement in the world to overthrow a government began in South Korea.

The ironic similarity between 4.19 and 4.29 does not escape most Korean Americans.

Los Angeles Koreatown has been important to me, even though I visit only a dozen times a year. Before Koreatown sprang up during the last decade and a half, I used to hang around the fringes of Chinatown, although I knew that this habit was pure pretense. For me, knowing that Los Angeles Koreatown existed made a difference; one of my closest friends worked with the Black-Korean Alliance there, and I liked to think of it as a kind of "home"—however idealized and hypostatized—for the soul, an anchor, a potential refuge, a place in America where I could belong without ever being asked, "Who are you and what are you doing here? Where did you come from and when are you going back?"

5   ˜ Many of us watched in horror the destruction of Koreatown and the systematic targeting of Korean shops in South Central Los Angeles after the Rodney King verdict. Seeing those buildings in flames and those anguished Korean faces, I had the terrible thought that there would be no belonging and that we were, just as I had always suspected, a people destined to carry our *han* around with us wherever we went in the world. The destiny (*p'aljja*) that had spelled centuries of extreme suffering from invasion, colonization, war, and national division had smuggled itself into the U.S. with our baggage.

AFRICAN AMERICAN AND KOREAN AMERICAN CONFLICT

As someone whose social consciousness was shaped by the African American–led civil rights movement of the 1960s, I felt that I was watching our collective dreams for a just society disintegrating, cast aside as naive and irrelevant in the bitter and embattled 1990s. It was the courageous African American women and men of the 1960s who had redefined the meaning of "American," who had first suggested that a person like me could reject the false choice between being treated as a perpetual foreigner in my own birthplace, on the one hand, and relinquishing my identity for someone else's ill-fitting and impossible Anglo American one on the other. Thanks to them, I began to discern how institutional racism works and why Korea was never mentioned in my world-history textbooks. I was able to see how others besides Koreans had been swept aside by the dominant culture. My American education offered nothing about Chicanos or Latinos, and most of what I was taught about African and Native Americans was distorted to justify their oppression and vindicate their oppressors.

I could hardly believe my ears when, during the weeks immediately following *sa-i-ku,* I heard African American community leaders suggesting that Korean American merchants were foreign intruders deliberately trying to stifle African American economic development, when I knew that they had bought those liquor stores at five times gross receipts from African American owners, who had previously bought them at two times gross receipts from Jewish owners after Watts. I saw anti-Korean flyers that were being circulated by African American political candidates and read about South Central residents petitioning against the reestablishment of swap meets, groups of typically Korean immigrant-operated market stalls. I was disheartened with Latinos who related the pleasure they felt while looting Korean stores that they believed "had it coming" and who claimed that it was because of racism that more Latinos were arrested during *sa-i-ku* than Asian Americans. And I was filled with despair when I read about Chinese Americans wanting to dissociate themselves from us. According to one Chinese American reporter assigned to cover Asian American issues for a San Francisco daily, Chinese and Japanese American shopkeepers, unlike Koreans, always got along fine with African Americans in the past. "Suddenly," admitted another Chinese American, "I am scared to be Asian. More specifically, I am afraid to be mistaken for Korean." I was enraged when I overheard European Americans discussing the conflicts as if they were watching a dogfight or a boxing match. The situation reminded me of the Chinese film *Raise the Red Lantern,* in which we never see the husband's face. We only hear his mellifluous voice as he benignly admonishes his four wives not to fight among themselves. He can afford to be kind and pleasant because the structure that pits his wives against each other is so firmly in place that he need never sully his hands or even raise his voice.

BATTLEGROUND LEGACY

Korean Americans are squeezed between black and white and also between U.S. and South Korean political agendas. Opportunistic American and South Korean presidential candidates toured the burnt ruins, posing for the television cameras but delivering nothing of substance to the victims. Like their U.S. counterparts, South Korean news media seized upon *sa-i-ku,* featuring sensational stories that depicted the problem as that of savage African Americans attacking innocent Koreans for no reason. To give the appearance of authenticity, Seoul newspapers even published articles using the names of Korean Americans who did not in fact write them.

Those of us who chafe at being asked whether we are Chinese or Japanese as if there were no other possibilities or who were angered when the news media sought Chinese and Japanese but not Korean American views during *sa-i-ku* are sensitive to an invisibility that seems particular to us. To many Americans, Korea is but the gateway to or the bridge between China and Japan, or a crossroads of major Asian conflicts.

10   It can certainly be said that, although little known or cared about in the Western world, Korea has been a perennial battleground. Besides the Mongols and the Manchus, there were the *Yaájin* (Jurched), the *Koran* (Khitan), and the *Waega* (Wäkö) invaders. In relatively recent years, there was the war between China and Japan that ended in 1895 and the war between Japan and Russia in 1905; both of which were fought on Korean soil and resulted in extreme suffering for the Korean people. Japan's 36 years of brutal colonial rule ended with the U.S. and what was then the Soviet Union dividing the country in half at the 38th parallel. Thus, Korea was turned into a Cold War territory that ulti-mately became a battleground for world superpowers during the conflict of 1950–53.

BECOMING AMERICAN

One of the consequences of war, colonization, national division, and superpower economic and cultural domination has been the migration of Koreans to places like Los Angeles, where they believed their human rights would be protected by law. After all, they had received U.S.-influenced political educations. They started learning English in the seventh grade. They all knew the story of the poor boy from Illinois who became president. They all learned that the U.S. Constitution and Bill of Rights protected the common people from violence and injustice. But they who grew up in Korea watching *Gunsmoke, Night Rider,* and *McGyver* dubbed in Korean were not prepared for the black, brown, red, and yellow America they encountered when they disembarked at the Los Angeles International Airport. They hadn't heard that there is no equal justice in the U.S. They had to learn about American racial hierarchies. They did not realize that, as immigrants of color, they would never attain political voice or visibility but would instead be used to uphold the inequality and the racial hierarchy they had no part in creating.

Most of the newcomers had underestimated the communication barriers they would face. Like the Turkish workers in Germany described in John Berger and Jean Mohr's *A Seventh Man,* their toil amounted to only a pile of gestures and the English they tried to speak changed and turned against them as they spoke it. Working 14 hours a day, six or seven days a week, they rarely came into sustained contact with English-speaking Americans and almost never had time to study English. Not feeling at ease with English, they did not engage in informal conversations easily with non-Koreans and were hated for being curt and rude. They did not attend churches or do business in banks or other enterprises where English was required. Typically, the immigrant, small-business owners utilized unpaid family labor instead of hiring people from local communities. Thanks to Eurocentric American cultural practices, they knew little or nothing good about African Americans or Latinos, who in turn and for similar reasons knew little or nothing good about them. At the same time, Korean shopowners in South Central and Koreatown were affluent compared with the impoverished residents, whom they often exploited as laborers or looked down upon as fools with an aversion to hard work. Most Korean immigrants did not even know that they were among the many direct beneficiaries of the African American–led civil rights movement, which helped pave the way for the 1965 immigration reforms that made their immigration possible.

Korean-immigrant views, shaped as they were by U.S. cultural influences and official, anticommunist, South Korean education, differed radically from those of many poor people in the communities Korean immigrants served: unaware of the shameful history of oppression of nonwhite immigrants and other people of color in the U.S., they regarded themselves as having arrived in a meritocratic "land of opportunity" where a person's chances for success are limited only by individual lack of ability or diligence. Having left a homeland where they foresaw their talents and hard work going unrecognized and unrewarded, they were desperate to believe that the "American dream" of social and economic mobility through hard work was within their reach.

SA-I-KU

What they experienced on 29 and 30 April was a baptism into what it really means for a Korean to "become American" in the 1990s. In South Korea, there is no 911, and no one really expects a fire engine or police car if there is trouble. Instead, people make arrangements with friends and family for emergencies. At the same time, guns are not part of Korean daily life. No civilian in South Korea can own a gun. Guns are the exclusive accoutrement of the military and police who enforce order for those who rule the society. When the Korean Americans in South Central and Koreatown dialed 911, nothing happened. When their stores and homes were being looted and burned to the

ground, they were left completely alone for three horrifying days. How betrayed they must have felt by what they had believed was a democratic system that protects its people from violence. Those who trusted the government to protect them lost everything; those who took up arms after waiting for help for two days were able to defend themselves. It was as simple as that. What they had to learn was that, as in South Korea, protection in the U.S. is by and large for the rich and powerful. If there were a choice between Westwood and Koreatown, it is clear that Koreatown would have to be sacrificed. The familiar concept of privilege for the rich and powerful would have been easy for the Korean immigrant to grasp if only those exhortations about democracy and equality had not obfuscated the picture. Perhaps they should have relied even more on whatever they brought with them from Korea instead of fretting over trying to understand what was going on around them here. That Koreatown became a battleground does seem like the further playing out of a tragic legacy that has followed them across oceans and continents. The difference is that this was a battle between the poor and disenfranchised and the invisible rich, who were being protected by a layer of clearly visible Korean American human shields in a battle on the buffer zone.

15   This difference is crucial. Perhaps the legacy is not one carried across oceans and continents but one assumed immediately upon arrival, not the curse of being Korean but the initiation into becoming American, which requires that Korean Americans take on this country's legacy of five centuries of racial violence and inequality, of divide and rule, of privilege for the rich and oppression of the poor. Within this legacy, they have been assigned a place on the front lines. Silenced by those who possess the power to characterize and represent, they are permitted to speak only to reiterate their acceptance of this role.

SILENCING THE KOREAN AMERICAN VOICE

Twelve years ago, in Kwangju, South Korea, hundreds of civilians demonstrating for constitutional reform and free elections were murdered by U.S.-

supported and -equipped South Korean elite para-troopers. Because I recorded it and played it over and over again, searching for a sign or a clue, I remember clearly how what were to me heartrendingly tragic events were represented in the U.S. news media. For a few fleeting moments, images of unruly crowds of alien-looking Asians shouting unintelligible words and phrases and wearing white headbands inscribed with unintelligible characters flickered across the screen. The Koreans were made to seem like insane people from another planet. The voice in the background stated simply that there were massive demonstrations but did not explain what the protests were about. Nor was a single Korean ever given an opportunity to speak to the camera.

The next news story was about demonstrations for democracy in Poland. The camera settled on individuals' faces which one by one filled the screen as each man or woman was asked to explain how he or she felt. Each Polish person's words were translated in a voice-over or subtitle. Solidarity leader Lech Walesa, who was allowed to speak often, was characterized as a heroic human being with whom all Americans could surely identify personally. Polish Americans from New York and Chicago to San Francisco, asked in man-on-the-street interviews about their reactions, described the canned hams and blankets they were sending to Warsaw.

This was for me a lesson in media representation, race, and power politics. It is a given that Americans are encouraged by our ideological apparatuses to side with our allies (here, the Polish resisters and the anti-communist South Korean government) against our enemies (here, the communist Soviet Union and protesters against the South Korean government). But visual-media racism helps craft and reinforce our identification with Europeans and whites while distancing us from fearsome and alien Asiatic hordes.

In March of last year, when two delegates from North Korea visited the Bay Area to participate in community-sponsored talks on Korean reunification, about 800 people from the Korean American community attended. The meeting was consummately newsworthy, since it was the first time in history that anyone from North Korea had ever been in California for more than 24 hours just passing through. The event was discussed for months in the Korean-language media—television, radio, and newspapers. Almost every Korean-speaking person in California knew about it. Although we sent press releases to all the commercial and public radio and television stations and to all the Bay Area newspapers, not a single mainstream media outfit covered the event. However, whenever there was an African American boycott of a Korean store or whenever conflict surfaced between Korean and African Americans, community leaders found a dozen microphones from all the main news media shoved into their faces, as if they were the president's press secretary making an official public pronouncement. Fascination with interethnic conflicts is rooted in the desire to excuse or minimize white racism by buttressing the mistaken notion that all human beings are "naturally" racist, and when Korean and African Americans allow themselves to be distracted by these interests, their attention is deflected from the social hierarchies that give racism its destructive power.

20   Without a doubt, the U.S. news media played a major role in exacerbating the damage and ill will toward Korean Americans, first by spotlighting tensions between African Americans and Koreans above all efforts to work together and as opposed to many other newsworthy events in these two communities, and second by exploiting racist stereotypes of Koreans as unfathomable aliens, this time wielding guns on rooftops and allegedly firing wildly into crowds. In news programs and on talk shows, African and Korean American tensions were discussed by blacks and whites, who pointed to these tensions as the main cause of the uprising. I heard some European Americans railing against rude and exploitative Korean merchants for ruining peaceful race relations for everyone else. Thus, Korean Americans were used to deflect attention from the racism they inherited and the economic injustice and poverty that had been already well woven into the fabric of American life, as evidenced by a judicial system that could allow not only the Korean store

owner who killed Latasha Harlins but also the white men who killed Vincent Chin and the white police who beat Rodney King to go free, while Leonard Peltier still languishes in prison.

As far as I know, neither the commercial nor the public news media has mentioned the many Korean and African American attempts to improve relations, such as joint church services, joint musical performances and poetry readings, Korean merchant donations to African American community and youth programs, African American volunteer teachers in classes for Korean immigrants studying for citizenship examinations, or Korean translations of African American history materials.

While Korean immigrants were preoccupied with the mantra of day-to-day survival, Korean Americans had no voice, no political presence whatsoever in American life. When they became the targets of violence in Los Angeles, their opinions and views were hardly solicited except as they could be used in the already-constructed mainstream discourse on race relations, which is a sorry combination of blaming the African American and Latino victims for their poverty and scapegoating the Korean Americans as robotic aliens who have no "real" right to be here in the first place and therefore deserve whatever happens to them.

THE *NEWSWEEK* EXPERIENCE

In this situation, I felt compelled to respond when an editor from the "My Turn" section of *Newsweek* magazine asked for a 1000-word personal essay. Hesitant because I was given only a day and a half to write the piece, not enough time in light of the vastness of American ignorance about Koreans and Korean Americans, I decided to do it because I thought I could not be made into a sound bite or a quote contextualized for someone else's agenda.

I wrote an essay accusing the news media of using Korean Americans and tensions between African and Korean Americans to divert attention from the roots of racial violence in the U.S. I asserted that these lie not in the Korean-

immigrant-owned corner store situated in a community ravaged by poverty and police violence, but reach far back into the corridors of corporate and government offices in Los Angeles, Sacramento, and Washington, D.C. I suggested that Koreans and African Americans were kept ignorant about each other by educational and media institutions that erase or distort their experiences and perspectives. I tried to explain how racism had kept my parents from ever really becoming Americans, but that having been born here, I considered myself American and wanted to believe in the possibility of an American dream.

The editor of "My Turn" did everything he could to frame my words with his own viewpoint. He faxed his own introductory and concluding paragraphs that equated Korean merchants with cowboys in the Wild West and alluded to Korean/African American hatred. When I objected, he told me that my writing style was not crisp enough and that as an experienced journalist, he could help me out. My confidence wavered, but ultimately I rejected his editing. Then he accused me of being overly sensitive, confiding that I had no need to be defensive—because his wife was a Chinese American. Only after I had decided to withdraw the piece did he agree to accept it as I wrote it.

25   Before I could finish congratulating myself on being able to resist silencing and the kind of decontextualization I was trying to describe in the piece, I started receiving hate mail. Some of it was addressed directly to me, since I had been identified as a University of California faculty member, but most of it arrived in bundles, forwarded by *Newsweek*. Hundreds of letters came from all over the country, from Florida to Washington state and from Massachusetts to Arizona. I was unprepared for the hostility expressed in most of the letters. Some people sent the article, torn from the magazine and covered with angry, red-inked obscenities scratched across my picture. "You should see a good doctor," wrote someone from Southern California, "you have severe problems in thinking, reasoning, and adjusting to your environment."

A significant proportion of the writers, especially those who identified themselves as descendants of immigrants from Eastern Europe, wrote *Newsweek* that they were outraged, sickened, disgusted, appalled, annoyed, and angry at the magazine for providing an arena for the paranoid, absurd, hypocritical, racist, and childish views of a spoiled, ungrateful, whining, bitching, un-American bogus faculty member who should be fired or die when the next California earthquake dumps all of the "so-called people of color" into the Pacific Ocean.

I was shocked by the profound ignorance of many writers' assumptions about the experiences and perspectives of American people of color in general and Korean and other Asian Americans in particular. Even though my essay revealed that I was born in the U.S. and that my parents had lived in the U.S. for more than six decades, I was viewed as a foreigner without the right to say anything except words of gratitude and praise about America. The letters also provided some evidence of the dilemma Korean Americans are placed in by those who assume that we are aliens who should "go back" and at the same time berate us for not rejecting "Korean American identity" for "American identity."

How many Americans migrate to Korea? If you are so disenchanted, Korea is still there. Why did you ever leave it? Sayonara.

Ms. Kim appears to have a personal axe to grind with this country that has given her so much freedom and opportunity....I should suggest that she move to Korea, where her children will learn all they ever wanted about that country's history.

[Her] whining about the supposedly racist U.S. society is just a mask for her own acute inferiority complex. If she is so dissatisfied with the United States why doesn't she vote with her feet and leave? She can get the hell out and return to her beloved Korea—her tribal afinity [sic] where her true loyalty and consciousness lies [sic].

You refer to yourself as a Korean American and yet you have lived all your life in the United States...you write about racism in this country and yet you are the biggest racist by your own written words. If you cannot accept the fact that you are an American, maybe you should be living your life in Korea.

My stepfather and cousin risked their lives in the country where your father is buried to ensure the ideals of our country would remain. So don't expect to find a sympathetic ear for your pathetic whining.

Many of the letter writers assumed that my family had been the "scum" of Asia and that I was a college teacher only because of American justice and largesse. They were furious that I did not express gratitude for being saved from starvation in Asia and given the opportunity to flourish, no doubt beyond my wildest dreams, in America.

Where would she be if her parents had not migrated to the United States? For a professor at Berkeley University [sic] to say the American dream is only an empty promise is ludicrous. Shame, shame, shame on Elaine!

[Her father and his family] made enough money in the USA to ship his corpse home to Korea for burial. Ms. Kim herself no doubt has a guaranteed life income as a professor paid by California taxpayers. Wouldn't you think that she might say kind things about the USA instead of whining about racism?

At the same time some letters blamed me for expecting "freedom and opportunity":

It is wondrous that folks such as you find truth in your paranoia. No one ever promised anything to you or your parents.

30   Besides providing indications of how Korean Americans are regarded, the letters revealed a great deal about how American identity is thought of. One California woman explained that although her grandparents were Irish immigrants, she was not an Irish American, because "if you are not with us, you are against us." A Missouri woman did not seem to realize that she was conflating race and nationality and confusing "nonethnic" and "nonracial," by which she seems to have meant "white," with "American." And, although she insists that it is impossible to

be both "black" and "American," she identifies herself at the outset as a "white American."

I am a white American. I am proud to be an American. You cannot be black, white, Korean, Chinese, Mexican, German, French, or English or any other and still be an American. Of course the culture taught in schools is strictly American. That's where we are and if you choose to learn another [culture] you have the freedom to settle there. You cannot be a Korean American which assumes you are not ready to be an AMERICAN. Do you get my gist?

The suggestion that more should be taught in U.S. schools about America's many immigrant groups and people of color prompted many letters in defense of Western civilization against non-Western barbarism:

You are dissatisfied with current school curricula that excludes Korea. Could it possibly be because Korea and Asia for that matter has [sic] not had...a noticeable impact on the shaping of Western culture, and Korea has had unfortunately little culture of its own?

Who cares about Korea, Ms. Kim?...And what enduring contributions has the Black culture, both here in the US and on the continent contributed to the world, and mankind? I'm from a culture, Ms. Kim, who put a man on the moon 23 years ago, who established medical schools to train doctors to perform open heart surgery, and...who created a language of music so that musicians, from Beethoven to the Beatles, could easily touch the world with their brilliance forever and ever and ever. Perhaps the dominant culture, whites obviously, "swept aside Chicanos... Latinos... African Americans... Koreans," because they haven't contributed anything that made— be mindful of the cliche—a world of difference?

Koreans' favorite means of execution is decapitation...Ms. Kim, and others like her, came here to escape such injustice. Then they whine at riots to which they have contributed by their own fanning of flames of discontent....Yes! Let us all study more about Oriental culture! Let us put matters into proper perspective.

Fanatical multiculturalists like you expect a country whose dominant culture has been formed and influenced by Europe..., nearly 80%

of her population consisting of persons whose ancestry is European, to include the history of every ethnic group who has ever lived here. I truly feel sorry for you. You and your bunch need to realize that white Americans are not racists....We would love to get along, but not at the expense of our own culture and heritage.

Kim's axe-to-grind confirms the utter futility of race-relations—the races were never meant to live together. We don't get along and never will....Whats [sic] needed is to divide the United States up along racial lines so that life here can finally become livable.

What seemed to anger some people the most was their idea that, although they worked hard, people of color were seeking handouts and privileges because of their race, and the thought of an ungrateful Asian American siding with African Americans, presumably against whites, was infuriating. How dare I "bite the hand that feeds" me by siding with the champion "whiners who cry 'racism'" because to do so is the last refuge of the "terminally incompetent"?

The racial health in this country won't improve until minorities stop erecting "me first" barriers and strive to be Americans, not African Americans or Asian Americans expecting privileges.

Ms. Kim wants preferential treatment that immigrants from Greece-to-Sweden have not enjoyed....Even the Chinese...have not created any special problems for themselves or other Americans. Soon those folk are going to express their own resentments to the insatiable demands of the Blacks and other colored peoples, including the wetbacks from Mexico who sneak into this country then pilfer it for all they can.

The Afroderived citizens of Los Angeles and the Asiatic derivatives were not suffering a common imposition....The Asiatics are trying to build their success. The Africans are sucking at the teats of entitlement.

As is usual with racists, most of the writers of these hate letters saw only themselves in their notions about Korea, America, Korean Americans, African Americans. They felt that their own sense of American identity was being threatened and that they were being blamed as individuals for U.S. racism. One man, adept at manipulating various fonts on his word processor, imposed his preconceptions on my words:

Let me read between the lines of your little hate message:
...."The roots...stretch far back into the corridors of corporate and government offices in Los Angeles, Sacramento, and Washington, D.C."
All white America and all American institutions are to blame for racism.
...."I still want to believe the promise is real."
I have the savvy to know that the American ideals of freedom and justice are a joke but if you want to give me what I want I'm willing to make concessions.
Ms. Kim,...if you want to embody the ignorant, the insecure, and the emotionally immature, that's your right! Just stop preaching hate and please, please, quit whining.
Sincerely, A proud White American teaching my children not to be prejudicial

Especially since my essay had been subdued and intensely personal, I had not anticipated the fury it would provoke. I never thought that readers would write over my words with their own. The very fact that I used words, and English words at that, particularly incensed some: one letter writer complained about my use of words and phrases like "mani-festation" and "zero-sum game," and "suzerain relationship," which is the only way to describe Korea's relationship with China during the T'ang Dynasty. "Not more than ten people in the USA know what [these words] mean," he wrote. "You are on an ego trip." I wondered if it made him particularly angry that an Asian American had used those English words, or if he would make such a comment to George Will or Jane Bryant Quinn.

35   Clearly I had encountered part of America's legacy, the legacy that insists on silencing certain voices and erasing certain presences, even if it means deportation, internment, and outright murder. I should not have been surprised by what happened in Koreatown or by the ignorance and hatred expressed in the letters to *Newsweek*, any more than African Americans should have been surprised by the Rodney King verdict. Perhaps the news media, which constituted *sa-i-ku* as news, as an extraordinary event in no way continuous with our everyday lives, made us forget for a moment that as people of color many of us simultaneously inhabit two Americas: the America of our dreams and the America of our experience.

Who among us does not cling stubbornly to the America of our dreams, the promise of a multicultural democracy where our cultures and our differences might be affirmed instead of distorted in an effort to destroy us?

After *sa-i-ku,* I was able to catch glimpses of this America of my dreams because I received other letters that expressed another American legacy. Some people identified themselves as Norwegian or Irish Americans interested in combating racism. Significantly, while most of the angry mail had been sent not to me but to *Newsweek*, almost all of the sympathetic mail, particularly the letters from African Americans, came directly to me. Many came from Korean Americans who were glad that one of their number had found a vehicle for self-expression. Others were from Chinese and Japanese Americans who wrote that they had had similar experiences and feelings. Several were written in shaky longhand by women fervently wishing for peace and understanding among people of all races. A Native American from Nashville wrote a long description of cases of racism against African, Asian, and Native Americans in the U.S. criminal-justice system. A large number of letters came from African Americans, all of them supportive and sympathetic—from judges and professors who wanted better understanding between Africans and Koreans to poets and laborers who scribbled their notes in pencil while on breaks at work. One man identified himself as a Los Angeles African American whose uncle had married a Korean woman. He stated that as a black man in America, he knew what other people feel when they face injustice. He ended his letter apologizing for his spelling and grammar mistakes and asking for materials to read on Asian Americans. The most touching letter I received was written by a prison inmate who had served twelve years of a 35-to-70-year sentence for armed robbery during which no physical injuries occurred. He wrote:

I've been locked in these prisons going on 12 years now…and since being here I have studied fully the struggles of not just blacks, but all people of color. I am a true believer of helping "your" people "first," but also the helping of all people no matter where there at or the color of there skin. But I must be truthful, my struggle and assistance is truly on the side of people of color like ourselves. But just a few years ago I didn't think like this.

I thought that if you wasn't black, then you was the enemy, but…many years of this prison madness and much study and research changed all of this….[I]t's not with each other, blacks against Koreans or Koreans against blacks. No, this is not what it's about. Our struggle(s) are truly one in the same. What happened in L.A. during the riot really hurt me, because it was no way that blacks was suppose to do the things to your people, my people (Koreans) that they did. You're my sister, our people are my people. Even though our culture may be somewhat different, and even though we may worship our God(s) different…white-Amerikkka [doesn't] separate us. They look at us all the same. Either you're white, or you're wrong….I'm just writing you to let you know that, you're my sister, your people's struggle are my people's struggle.

This is the ground I need to claim now for Korean American resistance and recovery, so that we can become American without dying of *han*.

Although the sentiments expressed in these letters seemed to break down roughly along racial lines—that is, all writers who were identifiably people of color wrote in support—and one might become alarmed at the depth of the divisions they imply, I like to think that I have experienced the desire of many Americans, especially Americans of color, to do as Rodney King pleaded on the second day of *sa-i-ku:* "We're all stuck here for awhile….Let's try to work it out."

40   In my view, it's important for us to think about *all* of what Rodney King said and not just the words "we all can get along," which have

been depoliticized and transformed into a Disneyesque catchphrase for Pat Boone songs and roadside billboards in Los Angeles. It seems to me the emphasis is on the being "stuck here for awhile" together as we await "our day in court."

Like the African American man who wrote from prison, the African American man who had been brutally beaten by white police might have felt the desire to "love everybody," but he had to amend—or rectify—that wish. He had to speak last about loving "people of color." The impulse to "love everybody" was there, but the conditions were not right. For now, the most practical and progressive agenda may be people of color trying to "work it out."

FINDING COMMUNITY THROUGH NATIONAL CONSCIOUSNESS

The place where Korean and American legacies converge for Korean Americans is the exhortation to "go home to where you belong."

One of the letters I received was from a Korean American living in Chicago. He had read a translation of my essay in a Korean language newspaper. "Although you were born in the U.S.A.," he wrote, noticing what none of the white men who ordered me to go back to "my" country had, "your ethnical background and your complexion belong to Korea. It is time to give up your U.S. citizenship and go to Korea."

Some ruined merchants are claiming that they will pull up stakes and return to Korea, but I know that this is not possible for most of them. Even if their stores had not been destroyed, even if they were able to sell their businesses and take the proceeds to Korea, most of them would not have enough to buy a home or business there, since both require total cash up front. Neither would they be able to find work in the society they left behind because it is plagued by recession, repression, and fierce economic competition.

45   Going back to Korea. The dream of going back to Korea fed the spirit of my father, who came to Chicago in 1926 and lived in the United States for 63 years, during which time he never became a U.S. citizen, at first because the law did not allow it and later because he did not want to.

He kept himself going by believing that he would return to Korea in triumph one day. Instead, he died in Oakland at 88. Only his remains returned to Korea, where we buried him in accordance with his wishes.

Hasn't the dream of going back home to where you belong sustained most of America's unwanted at one time or another, giving meaning to lives of toil and making it possible to endure other people's hatred and rejection? Isn't the attempt to find community through national consciousness natural for people refused an American identity because racism does not give them that choice?

Korean national consciousness, the resolve to resist and fight back when threatened with extermination, was all that could be called upon when the Korean Americans in Los Angeles found themselves abandoned. They joined together to guard each other's means of livelihood with guns, relying on Korean-language radio and newspapers to communicate with and help each other. On the third day after the outbreak of violence, more than 30,000 Korean Americans gathered for a peace march in downtown L.A. in what was perhaps the largest and most quickly organized mass mobilization in Asian American history. Musicians in white, the color of mourning, beat traditional Korean drums in sorrow, anger, and celebration of community, a call to arms like a collective heartbeat. I believe that the mother of Edward Song Lee, the Los Angeles–born college student mistaken for a looter and shot to death in the streets, has been able to persevere in great part because of the massive outpouring of sympathy expressed by the Korean American community that shared and understood her *han*.

I have been critical lately of cultural nationalism as detrimental to Korean Americans, especially Korean American women, because it operates on exclusions and fosters intolerance and uniformity of thought while stifling self-criticism and encouraging sacrifice, even to the point of suicide. But *sa-i-ku* makes me think again: what remains for those who are left to stand alone? If Korean Americans refuse to be victims or political pawns in the U.S. while rejecting the

exhortation that we go back to Korea where we belong, what will be our weapons of choice?

In the darkest days of Japanese colonial rule, even after being stripped of land and of all economic means of survival, Koreans were threatened with total erasure when the colonizers rewrote Korean history, outlawed the Korean language, forced the subjugated people to worship the Japanese emperor, and demanded that they adopt Japanese names. One of the results of these cultural-annihilation policies was Koreans' fierce insistence on the sanctity of Korean national identity that persists to this day. In this context, it is not difficult to understand why nationalism has been the main refuge of Koreans and Korean Americans.

50   While recognizing the potential dangers of nationalism as a weapon, I for one am not ready to respond to the antiessentialists' call to relinquish my Korean American identity. It is easy enough for the French and Germans to call for a common European identity and an end to nationalisms, but what of the peoples suppressed and submerged while France and Germany exercised their national prerogatives? I am mindful of the argument that the resurgence of nationalism in Europe is rooted in historical and contemporary political and economic inequality among the nations of Europe. Likewise, I have noticed that many white Americans do not like to think of themselves as belonging to a race, even while thinking of people of color almost exclusively in terms of race. In the same way, many men think of themselves as "human beings" and of women as the ones having a gender. Thus crime, small businesses, and all Korean-African American interactions are seen and interpreted through the lens of race in the same dominant culture that angrily rejects the use of the racial lens for viewing yellow/white or black/white interactions and insists suddenly that we are all "American" whenever we attempt to assert our identity as people of color. It is far easier for Anglo Americans to call for an end to cultural nationalisms than for Korean Americans to give up national consciousness, which makes it possible to survive the vicious racism that would deny our existence as either Korean Americans or Americans.

Is there anything of use to us in Korean nationalism? During one thousand years of Chinese suzerainty, the Korean ruling elite developed a philosophy called *sadaejui,* or reliance of the weak on the strong. In direct opposition to this way of thought is what is called *jaju* or *juche sasang,* or self-determination. Both *sadaejui* and *juche sasang* are ways of dealing with unequal power relationships and resisting the transformation of one's homeland into a battlefield for others, but *sadaejui* has never worked any better for Koreans than it has for any minority group in America. *Juche sasang,* on the other hand, has the kind of oppositional potential needed in the struggle against silence and invisibility. From Korean national consciousness, we can recover this fierce refusal to accept subjugation, which is the first step in the effort to build community, so that we can work with others to challenge the forces that would have us annihilate each other instead of our mutual oppression.

What is clear is that we cannot "become American" without dying of *han* unless we think about community in new ways. Self-determination does not mean living alone. At least for now, that may mean mining the rich and haunted lode of Korean national consciousness while we struggle to understand how our fate is entwined with the fate of others lying prostrate before the triumphal procession of the winners of History. During the past fifteen years or so, many young Korean nationalists have been studying the legacies of colonialism and imperialism that they share with peoples in many Asian, African, and Latin American nations. At the same time that we take note of this work, we can also try to understand how nationalism and feminism can be worked together to demystify the limitations and reductiveness of each as a weapon of empowerment. If Korean national consciousness is ever to be such a weapon for us, we must use it to create a new kind of nationalism-in-internationalism to help us call forth a culture of survival and recovery, so that our *han* might be released and we might be freed to dream fiercely of different possibilities.

NOTE

1. I am deeply indebted to the activists in the Los Angeles Korean American community, especially Bong Hwan Kim and Eui-Young Yu, whose courage and commitment to the empowerment of the disenfranchised, whether African American, Latino, or Korean American, during this crisis in Los Angeles has been a continuous source of inspiration for me. I would also like to thank Barry Maxwell for critically reading this manuscript and offering many insightful suggestions; my niece Sujin Kim, David Lloyd, and Caridad Souza for their encouragement; and Mia Chung for her general assistance.

SUGGESTIONS FOR DISCUSSION

1. Elaine H. Kim describes *han* as a Korean term for "the sorrow and anger that grow from the accumulated experiences of oppression." Why do you think has she titled her chapter "Home Is Where the 'Han' Is"? How does the notion of *han* inform Kim's line of thought throughout the chapter?

2. Kim presents the Korean American community as one that is "squeezed between black and white and also between U.S. and South Korean political agendas." Explain what Kim means by this "squeeze." What are the effects of this "interstitial position [of Korean Americans] in the American discourse of race"? In what sense have African American and Korean American conflicts been used to justify the racial divisions in contemporary America? How and by whom?

3. Kim compares the television coverage of South Korean demonstrations for constitutional reform and free elections with the coverage of the prodemocratic Solidarity movement in Poland. How does she explain the differences in coverage? How in a more general sense

does the media represent minority communities of Asian Americans, African Americans, Latinos, and so on? What are the effects of these representations on social, cultural, and political life in contemporary America?

SUGGESTIONS FOR WRITING

1. Kim suggests that minority groups such as Korean Americans are silenced or incorporated into a drama of interethnic conflict (thereby showing how all humans are "naturally" racist) by the media. Write an essay that analyzes how a particular minority or ethnic group is represented by the media—on the news, in films, or in television shows. What are the social, cultural, and political effects of such representations?

2. Use the letters from *Newsweek* readers that Kim quotes to write an essay that analyzes the responses that she received to her "My Turn" column, which appeared in *Newsweek* on May 18, 1992. First of all, go to the library and read the column. Then reread the responses that she quotes in the essay, both positive and negative. The point of your essay is not simply to dismiss (or denounce) the responses that are racist or ethnocentric, though some of them certainly are. The point is to identify what the letters indicate about deeply entrenched beliefs and attitudes about the nature of American culture, the position of immigrants, the multicultural debates, and so on. Consider how readers are making sense of the realities of contemporary America.

3. Notice how Kim develops her own position of being "squeezed," caught between the lessons that she learned from the African American–led civil rights movement and her feelings of dismay and sorrow at anti-Korean sentiments expressed by African Americans in Los Angeles. Along the same lines, she is also caught between her desire to affirm her Korean identify and her anger that the South Korean media depicted the Los Angeles uprising as "savage African Americans attacking innocent Koreans for no reason." Use Kim's essay as a model to write an essay where you describe and analyze how you are, or have been, in some sense "squeezed," caught in the middle. In this essay, explain carefully how you were caught in the middle, between which communities and contending forces. Explain also what conflicting loyalties you experienced and what you did (or did not do) to deal with the "squeeze" that you felt.

HOW TO TAME A WILD TONGUE

Gloria Anzaldúa

Gloria Anzaldúa writes in a language that grows out of the multiple cultures in the American Southwest—a mosaic of English (both standard and slang), Spanish (both Castilian and Mexican), northern Mexican and Chicano Spanish dialects, Tex-Mex, *Pachuco* (the vernacular of urban zoot suiters), and the Aztec language Nahuatl. The following selection is a chapter from her book, *Borderlands/La Frontera* (1987). As the title of her book indicates, Anzaldúa sees herself as a "border woman." "I grew up between two cultures," she says, "the Mexican (with a heavy Indian influence) and the Anglo (as a member of a colonized people in our own territory). I have been straddling that *tejas*-Mexican border, and others, all my life." Anzaldúa's "borderland" refers to those places "where two or more cultures edge each other, where people of different races occupy the same territory, where under, lower, middle, and upper classes touch, where the space between two individuals shrinks with intimacy."

SUGGESTION FOR READING As you read, you will notice how Gloria Anzaldua combines English and Spanish in a sentence or a paragraph. Consider the effects of Anzaldua's prose and how it locates you as a reader on the border where two cultures and languages touch.

1   We're going to have to control your tongue," the dentist says, pulling out all the metal from my mouth. Silver bits plop and tinkle into the basin. My mouth is a motherlode. The dentist is cleaning out my roots. I get a whiff of the stench when I gasp. "I can't cap that tooth yet, you're still draining," he says.

"We're going to have to do something about your tongue," I hear the anger rising in his voice. My tongue keeps pushing out the wads of cotton, pushing back the drills, the long thin needles. "I've never seen anything as strong or as stubborn," he says. And I think, how do you tame a wild tongue, train it to be quiet, how do you bridle and saddle it? How do you make it lie down?

> Who is to say that robbing a people of its language is less violent than war?
>
> *Ray Gwyn Smith[1]*

I remember being caught speaking Spanish at recess—that was good for three licks on the knuckles with a sharp ruler. I remember being sent to the corner of the classroom for "talking back" to the Anglo teacher when all I was trying to do was tell her how to pronounce my name. "If you want to be American, speak 'American.' If you don't like it, go back to Mexico where you belong."

"I want you to speak English. *Pa' hallar buen trabajo tienes que saber hablar el inglés bien. Qué vale toda tu educatión si todavía hablas inglés con un* 'accent,'" my mother would say, mortified that I spoke English like a Mexican. At Pan American University, I and all Chicano students were required to take two speech classes. Their purpose: to get rid of our accents.

5   Attacks on one's form of expression with the intent to censor are a violation of the First Amendment. *El Anglo con care de inocente nos arrancó la lengua.* Wild tongues can't be tamed, they can only be cut out.

OVERCOMING THE TRADITION OF SILENCE

Ahogadas, escupimos el oscuro. Peleando con nuestra propia sombra el silencio nos sepulta.

En boca cerrada no entran moscas. "Flies don't enter a closed mouth" is a saying I kept hearing when I was a child. *Ser habladora* was to be a gossip and a liar, to talk too much. *Muchachitas bien criadas,* well-bred girls don't answer back. *Es una falta de respeto* to talk back to one's mother or father. I remember one of the sins I'd recite to the priest in the confession box the few times I went to confession: talking back to my mother, *hablar pa' 'tras, repelar. Hocicona, repelona, chismosa,* having a big mouth, questioning, carrying tales are all signs of being *mal criada.* In my culture they are all words that are derogatory if applied to women—I've never heard them applied to men.

The first time I heard two women, a Puerto Rican and a Cuban, say the word "*nosotras,*" I was shocked. I had not known the word existed. Chicanas use *nosotros* whether we're male or female. We are robbed of our female being by the masculine plural. Language is a male discourse.

> And our tongues have become dry the wilderness has dried out our tongues and we have forgotten speech.
>
> *Irena Klepfisz[2]*

Even our own people, other Spanish speakers *nos quieren poner candados en la boca.* They would hold us back with their bag of *reglas de academia.*

OYÉ COMO LADRA: EL LENGUAJE DE LA FRONTERA

Quien tiene boca se equivoca.

Mexican saying

"*Pocho,* cultural traitor, you're speaking the oppressor's language by speaking English, you're ruining the Spanish language," I have been accused by various Latinos and Latinas. Chicano Spanish is considered by the purist and by most Latinos deficient, a mutilation of Spanish.

10   But Chicano Spanish is a border tongue which developed naturally. Change, *evolución, enriquecimiento de palabras nuevas por invención o adopción* have created variants of Chicano Spanish, *un nuevo lenguaje. Un lenguaje que corresponde a un modo de vivir.* Chicano Spanish is not incorrect, it is a living language.

For a people who are neither Spanish nor live in a country in which Spanish is the first language; for a people who live in a country in which English is the reigning tongue but who are not Anglo; for a people who cannot entirely identify with either standard (formal, Castilian) Spanish nor standard English, what recourse is left to them but to create their own language? A language which they can connect their identity to, one capable of communicating the realities and values true to themselves—a language with terms that are neither *español ni inglés,* but both. We speak a patois, a forked tongue, a variation of two languages.

Chicano Spanish sprang out of the Chicanos' need to identify ourselves as a distinct people. We need a language with which we could communicate with ourselves, a secret language. For some of us, language is a homeland closer than the Southwest—for many Chicanos today live in the Midwest and the East. And because we are a complex, heterogeneous people, we speak many languages. Some of the languages we speak are

1. Standard English
2. Working-class and slang English
3. Standard Spanish
4. Standard Mexican Spanish
5. North Mexican Spanish dialect
6. Chicano Spanish (Texas, New Mexico, Arizona, and California have regional variations)
7. Tex-Mex
8. *Pachuco* (called *caló*)

My "home" tongues are the languages I speak with my sister and brothers, with my friends. They are the last five listed, with 6 and 7 being closest to my heart. From school, the media, and job situations, I've picked up standard and working class English. From Mamagrande Locha and from reading Spanish and Mexican literature, I've picked up Standard Spanish and Standard Mexican Spanish. From *los recién llegados,* Mexican immigrants, and *braceros,* I learned the North Mexican dialect. With Mexicans I'll try to speak either Standard Mexican Spanish or the North Mexican dialect. From my parents and Chicanos living in the Valley, I picked up Chicano Texas Spanish, and I speak it with my mom, younger brother (who married a Mexican and who rarely mixes Spanish with English), aunts, and older relatives.

With Chicanas from *Nuevo México* or *Arizona* I will speak Chicano Spanish a little, but often they don't understand what I'm saying. With most California Chicanas I speak entirely in English (unless I forget). When I first moved to San Francisco, I'd rattle off something in Spanish, unintentionally embarrassing them. Often it is only with another Chicana *tejano* that I can talk freely.

15   Words distorted by English are known as anglicisms or *pochismos.* The *pocho* is an anglicized Mexican or American of Mexican origin who speaks Spanish with an accent characteristic of North Americans and who distorts and reconstructs the language according to the influence of English.[3] Tex-Mex, or Spanglish, comes most naturally to me. I may switch back and forth from English to Spanish in the same sentence or in the same word. With my sister and my brother Nune and with Chicano *tejano* contemporaries I speak in Tex-Mex.

From kids and people my own age I picked up *Pachuco*. *Pachuco* (the language of the zoot suiters) is a language of rebellion, both against Standard Spanish and Standard English. It is a secret language. Adults of the culture and outsiders cannot understand it. It is made up of slang words from both English and Spanish. *Ruca* means girl or woman, *vato* means guy or dude, *chale* means no, *simón* means yes, *churro* is sure, talk is *periquiar, pigionear* means petting, *que gacho* means how nerdy, *ponte águila* means watch out, death is called *la pelona*. Through lack of practice and not having others who can speak it, I've lost most of the *Pachuco* tongue.

CHICANO SPANISH

Chicanos, after 250 years of Spanish/Anglo colonization, have developed significant differences in the Spanish we speak. We collapse two adjacent vowels into a single syllable and sometimes shift the stress in certain words such as *maíz/maiz, cohete/cuete*. We leave out certain consonants when they appear between vowels: *lado/lao, mojado/mojao*. Chicanos from South Texas pronounce *f* as *j* as in *jue* (*fue*). Chicanos use "archaisms," words that are no longer in the Spanish language, words that have been evolved out. We say *semos, truje, haiga, ansina,* and *naiden*. We retain the "archaic" *j,* as in *jalar,* that derives from an earlier *h* (the French *halar* or the Germanic *halon* which was lost to standard Spanish in the sixteenth century), but which is still found in several regional dialects such as the one spoken in South Texas. (Due to geography, Chicanos from the Valley of South Texas were cut off linguistically from other Spanish speakers. We tend to use words that the Spaniards brought over from Medieval Spain. The majority of the Spanish colonizers in Mexico and the Southwest came from Extremadura—Hernán Cortés was one of them—and Andalucía. Andalucians pronounce *ll* like a *y,* and their *d*'s tend to be absorbed by adjacent vowels: *tirado* becomes *tirao*. They brought *el lenguaje popular, dialectos y regionalismos*.)[4]

Chicanos and other Spanish speakers also shift *ll* to *y* and *z* to *s*.[5] We leave out initial syllables, saying *tar* for *estar, toy* for *estoy, hora* for

ahora (*cubanos* and *puertorriqueños* also leave out initial letters of some words). We also leave out the final syllable such as *pa* for *para*. The intervocalic *y,* the *ll* as in *tortilla, ella, botella,* gets replaced by *tortia* or *tortiya, ea, botea*. We add an additional syllable at the beginning of certain words: *atocar* for *tocar, agastar* for *gastar*. Sometimes we'll say *lavaste las vacijas,* other times *lavates* (substituting the *ates* verb endings for the *aste*).

We used anglicisms, words borrowed from English: *bola* from ball, *carpeta* from carpet, *máchina de lavar* (instead of *lavadora*) from washing machine. Tex-Mex argot, created by adding a Spanish sound at the beginning or end of an English word such as *cookiar* for cook, *watchar* for watch, *parkiar* for park, and *rapiar* for rape, is the result of the pressures on Spanish speakers to adapt to English.

20   We don't use the word *vosotros/as* or its accompanying verb form. We don't say *claro* (to mean yes), *imagínate,* or *me emociona,* unless we picked up Spanish from Latinas, out of a book, or in a classroom. Other Spanish-speaking groups are going through the same, or similar, development in their Spanish.

LINGUISTIC TERRORISM

Deslenguadas. Somos los del español deficiente. We are your linguistic nightmare, your linguistic aberration, your linguistic *mestisaje,* the subject of your *burla*. Because we speak with tongues of fire we are culturally crucified. Racially, culturally, and linguistically *somos huérfanos*—we speak an orphan tongue.

Chicanas who grew up speaking Chicano Spanish have internalized the belief that we speak poor Spanish. It is illegitimate, a bastard language. And because we internalize how our language has been used against us by the dominant culture, we use our language differences against each other.

Chicana feminists often skirt around each other with suspicion and hesitation. For the longest time I couldn't figure it out. Then it dawned on me. To be close to another Chicana is like looking into the mirror. We are afraid of what we'll see there. *Pena*. Shame. Low estimation of self. In childhood we are told that our language is wrong. Repeated attacks on our native tongue diminish our sense of self. The attacks continue throughout our lives.

Chicanas feel uncomfortable talking in Spanish to Latinas, afraid of their censure. Their language was not outlawed in their countries. They had a whole lifetime of being immersed in their native tongue; generations, centuries in which Spanish was a first language, taught in school, heard on radio and TV, and read in the newspaper.

If a person, Chicana or Latina, has a low estimation of my native tongue, she also has a low estimation of me. Often with *mexicanas y latinas* we'll speak English as a neutral language. Even among Chicanas we tend to speak English at parties or conferences. Yet, at the same time, we're afraid the other will think we're *agringadas* because we don't speak Chicano Spanish. We oppress each other trying to out-Chicano each other, vying to be the "real" Chicanas, to speak like Chicanos. There is no one Chicano language just as there is no one Chicano experience. A monolingual Chicana whose first language is English or Spanish is just as much a Chicana as one who speaks several variants of Spanish. A Chicana from Michigan or Chicago or Detroit is just as much a Chicana as one from the Southwest. Chicano Spanish is as diverse linguistically as it is regionally.

25   By the end of this century, Spanish speakers will comprise the biggest minority group in the United States, a country where students in high schools and colleges are encouraged to take French classes because French is considered more "cultured." But for a language to remain alive it must be used.[6] By the end of this century English, and not Spanish, will be the mother tongue of most Chicanos and Latinos.

So, if you want to really hurt me, talk badly about my language. Ethnic identity is twin skin to linguistic identity—I am my language. Until I can take pride in my language, I cannot take pride in myself. Until I can accept as legitimate Chicano Texas Spanish, Tex-Mex, and all the other languages I speak, I cannot accept the legitimacy of myself. Until I am free to write bilingually and to switch codes without having always to translate, while I still have to speak English or

Spanish when I would rather speak Spanglish, and as long as I have to accommodate the English speakers rather than having them accommodate me, my tongue will be illegitimate.

I will no longer be made to feel ashamed of existing. I will have my voice: Indian, Spanish, white. I will have my serpent's tongue—my woman's voice, my sexual voice, my poet's voice. I will overcome the tradition of silence.

My fingers
move sly against your palm
Like women everywhere, we speak in code...

Melanie Kaye/Kantrowitz[7]

"VISTAS," CORRIDOS, Y COMIDA: MY NATIVE TONGUE

In the 1960s, I read my first Chicano novel. It was *City of Night* by John Rechy, a gay Texan, son of a Scottish father and a Mexican mother. For days I walked around in stunned amazement that a Chicano could write and could get published. When I read *I Am Joaquín*[8] I was surprised to see a bilingual book by a Chicano in print. When I saw poetry written in Tex-Mex for the first time, a feeling of pure joy flashed through me. I felt like we really existed as a people. In 1971, when I started teaching High School English to Chicano students, I tried to supplement the required texts with works by Chicanos, only to be reprimanded and forbidden to do so by the principal. He claimed that I was supposed to teach "American" and English literature. At the risk of being fired, I swore my students to secrecy and slipped in Chicano short stories, poems, a play. In graduate school, while working toward a Ph.D., I had to "argue" with one adviser after the other, semester after semester, before I was allowed to make Chicano literature an area of focus.

Even before I read books by Chicanos or Mexicans, it was the Mexican movies I saw at the drive-in—the Thursday night special of $1.00 a carload—that gave me a sense of belonging. *"Vámonos a las vistas,"* my mother would call out and we'd all—grandmother, brothers, sister, and cousins—squeeze into the car. We'd wolf down cheese and bologna white bread sandwiches while watching Pedro Infante in melodramatic tearjerkers like *Nosotros los pobres,* the first "real" Mexican movie (that was not an imitation of European movies). I remember seeing *Cuando los hijos se van* and surmising that all Mexican movies played up the love a mother has for her children and what ungrateful sons and daughters suffer when they are not devoted to their mothers. I remember the singing-type "westerns" of Jorge Negrete and Miquel Aceves Mejía. When watching Mexican movies, I felt a sense of homecoming as well as alienation. People who were to amount to something didn't go to Mexican movies, or bailes, or tune their radios to *bolero, rancherita,* and *corrido* music.

30   The whole time I was growing up, there was *norteño* music sometimes called North Mexican border music, or Tex-Mex music, or Chicano music, or *cantina* (bar) music. I grew up listening to *conjuntos,* three- or four-piece bands made up of folk musicians playing guitar, *bajo sexto,* drums, and button accordion, which Chicanos had borrowed from the German immigrants who had come to Central Texas and Mexico to farm and build breweries. In the Rio Grande Valley, Steve Jordan and Little Joe Hernández were popular, and Flaco Jiménez was the accordion king. The rhythms of Tex-Mex music are those of the polka, also adapted from the Germans, who in turn had borrowed the polka from the Czechs and Bohemians.

I remember the hot, sultry evenings when *corridos*—songs of love and death on the Texas-Mexican borderlands—reverberated out of cheap amplifiers from the local *cantinas* and wafted in through my bedroom window.

Corridos first became widely used along the South Texas/Mexican border during the early conflict between Chicanos and Anglos. The *corridos* are usually about Mexican heroes who do valiant deeds against the Anglo oppressors. Pancho Villa's song, "*La cucaracha,*" is the most famous one. *Corridos* of John F. Kennedy and his death are still very popular in the Valley. Older Chicanos remember Lydia Mendoza, one of the great bor-

der *corrido* singers who was called *la Gloria de Tejas.* Her "*El tango negro,*" sung during the Great Depression, made her a singer of the people. The ever-present *corridos* narrated one hundred years of border history, bringing news of events as well as entertaining. These folk musicians and folk songs are our chief cultural mythmakers, and they made our hard lives seem bearable.

I grew up feeling ambivalent about our music. Country-western and rock-and-roll had more status. In the fifties and sixties, for the slightly educated and *agringado* Chicanos, there existed a sense of shame at being caught listening to our music. Yet I couldn't stop my feet from thumping to the music, could not stop humming the words, nor hide from myself the exhilaration I felt when I heard it.

There are more subtle ways that we internalize identification, especially in the forms of images and emotions. For me food and certain smells are tied to my identity, to my homeland. Woodsmoke curling up to an immense blue sky; woodsmoke perfuming my grandmother's clothes, her skin. The stench of cow manure and the yellow patches on the ground; the crack of a .22 rifle and the reek of cordite. Homemade white cheese sizzling in a pan, melting inside a folded *tortilla.* My sister Hilda's hot, spicy *menudo, chile colorado* making it deep red, pieces of *panza* and hominy floating on top. My brother Carito barbequing *fajitas* in the backyard. Even now and 3,000 miles away, I can see my mother spicing the ground beef, pork, and venison with chile. My mouth salivates at the thought of the hot steaming *tamales* I would be eating if I were home.

SI LE PREGUNTAS A MI MAMÁ, "¿QUÉ ERES?"

Identity is the essential core of who we are as individuals, the conscious experience of the self inside.

Gershen Kaufman[9]

35   *Nosotros los* Chicanos straddle the borderlands. On one side of us, we are constantly exposed to the Spanish of the Mexicans, on the

other side we hear the Anglos' incessant clamoring so that we forget our language. Among ourselves we don't say *nosotros los americanos, o nosotros los españoles, o nosotros los hispanos*. We say *nosotros los mexicanos* (by *mexicanos* we do not mean citizens of Mexico; we do not mean a national identity, but a racial one). We distinguish between *mexicanos del otro lado* and *mexicanos de este lado*. Deep in our hearts we believe that being Mexican has nothing to do with which country one lives in. Being Mexican is a state of soul—not one of mind, not one of citizenship. Neither eagle nor serpent, but both. And like the ocean, neither animal respects borders.

Dime con quien andas y te diré quien eres.

(Tell me who your friends are and I'll tell you who you are.)

Mexican saying

Si le preguntas a mi mamá, "¿Qué eres?" te dirá, "Soy mexicana." My brothers and sister say the same. I sometimes will answer "soy mexicana" and at others will say "soy Chicana" o "soy tejana." But I identified as "Raza" before I ever identified as "mexicana" or "Chicana."

As a culture, we call ourselves Spanish when referring to ourselves as a linguistic group and when copping out. It is then that we forget our predominant Indian genes. We are 70–80 percent Indian.[10] We call ourselves Hispanic[11] or Spanish American or Latin American or Latin when linking ourselves to other Spanish-speaking peoples of the Western hemisphere and when copping out. We call ourselves Mexican American[12] to signify we are neither Mexican nor American, but more the noun "American" than the adjective "Mexican" (and when copping out).

Chicanos and other people of color suffer economically for not acculturating. This voluntary (yet forced) alienation makes for psychological conflict, a kind of dual identity—we don't identify with the Anglo-American cultural values and we don't totally identify with the Mexican cultural values. We are a synergy of two cultures with various degrees of Mexicanness or Angloness. I have so internalized the borderland conflict that some-

times I feel like one cancels out the other and we are zero, nothing, no one. *A veces no soy nada ni nadie. Pero hasta cuando no lo soy, lo soy.*

When not copping out, when we know we are more than nothing, we call ourselves Mexican, referring to race and ancestry; *mestizo* when affirming both our Indian and Spanish (but we hardly ever own our Black) ancestry; Chicano when referring to a politically aware people born and/or raised in the United States; *Raza* when referring to Chicanos; *tejanos* when we are Chicanos from Texas.

40   Chicanos did not know we were a people until 1965 when Cesar Chavez and the farmworkers united and *I Am Joaquín* was published and *la Raza Unida* party was formed in Texas. With that recognition, we became a distinct people. Something momentous happened to the Chicano soul—we became aware of our reality and acquired a name and a language (Chicano Spanish) that reflected that reality. Now that we had a name, some of the fragmented pieces began to fall together—who we were, what we were, how we had evolved. We began to get glimpses of what we might eventually become.

Yet the struggle of identities continues, the struggle of borders is our reality still. One day the inner struggle will cease and a true integration take place. In the mean-time, *tenémos que hacer la lucha. ¿Quién está protegiendo los ranchos de mi gente? ¿Quién está tratando de cerrar la fisura entre la india y el blanco en nuestra sangre? El Chicano, si, el Chicano que anda como un ladrón en su propia casa.*

Los Chicanos, how patient we seem, how very patient. There is the quiet of the Indian about us.[13] We know how to survive. When other races have given up their tongue we've kept ours. We know what it is to live under the hammer blow of the dominant *norteamericano* culture. But more than we count the blows, we count the days the weeks the years the centuries the aeons until the white laws and commerce and customs will rot in the deserts they've created, lie bleached. *Humildes* yet proud, *quietos* yet wild, *nosotros los mexicanos-Chicanos* will walk by the crumbling ashes as we go about our business. Stubborn, persevering, impenetrable as stone, yet possessing a malleability that renders us unbreakable, we, the *mestizas* and *mestizos,* will remain.

NOTES

1. Ray Gwyn Smith, *Moorland Is Cold Country,* unpublished book.
2. Irena Klepfisz, "*Di rayze aheym*/The Journey Home," in *The Tribe of Dina: A Jewish Women's Anthology,* Melanie Kaye/Kantrowitz and Irena Klepfisz, eds. (Montpelier, VT: Sinister Wisdom Books, 1986), 49.
3. R. C. Ortega, *Dialectologia Del Barrio,* trans. Hortencia S. Alwan (Los Angeles, CA: R. C. Ortega Publisher & Bookseller, 1977), 132.
4. Eduardo Hernández-Chávez, Andrew D. Cohen, and Anthony F. Beltramo, *El Lenguaje de los Chicanos: Regional and Social Characteristics of Language Used by Mexican Americans* (Arlington, VA: Center for Applied Linguistics, 1975), 39.
5. Hernández-Chávez, xvii.
6. Irena Klepfisz, "Secular Jewish Identity: Yidishkayt in America," in *The Tribe of Dina,* Kaye/Kantrowitz and Klepfisz, eds., 43.
7. Melanie Kaye/Kantrowitz, "Sign," in *We Speak in Code: Poems and Other Writings* (Pittsburgh, PA: Motheroot Publications, Inc., 1980), 85.
8. Rodolfo Gonzales, *I Am Joaquín/Yo Soy Joaquín* (New York, NY: Bantam Books, 1972). It was first published in 1967.
9. Gershen Kaufman, *Shame: The Power of Caring* (Cambridge, MA: Schenkman Books, Inc., 1980), 68.
10. John R. Chávez, *The Lost Land: The Chicano Images of the Southwest* (Albuquerque, NM: University of New Mexico Press, 1984), 88–90.
11. "Hispanic" is derived from *Hispanis* (*España,* a name given to the Iberian Peninsula in ancient times when it was a part of the Roman Empire) and is a term designated by the U.S. government to make it easier to handle us on paper.
12. The Treaty of Guadalupe Hidalgo created the Mexican American in 1848.
13. Anglos, in order to alleviate their guilt for dispossessing the Chicano, stressed the Spanish part of us and perpetrated the myth of the Spanish Southwest. We have accepted the fiction that we are Hispanic, that is Spanish, in order to accommodate ourselves to the dominant culture and its abhorrence of Indians. Chávez, 88–91.

SUGGESTIONS FOR DISCUSSION

1. Compare your experience of reading Gloria Anzaldúa's polyglot prose with the experiences of others in your class. As we have suggested, the purpose of Anzaldúa's mix of language is to recreate the conditions of the borderland, where the use of one language leaves out or excludes those who know only the other language. But what are readers to do with such prose? If you don't know Spanish, how did you try to make sense of the Spanish words and phrases Anzaldúa uses? Even if you do know Spanish, are you familiar with the terms that she draws from regional dialects? What does your experience reading "How to Tame a Wild Tongue" reveal to you about the nature of cultural encounters at the borderlands?

2. Anzaldúa has composed the chapter "How to Tame a Wild Tongue" like a mosaic, in which she juxtaposes seven separate sections without offering an overarching statement of purpose or meaning to unify the sections. At the same time, the sections do seem to go together in an associative, nonlinear way. Look back over the sections of the chapter to identify how (or whether) the separate parts work together to form a whole. What in your view is the principle of combination that links them together?

3. How is Anzaldúa's representation of the border similar to and different from the one you find in Amitava Kumar's "Passport Photos"?

SUGGESTIONS FOR WRITING

1. Write an essay describing and analyzing your experience reading "How to Tame a Wild Tongue." How do the mix of languages and the fragmentary character of the text put special demands on you as a reader? How and in what sense is this reading experience equivalent to what Anzaldúa calls the "borderland"? What does your position as a reader on the border reveal to you about the nature of encounters across cultures in multicultural America?

2. Write an essay that compares Anzaldúa's position as a *mestiza* of the borderlands to Elaine H. Kim's position as "squeezed" between Anglos and African Americans and Latinos. To what extent are their experiences similar? In what respects do they differ? Don't settle in your essay for just describing differences and similarities. The issue is how you explain what they have in common and what makes them different. What, in your view, is the significance of these similarities and differences?

3. Use Anzaldúa's chapter as a model to write your own essay about the contradictory and conflicting meanings of language use and cultural expression in your life. This assignment is meant to be an experiment in writing that asks you to emulate Anzaldúa in incorporating multiple voices, dialects, slangs, and languages and in composing by way of a collage that juxtaposes fragments of thought and experience instead of developing a linear piece of writing with a main point and supporting evidence. To develop ideas for this essay, you might begin by thinking of the different voices, musics, foods, and other cultural forms that are part of your experience, the conflicting ways of life that you have lived, and the multiple identities that you inhabit.

Case Study: The Politics of World English

In "English: Out to Conquer the World," an article that appeared in *U.S. News and World Report* (February 18, 1985), Susanna McBee presents a view of the role of English that is now commonplace. "English," she writes, "has become to the modern world what Latin was to the ancients, dominating the planet as the medium of exchange in science, technology, commerce, tourism, diplomacy, and pop culture. Indeed so wide is its sweep that 345 million people use English as their first language and an additional 400 million as their second."

There is little question that English has become a world language. It is the common language of many multinational corporations and international agencies as well as the medium for 80 percent of the information stored in computers world wide. What is not so clear, however, is exactly what the "domination" of English as a global language means for peoples, cultures, and other languages around the world. That is the question addressed in this case study.

Assembled here is a set of readings that will enable you to explore the meaning of English as a world language from several angles. First is Alastair Pennycock's analysis of the claims made on behalf of English, "Our Marvellous Tongue," and the responses of students he taught in Hong Kong to learning English as a second language. Then, a Perspectives feature appears that pairs the views of two important African writers, Chinua Achebe and Ngũgĩ wa Thiong'o, the first who writes in English and the second who writes in the African language Gĩkũyũ.

OUR MARVELLOUS TONGUE: The Wondrous Spread of English

Alastair Pennycock

Alastair Pennycock teaches critical applied linguistics at the University of Melbourne. The following reading consists of two excerpts from his book *English and the Discourses of Colonialism* (1998). In the first excerpt, he looks at the continuity of claims about the "wondrous spread of English" in the nineteenth and twentieth centuries. In the second, he looks at how the experiences of his students learning English in Hong Kong "seemed to replay colonial relations."

SUGGESTION FOR READING   Alastair Pennycock identifies three main arguments in praise of English. Make sure you underline or otherwise note each of the three. Notice how he evaluates these arguments. Then he presents the views of his students in Hong Kong. Pay attention here to the implications he draws from their writings about learning English.

1   The nineteenth century was a time of immense British confidence in their own greatness, and writing on English abounded with glorifications of English and its global spread. Guest (1838/1882) argued that English was 'rapidly becoming the great medium of civilization, the language of law and literature to the Hindoo, of commerce to the African, of religion to the scattered islands of the Pacific' (p. 703). Trench (1881, p. 44) quotes Jacob Grimm, the German linguist, as stating in 1832 that 'the English language ...may with all right be called a world-language; and, like the English people, appears destined hereafter to prevail with a sway more extensive even than its present over all the portions of the globe'. According to Read:

> Ours is the language of the arts and sciences, of trade and commerce, of civilization and religious liberty.... It is a store-house of the varied knowledge which brings a nation within the pale of civilization and Christianity.... Already it is the language of the Bible.... So prevalent is this language already become, as to betoken that it may soon become the language of international communication for the world.
>
> *(1849, p. 48, cited in Bailey, 1991, p. 116)*

Meiklejohn (1891, p. 6, cited in Crowley, 1989) stated the connection between Empire and the spread of English very explicitly: 'The sun never sets on the British dominions; the roll of the British drum encircles the globe with a belt of sound; and the familiar utterances of English speech are heard on every continent and island, in every sea and ocean, in the world' (cited in Crowley, 1989, p. 74). George suggested that:

> other languages will remain, but will remain only as the obscure Patois of the world, while English will become the grand medium for all the business of government, for commerce, for law, for science, for literature, for philosophy, and divinity. Thus it will really be a universal language for the great material and spiritual interests of mankind.
>
> *(1867, p. 6)*

For de Quincey, like George, it was a question not only of English spreading widely but also of replacing other languages: 'The English language is travelling fast towards the fulfillment of its destiny ..., running forward towards its ultimate mission of eating up, like Aaron's rod, all other languages' (de Quincey, 1862, pp. 149–50). Finally, some writers, such as Axon (1888) boldly predicted the course of this spread over the next century: 'it is as likely as anything prospective can be in human affairs, that the Englishry of 1980 will amount to about 1,000,000,000 souls.... [A]ll these people will speak the same language, read the same books, and be influenced by the same leading ideas' (Axon, 1888, p. 204; cited in Bailey, 1991, p. 113).

A similar tenor to discussions of English and its global spread can frequently be found today, though with a number of interesting developments. Although the fervent triumphalism that appears so evident in these earlier descriptions of the spread of Empire and English is a less acceptable aspect of more recent discourses on the spread of English, I would like to suggest that the same celebratory tone seems to underlie recent, supposedly neutral, descriptions of English. Thus, it is interesting to compare Rolleston's (1911) description of the spread of English with Crystal's (1987) from *The Cambridge Encyclopedia of Language*:

The British flag waves over more than one-fifth of the habitable globe, one-fourth of the human race acknowledge the sway of the British Monarch, more than one hundred princes render him allegiance. The English language is spoken by more people than that of any other race, it bids fair to become at some time the speech of the globe, and about one-half of the world's ocean shipping trade is yet in British hands.

(1911, p. 75)

English is used as an official or semi-official language in over 60 countries, and has a prominent place in a further 20. It is either dominant or well established in all six continents. It is the main language of books, newspapers, airports and air-traffic control, international business and academic conferences, science, technology, medicine, diplomacy, sports, international competitions, pop music, and advertising. Over two-thirds of the world's scientists write in English. Three quarters of the world's mail is written in English. Of all the information in the world's electronic retrieval systems, 80% is stored in English. English radio programmes are received by over 150 million in 120 countries.

(Crystal, 1987, p. 358)

5   The similarities become more obvious when we turn to other books and articles on English.

Bryson's (1990) book *Mother Tongue: The English Language* starts thus: 'More than 300 million people in the world speak English and the rest, it sometimes seems, try to' (p. 1). He goes on:

For better or worse, English has become the most global of languages, the lingua franca of business, science, education, politics, and pop music. For the airlines of 157 nations (out of 168 in the world), it is the agreed international language of discourse. In India, there are more than 3,000 newspapers in English. The six member nations of the European Free Trade Association conduct all their business in English, even though not one of them is an English-speaking country.

(p. 2)

and so on. 'For non-English speakers everywhere, English has become the common tongue' (p. 3). Claiborne (1983) opens his book *The life and times of the English language: The history of our marvellous tongue* with:

By any standard, English is a remarkable language. It is, to begin with, the native tongue of some 300,000,000 people—the largest speech community in the world except for Mandarin Chinese. Even more remarkable is its geographic spread, in which it is second to none; its speakers range from Point Barrow, Alaska, to the Falkland Islands; from the Shetland Islands to Capetown at the Southern tip of Africa; from Hong Kong to Tasmania ...English is also by far the most important 'second language' in the world. It is spoken by tens of millions of educated Europeans and Japanese, is the most widely studied foreign tongue in both the USSR and China, and serves as an 'official' language in more than a dozen other countries whose populations total more than a thousand million ...English is the lingua franca of scientists, of air pilots and traffic controllers around the world, of students hitchhiking around Europe, and of dropouts meditating in India and Nepal.

(pp. 1–2)

and so on and so on. Finally, in a newspaper article (from *The Times* of London) under the title

'The triumph of English' Jenkins (1995) reiterates much of the same list:

> When the Warsaw Pact was wound up it was wound up in English. When the G7 meets, it meets in English.... English is the global computer language. It is the language of news gathering and world entertainment. The only substantial world body that struggles to keep going in a 'foreign' tongue is the French-speaking European Commission in Brussels. With luck, enlargement will put an end to that.

These seemingly celebratory descriptions of the global spread of English are tied to more explicit benefits in certain versions of this story. Burnett (1962), for example, draws the connection between the use of English and being 'civilized'

> Today English is written, spoken, broadcast, and understood on every continent, and it can claim a wider geographical range than any other tongue. There are few civilized areas where it has any competition as the lingua franca—the international language of commerce, diplomacy, science, and scholarship.
>
> *(p. 12)*

The connection to civilization is of course a common one (see many other quotes in this chapter), and gets replayed constantly. Here is Jespersen, who Randolph Quirk describes as 'the most distinguished scholar of the English language who has ever lived' (1982, p. iii), arguing that we may compare languages according to their logic: 'there is perhaps no language in the civilised world that stands so high as English' (1938/1982, p. 12). This argument takes on a slightly different tone in Robert Burchfield's (1985) *The English Language* when he argues that:

> English has also become a lingua franca to the point that any literate, educated person on the face of the globe is in a very real sense deprived if he does not know English. Poverty, famine, and disease are instantly recognized as the cruellest and least excusable forms of deprivation. Linguistic deprivation is a less easily noticed condition, but one nevertheless of great significance.
>
> *(pp. 160–1)*

10 According to Jenkins (1995), attempts to introduce artificial languages have failed because 'English has triumphed. Those who do not speak it are at a universal disadvantage against those who do. Those who deny this supremacy merely seek to keep the disadvantaged deprived.' As we shall see later, this notion of 'linguistic deprivation' for those who do not speak English and even for those who do not speak it as a native language starts to have very particular significance within this discourse.

At times, too, the descriptions of this global spread start to use terms even more reminiscent of the prose of George (1867) or de Quincey (1862) and their talk of 'destiny' and the inevitable spread of English being like a mighty river flowing towards the sea. An editorial in *The Sunday Times* (UK) (10 July 1994), responding to the attempts in France to limit the use of English in various public domains, thunders against the French for opposing the 'European lingua franca which will inevitably be English'. To oppose English is pointless, the editorial warns, since 'English fulfills its own destiny as Churchill's 'ever-conquering language'. With every shift in international politics, every turn of the world's economies, every media development and every technological revolution, English marches on'. The editorial then returns to slightly more sober language:

> No other country in Europe works itself into such a frenzy about the way English eases the paths of multi-national discussion and assumes an ever-growing role as the language of power and convenience. The Germans, Spanish and Italians have accepted the inevitable. So, further afield, have the Russians, Chinese and Japanese. If you want to get ahead, you have to speak English. Two billion people around the world are believed to have made it their second language. Add that to 350m native English speakers in the United States, Britain and the Commonwealth, and you have an unstoppable force.

After these remarkable claims for the global spread of English and its inevitable path towards ascendancy, the editorial goes on to reassert that France must acknowledge 'the dominance of

Anglo-American English as the universal language in a shrinking world', and that 'no amount of protectionist legislation and subsidies can shut out the free market in the expression of ideas'. 'Britain,' it asserts, 'must press ahead with the propagation of English and the British values which stand behind it' with the British Council ('Once a target for those unable to see no further than the end of their nose, it now runs a successful global network with teaching as its core activity in 108 countries'), the BBC (which 'is told to exploit its reputation and products abroad as never before') helping with 'the onward march of the English language'. As we shall see, this juxtaposition of the spread of English with the protectionism of the *Académie Française* is a frequently repeated trope of these discourses.

An article in *U.S. News & World Report* (18 February 1985) called 'English: Out to conquer the world' starts with the usual cataloguing of the spread of English:

> When an Argentine pilot lands his airliner in Turkey, he and the ground controller talk in English. When German physicists want to alert the international scientific community to a new discovery, they publish their findings in English-language journals. When Japanese executives cut deals with Scandinavian entrepreneurs in Bangkok, they communicate in English.
>
> *(p. 49)*

and so on and so on. The article also derides those who would oppose the 'inevitable' spread of English, for 'English marches on. "If you need it, you learn it," says one expert'. Despite various attempts to counter the spread of English, 'the world's latest lingua franca will keep spreading. "It's like the primordial ooze," contends James Alatis, …"its growth is in inexorable and inevitable"' (p. 52). According to Burchfield (1985):

> The English language is like a fleet of juggernaut trucks that goes on regardless. No form of linguistic engineering and no amount of linguistic legislation will prevent the cycles of change that lie ahead. But English as it is spoken and written by native speakers looks like remaining a communicative force, however slightly or severely beyond the grasp of foreigners, and changed in whatever agreeable or disagreeable manner, for many centuries to come.
>
> *(p. 173)*

15   Finally, here is Claiborne (1983) again:

> From century to century the great river of English has flowed on, fed by all these streams [the languages of 'copper-hued Native Americans, blacks kidnapped into bondage, liquid-eyed Indian rajahs and craftsmen, narrow-eyed Malay pirates and merchants of Cathay'], and itself an inexhaustible source of song and story, of comedy and tragedy, of histories, sermons, orations and manifestos and of mere polite—or impolite—conversation. As it enriched the lives of past generations, so it will continue to enrich the lives of our children and their children's children—provided we take care that they learn how to understand and appreciate it.
>
> *(p. 292)*

Clearly, there is quite remarkable continuity in the writing on the global spread of English. Bailey (1991) comments that 'the linguistic ideas that evolved at the acme of empires led by Britain and the United States have not changed as economic colonialism has replaced the direct, political management of third world nations. English is still believed to be the inevitable world language' (p. 121). Viswanathan (1989) observes that constructions of the inferior Other and the superior Self arose not so much out of a position of strength and confidence as from a position of vulnerability and beleaguerment. Such constructions produced rather than reflected a confidence in English and the continued use of such cultural images needs to be seen as having the same productive force. It is more important, then, to look beyond arguments about the descriptive adequacy of such statements—are these statements true or false?—and rather to look at their productive force and the conditions of possibility of their production. Thus my interest here is in exploring not so much whether such discourses are in some sense *true* but rather what such discourses *produce*, what, in a Foucauldian (e.g. 1980) sense are their *truth effects*. And I want to argue that it is in the adherence of such discourses to English that we can see the continuing effects of the cultural constructs of colonialism.

IN PRAISE OF ENGLISH

If there are many similarities in the ways the spread of English has been both exhorted and applauded over the last hundred years, there are also interesting similarities in the way the language itself has been praised as a great language. Nineteenth-century writing on English abounded with glorifications of the language, suggesting that on the one hand the undeniable excellence of British institutions, ideas and culture must be reflected in the language and on the other, that the undeniably superior qualities of English must reflect a people and a culture of superior quality. Thus, the Reverend James George, for example, arguing that Britain had been 'commissioned to teach a noble language embodying the richest scientific and literary treasures,' asserted that 'As the mind grows, language grows, and adapts itself to the thinking of the people. Hence, a highly civilized race, will ever have, a highly accomplished language. The English tongue, is in all senses a very noble one. I apply the term noble with a rigorous exactness' (George, 1867, p. 4). And Archbishop Trench, discussing the ancestral legacy of English, asked:

> What can more clearly point out their native land and ours as having fulfilled a glorious past, as being destined for a glorious future, than that they should have acquired for themselves and for those who came after them a clear, a strong, a harmonious, a noble language? For all this bears witness to corresponding merits in those that speak it, to clearness of mental vision, to strength, to harmony, to nobleness in them who have gradually shaped and fashioned it to be the utterance of their inmost life and being.
>
> *(Trench, 1881, p. 3)*

A key argument in the demonstration of the superior qualities of English was in the breadth of its vocabulary, an argument which, as we shall see, is still used widely today.

The article 'English out to conquer the world' asks how English differs from other languages: 'First, it is bigger. Its vocabulary numbers at least 750,000 words. Second-ranked French is only two thirds that size. English has been growing fast for 1,000 years, promiscuously borrowing words from other lands' (1985, p. 53). According to Bryson (1990), the numbers of words listed in *Webster's Third New International Dictionary* (450,000) and the *Oxford English Dictionary* (615,000) are only part of the total number of English words since 'technical and scientific terms would add millions more'. Looking at which terms are actually commonly made use of, Bryson suggests that about '200,000 English words are in common use, more than in German (184,000) and far more than in French (a mere 100,000)' (p. 3). Claiborne (1983) asserts that 'For centuries, the English-speaking peoples have plundered the world for words, even as their military and industrial empire builders have plundered it for more tangible goods'. This plundering has given English:

> the largest, most variegated and most expressive vocabulary in the world. The total number of English words lies somewhere between 400,000— the number of current entries in the largest English dictionaries—and 600,000—the largest figure that any expert is willing to be quoted on. By comparison, the biggest French dictionaries have only about 150,000 entries, the biggest Russian ones a mere 130,000,000.
>
> *(p. 3)*

20   Jenkins (1995) explains that:

> English has not won the battle to be the world's language through a trial of imperial strength. As the American linguist Braj Kachru points out, English has achieved its hegemony through its inherent qualities, by 'its propensity for acquiring new identities …its range of varieties and above all its suitability as a flexible medium for literary and other types of creativity'.

The subtitle to Jenkins' article ('The triumph of English') is 'Our infinitely adaptable mother tongue is now the world's lingua franca—and not before time.'

Apart from clearly supporting a simple argument about the superiority of English, this view of the richness of English puts into play several other images of English that are extremely important: the notion of English as some pure, Anglo-Saxon language, the idea that English and English-speakers have always been open, flexible and integrationist, and the belief that because of their vast vocabulary, speakers of English are the ablest thinkers. The first of these emerges in 'English out to conquer the world' when the article suggests that 'All-told, 80 percent of the word stock is foreign-born' (p. 53). The implications of this statement seem to be that that 'English' refers to a language of Anglo-Saxon purity, a language that despite all its borrowings and enrichments is, at its heart, an Anglo-Saxon affair. This effort to construct some clear Anglo Saxon lineage for English has a long history (see Bailey, 1991; Crowley, 1989). Writing in 1901, Earle argued that:

> We do not want to discard the rich furniture of words which we have inherited from our French and classic eras; but we wish to wear them as trophies, as the historic blazon of a great career, for the demarcation and amplification of an imperial language whose thews and sinews and vital energies are essentially English.
>
> *(cited in Crowley, 1989, p. 74)*

According to Burnett (1962), 'the long process of creating the historic seedbed of the English language actually began with the arrival of the first Indo-European elements from the continent' (p. 75). Claiborne (1983) goes further and claims that 'the story of the life and times of English' can be traced from 'eight thousand years ago to the present' (p. 5). Although both these claims—that 80 per cent of English could be foreign and that the language can be traced back over 8,000 years—seem perhaps most remarkable for the bizarreness of their views, they also need to be taken very seriously in terms of the cultural constructions they produce, namely a view of English as some ethnically pure Anglo-Saxon or Aryan language. Bailey (1991) comments that '"Restoring" a racially pure lan-

guage to suit a racially "primitive" nation is an idea that reached its most extreme and dreadful consequence in Hitler's Reich, and its appearance in images of English has not been sufficiently acknowledged' (p. 270).

The second image that emerges here is that to this core of Anglo-Saxon has been added—like tributaries to the great river of English, as many writers like to describe this—words from languages around the world, suggesting that English and British people have always been flexible and keen to borrow from elsewhere to enrich the language. This image of English is then used to deride other languages for their lack of breadth and, especially when people have sought to safeguard languages from the incursions of English, to claim that English is democratic while other languages are not. Most commonly this argument is used against the French for their attempts to legislate against the use of English words. In the editorial 'Lingua Britannica' in *The Sunday Times* (10 July 1994), the French are attacked for their defensiveness and xenophobia: 'It is sad to see the French, with their great cultural heritage, being so defensive.... While France seeks to bring the shutters down against alien intrusions of its cultural heritage, the BBC is told to exploit its reputation and products abroad as never before. Who are the xenophobes here?' Who, indeed?

25 Thus, the image of English as a great borrowing language is used against any attempts to oppose the spread of English, the argument being that the diverse vocabulary of English is a reflection of the democratic and open nature of the British people, and that reactions against English are nothing but evidence that other people are less open and democratic. 'English need not be protected by French Academies, Canadian constitutions or Flemish language rioters,' Jenkins (1995) tells us. 'The world must just take a deep breath and admit that it has a universal language at last.' But Jenkins is of course merely repeating an old image of English, one that the linguist Jespersen was quite happy with: 'The English language would not have been what it is

if the English had not been for centuries great respecters of the liberties of each individual and if everybody had not been free to strike out new paths for himself.' (Jespersen, 1938/1982, p. 14). And this linguistic democracy is, as ever, far superior to the narrow-minded protectionism of the French:

the English have never suffered an Academy to be instituted among them like the French of Italian Academies...In England every writer is, and has always been, free to take his words where he chooses, whether from the ordinary stock of everyday words, from native dialects, from old authors, or from other languages, dead or living.

(1938/1982, p. 15)

The notion of English as a great borrowing language also seems to suggest a view of colonial relations in which the British intermingled with colonized people, enriching English as they communed with the locals. Such a view, however, is hardly supported by colonial history. Kiernan (1969) mentions Macartney's observation of the British 'besetting sin of contempt for the rest of mankind' and that 'while other foreigners at Canton mingled socially with the Chinese, the British kept aloof' (p. 148). Kiernan goes on to suggest that 'the *apartheid* firmly established in India was transferred in a great measure to China. Everyone has heard of the "Dogs and Chinese not admitted" notice in the park' (p. 156). In Hong Kong, he points out, 'the position of the Chinese as subjects under British rule increased British haughtiness'. He quotes Bowring in 1858 as observing that 'the separation of the native population from the European is nearly absolute; social intercourse between the races wholly unknown' (p. 156). As Metcalf (1995) shows with respect to India, this apartheid policy extended to the division of cities, with railway lines often built to separate the 'native areas' from the white preserves, and houses built with extensive verandahs, gardens and gateways in order to keep the colonized at bay. These observations are backed up by Wesley-Smith's (1994) analysis of 'anti-Chinese legislation' in Hong Kong. Looking at the 'considerable body of race-based discriminatory legislation' in Hong

Kong, Wesley-Smith points to one of the central aims of much of this legislation: the separation of Chinese and Europeans. In 1917, Governor May (who had replaced Lugard, see Chapter 4) wrote to the secretary of state about the importance of maintaining the Peak area as an all-European reserve: 'It would be little short of a calamity if an alien and, by European standards, semi-civilized race were allowed to drive the white man from the one area in Hong Kong, in which he can live with his wife and children in a white man's healthy surroundings' (cited in Wesley-Smith, p. 100).

If, then, the British tended to mingle with colonized or other people far less than did other Europeans, it is unlikely that the English language was in fact such an open, borrowing language as is claimed. Indeed, Bailey (1991) argues that the British 'sense of racial superiority made English voyagers less receptive to borrowings that had not already been, in part, authenticated by other European travelers' (p. 61). Thus, he goes on:

Far from its conventional image as a language congenial to borrowings from remote languages, English displays a tendency to accept exotic loanwords mainly when they first have been adopted by other European languages or when presented with marginal social practices or trivial objects. Anglophones who have ventured abroad have done so confident of the superiority of their culture and persuaded of their capacity for adaptation, usually without accepting the obligations of adapting. Extensive linguistic borrowing and language mixing arise only when there is some degree of equality between or among languages (and their speakers) in a multilingual setting. For the English abroad, this sense of equality was rare.

(p. 91)

There are, therefore, serious questions to be asked about the image democratic English put into play by the construction of English as a borrowing language. Indeed, the constant replaying of this image of English as an open and borrowing language, reflecting an open and borrowing people, is a cultural construct of colonialism that is in direct conflict with the colonial evidence.

The third, and probably most insidious, view produced by the insistence on English having a far larger vocabulary than other languages relates to thought. Having stated that English has more words than German or French Bryson (1990) goes on to argue that:

> The richness of the English vocabulary, and the wealth of available synonyms, means that English speakers can often draw shades of distinction unavailable to non-English speakers. The French, for example, cannot distinguish between house and home, between mind and brain, between man and gentleman, between 'I wrote' and 'I have written'. The Spanish cannot differentiate a chairman from a president, and the Italians have no equivalent of wishful thinking. In Russia there are no native words for efficiency, challenge, engagement ring, have fun, or take care.
>
> *(pp. 3–4)*

30   Now it is important to note here that this is not merely an argument that different languages cut the world up differently but rather that English, with its larger vocabulary, cuts the world up better. Claiborne (1983), having also claimed a larger vocabulary for English than for other languages, goes on to suggest that 'Like the wandering minstrel in *The Mikado*, with songs for any and every occasion, English has the right word for it—whatever 'it' may be' (p. 4). Thus:

> It is the enormous and variegated lexicon of English, far more than the more numbers and geographical spread of its speakers, that truly makes our native tongue marvellous makes it, in fact, a medium for the precise, vivid and subtle expression of thought and emotion that has no equal, past or present.
>
> *(p. 4)*

In case the implications of this are not clear, Claiborne goes on to claim that English is indeed 'not merely a great language but the greatest' (p. 4) and that 'Nearly all of us do our thinking in words, which symbolize objects and events (real or imagined) …' (p. 6). Clearly, then, in this view, if you are a speaker of English, you are better equipped than speakers of other languages to think about the world. In this view, English is a window

on the world. According to Burnett (1962), 'not only in Asia and Africa, but in Europe, crisscrossed by linguistic frontiers and dissected by deep-rooted cultural loyalties, people of all classes now look to English as a window, a magic casement opening on every horizon of loquacious men' (pp. 20–21).

Such a view, as Cohn (1996) points out, has a long history. Looking at colonial views of language in India, Cohn suggest that 'Meaning for the English was something attributed to a word, a phrase, or an object, which could be determined and translated, at best with a synonym that had a direct referent to something in what the English thought of as a "natural" world' (pp. 18–19). There was, then, an abiding view that there was a natural world, with a natural system for naming it: English. Fernando (1986) has pointed to the dual fallacies contained in this view:

> one is the influential and peculiarly Western notion that 'Language' is capable of describing the whole of nature alone: nature can be put entirely and completely into words. The other submerged assumption is that English, particularly, is capable of doing this, that other languages—usually Asian ones—do not have the full range of concepts necessary for the purpose.
>
> *(p. 108)*

What is interesting here is the availability of this belief in contemporary books on English.

If writers on English are not praising its supposedly vast vocabulary, another direction in which they often turn is towards its supposedly simple grammar. This argument, too, is an old one:

> In its easiness of grammatical construction, in its paucity of inflection, in its almost total disregard of the distinctions of gender excepting those of nature, in the simplicity and precision of its terminations and auxiliary verbs, not less than in the majesty, vigour and copiousness of its expression, our mother-tongue seems well adapted by *organization* to become the language of the world.
>
> *(Review of Bradshaw's Scheme, 1848; cited in Bailey, 1991, p. 108)*

35   Jenkins (1995) argues that the global adoption of English is a result of the adaptability and

simplicity of English: 'English has few inflections, endings or cases. Its grammar is based on simple word order. It has no clicks, tones or implosives.' After arguing that English has a greater vocabulary than other languages, and also that it is more flexible than other languages (another old favourite), Bryson (1990) goes on to argue for its simplicity. This takes a number of forms, such as simplicity of spelling and pronunciation: 'English is said to have fewer of the awkward consonant clusters and singsong tonal varieties that make other languages so difficult to master' (p. 6); uninflected pronouns: 'In German, if you wish to say *you*, you must choose between seven words: *du, dich, dir, Sie Ilmen, ihr*, and *euch*. This can cause immense social anxiety.... In English we avoid these problems by relying on just one form: *you*' (p. 8); gender and articles: 'English is mercifully free of gender.... In this regard English is a godsend to students everywhere. Not only have we discarded problems of gender with definite and indefinite articles, we have often discarded the articles themselves' (p. 8); and conciseness in words: 'German is full of jaw-crunching words like *Geisteswissenschaffeten* (sic) (a social worker).... English, in happy contrast, favours crisp truncations: IBM, laser, NATO' (p. 9).

Such arguments recall the work of the linguist Jespersen (1938/1982), who asserts in the introduction to his book on *Growth and structure of the English language* that 'there is one expression that continually comes to mind whenever I think of the English language and compare it with others: it seems to me positively and expressly *masculine*, it is the language of a grown-up man and has very little childish and feminine about it' (p. 2). It is worth noting here, I think, how such constructions of English replicate the colonial constructions of the Other as childlike and feminine (see Chapter 2). Jespersen then goes on, at pains to show that he is engaged in the scientific study of language, to demonstrate his reasons for making such a claim. English has 'business-like, virile qualities,' he argues, which 'manifest themselves in such things as word-order' (p. 10). And such 'business-like shortness' (one of the masculine characteristics

of English) can be found in such 'convenient abbreviations' of words and sentences that are so common in English (1938/1982, p. 7).

There are a number of points worth observing about these general arguments. The first question we might want to ask is why is it good on the one hand to have a supposedly vast and complex vocabulary and on the other a simple grammar? There would seem to be an equally valid argument (though equally problematic in other ways) that complex grammars are a sign of complex thinking. The point, of course, is that such apparent contradictions do not matter: there is no underlying rationale to the argument that English supposedly has more words than other languages or a less complex grammar; the issue is that English is better than other languages and that any evidence of difference can then be used to support that argument. It is also worth noting here that these arguments are not only ethnocentric in terms of their position relative to English and other languages, but also very Eurocentric: apart from the reference to the 'singsong tonal variations' of other languages, comparisons are almost always with European languages. Articles, grammatical gender, word classes, inflections, pronouns and so on are all played out in different combinations and varieties in other languages around the world.

But one significant implication of this supposed simplicity of English is that it makes it easy to learn: 'The current extraordinary spread of the English language around the world would never have begun, despite all the forces of history and all the facilities for its propagation, if English were a difficult language to learn' (Burnett, 1962, p. 27). For Burnett, this includes a general simplicity and elegance at all levels:

It excels by reason of its basically simple rudiments—a hard core of perhaps one thousand energetic words which fill all the needs of ordinary communication, a few tolerant rules governing their use, and a logical underlying skeletal structure—which can be taught and learned more quickly than is possible in any other language spoken on earth today.

(Burnett, 1962, p. 27)

But, whether the language supposedly has a vast vocabulary and simple grammar, or in the above example, 'one thousand energetic words' and 'a few tolerant rules' it is easy to learn. Indeed, beneath the centrepiece of Jenkins' article—a picture of two white men in the clothes of the church talking to a group of Africans —is the explanation 'A missionary at work in Africa, circa 1800: more than a billion people are now thought to be English-speakers, so easy is the language to learn.' The spread of English, therefore, is not a result of politics or economics but of the simplicity of English. On the one hand, then, English is a language richer and more complex than any other, a language that allows for better and more precise representations of the world. On the other hand, it is a simple and clear language that is easier to learn than any other. I am not as interested in pulling apart these arguments (to explain the extraordinary inaccuracies in these articles and books or to supply counterexamples, would fill dozens more pages) as I am in looking at their historical continuity and what they produce in terms of images of English.

• • •

40 Resistance, as the literature on this notion suggests (see, for example, Giroux, 1983; Harlow, 1987), is not an easy and automatically beneficial space. In order to explore this more, I shall turn to some writing by students of mine in Hong Kong. This writing was in response to my request to various first year undergraduate students at the University of Hong Kong to reflect on their 'relationship to English'. What is interesting here is that while few students articulated a clear sense of English as a colonial language, their experiences with the language seemed to replay colonial relations in terms of the imposition of English, their rejection of it, and their unwilling accommodation to the language. What we see here, then, is an embodied relationship to English, a struggle and an accommodation with English, and yet little available discourse for articulating this relationship.

Probably the most striking aspect of this relationship is the deep-seated vehemence towards English that many of the students felt when they moved from elementary school (where English

Missionaries at work in Southern Africa

was a subject but not a medium) to secondary school, where suddenly they were confronted by classes taught in English. The force of some of this language shows how English is being written onto the bodies of these students:

> When I finished my primary school, I entered an academic secondary school. I had to speak and listen to English in all subjects except Chinese and Chinese History. It was a hard time for me indeed. I could not understand what the teachers said for nearly one month since I was used to speaking and listening to Cantonese during the lesson in primary school. Besides, I found that the textbooks were all written in English. Whatever I tried my best to read the book, I could not grasp the meaning of many words. Every word looked like a monster, I wanted to kill them.
>
> *(Lilian Yeung)*

One obvious interpretation of this and some of the following statements is that since it is very hard to study through the medium of a second language, these students are recalling the difficulty of those early months. I want to suggest, however, that there is a slightly different way of reading these statements since it seems to me that these students are describing not merely a difficult period of learning but a process almost of brutalization. What I think emerges from a lot of these accounts is the start of a difficult and sometimes almost violent relationship to English:

> From time to time, English, in my mind, has turned sour. It is tough and also dull.... I hate English. I know nothing about the meaning of some pattern of expression although I am familiar with them. Suddenly, my mind has been engulfed by those English words!
>
> *(Lawrence Ho)*

> At that time (secondary school) I met frustration after frustration because every subject other than Chinese and Chinese History were taught in English. Worse still, during assembly English was used instead of Cantonese. It was a real harsh time for me to adapt to the new environment. Although I hated English, I had to overcome it.
>
> *(Veronica Chow)*

> The first two years of my English studies were really a nightmare to me.
>
> *(Lucetta Kam)*

> I encountered many many difficulties in learning English. When I read English articles, I didn't understand because of the abundant vocabularies. When I wrote, I made many grammatical and spelling mistakes. When I listened, I couldn't hear a word. When I spoke, I hardly said a word. Therefore, at the beginning, attending English lessons was just like going to hell. But, when time goes by, I start realising the merits of learning English.
>
> *(Anita Tang Wing Kin)*

> As a secondary student in an English grammar school, I usually avoided reading English articles. Other than English newspapers and magazines, I hated reading the English version of notices or announcements, too.
>
> *(Wong Kam Hon)*

> There was a period when I hate English. Which is the first few months in my secondary school.
>
> *(Teresa Wan Hang Yee)*

> I hated English. It brought me a lot of troubles in my study.
>
> *(Priscilla Tang Man Ki)*

> If you want to enter a higher school or to get a higher position, a good command of English is a must. Therefore, parents and teachers put much pressure on the students. They force the students to do a lot of extra work. To these students, English is no longer an interesting language, but a nightmare.
>
> *(Amy Chan Fung)*

> The teachers also encouraged us to put up our hands in class to answer questions in English, in order to train our speaking skills. Punishment would also be given for those who spoke Cantonese in class. As a result, silence prevailed throughout all English lessons.
>
> *(Lily Tsang)*

As I said, it might be possible to interpret these comments simply in terms of the educational difficulties faced by these students when they switched to English-medium secondary schools. Even from within this interpretation, however, it would have to be acknowledged that the students' remarks display a remarkable degree of vehemence towards English that would likely effect many of their learning experiences. But I want to suggest that this relationship of 'hatred' and of 'nightmares' is more profoundly linked to the colonial context of English, to the physical imposition of English on these students.

Another significant theme that arises from these essays is a questioning of the role of English in their lives. As many students suggest, it exists only as a language used for academic purposes and has little relevance to their daily lives. In this context, some students question the explanations given them by their teachers for learning English, since it seems perfectly possible to live one's life in Hong Kong with a knowledge only of Cantonese.

English rarely applies in our daily lives.

(Joanna Lui)

When I was born, I was a Chinese—a purely Chinese. Cantonese is my mother language. People I met are all Chinese—Hong Kong people. We communicate in Cantonese, but never English. Therefore, English, for myself, is only one academic subject which I must study well so as to pass the examinations and for further education.

(Joanne Ng Pui King)

The importance of English is even more obvious in the university. All the lectures and tutorials are taught in English. It is impossible for you to not understand English and survive in the university. I start doubting if Cantonese is our official language.

(Anita Tang Wing Kin)

It is rather ironic, students have to use double efforts for their studies since homeworks and tests are to be handed in English, but it is the idea in Cantonese that deep in their minds.

(Wan Wing Sze)

To me, English is mainly a tool for learning in school, not for communication in daily lives. As all my friends are Chinese, it is a general and straight thing for us to use Cantonese to communicate with others. Otherwise, one would think that you are quite arrogant as you speak lots of English which seems to be unnecessary.

(Wan Wing Sze)

I found English was meaningless to me and I didn't have good marks in this subject.

(Angela Chui Wing Yu)

It seemed that my relationship to English was confined to studies.

(Spencer Tse)

Why can my mother still fuse into the community without English?

(Wong Kam Hong)

What I mean is that English seems to be useless in our daily life. Outside the school, it is the world of Cantonese. When talking, Cantonese is the only language to communicate. When watching TV, most people would like to choose Chinese programmes. Even inside the school, I find that some teachers use Cantonese to teach English in English classes. Less practices and communication in English make me think that English is of no use. Why don't we cancel the subject? It's just a burden to me.

(Peg Lau Pui Man)

45   Once again, it might be possible to interpret such comments as expressing a lack of useful contexts in which to use English: English is not relevant to students' daily lives and therefore they lack both the incentive and the opportunity to develop English skills beyond the confines of the classroom. While this interpretation is no doubt useful, and indeed points to the important way in which students develop a split between English as academic language and Cantonese as everyday language, it does not seem to adequately address the ways in which these relationships between the everyday (private) and the academic, political and social domains (public) are also part of a colonial divide. This was more clearly articulated in the following comment:

As I grew up, I began to question why every Chinese student in Hong Kong has to learn

English and uses English in nearly all subjects.... Why did not the school teach us Putonghua, the official spoken language used by most Chinese? Although I and my classmates did not ask such questions directly to our teachers, they often told us that English is very important in Hong Kong and we should sharpen our language ability for our future career and studies. Hence, it is the reason why we are required to learn the language according to them. But we believed that the main reason of teaching English in school was that we were living in Hong Kong, a British colony. Our belief and the difficulty of English made me lose interest in this language so I always fell asleep in English lessons.

(Brian Chui Shiu Bong)

Significantly, however, these comments have all been written by students for whom learning English has been a relatively successful exercise: they have not only done well enough in English to avoid the cut-off point at the end of form five (continuing into form six is dependent on passing an English exam) but they have also continued to the exclusive and English-only context of Hong Kong University. Thus, these students not only recall the pain of being forced to study in English and the general frustration at the strange role English comes to play in their lives, but they are also very acutely aware of the implications of their success in English. It is important to recall, therefore, that these statements are made by students who have 'made it' with English. Outside the walls of Hong Kong University there is a vast majority for whom there has been no easy accommodation with the language. For my students, however, there has quite often been a certain shift in affections:

In short, my attitude towards English has changed a lot. Before, I treated her as an enemy but now she has become my intimate.

(Mona Lee Siu Ling)

In my childhood it acted as my enemy. It was always my obstacle in my studies.... Gradually, now, English has become my lover.

(Stella Cheung Man Sze)

English in Hong Kong stands for authority and studying it will probably lead to a better prospect like better job opportunities, higher living standards etc.

(Simon Fu)

Learning in one language and talking in another is a common phenomenon for all non-English speaking countries. But we still have to learn English. After all, it is an influential language in the world.

(Anita Tang Wing Kin)

Even though English is not always being used in our daily life at this stage, we must face the reality that it is very useful in the outside world. Therefore, we should learn more about English to express ourselves for future use.

(Peg Lau Pui Man)

Most of the elder people of Hong Kong are not very familiar with English. They regard English as a conqueror. They think it attacks the Chinese culture. On the other hand, most youngsters consider English as God simply because having a good English foundation will guarantee a good job and a promising future.

(Stella Cheung Man Sze)

There is, then, a strange ambivalence towards English, even amongst these students for whom ability in English is almost certain to lead to future prosperity. This difficulty is perhaps best articulated in the following extract:

Sometimes it comes to my mind that the compulsory learning of English in schools is one of the British government's political strategies. When the number of natives in the colony far outnumbers the British rulers, policies like intermarriage are more efficient to control the colony. By enforcing the compulsory education, more people in Hong Kong are ready to accept the British culture, customs and of course, the government policy. And if the majority of the English speakers in Hong Kong regard the language as superior to Chinese, it is reasonable or rational for them to support the government policy. In other words, the teaching of English is a kind of cultural intrusion in Hong Kong and may be regarded as a political weapon. Whenever I think about this, I will be very upset because all of the students are under the control of the Education Department which put too much stress on English. Students are just like the slaves of the Department because they follow and obey exactly what the examination requirement said.

However, the above assumption does not affect my decision about taking the degree course of English. I love English simply because the language is fascinating. It is easy to learn English but difficult to master it well. Moreover, English is widely used in the world and because the territory is an international trade centre, many jobs require candidates possessing a good command of English. Therefore, I cannot deny that studying English can secure my future prospect.

(Eva Ma Wai Yin)

There are several implications I want to draw from these statements about English. First, they constitute a good example of what I (1994b) have called the 'worldliness' of English. They suggest an almost material nature to language as students struggle to deal with its presence in their lives and their bodies. Second, these statements raise interesting questions to do with resistance. Amongst most of these students there seems little available discursive possibility to articulate resistance to English in English. They tell of the pain of English, the nightmare of English, the usefulness of English, the love of English; but few seem to have available means of articulating a resistance to English. It is only in the words of this last student that we can see an understanding of English as 'cultural intrusion' and a 'political weapon'.

And finally, the patterns of colonialism are indeed replayed through relationships to English in Hong Kong. This ambivalent relationship, acknowledging on the one hand that English is a language of colonial authority and a cultural intrusion but on the other hand that it is the language of success and a language one may come to love, is one that can be found constantly in colonial contexts. From Chinua Achebe (1975) to C.L.R. James (1963), this is one of the fundamental dilemmas of colonialism and postcolonialism:

how does one establish a relationship to the languages and cultures of the colonizers when they represent both colonial oppression and the possibilities for anti-colonial struggle? How does one work with a language that one may both hate as a language imposed in school and love as a language one has come to work with?

50   Thus, although these students generally have an unarticulated and ambivalent relationship to colonialism itself, the kind of ambivalences they seem to face with English echo many of the comments made about the postcolonial problematic of opposing the economies, political structures, cultures and languages of colonialism while at the same time doing so in and through a colonial language that has been part of one's social and educational life and which also allows access to a global audience. In his essay 'Biggles, Mau Mau and I', for example, Ngùgiwa Thiong'o (1993) recalls the 'dance of contradictions' (p. 138) he faced when he read and enjoyed Biggles' exciting escapades with the RAF, for it was this same RAF that was bombing the Mau Mau independence fighters in Kenya for whom his brother was fighting. Confronted for many years by the contradictions involved in writing in the language that was also the language of neocolonial oppression in Kenya, Ngùgì eventually vowed to give up writing in English and to write first in Gikuyu. Other writers have not had, or have not chosen to adopt, such an option and have continued to live with these contradictions. In his autobiographical work *Beyond a Boundary*, the Caribbean writer and political activist C.L.R. James (1963) recalls his love of the nineteenth-century British novelist Thackeray and of cricket during his school years. Although he later came to understand 'the limitation on spirit, vision and self-respect which was imposed on us by the fact that our masters, our curriculum, our code of morals, *everything* began from the basis that Britain was the source of all light and leading, and our business was to admire, wonder, imitate, learn' (pp. 38–9), he still acknowledges his 'inexhaustible passion' for cricket and English literature (p. 43).

SUGGESTIONS FOR DISCUSSION

1. What are the main arguments Pennycock identifies that people have made in praise of English? Notice that Pennycock, as he says, is "not as interested in pulling apart these arguments" by refuting them or giving counterexamples as he is in "looking at their historical continuity and what they produce in terms of images of English." What does he see as the "historical continuity" and the "images" of English? What functions, politically and culturally, do the continuity and images perform? Can you think of examples from your own experience of arguments in praise of English and the role they play?

2. Reread the comments of Pennycock's students about their experience learning English. What generalizations does Pennycock draw from their writings? Are there further or different generalizations you would draw? Explain the relationship of your thinking about the students' writings to Pennycock's.

3. Consider the "fundamental dilemma of colonialism and postcolonialism" Pennycock discusses in the final two paragraphs. What exactly is the dilemma here?

PERSPECTIVES: **African Writing, the Mother Tongue, and the English Language**

In the 1960s, the first decade of political independence for African nation-states such as Ghana, Nigeria, and Kenya, a debate emerged among African writers about whether to produce literary works in the European languages (English, French, Portuguese, Afrikaans) of the former colonial order or in native African languages. The debate centered in many respects around this question: Do the European languages such as English inevitably carry with them the cultural values of colonialism or can the European languages be Africanized to serve the aims of national self-determination and communication among ethnic groups in the new African nations?

Presented here are two of the most forceful speakers in this debate—the Nigerian novelist and critic Chinua Achebe and the Kenyan writer Ngũgĩ wa Thiong'o.

THE AFRICAN WRITER AND THE ENGLISH LANGUAGE

Chinua Achebe

Chinua Achebe is a Nigerian writer whose prize-winning novels include *Things Fall Apart* (1958), *Arrow of God* (second edition 1971), and *Anthills of the Savannah* (1988). This essay was written in 1964 and reprinted in the collection *Morning Yet on Creation Day* (1971).

SUGGESTION FOR READING Notice how Chinua Achebe uses the Conference of African Writers of English Expression, held in Makerere in 1952, to establish the context of issues he addresses in the essay. As you read, pay attention to what issues Achebe points to and how he positions himself in relation to them.

1   In June 1952, there was a writers' gathering at Makerere, impressively styled: 'A Conference of African Writers of English Expression'. Despite this sonorous and rather solemn title, it turned out to be a very lively affair and a very exciting and useful experience for many of us. But there was something which we tried to do and failed—that was to define 'African literature' satisfactorily.

Was it literature produced *in* Africa or *about* Africa? Could African literature be on any subject, or must it have an African theme? Should it embrace the whole continent or south of the Sahara, or just *Black* Africa? And then the question of language. Should it be in indigenous African languages or should it include Arabic, English, French, Portuguese, Afrikaans, et cetera?

In the end we gave up trying to find an answer, partly—I should admit—on my own instigation. Perhaps we should not have given up so easily. It seems to me from some of the things I have since heard and read that we may have given the impression of not knowing what we were doing, or worse, not daring to look too closely at it.

A Nigerian critic, Obi Wali, writing in *Transition* 10 said: 'Perhaps the most important achievement of the conference …is that African literature as now defined and understood leads nowhere.'

5   I am sure that Obi Wali must have felt triumphantly vindicated when he saw the report of a different kind of conference held later at Fourah Bay to discuss African literature and the University curriculum. This conference produced a tentative definition of African literature as follows: 'Creative writing in which an African setting is authentically handled or to which experiences originating in Africa are integral.' We are told specifically that Conrad's *Heart of Darkness* qualifies as African literature while Graham Greene's *Heart of the Matter* fails because it could have been set anywhere outside Africa.

A number of interesting speculations issue from this definition which admittedly is only an interim formulation designed to produce an indisputably desirable end, namely, to introduce African students to literature set in their environment. But I could not help being amused by the curious circumstance in which Conrad, a Pole, writing in English could produce African literature while Peter Abrahams would be ineligible should he write a novel based on his experiences in the West Indies.

What all this suggests to me is that you cannot cram African literature into a small, neat definition. I do not see African literature as one unit but as a group of associated units—in fact the sum total of all the *national* and *ethnic* literatures of Africa.

A national literature is one that takes the whole nation for its province and has a realized or potential audience throughout its territory. In other words a literature that is written in the *national* language. An ethnic literature is one which is available only to one ethnic group within the nation. If you take Nigeria as an example, the national literature, as I see it, is the literature written in English; and the ethnic literatures are in Hausa, Ibo, Yoruba, Efik, Edo, Ijaw, etc., etc.

Any attempt to define African literature in terms which overlook the complexities of the African scene at the material time is doomed to failure. After the elimination of white rule shall have been completed, the single most important fact in Africa in the second half of the twentieth century will appear to be the rise of individual nation-states. I believe that African literature will follow the same pattern.

10   What we tend to do today is to think of African literature as a newborn infant. But in fact what we have is a whole generation of newborn infants. Of course, if you only look cursorily, one infant is pretty much like another; but in reality each is already set on its own separate journey. Of course, you may group them together on the basis of anything you choose—the color of their hair, for instance. Or you may group them together on the basis of the language they will speak or the religion of their fathers. Those would all be valid distinctions; but they could not begin to account fully for each individual person carrying, as it were, his own little, unique lodestar of genes.

Those who in talking about African literature want to exclude North Africa because it belongs to a different tradition surely do not suggest that Black Africa is anything like homogeneous. What does Shabaan Robert have in common with Christopher Okigbo or Awoonor-Williams? Or Mongo Beti of Cameroun and Paris with Nzekwu of Nigeria? What does the champagne-drinking upper-class Creole society described by Easmon of Sierra Leone have in common with the rural folk and fishermen of J. P. Clark's plays? Of course, some of these differences could be accounted for on individual rather than national grounds, but a good deal of it is also environmental.

I have indicated somewhat offhandedly that the national literature of Nigeria and of many other countries of Africa is, or will be, written in English. This may sound like a controversial statement, but it isn't. All I have done has been to look at the reality of present-day Africa. This 'reality' may change as a result of deliberate, e.g. political, action. If it does, an entirely new situation will arise, and there will be plenty of time to examine it. At present it may be more profitable to look at the scene as it is.

What are the factors which have conspired to place English in the position of national language in many parts of Africa? Quite simply the reason is that these nations were created in the first place by the intervention of the British, which, I hasten to add, is not saying that the peoples comprising these nations were invented by the British.

The country which we know as Nigeria today began not so very long ago as the arbitrary creation of the British. It is true, as William Fagg says in his excellent new book *Nigerian Images*, that this arbitrary action has proved as lucky in terms of African art history as any enterprise of the fortunate Princess of Serendip. And I believe that in political and economic terms too this arbitrary creation called Nigeria holds out great prospects. Yet the fact remains that Nigeria was created by the British—for their own ends. Let us give the devil his due: colonialism in Africa disrupted many things, but it did create big political units where there were small, scattered ones before. Nigeria

had hundreds of autonomous communities ranging in size from the vast Fulani Empire founded by Usman dan Fodio in the north to tiny village entities in the east. Today it is one country.

15   Of course there are areas of Africa where colonialism divided up a single ethnic group among two or even three powers. But on the whole it did bring together many peoples that had hitherto gone their several ways. And it gave them a language with which to talk to one another. If it failed to give them a song, it at least gave them a tongue, for sighing. There are not many countries in Africa today where you could abolish the language of the erstwhile colonial powers and still retain the facility for mutual communication. Therefore those African writers who have chosen to write in English or French are not unpatriotic smart alecks with an eye on the main chance—outside their own countries. They are by-products of the same process that made the new nation-states of Africa.

You can take this argument a stage further to include other countries of Africa. The only reason why we can even talk about African unity is that when we get together we can have a manageable number of languages to talk in—English, French, Arabic.

The other day I had a visit from Joseph Kariuki of Kenya. Although I had read some of his poems and he had read my novels, we had not met before. But it didn't seem to matter. In fact I had met him through his poems, especially through his love poem 'Come away my love', in which he captures in so few words the trials and tensions of an African in love with a white girl in Britain:

Come away, my love, from streets
Where unkind eyes divide
And shop windows reflect our difference.

By contrast, when in 1960 I was traveling in East Africa and went to the home of the late Shabaan Robert, the Swahili poet of Tanganyika, things had been different. We spent some time talking about writing, but there was no real contact. I knew from all accounts that I was talking to an important writer, but of the nature of his work I had no idea. He gave me two books of his poems which I treasure but cannot read—until I have learned Swahili.

And there are scores of languages I would want to learn if it were possible. Where am I to find the time to learn the half dozen or so Nigerian languages, each of which can sustain a literature? I am afraid it cannot be done. These languages will just have to develop as tributaries to feed the one central language enjoying nationwide currency. Today, for good or ill, that language is English. Tomorrow it may be something else, although I very much doubt it.

20   Those of us who have inherited the English language may not be in a position to appreciate the value of the inheritance. Or we may go on resenting it because it came as part of a package deal which included many other items of doubtful value and the positive atrocity of racial arrogance and prejudice which may yet set the world on fire. But let us not in rejecting the evil throw out the good with it.

Some time last year I was traveling in Brazil meeting Brazilian writers and artists. A number of the writers I spoke to were concerned about the restrictions imposed on them by their use of the Portuguese language. I remember a woman poet saying she had given serious thought to writing in French! And yet their problem is not half as difficult as ours. Portuguese may not have the universal currency of English or French but at least it is the national language of Brazil with her eighty million or so people, to say nothing of the people of Portugal, Angola, Mozambique, etc.

Of Brazilian authors I have only read, in translation, one novel by Jorge Amado, who is not only Brazil's leading novelist but one of the most important writers in the world. From that one novel, *Gabriella*, I was able to glimpse something of the exciting Afro-Latin culture which is the pride of Brazil and is quite unlike any other culture. Jorge Amado is only one of the many writers Brazil has produced. At their national writers' festival there were literally hundreds of them. But the work of the vast majority will be closed to the rest of the world forever, including no doubt the work of some excellent writers. There is certainly a great advantage to writing in a world language.

I think I have said enough to give an indication of my thinking on the importance of the world language which history has forced down our throats. Now let us look at some of the most serious handicaps. And let me say straightaway that one of the most serious handicaps is *not* the one people talk about most often, namely, that it is impossible for anyone ever to use a second language as effectively as his first. This assertion is compounded of half truth and half bogus mystique. Of course, it is true that the vast majority of people are happier with their first language than with any other. But then the majority of people are not writers. We do have enough examples of writers who have performed the feat of writing effectively in a second language. And I am not thinking of the obvious names like Conrad. It would be more germane to our subject to choose African examples.

The first name that comes to my mind is Olauda Equiano, better known as Gustavus Vassa, the African. Equiano was an Ibo, I believe from the village of Iseke in the Orlu division of Eastern Nigeria. He was sold as a slave at a very early age and transported to America. Later he bought his freedom and lived in England. In 1789 he published his life story, a beautifully written document which, among other things, set down for the Europe of his time something of the life and habit of his people in Africa, in an attempt to counteract the lies and slander invented by some Europeans to justify the slave trade.

25   Coming nearer to our times, we may recall the attempts in the first quarter of this century by West African nationalists to come together and press for a greater say in the management of their own affairs. One of the most eloquent of that band was the Honorable Casely Hayford of the Gold Coast. His presidential address to the National Congress of British West Africa in 1925 was memorable not only for its sound common sense but as a fine example of elegant prose. The governor of Nigeria at the time was compelled to

take notice and he did so in characteristic style: he called Hayford's Congress 'a self-selected and self-appointed congregation of educated African gentlemen'. We may derive some amusement from the fact that British colonial administrators learned very little in the following quarter of a century. But at least they *did* learn in the end— which is more than one can say for some others.

It is when we come to what is commonly called creative literature that most doubt seems to arise. Obi Wali, whose article 'Dead end of African Literature' I referred to, has this to say:

until these writers and their Western midwives accept the fact that any true African literature must be written in African languages, they would be merely pursuing a dead end, which can only lead to sterility, uncreativity and frustration.

But far from leading to sterility, the work of many new African writers is full of the most exciting possibilities.

Take this from Christopher Okigbo's 'Limits':

Suddenly becoming talkative
    like weaverbird
Summoned at offside of
    dream remembered
Between sleep and waking
I hand up my egg-shells
To you of palm grove,
Upon whose bamboo towers hang
Dripping with yesterupwine
A tiger mask and nude spear....

Queen of the damp half light,
    I have had my cleansing.

Emigrant with air-borne nose,
    The he-goat-on-heat.

Or take the poem, 'Night Rain', in which J.P. Clark captures so well the fear and wonder felt by a child as rain clamors on the thatch roof at night and his mother, walking about in the dark, moves her simple belongings

Out of the run of water
That like ants filing out of the wood
Will scatter and gain possession
Of the floor....

30   I think that the picture of water spreading on the floor 'like ants filing out of the wood' is beautiful. Of course if you had never made fire with faggots, you may miss it. But Clark's inspiration derives from the same source which gave birth to the saying that a man who brings home ant-ridden faggots must be ready for the visit of lizards.

I do not see any signs of sterility anywhere here. What I do see is a new voice coming out of Africa, speaking of African experience in a world-wide language. So my answer to the question *Can an African ever learn English well enough to be able to use it effectively in creative writing?* is certainly yes. If on the other hand you ask: *Can he ever learn to use it like a native speaker?* I should say, I hope not. It is neither necessary nor desirable for him to be able to do so. The price a world language must be prepared to pay is submission to many different kinds of use. The African writer should aim to use English in a way that brings out his message best without altering the language to the extent that its value as a medium of international exchange will be lost. He should aim at fashioning out an English which is at once universal and able to carry his peculiar experience. I have in mind here the writer who has something new, something different to say. The nondescript writer has little to tell us, anyway, so he might as well tell it in conventional language and get it over with. If I may use an extravagant simile, he is like a man offering a small, nondescript routine sacrifice for which a chick, or less, will do. A serious writer must look for an animal whose blood can match the power of his offering.

In this respect Amos Tutuola is a natural. A good instinct has turned his apparent limitation in language into a weapon of great strength—a half-strange dialect that serves him perfectly in the evocation of his bizarre world. His last book, and to my mind, his finest, is proof enough that one can make even an imperfectly learned second language do amazing things. In this book, *The Feather Woman of the Jungle*, Tutuola's superb storytelling is at last cast in the episodic form which he handles best instead of being painfully stretched on the rack of the novel.

From a natural to a conscious artist: myself, in fact. Allow me to quote a small example from *Arrow of God*, which may give some idea of how I approach the use of English. The Chief Priest in the story is telling one of his sons why it is necessary to send him to church:

> I want one of my sons to join these people and be my eyes there. If there is nothing in it you will come back. But if there is something there you will bring home my share.
>
> The world is like a Mask, dancing. If you want to see it well you do not stand in one place. My spirit tells me that those who do not befriend the white man today will be saying *had we known* tomorrow.

Now supposing I had put it another way. Like this for instance:

> I am sending you as my representative among these people—just to be on the safe side in case the new religion develops. One has to move with the times or else one is left behind. I have a hunch that those who fail to come to terms with the white man may well regret their lack of foresight.

35   The material is the same. But the form of the one is *in character* and the other is not. It is largely a matter of instinct, but judgment comes into it too.

You read quite often nowadays of the problems of the African writer having first to think in his mother tongue and then to translate what he has thought into English. If it were such a simple, mechanical process, I would agree that it was pointless—the kind of eccentric pursuit you might expect to see in a modern Academy of Lagado; and such a process could not possibly produce some of the exciting poetry and prose which is already appearing.

One final point remains for me to make. The real question is not whether Africans *could* write in English but whether they *ought* to. Is it right that a man should abandon his mother tongue for someone else's? It looks like a dreadful betrayal and produces a guilty feeling.

But for me there is no other choice. I have been given this language and I intend to use it. I hope, though, that there always will be men, like the late Chief Fagunwa, who will choose to write in their native tongue and insure that our ethnic literature will flourish side by side with the national ones. For those of us who opt for English, there is much work ahead and much excitement.

Writing in the London *Observer* recently, James Baldwin said:

> My quarrel with the English language has been that the language reflected none of my experience. But now I began to see the matter another way.... Perhaps the language was not my own because I had never attempted to use it, had only learned to imitate it. If this were so, then it might be made to bear the burden of my experience if I could find the stamina to challenge it, and me, to such a test.

40   I recognize, of course, that Baldwin's problem is not exactly mine, but I feel that the English language will be able to carry the weight of my African experience. But it will have to be a new English, still in full communion with its ancestral home but altered to suit its new African surroundings.

THE LANGUAGE OF AFRICAN LITERATURE

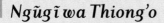

Ngũgĩ wa Thiong'o

Ngũgĩ wa Thiong'o is a Kenyan writer who wrote several novels in English, including *Weep Not, Child* (1964), *A Grain of Wheat* (1967), and *Petals of Blood* (1977). In 1977, however, Ngũgĩ began writing novels, plays, and children's books in this mother tongue, the African language Gĩkũyũ. Here are excerpts from his essay "The Language of African Literature," in which he explains why he changed languages. The essay appears in the collection *Decolonising the Mind* (1986).

SUGGESTION   Notice that Ngũgĩ wa Thiong'o quotes Chinua Achebe twice in this selection—once in the
FOR READING   opening section and then in the closing section. As you read, consider how Ngũgĩ wa Thiong'o
uses these quotes to position himself in relation to Achebe.

II

1   Why, we may ask, should an African writer, or
any writer, become so obsessed by taking from
his mother-tongue to enrich other tongues? Why
should he see it as his particular mission? We
never asked ourselves: how can we enrich our
languages? How can we 'prey' on the rich
humanist and democratic heritage in the struggles of other peoples in other times and other
places to enrich our own? Why not have Balzac,
Tolstoy, Sholokov, Brecht, Lu Hsun, Pablo Neruda,
H. C. Anderson, Kim Chi Ha, Marx, Lenin, Albert
Einstein, Galileo, Aeschylus, Aristotle and Plato in
African languages? And why not create literary
monuments in our own languages? Why in other
words should Gabriel Okara not sweat it out to
create in Ijaw, which he acknowledged to have
depths of philosophy and a wide range of ideas
and experiences? What was our responsibility to
the struggles of African peoples? No, these questions were not asked. What seemed to worry us
more was this: after all the literary gymnastics of
preying on our languages to add life and vigour
to English and other foreign languages, would the
result be accepted as good English or good
French? Will the owner of the language criticise
our usage? Here we were more assertive of our
rights! Chinua Achebe wrote:

> I feel that the English language will be able to
> carry the weight of my African experience. But it
> will have to be a new English, still in full
> communion with its ancestral home but altered
> to suit new African surroundings.

Gabriel Okara's position on this was representative of our generation:

> Some may regard this way of writing English as
> a desecration of the language. This is of course
> not true. Living languages grow like living things,
> and English is far from a dead language. There
> are American, West Indian, Australian, Canadian
> and New Zealand versions of English. All of them

add life and vigour to the language while
reflecting their own respective cultures. Why
shouldn't there be a Nigerian or West African
English which we can use to express our own
ideas, thinking and philosophy in our own way?

How did we arrive at this acceptance of 'the
fatalistic logic of the unassailable position of English in our literature', in our culture and in our politics? What was the route from the Berlin of 1884
via the Makerere of 1962 to what is still the prevailing and dominant logic a hundred years later?
How did we, as African writers, come to be so fee-
ble towards the claims of our languages on us and
so aggressive in our claims on other languages,
particularly the languages of our colonisation?

Berlin of 1884 was effected through the
sword and the bullet. But the night of the sword
and the bullet was followed by the morning of the
chalk and the blackboard. The physical violence
of the battlefield was followed by the psychological violence of the classroom. But where the former was visibly brutal, the latter was visibly
gentle, a process best described in Cheikh Hami-
dou Kane's novel *Ambiguous Adventure* where he
talks of the methods of the colonial phase of
imperialism as consisting of knowing how to kill
with efficiency and to heal with the same art.

> On the Black Continent, one began to
> understand that their real power resided not at
> all in the cannons of the first morning but in
> what followed the cannons. Therefore behind
> the cannons was the new school. The new
> school had the nature of both the cannon and
> the magnet. From the cannon it took the
> efficiency of a fighting weapon. But better than
> the cannon it made the conquest permanent.
> The cannon forces the body and the school
> fascinates the soul.

5   In my view language was the most important
vehicle through which that power fascinated and
held the soul prisoner. The bullet was the means
of the physical subjugation. Language was the

means of the spiritual subjugation. Let me illustrate this by drawing upon experiences in my own education, particularly in language and literature.

III

I was born into a large peasant family: father, four wives and about twenty-eight children. I also belonged, as we all did in those days, to a wider extended family and to the community as a whole.

We spoke Gĩkũyũ as we worked in the fields. We spoke Gĩkũyũ in and outside the home. I can vividly recall those evenings of storytelling around the fireside. It was mostly the grown-ups telling the children but everybody was interested and involved. We children would re-tell the stories the following day to other children who worked in the fields picking the pyrethrum flowers, tea-leaves or coffee beans of our European and African landlords.

The stories, with mostly animals as the main characters, were all told in Gĩkũyũ. Hare, being small, weak but full of innovative wit and cunning, was our hero. We identified with him as he struggled against the brutes of prey like lion, leopard, hyena. His victories were our victories and we learnt that the apparently weak can outwit the strong. We followed the animals in their struggle against hostile nature—drought, rain, sun, wind—a confrontation often forcing them to search for forms of cooperation. But we were also interested in their struggles amongst themselves, and particularly between the beasts and the victims of prey. These twin struggles, against nature and other animals, reflected real-life struggles in the human world.

Not that we neglected stories with human beings as the main characters. There were two types of characters in such human-centred narratives: the species of truly human beings with qualities of courage, kindness, mercy, hatred of evil, concern for others; and a man-eat-man two-mouthed species with qualities of greed, selfishness, individualism and hatred of what was good for the larger co-operative community. Co-operation as the ultimate good in a community was

a constant theme. It could unite human beings with animals against ogres and beasts of prey, as in the story of how dove, after being fed with castor-oil seeds, was sent to fetch a smith working far away from home and whose pregnant wife was being threatened by these man-eating two-mouthed ogres.

10   There were good and bad story-tellers. A good one could tell the same story over and over again, and it would always be fresh to us, the listeners. He or she could tell a story told by someone else and make it more alive and dramatic. The differences really were in the use of words and images and the inflexion of voices to effect different tones.

We therefore learnt to value words for their meaning and nuances. Language was not a mere string of words. It had a suggestive power well beyond the immediate and lexical meaning. Our appreciation of the suggestive magical power of language was reinforced by the games we played with words through riddles, proverbs, transpositions of syllables, or through nonsensical but musically arranged words. So we learnt the music of our language on top of the content. The language, through images and symbols, gave us a view of the world, but it had a beauty of its own. The home and the field were then our pre-primary school but what is important, for this discussion, is that the language of our evening teach-ins, and the language of our immediate and wider community, and the language of our work in the fields were one.

And then I went to school, a colonial school, and this harmony was broken. The language of my education was no longer the language of my culture. I first went to Kamaandura, missionary run, and then to another called Maanguuũ run by nationalists grouped around the Gĩkũyũ Independent and Karinga Schools Association. Our language of education was still Gĩkũyũ. The very first time I was ever given an ovation for my writing was over a composition in Gĩkũyũ. So for my first four years there was still harmony between the language of my formal education and that of the Limuru peasant community.

It was after the declaration of a state of emergency over Kenya in 1952 that all the schools run by patriotic nationalists were taken over by the colonial regime and were placed under District Education Boards chaired by Englishmen. English became the language of my formal education. In Kenya, English became more than a language: it was *the* language, and all the others had to bow before it in deference.

Thus one of the most humiliating experiences was to be caught speaking Gĩkũyũ in the vicinity of the school. The culprit was given corporal punishment—three to five strokes of the cane on bare buttocks—or was made to carry a metal plate around the neck with inscriptions such as I AM STUPID or I AM A DONKEY. Sometimes the culprits were fined money they could hardly afford. And how did the teachers catch the culprits? A button was initially given to one pupil who was supposed to hand it over to whoever was caught speaking his mother tongue. Whoever had the button at the end of the day would sing who had given it to him and the ensuing process would bring out all the culprits of the day. Thus children were turned into witch-hunters and in the process were being taught the lucrative value of being a traitor to one's immediate community.

15   The attitude to English was the exact opposite: any achievement in spoken or written English was highly rewarded; prizes, prestige, applause; the ticket to higher realms. English became the measure of intelligence and ability in the arts, the sciences, and all the other branches of learning. English became *the* main determinant of a child's progress up the ladder of formal education.

As you may know, the colonial system of education in addition to its apartheid racial demarcation had the structure of a pyramid: a broad primary base, a narrowing secondary middle and an even narrower university apex. Selections from primary into secondary were through an examination, in my time called Kenya African Preliminary Examination, in which one had to pass six subjects ranging from Maths to Nature Study and Kiswahili. All the papers were written in English. Nobody could pass the exam who failed the English language paper no matter how brilliantly he had done in the other subjects. I remember one boy in my class of 1954 who had distinctions in all subjects except English, which he had failed. He was made to fail the entire exam. He went on to become a turn boy in a bus company. I who had only passes but a credit in English got a place at the Alliance High School, one of the most elitist institutions for Africans in colonial Kenya. The requirements for a place at the University, Makerere University College, were broadly the same: nobody could go on to wear the undergraduate red gown, no matter how brilliantly they had performed in all the other subjects, unless they had a credit—not even a simple pass!—in English. Thus the most coveted place in the pyramid and in the system was only available to the holder of an English language credit card. English was the official vehicle and the magic formula to colonial elitedom.

Literary education was now determined by the dominant language while also reinforcing that dominance. Orature (oral literature) in Kenyan languages stopped. In primary school I now read simplified Dickens and Stevenson alongside Rider Haggard. Jim Hawkins, Oliver Twist, Tom Brown—not Hare, Leopard and Lion—were now my daily companions in the world of imagination. In secondary school Scott and G. B. Shaw vied with more Rider Haggard, John Buchan, Alan Paton, Captain W. E. Johns. At Makerere I read English: from Chaucer to T. S. Eliot with a touch of Graham Greene.

Thus language and literature were taking us further and further from ourselves to other selves, from our world to other worlds.

What was the colonial system doing to us Kenyan children? What were the consequences of, on the one hand, this systematic suppression of our languages and the literature they carried, and on the other the elevation of English and the literature it carried? To answer those questions, let me first examine the relationship of language to human experience, human culture and the human perception of reality.

VII

20 But African languages refused to die. They would not simply go the way of Latin to become the fossils for linguistic archaeology to dig up, classify, and argue about at international conferences.

These languages, these national heritages of Africa, were kept alive by the peasantry. The peasantry saw no contradiction between speaking their own mother-tongues and belonging to a larger national or continental geography. They saw no necessary antagonistic contradiction between belonging to their immediate nationality, to their multinational state along the Berlin-drawn boundaries, and to Africa as a whole. These people happily spoke Wolof, Hausa, Yoruba, Ibo, Arabic, Amharic, Kiswahili, Gĩkũyũ, Luo, Luhya, Shona, Ndebele, Kimbundu, Zulu or Lingala without this fact tearing the multinational states apart. During the anti-colonial struggle they showed an unlimited capacity to unite around whatever leader or party best and most consistently articulated an anti-imperialist position. If anything it was the petty-bourgeoisie, particularly the compradors, with their French and English and Portuguese, with their petty rivalries, their ethnic chauvinism, which encouraged these vertical divisions to the point of war at times. No, the peasantry had no complexes about their languages and the cultures they carried!

In fact when the peasantry and the working class were compelled by necessity or history to adopt the language of the master, they Africanised it without any of the respect for its ancestry shown by Senghor and Achebe, so totally as to have created new African languages, like Krio in Sierra Leone or Pidgin in Nigeria, that owed their identities to the syntax and rhythms of African languages. All these languages were kept alive in the daily speech, in the ceremonies in political struggles, above all in the rich store of orature—proverbs, stories, poems and riddles.

The peasantry and the urban working class threw up singers. These sang the old songs or composed new ones incorporating the new experiences in industries and urban life and in working-class struggle and organisations. These singers pushed the languages to new limits, renewing and reinvigorating them by coining new words and new expressions, and in generally expanding their capacity to incorporate new happenings in Africa and the world.

The peasantry and the working class threw up their own writers, or attracted to their ranks and concern intellectuals from among the petty-bourgeoisie, who all wrote in African languages. It is these writers like Heruy Wäldä Sellassie, Germacäw Takla Hawaryat, Shabaan Robert, Abdullatif Abdalla, Ebrahim Hussein, Euphrase Kezilahabi, B. H. Vilakazi, Okot p'Bitek, A. C. Jordan, P. Mboya, D. O. Fagunwa, Mazisi Kunene and many others rightly celebrated in Albert Gérard's pioneering survey of literature in African languages from the tenth century to the present, called *African Language Literatures* (1981), who have given our languages a written literature. Thus the immortality of our languages in print has been ensured despite the internal and external pressures for their extinction. In Kenya I would like to single out Gakaara we Wanjaū, who was jailed by the British for the ten years between 1952 and 1962 because of his writing in Gĩkũyũ. His book, *Mwandĩki wa Mau Mau Ithaamĩrioinĩ*, a diary he secretly kept while in political detention, was published by Heinemann Kenya and won the 1984 Noma Award. It is a powerful work, extending the range of the Gĩkũyũ language prose, and it is a crowning achievement to the work he started in 1946. He has worked in poverty, in the hardships of prison, in post-independence isolation when the English language held sway in Kenya's schools from nursery to University and in every walk of the national printed world, but he never broke his faith in the possibilities of Kenya's national languages. His inspiration came from the mass anti-colonial movement of Kenyan people, particularly the militant wing grouped around Mau Mau or the Kenya Land and Freedom Army, which in 1952 ushered in the era of modern guerrilla warfare in Africa. He is the clearest example of those writers thrown up by the mass political movements of an awakened peasantry and working class.

25   And finally from among the European-language-speaking African petty-bourgeoisie there emerged a few who refused to join the chorus of those who had accepted the 'fatalistic logic' of the position of European languages in our literary being. It was one of these, Obi Wali, who pulled the carpet from under the literary feet of those who gathered at Makerere in 1962 by declaring in an article published in *Transition* (10, September 1963), 'that the whole uncritical acceptance of English and French as the inevitable medium for educated African writing is misdirected, and has no chance of advancing African literature and culture', and that until African writers cultural level continuing that neo-colonial slavish and cringing spirit? What is the difference between a politician who says Africa cannot do without imperialism and the writer who says Africa cannot do without European languages?

While we were busy haranguing the ruling circles in a language which automatically excluded the participation of the peasantry and the working class in the debate, imperialist culture and African reactionary forces had a field day: the Christian bible is available in unlimited quantities in even the tiniest African language. The comprador ruling cliques are also quite happy to have the peasantry and the working class all to themselves: distortions, dictatorial directives, decrees, museum-type fossils paraded as African culture, feudalistic ideologies, superstitions, lies, all these backward elements and more are communicated to the African masses in their own languages without any challenges from those with alternative visions of tomorrow who have deliberately cocooned themselves in English, French and Portuguese. It is ironic that the most reactionary African politician, the one who believes in selling Africa to Europe, is often a master of African lan-

guages; that the most zealous of European missionaries who believed in rescuing Africa from itself, even from the paganism of its languages, were nevertheless masters of African languages, which they often reduced to writing. The European missionary believed too much in his mission of conquest not to communicate it in the languages most readily available to the people: the African writer believes too much in 'African literature' to write it in those ethnic, divisive and underdeveloped languages of the peasantry!

The added irony is that what they have produced, despite any claims to the contrary, is not African literature. The editors of the Pelican Guides to English literature in their latest volume were right to include a discussion of this literature as part of twentieth-century English literature, just as the French Academy was right to honour Senghor for his genuine and talented contribution to French literature and language. What we have created is another hybrid tradition, a tradition in transition, a minority tradition that can only be termed as Afro-European literature; that is, the literature written by Africans in European languages. It has produced many writers and works of genuine talent: Chinua Achebe, Wole Soyinka, Ayi Kwei Armah, Sembene Ousmane, Agostino Neto, Sédar Senghor and many others. Who can deny their talent? The light in the products of their fertile imaginations has certainly illuminated important aspects of the African being in its continuous struggle against the political and economic consequences of Berlin and after. However, we cannot have our cake and eat it! Their work belongs to an Afro-European literary tradition which is likely to last for as long as Africa is under this rule of European capital in a neo-colonial set-up. So Afro-European literature can be defined as literature written by Africans in European languages in the era of imperialism.

But some are coming round to the inescapable conclusion articulated by Obi Wali with such polemical vigour twenty years ago: African literature can only be written in African languages, that is, the languages of the African peasantry and working class, the major alliance of classes in each of our nationalities and the agency for the coming inevitable revolutionary break with neo-colonialism.

IX

I started writing in Gĩkũyũ language in 1977 after seventeen years of involvement in Afro-European literature, in my case Afro-English literature. It was then that I collaborated with Ngũgĩ wa Mĩriĩ in the drafting of the playscript *Ngaahika Ndeenda* (the English translation was *I Will Marry When I Want*). I have since published a novel in Gĩkũyũ, *Caitaani Mũtharabainĩ* (English translation: *Devil on the Cross*), and completed a musical drama, *Maitũ Njugĩra* (English translation: *Mother Sing for Me*), three books for children, *Njamba Nene na Mbaathi i Mathagu, Bathitoora ya Njamba Nene, Njamba Nene na CibũKĩng'ang'i*, as well as another novel manuscript: *Matigari Ma Njirũũngi*. Wherever I have gone, particularly in Europe, I have been confronted with the question: why are you now writing in Gĩkũyũ? Why do you now write in an African language? In some academic quarters I have been confronted with the rebuke, 'Why have you abandoned us?' It was almost as if, in choosing to write in Gĩkũyũ, I was doing something abnormal. But Gĩkũyũ is my mother tongue! The very fact that what common sense dictates in the literary practice of other cultures is being questioned in an African writer is a measure of how far imperialism has distorted the view of African realities. It has turned reality upside down: the abnormal is viewed as normal and the normal is viewed as abnormal. Africa actually enriches Europe: but Africa is made to believe that it needs Europe to rescue it from poverty. Africa's natural and human resources continue to develop Europe and America: but Africa is made to feel grateful for aid from the same quarters that still sit on the back of the continent. Africa even produces intellectuals who now rationalise this upside-down way of looking at Africa.

30   I believe that my writing in Gĩkũyũ language, a Kenyan language, an African language, is part and parcel of the anti-imperialist struggles of Kenyan and African peoples. In schools and uni-versities our Kenyan languages—that is the languages of the many nationalities which make up Kenya—were associated with negative qualities of backwardness, underdevelopment, humiliation and punishment. We who went through that school system were meant to graduate with a hatred of the people and the culture and the values of the language of our daily humiliation and punishment. I do not want to see Kenyan children growing up in that imperialist-imposed tradition of contempt for the tools of communication developed by their communities and their history. I want them to transcend colonial alienation.

Colonial alienation takes two interlinked forms: an active (or passive) distancing of oneself from the reality around; and an active (or passive) identification with that which is most external to one's environment. It starts with a deliberate disassociation of the language of conceptualisation, of thinking, of formal education, of mental development, from the language of daily interaction in the home and in the community. It is like separating the mind from the body so that they are occupying two unrelated linguistic spheres in the same person. On a larger social scale it is like producing a society of bodiless heads and headless bodies.

So I would like to contribute towards the restoration of the harmony between all the aspects and divisions of language so as to restore the Kenyan child to his environment, understand it fully so as to be in a position to change it for his collective good. I would like to see Kenyan peoples' mother-tongues (our national languages!) carry a literature reflecting not only the rhythms of a child's spoken expression, but also his struggle with nature and his social nature. With that harmony between himself, his language and his environment as his starting point, he can learn other languages and even enjoy the positive humanistic, democratic and revolutionary elements in other people's literatures and cultures without any complexes about his own language, his own self, his environment. The all-Kenya national language (i.e. Kiswahili); the other national languages (i.e. the languages of the nationalities like Luo, Gīkūyū, Maasai, Luhya, Kallenjin, Kamba, Mijikenda, Somali, Galla, Turkana, Arabic-speaking people, etc.); other African languages like Hausa, Wolof, Yoruba, Ibo, Zulu, Nyanja, Lingala, Kimbundu; and foreign languages—that is foreign to Africa—like English, French, German, Russian, Chinese, Japanese, Portuguese, Spanish will fall into their proper perspective in the lives of Kenyan children.

Chinua Achebe once decried the tendency of African intellectuals to escape into abstract universalism in the words that apply even more to the issue of the language of African literature:

Africa has had such a fate in the world that the very adjective *African* can call up hideous fears of rejection. Better then to cut all the links with this homeland, this liability, and become in one giant leap the universal man. Indeed I understand this anxiety. *But running away from oneself seems to me a very inadequate way of dealing with an anxiety* [italics mine]. And if writers should opt for such escapism, who is to meet the challenge?

Who indeed?

35   We African writers are bound by our calling to do for our languages what Spenser, Milton and Shakespeare did for English; what Pushkin and Tolstoy did for Russian; indeed what all writers in world history have done for their languages by meeting the challenge of creating a literature in them, which process later opens the languages for philosophy, science, technology and all the other areas of human creative endeavours.

But writing in our languages per se—although a necessary first step in the correct direction—will not itself bring about the renaissance in African cultures if that literature does not carry the content of our people's anti-imperialist struggles to liberate their productive forces from foreign control; the content of the need for unity among the workers and peasants of all the nationalities in their struggle to control the wealth they produce and to free it from internal and external parasites.

In other words writers in African languages should reconnect themselves to the revolutionary traditions of an organised peasantry and working class in Africa in their struggle to defeat imperialism and create a higher system of democracy and socialism in alliance with all the other peoples of the world. Unity in that struggle would ensure unity in our multi-lingual diversity. It would also reveal the real links that bind the people of Africa to the peoples of Asia, South America, Europe, Australia and New Zealand, Canada and the USA.

But it is precisely when writers open out African languages to the real links in the struggles of peasants and workers that they will meet their biggest challenge. For to the comprador-ruling regimes, their real enemy is an awakened peasantry and working class. A writer who tries to communicate the message of revolutionary unity and hope in the languages of the people becomes a subversive character. It is then that writing in African languages becomes a subversive or treasonable offence with such a writer facing possibilities of prison, exile or even death. For him there are no 'national' accolades, no new year honours, only abuse and slander and innumerable lies from the mouths of the armed power of a ruling minority—ruling, that is, on behalf of US-led imperialism—and who see in democracy a real threat. A democratic participation of the people in the shaping of their own lives or in discussing their own lives in languages that allow for mutual comprehension is seen as being dangerous to the good government of a country and its institutions. African languages addressing themselves to the lives of the people become the enemy of a neo-colonial state.

SUGGESTIONS FOR DISCUSSION

1. Chinua Achebe answers "certainly yes" to "the question *Can an African ever learn English well enough to be able to use it effectively in creative writing?*" But to the question "*Can he ever learn to use it like a native speaker?*" Achebe says, "I hope not." Explain Achebe's response to the second question. What does it reveal about his attitude toward the English language and the role he sees for it in African writing?

2. Ngũgĩ wa Thiong'o began his literary career writing what he calls "Afro-European literature" in English. How does he explain his decision to write in his mother tongue, Gĩkũyũ? Consider here not only what Ngũgĩ says explicitly about his decision but also how he recreates his own past growing up and in school and how he describes the situation of African literature.

3. Compare Achebe's and Ngũgĩ's view of language and culture. Consider, for example, how much power each ascribes to language, whether English or African, in conveying cultural values and determining cultural identities. Is the relationship between language and culture fixed or is it fluid and malleable? What do you see as the main similarities and differences in the two writers' views? What do you see as the significance of their debate?

CASE STUDY: SUGGESTIONS FOR WRITING

1. The selections in the Case Study, from one perspective or another, consider the spread of English to "non native speakers" in Asia and Africa. From the evidence you can find in these readings and any others in the chapter, how would you evaluate the diffusion of English? Consider, to begin with, arguments Pennycock presents in "Our Marvellous Tongue" that seek to explain the spread of English. Then consider the experience of Asian students and African writers. How do they clash or mesh with explanations of English's role as a world language? What do these various perspectives reveal about English's relationship to non native speakers?

2. Write an analysis of the debate between Achebe and Ngugi. You may side with one or the other, if you wish, but it's not really necessary for this assignment. The main thing is for you to bring out the meaning and significance in their positions and underlying assumptions. What is at stake in the debate for how we understand the relationship between language and culture? Draw on the selections from Pennycock in the Case Study, Gloria Anzaldúa's "How to Tame a Wild Tongue," and any other reading in the chapter as you see fit.

3. The Case Study suggests that English not only has spread throughout the world but that it changes as it spreads. Accordingly, when we talk about English, we are actually talking not so much about a single language as about a variety of Englishes. Consider the various Englishes you have encountered where you live or grew up. Draw on readings in this chapter, as well as June Jordan's "Nobody Mean More to Me Than You and the Future Life of Willie Jordan," to write an essay that examines the meaning of these various Englishes to the people who speak them and the relationship of these various Englishes to the standard of English you learn in school.

CULTURE AND IMPERIALISM

Edward W. Said

Edward W. Said is University Professor at Columbia University and one of the leading literary and cultural critics in the world today. His book *Orientalism* (1978) is a groundbreaking analysis of European representations of the Arab world and a founding work in postcolonial studies. The following excerpts, "American Ascendancy: The Public Space at War" and "Movements and Migrations," come from the final chapter of *Culture and Imperialism* (1994). After examining the logic of colonialism in Western culture and literature,

Said turns at the end of his book to the persistent legacy of imperialism in the late twentieth century and the possibility of more hopeful and humane relations between the West and the formerly colonized world.

SUGGESTION   Read the two excerpts in relation to each other. Notice how Said first establishes the continu-
FOR READING   ity of imperialism in the contemporary United States and in the next section considers the possibilities of change.

AMERICAN ASCENDANCY: THE PUBLIC SPACE AT WAR

1 Imperialism did not end, did not suddenly become "past," once decolonization had set in motion the dismantling of the classical empires. A legacy of connections still binds countries like Algeria and India to France and Britain respectively. A vast new population of Muslims, Africans, and West Indians from former colonial territories now resides in metropolitan Europe; even Italy, Germany, and Scandinavia today must deal with these dislocations, which are to a large degree the result of imperialism and decolonization as well as expanding European population. Also, the end of the Cold War and of the Soviet Union has definitively changed the world map. The triumph of the United States as the last superpower suggests that a new set of force lines will structure the world, and they were already beginning to be apparent in the 1960s and '70s.

Michael Barratt-Brown, in a preface to the 1970 second edition of his *After Imperialism* (1963), argues "that imperialism is still without question a most powerful force in the economic, political and military relations by which the less economically developed lands are subjected to the more economically developed. We may still look forward to its ending." It is ironic that descriptions of the new form of imperialism have regularly employed idioms of gigantism and apocalypse that could not have as easily been applied to the classical empires during their heyday. Some of these descriptions have an extraordinarily dispiriting inevitability, a kind of galloping, engulfing, impersonal, and deterministic quality. Accumulation on a world scale; the world capitalist system; the development of

underdevelopment; imperialism and dependency, or the structure of dependence; poverty and imperialism: the repertory is well-known in economics, political science, history, and sociology, and it has been identified less with the New World Order than with members of a controversial Left school of thought. Nevertheless the cultural implications of such phrases and concepts are discernible—despite their oft-debated and far from settled nature—and, alas, they are undeniably depressing to even the most untutored eye.

What are the salient features of the re-presentation of the old imperial inequities, the persistence, in Arno Mayer's telling phrase, of the old regime? One certainly is the immense economic rift between poor and rich states, whose basically quite simple topography was drawn in the starkest terms by the so-called Brandt Report, *North-South: A Program for Survival* (1980). Its conclusions are couched in the language of crisis and emergency: the poorest nations of the Southern Hemisphere must have their "priority needs" addressed, hunger must be abolished, commodity earnings strengthened; manufacturing in the Northern Hemisphere should permit genuine growth in Southern manufacturing centers, transnational corporations should be "restricted" in their practices, the global monetary system should be reformed, development finance should be changed to eliminate what has been accurately described as "the debt trap." The crux of the matter is, as the report's phrase has it, power-sharing, that is, giving the Southern countries a more equitable share in "power and decision-making within monetary and financial institutions."

It is difficult to disagree with the report's diagnosis, which is made more credible by its balanced tone and its silent picture of the untrammelled rapacity, greed, and immorality of the North, or even with its recommendations. But how will the changes come about? The post-war classifications of all the nations into three "worlds"—coined by a French journalist—has largely been abandoned. Willy Brandt and his colleagues implicitly concede that the United Nations, an admirable organization in principle, has not been adequate to the innumerable regional and global conflicts that occur with increasing frequency. With the exception of the work of small groups (e.g., the World Order Models Project), global thinking tends to reproduce the superpower, Cold War, regional, ideological, or ethnic contests of old, even more dangerous in the nuclear and post-nuclear era, as the horrors of Yugoslavia attest. The powerful are likely to get more powerful and richer, the weak less powerful and poorer; the gap between the two overrides the former distinctions between social-ist and capitalist regimes that, in Europe at least, have become less significant.

5   In 1982 Noam Chomsky concluded that dur-ing the 1980s

> the "North-South" conflict will not subside, and new forms of domination will have to be devised to ensure that privileged segments of Western industrial society maintain substantial control over global resources, human and material, and benefit disproportionately from this control. Thus it comes as no surprise that the reconstitu-tion of ideology in the United States finds echoes throughout the industrial world....But it is an absolute requirement for the Western system of ideology that a vast gulf be established between the civilized West, with its traditional commitment to human dignity, liberty, and self-determination, and the barbaric brutality of those who for some reason—perhaps defective genes—fail to appreciate the depth of this his-toric commitment, so well revealed by America's Asian wars, for example?

Chomsky's move from the North-South dilemma to American, and Western, dominance is, I think, basically correct, although the decrease in American economic power; the urban, economic, and cultural crisis in the United States; the ascendancy of Pacific Rim states; and the confusions of a multipolar world have muted the stridency of the Reagan period. For one it underlines the continuity of the ideological need to consolidate and justify domination in cultural terms that has been the case in the West since the nineteenth century, and even earlier. Second, it accurately picks up the theme based on repeated projections and theorizations of Amer-ican power, sounded in often very insecure and therefore overstated ways, that we live today in a period of American ascendancy...

Today the United States is triumphalist inter-nationally, and seems in a febrile way eager to prove that it is number one, perhaps to offset the recession, the endemic problems posed by the cities, poverty, health, education, production, and the Euro-Japanese challenge. Although an Amer-ican, I grew up in a cultural framework suffused with the idea that Arab nationalism was all-important, also that it was an aggrieved and unfulfilled nationalism, beset with conspiracies, enemies both internal and external, obstacles to overcome for which no price was too high.

My Arab environment had been largely colo-nial, but as I was growing up you could travel overland from Lebanon and Syria through Pales-tine to Egypt and points west. Today that is impossible. Each country places formidable obstacles at the borders. (And for Palestinians, crossing is an especially horrible experience, since often the countries who support Palestine loudly treat actual Palestinians the worst.) Arab nationalism has not died, but has all too often resolved itself into smaller and smaller units. Here too linkage comes last in the Arab setting. The past wasn't better, but it was more healthily interlinked, so to speak; people were actually connected to one another, rather than staring at one another over fortified frontiers. In many schools you would encounter Arabs from every-where, Muslims and Christians, plus Armenians, Jews, Greeks, Italians, Indians, Iranians, all mixed up, all under one or another colonial regime, but interacting as if it were natural to do so. Today state nationalisms fracture into clan or sectarian ones. Lebanon and Israel are perfect examples of what has happened: the desirability of rigid cantonization in one form or another is present nearly everywhere as a group feeling if not practice, and is subsidized by the state, with its bureaucracies and secret polices. Rulers are clans, families, cliques, closed circles of aging oligarchs, almost mythologically immune, like García Márquez's autumnal patriarch, to new blood or change.

10   The effort to homogenize and isolate populations in the name of nationalism (*not* liberation) has led to colossal sacrifices and failures. In most parts of the Arab world, civil society (universities, the media, and culture broadly speaking) has been swallowed up by political society, whose main form is the state. One of the great achievements of the early post-war Arab nationalist governments was mass literacy: in Egypt the results were dramatically beneficial almost beyond imagining. Yet the mixture of accelerated literacy and tub-thumping ideology exactly bears out Fanon's fears. My impression is that more effort is spent in sustaining the connection, bolstering the idea that to be Syrian, Iraqi, Egyptian, or Saudi is a sufficient end, rather than in thinking critically, even audaciously, about the national program itself. Identity, always identity, over and above knowing about others.

In this lopsided state of affairs, militarism gained far too many privileges in the Arab world's moral economy. Much of the reason has to do with the sense of being unjustly treated, for which Palestine was not only a metaphor but a reality. But was the only answer military force, huge armies, brassy slogans, bloody promises, and, along with that, endless concrete instances of militarism, starting with catastrophically lost wars at the top and working down to physical punishment and menacing gestures at the bottom? I do not know a single Arab who would demur in private, or who would not readily agree that the state's monopoly on coercion has almost completely eliminated democracy in the Arab

world, introduced immense hostility between rulers and ruled, placed much too high value on conformity, opportunism, flattery, and getting along rather than on risking new ideas, criticism, or dissent.

Taken far enough this produces exterminism, the notion that if you do not get your way or something displeases you it is possible simply to blot it out. That notion was surely in some way behind Iraq's aggression against Kuwait. What sort of muddled and anachronistic idea of Bismarckian "integration" was it to wipe out a country and smash its society with "Arab unity" as the goal? The most disheartening thing was that so many people, many of them victims of the same brutal logic, appear to have supported the action and sympathized not at all with Kuwait. Even if one grants that Kuwaitis were unpopular (does one have to be popular not to be exterminated?) and even if Iraq claimed to champion Palestine in standing up to Israel and the United States, surely the very idea that a nation should be obliterated along the way is a murderous proposition, unfit for a great civilization. It is a measure of the dreadful state of political culture in the Arab world today that such exterminism is current.

Oil, however much it may have brought development and prosperity—it did—where it was associated with violence, ideological refinement, political defensiveness, and cultural dependency on the United States created more rifts and social problems than it healed. For anyone who thinks of the Arab world as possessing a plausible sort of internal cohesion, the general air of mediocrity and corruption that hangs over this region that is limitlessly wealthy, superbly endowed culturally and historically, and amply blessed with gifted individuals is an immense puzzle and of course disappointment.

Democracy in any real sense of the word is nowhere to be found in the still "nationalistic" Middle East: there are either privileged oligarchies or privileged ethnic groups. The large mass of people is crushed beneath dictatorship or unyielding, unresponsive, unpopular government. But the notion that the United States is a virtuous innocent in this dreadful state of affairs is unacceptable, as is the proposition that the Gulf War was not a war between George Bush and Saddam Hussein—it most certainly was—and that the United States acted solely and principally in the interests of the United Nations. At bottom it was a personalized struggle between, on the one hand, a Third World dictator of the kind that the United States has long dealt with (Haile Selassie, Somoza, Syngman Rhee, the Shah of Iran, Pinochet, Marcos, Noriega, etc.), whose rule it encouraged, whose favors it long enjoyed, and, on the other, the president of a country which has taken on the mantle of empire inherited from Britain and France and was determined to remain in the Middle East for its oil and for reasons of geo-strategic and political advantage.

15   For two generations the United States has sided in the Middle East mostly with tyranny and injustice. No struggle for democracy, or women's rights, or secularism and the rights of minorities has the United States officially supported. Instead one administration after another has propped up compliant and unpopular clients, and turned away from the efforts of small peoples to liberate themselves from military occupation, while subsidizing their enemies. The United States has prompted unlimited militarism and (along with France, Britain, China, Germany, and others) engaged in vast arms sales everywhere in the region, mostly to governments which were driven to more and more extreme positions as a result of the United States' obsession with, and exaggeration of the power of Saddam Hussein. To conceive of a post-war Arab world dominated by the rulers of Egypt. Saudi Arabia, and Syria, all of them working in a new Pax Americana as part of the New World Order is neither intellectually nor morally credible.

There has not yet developed a discourse in the American public space that does anything more than identify with power, despite the dangers of that power in a world which has shrunk so small and has become so impressively interconnected. The United States cannot belligerently presume the right, with 6 percent of the world's population, to consume 30 percent of the world's energy, for example. But that is not all. For decades in America there has been a cultural war against the Arabs and Islam: appalling racist caricatures of Arabs and Muslims suggest that they are all either terrorists or sheikhs, and that the region is a large arid slum, fit only for profit or war. The very notion that there might be a history, a culture, a society—indeed many societies—has not held the stage for more than a moment or two, not even during the chorus of voices proclaiming the virtues of "multiculturalism." A flow of trivial instant books by journalists flooded the market and gained currency for a handful of dehumanizing stereotypes, all of them rendering the Arabs essentially as one or another variant of Saddam. As to the unfortunate Kurdish and Shi'ite insurgents, who were first encouraged by the United States to rise up against Saddam, then abandoned to his merciless revenge, they are scarcely remembered, much less mentioned.

After the sudden disappearance of Ambassador April Glaspie, who had long experience in the Middle East, the American administration had hardly any highly placed professional with any real knowledge or experience of the Middle East, its languages or its peoples. And after the systematic attack on its civilian infrastructure, Iraq is still being destroyed—by starvation, disease, and desperation—not because of its aggression against Kuwait, but because the United States wants a physical presence in the Gulf and an excuse to be there, wants to have direct leverage on oil to affect Europe and Japan, because it wishes to set the world agenda, because Iraq is still perceived as a threat to Israel.

Loyalty and patriotism should be based on a critical sense of what the facts are, and what, as residents of this shrinking and depleted planet, Americans owe their neighbors and the rest of mankind. Uncritical solidarity with the policy of the moment, especially when it is so unimaginably costly, cannot be allowed to rule.

Desert Storm was ultimately an imperial war against the Iraqi people, an effort to break and kill them as part of an effort to break and kill Saddam Hussein. Yet this anachronistic and singularly bloody aspect was largely kept from the American television audience, as a way of maintaining its image as a painless Nintendo exercise, and the image of Americans as virtuous, clean warriors. It might have made a difference even to Americans who are not normally interested in history to know that the last time Baghdad was destroyed was in 1258 by the Mongols, although the British furnish a more recent precedent for violent behavior against Arabs.

MOVEMENTS AND MIGRATIONS

20 For all its apparent power, this new overall pattern of domination, developed during an era of mass societies commanded at the top by a powerfully centralizing culture and a complex incorporative economy, is unstable. As the remarkable French urban sociologist Paul Virilio has said, it is a polity based on speed, instant communication, distant reach, constant emergency, insecurity induced by mounting crises, some of which lead to war. In such circumstances the rapid occupation of real as well as public space—colonization—becomes the central militaristic prerogative of the modern state, as the United States showed when it dispatched a huge army to the Arabian Gulf, and commandeered the media to help carry out the operation. As against that, Virilio suggests that the modernist project of liberating language/speech (*la libération de la parole*) has a parallel in the liberation of critical spaces—hospitals, universities, theaters, factories, churches, empty buildings; in both, the fundamental transgressive act is to inhabit the normally uninhabited. As examples, Virilio cites the cases of people whose current status is the consequence either of decolonization (migrant workers, refugees, *Gastarbeiter*) or of major demographic and political shifts (Blacks, immigrants, urban squatters, students, popular insurrections, etc.). These constitute a real alternative to the authority of the state.

If the 1960s are now remembered as a decade of European and American mass demonstrations (the university and anti-war uprisings chief among them), the 1980s must surely be the decade of mass uprisings outside the Western metropolis. Iran, the Philippines, Argentina, Korea, Pakistan, Algeria, China, South Africa, virtually all of Eastern Europe, the Israeli-occupied territories of Palestine: these are some of the most impressive crowd activated sites, each of them crammed with largely unarmed civilian populations, well past the point of enduring the imposed deprivations, tyranny, and inflexibility of governments that had ruled them for too long. Most memorable are, on the one hand, the resourcefulness and the startling symbolism of the protests themselves (the stone-throwing Palestinian youths, for example, or the swaying dancing South African groups, or the wall-traversing East Germans) and, on the other, the offensive brutality or collapse and ignominious departure of the governments.

Allowing for great differences in ideology, these mass protests have all challenged something very basic to every art and theory of government, the principle of confinement. To be governed people must be counted, taxed, educated, and of course ruled in regulated places (house, school, hospital, work site), whose ultimate extension is represented at its most simple and severe by the prison or mental hospital, as Michel Foucault argued. True, there was a carnivalesque aspect to the milling crowds in Gaza or in Wenceslas and Tiananmen squares, but the consequences of sustained mass unconfinement and unsettled existence were only a little less dramatic (and dispiriting) in the 1980s than before. The unresolved plight of the Palestinians speaks directly of an undomesticated cause and a rebellious people paying a very heavy price for their resistance. And there are other examples: refugees and "boat people," those unresting and vulnerable itinerants; the starving populations of the Southern Hemisphere; the destitute but insistent homeless who, like so many Bartlebys, shadow the Christmas shoppers in Western cities; the undocumented immigrants and exploited "guest workers" who provide cheap and usually seasonal labor. Between the extremes of discontented, challenging urban mobs and the floods of semi-forgotten, uncared-for people, the world's secular and religious authorities have sought new, or renewed, modes of governance.

None has seemed so easily available, so conveniently attractive as appeals to tradition, national or religious identity, patriotism. And because these appeals are amplified and disseminated by a perfected media system addressing mass cultures, they have been strikingly, not to say frighteningly effective. When in the spring of 1986 the Reagan administration decided to deal "terrorism" a blow, the raid on Libya was timed to occur exactly as prime-time national evening news began. "America strikes back" was answered resoundingly throughout the Muslim world with bloodcurdling appeals to "Islam," which in turn provoked an avalanche of images, writings, and postures in the "West" underscoring the value of "our" Judeo-Christian (Western, liberal, democratic) heritage and the nefariousness, evil, cruelty, and immaturity of theirs (Islamic, Third World, etc.)...

The major task, then, is to match the new economic and socio-political dislocations and configurations of our time with the startling realities of human interdependence on a world scale. If the Japanese, East European, Islamic, and Western instances express anything in common, it is that a new critical consciousness is needed, and this can be achieved only by revised attitudes to education. Merely to urge students to insist on one's own identity, history, tradition, uniqueness may initially get them to name their basic requirements for democracy and for the right to an assured, decently humane existence. But we need to go on and to situate these in a geography of other identities, peoples, cultures, and then to study how, despite their differences, they have always overlapped one another, through unhierarchical influence, crossing, incorporation, recollection, deliberate forgetfulness, and, of course, conflict. We are nowhere near "the end of history," but we are still far from free from monop-

olizing attitudes toward it. These have not been much good in the past—notwithstanding the rallying cries of the politics of separatist identity, multiculturalism, minority discourse—and the quicker we teach ourselves to find alternatives, the better and safer. The fact is, we are mixed in with one another in ways that most national systems of education have not dreamed of. To match knowledge in the arts and sciences with these integrative realities is, I believe, the intellectual and cultural challenge of moment.

25   The steady critique of nationalism, which derives from the various theorists of liberation I have discussed, should not be forgotten, for we must not condemn ourselves to repeat the imperial experience. In the redefined and yet very close contemporary relationship between culture and imperialism, a relationship that enables disquieting forms of domination, how can we sustain the liberating energies released by the great decolonizing resistance movements and the mass uprisings of the 1980s? Can these energies elude the homogenizing processes of modern life, hold in abeyance the interventions of the new imperial centrality?...

...Surely it is one of the unhappiest characteristics of the age to have produced more refugees, migrants, displaced persons, and exiles than ever before in history, most of them as an accompaniment to and, ironically enough, as afterthoughts of great post-colonial and imperial conflicts. As the struggle for independence produced new states and new boundaries, it also produced homeless wanderers, nomads, and vagrants, unassimilated to the emerging structures of institutional power, rejected by the established order for their intransigence and obdurate rebelliousness. And insofar as these people exist between the old and the new, between the old empire and the new state, their condition articulates the tensions, irresolutions, and contradictions in the overlapping territories shown on the cultural map of imperialism.

There is a great difference, however, between the optimistic mobility, the intellectual liveliness, and "the logic of daring" described by the various theoreticians on whose work I have drawn, and the massive dislocations, waste, misery, and horrors endured in our century's migrations and mutilated lives. Yet it is no exaggeration to say that liberation as an intellectual mission, born in the resistance and opposition to the confinements and ravages of imperialism, has now shifted from the settled, established, and domesticated dynamics of culture to its unhoused, decentered, and exilic energies, energies whose incarnation today is the migrant, and whose consciousness is that of the intellectual and artist in exile, the political figure between domains, between forms, between homes, and between languages. From this perspective then all things are indeed counter, original, spare, strange. From this perspective also, one can see "the complete consort dancing together" contrapuntally. And while it would be the rankest Panglossian dishonesty to say that the bravura performances of the intellectual exile and the miseries of the displaced person or refugee are the same, it is possible, I think, to regard the intellectual as first distilling then articulating the predicaments that disfigure modernity—mass deportation, imprisonment, population transfer, collective dispossession, and forced immigrations.

"The past life of emigrés is, as we know, annulled," says Adorno in *Minima Moralia*, subtitled *Reflections from a Damaged Life (Reflexionen aus dem beschädigten Leben)*. Why? "Because anything that is not reified, cannot be counted and measured, ceases to exist" or, as he says later, is consigned to mere "background." Although the disabling aspects of this fate are manifest, its virtues or possibilities are worth exploring. Thus the emigré consciousness—a mind of winter, in Wallace Stevens's phrase—discovers in its marginality that "a gaze averted from the beaten track, a hatred of brutality, a search for fresh concepts not yet encompassed by the general pattern, is the last hope for thought." Adorno's general pattern is what in another place he calls the "administered world" or, insofar as the irresistible dominants in culture are concerned, "the consciousness industry." There is then not just the negative advantage of refuge in the emigré's

eccentricity; there is also the positive benefit of challenging the system, describing it in language unavailable to those it has already subdued:

> In an intellectual hierarchy which constantly makes everyone answerable, unanswerability alone can call the hierarchy directly by its name. The circulation sphere, whose stigmata are borne by intellectual outsiders, opens a last refuge to the mind that it barters away, at the very moment when refuge no longer exists. He who offers for sale something unique that no one wants to buy, represents, even against his will, freedom from exchange.

30   These are certainly minimal opportunities, although a few pages later Adorno expands the possibility of freedom by prescribing a form of expression whose opacity, obscurity, and deviousness—the absence of "the full transparency of its logical genesis"—move away from the dominant system, enacting in its "inadequacy" a measure of liberation:

> This inadequacy resembles that of life, which describes a wavering, deviating line, disappointing by comparison with its premises, and yet which only in this actual course, always less than it should be, is able, under given conditions of existence, to represent an unregimented one.

Too privatized, we are likely to say about this respite from regimentation. Yet we can rediscover it not only in the obdurately subjective, even negative Adorno, but in the public accents of an Islamic intellectual like Ali Shariati, a prime force in the early days of the Iranian Revolution, when his attack on "the true, straight path, this smooth and sacred highway"—organized orthodoxy—contrasted with the deviations of constant migration:

> man, this dialectical phenomenon, is compelled to be always in motion…. Man, then, can never attain a final resting place and take up residence in God…. How disgraceful, then, are all fixed standards. Who can ever fix a standard? Man is a "choice," a struggle, a constant becoming. He is an infinite migration, a migration within himself, from clay to God; he is a migrant within his own soul.

Here we have a genuine potential for an emergent non-coercive culture (although Shariati speaks only of "man" and not of "woman"), which in its awareness of concrete obstacles and concrete steps, exactness without vulgarity, precision but not pedantry, shares the sense of a beginning which occurs in all genuinely radical efforts to start again—for example, the tentative authorization of feminine experience in Virginia Woolf's *A Room of One's Own*, or the fabulous reordination of time and character giving rise to the divided generations of *Midnight's Children*, or the remarkable universalizing of the African-American experience as it emerges in such brilliant detail in Toni Morrison's *Tar Baby* and *Beloved*. The push or tension comes from the surrounding environment—the imperialist power that would otherwise compel you to disappear or to accept some miniature version of yourself as a doctrine to be passed out on a course syllabus. These are not new master discourses, strong new narratives, but, as in John Berger's program, another way of telling. When photographs or texts are used merely to establish identity and presence—to give us merely representative images of *the* Woman, or *the* Indian—they enter what Berger calls a control system. With their innately ambiguous, hence negative and anti-narrativist way-wardness *not* denied, however, they permit unregimented subjectivity to have a social function: "fragile images [family photographs] often carried next to the heart, or placed by the side of the bed, are used to refer to that which historical time has no right to destroy."

From another perspective, the exilic, the marginal, subjective, migratory energies of modern life, which the liberationist struggles have deployed when these energies are too toughly resilient to disappear, have also emerged in what Immanuel Wallerstein calls "anti-systemic movements." Remember that the main feature of imperialist expansion historically was accumulation, a process that accelerated during the twentieth century. Wallerstein's argument is that at bottom capital accumulation is irrational; its additive, acquisitive gains continue unchecked even though its costs—in maintaining the process, in paying for wars to protect it, in "buying off" and co-opting "intermediate cadres," in living in an atmosphere of permanent crisis—are exorbitant, not worth the gains. Thus, Wallerstein says, "the very superstructure [of state power and the national cultures that support the idea of state power] that was put in place to maximize the free flow of the factors of production in the world-economy is the nursery of national movements that mobilize against the inequalities inherent in the world system." Those people compelled by the system to play subordinate or imprisoning roles within it emerge as conscious antagonists, disrupting it, proposing claims, advancing arguments that dispute the totalitarian compulsions of the world market. Not everything can be bought off.

All these hybrid counter-energies, at work in many fields, individuals, and moments provide a community or culture made up of numerous anti-systemic hints and practices for collective human existence (and neither doctrines nor complete theories) that is not based on coercion or domination. They fuelled the uprisings of the 1980s, about which I spoke earlier. The authoritative, compelling image of the empire, which crept into and overtook so many procedures of intellectual mastery that are central in modern culture, finds its opposite in the renewable, almost sporty discontinuities of intellectual and secular impurities—mixed genres, unexpected combinations of tradition and novelty, political experiences based on communities of effort and interpretation (in the broadest sense of the word) rather than classes or corporations of possession, appropriation, and power.

I find myself returning again and again to a hauntingly beautiful passage by Hugo of St. Victor, a twelfth-century monk from Saxony:

> It is therefore, a source of great virtue for the practiced mind to learn, bit by bit, first to change about in visible and transitory things, so that afterwards it may be able to leave them behind altogether. The person who finds his homeland sweet is still a tender beginner; he to whom

every soil is as his native one is already strong; but he is perfect to whom the entire world is as a foreign place. The tender soul has fixed his love on one spot in the world; the strong person has extended his love to all places; the perfect man has extinguished his.

Erich Auerbach, the great German scholar who spent the years of World War Two as an exile in Turkey, cites this passage as a model for anyone—man *and* woman—wishing to transcend the restraints of imperial or national or provincial limits. Only through this attitude can a historian, for example, begin to grasp human experience and its written records in all their diversity and particularity; otherwise one would remain committed more to the exclusions and reactions of prejudice than to the negative freedom of real knowledge. But note that Hugo twice makes it clear that the "strong" or "perfect" person achieves independence and detachment by *working through* attachments, not by rejecting them. Exile is predicated on the existence of, love for, and a real bond with one's native place; the universal truth of exile is not that one has lost that love or home, but that inherent in each is an unexpected, unwelcome loss. Regard experiences then *as if* they were about to disappear: what is it about them that anchors or roots them in reality? What would you save of them, what would you give up, what would you recover? To answer such questions you must have the independence and detachment of someone whose homeland is "sweet," but whose actual condition makes it impossible to recapture that sweetness, and even less possible to derive satisfaction from substitutes furnished by illusion or dogma, whether deriving from pride in one's heritage or from certainty about who "we" are.

40   No one today is purely *one* thing. Labels like Indian, or woman, or Muslim, or American are not more than starting-points, which if followed into actual experience for only a moment are quickly left behind. Imperialism consolidated the mixture of cultures and identities on a global scale. But its worst and most paradoxical gift was to allow people to believe that they were only, mainly, exclusively, white, or Black, or Western, or Oriental. Yet just as human beings make their own history, they also make their cultures and ethnic identities. No one can deny the persisting continuities of long traditions, sustained habitations, national languages, and cultural geographies, but there seems no reason except fear and prejudice to keep insisting on their separation and distinctiveness, as if that was all human life was about. Survival in fact is about the connections between things; in Eliot's phrase, reality cannot be deprived of the "other echoes [that] inhabit the garden." It is more rewarding—and more difficult—to think concretely and sympathetically, contrapuntally, about others than only about "us." But this also means not trying to rule others, not trying to classify them or put them in hierarchies, above all, not constantly reiterating how "our" culture or country is number one (or *not* number one, for that matter). For the intellectual there is quite enough of value to do without *that*.

SUGGESTIONS FOR DISCUSSION

1. Edward W. Said says that one of the key links between justifications of the United States as a superpower today and justifications of Western imperialism in the nineteenth century (and earlier) is the consensus among Americans that "it is up to 'us' to right the wrongs of the world." Who is the "us" in the sentence—all Americans or just some? Who then implicitly would "they" be—the rest of the world or just some people? What is the relation between "us" and "them"? What must Americans assume to believe it is up to "us"? Is this a justifiable assumption? What would Said say? What do you say? Given the situation in world politics when you read this selection, how would you extend Said's analysis?

2. As you can see, Said is highly critical of the United States' role in world politics. But he is also critical of the postcolonial Arab and Islamic world. What is the nature of this criticism? How is it linked to his criticism of the United States?

3. In "Movements and Migrations," Said is looking for forces of hope, liberation, and change. Where does he find such forces? Can you add further examples? What makes them possible agents of change?

SUGGESTIONS FOR WRITING

1. Write an analysis of Said's line of reasoning that connects U.S. power in the late twentieth century to the imperialism of the West in the nineteenth century. Begin with Said's claim that "[i]mperialism did not end, did not suddenly become 'past,' once decolonization had set in motion the dismantling of the classical empires." Explain what he sees as the persistence of the imperial legacy. You may agree or disagree with Said's analysis. But instead of arguing with him or supporting him, identify his underlying assumptions, locate your own assumptions, and compare them with Said's. What do you see as the significance of differences and similarities?

2. As this edition of *Reading Culture* goes to press in April 2003, U.S. troops have just captured Baghdad and other Iraqi cities. It is difficult to predict what will be happening in world politics at the time you read this selection. Write an essay that explains how you think Said would extend his analysis of the United States as a superpower and the continuity of the imperial legacy. Assess the usefulness of Said's perspective to understanding the situation in the world. What alternative perspectives are available? What do you see as their usefulness in comparison with Said's?

3. Said closes the section "Movements and Migrations" with a reflection on a passage by Hugo of St. Victor, a twelfth-century Saxon monk. Write an essay that explores Said's use of this passage. How does he interpret the passage? How does he connect it to the line of thinking in "Movements and Migrations"? How does he make the passage speak to the postcolonial situation and the legacy of imperialism?

CLASSIC READING

THE SOULS OF OUR STRIVING

W.E.B. Du Bois

W.E.B. Du Bois (1868–1963) was the cofounder of the National Association for the Advancement of Colored People in 1909, a prolific author on issues of race, and a political and intellectual leader of the African American struggle for equal rights. Toward the end of his life, Du Bois grew increasingly disillusioned with the United States. At the age of ninety-one, he renounced his American citizenship and lived in exile in Ghana until his death in 1963. The following selection comes from a time much earlier in Du Bois' life. "The Souls of Our Striving" is the opening chapter of his classic work *The Souls of Black Folk*, published in 1903.

SUGGESTION FOR READING In this opening chapter, Du Bois presents the idea of "double consciousness"—a concept that has become widely influential in explaining the relations between whites and African Americans in the United States and colonizers and the colonized throughout the world. He sets the context from the beginning sentence by dividing "me and the other world." Notice how this lays the groundwork for the third paragraph, in which Du Bois first mentions "double consciousness."

O water, voice of my heart, crying in the sand,
   All night long crying with a mournful cry,
As I lie and listen, and cannot understand
      The voice of my heart in my side or the
voice of the sea,
   O water, crying for rest, is it I, is it I?
    All night long the water is crying to me.

Unresting water, there shall never be rest
   Till the last moon droop and the last tide fail,
And the fire of the end begin to burn in the west;
    And the heart shall be weary and wonder
and cry like the sea,
   All life long crying without avail,
    As the water all night long is crying to me.
                    Arthur Symons.

1 Between me and the other world there is ever an unasked question: unasked by some through feelings of delicacy; by others through the difficulty of rightly framing it. All, nevertheless, flutter round it. They approach me in a half-hesitant sort of way, eye me curiously or compassionately, and then, instead of saying directly, How does it feel to be a Problem? they say, I know an excellent colored man in my town; or, I fought at Mechanicsville; or, Do not these Southern outrages make your blood boil? At these I smile, or am interested, or reduce the boiling to a simmer, as the occasion may require. To the real question, How does it feel to be a problem? I answer seldom a word.

And yet, being a problem is a strange experience,—peculiar even for one who has never been anything else, save perhaps in babyhood and in Europe. It is in the early days of rollicking boyhood that the revelation first bursts upon one, all in a day, as it were. I remember well when the shadow swept across me. I was a little thing, away up in the hills of New England, where the dark Housatonic winds between Hoosac and Taghkanic to the sea. In a wee wooden schoolhouse, something put it into the boys' and girls' heads to buy gorgeous visiting-cards—ten cents a package—and exchange. The exchange was merry, till one girl, a tall newcomer, refused my card,—refused it peremptorily, with a glance. Then it dawned upon me with a certain suddenness that I was different from the others; or like, mayhap, in heart and life and longing, but shut out from their world by a vast veil. I had thereafter no desire to tear down that veil, to creep through; I held all beyond it in common contempt, and lived above it in a region of blue sky and great wandering shadows. That sky was bluest when I could beat my mates at examination-time, or beat them at a foot-race, or even beat their stringy heads. Alas, with the years all this fine contempt began to fade; for the words I longed for, and all their dazzling opportunities, were theirs, not mine. But they should not keep these prizes, I said; some, all, I would wrest from them. Just how I would do it I could never decide: by reading law, by healing the sick, by telling the wonderful tales that swam in my head,—some way. With other black boys the strife was not so fiercely sunny: their youth shrunk into tasteless sycophancy, or into silent hatred of the pale world about them and mocking distrust of everything white; or wasted itself in a bitter cry, Why did God make me an outcast and a stranger in mine own house? The shades of the prison-house closed round about us all: walls strait and stubborn to the whitest, but relentlessly narrow, tall, and unscalable to sons of night who must plod darkly on in resignation, or beat unavailing palms against the stone, or steadily, half hopelessly, watch the streak of blue above.

After the Egyptian and Indian, the Greek and Roman, the Teuton and Mongolian, the Negro is a sort of seventh son, born with a veil, and gifted with second-sight in this American world,—a world which yields him no true self-consciousness, but only lets him see himself through the revelation of the other world. It is a peculiar sensation, this double-consciousness, this sense of always looking at one's self through the eyes of others, of measuring one's soul by the tape of a world that looks on in amused contempt and pity. One ever feels his twoness,—an American, a Negro; two souls, two thoughts, two unreconciled strivings; two warring ideals in one dark body, whose dogged strength alone keeps it from being torn asunder.

The history of the American Negro is the history of this strife,—this longing to attain self-conscious manhood, to merge his double self into a better and truer self. In this merging he wishes neither of the older selves to be lost. He would not Africanize America, for America has too much to teach the world and Africa. He would not bleach his Negro soul in a flood of white Americanism, for he knows that Negro blood has a message for the world. He simply wishes to make it possible for a man to be both a Negro and an American, without being cursed and spit upon by his fellows, without having the doors of Opportunity closed roughly in his face.

5   This, then, is the end of his striving: to be a co-worker in the kingdom of culture, to escape both death and isolation, to husband and use his best powers and his latent genius. These powers of body and mind have in the past been strangely wasted, dispersed, or forgotten. The shadow of a mighty Negro past flits through the tale of Ethiopia the Shadowy and of Egypt the Sphinx. Through history, the powers of single black men flash here and there like falling stars, and die sometimes before the world has rightly gauged their brightness. Here in America, in the few days since Emancipation, the black man's turning hither and thither in hesitant and doubtful striving has often made his very strength to lose effectiveness, to seem like absence of power, like weakness. And yet it is not weakness,—it is the contradiction of double aims. The double-aimed struggle of the black artisan—on the one hand to escape white contempt for a nation of mere hewers of wood and drawers of water, and on the other hand to plough and nail and dig for a poverty-stricken horde—could only result in making him a poor craftsman, for he had but half a heart in either cause. By the poverty and ignorance of his people, the Negro minister or doctor was tempted toward quackery and demagogy; and by the criticism of the other world, toward ideals that made him ashamed of his lowly tasks. The would-be black *savant* was confronted by the paradox that the knowledge his people needed was a twice-told tale to his white neighbors, while the knowledge which would teach the white world was Greek to his own flesh and blood. The innate love of harmony and beauty that set the ruder souls of his people a-dancing and a-singing raised but confusion and doubt in the soul of the black artist; for the beauty revealed to him was the soul-beauty of a race which his larger audience despised, and he could not articulate the message of another people. This waste of double aims, this seeking to satisfy two unreconciled ideals, has wrought sad havoc with the courage and faith and deeds of ten thousand thousand people,—has sent them often wooing false gods and invoking false means of salvation, and at times has even seemed about to make them ashamed of themselves.

Away back in the days of bondage they thought to see in one divine event the end of all doubt and disappointment; few men ever worshipped Freedom with half such unquestioning faith as did the American Negro for two centuries. To him, so far as he thought and dreamed, slavery was indeed the sum of all villainies, the cause of all sorrow, the root of all prejudice; Emancipation was the key to a promised land of sweeter beauty than ever stretched before the eyes of wearied Israelites. In song and exhortation swelled one refrain—Liberty; in his tears and curses the God he implored had Freedom in his right hand. At last it came,—suddenly, fearfully, like a dream. With one wild carnival of blood and passion came the message in his own plaintive cadences:—

"Shout, O children!
Shout, you're free!
For God has bought your liberty!"

Years have passed away since then,—ten, twenty, forty; forty years of national life, forty years of renewal and development, and yet the swarthy spectre sits in its accustomed seat at the Nation's feast. In vain do we cry to this our vastest social problem:—

"Take any shape but that, and my firm nerves
Shall never tremble!"

The Nation has not yet found peace from its sins; the freedman has not yet found in freedom his promised land. Whatever of good may have come in these years of change, the shadow of a deep disappointment rests upon the Negro people,—a disappointment all the more bitter because the unattained ideal was unbounded save by the simple ignorance of a lowly people.

The first decade was merely a prolongation of the vain search for freedom, the boon that seemed ever barely to elude their grasp,—like a tantalizing will-o'-the-wisp, maddening and misleading the headless host. The holocaust of war, the terrors of the Ku-Klux Klan, the lies of carpet-baggers, the disorganization of industry, and the contradictory advice of friends and foes, left the bewildered serf with no new watchword beyond the old cry for freedom. As the time flew, however, he began to grasp a new idea. The ideal of liberty demanded for its attainment powerful means, and these the Fifteenth Amendment gave him. The ballot, which before he had looked upon as a visible sign of freedom, he now regarded as the chief means of gaining and perfecting the liberty with which war had partially endowed him. And why not? Had not votes made war and emancipated millions? Had not votes enfranchised the freedmen? Was anything impossible to a power that had done all this? A million black men started with renewed zeal to vote themselves into the kingdom. So the decade flew away, the revolution of 1876 came, and left the half-free serf weary, wondering, but still inspired. Slowly but steadily, in the following years, a new vision began gradually to replace the dream of political power,—a powerful movement, the rise of another ideal to guide the unguided, another pillar of fire by night after a clouded day. It was the ideal of "book-learning"; the curiosity, born of compulsory ignorance, to know and test the power of the cabalistic letters of the white man, the longing to know. Here at last seemed to have been discovered the mountain path to Canaan; longer than the highway of Emancipation and law, steep and rugged, but straight, leading to heights high enough to overlook life.

10   Up the new path the advance guard toiled, slowly, heavily, doggedly; only those who have watched and guided the faltering feet, the misty minds, the dull understandings, of the dark pupils of these schools know how faithfully, how piteously, this people strove to learn. It was weary work. The cold statistician wrote down the inches of progress here and there, noted also where here and there a foot had slipped or some one had fallen. To the tired climbers, the horizon was ever dark, the mists were often cold, the Canaan was always dim and far away. If, however, the vistas disclosed as yet no goal, no resting-place, little but flattery and criticism, the journey at least gave leisure for reflection and self-examination; it changed the child of Emancipation to the youth with dawning self-consciousness, self-realization, self-respect. In those sombre forests of his striving his own soul rose before him, and he saw himself,—darkly as through a veil; and yet he saw in himself some faint revelation of his power, of his mission. He began to have a dim feeling that, to attain his place in the world, he must be himself, and not another. For the first time he sought to analyze the burden he bore upon his back, that dead-weight of social degradation partially masked behind a half-named Negro problem. He felt his poverty; without a cent, without a home, without land, tools, or savings, he had entered into competition with rich, landed, skilled neighbors. To be a poor man is hard, but to be a poor race in a land of dollars is the very bottom of hardships. He felt the weight of his ignorance,—not simply of letters, but of life, of business, of the humanities; the accumulated sloth and shirking and awkwardness of decades and centuries shackled his hands and feet. Nor was his burden all poverty and ignorance. The red stain of bastardy, which two centuries of systematic legal defilement of Negro women had stamped upon his race, meant not only the loss of ancient African chastity, but also the hereditary weight of a mass of corruption from white adulterers, threatening almost the obliteration of the Negro home.

A people thus handicapped ought not to be asked to race with the world, but rather allowed to give all its time and thought to its own social problems. But alas! while sociologists gleefully count his bastards and his prostitutes, the very soul of the toiling, sweating black man is darkened by the shadow of a vast despair. Men call the shadow prejudice, and learnedly explain it as the natural defence of culture against barbarism, learning against ignorance, purity against crime, the "higher" against the "lower" races. To which the Negro cries Amen! and swears that to so much of this strange prejudice as is founded on just homage to civilization, culture, righteousness, and progress, he humbly bows and meekly does obeisance. But before that nameless prejudice that leaps beyond all this he stands helpless, dismayed, and well-nigh speechless; before that personal disrespect and mockery, the ridicule and systematic humiliation, the distortion of fact and wanton license of fancy, the cynical ignoring of the better and the boisterous welcoming of the worse, the all-pervading desire to inculcate disdain for everything black, from Toussaint to the devil,—before this there rises a sickening despair that would disarm and discourage any nation save that black host to whom "discouragement" is an unwritten word.

But the facing of so vast a prejudice could not but bring the inevitable self-questioning, self-disparagement, and lowering of ideals which ever accompany repression and breed in an atmosphere of contempt and hate. Whisperings and portents came borne upon the four winds: Lo! we are diseased and dying, cried the dark hosts; we cannot write, our voting is vain; what need of education, since we must always cook and serve? And the Nation echoed and enforced this self-criticism, saying: Be content to be servants, and nothing more; what need of higher culture for half-men? Away with the black man's ballot, by force or fraud,—and behold the suicide of a race! Nevertheless, out of the evil came something of good,—the more careful adjustment of education to real life, the clearer perception of the Negroes' social responsibilities, and the sobering realization of the meaning of progress.

So dawned the time of *Sturm und Drang*: storm and stress to-day rocks our little boat on the mad waters of the world-sea; there is within and without the sound of conflict, the burning of body and rending of soul; inspiration strives with doubt, and faith with vain questionings. The bright ideals of the past,—physical freedom, political power, the training of brains and the training of hands,—all these in turn have waxed and waned, until even the last grows dim and overcast. Are they all wrong,—all false? No, not that, but each alone was over-simple and incomplete,—the dreams of a credulous race-childhood, or the fond imaginings of the other world which does not know and does not want to know our power. To be really true, all these ideals must be melted and welded into one. The training of the schools we need to-day more than ever,—the training of deft hands, quick eyes and ears, and above all the broader, deeper, higher culture of gifted minds and pure hearts. The power of the ballot we need in sheer self-defence,—else what shall save us from a second slavery? Freedom, too, the long-sought, we still seek,—the freedom of life and limb, the freedom to work and think, the freedom to love and aspire. Work, culture, liberty,—all these we need, not singly but together, not successively but together, each growing and aiding each, and all striving toward that vaster ideal that swims before the Negro people, the ideal of human brotherhood, gained through the unifying ideal of Race; the ideal of fostering and developing the traits and talents of the Negro, not in opposition to or contempt for other races, but rather in large conformity to the greater ideals of the American Republic, in order that some day on American soil two world-races may give each to each those characteristics both so sadly lack. We the darker ones come even now not altogether empty-handed: there are to-day no truer exponents of the pure human spirit of the Declaration of Independence than the American Negroes; there is no true American music but the wild sweet melodies of the Negro slave; the American fairy tales and folk-lore are Indian and African; and, all in all, we black men seem the sole oasis of simple faith and reverence in a dusty desert of dollars and smartness. Will America be poorer if she replace her brutal dyspeptic blundering with light-hearted but determined Negro humility? or her coarse and cruel wit with loving jovial good-humor? or her vulgar music with the soul of the Sorrow Songs?

Merely a concrete test of the underlying principles of the great republic is the Negro Problem, and the spiritual striving of the freedmen's sons is the travail of souls whose burden is almost beyond the measure of their strength, but who bear it in the name of an historic race, in the name of this the land of their fathers' fathers, and in the name of human opportunity.

15   And now what I have briefly sketched in large outline let me on coming pages tell again in many ways, with loving emphasis and deeper detail, that men may listen to the striving in the souls of black folk.

SUGGESTIONS FOR DISCUSSION

1. What does Du Bois mean by "double consciousness"? What is he trying to explain? How does he define the term? What examples does he offer? Does the term have relevance for social life in the United States today? Where would you look for evidence of "always looking at one's self through the eyes of others?" What are the effects?

2. At the end of this chapter, Du Bois says that the "Negro Problem" is a "concrete test of the underlying principles of the great republic." What does he mean here? Exactly how does the question of race in the United States "test" the nation's principles? In another part of *The Souls of Black Folks*, Du Bois claims more widely that the "problem of the Twentieth Century is the problem of the color line." Now that you are living in a postcolonial world in the twenty-first century, what is the current status of the "problem of the color line"—in the United States and internationally?

3. Du Bois' notion of "double consciousness" is recalled by the opening sentence of the final paragraph in Said's "Movements and Migrations": "No one is purely *one* thing." To what extent are Du Bois and Said getting at the same thing? To what extent do they differ? What do you see as the significance of their differences and similarities?

SUGGESTIONS FOR WRITING

1. In the contemporary world of visual images and the mass media, viewers are constantly encountering representations of nonwhites, whether American racial minorities or people of color from around the world. Pick an example from an ad, a film, a television show, or elsewhere. Write an essay that uses Du Bois' concept of "double consciousness" to analyze the representation as a "revelation of the other world," where the dominant white culture presents nonwhites with images of themselves. Take into account here how the dominant culture defines others and what the effects might be.

2. Many of the other readings in this chapter, in one way or another, take up notions similar to Du Bois' concept of "double consciousness" such as in the image of the border that turns up in Amitava Kumar, in Elaine Kim's sense of being caught in the middle, or in the relations of African writers with the English language. Pick one or more of the other readings in this chapter and write an essay that compares the sense, in Said's words, of not being "purely *one* thing" with Du Bois' notion of "double consciousness."

3. Write an essay in which you locate yourself in a postcolonial world. Draw on your ancestry and family history, but do not simply report on the paths of migration and patterns of settlement that brought you to where you are today. Answer this question: In an era of globalization and the movements of people, where and how do you fit in? Think in terms of how culture is changing in the United States and the world—in part becoming more stan-

dardized and more Americanized, in part more diverse and polycultural. Think in terms of your identity and the identity of those around you. Can you say you are "purely *one* thing," or is the identity of you and others more complicated and perhaps more contradictory?

CHECKING OUT THE WEB

1. The island of Puerto Rico has had a complicated relationship with the United States ever since the United States acquired it from Spain as a result of the Spanish American War of 1898. It is officially a commonwealth, but some think it is really a colony whereas others believe it should be the fifty-first state. To investigate the relationship between the United States and Puerto Rico, research the controversy over the naval base and training exercises at Vieques in Puerto Rico. A good place to start is http://www.viequelibre.org, which includes photo essays and background information. Check out this site and others. Come to class prepared to discuss what's at stake in the Vieques controversy and what the implications are for the status of Puerto Rico.

2. Frantz Fanon (1925–1961) was born in Martinique, studied medicine in France, and then became a partisan of the Algerian struggle against France for national independence. He is considered one of the first and most important postcolonial theorists. Do a Web search to find out who he was and what his influence has been on current thinking about the nature of colonialism and about relations between formerly colonized people and their former colonial powers.

3. South Africa has recognized 11 official languages. Prepare a report that explains South Africa's linguistic diversity and examines various approaches to language policy and nation-building. The Pan South African Language Board (PANSALB) has good background information at its website http://www.pansalb.org.za. For information on language planning and nation-building, see Project for the Study of Alternative Education in South Africa at its website http://web.uct.ac.za/depts/praesa/index.htm.

VISUAL CULTURE

Coco Fusco and Guillermo Gómez-Peña: Postcolonial Representation

Coco Fusco and Guillermo Gómez-Peña are writers, critics, and performance artists who call into question representations in popular culture and the media of Latino cultures, the U.S.–Mexican border, globalization, and national identity. Their techniques, which resemble those of "rewriting the image" in Chapter 4, involve exaggerating common images to expose the ethnocentric stereotyping and scapegoating that creates the "we" and "they" of mainstream America and its cultural Others. Here are three examples of their work.

TWO UNDISCOVERED AMERINDIANS VISIT THE WEST
The cage performance pictured here, in which Fusco and Gómez-Peña are "undiscovered Amerindians" from an island in the Gulf of Mexico, is part of a larger interdisciplinary arts project including multimedia, installation, and experimental radio soundtrack that premiered at the Walker Art Center in Minneapolis in 1992 and subsequently appeared in Madrid, London, and Washington, D.C.

BETTER YET WHEN DEAD

Coco Fusco's performance installation raises questions about why Latina artists such as Selena, Ar Mendieta, Sara Gomez, Frida Kahlo, and Sor Juana become celebrated figures once they are dead. The installation, which premiered in 1997, resembles a funeral parlor in which the spectators become guests at a wake.

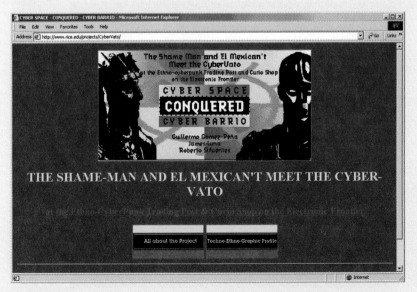

THE SHAME MAN AND EL MEXICAN'T MEET CYBERVATO.

This arts project, created by Gómez-Peña, James Luna, and Roberto Sifuentes, included a performance and installation at Rice University in 1995 as well as a Web site, http://www.rice.edu/projects/CyberVato. In this project, the artists invent hybrid identities to parody common notions of ethnicity and cyber culture.

SUGGESTIONS FOR DISCUSSION

1. Coco Fusco and Guillermo Gómez-Peña's cage performance in "Two Undiscovered Amerindians Visit the West" puts spectators in the uncomfortable position of viewing the "undiscovered Amerindians" as exotic curiosities. Notice particularly the image of a family posing in front of the cage while someone takes its picture. What commentary does the cage performance make about American history? What does it tell about representations of American Indians?

2. Visit Coco Fusco's Virtual Laboratory at http://www.thing.net/~cocofusco , and on the home page, click on "Performances" for descriptions of performance art projects Fusco has created. Check out "Better Yet When Dead" and the other performances. How would you describe Fusco's method as an artist? What do you see her trying to do? In what ways do her performances involve the audience?

3. Visit "The Shame Man and El Mexican't Meet the CyberVato" Web site. Click on "Techno-Ethno-Graphic Profile" and check out the various questionnaires it leads to. What kind of position do the questions put you in? Do you think this is really a survey? Are you supposed to answer or think about the logic of the questions? What is the relationship between the questionnaires and the larger themes of this arts project?

SUGGESTED ASSIGNMENT

Design your own instance of performance art. Follow Coco Fusco and Guillermo Gomez-Pena's example by involving the audience directly in issues such as cultural representation, stereotyping, and scapegoating.

MINING THE ARCHIVE

Nineteenth-Century Orientalist Painting

The Snake Charmer by Jean-Leon Gérôme, c. 1880. Oil on canvas. Acc: 1955.51. Sterling and Francine Clark Art Institute, Williamstown, Massachusetts.

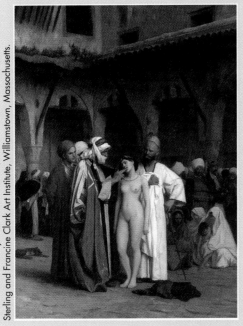

The Slave Market by Jean-Leon Gérôme, 1866. Oil on canvas. Acc: 1955.53. Sterling and Francine Clark Art Institute, Williamstown, Massachusetts.

Representations of the Arab world in North Africa and the Middle East were favorite subjects in nineteenth-century European art. Often called Orientalist painting, with its scenes of Turkish baths, snake charmers, slave markets, and harems, this style represented Arab culture as exotic and alien. As you can see from the two paintings reproduced here— "The Slave Market" and "The Snake Charmer" by Jean-Leon Gerome, perhaps the most important nineteenth-century French painter of Orientalist subjects—Orientalist art offered European viewers the titillation of sexual power and forbidden pleasures while assuring them such unthinkable desires and practices belonged to an Oriental Other, not to "us."

Nineteenth-century Orientalist painting forms an important archive for understanding how representations of Arab culture were quite literally fantastic figments of the European imagination. An art museum near you may have Orientalist paintings in its collection. There are also several excellent books that have plenty of examples of paintings, such as the exhibition catalogue *The Orientalists: Delacroix to Matisse: The Allure of North Africa and the Near East* (Ed. MaryAnne Stevens. London: Thames and Hudson, 1984) and Web sites you can find by entering "orientalism" and "art" in your search engine. Look for definitions of the term *Orientalism* so that you understand how art historians and cultural critics use it.

As you look at the paintings, consider what they reveal about Western representations of the Arab world and how these representations continue to shape perceptions today. For example, compare images of the Arab world that appear in nineteenth-century paintings and in *National Geographic*. Linda Street's book *Veils and Daggers: A Century of National Geographic's Representation of the Arab World* (Philadelphia: Temple UP, 2000) is a good source for this project.

Credits

Text Credits

Introduction

Williams, Raymond. From "Culture is Ordinary" from *Resources of Hope: Culture, Democracy, Socialism* by Raymond Williams. Copyright © 1989 by the Estate of Raymond Williams. Reprinted by permission of Verso.

Chapter 1

Downie, Leonard Jr. "News Values" from *The News About the News* by Leonard Downie Jr. and Robert G. Kaiser, copyright © 2002 by Leonard Downie and Robert G. Kaiser. Used by permission of Alfred A. Knopf, a division of Random House, Inc.

Rutenberg, Jim. "Fox Portrays a War of Good and Evil, and Many Applaud." Copyright © 2001 by The New York Times Company. Reprinted by permission.

Uricchio, William. "Television Conventions" from *Re:constructions*, September 16, 2001. Reprinted by permission of William Uricchio.

Re:constructions web page reprinted by permission of MIT Comparative Media Studies.

Lertola, Joe. "Parched Land." Time, Sept. 16, 2002. Copyright © Time, Inc. Reprinted by permission.

Chapter 2

Naylor, Gloria. "Kiswana Browne" from *The Women of Brewster Place* by Gloria Naylor, copyright © 1980, 1982 by Gloria Naylor. Used by permission of Viking Penguin, a division of Penguin Putnam, Inc.

Marsh, Dave. From "Introduction" from *Fortunate Son* by Dave Marsh, 1986, pp. xv–xxvi. Copyright © 1985 by Duke and Duchess Ventures, Inc. Reprinted by permission of the author.

Grossberg, Lawrence. "Youth and American Identity" [editor's title] from *It's a Sin: Essays on Postmodernism, Politics, and Culture* by Lawrence Grossberg. Copyright © 1988 by Lawrence Grossberg. Reprinted by permission of Power Publications and the author.

Gaines, Donna. Excerpt from *Teenage Wasteland* by Donna Gaines, 1992, pp. 33–38. Copyright © 1990, 1991 by Donna Gaines. Reprinted by permission of the author.

Hine, Thomas. "Goths in Tomorrowland" from *The Rise and Fall of the American Teenager* by Thomas Hine. Copyright © 1999 by Thomas Hine. Reprinted by permission of HarperCollins Publishers Inc.

Pope, Mike. "Gen X's Enduring Legacy: The Internet." Originally published in the *Tallahassee Democrat* 10/28/2001. Reprinted by permission of the *Tallahassee Democrat*.

Hochschild, Arlie Russell. "Coming of Age, Seeking an Identity." Copyright © 2000 by The New York Times Co. Reprinted by permission.

Kantrowitz, Barbara and Keith Naughton. "Generation 9-11." Copyright © 2001 Newsweek, Inc. All rights reserved. Reprinted by permission.

Chambers, Veronica and Yahlin Chang. "Raging Teen Hormones" from "Highschool Confidential." Copyright © 1999 Newsweek, Inc. All rights reserved. Reprinted by permission.

Ginsberg, Allen. All lines from "Howl" from *Collected Poems 1947–1980* by Allen Ginsberg. Copyright © 1955 by Allen Ginsberg. Reprinted by permission of HarperCollins Publishers, Inc.

Gilbert, James. "Juvenile Delinquency Films" from *A Cycle of Outrage: America's Reaction to the Juvenile Delinquent in the 1950s* by James Gilbert. Copyright © 1986 by Oxford University Press, Inc. Used by permission of Oxford University Press, Inc.

Crafts, S. D. et al. Excerpts from pp. 52–3, 113, 115–7, 181–4 from *My Music* © 1993 by Wesleyan University Press, reprinted by permission of Wesleyan University Press.

Chapter 6

Lopez, Barry. "Borders" reprinted by permission of Sterling Lord Literistic, Inc. Copyright © 1988 by Barry Holstun Lopez.

Fiske, John. "Shopping for Pleasure: Malls, Power and Resistance" pp. 13–18 from *Reading the Popular* by John Fiske. Reprinted by permission of Routledge, Ltd.

Davis, Mike. "Fortress Los Angeles: The Militarization of Urban Space" by Mike Davis from *Variations of a Theme Park* edited by Mike Sorkin. Compilation copyright © 1992 by Michael Sorkin. Copyright © 1992 by Mike Davis. Reprinted by permission of Hill & Wang, a division of Farrar, Straus and Giroux, LLC.

Davis, Murphy. "Woodruff Park and the Search for Common Ground" from *A Work of Hospitality: The Open Door Reader.* Copyright © 2002 by The Open Door Community. Reprinted by permission of the author.

Cockcroft, Eva Sperling and Holly Barnet Sanchez. Excerpts from the SPARC book, *Signs from the Heart: California Chicano Murals.* Segments written by Eva Sperling Cockcroft and Holly Barnet-Sanchez. Reprinted by permission of SPARC.

Muschamp, Herbert. "The Commemorative Beauty of Tragic Wreckage." Copyright © 2001 by The New York Times Company. Reprinted by permission.

Silverstein, Larry. "Rebuild at Ground Zero." Appeared in *The Wall Street Journal,* September 23, 2002. Copyright © 2002 Dow Jones & Company, Inc. All rights reserved. Reprinted by permission of Dow Jones & Company and Larry Silverstein.

Jacobs, Jane. "The Uses of Sidewalks: Safety" from *The Death and Life of Great American Cities* by Jane Jacobs, copyright © 1961 by Jane Jacobs. Used by permission of Random House, Inc.

Chapter 7

Brunvand, Jan Harold. "The Hook" from *The Vanishing Hitchhiker: American Urban Legends and Their Meaning* by Jan Harold Brunvand.

Turner, Patricia A. From *I Heard It Through the Grapevine: The Rhetoric of Rumor in Black Culture* by Patricia A. Turner. Copyright © 1993 The Regents of The University of California. Reprinted by permission.

King, Stephen. "Why We Crave Horror Movies" by Stephen King. Reprinted with permission. Copyright © 1982 by Stephen King. All rights reserved. Originally appeared in *Playboy,* (1982).

Scott, A. O. "The Hunger for Fantasy, An Empire to Feed It." Copyright © 2002 by The New York Times Company. Reprinted by permission.

Taken from the ROGER EBERT column by Roger Ebert © 2002. Dist. by UNIVERSAL PRESS SYNDICATE. Reprinted with permission. All rights reserved.

Chabon, Michael. From *The Amazing Adventures of Kavalier and Clay* by Michael Chabon, copyright © 2000 by Michael Chabon. Used by permission of Random House, Inc.

Warshow, Robert. "The Gangster as Tragic Hero" from *The Immediate Experience* by Robert Warshow from *The Immediate Experience.* Copyright © 1962 by Robert Warshow. Reprinted by permission.

Chapter 8

Cisneros, Sandra. "The First Job" from *The House on Mango Street.* Copyright © 1984 by Sandra Cisneros. Published by Vintage Books, a division of Random House, Inc. and in hardcover by Alfred A. Knopf in 1994. Reprinted by permission of Susan Bergholz Literary Services, New York. All rights reserved.

Adams, Scott. Pages 11–15 from *The Dilbert Principle* by Scott Adams. Copyright © 1996 by United Features Syndicate, Inc. Reprinted by permission of HarperCollins Publishers, Inc.

Hochschild, Arlie Russell. "Work: The Great Escape" adapted from *The Time Bind: When Work Becomes Home and Home Becomes Work* by Arlie Russell Hochschild. First published in *The New York Times Magazine,* © 1997 by Arlie Russell Hochschild. Reprinted by permission of Henry Holt and Company, LLC.

Ehrenreich, Barbara. "Nickel-and-Dimed" by Barbara Ehrenreich. Copyright © 1999 by Barbara Ehrenreich. Reprinted by permission of International Creative Management.

Kristof, Nicholas D. and Sheryl WuDunn. "Two Cheers for Sweatshops" from *Thunder From the East* by Nicholas D. Kristof and Sheryl WuDunn, copyright © 2000 by Nicholas D. Kristof and Sheryl WuDunn. Used by permission of Alfred A. Knopf, a division of Random House, Inc.

Hayden, Tom and Charles Kernaghan. "Pennies an Hour and No Way Up" Originally published in *The New York Times,* July 6, 2002. Reprinted by permission of The New York Times Co.

Olson, Tillie. "I Stand Here Ironing," copyright © 1956, 1957, 1960, 1961 by Tillie Olson, from *Tell Me a Riddle* by Tillie Olsen, Introduction by John Leonard. Used by permission of Dell Publishing, a division of Random House, Inc.

Spradley, J. From *The Cocktail Waitress: Women's Work in a Man's World* by J. Spradley. Copyright © 1975. Reprinted by permission of the McGraw-Hill Companies.

Chapter 9

Gordon, Mary. "More Than Just a Shrine." Copyright © 1985 by the New York Times Co. Reprinted by permission.

Tompkins, Jane. "Indians' Textualism, Morality and the Problem of History." *Critical Inquiry,* 13:1 (1986): pp. 101–119. Copyright © 1986 by The University of Chicago Press. Reprinted by permission of the University of Chicago Press.

Phillips, Christopher. "Necessary Fictions: Warren Neidich's Early American Cover-ups" from *American History Reinvented: Photographs of Warren Neidich.* Essay copyright © 1989 by Christopher Phillips. Reprinted by permission of the author.

Neidach, Warren. "Contra-Curtis: Early American Cover-Ups" #2, 5, 9 and 14 from *American History Reinvented: Photographs by Warren Neidich.* Reprinted by permission of Warren Neidich.

Tindall, George B. and David E. Shi. "The Tragedy of Vietnam" from *America: A Narrative History, Brief Second Edition* by George B. Tindall with David E. Shi. Copyright © 1989, 1988, 1984 by W. W. Norton & Company, Inc. Used by permission of W. W. Norton & Company, Inc.

Baritz, Loren. "God's Country and American Know-How" from *Backfire* by Loren Baritz. Copyright © 1985 by Loren Baritz. Reprinted by permission of Gerard McCauley Literary Agency.

Terry, Wallace. "Private First Class Reginald 'Malik' Edwards" from *Bloods* by Wallace Terry, copyright © 1984 by Wallace Terry. Used by permission of Random House, Inc.

Hass, Kristin Ann. "Making Memory of War: Building the Vietnam Veterans Memorial" from *Carried to the Wall: American Memory and The Vietnam Veteran's Memorial* by Kristin Ann Hass. Copyright 9c) 1998 by the Regents of the University of California. Reprinted by permission of the Regents of the University of California and the University of California Press.

Sturken, Marita. "Spectacle of Memory and Amnesia" Remembering the Persian Gulf War" from *Tangled Memories: The Vietnam War, the AIDS Epidemic, and the Politics of Remembering* by Marita Sturken. Reprinted by permission of the University of California Press.

Mead, Margaret. "We Are All Third Generation" from *And Keep Your Powder Dry* by Margaret Mead. Copyright 1942. Reprinted courtesy of the Institute for Intercultural Studies, Inc., New York.

Trachtenberg, Alan. Excerpt from *Preface* from *Reading American Photographs: Images as History From Matthew Brady to Walker Evans* by Alan Trachtenberg. Copyright © 1989 by Allen Trachtenberg. Reprinted by permission of Hill & Wang, a division of Farrar, Straus and Giroux, LLC.

Chapter 10

Kumar, Amitava. "The Shame of Arrival" from *Passport Photos*, copyright © 2000. Reprinted by permission of the University of California Press.

Kim, Elaine H. "Home is Where the Han Is: A Korean American Perspective on the Los Angeles Upheavals" by Elaine H. Kim from *Reading Rodney King, Reading Urban Uprising*, 1993. Reprinted by permission of the author.

Anzaldúa, Gloria. "How To Tame a Wild Tongue" from *Borderlands/La Frontera: The New Mestiza.* Copyright © 1987, 1999 by Gloria Anzaldúa. Reprinted by permission of Aunt Lute Books.

Pennycook, Alastair. "Our Marvelous Tongue" pp. 133–146 and 207–214 from *English and the Discourse of Colonialism* by Alistair Pennycook. Reprinted by permission of Routledge, Ltd.

Achebe, Chinua. "The African Writer and the English Language" from *Morning Yet on Creation Day* by Chinua Achebe, copyright © 1975 by Chinua Achebe. Used by permission of Doubleday, a division of Random House, Inc. and Harold Ober Associates, Inc.

"The Language of African Literature" reprinted from *Decolonizing the Mind: The Politics of Language in African Literature* by Ngugi wa Thiong'o. Copyright © 1986 by Ngugi wa Thiong'o. Published by Heinemann, a division of Reed Elsevier, Inc., Portsmouth, NH. www.heinemann.com.

Said, Edward W. From *Culture and Imperialism* by Edward W. Said, copyright © 1993 by Edward W. Said. Used by permission of Alfred A. Knopf, a division of Random House, Inc.

Cyber Space Conquered web page reprinted by permission of Guillermo Goméz-Peña.

Photo credits

Introduction   Page 2: ©The Absolut Company.

Chapter 1   Page 16: ©Tom Tomorrow

Page 23: (Top Right): Reprinted by permission of the *Wall Street Journal*, ©2003 Dow Jones & Company, Inc. All Rights Reserved Worldwide. **Page 23 (Bottom Left):** Copyright 2003, USA TODAY. Reprinted with permission. **Page 23 (Bottom Right):** Globe Editorial, Inc. **Page 27 (Top Left):** *Time* Magazine, Copyright Time Inc./TimePix **Page 27 (Top Right):** *Time* Magazine, Copyright Time Inc./TimePix **Page 27 (Bottom Left):** Roberto Brosan/*Time* Magazine, Copyright Time Inc./TimePix **Page 27 (Bottom Right):** *Time* Magazine, Copyright Time Inc./TimePix

Chapter 2   Page 93 (All) Courtesy The Everett Collection **Page 102** Nina Leen/*Life* Magazine, Copyright Time Inc./TimePix

Chapter 3   Page 103: Courtesy of Teachers College, Columbia University **Page 163 (Top):** Courtesy of Hampton University Archives **Page 164:** Jane Addams Memorial Collection (JAMC neg. 613), Special Collections, The University Library, The University of Illinois at Chicago **Page 172 (Top):** From *THE NEW FUN WITH DICK AND JANE* by William S. Gray, et al., illustrated by Keith Ward and Eleanor Campbell. Copyright 1951 by Scott, Foresman and Company. Reprinted by permission of Addison-Wesley Educational Publishers, Inc.

Chapter 4   Page 175: Courtesy of Craig Frazier **Page 177:** Courtesy of Coach **Page 178:** The mark JEEP® is a registered trademark of DaimlerChrysler Corporation and the JEEP advertisement is used with permission. **Page 179:** Concept by Tibor Kalman, Courtesy of *Colors* Magazine **Page 188 (Left and Right):** ©The Procter & Gamble Company. Used by permission. **Page 189 (Left):** ©The Procter & Gamble Company. Used by permission. **Page 191:** Courtesy of Reebok, Photography by Nadav Kander **Page 192 (Left):** Courtesy of the American Dairy Farmers and Milk Processors **Page 192 (Right):** Courtesy of American Indian College Fund **Page 193:** Reprinted with the permission of The Pillsbury Company who has ownership of the Häagen-Dazs trademark. **Page 203 (Left):** Erich Lessing/Art Resource, NY **Page 203 (Right):** Cameraphoto/Art Resource, NY **Page 204 (Top):** Photograph by Hervé Lewandoswki. Réunion des Musées Nationaux/Art Resource, NY **Page 204 (Bottom):** Courtesy of Guerrilla Girls **Page 205 (Top and Bottom):** Image courtesy of www.adbusters.org **Page 207:** The Candie's Foundation **Page 208 (Left and Right):** Courtesy of National Archives

Page 209 (Top): RAJ Publications, Lakewood, CO. **Page 209 (Bottom):** Paul Martin Lester **Page 218:** Private Collection

Chapter 5   Page 226 (Left): Used with permission of Family Dog Productions/Chet Helms. **Page 226 (Right):** Courtesy of Nirvana L.L.C. **Page 227 (Bottom):** Courtesy of Mike Szabo and N.A.S.A. **Page 238 (Left):** Photo courtesy of Apple Computer, Inc. **Page 238 (Right):** Courtesy of ACCO Brands, Inc. **Page 239 (Left):** The Gillette Company **Page 239 (Right):** *Nesstalgia* by Arlen Ness. Courtesy of Arlen Ness Enterprises, Inc. Photography by Carmina Besson. **Page 263:** AP/Wide World Photos

Chapter 6   Page 305: Joseph Szkodzinski **Page 307 (Top):** Courtesy of Henry Chalfant, from *Subway Art*, by Martha Cooper and Henry Chalfant. **Page 307 (Bottom):** CORBIS **Page 310:** Hancock Historic Preservation Committee **Page 311:** Hancock Historic Preservation Committee

Chapter 7   Page 355: ©2000 Atlantic Syndication Partners. Reprinted by permission.

Chapter 8   Page 393 (Left): Courtesy National Archives, ARC Identifier: 514416 **Page 393 (Right):** Courtesy National Archives, NWDNS-179-WP-1563 **Page 395 (Left):** © Gordon Parks **Page 404:** Bettmann/CORBIS

Chapter 9   Page 428: Library of Congress **Page 451 (Top):** Getty Images **Page 451 (Bottom Left):** Tom Carter/PhotoEdit **Page 451 (Bottom Right):** Wolfgang Kaehler/CORBIS **Page 465:** CNN/Getty Images **Page 481 (Top):** Bettmann/CORBIS **Page 481 (Bottom):** Library of Congress **Page 482 (Top and Bottom):** AP/Wide World Photos **Page 485 (Top):** AP/Wide World Photos **Page 485 (Bottom):** John Filo/Hulton | Archive Photos/ Getty Images **Page 486 (Top):** AP/Wide World Photos **Page 486 (Bottom):** Bettmann/CORBIS **Page 490 (Top and Bottom):** Albany Civil Rights Movement Museum

Chapter 10   Page 491: For maps and other related teaching materials contact: ODT, Inc., P.O. Box 134, Amherst, MA 01004, USA, 800-736-1293. **Page 494:** Photography by Amitava Kumar **Page 499:** Photography by Amitava Kumar **Page 500–501:** Photography by Amitava Kumar **Page 535:** Mary Evans Picture Library **Page 570 (Top):** Courtesy of Coco Fusco, Unknown photographer **Page 570 (Bottom):** Courtesy of Coco Fusco, Photography by Peter Barker **Page 571 (Top):** Courtesy of Coco Fusco, *Better Yet When Dead*, performance, 1996–97

Index

Note to reader: All titles (of text selections, books, magazines, newspapers, television shows, movies, and songs) are printed in italic type. Names of authors of text selections are printed in bold type. Names of images are printed in regular type.